The Elements of Conveyancing

AUSTRALIA
The Law Book Company Ltd.
Sydney : Melbourne : Brisbane

CANADA AND U.S.A.
The Carswell Company Ltd.
Agincourt, Ontario

INDIA
N. M. Tripathi Private Ltd.
Bombay

ISRAEL
Steimatzky's Agency Ltd.
Jerusalem : Tel Aviv : Haifa

MALAYSIA : SINGAPORE : BRUNEI
Malayan Law Journal (Pte) Ltd.
Singapore

NEW ZEALAND
Sweet & Maxwell (N.Z.) Ltd.
Wellington

PAKISTAN
Pakistan Law House
Karachi

The Elements of Conveyancing

By

E. G. BOWMAN, M.A., LL.B. (Cantab.)
of Lincoln's Inn, Barrister

and

E. L. G. TYLER, M.A. (Oxon.)
of Lincoln's Inn and the Northern Circuit, Barrister;
and of the Faculty of Law, University of Liverpool

LONDON
SWEET & MAXWELL LIMITED
1972

ALSO BY E. L. G. TYLER

FISHER AND LIGHTWOOD'S LAW OF MORTGAGE (8th ed.)
FAMILY PROVISION

Published in 1972 by
Sweet & Maxwell Limited of
11 New Fetter Lane London
and printed in Great Britain
by The Eastern Press Limited
of London and Reading

SBN   Hardback 421 13590 5
      Paperback 421 13390 2

PREFACE

OLDER readers will be familiar with Burnett's *The Elements of Conveyancing*, a book which served many candidates for the Conveyancing paper in the Bar Examinations well. The last edition of that work (1952) is now out of print and out of date. The publishers felt that it should be brought up to date and at the same time given a new character. The present book, while following the general pattern and retaining and adapting parts of *Burnett*, is a new book. We have written the book with the Law Society's Examinations in mind, though it should prove useful to those taking other professional examinations (including the Bar Examinations) and to those studying conveyancing as part of a University course.

The book deals with conveyancing not only in the narrow sense which comprises contracts and deeds of conveyance, but also in the wider sense which includes leases, mortgages, settlements and wills, as all these topics are likely to be of regular concern to the practitioner. Indeed, we have attempted a practical approach throughout. We have, therefore, included brief comments on such matters as the tax implications of transactions and stressed, as in the introductory chapter, the realities of ordinary day-to-day conveyancing transactions as well as the legal principles involved. We have dealt in some detail with, for example, options, conditional sales, estate agents, town and country planning, fixtures and fittings, defective premises, notice to complete, the matters most commonly encountered on investigating title, sub-sales and instalment sales, the advantages of a mortgage to an individual taxpayer, the use of mortgages in property development and discretionary trusts.

We have placed special emphasis on such matters as inquiries and searches before contract, the contents of the standard sets of general conditions of sale, registration of land charges and registration of title, statutory protection for tenants and trusts for sale. On the other hand, we have tried to minimise the amount of space devoted to topics which have little relevance to the average practitioner's work, such as the trusts of a strict settlement. At the end of the book there is a short collection of precedents which, it is hoped, will help to bring the subject to life and to give some insight into the art of drafting.

We have assumed that the reader has a knowledge of the law of contract and real property, and a basic knowledge of revenue law, though not essential, would be useful.

v

We should emphasise that this book deals with the *elements* of conveyancing. It will be seen that the first part of the book dealing with contracts for the sale of land is rather more detailed than the rest. In our view we feel that, at this stage, it is more important that the student should master the law and practice of conveyancing contracts rather than the various conveyancing transactions, which, if dealt with in depth, would have extended the length of the book beyond the limits permitted. We have, however, referred to the more specialised works where appropriate and the reader should turn to these for further assistance.

We should, perhaps, explain our methods of working. Mr. Tyler has been chiefly responsible for the chapters on contracts for the sale of land (Chapters 1 to 9 inclusive) and on mortgages (Chapter 12). Mr. Bowman has undertaken the remainder. We hope that any difference in style is not too disconcerting. We have had an opportunity of commenting on each other's work and accept joint and several liability for the whole.

We should like to record our thanks to Mr. V. G. H. Hallett for allowing us to base our precedents on some of those in his *Conveyancing Precedents* and for his kindness in perusing and commenting on them for us.

Mr. Tyler would also like to thank Mr. R. O. Griffith whose careful examination of the manuscript of Chapters 1 to 9 and Chapter 12 has been most valuable, and Mr. J. W. Grey, who has perused and commented upon parts of the manuscript. Finally, we should both like to thank those involved in the preparation of the typescript, in particular Mrs. J. Bennett.

We have endeavoured in this book to state the law as it was at July 1, 1972.

E. G. B.
E. L. G. T.

July, 1972

CONTENTS

Preface v

Table of Cases xi

Table of Statutes xxi

*Table of References to the Law Society's and National Conditions
of Sale* xxxi

1. INTRODUCTORY 1

2. CONTRACT FOR THE SALE OF LAND GENERALLY . . . 8
    I. Existence and Validity of the Contract 8
    II. Statutory Requirements of the Contract 15
    III. Agreements for Leases 24
    IV. Contracts for Sale of Registered Land 24
    V. Variation and Rectification of the Contract . . . 24
    VI. Registration of the Contract 25
    VII. Options 28
    VIII. Estate Agents 31

3. INQUIRIES AND SEARCHES BEFORE CONTRACT . . . 34
    I. Preliminary Inquiries 34
    II. Local Searches and Inquiries of Local Authorities . . 39
    III. Land Charges Searches 43
    IV. Land Registry Search 44
    V. Town and Country Planning 44

4. INFORMAL CONTRACTS FOR THE SALE OF LAND . . . 59
    I. Open Contracts for the Sale of Land made otherwise
        than by Correspondence 59
    II. Open Contracts for the Sale of Land made by Corres-
        pondence 65
    III. Advantages and Disadvantages of an Open Contract . 69

5. FORMAL CONTRACTS FOR SALE OF LAND 71
    I. Particulars of Sale 71
    II. Conditions of Sale 84
    III. Leasehold Enfranchisement 113
    IV. Compulsory Purchase 116

6. INVESTIGATION OF TITLE 119
    I. The Abstract of Title 119
    II. Requisitions 131
    III. The Vendor's Title 136
    IV. Notice and Searches 148
    V. Registered Land 163
    VI. Inspection of the Property 186
    VII. Investigation of Title by Mortgagee . . . 187
    VIII. Investigation of Title to Leaseholds . . . 187

7. EFFECT OF CONTRACT PENDING COMPLETION . . . 189
    I. The Position of the Parties Generally . . . 189
    II. The Effect of the Death of Either Party . . 191
    III. The Effect of the Bankruptcy of Either Party . 192
    IV. Liens of Vendor and Purchaser 193
    V. Sub-Sales 195
    VI. Instalment Sales 196
    VII. Stamp Duty on Contract 197
    VIII. Vendor and Purchaser Summons 198

8. REMEDIES 200

9. COMPLETION 206
    I. Meaning of Completion 206
    II. Preparation and Execution of Conveyance . . 206
    III. Actual Completion 210
    IV. Matters Subsequent to Completion . . . 213
    V. Registration of Title 214

10. CONVEYANCES AND TRANSFERS 221
    I. Unregistered Land: Conveyances 221
    II. Registered Land: Transfers 240
    III. Husband and Wife 243

11. LEASES 245
    I. Agreements for Leases and Leases . . . 245
    II. Implied Terms 248
    III. Express Contents of Leases 252
    IV. Assignments 267
    V. Taxation 269
    VI. Special Cases 270

12. MORTGAGES 292
    I. Form 292
    II. The Contents of a Mortgage 303

III. Second Mortgages 327
IV. Sub-Mortgages 328
V. Registration of Charges 329
VI. Transfer of Mortgages 331
VII. Termination of Mortgages 333
VIII. Use of Mortgages 338
IX. Obtaining the Mortgage 341

13. SETTLEMENTS: GENERAL CONSIDERATIONS 342
I. Settlements of Land 342
II. Trusts of Personalty 345
III. Discretionary Trusts and Protective Trusts . . . 345
IV. Taxation 348

14. STRICT SETTLEMENTS 351
I. Meaning of " Settlement " 351
II. Meaning of " Tenant for Life " and " Statutory Owner " 353
III. The " Trustees of the Settlement " 356
IV. Creation of Settlements 358
V. Powers of Tenant for Life and Statutory Owner . . 361
VI. Change of Ownership 367
VII. Deed of Discharge 369

15. TRUSTS FOR SALE 371
I. Form of Trust for Sale 371
II. The Trusts 371
III. Appointment, Disclaimer and Retirement of Trustees . 372
IV. Sale by Trustees 376
V. Powers of Trustees 378
VI. A Note on Discretionary Trusts 381

16. WILLS 383
I. Reasons for Making a Will 383
II. Capacity 384
III. Formalities 385
IV. Revocation 389
V. Contents of a Will 391
VI. Taxation 398
VII. Incidence of Debts and Estate Duty 399
VIII. Assents 400

APPENDIX: PRECEDENTS 403

Index 445

A*

TABLE OF CASES

ABDULLAH v. Shah 190
Aberfoyle Plantations Ltd. v.
  Cheng (P.C.) 13, 14
Abernethie v. Kleiman (A. M. &
  J.) Ltd. 282
Adams v. Gibney 250
——— v. Taunton 373
Addiscombe Garden Estates Ltd.
  v. Crabbe 282
Ajit v. Sammy 110
Aldin v. Latimer Clark Muir-
  head & Co. 250
Alefounder's Will Trusts, Re ... 359
Allen v. Smith 79
Allhusen v. Whittell 442
Anderton & Milner's Contract,
  Re 246
Andrew v. Bridgman 261
Angel v. Jay 35
Anstee, In b. 386
Appah v. Parncliffe Investments
  Ltd. 17
Arbib and Class's Contract, Re 102
Archer, Re 386
Arlesford and Co. v. Servansingh 269
Arnold v. Arnold 76
Ashburner v. Sewell 80
Ashby, Re 347
Astra Trust v. Adams 13
Atkinson and Horsell's Contract,
  Re 93, 122
Att.-Gen. v. Smith 51
Auerbach v. Nelson 18, 20
Austerberry v. Corporation of
  Oldham 236
Avard, Re 30

BAILEY, Re 385
——— v. Barnes 150
Bain v. Fothergill 203
Baines v. Tweddle 103
Baker and Selmon's Contract, Re 120
Balfour v. Kensington Gardens
  Mansions Ltd. 262
Ballard v. Shutt 106
Ballard's Conveyance, Re 237
Bangor (Bishop of) v. Parry 138
Banister, Re, Broad v. Munton 85,
                                 92, 93
Banks v. Goodfellow 384
——— v. Ripley 235
Bannister v. Bannister 15
Barber v. Wolfe 112, 204
Barclays Bank v. Taylor 299
Barker v. Barker 311
——— v. Illingworth 318
Barleycorn Enterprises Ltd., Re 142

Barr's Contract, Re 110, 111
Barrell, ex p. See Re Parnell.
Barrington v. Lee 32
Barrow v. Isaacs 262, 264
Barry v. Butlin 384
Barsht v. Tagg 107
Basma v. Weekes 18
Bastable, Re 192
Batchelor v. Murphy 30
Bateman v. Hunt 329
Bayley-Worthington and Cohen's
  Contract, Re 106
Baynes & Co. v. Lloyd & Sons 250
Beale's Settlement Trusts, Re ... 345
Beard v. Porter 203
Beardman v. Wilson 261
Beauchamp's Trusts, Re 354
Becker v. Partridge 60, 76, 79
Beckett v. Nurse 21
Beckett's Settlement, Re 380
Beesly v. Hallwood Estates Ltd. 15,
                             26, 208, 209
Belcham and Gawley's Contract,
  Re 75, 80, 81
Belcher and Green v. M'Intosh 257
Bell v. Fothergill 390
——— v. Marsh 72
Bellamy v. Debenham 10, 79
Bendles Motors Ltd. v. Bristol
  Corporation 46
Bennett v. Stone 106, 107
Bentall, Horsley and Baldry v.
  Vicary 33
Bercovitz, In the Estate of 386
Berkeley (Earl), Re 396
Bernays v. Prosser 288
Berridge and Another v. Ward ... 231
Beyfus v. Lodge 79, 89
Beyfus and Masters' Contract, Re 96
Bigg v. Boyd Gibbins Ltd. 8, 10
Biggs v. Hoddinott 312
Billing v. Pill 16
Billyack v. Leyland Construction
  Co. Ltd. 82
Birch v. Paramount Estates Ltd. 82
Birchall, Re 373
Birmingham, Re 192, 193
Birmingham Citizens Permanent
  Building Society v. Caunt ... 323
Birmingham Corporation v. Min-
  ister of Housing and Local
  Government and Habib Ullah 46
Bisset v. Wilkinson 73
Blaiberg v. Keeves 71
Blaiberg and Abraham's Con-
  tract, Re 310
Blewitt, In the Goods of 388
Bligh v. Martin 200

A**

Bolton v. London School Board   123
Bolton Partners v. Lambert   12
Bonnewell v. Jenkins   12
Booth, Re   390
Borman v. Griffith 233, 253
Born v. Turner   319
Bottomley v. Bannister   82
Bowes-Lyon v. Green   283
Bowman v. Hyland   104
Boyle's Claim, Re   173
Bracey v. Read   282
Bradley v. Carritt   312
Bramwell's Contract, Re ... 95, 199
Branca v. Cobarro   12
Brandon v. Robinson   346
Bravda, In the Estate of, Bravda
  v. Bravda   388
Braybrooks v. Whaley   203
Breed v. Cluett   83
Brew Brothers v. Snax (Ross) ...   257
Brewer and Hanken's Contract,
  Re   80
Brewer Street Investments v.
  Barclays Woollen Co.   194
Bridges v. Mees   190
Bridgett and Hayes' Contract, Re   368
Brine and Davies' Contract, Re   76,
                           79, 93, 199
British and Benningtons Ltd. v.
  N.W. Cachar Tea Co.   25
Brocklesby v. Temperance Build-
  ing Society   333
Brooke v. Pearson   347
Brown v. Gould 19, 30
—— v. Liverpool Corporation ...   251
—— v. Raphael   73
Brunner v. Greenslade   238
Bryant and Barningham's Con-
  tract, Re 91, 119
Brynlea Property Investments
  Ltd. v. Ramsay   113
Buchanan-Wollaston's Convey-
  ance, Re   377
Buckinghamshire County Council
  v. Callingham   46
Budd-Scott v. Daniel   250
Bull v. Hutchens   151
Burgess v. Cox 19, 20, 21
Burrell and Kinnard v. Att.-Gen.   349
Burroughs-Fowler, Re   347
Burt v. Claude Cousins and Co.
  Ltd.   32
Buswell v. Goodwin   251
Butcher v. Nash   18
Butler v. Mountview Estates Ltd.   96,
                               97, 229
Button's Lease, Re 28, 30

CABELLERO v. Henty   101
Calgary & Edmonton Land Co.
  Ltd. v. Discount Bank (Over-
  seas) Ltd.   27
Canas Property Co. Ltd. v. K. L.
  Television Services   264
Caney v. Leith   13
Capital Finance Co. Ltd. v.
  Stokes 194, 296, 303, 330

Capital Investments Ltd. v. Wed-
  nesfield U.D.C. 117, 154
Carlish v. Salt   78
Carter v. Butcher   6
Carter and Kenderdine's Con-
  tract, Re   148
Castellain v. Preston   190
Castle v. Wilkinson   75
Catling, Re   354
—— v. King   18
Cato v. Thompson   80
Caunce v. Caunce 147, 148, 150
Cavalier v. Pope   82
Chalcraft, In b. 385, 387
Chaney v. Maclow   11
Chaproniere v. Lambert 23, 245
Charterbridge Corpn. Ltd. v.
  Lloyds Bank Ltd.   301
Chatsworth Properties Ltd. v.
  Effiom   315
Chatterly v. Nicholls   12
Cheshire County Council v.
  Woodward   46
Chesterfield, Re   442
Chillingworth v. Esche ... 12, 13, 32,
                                   89
Chowood v. Lyall   173
Church of England Building
  Society v. Piskor   303
City and Westminster Properties
  (1934) Ltd. v. Mudd   15
City Permanent Building Society
  v. Miller   170
Cityland and Property (Holdings)
  Ltd. v. Dabrah ... 306, 307, 308,
                        311, 338, 432
Claridge v. Tingey. See Re Sea
  View Gardens.
Clark, Re   385
—— v. Barnes   233
Clarke v. Hall   290
—— v. Ramuz   189
Clarkson v. Henderson   307
Clayton v. Blakey   247
—— v. Clayton   65
—— v. Leech   74
Clifton v. Palumbo   8
Coats Patons (Retail) Ltd. v.
  Birmingham Corporation   42
Cockwell v. Romford Sanitary
  Steam Laundry Ltd.   31
Cohen v. Roche 19, 20
Coleman, In the Estate of   389
——, Re   347
Coleshill & District Investment
  Co. Ltd. v. Minister of Housing
  and Local Government   46
Colling, Re   385
Collins Will Trusts, Re   394
Compton v. Bagley   65
Conquest v. Ebbetts   258
Cook, In the Estate of   385
—— v. Greendon Investments ...   305
—— v. Taylor   97
Cooke v. Soltau   131
Coombs v. Wilkes   18
Coope v. Ridout   12
Cooper v. Critchley   17
—— v. Phibbs   200

Copelin's Contract, Re 63
Cordell v. Second Clanfield Pro-
    perties 235
Cordingley v. Cheesborough ... 96
Coslake v. Till 109
Costagliola v. Bunting 290
Cottrill v. Steyning and Little-
    hampton Building Society 203
Cowley v. Watts 18
Cox and Neve's Contract, Re ... 59,
                                        149
Craddock Bros. v. Hunt 25
Cradock v. Scottish Provident
    Institution 297
Craig, Re 385
Craven Settled Estates, Re 365
Cromwell Property Investment
    Co. v. Western and Toovey ... 333
Cruse v. Mount 251
Crusoe d. Blencowe v. Bugby ... 261
Cuckmere Brick Co. Ltd. v.
    Mutual Finance Ltd. 320
Cumberland Consolidated Hold-
    ings Ltd. v. Ireland 97, 189
Cumberland Court (Brighton)
    Ltd. v. Taylor 111, 223, 294,
                                        336
Cunard's Trustees v. Inland Rev-
    enue Commissioners 396
Cunliffe v. Goodman 285
Curling v. Austin 95
Curtis Moffat Ltd. v. Wheeler ... 13,
                                        195

DADDS, In the Goods of ... 390, 391
Dances Way, West Town, Hay-
    ling Island, Re 170, 171, 172
Daniel, Re 204
Daniels v. Trefusis 19, 23
Dartstone v. Cleveland Petroleum
    Co. 155
Davey v. Harrow Corporation ... 231
David v. Sabin 228
Davies, In b. 389, 391
—— v. Davies 249
—— v. Sweet 18
Davstone Estates Ltd.'s Leases,
    Re 257
Davy v. Turner 307
Day v. Singleton 203
De Lassalle v. Guildford 14
De Soysa v. De Pless Pol 246
De Visme v. De Visme 106
Dearle v. Hall 169, 213
Debenham and Mercer's Con-
    tract, Re 87
Deighton and Harris' Contract,
    Re 104
Delaney v. Smith 22
Dellafiora v. Lester 32
Dennis Reed Ltd. v. Goody ... 32, 33
Dewar v. Mintoft 20
D'Eyncourt v. Gregory 16
Diamond v. Campbell-Jones 203
Dibble (H.E.) Ltd. v. Moore ... 16
Dimes v. Scott 442
Dimmock v. Hallett 77
District Bank Ltd. v. Luigi Grill 80
—— v. Webb 305

Dixon v. Solicitor to the Trea-
    sury 391
—— v. Winch 333
Doe d. Rigg v. Bell 247
—— d. Wetherell v. Bird 260
—— d. Mitchinson v. Carter ... 263
—— d. Musto v. Gladwin 260
—— d. Bish v. Keeling 260
—— d. Wright v. Manifold 387
—— d. Harris v. Masters 263
—— d. Gatehouse v. Rees 267
Doland's Will Trusts, Re 388
Dolphin's Conveyance, Re ... 147, 238
Don Lodge Motel Ltd. v. Inver-
    cargil Licensing Trust 25
D'Oyley Downs Ltd. v. Galloway 19
Drake v. Gray 237
Drax, Re 307, 433
Drewery v. Ware-Lane 33
D'Silva v. Lister House Develop-
    ment Ltd. 15, 208, 209, 245
Du Sautoy v. Symes 26, 27, 28,
                                30, 159
Duce and Boots Cash Chemists
    (Southern) Ltd.'s Contract, Re 137
Duddell v. Simpson 103
Dudley and District Benefit
    Building Society v. Gordon ... 326
Dunn v. Blackdown Properties
    Ltd. 415
Durance, In the Goods of 390
Duthy and Jesson's Contract, Re 64
Dutton v. Bognor Regis U.D.C. 82

EAGON v. Dent 27, 30, 212
East Barnet U.D.C. v. British
    Transport Commission 46
Eastern Telegraph Co. v. Dent 262
Eastwood v. Ashton 230
Ebbetts v. Conquest 258
Eccles v. Bryant 10, 12, 15
—— v. Cheyne 394
Eckersley v. Platt 390
Edler v. Auerbach 77
Egerton v. Esplanade Hotels
    (London) 265
Egmont (Earl of) v. Smith 190, 195
Elias v. Mitchell 17, 181
Elliott and H. Elliott (Builders)
    Ltd. v. Pierson 202
Ellis v. Rowbotham 107
Elliston v. Reacher 238
Engall's Agreement, Re 27, 110
Engell v. Fitch 97, 203
Englefield Holdings Ltd. and Sin-
    clair's Contract, Re ... 77, 79, 96
Erskine's Settlement Trusts, Re ... 379
Esdaile v. Stephenson 106
Essex v. Daniell 112
Essex County Council v. Essex
    Inc. Congregational Church
    Union 57
Esso Petroleum Co. Ltd. v. Har-
    per's Garage (Stourport) Ltd. 312
Ethel and Mitchell and Butler's
    Contract, Re 235
Eva v. Morrow 109
Evans v. Prothero 20

Evans v. Vaughan 250
Evans' Contract, Re 183, 199
Eyre v. Rea 259

Fairclough v. Swan Brewery
  Co. Ltd. 309
Farr, Smith and Co. Ltd. v.
  Messers Ltd. 20
Farrer v. Lacey, Harland and
  Co. 90
Fawcett and Holmes' Contract,
  Re 75
Fawcett Properties Ltd. v. Buck-
  inghamshire County Council ... 49
Fay v. Miller, Wilkins & Co. ... 18, 228
Figgis, Re 397
Filby v. Hounsell 19
Finklekraut v. Monohan 89, 111, 204
Finn, In b. 385
Fitch Lovell v. I.R.C. 195
Flather v. Hood 289
Fletcher v. Ashburner 192
—— v. Lancashire, etc., Pty.
  Co. 106
Flexman v. Corbett 24
Flight v. Bolland 202
—— v. Booth 73, 74, 76, 96
Flinn v. Pountain 201
Flower v. Hartopp 95
Flureau v. Thornhill 203
Ford and Hill, Re 135
Formby v. Barker 237
Forsey and Hollebone's Contract,
  Re 39, 43, 80
Four-maids Ltd. v. Dudley Mar-
  shall (Properties) Ltd. 323
Fox v. Swann 263
Freeman v. Pope 148
Frend v. Buckley 61
Frewen, Re 354, 355
Frost's Application, Re 114
Furneaux and Aird's Contract, Re 194

Gallenga's Will Trusts, Re 354, 355
Gallie v. Lee. See Saunders v.
  Anglia Building Society.
Gardner v. Blaxill 31
—— v. Coutts & Co. 196
Gartside v. I.R.C. 346, 349
—— v. Silkstone etc. Co. 130
Gavaghan v. Edwards ... 9, 19, 108
Gaze v. Gaze 387
Gee, In b. 386
George Wimpey & Co. v. Sohn.
  See Wimpey (George) & Co.
  v. Sohn.
Georgiades v. Edward Wolfe &
  Co. Ltd. 153
Gibson, In the Estate of 387
Gilchester Properties Ltd. v.
  Gomm 15, 35, 36, 77
Gilliat v. Gilliat 88
Gilligan, In the Goods of 390
Gissing v. Gissing 147, 244
Gladstone v. Bower 289
Glass v. Kencakes 265

Gloag and Miller's Contract, Re 80, 105
Goddard's Case 221
Goldberg v. Edwards 233
Golden Bread Co. v. Hemmings 189, 190
Goldsmith (F.) (Sicklemere) v.
  Baxter 18
Goody v. Baring 3, 38
Gordon-Cumming v. Houlds-
  worth 72
Gosling v. Woolf 60
Goss v. Nugent 21, 25
Grace Rymer Investments Ltd.
  v. Waite 303, 316
Graham & Scott (Southgate) Ltd.
  v. Oxlade 13, 32
Grand Junction Co. Ltd. v. Bates 294
Grangeside Properties Ltd. v.
  Collingwoods Securities Ltd. 293
Gray v. Fowler 102
Great Western Ry. v. Fisher ... 229
Greater London Council v. Con-
  nolly 256
Greaves v. Tofield 201
Green v. Sevin 110
—— v. Whitehead 127, 138
Greenhalgh v. Brindley 79
Greenwood v. Turner 202
Gregson v. Cyril Lord Ltd. 285
Griffiths v. Young ... 10, 15, 19, 21
Grindell v. Bass 20
Grist v. Bailey 200
Groffman, Re 387
Grover & Grover Ltd. v.
  Mathews 191
Gutteridge v. Munyard 257

Hadley v. Baxendale 203
Haedicke and Lipski's Contract,
  Re 79
Hailes and Hutchinson's Con-
  tract, Re 120
Halifax Building Society v.
  Keighley 312
Hall v. Burnell 112, 203
—— v. Heward 331
—— v. Meyrick 390
Hall & Co. Ltd. v. Shoreham-
  by-Sea Urban District Council 49
Hamilton-Snowball's Conveyance,
  Re 190
Hampshire v. Wickens 24, 246
Hancock v. Brazier (B. W.)
  (Anerley) Ltd. 81, 82, 212
Hanley Theatre of Varieties v.
  Broadbent 306
Harari's Settlement Trusts, Re ... 378
Harding v. Metropolitan Ry. ... 192
Hare v. Nicoll 31
Hargreaves and Thompson's Con-
  tract, Re 199
Hargreaves Transport Ltd. v.
  Lynch 14
Harmes v. Hinkson 384
Harold Wood Brick Co. v.
  Ferris 109, 112
Harris' Settlement, Re 380

Harrison *v.* Wells 222
Hart, *Re, ex p.* Green 148
—— *v.* Rogers 259
Harvey *v.* Facey 8
—— *v.* Pratt 24
Hasham *v.* Zenab 110, 201
Havens *v.* Middleton 260
Hawkesworth *v.* Turner 17
Hawkins *v.* Price 19
Haynes, *Re* 365
Haywood *v.* Brunswick Building
  Society 237
Hazle's Settled Estates, *Re* 354
Heath *v.* Crealock 223
Hedley Byrne & Co. Ltd. *v.*
  Heller & Partners Ltd. 31, 35
Henshall *v.* Fogg 108
Henthorn *v.* Fraser 9
Hetling and Merton's Contract,
  Re 106
Hewitt's Contract, *Re* 106, 107
Hewson *v.* Shelley 138
Heywood *v.* B.D.C. Properties
  Ltd. 27
—— *v.* —— (No. 2) 151
Hickman *v.* Peacey 131
High Street, Deptford, No. 139,
  Re 173
Highett and Bird's Contract, *Re* 62,
                          96, 100, 206
Higinbotham *v.* Holmes 347
Hill *v.* Barclay 264
—— *v.* Hill 20, 30
Hillingdon Estates Co. *v.* Stone-
  field Estates Ltd. 97, 190
Hinckley and Country Building
  Society *v.* Henny 326
Hissett *v.* Reading Roofing Co.
  Ltd. 97, 212, 213
Hodgens *v.* Keen 90
Hodgson *v.* Marks 171, 187
Hoffman *v.* Fineberg 265
Holland, *Re* 20, 391
—— *v.* Hodgson 16
Hollington Bros. Ltd. *v.* Rhodes 15, 27
Holloway *v.* York 193
Holmes *v.* Penney 347
Holyland *v.* Lewin 394
Hoole *v.* Smith 319
Hooper *v.* Bourne 116
Hopgood *v.* Brown 72, 230
Hopkins' Lease, *Re* 255
Hopwood *v.* Hough 197
Horgan, *Re* 392
Horton *v.* Kurzke 202
Hoskins *v.* Woodham 82
Houlder Bros. & Co. Ltd. *v.*
  Gibbs 262
Howe *v.* Smith 89, 204
Hoyle, *Re* 20
Hudson *v.* Temple 109
Hughes *v.* Parker 76, 78
—— *v.* Waite 316
Hulme *v.* Brigham 16
Hunt *v.* Luck 186
Hunt (Charles) Ltd. *v.* Palmer 76, 89

Hussey *v.* Horne-Payne 10, 13
Hutton *v.* Watling 17, 29
Hyde *v.* Wrench 9

IDEAL FILM RENTING CO. *v.*
  Nielsen 262
I.R.C. *v.* Bernstein 380
Inns, *Re* 345
Introductions Ltd., *Re* 301
Irani Finance Ltd. *v.* Singh ... 17, 151
Iron Trades Employers' Insurance
  Association Ltd. *v.* Union Land
  and House Investors Ltd. 315
Itter, *In b.* 388
Ives (E.R.) Investments Ltd. *v.*
  High 12, 156

J. W. CAFÉS LTD. *v.* Brownlow
  Trust Ltd. 203
Jackson *v.* Jackson 377
Jackson and Haden's Contract,
  Re 102, 103, 104
Jackson and Woodburn's Con-
  tract, *Re* 199
Jacobs *v.* Revell 74, 89, 93, 96
James Macara Ltd. *v.* Barclay.
  See Macara (James) Ltd. *v.*
  Barclay.
Jameson, *Re* 391
—— *v.* Kinmel Bay Land Co.
  Ltd. 17, 213
Jaques *v.* Lloyd D. George and
  Partners 33
Jared *v.* Clements 150
Jarvis *v.* Jarvis 17
Jeff's Transfer, *Re* (No. 2) 237
Jelbert *v.* Davis 140
Jenkins *v.* Gaisford 385
Jenner *v.* Jenner 224
Jennings *v.* Tavener 81
Jennings' Trustee *v.* King 193
Joel *v.* Montgomery & Taylor ... 105
Johnson *v.* Humphrey 108
Johnson and Tustin, *Re* 64, 124
Johnston *v.* Boyes 90, 211
Johnstone *v.* Holdway 235
Joliffe *v.* Baker 74
Jones *v.* Challenger 377
—— *v.* Gardiner 203
—— *v.* Herxheimer 259
—— *v.* King 229
—— *v.* Lipman 119, 201
—— *v.* Mudd 105
Jopling *v.* I.R.C. 138
Joscelyne *v.* Nissen 25
Joyner *v.* Weeks 259
Judd and Poland and Skelcher's
  Contract, *Re* 100

KAMMINS BALLROOMS CO. LTD.
  v. Zenith Investments (Tor-
  quay) Ltd. 284
Keeble and Stillwell's Fletton
  Brick Co., *Re* 105
Keeves *v.* Dean 272

Keller (Samuel) Holdings Ltd. v.
  Martins Bank Ltd. 333
Kemp v. Lester 326
Kempthorne, Re 31
Kennewell v. Dye 31
Kenny v. Preen 250
Kent County Council v. Ken-
  worthy. See Kingsway Invest-
  ments (Kent) Ltd. v. Kent C.C.
Kent County Council v. Kings-
  way Investments (Kent) Ltd.
  See Kingsway Investments
  (Kent) Ltd. v. Kent County
  Council.
Kestell v. Langmaid 290
Kimbers & Co. v. I.R.C. 214
Kine v. Balfe 245
King, Re 175
King, Re, Robinson v. Gray 260, 269
—— v. O'Shee 15
—— v. Victor Parsons & Co. ... 82
King's Will Trusts, Re 34, 401
Kingsway Investments (Kent) Ltd.
  v. Kent County Council 49
Kingswood Estate Co. Ltd. v.
  Anderson 23, 245
Kirby v. Harrogate School Board 116
Kitcat v. King 389
Kitchin, Re, ex p. Punnett 327
Knibbs, In the Estate of 389
Knight Sugar Co. v. The Alberta
  Railway and Irrigation Co. ... 213
Knightsbridge Estates Trusts Ltd.
  v. Byrne 309, 312
Koenigsblatt v. Sweet 19
Kreglinger v. New Patagonia
  Meat & Cold Storage Co. Ltd. 311
Kuypers, Re 391

LACE v. Chantler 253, 255
Ladyman v. Wirral Estates Ltd. 253
Lake v. Bennett 278
—— v. Bushby 38
Lancashire & Yorkshire Rever-
  sionary Interest Co. Ltd. v.
  Crowe 317
La Salle Recreations v. Canadian
  Camdex Investments 17
Lavery v. Pursell 17, 18
Lawes v. Bennett 31
Lawrence v. Cassel 212
Lee v. Barrey 217
—— v. Gaskell 17
—— v. Rayson 77, 95
Lee-Parker v. Izzet (No. 2) 14
Leeman v. Stocks 11, 19
Leeming, Re 392
Leigh v. Taylor 16, 17
Leighton's Conveyance, Re 173
Lester v. Foxcroft 22
Letterstedt v. Broers 376
Lever Finance Ltd. v. Needle-
  man's Property Trustee 213, 299,
                               315, 318
—— v. Westminster (City) Lon-
  don Borough Council 46
Levy v. Stogdon 202

Lewis v. Brass 9
—— v. Harries 113
—— v. Love (Frank) Ltd. 312
—— v. Plunket 65, 338
Lewis & Son (Jenkin, R.) v.
  Kerman 290
Lindsay and Forder's Contract,
  Re 72, 75
Lipman Wallpapers Ltd. v.
  Mason & Hodghton Ltd. 14
Lister v. Lane 257
Lloyd, Re 297
—— v. Stanbury 203
Lloyds Bank Ltd. v. Margolis 306, 318
Lock v. Bell 109
—— v. Pearce 265
Lockett v. Norman Wright 12
Lockharts Ltd. v. Bernard Rosen
  & Co. 62, 97
London and Cheshire Insurance
  Co. Ltd. v. Laplagrene Property
  Co. Ltd. ... 171, 186, 193, 194, 225
London and County (A. & D.)
  Ltd. v. Wilfred Sportsman Ltd. 144,
                                   269
London and County Banking Co.
  v. Goddard 297
London and South Western Ry.
  Co. v. Gomm 29
London Corporation v. Cusack-
  Smith 57
London County and Westminster
  Bank v. Tompkins 297
London County Freehold and
  Leasehold Properties Ltd. v.
  Berkeley Property and Invest-
  ment Co. Ltd. 35
London Investment etc. Co. v.
  Ember Estates 76, 78
Londonderry's Settlement, Re ... 382
Long, In the Estate of 386
—— v. Miller 20
Longlands Farm, Re 14, 28
Longmuir v. Kew 30
Lord and Fullerton's Contract,
  Re 373
Lovesy v. Palmer 18
Low v. Fry 22, 89
Lowe v. Hope 89, 204
Lower v. Sorrell 289
Lurcott v. Wakeley 257
Lynch v. Thorne 82
Lyne-Stephens and Scott-Miller's
  Contract, Re 190
Lysaght v. Edwards 189

MACARA (JAMES) LTD. v. Barclay 97
McCarrick v. Liverpool Corpora-
  tion 251
McCarthy & Stone Ltd. v. Hodge
  (Julian S.) & Co. Ltd. 325
Mackreth v. Symmons 193
Maclay v. Dixon 272
McManus v. Cooke 23
McPhail v. Doulton 381
Maddison v. Alderson 23
Mahon v. Ainscough 36

Makin v. Watkinson 259
Malins v. Freeman 202
Mallot v. Wilson 373
Manchester Diocesan Council for
    Education v. Commercial and
    General Investments Ltd. ... 9, 10
Manchester Ship Canal Co. v.
    Manchester Racecourse Co. ... 28
Manfield & Sons Ltd. v. Botchin 282
Manning v. Turner 143
Manser v. Back 75
Maples v. I.R.C. 195
Margravine of Anspach v. Noel 135
Markham v. Paget 250
Marks v. Board 13
—— v. Lilley 109, 201
Marquess of Zetland v. Driver 237
Marsden v. Heyes (Edward) Ltd. 249
Marsh and Earl Granville, Re 79,
    92, 202
Marshall v. Taylor 231
Marten v. Flight Refuelling Ltd. 146
Maskell v. Ivory 202
Matthews (C. & M.) Ltd. v.
    Marsden Building Society 322
May v. Belville 208, 234
Mayo, Re 375
Mayson v. Clouet 90, 197
Mendl v. Smith 307
Merrett and Schuster, Re 104
Micklethwaite v. Newlay Bridge
    Co. 231
Midland Railway Co.'s Agree-
    ment, Re 254
Miles v. Bull 157
—— v. —— (No. 2) 15
Miller v. Cannon Hill Estates
    Ltd. 81
Mills, Re 391
Milner v. Staffordshire Congrega-
    tional Union 138
Ministry of Housing and Local
    Government v. Sharp 42, 56
Mint v. Good 250
Mitchell v. Beacon Estates (Fins-
    bury Park) Ltd. 79
Molton Finance Co. Ltd., Re ... 330
Molyneux v. Hawtrey 76, 79
Monnickendam v. Leanse...12, 22, 89
Monro v. Taylor 190
Montacute (Viscountess) v. Max-
    well 22
Monti v. Barnes 16
Moore v. Frowd 381
Moore and Hulm's Contract, Re 334
Morgan v. Liverpool Corporation 251
—— v. Milman 19
Morgan's Lease, Re 9
Moritz v. Knowles 25
Morris v. Baron & Co. ....
Moss Empires Ltd. v. Olympia
    (Liverpool) Ltd. 259
Moxon's Will Trusts, Re 380
Muller v. Trafford 29, 30
Mumford v. Collier 326
Mumford Hotels Ltd. v. Wheler 260
Musgrave, Re 354

NAAS v. Westminster Bank Ltd. 208,
    209
Nash v. Wooderson 76
Nathan, Re, ex p. Stapleton 193
National Provincial Bank Ltd. v.
    Ainsworth 147, 171, 186
—— v. Allen 17, 151
—— v. Hastings Car Mart Ltd. 186
National Provincial Bank and
    Marsh, Re 93
Neale v. Merrett 9
Newton v. Clarke 387
Nichols v. Walters 144
Nichols and Von Joel's Contract,
    Re 199
Nisbet and Pott's Contract, Re 70
    122, 149, 237
Nives v. Nives 193
Noakes & Co. Ltd. v. Rice 312
North v. Loomes 19, 21
Northchurch Estates Ltd. v.
    Daniels 255
Northern Counties of England
    Fire Insurance Co. v. Whipp 149
Norwich Union Life Insurance
    Society v. Preston 97
Nottidge v. Dering 229
Nottingham Patent Brick and
    Tile Co. v. Butler 79, 93
Nye (C.L.) Ltd., Re 330

OAK CO-OPERATIVE BUILDING
    SOCIETY v. Blackburn ... 158, 159
Oakes v. Commissioner of Stamp
    Duties of New South Wales ... 348
Oates v. Frith 256
Ogilvie v. Foljambe 18
Olney v. Bates 394
Ossemsley Estates Ltd., Re ... 76, 78
Otto v. Bolton 82
Owen, Re 297

PAGE v. Midland Ry. Co. 229
Paget v. Marshall 200
Paget's Settled Estates, Re 365
Pain v. Coombs 245
Paine v. Meller 190
Palin v. Ponting 386
Palmer v. Johnson 74, 96, 212
—— v. Lark 105
Parfitt v. Lawless 385
Parkash v. Irani Finance Ltd. ... 182,
    300, 336
Parker v. Clark 23
—— v. Judkin 228
—— v. Taswell 247
Parkus v. Greenwood 255
Parnell, Re ex p. Barrell 193
Patman v. Harland 62
Patrick and Lyon Ltd., Re 142
Pattle v. Anstruther 18
Pawley and London Provincial
    Bank, Re 146
Pawson v. Revell 314, 316
Payne v. Cardiff R.D.C. 39, 318
—— v. Cave 8, 88

Pearce v. Bastable's Trustee 192
—— v. Bulteel 148
—— v. Gardner 20
Pearlberg v. May 107
Pearson, Re 389, 393
Peat v. Gresham Trust Ltd. 142
Peck v. Anicar Properties Ltd. 114, 278

Peck and The School Board for London's Contract, Re 233
Pemsel and Wilson v. Tucker ... 79
Penn v. Dunn 157
Penniall v. Harborne 260
Perry v. Sharon Development Co. Ltd. 81
—— v. Suffields Ltd. 10
Pettit, Re 396
—— v. Pettit 147, 244
Phillips v. Butler 11
—— v. Lamdin 109, 189
—— v. Silvester 189
Pilkington v. I.R.C. 380
—— v. Wood 228
Pimms v. Tallow Chandlers Company 262
Plant v. Bourne 18
Plews v. Samuel 107
Pooley, Re 388
Pope v. Westacott 211
Portman Building Society v. Gallwey 323
Poster v. Slough Estates Ltd. ... 156
Potter v. Duffield 18
Powell v. Marshall Parkes & Co. 109, 192

Power, Re 379
Practice Direction (1953) 386
Premor Ltd. v. Shaw Brothers ... 305
Proctor v. Pugh 102, 104
Propert v. Parker 246
Property and Bloodstock Ltd. v. Emerton 13, 318
Prytherch v. Williams 331
Public Trustee v. Lawrence 316, 319
—— v Pearlberg 102, 203
Puckett and Smith's Contract, Re 80, 81
Pulbrook v. Lawes 22
Punnett, Ex p. See Kitchen, Re.
Pyke v. Peters 336

Quinion v. Horne 102

R. v. Minister of Housing and Local Government, ex p. Chichester R.D.C. 57
Rafferty v. Schofield 190
Rawlinson v. Ames 23, 245
Rawlplug Co. Ltd. v. Kamvale Properties Ltd. 27
Rayleigh Weir Stadium, Re 26, 154
Rayner v. Preston 190
Refuge Assurance Co. Ltd. v. Pearlberg 323
Regent Oil Co. Ltd. v. Gregory (J. A.) (Hatch End) Ltd. 326

Reid v. Dawson 288
Reohorn v. Barry Corporation ... 285
Reynold's Will Trusts, Re 394
Rhodes v. Dalby 314, 316
Richards v. Phillips 88
—— v. Powell 10
Richards (A.) Builders Ltd. v. White 82
Richardson, Re 333
Rider v. Ford 29
Ridley v. Osler 74, 77
Riggs, Re, ex p. Lovell 263
Riley to Streatfield, Re 107
Riley v. Troll 12
Roberts v. Leicestershire County Council 25
Robertson's Application, Re 114
Rochefoucauld v. Boustead 22
Rochford v. Hackman 346
Rogers v. Hosegood 237
—— v. Rice 265
Rose v. Watson 194
Rossdale v. Denny 12
Rossiter v. Miller 12, 18
Rourke v. Robinson 338
Rousou v. Photi 251
Routledge v. Grant 8
Rowland, Re 131, 395
Royal Victoria Pavilion, Ramsgate, Re 237
Royce's Will Trusts, Re 388
Rudd v. Lascelles 74, 81
Rugby School Governors v. Tannahill 265
Russ and Brown's Contract, Re 76
Russel, In b. 390
—— v. Russel 296
Russell v. Archdale 146, 237
Rutherford v. Acton-Adams ... 74
—— v. Maurer 288
—— v. Rutherford 156, 157
Ryan v. Pilkington 32
Rye v. Rye 252

Sainsbury v. Inland Revenue Commissioners 346, 349
Sallis v. Jones 390
Salt v. Marquis of Northampton 312
Samuel v. Jarrah Timber and Wood Paving Corpn. Ltd. ... 312
Sandbach and Edmondson's Contract, Re 93, 199
Sands to Thompson, Re 334
Saner v. Bilton 250
Sanson v. Rhodes 108
Sarson v. Roberts 251
Saunders v. Anglia Building Society 200
Schaeffer v. Schuhmann 383
Scheggia v. Gradwell 32
Schlisselman v. Rubin 77
Scott v. Bradley 19, 21
Scott and Alvarez's Contract, Re 63, 89, 92
Scott and Coutts and Co. v. I.R.C. 349
Sea View Gardens, Re 173

Seddon v. North Eastern Salt Co. Ltd. 35
Segal Securities Ltd. v. Thoseby 267
Selkirk v. Romar Investments Ltd. 19, 102, 103
Selwyn v. Garfit 319
Sharman and Meade's Contract, Re 230
Sharman's Will Trust, Re 373
Sharp v. Coates 26, 154
Sheggia v. Gradwell. See Scheggia v. Gradwell.
Shell-Mex and B.P. Ltd. v. Manchester Garages Ltd. 282
Shepherd v. Croft 80, 81
Sherwin v. Shakespear 106
Shiloh Spinners Ltd. v. Harding 26, 154, 156
Shires v. Glascock 387
Shuttleworth v. Clews 112, 204
Sidney v. Buddery 79
Sikes, Re 394
Sim v. Griffiths 15
Simpson v. Foxon 389
―― v. Geoghegan 335, 336
―― v. Sadd 135
Skelton v. Younghouse 30
Smallman v. Smallman 13
Smart, In b. 386
Smiley v. Townshend 259
Smith v. Barton 31
―― v. City Petroleum Co. Ltd. 16
―― v. Hamilton ... 89, 109, 110, 204
―― v. Jones (1952) 19
―― v. ―― (1954) 186
―― v. Land and House Property Corpn. 76
―― v. Mansi ... 3, 8, 10, 15, 18, 19, 87
―― v. Marrable 251
―― v. Morgan 9, 19, 30
―― v. Smith 387
Smith and Olley v. Townsend 13, 78
Smith's Lease, Re, Smith v. Richards 262
Soper v. Arnold 89
Sopher v. Mercer 311
South African Territories v. Wallington 187
Southby v. Hutt 135
Southerden, In the Estate of ... 391
Sparrow and James' Contract, Re 230
Spector v. Ageda 305
Spencer and Hauser's Contract, Re 91, 120
Spencer Cooper, Re 400, 441
Spencer's Case 268
Spiller v. Bolton 78
Spindler and Mear's Contract, Re 102
Spoor v. Green 229
Spottiswoode, Ballantyne & Co. Ltd. v. Doreen Appliances Ltd. 12
Spracklan's Estate, Re 390
Standard Pattern Co. Ltd. v. Ivey 264
Starr-Bowkett Building Society and Sibun's Contract, Re 103
Stephens v. Taprell 390
Stickney v. Keeble 65, 109
Stilwell v. Blackman 238

Stirrup's Contract, Re 230
Stock v. Wanstead and Woodford B.C. 42, 56
Stockloser v. Johnson 197
Stokes v. Whicher 20
Stone and Saville's Contract, Re 120, 199
Strand Securities Ltd. v. Caswell 171, 217
Strode v. Parker 307
Stromdale and Ball Ltd. v. Burden 207
Stroud Building Society v. Delamont 315
Stucley, Re 193, 194
Stylo Shoes v. Prices Tailors ... 284
Suarez, Re 175
Sugden v. Lord St. Leonards ... 391
Surplice v. Farnsworth 259
Sutton v. Sutton 306
Sweet v. Meredith 135
Sweet and Maxwell Ltd. v. Universal News Services Ltd. 24
Sykes, In b. 388
―― v. Giles 11
―― v. Midland Bank Executor and Trustee Co. Ltd. 188
Symes v. Green 384
Syrett v. Egerton 311

Tamplin v. James 200, 202
Tanner v. Smith 102
Tanqueray-Willaume and Landau, Re 102, 145
Taunton & West of England Perpetual Benefit Building Society and Robert's Contract, Re ... 62
Taylor v. Ellis 315
―― v. Taylor 151, 154
Terrene Ltd. v. Nelson 78
Terry and White's Contract, Re 74, 96
Texaco Ltd. v. Mulberry Filling Station Ltd. 312
Thatcher v. Pearce (C. H.) & Sons (Contractors) Ltd. 264
Thirkell v. Cambi 20
Thomas v. Dering 75
―― v. Jones 384
―― v. Kensington 204
―― v. Rose 26, 153, 154
Thompson v. McCullough 209
―― v. Salah 315
Thompson and Cotterell's Contract, Re 76
Thomson's Mortgage Trusts, Re 322
Thorn v. Dickins 385
Thorne v. Heard and Marsh ... 150
Tickner v. Buzzacott 267
Tilley v. Thomas 109
Timmins v. Moreland Street Property Co. Ltd. 18, 20, 21, 76
Tollhurst v. Associated Portland Cement Manufacturing (1900) Ltd. 195
Torrance v. Bolton 71
Tredegar v. Harwood 260, 262
Treloar v. Bigge 262
Tulk v. Moxhay 237

Turley v. Mackay 26, 154
Turner v. Forwood 224
——— v. Moon 229
——— v. Smith 333
Turner's Will Trusts, Re 379

UNION OF LONDON AND SMITH'S
  BANK LTD.'S CONVEYANCE, Re,
  Miles v. Easter 237, 238
United Dominions Trust Ltd. v.
  Kirkwood 305
United Realisation Co. v. I.R.C. 296
United States of America v.
  Motor Trucks Ltd. 25
Usher's Brewery Ltd. v. King
  (P. S.) & Co. (Finance) Ltd. 144, 294

VAN PRAAGH v. Everidge 202
Venn and Furze's Contract, Re 145
Verrall v. Farnes 288
Verrell's Contract, Re 145
Vincent v. Premo Enterprises Ltd. 209
Viscountess Montacute v. Max-
  well 22
Von Hatzfeldt-Wildenburg v.
  Alexander 12

WAKEHAM v. Mackenzie 23
Wakeman, Re 378
Wales v. Carr 187
Walker, In the Estate of 384
Waller v. Waller 147
Wallingford v. Mutual Society ... 307
Wallington v. Townsend 72
Wallis and Barnard, Re 199
Wallis and Grout's Contract, Re 123
Walsh v. Lonsdale 247, 248
Want v. Stallibrass 102
Ward v. Kirkland 233
Waring v. London and Man-
  chester Assurance Co. Ltd. ... 318
Warren v. Keen 250
Watford Corporation and Ware's
  Contract, Re 189
Watkins, Re, Watkins v. Watkins
  (1953) 129
Watson v. Burton 73, 74, 75
Watteau v. Fenwick 31
Wayland, Re 389
Webb, In the Goods of 387
——— v. Bevis (Frank) Ltd. 16
——— v. Pollmount Ltd. 29, 171, 186
Webber v. Minister of Housing
  and Local Government 46
Webster v. Cecil 200
Wedd v. Porter 249
Weg Motors Ltd. v. Hales ... 29, 30
Weinbergs Weatherproofs v. Rad-
  cliffe Paper Mill Co. 283
Weldsted's Will Trusts, Re 378
West v. Gwynne 261
West (Richard) and Partners
  (Inverness) v. Dick 14
West Country Cleaners (Fal-
  mouth) v. Saly 31
Westminster (Duke of) v. Swin-
  ton 265

Weston and Thomas' Contract,
  Re 102
Wheeldon v. Burrows 232, 233
Wheeler v. Mercer 282
White, Re 386
——— v. Bijou Mansions Ltd. 62, 181
——— v. City of London Brewery
  Co. 324
——— v. Metcalf 324
White and Smith's Contract, Re 79
White Rose Cottage, Re 182, 296, 298,
                              300, 322
White's Charities, Re 231
Whitlock's Case 256
Wilkes v. Spooner 149, 237
Wilkinson v. Hall 323
Williams v. Evans 90
——— v. Glenton 106
——— v. Greatrex 108, 202
——— v. Spargo 61
Williams and the Duchess of
  Newcastle's Contract, Re 65
Williamson v. Naylor 393
Willis, Re, ex p. Kennedy 326
Willson v. Greene 230
Wilson v. Kelland 330
——— v. Thomas 93, 199
Wilson and Stevens' Contract, Re 106
Wimpey (George) & Co. Ltd. v.
  Sohn 93
Windsor Refrigerator Co. Ltd. v.
  Branch Nominees Ltd. 209
Wing v. Angrave 131
Wingham, Re 389
Winn v. Bull 12
Wintle v. Nye 385
Wise v. Whitburn 129, 136
Wolf v. Crutchley 114
Woodall v. Clifton 29
Woodhouse & Co. Ltd. v. Kirk-
  land (Derby) Ltd. 140
Woolwich Equitable Building
  Society v. Marshall 27
——— v. Preston 326
Woolworth (F. W.) & Co. Ltd.
  v. Lambert 261
Worthing Corporation v. Heather 29
Wragg v. Lovett 20
Wright, Re, ex p. Landau v.
  The Trustee 263
——— v. Dean 27, 29, 30
——— v. Macadam 253
——— v. Wakeford 385
Wrigley v. Gill 307

XENOS v. Wickham 209

YANDLE & SONS v. Sutton 80
Yeovil Glove Co. Ltd., Re 142
Young v. Ashley Gardens Pro-
  perties Ltd. 262
——— v. Clarey 322
Young and Harston's Contract,
  Re 106

ZIMBLER v. Abrahams 247

TABLE OF STATUTES

1381 Forcible Entry Act (5 Ric.
      2, St. 1, c. 7) ... 263, 322
1391 Forcible Entry Act (15
      Ric. 2, c. 2) 263, 322
1429 Forcible Entry Act (8
      Hen. 6, c. 9) 263, 322
1535 Statute of Uses (27 Hen.
      8, c. 10) 234
1588 Forcible Entry Act (31
      Eliz. 1, c. 11) 263, 322
1623 Forcible Entry Act (21
      Jac. 1, c. 15) 263, 322
1677 Statute of Frauds (29 Car.
      2, c. 3)—
      ss. 1, 2 247
      s. 4 .... 15, 293
1774 Fires Prevention (Metro-
      polis) Act (14 Geo. 3,
      c. 78) 191
      s. 83 191
1835 Statutory Declarations Act
      (5 & 6 Will. 4, c. 62) 95
1837 Wills Act (7 Will. 4, c. 26 384
                          et seq.
      s. 7 384
      s. 9 .... 385, 386, 387
      s. 11 389
      ss. 15–17 388
      s. 18 390
      s. 20 .... 389, 390
      s. 21 388
      s. 22 391
      s. 24 394
      ss. 25, 32 393
      s. 33 .... 393, 397
1838 Small Tenements Recovery
      Act (1 & 2 Vict. c. 74) 326
1845 Land Clauses Consolida-
      tion Act (8 & 9 Vict.
      c. 18)—
      s. 6 116
      ss. 18, 75, 77, 84, 85 ... 117
      ss. 108 et seq. 117
      Real Property Act (8 & 9
      Vict. c. 106)—
      s. 3 .... 247, 248
      Satisfied Terms Act (8 & 9
      Vict. c. 112) 334
1852 Wills Act Amendment Act
      (15 & 16 Vict. c. 24) 386
      Common Law Procedure
      Act (15 & 16 Vict.
      c. 76)—
      s. 210 263
      s. 212 264
1860 Lord Cranworth's Act (23
      & 24 Vict. c. 145) ... 317
1867 Sale of Land by Auction
      Act (30 & 31 Vict.
      c. 48)—
      ss. 5, 6 88

1867 Policies of Assurance Act
      (30 & 31 Vict. c. 144) 301
1870 Apportionment Act (33 &
      34 Vict. c. 35)—
      s. 2 107
1873 Supreme Court of Judica-
      ture Act (36 & 37
      Vict. c. 66)—
      s. 25 (7) 109
          (11) 247
1874 Building Societies Act (37
      & 38 Vict. c. 42)—
      s. 42 334
      Vendor and Purchaser Act
      (37 & 38 Vict. c. 79) 60,
                          123
      s. 2 60
      s. 9 198
1875 Friendly Societies Act (38
      & 39 Vict. c. 60) ... 334
      Land Transfer Act (38 &
      39 Vict. c. 87) 164
1878 Bills of Sale Act (41 & 42
      Vict. c. 31) 326
1881 Conveyancing Act (44 &
      45 Vict. c. 41) ... 225, 235,
                          295, 310
      s. 3 (1) 61
          (3) 63
      s. 4 .... 321, 324
      s. 6 233
      s. 9 238
      s. 13 60
      s. 15 335
      s. 17 325
      s. 18 314
      s. 19 .... 312, 317
      s. 21 (3) 322
      s. 30 146
      s. 46 125
      s. 62 234
1882 Settled Land Act (45 & 46
      Vict. c. 38) 342, 343
      Conveyancing Act (45 &
      46 Vict. c. 39)—
      s. 12 335
      Bills of Exchange Act (45
      & 46 Vict. c. 61) 89
1884 Yorkshire Registries Act
      (47 & 48 Vict. c. 54)—
      s. 14 162
1889 Customs and Inland Re-
      venue Act (52 & 53
      Vict. c. 7)—
      s. 12 141
1891 Stamp Act (54 & 55 Vict.
      c. 39)—
      s. 5 224
      s. 14 (4) 213
      s. 15 .... 198, 213
          (2) 195, 213
      s. 58 (4) (5) 195

1891　Stamp Act (54 & 55 Vict.
　　　　c. 39)—*cont.*
　　　s. 59 198
　　　s. 86 (1) (2) 296
　　　s. 117 87
　　　Sched. 1 .... 239, 270
1894　Finance Act (57 & 58
　　　　Vict. c. 30)—
　　　s. 1 349
　　　s. 2 (1) (*b*) 348, 349
　　　　　(*c*) 348
　　　s. 5 (2) 399
　　　s. 8 (2) 141
　　　　(18) 143
　　　s. 9 (1) 141, 143
　　　　(6) 153
1896　Friendly Societies Act (59
　　　　& 60 Vict. c. 25) 334
1897　Land Transfer Act (60 &
　　　　61 Vict. c. 65) ... 145, 164,
　　　　　　　　　　　　　　180
　　　s. 2 (2) 146
　　　s. 3 136
　　　s. 20 166
1899　Small Dwellings Acquisi-
　　　　tion Act (62 & 63
　　　　Vict. c. 44) 337
1900　Moneylenders Act (63 &
　　　　64 Vict. c. 51) 305
1906　Public Trustee Act (6
　　　　Edw. 7, c. 55)—
　　　s. 5 (2) 376
1910　Finance (1909–10) Act (10
　　　　Edw. 7, c. 8)—
　　　s. 55 399
　　　s. 74 214
　　　　(5) 198
1911　Conveyancing Act (1 &
　　　　2 Geo. 5, c. 17)—
　　　s. 4 321
　　　s. 12 146
　　　Moneylenders Act (1 & 2
　　　　Geo. 5, c. 38) 305
1914　Finance Act (4 & 5 Geo.
　　　　5, c. 10)—
　　　s. 14 399
　　　Deeds of Arrangement
　　　　Act (4 & 5 Geo. 5,
　　　　c. 47) 152
　　　Bankruptcy Act (4 & 5
　　　　Geo. 5, c. 59)—
　　　s. 42 148
　　　s. 54 .... 192, 193
　　　　(6) 192
　　　ss. 137 (2), 139, 143 ... 129
1918　Wills (Soldiers and Sail-
　　　　ors) Act (8 & 9 Geo.
　　　　5, c. 58)—
　　　s. 1 389
1922　Law of Property Act (12
　　　　& 13 Geo. 5, c. 16)—
　　　s. 145, Sched. 15 255
1923　Small Dwellings Acquisi-
　　　　tion Act (s. 22 of the
　　　　Housing etc. Act 1923
　　　　(13 & 14 Geo. 5, c.
　　　　24)) 337

1925　Settled Land Act (15 &
　　　　16 Geo. 5, c. 18) 252,
　　　　　　　343, 344, 351 *et seq.*
　　　s. 1 (1) 351, 361
　　　　(7) 344, 353, 355
　　　ss. 2, 3 353
　　　s. 4 (1) 359
　　　　(2) 360
　　　　(3) 361
　　　ss. 5, 6 360
　　　s. 7 368
　　　　(2) 368
　　　　(4) 269
　　　s. 8 368
　　　　(4) 361, 368, 369
　　　s. 9 359
　　　s. 10 (1) (2) 360
　　　ss. 12, 13 359
　　　s. 17 370
　　　　(3) 370
　　　s. 18 (1) 222, 363
　　　s. 19 .... 353, 355
　　　s. 20 .... 352, 354, 355
　　　s. 23 356
　　　　(1) 365
　　　ss. 24, 26 355
　　　s. 27 130
　　　s. 29 139
　　　s. 30 356
　　　ss. 32–34 357
　　　s. 35 (1) (2) 357
　　　s. 36 .... 344, 355
　　　ss. 38 (1), 39 (1) (6) ... 362
　　　ss. 41–48 364
　　　s. 63 244
　　　s. 65 365
　　　s. 71 .... 364, 367
　　　s. 72 364
　　　s. 73 366
　　　　(1) 378
　　　s. 75 366
　　　　(1) 363
　　　ss. 83, 84 367
　　　s. 91 357
　　　s. 101 366
　　　　(5) 366
　　　s. 103 355
　　　s. 104 .... 365, 368, 369
　　　　(10) 369
　　　s. 105 369
　　　s. 106 .... 344, 365
　　　s. 108 .... 356, 365
　　　s. 109 365
　　　s. 110 (2) 357, 359, 363,
　　　　　　　　　　　　　370
　　　s. 117 (1) (ii) 366
　　　　(xxvi) 355
　　　　(xxviii) 353
　　　Sched. 2 358
　　　Sched. 3 .... 366, 367

　　　Trustee Act (15 & 16 Geo.
　　　　5, c. 19) 304
　　　s. 12 (1) (2) 377
　　　s. 14 374
　　　s. 15 381
　　　s. 16 304
　　　s. 18 145
　　　s. 23 (3) 211

1925   Trustee Act (15 & 16 Geo.
        5, c. 19)—*cont.*
       s. 25 127
       s. 31 379
            (2) (3) 379
       s. 32 380
       s. 33 347
            (3) 347
       s. 34 .... 243, 372
            (3) 372, 374
       s. 35 357
       s. 36 .... 297, 373
            (1) (2) 373
            (6) 374
       s. 37 374
            (1) 374
       s. 39 375
       s. 40 ... 139, 297, 375, 376
            (4) 375
       s. 63 322
       s. 64 357
       s. 69 (2) 379, 380

      Law of Property Act (15
        & 16 Geo. 5, c. 20)—
       s. 1 .... 236, 343, 358
            (1) 247
            (6) 130, 352
       s. 2 378
            (5) 155
       s. 5 334
       s. 10 123
       s. 11 162
       s. 15 130
       s. 17 (1) 155
       s. 19 130
       s. 22 (1) 355
       s. 25 176
       s. 26 (1) (2) 377
            (3) 376
       s. 27 .... 123, 149, 374, 378
            (2) 222
       s. 28 .... 252, 304
            (1) 244, 378
       s. 30 .... 345, 377
       s. 34 ... 91, 143, 243, 343, 376
       s. 35 .... 243, 343, 376
       s. 36 ... 91, 143, 243, 343, 376
            (2) 143
       s. 40 ... 7, 15, 16, 17, 18, 22,
                25, 245, 293, 296
            (2) 16, 22
       s. 41 109
       s. 42 (1) 86
            (2) 87
            (3) 64, 87
       s. 44 (1) 60
            (2) 60, 61
            (3) 61
            (4) 60
            (5) 61, 62
            (8) 60, 92
       s. 45 (1) 63, 223
            (2) (3) 62, 100
            (4) 64
            (5) 63, 124
            (6) 63, 123, 224
            (8) 65

1925   Law of Property Act (15 &
        16 Geo. 5, c. 20)—*cont.*
       s. 45 (9) 64, 211, 238
       s. 46 .... 10, 65
       s. 47 .... 190, 191
       s. 48 207
            (1) 87, 221
       s. 49 198
            (2) ... 89, 93, 202, 204
       s. 50 322
       s. 51 (2) 229
       s. 52 .... 247, 268
            (2) 400
       s. 53 247
            (1) (*c*) 301
       s. 54 247
       s. 55 (*d*) 22
       s. 57 221
       s. 60 (1) 236
       s. 62 ...... 99, 233, 253, 279
            (1) 16, 133, 231
            (2) (4) 233
       s. 63 .... 234, 279
       s. 64 238
            (2)–(4) (9) ... 238, 239
       s. 65 208
            (1) 235
      ss. 67, 68 225
       s. 69 .... 211, 225
       s. 73 207
       s. 74 208
       s. 75 207
       s. 76 ... 225 *et seq.*, 241, 310
            (1) 226
                (*c*) (*d*) 227
                (*e*) 228
                (*f*) ... 228, 279, 332,
                        434
            (2) 227, 332
            (6) 227
       s. 77 208
            (1) (*c*) 269, 420
               (*d*) 269, 421
       s. 79 .... 237, 268
       s. 84 .... 147, 236
            (1) (2) 147
      ss. 85 (1) (2), 86 (1) (2) 293
       s. 87 (1) 294
      ss. 88, 89 ...... 317, 321, 329
       s. 91 317
       s. 93 325
       s. 94 .... 325, 328, 371
       s. 95 336
            (3) 336
       s. 96 (2) 328
       s. 99 314
            (5)–(8) (11) 316
            (13) 314
            (17) 316
            (18) 314
            (19) 314, 316
       s. 100 314
            (12) 314
       s. 101 .... 317, 318
            (1) (ii) 312, 313
               (iii) 323
            (2) 321
            (3) (4) 318
       s. 103 318

1925 Law of Property Act (15
        & 16 Geo. 5, c. 20)—
        cont.
      s. 104 .... 321, 418
              (2) (3) 319
      ss. 105–107 322
      s. 108 (1)–(4) 313
      s. 109 324
              (8) 324
      s. 110 320
      s. 111 .... 304, 310
      s. 112 310
      s. 113 .... 310, 331
              (1) 304, 310
      s. 114 ...... 329, 331, 333
      s. 115 .... 335, 337
              (1) 435
              (2) 336, 435
              (3) 336
              (4) 337
              (6) 335
              (7) (9) (10) 337
      s. 116 334
      s. 117 (2) 295
      s. 123 .... 125, 126
      s. 124 126
      ss. 125–127 .... 125, 126
      s. 128 126
      s. 130 393
              (1) 236
      s. 136 .... 195, 213, 301
      s. 137 .... 154, 169, 213
      ss. 141, 142 269
      s. 143 267
      s. 144 261
      s. 146 .... 258, 265, 266
              (1) 258
              (4) 266
              (8) 265
              (9) (10) 266
      s. 147 259
      s. 148 267
      s. 149 (1) (2) 253
              (3) 29, 254
              (5) 254
              (6) 255
      s. 152 (1) 316
      s. 164 382
      s. 172 .... 148, 225
              (3) 148
      s. 173 225
      s. 177 390
      s. 183 135
              (1) (2) 135
      s. 184 .... 131, 395
      s. 196 320
      s. 197 162
      s. 198 ... 26, 40, 43, 150, 159
              (1) 247
      s. 199 .... 92, 150
      s. 200 150
      s. 205 319
              (1) (i) 265
                   (ii) 245, 253
                   (xvi) ... 329, 426
                   (xix) 16, 17
                   (xxix) 371
      s. 207 234

1925 Law of Property Act (15
        & 16 Geo. 5, c. 20)—
        cont.
      Sched. 1 358
      Sched. 2 332
              Part IX ... 225, 228
              Part X 269
      Sched. 4 295
      Sched. 5 .... 138, 295
      Sched. 7 234

      Land Registration Act (15
        & 16 Geo. 5, c. 21)
                        163 et seq.
      s. 2 167
      s. 3 .... 168, 170
      ss. 4–7 175
      s. 8 176
              (1)–(3) 168
      s. 9 175
      s. 10 176
      ss. 11, 12 175
      s. 13 .... 176, 217
      s. 16 218
      s. 18 168
      s. 19 (1) 242
              (2) 168
              (3) 241
      s. 20 (1) 177, 241, 242,
                           243, 303
              (2)–(4) 177
      s. 23 177
              (2) 178
      s. 24 .... 78, 178, 269
      s. 25 .... 244, 298
              (2) 298
      s. 26 299
      ss. 27 (1) (2), 28 298
      s. 29 299
      s. 33 333
      s. 34 (1) 299, 318
              (2)–(5) 299
      s. 36 .... 322, 329
      s. 37 243
              (3) 219
      s. 38 (1) 242
      s. 39 178
      s. 40 (1) 242
      s. 41 178
      s. 48 180
      s. 49 .... 171, 180, 299
              (1) 27
      s. 50 180
              (1) 180
              (2) 181
      s. 52 300
      s. 53 (1) (3) 181
      s. 54 .... 27, 299, 300
      s. 55 300
              (1) 181, 182
              (2) 182
      s. 57 182
      s. 58 (1) 27, 182
              (2)–(4) 182
      s. 60 (1) 163
      s. 61 (1) 179
              (3) 179, 182
              (4) 179
      s. 63 174

1925 Land Registration Act (15
        & 16 Geo. 5, c. 21)—
        cont.
      s. 64 .... 174, 242, 299
        (1) 27, 28
      s. 65 ...... 27, 28, 174, 299
      s. 66 .... 298, 300
      s. 70 (1) 29, 170, 303
        (2) (3) 170
      s. 74 171
      s. 77 176
        (1) (2) 176
        (3) (4) 177
      s. 82 .... 172, 173
        (3) 173
      s. 83 173
        (5) 173
      ss. 86 (1)–(3), 92 179
      s. 94 180
      s. 101 .... 169, 178
        (2) 300
      s. 102 169
      s. 106 298
        (1) (2) 299
        (4) 300
      ss. 110, 112 93
      s. 113 94
      s. 120 166
      s. 123 ... 166, 167, 168, 215
        (1) 167
      ss. 132–134 165
      ss. 144–145 166

      Land Charges Act (15 &
        16 Geo. 5, c. 22) 151
                          et seq.
      s. 1 (6) 158
      s. 2 151
      s. 3 .... 151, 152
      s. 4 151
        (1) 156
      s. 5 156
      ss. 6, 7 152
      s. 10 (1) (2) 26
        (5) 155, 163
        (6) 162
        (8) 27
      s. 11 .... 39, 153
      s. 11A 153
      s. 13 152
        (2) ... 26, 154, 155, 237,
                              247
        (3) 156
      s. 14 152
        (2) 155
      s. 15 40
        (1) 40
        (2) 39
      s. 16 .... 42, 158
      s. 17 .... 42, 158
        (3) 159
      s. 20 (8) 151, 159
      s. 23 (1) 41

      Administration of Estates
        Act (15 & 16 Geo. 5,
        c. 23)—
      s. 1 .... 145, 191, 333
        (1) 143

1925 Administration of Estates
        Act (15 & 16 Geo. 5,
        c. 23)—*cont.*
      s. 2 .... 191, 222, 333
      s. 2 (2) 146
      s. 3 .... 145, 222, 333
        (4) 143
      s. 8 146
      s. 22 (1) 367
      s. 24 368
      s. 33 .... 145, 222
      s. 34 .... 192, 399
      s. 35 399
      s. 36 .... 122, 136, 222
        (4) 400
        (5) (6) 136
        (7) 137
        (8) 145
        (11) 138
        (12) 145
      s. 37 .... 137, 222
      s. 39 .... 145, 222, 252
      s. 55 (1) (iii) 222
        (ix) 393
        (x) 394
      Sched. 1, Part 2 393

      Supreme Court of Judica-
        ture   (Consolidation)
        Act (15 & 16 Geo. 5,
        c. 49)—
      s. 43 22
      s. 160 .... 391, 392
      s. 162 367
      s. 165 392

1926 Law of Property (Amend-
        ment) Act (16 & 17
        Geo. 5, c. 11) ... 125, 266,
                          344, 353
      s. 1 352
      s. 4 160
        (2) 158
      s. 7 .... 143, 328
      Sched. ... 143, 222, 328, 376

1927 Moneylenders Act (17 &
        18 Geo. 5, c. 21) 305
      s. 6 305
      s. 10 (1) 307

      Landlord and Tenant Act
        (17 & 18 Geo. 5,
        c. 36)—
      s. 1 287
        (1), proviso 287
        (2) (3) 287
      ss. 3, 9, 17 (1)–(4) 287
      s. 18 259
        (2) 258, 265
      s. 19 (1) 261, 262
        (4) 261
      s. 20 421
      s. 21 287
      Part I 281, 286

1928 Administration of Justice
        Act (18 & 19 Geo. 5.
        c. 26)—
      s. 9 367

1931 Finance Act (21 & 22 Geo.
      5, c. 28)—
      s. 28, Sched. 2 214

1932 Agricultural Credits Act
      (22 & 23 Geo. 5,
      c. 35)—
      s. 2 309

1936 Land Registration Act (26
      Geo. 5 & 1 Edw. 8,
      c. 26) 164

      Tithe Act (26 Geo. 5 & 1
      Edw. 8. c. 43) 170

1938 Evidence Act (1 Geo. 6,
      c. 28)—
      s. 4 125

      Leasehold Property (Re-
      pairs) Act (1 Geo. 6,
      c. 34) 258, 270

      Inheritance (Family Provi-
      sion) Act (1 Geo. 6,
      c. 45) 383
      s. 1 (7) 383

1939 Limitation Act (2 & 3 Geo.
      6, c. 21) ... 122, 170, 173,
                          185, 299
      s. 2 (3) 229
           (7) 202
      s. 29 202

1940 Middlesex Deeds Act (3 &
      4 Geo. 6, c. 34) 162

1941 Landlord and Tenant (War
      Damage) (Amendment)
      Act (4 & 5 Geo. 6,
      c. 41) 189

1944 Validation of War-Time
      Leases Act (7 & 8
      Geo. 6, c. 34) ... 255, 256

1946 Coal Industry Nationalisa-
      tion Act (9 & 10 Geo.
      6, c. 59) 79

1947 Agriculture Act (10 & 11
      Geo. 6, c. 48) 287

      Town and Country Plan-
      ning Act (10 & 11
      Geo. 6, c. 51) ... 45, 52, 53

1948 Companies Act (11 & 12
      Geo. 6, c. 38)—
      s. 14 139
      s. 32 19
      s. 89 309
      s. 92 187
      s. 95 155
      ss. 95 et seq. 330
      ss. 97, 101 330
      s. 283 140
      ss. 320–322 142
      s. 455 302

1948 Agricultural Holdings Act
      (11 & 12 Geo. 6,
      c. 63) .... 287 et seq.
      s. 1 (1) (2) 288
      s. 2 (1) 288, 289
          (1), proviso 288
      s. 3 (1) (2) (4) 289
      s. 8 291
          (3) 291
      s. 9 291
      s. 17 250
      s. 23 (1) 289
          (1), proviso 289
      s. 24 (1) (2) 289
      s. 25 (1) 290
          (1), proviso 290
      s. 34 (1) 290
          (1), proviso 290
          (2) 290
      ss. 35–47, 56–58 291
      s. 65 290
      ss. 72, 74, 82 152
      s. 94 (1) 288
      Sched. 7 314

1949 Married Women (Restraint
      upon Anticipation)
      Act (12, 13 & 14 Geo.
      6, c. 78) 351, 354

1952 Intestates' Estates Act (15
      & 16 Geo. 6 & 1 Eliz.
      2, c. 64)—
      s. 1 (4) 131, 395

1953 Town and Country Plan-
      ning Act (1 & 2 Eliz.
      2, c. 16) 54

1954 Landlord and Tenant Act
      (2 & 3 Eliz. 2, c. 56) 258,
                          281 et seq.
      s. 2 (1) 276, 277
          (4) (5) 276
          (6) 277
      ss. 3, 4, 12 277
      s. 23 (1) (2) 282
          (3) 285
      s. 24 286
          (1) (2) 283
      s. 25 .... 283, 286
          (5) (6) 284
      s. 26 286
          (1) (2) (6) 284
      ss. 27–28 .... 283, 286
      s. 29 (2) (3) 284
      s. 30 284
          (1) 284
          (2) (3) 285
      ss. 31A, 32 (1), 33–35 .. 285
      s. 36 (4) 314
      s. 37 (1)–(3) 286
      s. 38 (1) 285
          (2) (3) 286
          (4) 285
      s. 43 282
      s. 45 281

1954 Landlord and Tenant Act
 (2 & 3 Eliz. 2, c. 56)
 —*cont.*
 ss. 47, 49, 63 (2) 287
 s. 69 (1) 282
 Part I .... 267 *et seq.*
 Part II 271, 281 *et seq.*, 315
 Part III 286

 Town and Country Plan-
 ning Act (2 & 3 Eliz.
 2, c. 72) 54

1956 Administration of Justice
 Act (4 & 5 Eliz. 2,
 c. 46)—
 s. 35 .... 17, 151

 Clean Air Act (4 & 5 Eliz.
 2, c. 52) 40

 Finance Act (4 & 5 Eliz. 2,
 c. 54)—
 s. 22 397

1957 Rent Act (5 & 6 Eliz. 2,
 c. 25) 365
 s. 16 423

 Occupiers' Liability Act (5
 & 6 Eliz. 2, c. 31) ... 251

 Finance Act (5 & 6 Eliz. 2,
 c. 49)—
 s. 38 143

 Housing Act (5 & 6 Eliz.
 2, c. 56)—
 s. 6 251

1958 Costs of Leases Act (6 &
 7 Eliz. 2, c. 52)—
 s. 1 87

 Finance Act (6 & 7 Eliz. 2,
 c. 56)—
 ss. 29 (1), 30 398
 s. 34 239

 Agriculture Act (6 & 7 Eliz.
 2, c. 71)—
 s. 3 290

1959 County Courts Act (7 & 8
 Eliz. 2, c. 22)—
 s. 103 22

 Highways Act (7 & 8 Eliz.
 2, c. 25)—
 s. 40 37
 ss. 108, 109 47
 ss. 173–192, 226 37
 Part IX 37

 Rights of Light Act (7 &
 8 Eliz. 2, c. 56)—
 s. 2 40

1959 Mental Health Act (7 &
 8 Eliz. 2, c. 72)—
 s. 149 377
 Sched. 7 377
 Sched. 8 355

1960 Corporate Bodies' Contracts Act (8 & 9 Eliz.
 2, c. 46) 19

 Charities Act (8 & 9 Eliz.
 2, c. 58)—
 s. 29 138
 ss. 35 (4), 38, 45 (6) 139

1961 Trustee Investments Act
 (9 & 10 Eliz. 2, c. 62) 304,
 366, 378

 Public Health Act (9 & 10
 Eliz. 2, c. 64)—
 s. 4 48

 Housing Act (9 & 10 Eliz.
 2, c. 65) 270
 s. 32 250
 s. 33 251

1962 Recorded Delivery Service
 Act (10 & 11 Eliz. 2,
 c. 27)—
 s. 1 .... 258, 320, 365
 (1) 265
 Sched. 365

 Building Societies Act (10
 & 11 Eliz. 2, c. 37)—
 s. 33 304
 s. 36 320
 s. 37 .... 334, 337, 435

 Town and Country Plan-
 ning Act (10 & 11
 Eliz. 2, c. 38)—
 ss. 74 *et seq.* 118

1963 Finance Act (c. 25)—
 ss. 55, 56 270
 Part V, Sched. 14 170

 Offices, Shops and Railway
 Premises Act (c. 41)—
 s. 42 251

 Wills Act (c. 44) 385

1964 Hire Purchase Act (c. 53) 327

 Perpetuities and Accumu-
 lations Act (c. 55)—
 s. 1 382
 ss. 3, 9 (1) (2), 10 29
 s. 13 382

 Housing Act (c. 56) 42
 s. 95 40

 Law of Property (Joint
 Tenants) Act (c. 63) 130,
 143
 ss. 1–3 144

1965 Compulsory Purchase Act
           (c. 56) 305
         s. 2 117
         s. 3 116
         ss. 5, 9, 11 117
         ss. 14 et seq. 117
         Sched. 1, para. 10 (1) .. 117
         Sched. 2, para. 2 117

      Hire Purchase Act (c. 66) 327

      Race   Relations   Act   (c.
           73)—
         s. 5 262

      Rent Act (c. 75)—
         s. 31 263

1966 Land Registration Act (c.
           39) 185
         s. 1 166
             (4) 173

1967 Misrepresentation Act (c.
           7)—
         s. 1 .... 35, 36, 201
         s. 2 201
             (1) 31, 35
             (2) 35, 36
         s. 3 ...... 36, 87, 95, 96, 98
         s. 5 35

      General Rate Act (c. 9)—
         ss. 49, 50 108

      Agriculture Act (c. 22)—
         s. 45 (7), Sched. 3, para.
             2 (1) 40

      Housing Subsidies Act (c.
           29)—
         Part II 307

      Decimal Currency Act (c.
           47) 198

      Finance Act (c. 54)—
         s. 27 239

      Matrimonial   Homes   Act
           (c. 75) 156, 158, 171
         s. 1 (1) 156
             (5) (7) (8) 157
             (9) 159
         s. 2 156
             (2) 157
             (7) 156, 157
             (8) 156
         s. 3 157
         s. 4 158
         s. 6 (1) (2) (3) 157
         Sched. 156

      Companies Act (c. 81)—
         s. 23 305

      Leasehold Reform Act (c.
           88) ... 113 et seq., 161, 277
                         et seq., 314
         s. 1 (1) 277, 278
             (2)–(4) 278

1967 Leasehold Reform Act (c.
           88)—cont.
         s. 2 278
             (3) 279
         s. 3 278
         s. 4 278
             (1) 278
         s. 5 (1) (2) (5) 114
         s. 7 278
             (7) 278
         s. 8 (1) 278
         s. 9 .... 114, 279
             (3) 116, 279
         s. 10 279
             (1) 279
         ss. 11, 12, 13 279
         s. 14 (1) 278, 279
         ss. 15 (1) (2), 16, 17 (1)–
             (4) 280
         s. 18 (1) 280
             (2) 281
             (3) 280
             (4) 281
         s. 19 281
         s. 20 (1) 280
         s. 21 (1) 279
         s. 27 114
         s. 37 (1) 280
         s. 41 (4) 281
         Sched. 2 .... 280, 281
         Sched. 3 113

1968 Rent Act (c. 23) ... 196, 197,
                     271 et seq., 314
         s. 1 (1) 271
         ss. 2 (1) (3), 3 (1) 272
         ss. 4, 5 271
         s. 6 (3) 272
         s. 7 273
             (2) 273
         s. 9 271
             (2) 271
         ss. 10, 11 274
         ss. 12 (1), 14 272
         ss. 20 (2) (3), 44 (3) ... 275
         ss. 52, 56 274
         ss. 67, 70–73 275
         s. 74 .... 43, 275
         ss. 75–77 276
         s. 78 276
             (1) 276
         s. 80 276
         ss. 94 et seq. 318
         s. 113 273
         Parts III, IV 274, 275
         Part V 274
         Part VI .... 275 et seq.
         Sched. 1 275
         Sched. 2 273
         Scheds. 3, 4 274
         Scheds. 5–7 275
         Scheds. 8, 9 274

      Wills Act (c. 28)—
         s. 1 388

      Trade Descriptions Act (c.
           29) 83

1968 Agricultural (Miscellaneous Provisions) Act (c. 34)—
s. 9 ... 291
s. 10 ... 290

Clean Air Act (c. 62) ... 40

Town and Country Planning Act (c. 72) ... 45, 46, 51, 52
s. 30 ... 118
Sched. 3, para. 2 (3) ... 118
Sched. 3A ... 118

1969 Finance Act (c. 32)—
ss. 19 et seq. ... 339
s. 36 ... 348, 349
s. 37 (1) (3) ... 349

Housing Act (c. 33)—
s. 71 ... 251
s. 82 ... 114, 299

Family Law Reform Act (c. 46)—
s. 1 ... 130, 352, 379
s. 3 ... 384
s. 7 ... 392
s. 15 ... 438, 443

Law of Property Act (c. 59)—
ss. 1, 2 ... 285
s. 4 (1) ... 283
ss. 5–7 ... 285
s. 11 ... 286
s. 12 ... 282
s. 16 ... 162
ss. 17, 21 ... 163
s. 23 ... 60
s. 24 ... 44, 150
s. 25 ... 160, 161, 162
(1) ... 161
(2) ... 150, 160, 161
(6) (7) ... 161
(8) ... 162
(9) (10) ... 161
s. 26 ... 155, 163, 330
s. 27 ... 153
s. 28 ... 147, 236
Part I ... 281

1970 Income and Corporation Taxes Act (c. 10)—
s. 19 ... 340
ss. 52–56 ... 107
s. 57 ... 107, 339
(1) ... 339
ss. 57 et seq. ... 339
ss. 58–64 ... 107
s. 67 ... 269
ss. 72–77, 80 (1), 82 (1) (3), 84 ... 270
s. 86 ... 108
s. 230 ... 396
s. 343 ... 339
s. 445 ... 349

1970 Finance Act (c. 24)—
s. 32 ... 198, 239, 270
Sched. 7 ... 198, 239

Administration of Justice Act (c. 31)—
s. 36 ... 323, 338
s. 37 ... 323, 326

Matrimonial Proceedings and Property Act (c. 45)—
s. 37 ... 147, 244
s. 38 ... 157

1971 Land Commission (Dissolution Act (c. 18) ... 195
s. 6 (1) ... 118

Coinage Act (c. 24)—
ss. 2, 3 ... 211

Administration of Estates Act (c. 25)—
ss. 8, 9 ... 384

Powers of Attorney Act (c. 27) ... 125 et seq.
ss. 1–4 ... 126
s. 5 ... 126
(1) (2) ... 126
(3) (4) ... 127
ss. 7, 9 ... 127

Land Registration and Land Charges Act (c. 54)—
s. 9 ... 158
s. 12 ... 165

Finance Act (c. 68)—
s. 32 ... 198, 239, 270
Sched. 7 ... 198, 239

Housing Act (c. 76)—
s. 71 ... 251

Town and Country Planning Act (c. 78) ... 44 et seq., 77
ss. 6, 7 (3)–(6), 8–19 ... 53
s. 22 (1)–(3) ... 46
s. 23 ... 44
(1) ... 47
(3) (5) ... 45
s. 24 ... 48
ss. 29, 30 ... 49
ss. 33 (1), 34 ... 50
s. 35 ... 55
s. 40 ... 47
ss. 42, 44 ... 49
s. 45 ... 50, 56
s. 51 ... 50
s. 53 ... 46
s. 54 ... 46, 47
(6) ... 47
ss. 55, 58, 60, 64 ... 47
ss. 67, 68, 74 ... 50

XXX

TABLE OF STATUTES

1971 Town and Country Plan-
       ning Act (c. 78)—cont.
      s. 87 51
          (1) 51
          (3) 45, 51
          (6) (7) 51
      ss. 88–91 51
      s. 94 52
      s. 147 (1) (2) 56
      s. 158 56
      s. 159–161 50
      s. 164 .... 50, 56
      ss. 180, 182, 193 57
      s. 196 58
      ss. 209, 211, 212, 215,
          277 47
      s. 290 57
      Sched. 8 55

1971 Town and Country Plan-
       ning Act (c. 78)—cont.
      Sched. 11 118

1972 Defective Premises Act (c.
       35) 82, 83, 251

      Finance Bill (c. 41) 213,
                 239, 270, 395, 399

      Town and Country Plan-
       ning   (Amendment)
       Bill 50, 53

      Land Charges Bill ... 151, 152,
                                  160

TABLE OF REFERENCES TO THE LAW
SOCIETY'S AND NATIONAL CONDITIONS
OF SALE

THE LAW SOCIETY'S CONDITIONS
(1953 ed.)
Condition 20 97
Condition 21 .... 34, 43, 97
Condition 22 97
Condition 33 213
Condition 36 111

THE LAW SOCIETY'S CONDITIONS
(1970 ed.) ...... 9, 84, 87 et seq.
Condition 1 (2) 111
Condition 2 97
          (2) 97
          (3) 98
          (4) 41, 98
Condition 3 (1) 97
          (2) 101
          (3) 101
Condition 4 99
          (2) (a) 96
             (c) 99
Condition 5 (1) 88, 90
          (2) 15, 90
Condition 6 .... 104, 191
Condition 7 101
          (1) (b) 94
Condition 8 99
          (1) (a) 99
             (b) 100
          (2) 100
          (3) 14, 100
          (4) 100
Condition 10 101
Condition 11 104
          (2) 414
          (4) 104, 195
Condition 12 95
Condition 13 95
          (1) 96
          (4) 96
Condition 14 105
          (1) 105
Condition 15 210
          (1) 108, 111
          (2) 108
Condition 16 105
          (1) (b) 107
          (2) 106
          (3) 107
          (4) 106
Condition 18 102
          (1) 103
Condition 19 .... 111, 113, 412
          (2) 110

THE LAW SOCIETY'S CONDITIONS
(1970 ed.)—cont.
Condition 19 (3) 111
          (4) 112
          (6) 111
Condition 20 (1) 87
          (2) 91
Special Condition 1 87

THE NATIONAL CONDITIONS (17th
ed., 1959)
Condition 13 43

THE NATIONAL CONDITIONS (18th
ed., 1969) .... 9, 84, 87 et seq.
Condition 2 87
Condition 3 91
Condition 4 (1) 108
          (2) 111, 210
          (3) 104, 195
Condition 5 108
Condition 6 105
          (1) (i) 107
             (ii) 107
          (2) (i) 106
Condition 7 105
          (3) 105
Condition 8 101
Condition 9 102
          (1) 103
Condition 10 (2) 100
          (4) 100
          (5) 14, 100
Condition 12 95
          (3) 96
Condition 13 .... 34, 39, 98
Condition 14 99
Condition 15 98
Condition 16 41
          (3) 98
          (4) 98
Condition 17 95
          (1) 96
Condition 18 101
Condition 19 104
          (6) 414
Condition 21 .... 104, 191
Condition 22 .... 111, 412
          (1) 110, 111, 113
          (2) 111
          (3) 112
Special Condition D 97

CHAPTER 1

INTRODUCTORY

The scope of conveyancing

Conveyancing is concerned with the transfer of property (in particular, real property). It is generally understood to include contracts for the sale of land, the various stages of investigation of title and the form and content of conveyances, leases, mortgages and some other documents. All these matters are dealt with in this book. We shall deal with settlements and wills as these are regular transactions for the conveyancer. In the space permitted, we have not attempted to deal with less familiar topics, such as bills of sale, and we have only made passing mention to such matters as assignments of choses in action and gifts.

The law relating to contract for the sale of land and conveyancing overlaps the law of contract and real property and we have, to some extent at least, assumed that the reader will have studied these subjects before he comes to conveyancing. Other subjects impinge on conveyancing, such as town and country planning and compulsory purchase, and we have touched on these briefly in so far as they are directly relevant to the discussion, for example, in connection with searches in the one case and notices to treat and conveyances on compulsory purchase in the other.

In a book of this size we can only hope, as the title suggests, to deal with the bare elements of such a broad subject, and we have tried to keep a happy medium between the technical and practical aspects of the subject. In the footnotes we shall indicate the larger and more detailed works [1] and the journals [2] where the reader will find further discussion. Most conveyancing transactions are completed without a hitch so it is important for the reader to keep in mind the whole time the various practical stages of the typical conveyancing transaction and not get too bogged down in the law, which he will generally only have to consider if something goes wrong. It may be convenient then to deal first with the various stages of a typical house purchase transaction. [3] We suggest this summary of the conveyancing

---

[1] Such as *Emmet on Title* (15th ed., 1967); Gibson's *Conveyancing* (20th ed., 1970); Farrand, *Contract and Conveyance* (1968).
[2] Such as *The Conveyancer* (cited as Conv.(N.S.)).
[3] See generally Moeran, *Practical Conveyancing* (5th ed., 1971); Table of procedure, *post*, p. 406; *The Legal Side of Buying a House* (a Consumers' Association publication).

1

process is read fast and lightly on the first reading and that the student returns to it when he has mastered the legal principles involved.

Usual procedure on sale of land

The first step is usually taken by the would-be vendor when he puts his house on the market. He may put the matter in the hands of an estate agent, who will advertise the property for sale. There will be a contract between the vendor and the agent, and in due course we shall discuss the potential liability of the vendor in respect of misrepresentations made by the agent [4] and deal with one aspect of the agent's right to commission.[5] If all goes well a purchaser will show interest and want to see the premises. Generally the vendor will show him round. The vendor will, of course, be anxious to sell, but he must beware of overselling his property, i.e. he must be careful what he says and not make any misrepresentation.[6] The purchaser should inspect the property as carefully as he can in the circumstances and, if he proceeds, have a proper survey carried out by a qualified surveyor.

We shall assume the purchaser agrees to buy. Sometimes where there is an estate agent involved he will insist on the purchaser signing a form of preliminary agreement and paying a deposit.[7] The agreement will generally be subject to a formal contract in which case there will be no binding contract until the parts have been exchanged. The only real advantage of such an agreement is that, if properly drawn, it will entitle the agent to his commission.[5] Any deposit paid to the agent will be released to the vendor on completion. Even if there is no estate agent involved, the parties generally agree " subject to contract," the effect of this formula being well known even to non-lawyers.[8]

It is usually only at the next stage that a solicitor comes into the picture. It is rare that he is instructed by either party before a sale has been agreed between them. The vendor usually informs his solicitors that he has agreed to sell, and asks the solicitors to act for him. The vendor's solicitors will then write to the purchaser, or, if his solicitors are known, to the purchaser's solicitors, stating that they understand that the parties have agreed the sale and that they will shortly be submitting a draft contract for approval. The terms of any correspondence between the parties or their solicitors are important because a contract may have to be sought in the correspondence if a formal contract is not made.[9] We might mention here that the

4 See *post,* p. 31.
5 See *post,* p. 32.
6 See *post,* p. 35.
7 In fact the payment will not be a deposit in the technical sense as there is still no contract. For deposits, see *post,* p. 89.
8 See *post,* p. 11. And see note 47, *post,* p. 7.
9 See *post,* p. 10.

practice of the same solicitor acting for both parties is a dangerous one, both for the client and the solicitor.[10]

The vendor's solicitors will then obtain the title deeds and prepare the draft contract. Usually the property will be mortgaged and the vendor's solicitor will have to obtain the deeds from the vendor's mortgagee (for example, a building society). The letter to the building society will generally contain the solicitor's undertaking to hold the deeds on behalf and on the instructions of the society. Notice of intention to redeem (*i.e.* pay off) the mortgage may be given at the same time.

Once the deeds have been obtained the draft contract can be prepared and submitted to the purchaser's solicitors for approval. Once approved the contract is *engrossed* (*i.e.* a fair copy is made). The contract usually consists of two copies of the agreement. The draft contract is in practice submitted in duplicate, so that one copy can be retained by the purchaser's solicitors and, assuming there are no major amendments, used as the engrossment. Each party's solicitors will submit an engrossment of the contract to the other for signature.

On receipt of the draft contract (or before if the property is easily identifiable and the appropriate local authorities known) the purchaser's solicitors will make a local land charges search and make inquiries of the local authorities.[11] The purchaser's solicitors will also submit *preliminary inquiries*, or enquiries before contract, to the vendor's solicitors. The purpose and contents of these inquiries are discussed subsequently.[12]

As soon as the purchaser's solicitors are satisfied with the vendor's replies to the preliminary inquiries, and the contract is agreed, the two parts of the contract can be exchanged.[13] Only then will there be a binding contract. A deposit, or the balance of a deposit, will be paid.[14]

If the purchaser is raising the purchase-money by an advance on mortgage, the contract should not be exchanged until the purchaser has a definite offer of an advance from the mortgagee.

After contract the vendor's solicitors submit an *abstract* (*i.e.* epitome [15] of the vendor's title) to the purchaser's solicitors, who will examine the title [16] and raise any inquiries on it by *requisition*. The purpose and form of requisitions are discussed later.[17] The purchaser's solicitors will usually submit to the vendor's solicitors a draft conveyance at the same time as the requisitions. If, as is usual, the purchaser

---

[10] See *Goody* v. *Baring* [1956] 1 W.L.R. 448; *Smith* v. *Mansi* [1963] 1 W.L.R. 26. And (1970) 67 L.S.Gaz. 330. The Law Society now propose to forbid the practice.
[11] See *post*, p. 39.
[12] *Post*, p. 34.
[13] *Post*, p. 15.
[14] *Post*, p. 89.
[15] See *post*, p. 119.
[16] *Post*, pp. 119 *et seq.*
[17] *Post*, p, 133.

is going to mortgage the property, his solicitors will in the meanwhile have submitted to the mortgagee's solicitors the preliminary inquiries and replies thereto, the contract and the abstract.

Once the draft conveyance is approved by the vendor's solicitors, the conveyance is engrossed by the purchaser's solicitors. In this case the fair copy is usually typed out onto good quality paper and the pages and any plan sewn together with ribbon. If the purchaser has to execute (*i.e.* sign, seal and deliver [18]) the deed, he will do so at this stage. However, it is only necessary for a purchaser to execute the deed if he has entered into any covenant with the vendor. The conveyance is then sent to the vendor's solicitors. Shortly before completion the purchaser's solicitors should make a search in the Land Charges Department.[19]

If there is to be a mortgage by the purchaser, the mortgagee's solicitors will meanwhile have investigated the purchaser-mortgagor's title and the mortgage engrossment will have been prepared. The mortgagee's cheque for the advance will be sent to the purchaser's solicitors.

It now remains only to complete. The vendor's solicitors will arrange a time and place for completion and indicate how the purchase-money is to be paid. Usually payment is made by banker's draft. Two drafts may be needed if the vendor has a mortgage to discharge, one in favour of the mortgagee, the other in the vendor's favour. The vendor's solicitors will supply the purchaser's solicitors with a *completion statement*,[20] which states how much is due and shows how the amount is made up. Before the date fixed for completion the vendor must execute the conveyance and provide his solicitors with the last receipts for rates, water rates and ground or chief rent (if any) to support the completion statement. The appointment for completion then takes place. It is often at the office of the solicitors to the vendor's mortgagee. The purchaser's solicitor will then compare the abstract against the original deeds (if this has not already been done). If he is satisfied, the title deeds, including, of course, the conveyance to the purchaser, are handed over with the keys of the property (if the purchaser has not already been allowed into possession), and the purchase-money is paid.[21]

After completion the purchaser's solicitor must see to the stamping of the conveyance [22] and, if the conveyance leads to first registration, he must apply for first registration.[23]

The vendor's solicitor sees to the discharge of the vendor's mortgage. As it may take some days to get back the discharged mortgage from

[18] *Post*, p. 207.
[19] *Post*, p. 159.
[20] *Post*, p. 210.
[21] *Post*, p. 211.
[22] *Post*, p. 213.
[23] *Post*, p. 214.

the mortgagee, on completion the vendor's solicitor usually gives the purchaser's solicitor an undertaking to see to the discharge.[24]

Where the land is registered the procedure is much the same, although the investigation of title will be somewhat simpler.[25]

In the above survey of a typical conveyancing transaction we have mentioned only the main points. The details are discussed in subsequent chapters.[26]

Future of conveyancing

From the above survey it can be seen that conveyancing is a complicated and necessarily expensive matter and, in recent years, there have been demands for drastic reform.[27] The main objections relate to cost and complexity. As to cost, there are, of course, votes to be had by promising cheaper house purchase and successive Governments have made such promises. There is good evidence that the cost of house purchase in England is in fact much cheaper than in, for example, the United States.[28] Moreover solicitors' costs are often less than those of some others involved in house purchase, such as estate agents.[29] Nevertheless solicitors' remuneration was subjected to the critical gaze of the former Prices and Incomes Board which produced three reports on the topic.[30] The general opinion of the Board was that most conveyancing costs were too high. Subsequently new Remuneration Orders were made which came into effect in 1971.[31]

It must be admitted that the repeated full examination of title in unregistered conveyancing each time the property is sold seems excessive. This is, of course, avoided to some extent once the land is registered, and solicitors' remuneration for registered conveyancing is on a somewhat lower scale than that for unregistered conveyancing. It is hoped that compulsory registration will cover the whole country by 1977.[32]

A number of proposals has been made by the profession itself to reduce conveyancing costs. One idea was the "Title Certificate Scheme," under which, after a final investigation of title by two solicitors on the next sale of certain property, a book or certificate (something like a car log-book) should be produced which would replace the title deeds, as in the case of registered land. The certificate was to be backed by insurance. On each subsequent sale a new

---

[24] *Post,* p. 211.
[25] *Post,* p. 183.
[26] And see the Table of procedure, *post,* p. 406.
[27] See generally (1969) 32 M.L.R. 477 *et seq.*
[28] See (1963) 27 Conv.(N.S.) 240, 246; (1966) 30 Conv.(N.S.) 194, 212 *et seq*; and *Which* report on conveyancing, 1970; (1970) 114 S.J. 19, 495.
[29] See (1966) 30 Conv.(N.S.) 81.
[30] See *e.g.* (1968) 112 S.J. 183; (1968) 118 New.L.J. 1214; (1969) 119 New.L.J. 113, 1124; (1969) December L.S.Gaz. la; (1971) 35 Conv.(N.S.) 143.
[31] But now conveyancing scale charges are to be abolished: see (1972) 122 New L.J. 390, 409; (1972) 69 L.S.Gaz. 381.
[32] See (1969) 32 M.L.R. 122.

certificate would be added covering the change in the title since the last sale.[33] The proposal was not without critics [34] and was dropped (after it had been considered by the Law Commission) in favour of a crash programme to extend compulsory registration.

The latest proposal is for title insurance similar to the conveyancing methods in some parts of the United States. Where the system operates, conveyancing has for the most part been taken out of the lawyers' hands by the insurance companies, who will indemnify a purchaser against a defective title. In practice, some sort of examination is made by the insurance company itself.[35] A similar scheme has recently been suggested, under which a large house building company plans to join with a building society in offering a registered transfer and charge to a purchaser for a £10 fee. Half of this fee would provide a premium on a defective title indemnity insurance and the other half would be for administrative expenses.[36]

Successive Governments have also helped to keep house purchase costs down by raising the limits for which the rate of stamp duty is nil or reduced if a certificate is given [37] and abolishing some duties, notably mortgage duty, altogether.[38]

As regards improvements in conveyancing procedures the Law Commission has issued several working papers and reports [39] suggesting improvements in both registered and unregistered conveyancing procedure. Some of these have led to amending legislation. The Root of Title Report and Land Charges Report, for instance, have resulted in the Law of Property Act 1969 which has gone some way towards simplifying conveyancing, by reducing the statutory length of title, etc.[40]

While the investigation of title itself may be simpler today than in the past, other parts of a conveyancing transaction have become more important. Defects in title (other than technical ones) are comparatively rare and one could, in most cases, start with a presumption that the title is satisfactory if it has passed through several hands. For this reason the risk to insurance companies under the title insurance schemes is small. A more important consideration than pure title

---

[33] See (1965) 29 Conv.(N.S.) 329; (1966) 30 Conv. 8 (in which another scheme is suggested).
[34] See *e.g.* (1965) 29 Conv. 419.
[35] See (1963) 27 Conv.(N.S.) 240; (1966) 30 Conv. 194.
[36] See (1971) 115 S.J. 85.
[37] See Finance Act 1967, s. 27 (1). See *post*, p. 213.
[38] See Finance Act 1971, s. 64. For the abolition of the 6d. duty on contracts, see Finance Act 1970, Sched. 7, para. 1 (2) (*a*). One cannot end this short discussion on conveyancing costs without mentioning the National House Owners' Society, which was formed by Mr. Carter to do conveyancing work for members at a cost of about one-third of the normal; see *Carter* v. *Butcher* [1966] 1 Q.B. 526; (1969) 32 M.L.R. 497, note 62; (1971) 68 L.S.Gaz. 584. There is no doubt that Mr. Carter's criticisms have had some effect; see *e.g.* (1970) 56 *Law Guardian* 23; (1970) 114 S.J. 278 and subsequent correspondence.
[39] See *e.g.* No. 9 (1967) Transfer of land: interim report on root of title to freehold land; No. 11 (1967) Transfer of land: report on restrictive covenants; No. 18 (1969) Transfer of land: report on land charges affecting unregistered land.
[40] See *post*, p. 60.

matters in recent years has been the planning matters (if any) affecting the property. Can the property be used for the purpose the would-be purchaser desires? Is there any likelihood of compulsory purchase? These (and others) are the problems that the conveyancer faces today. Most of these matters will be revealed by searches in the appropriate registers. Searches and inquiries are important topics and we have dealt with them in some detail in Chapter 3.

Another common task for the purchaser's solicitor is to assist his client in obtaining mortgage facilities. Today most houses are bought with the assistance of an advance on mortgage by a building society or other lender. We shall say something about obtaining a mortgage later.[41]

The conveyancer may also have to consider the tax and estate duty implications of the transaction. We shall deal with these in their proper context.[42]

There is no doubt in our view that conveyancing requires considerable skill and that those who undertake it are not overpaid for the work involved. It may not be the esoteric art it once was when the normal conveyance [43] related to some large settled estate to which there was a long and complicated title. New techniques of abstracting,[44] standard form documentation [45] and non-technical language in deeds [46] have all tended to disperse the mystery of the ancient art.

We shall now hope to reveal some of the mystery.[47]

---

[41] See *post*, p. 341.

[42] See *e.g. post*, pp. 270, 339, 348, 398.

[43] Which might be the hand-written indenture on waxed paper ostentatiously sealed and bound together now lying under the perspex top of the reader's coffee table or shading the bulb of his lamp.

[44] See *post*, p. 121.

[45] *e.g.* with regard to preliminary inquiries (*post*, p. 36) and requisitions (*post*, p. 134).

[46] See *e.g.* Parker's *Modern Conveyancing Precedents* (1964).

[47] Readers may be familiar with the recent public discussion on " gazumping " *i.e.* the practice of some vendors of reneging from an oral agreement for sale if some other person offers a higher price (see (1972) 36 Conv.(N.S.) 1; (1972) 116 S.J. 110). This problem has been put to the Law Commission which is at present (July 1972) considering " subject to contract " agreements. Any changes in the law must involve substantial amendments to the Law of Property Act 1925, s. 40, and this should be kept in mind in reading Chap. 2 and subsequent Chaps.

CHAPTER 2

CONTRACT FOR THE SALE OF LAND GENERALLY

I. EXISTENCE AND VALIDITY OF THE CONTRACT

Existence and validity generally

The existence and validity of a contract for the sale of land depend upon the ordinary rules of contract. For example, the parties must have capacity to contract and there must be offer and acceptance and consideration.[1] But there are also special peculiarities to a contract for the sale of land which arise from the nature of the subject matter. These are mentioned below. Sales of land may take place by private agreement or by auction. The same rules apply to contracts for the sale of registered land as for unregistered land.

Agreement—offer and acceptance

Because of the special nature of the contract the court will require (1) clear evidence of an intention by the parties to be bound, and (2) evidence that the matter has got beyond the stage of mere negotiation. A distinction has therefore to be drawn between a preliminary statement as to the price, which has no legal effect, and an offer.[2] In an auction sale it is the bid of a prospective purchaser which constitutes the offer.[3] An offer may be withdrawn at any time before it has been accepted.[4] If a prospective purchaser does not wish to commit himself immediately, his proper course, if the vendor is willing, is to enter into an option agreement.[5]

In a sale by auction, the contract is complete as soon as the hammer falls. This is the acceptance by the vendor's agent, the auctioneer, of the offer of the prospective purchaser. Sometimes the printed "auction particulars," distributed amongst those who attend at the auction, contain a provision that no offer once made by a bidder can be withdrawn. Probably this provision is not binding in law and the

---

[1] See generally Treitel, *The Law of Contract* (3rd ed.).
[2] *Clifton* v. *Palumbo* [1944] 2 All E.R. 497; *Harvey* v. *Facey* [1893] A.C. 552; and see *Smith* v. *Mansi* [1963] 1 W.L.R. 26; *Bigg* v. *Boyd Gibbins Ltd.* [1971] 1 W.L.R. 913.
[3] *Payne* v. *Cave* (1789) 3 Term Rep. 148.
[4] *Routledge* v. *Grant* (1828) 4 Bing. 653. But there may be a separate agreement to keep the offer open for a certain time, *e.g.* where a would-be purchaser pays a " holding fee." And see options, *post*, p. 28.
[5] See *post*, p. 28.

bidder can withdraw his offer at any moment before the hammer falls.[6]

The acceptance must be unqualified. A letter merely agreeing the price does not necessarily amount to an unqualified acceptance.[7] If the person accepting the offer introduces a new term into the agreement, this must be agreed to by the other party before a binding contract can arise.[8] This new term is a counter-offer which destroys the original offer.[9] The distinction between a conditional acceptance, in which case there is no binding contract,[10] and a conditional contract[11] should be noted.

Sometimes a particular mode of acceptance is prescribed. In these cases it is a question of construction whether acceptance only in the particular mode prescribed will conclude the contract, or, whether acceptance in any other mode, no less advantageous to the offeror, will also suffice.[12] Where an offer is made in terms which fix no time limit for acceptance, the offer must be accepted within a reasonable time, otherwise the offeror will be treated as having refused it.[12] When the acceptance is made through the post the contract is complete when the acceptance is posted.[13] It is undecided whether or not an acceptance once posted can be withdrawn by a speedier means of communication.[14]

An agreement to agree, as, for instance, where there is an agreement for a lease at a rent to be agreed, does not create a contract.[15]

Formal contracts

It is well known that there are certain statutory requirements to be fulfilled if a contract for the sale of land is to be enforceable.[16] Generally, a formal contract is prepared by the vendor's solicitor for approval by the purchaser's solicitor. The vendor's solicitor in the normal case will use one of the printed forms of agreement incorporating the standard conditions of sale.[17] If the property is a house on a large building estate, a standard form of contract will often have

---

6 See *post*, p. 11.
7 *Neale* v. *Merrett* [1930] W.N. 189.
8 *Lewis* v. *Brass* (1877) 3 Q.B.D. 667, at p. 672.
9 *Hyde* v. *Wrench* (1840) 3 Beav. 334.
10 But where the acceptance is conditional, the acceptor can, if the condition is one solely for his benefit, waive the condition at any time before the other party has repudiated the contract: *Moritz* v. *Knowles* [1899] W.N. 83.
11 See *post*, p. 13.
12 *Manchester Diocesan Council for Education* v. *Commercial and General Investments Ltd.* [1970] 1 W.L.R. 241.
13 *Henthorn* v. *Fraser* [1892] 2 Ch. 27, at p. 33. And see *post*, p. 15.
14 See Treitel, *The Law of Contract* (3rd ed.), p. 27.
15 See *Smith* v. *Morgan* [1971] 1 W.L.R. 803; *Gavaghan* v. *Edwards* [1961] 2 Q.B. 220 (completion date to be agreed). But if the formula and machinery for determining the rent or price are agreed there will be a binding contract; see the option cases, *post*, p. 30, note 28.
16 See *post*, p. 15.
17 *i.e.* the Law Society's Contract (1970 ed.), or a local law society's contract, or the National Conditions Contract (18th ed.); see *post*, p. 84. Students should obtain copies of these from their local Law Society and law stationers.

been specially prepared. Some firms of solicitors have their own printed or typed standard forms. A formal contract will generally be in two parts, *i.e.* there are two copies of the contract, and each party will sign one copy. The parts are then exchanged and the contract is complete when the exchange has been effected.[18] In other cases the procedure is less formal, as when the purchaser signs a contract prepared by an estate agent. If both parties are to sign one document, the contract is complete when signed by both parties.[19] On a sale by auction the purchaser sometimes signs a memorandum of agreement set out in the auction particulars.

In other cases there will be no formal contract of any sort at all and the agreement has to be sought in the correspondence between the parties or some other writing (if any) sufficient to satisfy the statutory requirements.

Contracts by correspondence

Here the contract is spelt out of the correspondence between the parties. The whole correspondence must be looked at to determine whether the correspondence, properly construed, establishes a contract, or whether it is no more than a record of the negotiations between the parties.[20] A completed offer and acceptance by correspondence cannot be affected by subsequent negotiations, unless those subsequent negotiations result in a new contract taking the place of the former.[21]

In some cases there is a clear contract to be found in the correspondence (for example, where there is an unconditional acceptance of an unconditional offer). But, nevertheless, the parties' solicitors proceed on the basis that a formal contract is necessary. If a formal contract is not subsequently completed, the parties will be able to rely on the contract in the correspondence. Indeed, even in the case where a formal contract is envisaged, and the sale falls through, the parties' advisers should still examine the correspondence, or any other documents, to see if a contract can be made out from them.

The statutory form of conditions of sale [22] applies to a contract by correspondence, unless excluded by the terms of the correspondence.

Open contracts

An open contract is a contract which does no more than specify the intention to sell and name the parties, the property and the price

---

[18] *Eccles* v. *Bryant* [1948] Ch. 93. As to formal contracts generally, see *post*, Chap. 4. For exchange of contracts, see *post*, p. 15.
[19] *Smith* v. *Mansi* [1963] 1 W.L.R. 26.
[20] *Hussey* v. *Horne-Payne* (1879) 4 App.Cas. 311. And see *Griffiths* v. *Young* [1970] 1 Ch. 675; *Manchester Diocesan Council etc., supra*; *Bigg* v. *Boyd Gibbins Ltd., supra*. As to the extent of the meaning of a contract by " correspondence," see Farrand, *Contract and Conveyance*, p. 68.
[21] *Bellamy* v. *Debenham* [1891] 1 Ch. 412; *Perry* v. *Suffields Ltd.* [1916] 2 Ch. 187; *Richards* v. *Powell* (1966) 110 S.J. 330.
[22] Law of Property Act 1925, s. 46. See *post*, Chap. 4.

or enable them to be ascertained. The contract is " open " because it does not exclude any of the terms which are implied by law in any contract for the sale of land.[23] The usual informal contract prepared by one or other of the parties or a contract by correspondence are examples. The advantages and disadvantages of an open contract are discussed in a later chapter.[24]

Oral contracts

As will be seen [25] a contract for the sale of land which is not in writing or evidenced in writing is *unenforceable* unless there is a sufficient act of part performance by the party claiming to enforce the agreement. An oral contract may become enforceable if the requisite memorandum subsequently becomes available.

Auction sales

The auctioneer is the agent of the vendor. When land is sold by auction, the contract is complete as soon as the hammer falls [26]; but until the contract has been reduced to writing or some note or memorandum made of it, it remains unenforceable. The sale is made subject to conditions of sale, usually incorporating one or the other of the standard sets of conditions, and these, together with the particulars of sale (which describe the property) and, in some cases, a memorandum of the sale for use by the purchaser, make up the " auction particulars."

The auctioneer's authority extends to signing the contract or memorandum on behalf of the vendor,[27] and, generally, he has authority to sign the contract on behalf of the purchaser, where, for example, the latter refuses to sign.[28] Neither the vendor nor the purchaser can withdraw this authority after the contract has been made.[29]

Unless there is anything to the contrary in the conditions of sale, the auctioneer's authority extends to receiving any deposit payable under the contract.[30]

" Subject to contract "

We have seen [31] that, if there is to be a binding contract following an offer, the acceptance must be unqualified. Frequently, the acceptance is conditional, in which case there can be no binding contract, and the matter remains in negotiation. It is everyday practice for intending vendors of property, who are accepting an offer, to make their acceptance " subject to contract " with the result that they are not then

23 For these terms, see *post*, Chap. 4.
24 *Post*, p. 69.
25 *Post*, p. 16.
26 *Ante*, p. 8.
27 *Leeman* v. *Stocks* [1951] Ch. 941.
28 *Chaney* v. *Maclow* [1929] 1 Ch. 461.
29 *Phillips* v. *Butler* [1945] Ch. 358.
30 *Sykes* v. *Giles* (1839) 5 M. & W. 645, 651. For estate agents, see *post*, p. 32.
31 *Ante*, p. 9.

bound until a subsequent formal contract has been exchanged.[32] Either party may resile until exchange of contracts, and, if a deposit has been paid, this will be recoverable.[33]   Where the formula " subject to contract " or " subject to formal contract " is used the preparation, approval and *exchange* of a *formal* contract is clearly made a condition precedent of the acceptance.[34]   And even where the expression " subject to formal contract *if the vendors shall so require* " was used, there was held to be no binding contract.[35]   Other expressions may or may not have the same effect depending on the intention of the parties.   It is a question of construction in each case whether there is (1) an already complete contract which is to be reduced into a more formal shape later or (2) an offer or acceptance which is conditional only and the parties do not intend to be bound until a formal document is, in fact, later executed.[36]   So an agreement expressed to be " a provisional agreement until a fully legalised agreement, drawn up by a solicitor . . . is signed " [37] is a binding contract, as the parties *intended to be bound* from the outset.

Other expressions

The cases illustrate the effect of other expressions.   There will be no contract if the acceptance is " subject to approval of title and terms of contract," [38] or " subject to title and contract." [39]   Similarly there will be no contract where the acceptance is " subject to suitable agreements being arranged between your solicitors and mine," [40] or " subject to the terms of a formal lease to be prepared by solicitors." [41]   But where the acceptance is in such terms as " we will have this agreement put into due form by a solicitor," [42] or where the vendor accepts the purchaser's offer, adding that he has asked his solicitor " to prepare a contract " [43] or " to prepare the necessary documents," [44] there will be a binding contract.

Effect of " subject to contract," etc.

Where the expression prevents the coming into existence of a binding contract, either party can withdraw.   In that case neither party

---

[32] *Eccles* v. *Bryant* [1948] Ch. 93.
[33] *Chillingworth* v. *Esche* [1924] 1 Ch. 97 (subject to a proper contract to be prepared by the vendor's solicitors); *cf. Monnickendam* v. *Leanse* (1923) 39 T.L.R. 445; *post*, p. 22.
[34] *Winn* v. *Bull* (1877) 7 Ch.D. 29; *Rossdale* v. *Denny* [1921] 1 Ch. 57.
[35] *Riley* v. *Troll* [1953] 1 All E.R. 966.
[36] *Rossdale* v. *Denny, supra*; and see *Rossiter* v. *Miller* (1878) 3 App.Cas. 1124, 1152; *Von Hatzfeldt-Wildenburg* v. *Alexander* [1912] 1 Ch. 284, at pp. 288, 289.
[37] *Branca* v. *Cobarro* [1947] K.B. 854.
[38] *Chatterley* v. *Nicholls* (1884) 1 T.L.R. 14.
[39] *Coope* v. *Ridout* [1921] 1 Ch. 291.
[40] *Lockett* v. *Norman-Wright* [1925] Ch. 56.
[41] *Spottiswoode, Ballantyne and Co. Ltd.* v. *Doreen Appliances Ltd.* [1942] 2 K.B. 32.
[42] *Rossiter* v. *Miller* (1878) 3 App.Cas. 1124, at p. 1143.
[43] *Bonnewell* v. *Jenkins* (1878) 8 Ch.D 70; *E. R. Ives Investments Ltd.* v. *High* [1967] 2 Q.B. 379.
[44] *Bolton Partners* v. *Lambert* (1889) 41 Ch.D. 295.

will have any remedy against the other, save to recover the possession of the property or repayment of any deposit paid.[45]

Conditional contracts

Where the acceptance is " subject to contract," there is no contract at all, and the matter remains in negotiation, until exchange of contracts.[46] Other expressions, like " subject to survey," [47] have the same effect. On the other hand, there are some expressions which give rise to an immediate binding contract, but the contract only becomes enforceable once a particular condition has been fulfilled. Unlike the " subject to contract " cases, the parties are not able to withdraw but must await the fulfilment of the condition. An acceptance " subject to the title being approved by our solicitors " has been held to constitute a binding contract. The words were construed as a condition that the title must be investigated and approved in the usual manner, subject to legally sustainable objections, but, as the vendor must in any case prove his title, the words added nothing and so did not prevent there being a binding contract.[48] But in a more recent case [49] where the agreement was " subject to the purchaser's solicitor approving the lease " there was held to be no enforceable contract unless and until the solicitor's approval was obtained.[50] On the other hand, where an agreement was " subject to answers to preliminary inquiries and subject to searches," there was, it seems, a potentially binding agreement, which, in the circumstances, failed, either for uncertainty or because the condition was not satisfied. In that case, the property had been purchased for industrial use, and the search showed that it was being zoned for residential purposes. The purchasers were entitled to recover their deposit.[51]

Conditions may be *precedent* or *subsequent*.[52] Where the contract is subject to a condition precedent, there is no binding contract until the condition is satisfied.[53] In this situation the contract exists but is, as it were, suspended until the condition is satisfied, if at all. On the other hand, where the condition is subsequent, there is immediately a binding contract and the relationship of vendor and purchaser will have been established between the parties.[54] In either case, once the

---

[45] *Chillingworth* v. *Esche, supra.*
[46] For exchange, see *post,* p. 15.
[47] *Marks* v. *Board* (1930) 46 T.L.R. 424; *Graham and Scott (Southgate) Ltd.* v. *Oxlade* [1950] 2 K.B. 257; *Astra Trust* v. *Adams* [1969] 1 Lloyd's Rep. 81.
[48] *Hussey* v. *Horne-Payne, supra.* And see *Smallman* v. *Smallman* [1971] 3 W.L.R. 588 (agreement subject to approval of court).
[49] *Caney* v. *Leith* [1937] 2 All E.R. 532; *Curtis Moffat Ltd.* v. *Wheeler* [1929] 2 Ch. 224.
[50] Any disapproval must be bona fides: *Caney* v. *Leith, supra.*
[51] *Smith and Olley* v. *Townsend* (1949) 1 P. & C.R. 28; (1950) 14 Conv.(N.S.) 307 at p. 308. See Farrand, *Contract and Conveyance,* p. 18.
[52] See generally, Treitel, *The Law of Contract,* p. 55.
[53] *Aberfoyle Plantations Ltd.* v. *Cheng* [1960] A.C. 115 (the condition being the renewal of certain leases).
[54] *Property and Bloodstock Ltd.* v. *Emerton* [1968] Ch. 94 (the condition being the landlord's consent to the assignment by a mortgagee under his power of sale).

B.

condition is satisfied, the contract becomes unconditional. If the condition is not satisfied, the contract will be void. The most common example of a conditional contract occurs on the sale of leaseholds where the sale is conditional upon the landlord's consent to the assignment being obtained.[55] If the necessary consent is not obtained the condition defeats the sale. Both the Law Society's and the National Conditions of Sale make the contract for the sale of leaseholds conditional on licence to assign being obtained (where this is required) and entitle the vendor to resile from the contract where the landlord withholds his consent.[56] Such a contract is, therefore, subject to a condition subsequent in the sense mentioned above.[57]

Another common condition nowadays is " subject to planning permission." This condition has given rise to several questions of construction, for example, as to how far the purchaser has to pursue his application for permission. It has been held that he is acting reasonably if he accepts the decision of the planning authority. He is under no obligation to appeal.[58] The condition may be satisfied if a conditional permission is obtained,[59] but not necessarily by an outline permission.[60]

Where the contract fixes a date by which the condition has to be met, it will be void [61] if the condition remains unsatisfied by that date and time is of the essence in this respect.[62] Where no date is specified, but the contract fixes a date for completion, the condition must be fulfilled by that date.[62] Where the contract fixes no date for completion, the condition must be fulfilled within a reasonable time.[63, 64]

Collateral contracts

Where a promise has been made by one party in consideration of the other party entering into a contract, the promise can be treated as a collateral and independent contract and will be enforceable even though not evidenced in writing. Thus, where a tenant refused to take a lease unless the landlord warranted that the drains were in order, the tenant was held entitled to sue on the warranty [65] and, similarly, where the tenant executed a lease in reliance on a promise

---

55 For covenants in leases against assignment, etc., see *post*, p. 261.
56 Law Society's Conditions, Condition 8 (3); National Conditions, Condition 10 (5); see *Lipman's Wallpapers Ltd.* v. *Mason & Hodghton Ltd.* [1969] 1 Ch. 20.
57 See generally (1970) 34 Conv.(N.S.) 332.
58 *Hargreaves Transport Ltd.* v. *Lynch* [1969] 1 W.L.R. 215.
59 *West (Richard) & Partners (Inverness) Ltd.* v. *Dick* [1969] 2 Ch. 424.
60 *Hargreaves Transport Ltd.* v. *Lynch, supra.*
61 It has been suggested that *voidable* is more correct, the contract only being void if the event is one the parties cannot influence: (1970) 34 Conv.(N.S.) at p. 334.
62 *Aberfoyle Plantations Ltd.* v. *Cheng, supra.*
63 *Ibid. Re Longlands Farm* [1968] 3 All E.R. 552 (three and a half years more than reasonable).
64 For " subject to finance " conditions, which are rarely encountered, because formal contracts will not usually be exchanged before the purchaser has had an offer of an advance from his building society (*ante*, p. 3); see Farrand, *Contract and Conveyance*, p. 20; *Lee-Parker* v. *Izzet (No. 2)* [1972] 1 W.L.R. 775.
65 *De Lassalle* v. *Guildford* [1901] 2 K.B. 215.

made by the landlord not to enforce a covenant in the lease.[66] Such a contract will not easily be presumed. A solicitor has no implied authority to bind his client to a collateral contract.[67]

Exchange of contracts

Where a contract is to be executed in two or more parts, and it is intended that each party shall sign one part, and that the parts shall be exchanged, there is, in the absence of contrary agreement,[68] no binding agreement until the parts have been physically exchanged.[69] Where the agreement is " subject to contract " the contract is not binding until the exchange.[70] Similarly, where there is an agreement to grant a lease " subject to the terms of a lease " there is no binding agreement until the lease is actually executed.[71]

Nowadays the parts of the contract are usually exchanged by post. In this case, in the absence of express provision in the contract, the exchange is probably not complete until each party has received the part signed by the other party.[72] The Law Society's Conditions [73] provide that the exchange is effective when the last part is actually posted. The National Conditions do not deal with the matter.

II. Statutory Requirements of the Contract

Law of Property Act 1925, s. 40 [74]

This section, which replaces in part the Statute of Frauds 1677, s. 4, provides that " no action may be brought upon any contract for the sale or other disposition of land or any interest in land, unless the agreement upon which such action is brought, or some memorandum or note thereof, is in writing, and signed by the party to be charged or by some other person thereunto by him lawfully authorised."

The section does not affect the formation or validity of the contract; it lays down a rule of evidence. It merely deals with the necessary evidence of a contract when it is sought to enforce it. The absence of

---

[66] *City and Westminster Properties* (1934) *Ltd.* v. *Mudd* [1959] Ch. 129; and see *Bannister* v. *Bannister* [1948] 2 All E.R. 133.
[67] *Gilchester Properties Ltd.* v. *Gomm* [1948] 1 All E.R. 493.
[68] See *Griffiths* v. *Young* [1970] Ch. 675.
[69] *Eccles* v. *Bryant* [1948] Ch. 93; *D'Silva* v. *Lister House Development Ltd.* [1971] Ch. 17. *Cf. Smith* v. *Mansi* [1963] 1 W.L.R. 26 (where one solicitor was acting for both parties and there was only one contract).
[70] *Eccles* v. *Bryant, supra*; *King* v. *O'Shee* (1951) E.G. 83 (where plaintiff purported to withdraw by telephone after posting his part but before defendant had posted his part and it was held no concluded exchange and either party might withdraw).
[71] *Hollington Bros. Ltd.* v. *Rhodes* [1951] 2 T.L.R. 691, 694; (1970) 34 Conv.(N.S.) 145. But once a lease under seal has been delivered as an escrow it is not recallable: *Beesly* v. *Hallwood Estates Ltd.* [1961] Ch. 105. For escrows, see *post*, p. 209.
[72] See *Eccles* v. *Bryant, supra*, at pp. 97, 98 (no binding contract until, at the earliest, the date of posting the later contract to be posted); *Sim* v. *Griffiths* (1963) 107 S.J. 462 (no contract where vendor died after receipt of purchaser's part but before her part was posted); and (1967) 117 New L.J. 855.
[73] Condition 5 (2).
[74] See generally Megarry and Wade, *The Law of Real Property* (3rd ed.), pp. 554 *et seq.* And for criticisms of the statutory requirements see (1967) 31 Conv.(N.S.) 182, 254; (1968) 118 New L.J. 103. And see *ante*, p. 7, note 47.

writing does not render an oral contract *void*, but merely makes it
unenforceable by action.   It is true that in most cases the effect is the
same as if the contract is void, but, as will be seen,[75] a deposit paid
under an unenforceable contract cannot be recovered and, as the necessary note or memorandum may be made at any time after the agreement and before the commencement of proceedings,[76] a contract
originally unenforceable may become enforceable if the necessary
memorandum is subsequently made.   The section does not affect the
law relating to part performance or sales by the court.[77]

Land or interest in land

Land is defined in wide terms by the Law of Property Act 1925,
s. 205 (1) (ix).   Only a few matters need to be mentioned in this context.
Readers may recall the distinction between *fructus naturales, i.e.*
natural crops, which generally form part of the land, and *fructus
industriales, i.e.* cultivated crops, which do not.[78]

Again, fixtures form part of the land, and a contract for the sale of
fixtures, even separate from the land, is within section 40.   Whether a
chattel becomes a fixture and so passes to the purchaser without express
mention depends on the circumstances of each particular case.[79]   The
degree of annexation and the object of annexation are both relevant,
the latter, perhaps, being the primary consideration nowadays.[80]   The
annexation must appear to be for the permanent and substantial
improvement of the land or building.   It must not be for a temporary
purpose, nor merely to enable the owner of the chattel to enjoy the
chattel *as a chattel*.[81]   It is not always clear whether a particular object
is a fixture or not, and it is always better to deal with the matter
expressly by inquiry[82] and agreement.[83]   Greenhouses standing on
their own weight, and not secured to the ground, are not fixtures.[84]
On the other hand, mill-looms nailed into beams built into the stone
floor become fixtures, even though they can easily be removed without
damage to the building.[85]   Statues forming part of an ornamental
garden, and standing merely by their own weight, have been held to be
fixtures,[86] as have dog grates substituted for an ordinary grate,[87] and

[75] *Post*, p. 22.
[76] *Post*, p. 20.
[77] Law of Property Act 1925, s. 40 (2).   See *post*, p. 22.
[78] See *e.g.* Treitel, *The Law of Contract*, p. 138.
[79] See generally Megarry and Wade, *The Law of Real Property* (3rd ed.), pp. 715
   et seq.   Note also Law of Property Act 1925, s. 62 (1); *Dibble Ltd.* v. *Moore*
   [1970] 2 Q.B. 181.
[80] *Leigh* v. *Taylor* [1902] A.C. 157, 162.
[81] See *Holland* v. *Hodgson* (1872) L.R. 7 C.P. 328, 335.
[82] *Post*, p. 37.
[83] *Post*, p. 90.
[84] *Dibble* v. *Moore, supra; Billing* v. *Pill* [1954] 1 Q.B. 70.
[85] *Holland* v. *Hodgson, supra; Smith* v. *City Petroleum Co. Ltd.* [1940] 1 All E.R.
   260; *Webb* v. *Frank Bevis Ltd.* [1940] 1 All E.R. 247; *Hulme* v. *Brigham* [1943]
   K.B. 152.
[86] *D'Eyncourt* v. *Gregory* (1866) L.R. 3 Eq. 382.
[87] *Monti* v. *Barnes* [1901] 1 Q.B. 205.

even fitted carpets.[88] But a tapestry attached to a framework of wood and canvas, which was nailed to a wall and then surrounded by a frame fastened to the wall, remained a chattel.[89] It should also be remembered that as between landlord and tenant, mortgagor and mortgagee, etc., certain fixtures are removable.[90] An agreement for the sale of *tenant's* fixtures is not within section 40, since it amounts merely to a renunciation of the tenant's right of removal.[91]

An undivided share in land, *i.e.* a beneficial interest in land subject to a trust for sale, has been held to be an interest within the section,[92] but this has been criticised, and must now be doubted in view of a recent decision [93] where it was held that a beneficial joint tenancy is not an interest in land capable of being made subject to a charging order under section 35 of the Administration of Justice Act 1956.[94] The trust for sale brings into operation the doctrine of conversion, so treating the land as personalty, even before it is sold.

A contract to grant a lease, or a contract for the sale or surrender of leaseholds, and a contract to grant a mortgage or an easement, are all within section 40. A contract to take or let furnished rooms is within the section if specific rooms are let, but not if the lodger is not to have exclusive occupation of any particular room.[95] A building contract is not within the section.[96]

An agreement relating to matters, some of which are within section 40 and some of which are outside, for example, where the goodwill and stock-in-trade of a business is sold with the land, is not enforceable, even in respect of those matters which do not relate to land, unless it can be construed as separate and severable contracts.[97]

Contents of memorandum

Where there is a formal contract [98] the requirements of the section will be satisfied. In other cases, the party seeking to enforce the contract will usually rely on some correspondence or documents that have passed between the parties as constituting the required note or

---

[88] *La Salle Recreations Ltd.* v. *Canadian Camdex Investments Ltd.* (1969) 4 D.L.R. (3d) 549.
[89] *Leigh* v. *Taylor, supra.*
[90] Megarry and Wade, pp. 718 *et seq.*
[91] *Lee* v. *Gaskell* (1876) 1 Q.B.D. 700; *cf. Jarvis* v. *Jarvis* (1893) 63 L.J.Ch. 10 (charge of tenant's fixtures within section).
[92] *Cooper* v. *Critchley* [1955] Ch. 431 (although expressly excluded by the definition in Law of Property Act 1925, s. 205 (1) (ix) unless contrary intention is shown).
[93] *Irani Finance Ltd.* v. *Singh* [1971] Ch. 59; and see (1969) 119 New L.J. 1156; (1971) 34 M.L.R. 441.
[94] *Cf. National Westminster Bank Ltd.* v. *Allen* [1971] 2 Q.B. 718; (1971) 121 New L.J. 724 (where the charging order was a single one against the two persons beneficially entitled); and *Elias* v. *Mitchell* [1972] 2 W.L.R. 740.
[95] *Appah* v. *Parncliffe Investments Ltd.* [1964] 1 W.L.R. 1064.
[96] *Jameson* v. *Kinmel Bay Land Co. Ltd.* (1931) 47 T.L.R. 593; *cf. Lavery* v. *Pursell* (1888) 39 Ch. 508.
[97] *Hawkesworth* v. *Turner* (1930) 46 T.L.R. 389.
[98] See *ante*, p. 9. In some cases it may be doubtful whether the document is the contract itself or only a memorandum thereof: see *Hutton* v. *Watling* [1948] Ch. 398.

memorandum. Here, the contract is oral, but there is written evidence
of it to satisfy section 40.

The note or memorandum must, in the case of a sale, show:

  (1) the names or description of the vendor and purchaser;
  (2) the subject-matter of the contract;
  (3) the consideration; and
  (4) any special terms agreed between the parties.

In the case of a contract to grant a lease, the rent, the length of
the term, and the date of its commencement must also be specified.[99]

The parties. The names of the vendor and the purchaser must
appear in the note or memorandum or there must be a sufficient
description of them to enable them to be identified. " The vendor," [1]
" my client," [2] or " the landlord " [3] are not sufficient, for they are only
referable to the contract, the existence of which is in question. But
" the proprietor," [4] " owner," [5] " mortgagee," [6] " personal representatives " [7] and " trustees for sale " [8] have been sufficient. Persons
answering those descriptions can be identified quite apart from the
existence of the contract. Parol evidence is admissible to explain
the description.[9]

The name or description of an agent acting for an undisclosed
principal is sufficient compliance with the section.[10] Where the agent
signs as such, evidence cannot be adduced to identify the principal.[11]

The subject-matter. Parol evidence is also admissible to explain
the description of the subject-matter. " My house," [12] " twenty-four
acres of land at Totmanslow," [13] the " property bought " on a
specified date [14] have all been held sufficient.[15] The property need
only be described in a physical sense. Where a freehold reversion is
sold, the memorandum need not state that the property is subject to
a lease.[16]

The consideration. The consideration must be stated. The price
must be either a fixed price or a price to be calculated on a fixed

[99] See *post,* p. 24.
[1] *Potter* v. *Duffield* (1874) L.R. 18 Eq. 4; *Lavery* v. *Pursell, supra.*
[2] *Lovesy* v. *Palmer* [1916] 2 Ch. 233.
[3] *Coombs* v. *Wilkes* [1891] 3 Ch. 77.
[4] *Rossiter* v. *Miller* (1878) 3 App.Cas. 1124; *Fay* v. *Miller, Wilkins and Co.* [1941]
    Ch. 360.
[5] *Butcher* v. *Nash* (1889) 61 L.T. 72.
[6] *Pattle* v. *Anstruther* (1893) 69 L.T. 175.
[7] *Fay* v. *Miller, Wilkins and Co., supra.*
[8] *Catling* v. *King* (1877) 5 Ch.D. 660.
[9] *Auerbach* v. *Nelson* [1919] 2 Ch. 383; *F. Goldsmith (Sicklemere) Ltd.* v. *Baxter*
    [1970] Ch. 85; and see (1969) 119 New L.J. 990.
[10] *Basma* v. *Weekes* [1950] A.C. 441; *Davies* v. *Sweet* [1962] 2 Q.B. 300.
[11] *Lovesy* v. *Palmer, supra.*
[12] *Cowley* v. *Watts* (1853) 17 Jur. 172. And see *Ogilvie* v. *Foljambe* (1817) 3 Mer. 53
    (Mr. Ogilvie's house).
[13] *Plant* v. *Bourne* [1897] 2 Ch. 281.
[14] *Auerbach* v. *Nelson, supra.*
[15] See also *Davies* v. *Sweet, supra; Smith* v. *Mansi* [1963] 1 W.L.R. 26 at p. 38.
[16] *Timmins* v. *Moreland Street Property Co. Ltd.* [1958] Ch. 110.

basis.[17] If no price is stated, an agreement to sell at a reasonable price is not implied.[18]

Special terms. If no special terms were agreed upon, a memorandum specifying the parties, the property, and the consideration, and including the necessary signature, will be sufficient. But if any other terms were agreed, these must appear in the memorandum, unless they were entirely for the benefit of one party who is prepared to waive them,[19] or to the detriment of the party seeking to enforce the contract and he is willing to perform them. Examples of other terms which have been considered are provisions relating to the date for completion and vacant possession[20] or a provision that the purchaser shall pay half the vendor's costs.[21]

Signature. The memorandum must be signed by the defendant or his agent. It need not be signed by both parties. If the memorandum is signed by, or on behalf of, one of the parties, but not the other, the party who signed can be sued, whereas the other cannot.[22] The section requires signature not subscription, *i.e.* the signature may be in any part of the note or memorandum, not necessarily at the end, provided it applies to the whole of the document.[23] It may be by initial or printed, typed or stamped.[24]

If, after signature, the memorandum is altered by the solicitor of the person who signed, the alterations may be ratified, and, if so, the signature will cover the alterations.[25]

Where it is alleged that the document was signed by the defendant's agent, it must be proved that the person signing had authority to do so. Written authority is not required[26] but is usually obtained. A signature made without authority may be ratified. But the agent must be authorised to *sign*: it is not enough that he was authorised to *negotiate* a sale. Nor is it enough that he is the purchaser's solicitor; either the solicitor must be *expressly* authorised to bind his client, or such authority must be necessarily implicit in the terms of his retainer.[27] A solicitor retained to defend an action usually has no authority to

---

[17] See *Smith* v. *Jones* [1952] 2 All E.R. 907; *Selkirk* v. *Romar Investments Ltd.* [1963] 1 W.L.R. 1415; *Smith* v. *Morgan* [1971] 1 W.L.R. 803; *Brown* v. *Gould* [1972] Ch. 53.
[18] *Morgan* v. *Milman* (1853) 3 De G.M. & G. 24 at p. 37.
[19] See *post*, p. 21. Oral evidence may be introduced to prove that there were other terms.
[20] *Hawkins* v. *Price* [1947] Ch. 645; *Burgess* v. *Cox* [1951] Ch. 383.
[21] *Scott* v. *Bradley* [1971] Ch. 850.
[22] *Filby* v. *Hounsell* [1896] 2 Ch. 737.
[23] *Leeman* v. *Stocks* [1951] Ch. 941.
[24] *Cohen* v. *Roche* [1927] 1 K.B. 169. For contracts by companies, see the Companies Act 1948, s. 32; for corporations, see Corporate Bodies' Contracts Act 1960.
[25] *Koenigsblatt* v. *Sweet* [1923] 2 Ch. 314; and see *D'oyly Downs Ltd.* v. *Galloway* [1970] N.Z.L.R. 1077.
[26] *Daniels* v. *Trefusis* [1914] 1 Ch. 788.
[27] *North* v. *Loomes* [1919] 1 Ch. 378; *Griffiths* v. *Young* [1970] 1 Ch. 675. A solicitor may be the agent of both parties, if so authorised: see *Gavaghan* v. *Edwards* [1961] 2 Q.B. 220; *Smith* v. *Mansi* [1963] 1 W.L.R. 26.

create a memorandum by repudiation, for example, by a letter denying liability, or otherwise.[28]   The authority of auctioneers has already been mentioned.[29]   Prima facie an estate agent has no authority to sell and express authority to sign a contract will be required.[30]

Form of memorandum

The written memorandum need not be formal.   There is no need for there to have been any intention to make a memorandum satisfying the section; indeed, many a memorandum is made unintentionally.

As the section merely states a rule of evidence, the memorandum may come into existence at any time.   Usually the contract will be made before the memorandum, but a memorandum may come into existence before the contract, as in the case of an offer in writing accepted orally (where, if he can prove his acceptance, the offeree will be able to sue the offeror).   A letter repudiating an admitted contract [31] and a pleading signed by counsel in proceedings other than for the enforcement of the contract,[32] have been held sufficient.   Other examples of documents held sufficient to constitute memoranda are a receipt,[33] an entry in an auctioneer's book,[34] a note in a rent-book,[35] a will,[36] and a recital in a marriage settlement.[37]

Memorandum may consist of several documents

The memorandum need not consist of one document.   It may be made out from several documents if the documents can be connected together, for example, from several letters in a correspondence.   It has been said that to connect two documents there must be an express or implied reference to the other so that oral evidence is confined merely to identification.[38]   A letter and the envelope in which it was posted, connected by parol evidence, have been treated as one document.[39]   But in many cases there will be no need for evidence to connect the documents, a visual comparison being sufficient to show they are connected.[40]   A document cannot ordinarily be treated as referring to another document not in existence at that time, unless they were virtually contemporaneous.[41]

---

[28] *Thirkell* v. *Cambi* [1919] 2 K.B. 590.
[29] *Ante,* p. 11.
[30] *Wragg* v. *Lovett* [1948] 2 All E.R. 968.
[31] *Dewar* v. *Mintoft* [1912] 2 K.B. 373; *cf. Thirkell* v. *Cambi, supra.*
[32] *Grindell* v. *Bass* [1920] 2 Ch. 487; *Farr, Smith and Co. Ltd.* v. *Messers Ltd.* [1928] 1 K.B. 397.
[33] *Evans* v. *Prothero* (1852) 1 De G.M. & G. 572; *Auerbach* v. *Nelson* [1919] 2 Ch. 383.
[34] *Cohen* v. *Roche* [1927] 1 K.B. 169.
[35] *Hill* v. *Hill* [1947] Ch. 231.
[36] *Re Hoyle* [1893] 1 Ch. 84.
[37] *Re Holland* [1902] 2 Ch. 360.
[38] *Long* v. *Millar* (1879) 4 C.P.D. 450; *Stokes* v. *Whicher* [1920] 1 Ch. 411.
[39] *Pearce* v. *Gardner* [1897] 1 Q.B. 688.
[40] *Burgess* v. *Cox* [1951] Ch. 383.
[41] *Timmins* v. *Moreland Street Property Co. Ltd.* [1958] Ch. 110.

The leading modern authority on these principles is *Timmins* v. *Moreland Street Property Co. Ltd.*[42] There was an oral contract for the sale of land, and the purchaser's agent made out a cheque for the deposit in favour of the vendor's solicitor. For this the vendor gave him a receipt in the following terms—" Received of (then followed the name of the purchaser) the sum of £3,000 as a deposit for the purchase of 6, 8 and 41, Boundary Street, Shoreditch (freehold) which I agree to sell at £39,000." It was held that there was no sufficient memorandum, because the cheque, which was the only document signed on behalf of the purchaser, contained no reference to any other document or any transaction other than the order for payment which the cheque itself constituted and which was not an order for payment to the vendor. Accordingly the cheque could not be linked with the receipt and the purchaser's action for breach of contract when the vendor repudiated the agreement failed.

Concluded contract necessary

Of course, it is only necessary to have to consider whether there is a sufficient memorandum if there is a concluded contract. Accordingly, where one party is claiming specific performance of a contract, the terms of which are contained in an alleged memorandum, the other party may be able to defend the action on the basis that there is not a sufficient memorandum, or that there was no concluded agreement and the parties were still in negotiation.

Memorandum must contain all terms

It is essential that the memorandum should contain all the terms of the oral contract which have been expressly agreed.[43] The omission of a single term is fatal.[44] Accordingly, if he can show that not all the terms orally agreed are contained in the memorandum, the defendant will have a good defence to an action for specific performance.[45] But, if the memorandum omits a stipulation which is for the benefit of one of the parties alone, that party can enforce the contract if he waives the stipulation.[46] Similarly, if the missing term is to the detriment of the party seeking to enforce the contract he can enforce the contract if he is willing to perform that term.[47]

Absence of memorandum

We have already seen[48] that the absence of a sufficient memorandum does not render an oral contract void, but merely unenforceable.

[42] [1958] Ch. 110; see (1958) 74 L.Q.R. 22; (1958) 16 C.L.J. 36. And see *Griffiths* v. *Young* [1970] 1 Ch. 675.
[43] *Beckett* v. *Nurse* [1948] 1 K.B. 535; *Burgess* v. *Cox* [1951] Ch. 383.
[44] But as to rectification, see *post*, p. 25.
[45] Oral evidence may be introduced to prove this. In the case of a formal contract extrinsic evidence is not admissible to contradict or vary its terms: *Goss* v. *Nugent* (1833) 2 L.J.K.B. 127.
[46] *North* v. *Loomes* [1919] 1 Ch. 378.
[47] *Scott* v. *Bradley* [1971] Ch. 850.
[48] *Ante*, p. 16.

Thus the vendor may keep any deposit paid by the purchaser if the purchaser defaults,[49] and, if the deposit is paid by cheque, the vendor may sue on the cheque.[50] Likewise, the purchaser may recover the deposit if the vendor defaults.[51] But a purchaser under an oral contract who had taken possession of the property *without the vendor's consent* and was subsequently ejected by him, was not entitled to rely on the contract in reply to the vendor's defence in an action by the purchaser for trespass.[52]

Cases in which writing is not essential

A contract for the sale of land may sometimes be enforced, although there is no memorandum in writing to satisfy section 40 of the Law of Property Act 1925, namely:
(1) where the sale is by order of the court [53];
(2) where the absence of writing is not pleaded in the defendant's defence to the action on the contract [54];
(3) where it would be a fraud on the part of the defendant to rely upon the absence of writing, for example, where by his fraud he prevented the oral agreement from being put in writing,[55] or
(4) where there has been a sufficient act of *part performance* [56] on the part of the plaintiff to take the case out of section 40 of the Law of Property Act 1925.

Part performance [57]

Although at common law the absence of a memorandum was fatal to an action for damages for breach of a contract for the sale of land, courts of equity would not allow the statute to be used as an engine of fraud and would decree specific performance of the contract at the suit of a plaintiff who, in part or in whole, had performed his obligations under the contract.[58] If the plaintiff could show to the court's satisfaction a sufficient act of part performance, he would be allowed to give evidence of the terms of the contract in respect of which the court would order specific performance. This is still the position [59] save that damages may now also be awarded,[60] though in

---

[49] *Monnickendam* v. *Leanse* (1923) 39 T.L.R. 445.
[50] *Low* v. *Fry* (1935) 152 L.T. 585. *Aliter* if there is no contract; see *ante*, p. 12.
[51] *Pulbrook* v. *Lawes* (1876) 1 Q.B.D. 284.
[52] *Delaney* v. *Smith* [1946] K.B. 393.
[53] See Law of Property Act 1925, s. 40 (2).
[54] The Rules of the Supreme Court require the defendant to plead expressly the failure to satisfy s. 40: R.S.C., Ord. 18, r. 8. The same applies in the county court: see County Courts Act 1959, s. 103.
[55] *Viscountess Montacute* v. *Maxwell* (1720) 1 P.Wms. 618.
[56] See *post.*
[57] See Megarry and Wade, *The Law of Real Property* (3rd ed.), pp. 569 *et seq.*
[58] *Lester* v. *Foxcroft* (1701) Colles P.C. 108; *Rochefoucauld* v. *Boustead* [1897] 1 Ch. 196.
[59] Law of Property Act 1925, ss. 40 (2), 55 (d).
[60] Judicature Act 1925, s. 43.

practice it is specific performance which is the remedy usually sought by the plaintiff.

It is not every act of part performance that is sufficient to take the case out of section 40 of the Law of Property Act 1925. The act must comply with the following conditions:

(1) There must be a valid oral contract capable of being proved by oral evidence [61]; and

(2) The act relied on must be an act on the part of the *plaintiff*, for example, if on the faith of an oral contract, and to suit the purchaser, a vendor makes structural alterations in the premises agreed to be sold, this may be an act of part performance which will enable the vendor to sue the purchaser for specific performance.[62] It will not, however, enable the purchaser to sue the vendor. Taking possession of the land with the vendor's consent is an act of part performance by both purchaser and vendor, the latter's giving up of possession being regarded as an act of part performance [63]; and

(3) The act relied on must be one that is referable to some contract and may be referred to the alleged one.[64] It must be a substantial act and not merely of an introductory nature; for example, examining the drains, valuing or surveying the premises, or delivering an abstract of title, are not sufficient acts of part performance. Taking possession by the purchaser is generally an act of part performance on his part, and, as already indicated, allowing him to take possession is an act of part performance on the part of the vendor. Where, however, the purchaser's possession is referable to some other state of things, for example, he is already in possession as tenant of his vendor, the possession will not of itself amount to an act of part performance.[65] The payment by the purchaser of a deposit, or even of the whole of the purchase price, is not usually in itself a sufficient act of part performance [66]; and

(4) The act relied on must make it a fraud on the part of the defendant to take advantage of the statute. The acts done by the plaintiff must be known to the defendant, and the plaintiff must have altered his position upon the strength of the contract.[67] The payment of money is not sufficient in this respect as it may be returned by the defendant to the plaintiff.

61 *Parker* v. *Clark* [1960] 1 W.L.R. 286; *Wakeham* v. *Mackenzie* [1968] 1 W.L.R. 1175; *cf. Maddison* v. *Alderson* (1883) 8 App.Cas. 467.
62 *Rawlinson* v. *Ames* [1925] Ch. 96; and see *Daniels* v. *Trefusis* [1914] 1 Ch. 788.
63 See Fry, *Specific Performance* (6th ed.), pp. 286, 287.
64 *Kingswood Estate Co. Ltd.* v. *Anderson* [1963] 2 Q.B. 169; *Wakeham* v. *Mackenzie* [1968] 1 W.L.R. 1175. See (1968) 32 Conv.(N.S.) 384.
65 *Maddison* v. *Alderson, supra.*
66 *Maddison* v. *Alderson, supra*; *Chaproniere* v. *Lambert* [1917] 2 Ch. 356.
67 *McManus* v. *Cooke* (1887) 35 Ch.D. 681, at p. 697; *Chaproniere* v. *Lambert, supra.*

III. Agreements for Leases

We shall see [68] that the distinction between leases and agreements for leases has become less important, and often the parties will rely on the agreement alone, and not follow it up with a formal lease.

Section 40 of the Law of Property Act 1925 applies to agreements for leases.[69] Any memorandum of a contract to grant a lease must contain the names of the parties, and description of the property, the rent, the length of term and the date of its commencement [70] and any special terms agreed.

If the terms of the agreement are so vague or indefinite that they cannot be ascertained with reasonable certainty, there will be no enforceable agreement.[71] An agreement that the lease should contain such covenants and conditions as should " be reasonably required by " the lessors was held to be sufficiently certain and the lessors could not insist on an absolute prohibition against underletting, etc.[72]

The agreement may provide for the insertion of " the usual covenants " in the lease.[73] What is meant by " the usual covenants " is discussed subsequently.[74] Because of the restricted meaning of the expression, it is desirable either that the agreed covenants be listed in summary form, or for reference to be made to the covenants in a specified form.

We have already seen that if a formal lease is envisaged by the parties, for example, where the agreement is " subject to the terms of a lease," there is no binding agreement until the lease is executed.[75]

IV. Contracts for Sale of Registered Land

A contract is required for the sale of registered land in just the same way as for unregistered land.[76] There are no differences in the *form* of the contract. There will be some differences in the *terms* of a formal contract and major differences in the investigation of title. These differences are mentioned in their appropriate contexts in subsequent chapters.

V. Variation and Rectification of the Contract

Variation

It is not uncommon for the terms of the written contract to be varied by agreement between the parties. If the transaction is completed satisfactorily, no difficulties will arise. But if the parties fall

---

[68] *Post,* p. 245.
[69] *Ante,* p. 17.
[70] *Harvey* v. *Pratt* [1965] 1 W.L.R. 1025.
[71] See *Sweet and Maxwell Ltd.* v. *Universal News Services Ltd.* [1964] 2 Q.B. 699.
[72] *Sweet and Maxwell Ltd.* v. *Universal News Services Ltd., supra.* For covenants against underletting, etc., see *post,* p. 261.
[73] See *Hampshire* v. *Wickens* (1878) 7 Ch.D. 555; *Flexman* v. *Corbett* [1930] 1 Ch. 672.
[74] *Post,* p. 246.
[75] *Ante,* p. 15.
[76] See Farrand, *Contract and Conveyance,* p. 151; (1969) 32 M.L.R. 121.

out, complications may follow. Parol variations are not admissible. Where the contract requires to be in writing or evidenced in writing under section 40 of the Law of Property Act 1925, a *partial* variation of the contract must itself satisfy the statutory formalities.[77] If not, the original contract without the variation will be enforced.[78]

This position is different where the original written contract is subsequently *discharged* by an oral agreement. In that case the oral agreement is effective to discharge the written contract. But if the oral agreement purports to substitute a new agreement, the latter will not be effective, as not being evidenced in writing it fails to satisfy the statutory formalities.[79]

Rectification

It will sometimes happen that owing to a mistake, the written contract does not accurately set forth the terms orally agreed upon by the parties, *i.e.* the mistake occurs in reducing the contract into writing. In such a case, if the parties cannot agree to amend the contract, the court, on the application of one of the parties to the contract, will admit parol evidence to prove the mistake and will rectify the written agreement so as to give true effect to the intention of the parties.[80] The agreement prior to the written contract need not be a completely concluded, binding contract; it is sufficient so long as there is an outward expression of accord between the parties.[81] Generally, the mistake must be mutual and not merely unilateral.[82] What usually happens in practice is that one party to the agreement opposes the inclusion of the omitted term, and refuses to perform the contract, so that the action will be for rectification and specific performance of the contract as rectified.[83]

Sometimes the mistake will have been carried forward into the conveyance, made pursuant to the contract. In that case, the court will rectify the conveyance.[84]

VI. REGISTRATION OF THE CONTRACT

Registration as estate contract

Contracts for the sale of land, and options to purchase, or to take or renew a lease, are registrable under the Land Charges Act 1925 as

---

[77] *Goss* v. *Nugent* (1833) 2 L.J.K.B. 127.
[78] *Morris* v. *Baron and Co.* [1918] A.C. 1; *British and Beningtons Ltd.* v. *N.W. Cachar Tea Co.* [1923] A.C. 48.
[79] *Morris* v. *Baron, supra*; *Don Lodge Motel Ltd.* v. *Invercargill Licensing Trust* [1970] N.Z.L.R. 1105.
[80] See generally, Snell's *Equity* (26th ed.), pp. 679 *et seq.*
[81] *Joscelyne* v. *Nissen* [1970] 2 Q.B. 86. Until this case the authorities had been in conflict on this point; see (1970) 120 New L.J. 330; (1971) 87 L.Q.R. 532.
[82] *A. Roberts and Co. Ltd.* v. *Leicestershire County Council* [1961] Ch. 555. See Snell, p. 684; *post*, p. 200.
[83] *Craddock Bros.* v. *Hunt* [1923] 2 Ch. 136; *United States of America* v. *Motor Trucks Ltd.* [1924] A.C. 196.
[84] *Craddock Bros.* v. *Hunt, supra.*

estate contracts. An estate contract is a land charge Class C (iv). It is defined by section 10 of the Land Charges Act 1925 as any contract by an estate owner or by a person entitled at the date of the contract to have a legal estate conveyed to him or create a legal estate, including a contract conferring either expressly or by statutory implication a valid option of purchase, a right of pre-emption or any other like right.[85] The definition therefore includes a contract to sell a legal estate, to grant a legal lease or to grant a legal mortgage.[86]

A land charge is registered in the name of the estate owner whose estate is intended to be affected.[87] The registration is effected by the purchaser or other grantee, application therefor being made to the Land Charges Department on the prescribed form.[88] In the case of a sub-sale, in addition to any registration by the purchaser, the sub-purchaser must register against the name of the head vendor.

A different method of protection applies where the title is registered.[89]

The purpose of registration is to give the purchaser priority should the vendor attempt to dispose of the land by sale or otherwise to another. Registration is deemed to constitute actual notice of the interest registered.[90] It is not the general practice to register a contract for sale as an estate contract. But the contract should be registered if completion is delayed, and in a number of other special circumstances, for example, when there is any suspicion as to the good faith of the vendor, or where the contract provides for payment by instalments,[91] or where a dispute arises between vendor and purchaser before completion.

Effect of non-registration

An estate contract created, or entered into, after 1925 is void against a purchaser of a legal estate in the land affected thereby for money or money's worth, unless registered before the completion of the purchase.[92] Accordingly, if the estate contract is not registered, and the vendor should sell and convey the property to another person, that person will, in the case of unregistered land, take the property free from the original purchaser's interest, even if he has express notice of it. In this case, the original purchaser's remedy will be in damages, either against the vendor for breach of contract, or against his own

---

85 This includes an option to renew contained in a lease: *Beesly* v. *Hallwood Estates Ltd.* [1961] Ch. 105. See also *Shiloh Spinners Ltd.* v. *Harding* [1972] Ch. 326 (right to re-enter under lease on breach of covenant).
86 See *Turley* v. *Mackay* [1944] Ch. 37; *Sharp* v. *Coates* [1949] 1 K.B. 285; *Re Rayleigh Weir Stadium* [1954] 1 W.L.R. 786; *Du Sautoy* v. *Symes* [1967] Ch. 1146; *Thomas* v. *Rose* [1968] 1 W.L.R. 1797. As to whether an oral agreement made enforceable by part performance is registrable, see (1955) 19 Conv.(N.S.) 99, 100.
87 Land Charges Act 1925, s. 10 (2). See *post*, p. 158.
88 See *post*, p. 158.
89 *Post*, p. 27.
90 Law of Property Act 1925, s. 198; see *post*, p. 150.
91 For sub-sales, see *post*, p. 195.
92 Land Charges Act 1925, s. 13 (2).

solicitors for negligence in failing to register the contract.[93] A lessee, who fails to protect an option to renew by registration, may, therefore, still recover damages against the original lessor although the option would be unenforceable for non-registration against a purchaser of the reversion. The lessor may, however, be entitled to be indemnified by the purchaser under the terms of the contract.[94] In the case of registered land, if the original purchaser or tenant, etc., is in possession, his interest under the contract of sale will be binding on the third person as an overriding interest.[95]

Vacating the registration

On applying for registration of an estate contract, the document creating the contract has to be mentioned in the application form. However, the validity of the contract is not determined by the Registry, and, in practice, unenforceable contracts are occasionally registered. Registration of an estate contract therefore affords an opportunity for an unscrupulous person who has negotiated a purchase, but does not have an enforceable contract, to put pressure on a vendor. The registration will prevent the vendor selling his land until such time as he has an order of the court vacating the registration.[96] In such circumstances, the vendor might be obliged to accept the unenforceable contract as binding rather than attempt to have the registration vacated.[97]

Where an estate contract has been registered, the purchaser's solicitor should see to the cancellation of the registration on completion.[98]

Registered land

Where the land is registered, the contract should be protected by notice [99] or restriction,[1] if the vendor will co-operate by lodging his land certificate at the Registry or, if not, by caution.[2] If the land is subject to a registered charge, the land certificate will already be deposited in the Registry,[3] in which case the purchaser should apply for

---

[93] *Wright* v. *Dean* [1948] Ch. 686; *Hollington Bros. Ltd.* v. *Rhodes* [1951] 2 All E.R. 578n.

[94] *Eagon* v. *Dent* [1965] 3 All E.R. 334.

[95] *Woolwich Equitable Building Society* v. *Marshall* [1952] Ch. 1; *Du Sautoy* v. *Symes* [1967] Ch. 1146. As to overriding interests, see *post*, p. 170.

[96] Land Charges Act 1925, s. 10 (8); and see *Re Engall's Agreement* [1953] 1 W.L.R. 977; *Heywood* v. *B.D.C. Properties Ltd.* [1963] 1 W.L.R. 975.

[97] See generally (1968) 118 New L.J. 1167.

[98] For the purchaser's duties and rights as to cancellation of land charge entries, see *Emmet on Title* (15th ed.), pp. 590, 591.

[99] Under Land Registration Act 1925, s. 49 (1) (*c*). This is the usual method where there has been a contract to sell by an applicant for first registration.

[1] Under *ibid.* s. 58 (1). For restrictions, notices and cautions, see *post*, pp. 180 *et seq.*

[2] Under *ibid.* s. 54. See *Rawlplug Co. Ltd.* v. *Kamvale Properties Ltd.* (1968) 112 S.J. 723; (1969) 20 P. & C.R. 32; also *Calgary & Edmonton Land Co. Ltd.* v. *Discount Bank (Overseas) Ltd.* [1971] 1 W.L.R. 81. If there is a sub-sale application should be made for the registration of a fresh caution by the sub-purchaser, the original caution being withdrawn.

[3] Under *ibid.* s. 65; see *post*, p. 299.

the entry of a notice; but this notice will not be effective against the chargee, unless he concurs in the application and lodges his charge certificate for the entry of the notice to be made in it.[4]

VII. OPTIONS

Nature of options

An option is an irrevocable offer, which, if properly exercised by the grantee, will become an enforceable contract. It is not in itself a contract or a conditional contract. No contract is concluded until the option is exercised.[5]

When used

If a developer or speculator is interested in a particular property or piece of land he may be unwilling to purchase it outright if the prospects are uncertain. The answer is to take an option on it for a small sum, if the vendor is willing to grant one. The effect of this is that the option-holder can then purchase the property at a later date if he wishes and the owner of the land cannot sell it to another, unless the option-holder consents. Another way of securing the same result is to enter into a conditional contract.[6] Options are often acquired, for example, over agricultural land near towns, on the off-chance that development will spread. If that happens, the grantee will exercise the option and so be able to acquire the land at what will usually be a modest price. He will then sell the land for building development, or develop the land himself, and hope to make a profit on the transaction. If the town does not develop in the manner anticipated, the option will not be exercised and the option-holder will suffer a small loss in so far as the option turns out to be worthless. Options are, of course, used in other contexts and in respect of other property, such as shares, and are quite often granted by will by a testator in favour of named beneficiaries.

Types of option

There are various types of option, the most common being found in leases. These may be either an *option to purchase* the reversion or an *option to renew* the lease, *i.e.* to take a further term. An option in respect of land not contained in a lease is called an *option in gross*. Examples are options to purchase or to take a lease. Somewhat similar to an option are a *right of pre-emption*[7] and a *right of first refusal*, which require the grantor of the option, if he wishes to sell his property, to offer it first to the grantee.

---

[4] Land Registration Act 1925, ss. 64 (1) (c), 65.
[5] *Re Button's Lease* [1964] Ch. 263; and see (1958) 74 L.Q.R. 242.
[6] See *ante*, p. 13. It may be a question of construction whether a document is an option or a conditional contract: see *Re Longlands Farm* [1968] 3 All E.R. 552.
[7] See *Manchester Ship Canal Co.* v. *Manchester Racecourse Co.* [1901] 2 Ch. 37; *Du Sautoy* v. *Symes* [1967] Ch. 1146.

Validity of option—rule against perpetuities

At common law the rule against perpetuities [8] applied to options to purchase simpliciter or to purchase the reversion, in so far as they created proprietary (as opposed to purely contractual) rights,[9] because the option might be exercised many years after its creation.[10] If the option was exercisable beyond the perpetuity period, it was not enforceable against a person other than the grantor or his personal representatives. The rule did not apply, however, to mere contractual rights, so that damages [11] or even specific performance [12] were obtainable against the grantor or his estate. Where the option was granted by will, and infringed the rule against perpetuities, it was entirely void.

The rule against perpetuities did not apply at common law to options to renew,[13] even where the lease was perpetually renewable.[14]

The position is different in respect of options in instruments coming into effect on or after July 16, 1964. Section 9 (1) of the Perpetuities and Accumulations Act 1964 provides that the rule against perpetuities shall not apply to an option given for valuable consideration to a lessee to purchase an interest reversionary (whether directly or indirectly) on the term of a lease (*i.e.* an option to purchase the reversion or to renew the lease) if (1) the option is exercisable only by the lessee or his successors in title and (2) it ceases to be exercisable at or before the expiration of one year following the determination of the lease. In any other case the option is void, even as between the original parties,[15] unless exercised within twenty-one years.[16]

Validity of option—protection by registration

If the option is to be binding upon a purchaser of the land subject to it, it must be protected by registration as a land charge,[17] or, in the case of registered land, by an appropriate entry in the register.[18] In the latter case, even if not protected by notice on the register it may be enforceable as an overriding interest where the grantee is in actual occupation.[19]

---

[8] See Megarry and Wade, *The Law of Real Property* (3rd ed.), pp. 264 *et seq.*
[9] A contract for the sale of land gives the purchaser an equitable interest in the land. An option gives the grantee an equitable interest in the land contingent on his exercise of the option.
[10] *London and South Western Ry.* v. *Gomm* (1882) 20 Ch.D. 562; *Woodall* v. *Clifton* [1905] 2 Ch. 257; *Rider* v. *Ford* [1923] 1 Ch. 541 (option to take lease).
[11] *Worthing Corpn.* v. *Heather* [1906] 2 Ch. 532; *Wright* v. *Dean* [1948] Ch. 686.
[12] *Hutton* v. *Watling* [1948] Ch. 398.
[13] *Muller* v. *Trafford* [1901] 1 Ch. 54; *Weg Motors Ltd.* v. *Hales* [1962] Ch. 49. An option to renew contained in a lease for a term exceeding 21 years is not invalidated by s. 149 (3) of the Law of Property Act 1925 (see *post*, p. 254), provided the new term is not limited to commence more than 21 years from the date of the lease creating it: *Weg Motors Ltd.* v. *Hales, supra.*
[14] For perpetually renewable leases after 1925, see *post*, p. 255.
[15] Perpetuities and Accumulations Act 1964, s. 10.
[16] Perpetuities and Accumulations Act 1964, ss. 9 (2), 3 (wait and see). For difficulties raised by these sections, see Megarry and Wade, *ubi supra.*
[17] As an estate contract; see *ante*, p. 25.
[18] By notice, etc.; see *ante*, p. 27.
[19] *Webb* v. *Pollmount* [1966] Ch. 584 (for overriding interests, see *post*, p. 170). Or under s. 70 (1) (*k*) of the Land Registration Act 1925, if the lease does not exceed 21 years.

Assignment of benefit of option

Subject to any express or implied limitation to the contrary, an option is assignable. If the option is intended to be personal to the grantee, this fact should be stated. Otherwise the option will be exercisable by anyone to whom the grantee assigns the benefit of it, unless there is some contrary indication in the document making it personal to the grantee, or, in the case of an option granted to a tenant, limiting the possible assignees to assignees of the term.[20] An option to renew contained in a lease touches and concerns the land and prima facie runs with it.[21] An option to purchase the reversion contained in a lease, although it does not touch and concern the land but is merely collateral, is also prima facie assignable.[22] In neither case is an express assignment of the option, in addition to an assignment of the term, necessary.[23] The benefit of an option in gross is also assignable unless there is a contrary intention in the document.[24]

Burden of option runs with the land

The burden of an option to renew runs with the reversion,[21] but it must, however, be registered as an estate contract,[17] or, in the case of registered land, be protected by an entry on the register,[18] to bind successors of the grantor. The tenant who has failed to protect his option will have an action for damages against the grantor,[25] even though he cannot force the option against the grantor's successors in title.[26] An option to purchase, whether contained in a lease or not, will only be enforceable against a purchaser of the land subject to the option if registered as an estate contract.[27]

Exercise of option

An option must be exercised in strict accordance with its terms,[28] unless the grantor waives his rights in this respect.[29] Hence the terms of the option should deal with the method of exercising it, for example,

---

[20] *Re Button's Lease* [1964] Ch. 263.
[21] *Muller* v. *Trafford* [1901] 1 Ch. 54; *Weg Motors Ltd.* v. *Hales* [1962] Ch. 49.
[22] *Batchelor* v. *Murphy* [1926] A.C. 63. But where a tenant holds over as a yearly tenant, or under the Rent Act, an option to purchase is not one of the terms of the original tenancy which will be incorporated in the new tenancy: *Longmuir* v. *Kew* [1960] 1 W.L.R. 862.
[23] *Griffith* v. *Pelton* [1958] Ch. 205.
[24] As to options in wills, see *Skelton* v. *Younghouse* [1942] A.C. 571.
[25] *Wright* v. *Dean* [1948] Ch. 686.
[26] See *Eagon* v. *Dent* [1965] 3 All E.R. 334; *Du Sautoy* v. *Symes* [1967] Ch. 1146. For the grantor's right of indemnity from a purchaser of the reversion, see *ante*, p. 27, footnote 94. To avoid this liability the option should contain a proviso that it shall become void unless protected by registration within a specified period (see *Encyclopaedia of Forms and Precedents* (4th ed.), Vol. 11, p. 341).
[27] An option in a will, not being given for value, is not registrable as a land charge, so it cannot bind a purchaser from the personal representatives.
[28] If the terms are uncertain it will be void: *Smith* v. *Morgan* [1971] 1 W.L.R. 803; *Brown* v. *Gould* [1972] Ch. 53; see (1971) 121 New L.J. 657. As to options in wills, see *Re Avard* [1948] Ch. 43.
[29] *Hill* v. *Hill* [1947] Ch. 231.

whether it is to be exercised by notice in writing,[30] and the time within which it is to be exercised.[31] Time is of the essence of the contract in the exercise of an option.[31]

An option to renew is generally made conditional on the tenant not being in breach of any of his covenants under the lease.[32]

Whether or not the exercise of the option will have the effect of determining the tenancy will depend on the terms of the option.[33]

Conversion

Where an option to purchase land is exercised after the death of the grantor the exercise of the option retrospectively converts the land into personalty.[34] The effect of the doctrine of conversion may be to defeat a testator's intention, as, for example, where there is a specific devise of realty subject to an option which is exercised after the testator's death. Here, the devise will lapse.[35]

VIII. ESTATE AGENTS

Many sales involve an estate agent. It is convenient to deal here with a number of points in relation to estate agents.

Misrepresentation

The vendor's estate agent in making statements about the property to be sold, or let, will be acting as the vendor's, or lessor's agent. Acting under express or implied authority, an estate agent's misrepresentation may make the vendor liable to the purchaser. An estate agent has implied or usual authority to make statements about the property being sold.[36] However, he owes a duty of care to the vendor.[37]

An estate agent is probably not directly liable to a purchaser or tenant under the Misrepresentation Act 1967, as section 2 (1) of the Act refers to a misrepresentation made to one party to a contract by *another party thereto*.[38] It is possible, however, that he may be liable under the principle enunciated in *Hedley Byrne & Co. Ltd.* v. *Heller and Partners Ltd.*[39] and the particulars of sale of most firms of estate agents now contain a disclaimer of liability for statements contained in them. The effect of this is probably to relieve the estate agent of any

---

[30] An option which provides for notice to the lessor is effectively exercised by notice to his personal representatives: *Kennewell* v. *Dye* [1949] Ch. 517. In the absence of a provision for notice an option to renew may be exercised by the tenant remaining in occupation and paying rent: *Gardner* v. *Blaxill* [1960] 1 W.L.R. 752.
[31] *Hare* v. *Nicoll* [1966] 2 Q.B. 130.
[32] *West Country Cleaners (Falmouth)* v. *Saly* [1966] 1 W.L.R. 1485.
[33] *Cockwell* v. *Romford Sanitary Steam Laundry Ltd.* [1939] 4 All E.R. 370.
[34] *Lawes* v. *Bennett* (1785) 1 Cox Eq. 167. See Snell's *Equity* (26th ed.), p. 520.
[35] See *Re Kempthorne* [1930] 1 Ch. 268.
[36] *Watteau* v. *Fenwick* [1893] 1 Q.B. 346.
[37] See *e.g. Smith* v. *Barton* (1866) 15 L.T. 294.
[38] *Post,* p. 35.
[39] *Post,* p. 35.

Hedley Byrne liability; and may relieve him of his duty of care to the vendor. But the disclaimer will not relieve the *vendor* of liability to the purchaser in respect of any misrepresentation made by the estate agent.[40]

Deposits

Estate agents commonly ask a prospective purchaser to sign some sort of agreement " subject to contract," and to pay a proportion of the purchase price as a " deposit." The capacity in which the estate agent holds the deposit will be of particular importance if, for example, the estate agent becomes bankrupt. If nothing is said as to the agent's capacity until contract, the estate agent will hold the deposit as agent for the vendor, who will be liable to repay it if the agent does not return it should the proposed sale fall through.[41] After contract he holds it in accordance with the terms of the contract.[42] A practice has grown up in recent years for the estate agent to take the deposit expressly as agent for the vendor, in which case if the estate agent absconds the purchaser will have to look to the vendor for the return of the money if the sale goes off.[43] The better practice (from the vendor's point of view) is for the money to be paid to the estate agent as " stakeholder " subject to contract. The effect of this is that the agent holds the money until contract as agent for the purchaser and thereafter in accordance with the terms of the contract.[44]

Commission

If the sale goes through, there is no doubt that the estate agent is entitled to his commission.[45] But if the sale is " subject to contract " and goes off, the position is not so clear. In every case it will depend on the terms of the contract between the vendor and estate agent. The contract may provide for the payment of commission on the signing of a " legally binding contract." [46] If it provides for payment of commission on introducing a person " ready, willing and able " to purchase, this means that there must be a firm offer, *i.e.* not one " subject to contract," [47] and the purchaser must not have refused to complete [48] and must be acceptable to the vendor.[49] Commission may

---

[40] (1968) 118 New L.J. 789; *cf.* (1967) 30 M.L.R. 369. For a form of exception clause, see *Precedents for the Conveyancer* (a collection of precedents issued with *The Conveyancer* journal), precedent 16–1.
[41] *Burt* v. *Claude Cousins & Co. Ltd.* [1971] 2 Q.B. 426; *cf. Barrington* v. *Lee* [1972] 1 Q.B. 326. And see (1972) 36 Conv.(N.S.) 5.
[42] *Chillingworth* v. *Esche* [1924] 1 Ch. 97.
[43] *Ryan* v. *Pilkington* [1959] 1 W.L.R. 403; *Burt* v. *Claude Cousins Ltd., supra.*
[44] *Chillingworth* v. *Esche, supra.* And see *per* Lord Denning M.R., in *Burt* v. *Claude Cousins Ltd., supra.*
[45] Although there may be disputes as to who is entitled to the commission where there are several estate agents acting.
[46] *Scheggia* v. *Gradwell* [1963] 1 W.L.R. 1049.
[47] *Graham and Scott (Southgate) Ltd.* v. *Oxlade* [1950] 2 K.B. 257.
[48] *Dennis Reed Ltd.* v. *Goody* [1950] 2 K.B. 277.
[49] *Dellafiora* v. *Lester* [1962] 1 W.L.R. 1208; *cf. Scheggia* v. *Gradwell, supra.*

be made payable on a prospective purchaser signing the agent's purchaser's agreement.[50]

Where a contract is signed but is repudiated by the vendor, the estate agent is entitled to his commission.[51]

[50] *Drewery and Drewery* v. *Ware-Lane* [1960] 1 W.L.R. 1204. See also *Jaques* v. *Lloyd D. George and Partners Ltd.* [1968] 1 W.L.R. 625; (1969) 119 New L.J. 407.

[51] See generally, *Dennis Reed Ltd.* v. *Goody, supra*; Treitel, *The Law of Contract*, pp. 654–658. If a " sole agent " is appointed, the principal cannot sell through another agent, but he can still sell himself; see *Bentall, Horsley and Baldry* v. *Vicary* [1931] 1 K.B. 253, where it was also suggested that a grant of a " sole right to sell " would deprive the principal selling to someone not introduced through the agent.

CHAPTER 3

INQUIRIES AND SEARCHES BEFORE CONTRACT

SAVE for technical defects,[1] the occasions when one finds a defective title are comparatively rare. Accordingly, in most cases, the investigation of title is, to some extent at least, a formality. More important in practice are the various searches and inquiries that have to be made before and after contract. In this chapter we shall deal with those inquiries and searches.

I. PRELIMINARY INQUIRIES

Purpose

It has, in comparatively recent times,[2] become the common practice for the purchaser's solicitor to make certain preliminary inquiries of the vendor, or his solicitor, before the contract has been entered into. These inquiries are known as " preliminary inquiries " or " enquiries before contract." [3] The purpose of such inquiries is to obtain information as to matters which the vendor might not otherwise be obliged to disclose,[4] such as the application of the Rent Act to any tenancies affecting the property, or the Town and Country Planning Acts or other related legislation.[5] Preliminary inquiries are also to some extent a reaction to the standard conditions of sale which generally favour the vendor.[6] The advantage of making such inquiries is that, in the event of the answers proving unsatisfactory, the purchaser is at liberty to discontinue his negotiations. Of course, where the purchaser has already entered into a contract before consulting his solicitor, there will be no place for preliminary inquiries, nor is it usually possible to make them in the case of a sale by auction. In rare cases, where the conditions of sale are so framed as to enable the purchaser to rescind the contract if the results of his inquiries are unsatisfactory, inquiries may be left until after the contract.[7]

Preliminary inquiries should not be confused with *requisitions* on

---

1 Such as those arising out of *Re King's Will Trusts*; see *post*, p. 401.
2 See (1950) 14 Conv.(N.S.) 226; (1964) 28 Conv.(N.S.) 28.
3 The use of " enquiries " or " inquiries " is a matter of preference.
4 See *post*, p. 78, as to the duty to disclose.
5 See *post*, p. 44, for town and country planning matters.
6 *Post*, p. 84.
7 The former Condition 21 of the previous edition of the Law Society's Conditions of Sale (1953 ed.) provided for exchange of contracts before local land charge searches, but had to be expressly incorporated. That condition has not been repeated in the latest edition. And see National Conditions, Condition 13, which applies if expressly incorporated.

title, the nature of which is different,[8] although to some extent they cover the same ground.

Remedies for incorrect answers

Answers to preliminary inquiries do not form part of the contract, but amount to representations. If a purchaser, after a contract has been made, discovers that the answers are incorrect, he will, subject to the conditions of sale,[9] have the following remedies:

(1) If the answer was made fraudulently, the purchaser will have an action for damages and he will be able to rescind the contract, even after completion[10];

(2) If the answer was not made fraudulently, but negligently, *i.e.* the vendor cannot prove that he had reasonable grounds to believe and did believe up to the time of the contract that the facts represented were true,[11] the purchaser will have an action for damages for misrepresentation under the Misrepresentation Act 1967,[12] whether or not the representation has become a term of the contract,[13] and will be able to rescind the contract, even after completion,[14] subject to the power of the court to award compensation in lieu thereof.[15] Because of the difficulty of proving fraud, the remedy under the Act will probably replace that for fraudulent misrepresentation in the normal case.

The purchaser may also have, in the alternative, an action for damages at common law under the principle enunciated in *Hedley Byrne and Co. Ltd.* v. *Heller and Partners Ltd.*[16]

(3) If the answer was neither fraudulent nor negligent, *i.e.* the vendor can prove that he had reasonable grounds to believe and did believe up to the time of the contract that the facts represented were true, then the purchaser will have a right to rescind the contract,[17]

---

[8] See *post*, p. 134.

[9] Law Society's Conditions, Condition 13; National Conditions, Condition 17; see *post*, p. 95.

[10] Alternatively, the purchaser may affirm the conveyance and have damages only: *London County Freehold & Leasehold Properties Ltd.* v. *Berkeley Property and Investment Co. Ltd.* [1936] 2 All E.R. 1039.

[11] Misrepresentation Act 1967, s. 2 (1). The terms " negligent " and " innocent " misrepresentation are not used in the Act.

[12] s. 2 (1). The Act applies where both the misrepresentation and the contract were made after April 22, 1967: s. 5. See (1967) 30 M.L.R. 369; (1967) 16 C.L.J. 239; (1967) 31 Conv.(N.S.) 234; (1967) 117 New L.J. 616; (1970) 67 L.S.Gaz. 183, 256, 287, 318; Treitel, *The Law of Contract*, 3rd ed., pp. 271 *et seq.*

[13] s. 1. Before the Act in the case of non-fraudulent misrepresentation the injured party only had an action for damages if the misrepresentation was incorporated in the contract.

[14] s. 1. Rescission after completion was not possible before the Act under the extensions of the rule in *Seddon* v. *North Eastern Salt Co. Ltd.* [1905] 1 Ch. 326; see *Angel* v. *Jay* [1911] 1 K.B. 666. It was also doubtful whether there was a right to rescission where the misrepresentation had become incorporated in the contract.

[15] s. 2 (2).

[16] [1964] A.C. 465. For the differences between the statutory and Hedley Byrne liability, see Treitel, pp. 285 *et seq.*

[17] *Cf. Gilchester Properties Ltd.* v. *Gomm* [1948] 1 All E.R. 493.

even after completion and whether or not the representation has been incorporated in the contract,[18] or, if the court thinks just, he will be entitled to compensation in lieu.[19]

These remedies for the purchaser explain the advantage to him of asking preliminary inquiries.

Answers to preliminary inquiries do not constitute warranties for breach of which an action for damages will lie.[20]   Nor does it seem that preliminary inquiries and the answers thereto will constitute a " collateral contract." [21]

It is quite common for the vendor's solicitor to attempt to limit his own, and his client's, liability in respect of the answers to preliminary inquiries, by the inclusion of such a clause as " These replies are given only on the basis that they do not form part of the agreement for sale and are not collateral to it, and that they do not constitute representations or amount to warranties."[22]   Such exclusions would appear to be possible, in spite of the limitation on exclusion clauses in the Misrepresentation Act.[23]

The inquiries

A standard form of preliminary inquiries is generally used, either one of the printed forms supplied by law stationers,[24] or a printed or typed and duplicated form prepared by a particular firm of solicitors for its own use.   The standard forms, of course, attempt to cover all eventualities.[25]   The solicitor should therefore eliminate or edit out all inquiries which are manifestly inapplicable to the particular purchase, such as those inquiries which deal with tenanted properties where vacant possession will be given, or those that refer to agricultural land where the property is a town house.   There are several advantages in using standard forms [26] but the generality of the questions tends to evasion by the vendor's solicitor in his answers.   There is a well-recognised string of phrases, such as " . . . as far as the vendor knows," or " please inspect," which are commonly used to qualify answers.[27] Where general questions are asked the answers are often worthless and the whole business becomes a waste of everybody's time.[28]   Specific questions will generally get specific answers.

18 Misrepresentation Act 1967, s. 1.
19 *Ibid.* s. 2 (2).   As to these remedies generally, see (1967) 117 New L.J. 975.
20 *Mahon* v. *Ainscough* [1952] 1 All E.R. 337.
21 *Gilchester Properties Ltd.* v. *Gomm, supra* (innocent overstatement as to rents).
22 (1967) 117 New L.J. 975; (1970) 67 L.S.Gaz. 318.
23 s. 3. The restrictions seem to be limited to exclusions in the *contract*.
24 Students should obtain the appropriate forms, *e.g.* from the Solicitors' Law Stationery Society Ltd., Conveyancing 29 (Long).
25 See generally (1961) 25 Conv.(N.S.) 336, 744; (1970) 120 New L.J. 610, 630; (1970) 63 *Law Guardian* 15, for commentary on the standard form inquiries.
26 Uniformity, time-saving, etc.
27 Mr. Carter (see *ante,* p. 6) has even suggested that the *answers* be printed on the printed forms; see letter in (1969) 48 *Law Guardian* 29.
28 See, *e.g.* the criticisms in the articles referred to in note 25 above and correspondence in the *Law Guardian* for 1969 and 1970.

Where the land is registered appropriate preliminary inquiries should be asked in exactly the same manner as in the case of unregistered land.

As to the actual layout of the form of preliminary inquiries, the inquiries are generally set out on the left-hand half of the paper, the right-hand half being used for the answers. As a matter of courtesy, the form of inquiries should be sent in duplicate so that the vendor's solicitor can retain one copy for reference.

Inquiries can be divided into *general inquiries* and *special inquiries*.

General inquiries relate to matters which arise in every case, such as the whereabouts of the documents of title; the various outgoings affecting the property (other than the usual general rates); easements affecting the property; public services and utilities; drainage rights; and, in the case of registered land, overriding interests.[29] Inquiries should also be directed to the legal status of roads and passages abutting the property (whether or not they have been adopted, *i.e.* taken over by the local authority[30]) and, in the case of new property, to whether provision has been made by the developer in respect of road charges.[31] An inquiry should be made with regard to the ownership of the various boundary structures. It is now common form to inquire whether the property is affected by woodworm, dry rot, etc., and to deal with fixtures and fittings.[32] Many items, such as carpets and curtains, will clearly not be fixtures and will not be included in the sale, unless expressly so provided. But other items, such as television aerials, electric fires, light fittings, built-in furniture and garden features, may well be fixtures (or at least the purchaser may think these are included in the sale). The position should be clarified by raising a preliminary inquiry as to such things. Garden plants, bushes and trees, form part of the land and pass without express mention, but are often taken away by the vendor. If there are any special plants and trees, for instance those in tubs, an inquiry should be made as to whether these will be left.

Special inquiries, on the other hand, will depend on the particular property involved. For example, where a property is tenanted, an

[29] For overriding interests, see *post*, p. 170.
[30] Inquiry as to this will also be made of the appropriate local authority or authorities (see *post*, p. 42). If they have not been adopted there will be a potential liability for road charges, for the cost of " making up " a street before it is adopted by the local authority is generally to be borne by the frontagers: Highways Act 1959, ss. 173–191. Where the highway has been taken over but has not been made up there is a potential liability for making up, but until making up there is nothing to be registered in the local land charges register so that a search there is not in itself sufficient protection.
[31] The developer has a choice of two alternative methods. He may enter into an agreement with the local authority under s. 40 of the Highways Act 1959, (a s. 40 agreement) or operate the so-called Advance Payments Code under s. 192 and Pt. IX of the 1959 Act; see further (1963) 27 Conv.(N.S.) 284, 375, 451.
[32] See *ante*, p. 16, for fixtures.

C

intending purchaser will want to know the nature and terms of the
tenancy, in particular, the rents receivable,[33] and, in the case of residential premises, inquiries will be directed towards ascertaining such
matters as whether the tenancy is *contractual* or *statutory* and if it is
controlled or *regulated*.[34]   Again, in the case of business premises,
inquiries will be directed to ascertain whether a claim for a new tenancy
has been made.[35]   With leasehold premises the intending purchaser
will want details of the lease, and will need to know whether consent
to an assignment is necessary and has been obtained.[36]   The intending
purchaser should inquire whether the covenants in the lease have been
complied with.[37]

The intending purchaser will want to know that he can use the
property for the purpose for which he wishes to buy it.   This will
involve inquiries as to planning matters.   These are discussed in a
subsequent section.   We shall also see in due course that as the vendor
must disclose incumbrances he must disclose to the purchaser any
planning matters, such as a temporary permission, which count as
incumbrances.[38]   Nor must the vendor make any misstatements as
to the planning use of the land, for example, he must not describe
agricultural land as building land.[39]

Practice points

Preliminary inquiries should be sent by the purchaser's solicitor as
soon as the draft contract is received.   Since the passing of the Misrepresentation Act 1967, it is all the more important that the replies
to the preliminary inquiries should be carefully considered by the
vendor and his solicitor.   The vendor should himself supply the
replies or, if he does not, the replies should be approved by him.   Time
can often be saved by the vendor's solicitor taking the vendor through
a printed form of preliminary inquiries as soon as he is instructed, so
that when the inquiries are received the vendor's solicitor will have the
answers to all or most of the questions raised.   A solicitor in
answering a purchaser's inquiries before contract will be acting as the
vendor's agent.

A solicitor is under an obligation to communicate the results of
inquiries and searches, so far as there is anything to communicate, to
his client.[40]

---

[33] It is professional negligence for the purchaser's solicitor not to inquire about
recoverable rent: *Goody* v. *Baring* [1956] 1 W.L.R. 448.   As to statements as to
the amount of rent receivable, see *post*, p. 77.
[34] *Post*, p. 271.
[35] *Post*, p. 284.
[36] *Post*, p. 261.
[37] *Post*, p. 100.
[38] *Post*, p, 79.
[39] *Post*, p. 77.

II. LOCAL SEARCHES AND INQUIRIES OF LOCAL AUTHORITIES

A. Local Searches

Generally

A search for local land charges is usually made by the purchaser, or his solicitor, before contract. In *Re Forsey and Hollebone's Contract*[41] it was suggested that a vendor was not under any duty to disclose matters registrable as local land charges, the existence of which the purchaser might discover by searching.[42] Despite this decision the general practice has been for vendors to disclose such matters[43] and for purchasers to make a local land charges search before contract. Provision may, however, be made for exchange of contracts before replies to local searches have been received.[44] As we shall see[45] inquiries are also made of the local authority, and the searches and inquiries should be made at the same time. The appropriate time is after the purchaser's solicitor has received the draft contract, but if the property is easily identifiable they can be made immediately he is instructed, and this will save time later.

Local land charges register

Provision is made under the Land Charges Act 1925, s. 15, for the registration of local land charges. Local land charges are charges acquired by local authorities under the provisions of various Acts. Originally, they were pecuniary charges, for example, those charges which arose under the Public Health Acts and Highways Acts, when the local authority had expended money for purposes under the relevant Act. Such charges have, in most respects, the same effect as a mortgage,[46] giving the local authority a power of sale in default of payment. Other pecuniary charges have been added over the years. The other type of local land charge arises under different Acts creating orders, notices, directions, etc., which are to be treated as local land charges. For example, various notices and orders under the Town and Country Planning Acts are so registrable.

The local land charge register is divided into twelve parts as follows:

> Part 1—Register of general financial charges.
> Part 2—Register of specific financial charges, *e.g.* road and drainage charges.
> Part 3—Register of planning charges, *e.g.* enforcement notices,[47] tree and building preservation orders.[48]

[41] [1927] 2 Ch. 379. See *post*, p. 43.
[42] See further (1964) 28 Conv.(N.S.) 114; and George, *Sale of Land*, p. 149.
[43] For contract conditions as to local land charges, see *post*, p. 97.
[44] National Conditions, Condition 13.
[45] *Post*, p. 42.
[46] Land Charges Act 1925, s. 15 (2) applying s. 11; and see *Payne* v. *Cardiff R.D.C.* [1932] 1 K.B. 241.
[47] As to these, see *post*, p. 51.
[48] As to these, see *post*, p. 47.

Part 4—Register of prohibitions and restrictions not falling within Parts I, II and III, *e.g.* a smoke control order under the
Clean Air Act 1956[49] or a combined drainage agreement
under some local Act.

Part 5—Register of charges for improvement of ways over
fenland.

Part 6—Register of compulsory purchase orders providing for
expedited completion.[50]

Part 7—Register of new towns orders.

Part 8—Register of civil aviation orders and directions.

Part 9—Register of opencast mining orders.

Part 10—Register of lists of buildings of special architectural or
historic interest.[51]

Part 11—Register of light obstruction notices under the Rights
of Light Act 1959, s. 2.

Part 12—Register of land drainage schemes.

The registers of local land charges are kept by the clerks of local
authorities. Outside Greater London certain charges are registered by
the clerk of the county, or county borough, council rather than the
clerk to the borough or district council and vice versa.[52] Accordingly,
searches must be made of both councils.

Registration

Registration must be effected by the proper officer of the local
authority, for example, the clerk of the borough council or the clerk
of the county council. Registration is deemed to constitute actual
notice.[53] If not registered before completion of a purchase, a local
land charge is void against a purchaser for money or money's worth of
a legal estate in the land.[54] But this protection does not apply to all
local land charges. Those in Parts 6 to 12 of the register, which are
not specifically to be regarded as local land charges, will bind a
purchaser *whether registered or not.* Some Acts creating local land
charges expressly provide for the Land Charges Act 1925, s. 15, to
apply,[55] but others are silent on the effect of non-registration.[56]

Unlike land charges registered in the register maintained at Kidbrooke by the Land Charges Department of H.M. Land Registry
(sometimes called " London land charges ") local land charges are

[49] As amended by the Housing Act 1964, s. 95, and the Clean Air Act 1968.
[50] See *post,* p. 117.
[51] See *post,* p. 46.
[52] Local Land Charges Rules 1966, r. 3.
[53] Law of Property Act 1925, s. 198; see *post,* p. 150.
[54] Land Charges Act 1925, s. 15 (1).
[55] See *e.g.* Agriculture Act 1967, s. 45 (7), Sched. 3, para. 2 (1).
[56] *e.g.* the Acts providing for registration of matters registrable in Parts 6–12 of the
Register. For a useful classification of land charges, in so far as they are incumbrances which require to be disclosed by the vendor, see George, *The Sale of Land*
p. 149.

registrable whether the title to the land is registered or not.[57] In the case of registered land, rights under local land charges, until they are registered as a charge with substantive registration or protected by being noted on the register of title, are overriding interests.[58]

Searches

Searches of the local land charges registers may be made personally, but an official search is preferable.[59] The search is made against the *land* (not as in the case of London land charges against the names of estate owners).

Application for an official search is made on a prescribed form [60] which must be properly completed and accompanied by the proper fee. The official search form is in duplicate, and must contain a sufficient description of the property, if necessary by reference to a plan (generally one plan is sufficient).

As already indicated,[61] searches may have to be made of more than one local authority, for example, of both a borough council, or urban district council, and the county council. In the case of a county borough, or London borough, only one search need be made.

A search is then made by the staff of the clerk of the appropriate local authority, and any entries on the registers should be duly noted on the search form. One copy of the form is then returned. This process generally takes about one to three weeks.[62]

It sometimes happens that a charge is registered between the time of search and the day of completion of the purchase. If a purchaser has obtained an official certificate of search, and then *completes* his purchase within fourteen days, he will be protected against any entry made in the meantime in the register otherwise than pursuant to a *priority notice* entered before the issue of the certificate.[63] Accordingly, in theory, the search should be made as near the completion date as possible. But in practice, a search before completion, in addition to the search before contract, is never made. As between the purchaser and the local authority, the purchaser's inquiries to the local authorities [64] will generally reveal any land charges likely to come into existence between contract and completion. As between the purchaser and the vendor, the conditions of sale generally provide for charges arising after contract to fall on the purchaser.[65]

[57] Land Charges Act 1925, s. 23 (1).
[58] As to overriding interests, see *post*, p. 170.
[59] Local Land Charges Rules 1966, rr. 23, 24.
[60] Form L.L.C.1 sold by branches of the Solicitors' Law Stationery Society Ltd. As in the case of any other standard conveyancing forms this should be obtained by the student.
[61] *Ante*, p. 40.
[62] See (1967) 117 New L.J. 1311 (the seven days suggested is optimistic).
[63] Local Land Charges Rules 1966, rr. 25, 26. And see *post*, p. 160.
[64] *Post*, p. 42.
[65] See Law Society's Conditions, Condition 2 (4); National Conditions, Condition 16.

As regards most matters an official certificate of search is conclusive in favour of a purchaser or intending purchaser as against
authorities or persons interested under or in respect of charges required
or allowed to be registered in the register.[66] So, where the official
certificate fails to reveal a charge which is, in fact, on the register, the
purchaser will take free of the charge,[67] provided he has applied for a
search in respect of the right land. But this protection does not apply
in respect of control orders registered under the Housing Act 1964,
in Part 4 of the register, nor necessarily in the case of charges
registered in Parts 6 to 12 of the register. In the latter case the matter
will turn on the words used in the Act creating the charge. So where,
in respect of a notice of payment of compensation registrable under
Part 6 of the register, the Town and Country Planning Act 1962, s. 112
(5), provided that the notice should be registered in the register of
local land charges, in such manner as may be prescribed, and the
Local Land Charges Rules applied section 17 of the Land Charges
Act 1925, it was held that the failure of the official certificate to reveal
a compensation notice, which had been registered, had the effect of
making the notice void against a purchaser.[68] If the effect of the
Act is not to make the certificate conclusive in the purchaser's favour,
he will take subject to the incumbrance, and sue the registrar for
damages for breach of statutory duty or negligence.

B. Inquiries of Local Authorities

It is the practice to send inquiries to the local authorities concerned
at the same time as the requisitions for an official search. These
inquiries will relate to matters within the knowledge of the local
authorities, but not registrable as local land charges. Local authorities
are not bound to answer such inquiries, but in practice they will do
so if the proper forms are used. These are forms agreed between the
Law Society and bodies representing local authorities and their
officials.[69] The form should be properly completed in duplicate and
accompanied by the appropriate fee. Some questions on the form
will clearly be inappropriate and should be deleted. It may be necessary to add further questions to the printed form.

The forms contain inquiries, *inter alia*, on the following matters:

  (1) Roads—whether the highways and footpaths abutting the
       property have been taken over, and whether there are any
       proposals in respect of the roads;

---

[66] Land Charges Act 1925, ss. 16, 17; Local Land Charges Rules 1966, r. 24 (6).
[67] *Stock* v. *Wanstead and Woodford Borough Council* [1962] 2 Q.B. 479. The incumbrancer will have to look to his remedy against the registrar.
[68] *Minister of Housing and Local Government* v. *Sharp* [1970] 2 Q.B. 223.
[69] Obtainable from branches of the Solicitors' Law Stationery Society Ltd. Form
Con.29A (inquiries of borough or district councils (other than London boroughs)),
Con.29B (county councils), Con.29C (county borough councils), Con.29D (London
borough councils or the Corporation of London). And see *Coats Patons (Retail) Ltd.*
v. *Birmingham Corporation* (1971) 68 L.S.Gaz. 398.

(2) Drainage and sewerage—whether there is a public sewer serving the property, or a combined drainage agreement;
(3) Building regulations—whether there has been any infringement;
(4) Furnished dwellings—the existence of any entries in registers of rent of furnished dwellings kept under the Rent Act 1968, s. 74;
(5) Town and country planning matters [70];
(6) Smoke control, etc.[71]

In addition to these formal inquiries it is often worthwhile for the purchaser to make a personal call at the town hall or council offices to inquire as to any matters affecting the property.

III.   LAND CHARGES SEARCHES

There was previously much controversy as to whether or not it was necessary for the purchaser to search in the register of land charges kept under the Land Charges Act 1925 before contract. He was in any event under some difficulty because that register is a *names* register, *i.e.* registration is against the names of estate owners, not against the land,[72] and he might not know the names of the vendor's predecessors in title. The strict view was that a search was necessary before contract. This was based on the decision in *Re Forsey and Hollebone's Contract.*[73] Under section 198 (1) of the Law of Property Act 1925, registration is deemed to constitute actual notice of any instrument or matter registered under the Land Charges Act. Eve J., at first instance in *Re Forsey and Hollebone's Contract,* held that an undisclosed planning resolution was not an incumbrance, and went on to say that even if it was, by virtue of section 198 of the Law of Property Act 1925, the purchaser was deemed to have notice of it.[74] This view has been strongly criticised [75] but has never been challenged in the courts, and a somewhat unsatisfactory Law Society Opinion [76] stated that a purchaser's solicitor would be exposing his client to risk if he omitted to search before contract against all persons who to the knowledge of the purchaser or his solicitor, gained in that transaction, were or had been since 1925 estate owners of the property.

However, the provisions of the contract might permit the purchaser to rescind if the vendor had not disclosed a land charge affecting the property.[77]

---

[70] See generally *post*, pp. 44 *et seq.*
[71] Students should obtain copies of the printed forms.
[72] See *post*, p. 158.
[73] [1927] 2 Ch. 379.
[74] At p. 387. The s. 198 point was not mentioned in the Court of Appeal.
[75] See Farrand, *Contract and Conveyance*, p. 56.
[76] See Law Society Digest, Vol. 1, Opinion No. 135. These opinions are opinions of the Law Society's Council on Conveyancing Practice.
[77] See the previous editions of the Law Society's and National Conditions, Conditions 21 and 13 respectively.

As regards contracts made on or after January 1, 1970, the Law
of Property Act 1969, s. 24, provides that a purchaser shall only be
deemed to have notice of land charges within his *actual* knowledge.[78]
Any stipulation in the contract which purports to exclude this provision
is void.   Accordingly, a search in the Land Charges Department of
the Land Registry in London is no longer necessary before contract,
as the purchaser will be able to rescind if the vendor does not disclose
a registered land charge.   The 1969 Act does not affect the position
with regard to local land charges, where the search must still be made
before contract.

IV.   LAND REGISTRY SEARCH

If there is any suspicion that the title to the property, agreed to be sold
as unregistered land, is registered, then an application for an official
search of the index map and parcels index should be made to the
appropriate District Land Registry.[79]   The certificate of search will
show whether or not the land is registered, and, if so, whether with
freehold or leasehold title, and whether there is any caution against
first registration.[80]

V.   TOWN AND COUNTRY PLANNING; PLANNING SEARCHES AND INQUIRIES [81]

We have seen in this chapter that many of the inquiries and searches
made before contract relate to planning matters.   The purchaser will
desire to know whether he can use the property for the purpose he
wants and whether or not the property is likely to be affected by
planning proposals.   It is convenient to deal here briefly with some
of the principal topics in the town and country planning legislation,
recently consolidated in the Town and Country Planning Act 1971,
with which a conveyancer will be concerned.[82]

A.   Use and Development

Use

A purchaser will want to know the *permitted use* of the property,[83]
because a change of use may constitute development for which planning
permission is required.[84]   In the case of a dwelling-house which is not
newly built, inquiry as to its use need only go back four years, because
a use enjoyed for four years cannot be prevented,[85] but it is still
common-form to inquire of the vendor as to the use of the property

---

[78] See *post*, p. 148.
[79] See *post*, p. 172.
[80] Land Registration Rules 1925, r. 286.   See *post*, p. 184.
[81] See (1964) 28 Conv.(N.S.) 27, 101.
[82] See generally Heap, *An Outline of Planning Law* (5th ed.).
[83] As to the controversy whether use is a matter of title, see *post*, p. 79.
[84] Town and Country Planning Act 1971, s. 23.   For development, see *post*, p. 46.
[85] *Post*, p. 45.

on July 1, 1948 (the date of the coming into operation of the Town
and Country Planning Act 1947), if the property is so old. The
permitted use of the property on that date will generally be the same
as the *existing, i.e.* actual, use at that date, but there are a number of
exceptions, for example, if the use was a temporary one, in which
case there is a right to revert to the normal use, or if the property
was used on occasions for a use other than the normal use.[86]

The purchaser will need to know from the vendor the *present* use
of the property. If this differs from the *permitted* use, he will have to
consider whether the change has been development requiring planning
permission from the local planning authority.[87] If so, he will want to be
sure planning permission has been obtained. If planning permission was
required, but was not obtained, there will have been a breach of
planning control and the local planning authority may take action
requiring the breach to be remedied by serving an *enforcement notice.*
Enforcement action is discussed subsequently.[88] All we shall say at
this stage is that before the Town and Country Planning Act 1968, an
enforcement notice had to be served within four years of the breach
of planning control to which it related.[89] Since the 1968 Act
the notice may be served at any time, subject to three important
exceptions, where it must still be served within four years. The
exceptional cases are:

(1) Building, engineering, mining or other operations carried out
    without permission;
(2) Failure to comply with any conditions or limitations subject to
    which planning permission for such operation was granted;
(3) Changing the use of any building to use as a single dwelling-
    house.[90]

This last exception is the only case of change of use which can become
protected by the passing of time. Accordingly, if the use of the
property at the time of the proposed purchase is as a single dwelling-
house, and that has been its use for the past four years, the purchaser
need not inquire further.

On the purchase of a new house the purchaser will need to
ascertain from the vendor that planning permission for the erection
of the house was obtained.

If the purchaser is buying the property for development, he will
generally need to know the permitted use on July 1, 1948, and the
present use. He should direct inquiries on these points to the vendor
before contract. He will then have to consider whether his proposals
require planning permission.

86 Town and Country Planning Act 1971, s. 23 (3) (5).
87 Generally the county council or county borough council. County councils may
   delegate certain functions to district councils. In some areas, *e.g.* National Parks,
   there may be a joint planning board.
88 *Post,* p. 51.
89 1962 Act, s. 45 (repealed by the 1968 Act).
90 1971 Act, s. 87 (3).

C*

Development

Development means the carrying out of building, engineering, mining or other *operations* in, on, over or under land,[91] or the making of any *material change of use*[92] of any buildings or other land.[93] Certain matters are not regarded as development, for example:

(1) The maintenance, improvement or other alteration to any building, being works which affect only the interior of a building[94] or do not materially affect the external appearance of the building;

(2) The use of a building or other land within the curtilage of a dwelling-house for any purpose incidental to the enjoyment of the dwelling-house as such; and

(3) A change of use within a Use Class Order.[95]

As regards (3), the Town and Country Planning (Uses Classes) Order 1963 sets out a number of use classes[96] and a change of use within the use class is not development. Permission is still required, however, for any building operations in connection with any change of use.

If it is uncertain whether the proposed development requires planning permission, application may be made to the local planning authority for a determination of the question.[97]

Building preservation orders, etc.

An intending developer will need to ascertain by local land charges searches and inquiries of local authorities whether the property is affected by listed building protection. And trees on the site may be subject to tree preservation orders. Section 54 of the 1971 Act enables the Secretary of State for the Environment to make lists of

---

[91] *See Buckinghamshire C.C.* v. *Callingham* [1952] 2 Q.B. 515 (model village a building operation); *Cheshire C.C.* v. *Woodward* [1962] 2 Q.B. 126 (installation of movable coal-hopper and conveyor not a building operation); *cf. Bendles Motors Ltd.* v. *Bristol Corporation* [1963] 1 W.L.R. 247 (installation of free-standing egg-vending machine in garage forecourt material change of use); *Coleshill and District Investment Co. Ltd.* v. *Minister of Housing and Local Government* [1969] 1 W.L.R. 746 (demolition an operation). And see (1971) 35 Conv.(N.S.) 399.

[92] See *East Barnet U.D.C.* v. *British Transport Commission* [1962] 2 Q.B. 484 (depot for coal used for cars; held no change); *Birmingham Corporation* v. *Minister of Housing and Local Government and Habib Ullah* [1964] 1 Q.B. 178 (change to multiple occupation of dwelling-house may be change of use); *Webber* v. *Minister of Housing and Local Government* [1968] 1 W.L.R. 29.

[93] Town and Country Planning Act 1971, s. 22 (1). The conversion of a single dwelling-house into two or more separate dwellings involves a material change of use: s. 22 (3) (*a*).

[94] But the creation of a basement is development: Town and Country Planning Act 1971, s. 22 (2) (*a*).

[95] Town and Country Planning Act 1971, s. 22 (2).

[96] Class I. Use of a shop for any purpose, *except* as a fried fish shop, tripe shop, pet food shop or shop for the sale of motor vehicles; Class II. Use of an office for any purpose; Class III. Light industrial building for any purpose; Class IV. General industrial building for any purpose; Classes V to IX refer to various special industrial uses. The remainder relate to hotels, schools, etc.

[97] Town and Country Planning Act 1971, s. 53; see *Lever Finance Ltd.* v. *Westminster (City) London Borough Council* [1971] 1 Q.B. 222.

[49] *Lake* v. *Bushby* [1949] 2 All E.R. 964.

buildings of architectural or historic interest. Before the 1968 Act the effect of such listing was to require the owner of a listed building to give notice to the local planning authority before the building was demolished or altered. The planning authority could then, if it acted in time, make a *building preservation order* to protect the building. Since the 1968 Act, all listed buildings are protected,[98] and no person may demolish or alter a listed building without first obtaining a *listed building consent* from the local planning authority or the Secretary of State.[99] A building not already listed may be protected by the local planning authority making a *building preservation notice.* This gives protection for six months to give time to ask the Secretary of State to list the building.[1]

Under the Town and Country Planning Act 1971, s. 277, local planning authorities may designate whole areas *conservation areas.* The effect of such designation is that all applications for planning permission have to be advertised and permission will generally only be granted for development consistent with the character of the area.

The local planning authority may, in the interests of amenity, make *tree preservation orders* prohibiting the felling, lopping, or wilful destruction of trees without the consent of the authority. If opposed, the order requires the confirmation of the Secretary of State, after considering any objections.[2]

Stopping up and diversion of highways

The stopping up, diversion, and extinguishment of highways, by order of the Secretary of State for the Environment, are authorised for particular purposes, for example, development.[3] Inquiries should be made of the local authority as to any schemes or proposals relating to highways or roads.

B. Planning Permission
Planning permission

If development is involved, planning permission will generally be necessary.[4] No permission is required for certain temporary or occasional uses existing on July 1, 1948.[5] Nor is express permission

[98] Town and Country Planning Act 1971, s. 54. The fact that a building has been listed is to be entered in the register of local land charges (subs. (6)).
[99] Town and Country Planning Act 1971, s. 55. Contravention of the section becomes a penalty of a fine and/or imprisonment.
[1] s. 58.
[2] s. 60.
[3] ss. 209, 211, 212. Section 215 lays down the relevant procedure. Local authorities may also apply for stopping up and diversion under the Highways Act 1959, ss. 108, 109. This order, in that case, is made by the magistrates' court.
[4] 1971 Act, s. 23 (1).
[5] But an occasional use must have occurred at least once before 1968: s. 23. And see ss. 40, 64 for certain cases where permission is deemed to be granted.

required where there is an order of the Secretary of State [6] permitting certain development.[7]

Orders may be special [8] or general. The current general order is the Town and Country Planning General Development Order 1963. This order specifies twenty-three classes of *permitted* development for which planning permission is not required. Class I deals with development within the curtilage of a dwelling-house, and covers the enlargement, improvement, etc., of the house. The enlargement must not exceed 1,750 cubic feet or one-tenth of the cubic content of the original house, whichever is the greater; and in the case of the latter there is an overall maximum of 4,000 cubic feet. No part of the new building must be either above or in front of the existing building. This class also includes the erection of garages, etc., and the erection of other buildings for a purpose incidental to the enjoyment of a house. So long as the new building does not obstruct the view of traffic on a corner or a junction, and does not involve constructional work on an access point to a classified road, planning permission is not required.[9]

Class II deals with the erection of fences (not exceeding four feet where the property fronts a road, or seven feet elsewhere) and the painting of the exterior of buildings.

There are twenty-one other classes, some of which deal with shops and business and industrial purposes. Save for these exceptional cases mentioned in the Classes, planning permission will be required.

In certain areas, for example conservation areas, the local planning authority can, with the approval of the Secretary of State, remove any specified development from the category of permitted development.

Application for permission

Application for planning permission is made to the local planning authority on the standard printed form, signed by the applicant or one of his professional advisers (for example, solicitor or architect) and accompanied by the necessary plans, and a certificate that the applicant is the owner (or lessee with ten or more years to run) or has given notice to such persons.[10]   In appropriate cases, for example, where it is proposed to erect a new house, the application for planning permission will generally be accompanied by an application under the Building Regulations for the approval of the proposed building.[11]   It should

---

[6] Formerly the Minister of Housing and Local Government. Since November 12, 1970, the Secretary of State for the Environment; see Secretary of State for Environment Order 1970 (S.I. 1970 No. 1681), art. 2.

[7] 1971 Act, s. 24.

[8] Made in respect of new airports, etc. And note the New Towns Special Development Order 1963 in respect of development carried out by the development corporations of new towns.

[9] General Development Order 1963, art. 3 (1). These are the so-called " standard conditions " which apply to most of the permitted developments.

[10] See generally Heap, *Outline of Planning Law* (5th ed.), pp. 97 *et seq.*

[11] Made under the provisions of the Public Health Act 1961, s. 4. The current regulations are contained in the Building Regulations 1965, as amended. They deal with the types of material which may be used, the strength of walls, drainage, etc.

be noted that approval under the Building Regulations may be required even in a case where planning permission is not needed. In a case where both planning permission and Building Regulations approval are required, it may happen that one will be granted and the other refused.

An application may be an outline application, as, for example, one to build a housing estate without stating the type of house or siting.[12] If the application is successful, an *outline permission* will be granted, and the permission will be subject to conditions, such as the approval of details about the siting and design of the buildings. Application for approval of these details must be made within three years of the granting of outline permission; and development must be begun within five years of the granting of the outline permission or two years of the final approval of plans, whichever is the later.[13]

Conditions on permission

A planning permission may be made subject to conditions,[14] for example as to access between the subject site and the highway. The conditions imposed must fairly and reasonably relate to the permitted development,[15] and the local authority must state their reasons for imposing the condition. If a condition is void, for example, for uncertainty or because it is *ultra vires*, the whole permission is invalid.[16]

Temporary permission

Permission may be given for development or change of use subject to removal of the development or discontinuance of the use on a certain date.[17]

Because the permission may be temporary or conditional, it is important to make preliminary inquiries as to these matters, and request the production of permissions so that they can be examined to see whether there are any conditions.

Lapse, revocation, etc., of permission

A planning permission granted before April 1, 1969, will lapse if development is not commenced within five years from that date. If permission was granted on or after April 1, 1969, the period is five years from the granting of the permission or such other period as may be specified by the local planning authority.[18]

If work is begun but is not completed, the local planning authority

12 General Development Order 1963, art. 5.
13 Town and Country Planning Act 1971, s. 42.
14 s. 29.
15 *Fawcett Properties Ltd.* v. *Buckinghamshire C.C.* [1961] A.C. 636.
16 *Hall & Co. Ltd.* v. *Shoreham-by-Sea U.D.C.* [1964] 1 W.L.R. 240; *Kingsway Investments (Kent) Ltd.* v. *Kent C.C.* [1971] A.C. 72.
17 Town and Country Planning Act 1971, s. 30.
18 s. 41. As to the lapsing of outline permission, see *supra*.

may, if they are of the opinion that the development will not be completed within a reasonable time, serve a *completion notice* specifying a period of not less than twelve months by which development must be completed, or otherwise the permission will no longer be valid.[19]

Planning permission may be revoked or modified before the works have been completed or the change of use effected, subject to compensation.[20] The local planning authority may also make an order requiring the discontinuance of any use or the alteration of any buildings or works, subject to the payment of compensation.[21]

Industrial and office development

There are special provisions applicable to industrial and office development. If an application for planning permission is for an industrial building with a floor space of over 10,000 square feet (or less in some areas) it must be accompanied by an Industrial Development Certificate obtained from the Department of Trade and Industry.[22] In London and certain other cases there is a similar control of new office development and the application must be accompanied by an Office Development Permit obtained from the Department of the Environment where the area exceeds 10,000 square feet.[23]

Advertisements

There are special provisions for the control of advertisements.[24]

Planning permission not personal to applicant

It should perhaps be pointed out that a planning permission is not generally personal to the applicant, but, unless it provides to the contrary, enures for the benefit of the land,[25] subject to lapse, etc., as mentioned above.

Register of permissions

The local land charges search and the inquiries of the local authority[26] will reveal what permissions have been granted, and what applications have been refused, in the past, so the intending developer will get a good idea as to whether or not permission will be granted for his own application. It should be noted that the register of applications for planning permission, maintained by the local planning authority,[27] is quite distinct from the local land charges register.

---

[19] Town and Country Planning Act 1971, s. 44.   [20] ss. 45, 164.
[21] *Ibid.* s. 51.
[22] *Ibid.* ss. 67, 68.
[23] *Ibid.* s. 74. " Office premises " are defined by s. 73. Control of Office Development (Exemption Limit) Order 1970. See Heap, *An Outline of Planning Law* (5th ed.), pp. 155 *et seq.* Town and Country Planning (Amendment) Bill 1972.
[24] Town and Country Planning (Control of Advertisements) Regulations 1969. See Heap, *ubi supra*, pp. 134 *et seq.*
[25] Town and Country Planning Act 1971, s. 33 (1).
[26] See *e.g.* inquiry 12 on Con. 29C.
[27] Under Town and Country Planning Act 1971, s. 34.

C. Enforcement Action

Enforcement notice

Where there has been a breach of planning control, *i.e.* if development requiring permission is carried out without planning permission, or if a condition in a planning permission is not complied with, then the local planning authority may serve an *enforcement notice* on both the owner and occupier of the premises, and any other person who has an interest which the authority thinks is materially affected by the notice.[28] The notice must specify (1) the matters alleged to constitute the breach of planning control; (2) the steps required to remedy the breach [29]; and (3) the period for compliance.[30] As we have already seen,[31] the authority was required to serve such a notice within four years of the breach of planning control to which it related. Since the 1968 Act, the notice may be served at *any* time, provided that no notice can now be served in respect of a breach which occurred before January 1, 1964.[32] We have already mentioned the three exceptions to this rule,[33] in which cases the enforcement notice must still be served within four years of the breach. There is a right of appeal against an enforcement notice to the Secretary of State on certain grounds.[34] Failure to comply with a notice is an offence punishable on summary conviction by a fine not exceeding £400 and a daily penalty of £50 if the offence continues after conviction.[35] There is no maximum fine if the conviction is on indictment. The local authority also has a right to enter on the land and do any necessary works required by the notice if those are not done, and to recover the cost from the owner.[36] The breach of planning control may also be prevented by injunction.[37]

An enforcement notice does not take effect until at least twenty-eight days after it is served and until any appeal against it is determined. It follows that the unauthorised development could meanwhile continue. The 1968 Act introduced a *stop notice*, the object of which is to maintain the status quo while the merits of the enforcement notice are considered. The notice prohibits any person on whom it is served from carrying out any of the operations specified in the notice. It is in effect supplemental to an enforcement notice and must refer to the relevant enforcement notice. Its validity stands or falls with that of the enforcement notice.[38]

---

[28] Town and Country Planning Act 1971, s. 87.
[29] This may involve demolition: s. 87 (7).
[30] s. 87 (6) (c).
[31] *Ante*, p. 45.
[32] s. 87 (1).
[33] s. 87 (3); *ante*, p. 45.
[34] s. 88.
[35] s. 89.
[36] s. 91.
[37] *Att.-Gen.* v. *Smith* [1958] 2 Q.B. 173.
[38] Town and Country Planning Act 1971, s. 90.

As an enforcement notice may now, in most cases, be served at any time after the breach, the 1968 Act introduced a *certificate of established use* to enable a landowner to record the fact that the current use of his land, though originally unauthorised, is safe from enforcement proceedings. It is only obtainable where the use began before 1964.[39]

D. Planning Proposals

Development plans

The intending purchaser will need to know whether the property is likely to be adversely affected by planning proposals. The development plan will give some indication of likely developments, such as roads.

Local planning authorities are under a duty to prepare a development plan. This has to be reconsidered every five years and may be amended at any time. Before the 1947 Town and Country Planning Act came into force, local authorities had been merely *empowered* to prepare planning schemes showing what development would be permitted in their areas. This procedure was unsatisfactory, and the 1947 Act introduced the system of development plans. Each local planning authority was required, under the Act, to carry out a survey of the whole of its area, and to prepare a development plan based on this survey by July 1, 1951, although this time limit was extended in most cases. These plans form a broad statement of planning policy. Unlike planning schemes under the old system, it is not the plan itself which authorises the development: planning permission must, in most cases, still be obtained. The plan, therefore, does no more than indicate the nature of the development intended to be permitted.[40]

The development plan consists of a basic map and written statement, together with such maps as may be appropriate. One of the principal features of the plan is the establishment of " zones " allocating land for agriculture, houses, shops, industry, etc. The plan also defines the proposed sites of specific projects, such as schools, open spaces or new roads.

Local searches will often reveal (under Part 3 of the Register) the existence of some planning schemes or development plan and inquiries should be made of the local authority as to whether any development plan affects the property.

This system of development plans operated effectively in a negative way by preventing undesirable development. In 1965 a new type of development plan to positively stimulate development and redevelopment was recommended, and effect was given to this recommendation by Part I of the Town and Country Planning Act 1968. Part I will come into force in different parts of the country gradually, beginning

[39] *Ibid.* s. 94.
[40] Before 1969 the plan also designated the land proposed to be acquired compulsorily.

with the large urban areas, so for some years to come there will be the two different systems operating.[41]

Structure plans

The new system also provides for a survey, followed by a report on the survey, and a *structure plan*.[42] The structure plan will set out the local planning authority's policy and general proposals in respect of the development and other use of land in its area (including measures for the improvement of the physical environment and the management of traffic). The local planning authority is also required to have regard to current policies for the economic planning and development of the region as a whole.[43]

The structure plan will also indicate *action areas*, in which comprehensive treatment is intended within the near future, *i.e.* not more than ten years. The treatment referred to may be development, redevelopment, or improvement: thus the concept of an action area is wider than that of an area of comprehensive development under the earlier legislation.[44]

The form of structure plans will be different from that of development plans. The structure plan will consist of a written statement describing the authority's proposals, accompanied by such diagrams, illustrations and other descriptive matter as may be considered appropriate.[45] A structure plan needs the Secretary's approval. It *may* be supplemented by *local plans* for parts of the authority's area and *must* be so supplemented for any action area. A local plan consists of a map and written statement. More often the Secretary's approval is not required for it.[46]

The Act also provides elaborate provision for public participation or objection.[47]

Effect of development plans

We have already seen that a development plan does not confer any right of development. On the other hand, if the proposed development accords with the provisions of the plan, there will be a good chance that planning permission will be granted. But even if the development does not accord with the plan, permission may be given.

E. Compensation

Generally

The effect of the Town and Country Planning Act 1947 was to restrict the owner of land to the enjoyment of its existing use on July 1,

---

41 See generally, Heap, *The New Town Planning Procedures*; [1971] J.P.L. 605, 674.
42 Town and Country Planning Act 1971, ss. 6, 7.
43 *Ibid*. s. 7 (3) (4).   44 *Ibid*. s. 7 (5).
45 *Ibid*. s. 7 (6).
46 *Ibid*. s. 11.
47 *Ibid*. ss. 8–10, 12–19. But see now Town and Country Planning (Amendment) Bill 1972.

1948. Thereafter planning permission was required for any development. In effect the Act nationalised the development value of all land, but not the land itself. The landowner was entitled to compensation for loss of development rights on a once-for-all basis against a compensation fund of £300 million set aside for this purpose. Claims, which could not be made after July 30, 1949, were based on the development value of the land, *i.e.* the difference between the " restricted " and " unrestricted " values on July 1, 1948. The " unrestricted " value was that which the property would have had if the Act had not been passed. The " restricted " value was its value on the basis that permission would not be granted for development (other than Third, now Eighth, Schedule development which is described below).

If the owner wished to develop his land, he required planning permission. If permission was granted, he had to pay a *development charge* equal to the increase in the value of the land caused by the grant of planning permission. Certain minor developments were exempt from the payment of development charge. If planning permission was refused, no compensation was payable because the owner no longer possessed the development rights. On compulsory purchase compensation was limited to existing use value.

These financial provisions were unpopular, and the system failed partly because landowners refused to sell at existing use value and so land prices continued to rise. Development charges were abolished by the Town and Country Planning Act 1953 and the provisions for compensation were repealed by that Act and another in the following year.

Unexpended balance of established development value

Claims established against the £300 million compensation fund were never paid out because of the changes in the system. By the 1954 Act, an established claim against the fund was made available to provide compensation when planning permission was subsequently refused or granted subject to conditions. The established claim, reduced in some cases by payment under Parts I and V of the 1954 Act, was converted into the *unexpended balance of established development value.*[48] This provides the basis of compensation on restrictions on development, other than Eighth Schedule development, imposed after January 1, 1955. We shall now consider the three cases in which compensation is payable for planning restrictions.[49]

The refusal of planning permission or the grant of permission subject to conditions may give rise to a right to compensation in the following cases.

[48] The established claim, reduced by any payments already made and by the value of any new development carried out after July 1, 1948, is increased by one-seventh representing interest at 3·5 per cent. from 1948 to 1955.
[49] See Heap, *An Outline of Planning Law*, pp. 227 *et seq.*

(i) *Compensation for refusal or conditional grant of planning permission where the development is deemed to be within the existing use*

Certain types of development (as extended, now contained in the Eighth Schedule to the 1971 Act) were exempt from development charge. Eighth Schedule development is development consistent with, or required for the existing use of the land or building in question, for example, rebuilding or extension of existing premises. There are two parts to this Schedule. Part I specifies development *not* ranking for compensation under section 169 of the Act, and comprises rebuilding (within certain limits), and the use as two or more separate dwellings of any building used at a material date as a single dwelling. Part II specifies development which *does* rank for compensation, which includes the enlargement or other alteration of premises and a change of use from one purpose to another within any use-class specified in the Use-Classes for Third Schedule Purposes Order 1948.

Where planning permission has been refused, or granted subject to conditions in respect of development within Part II of the Eighth Schedule, compensation will be payable by the *local planning authority*, if the value of the interest, in respect of which the claim is made, is less than it would have been but for the Secretary of State's decision.[50] It should be noted that to establish his rights to compensation, the claimant must first have appealed to the Secretary of State against the decision of the local planning authority.[51]

(ii) *Compensation for refusal or conditional grant of planning permission for new development*

Compensation is payable by the *State* under Part VII of the 1971 Act for restrictions on new developments (*i.e.* development other than Eighth Schedule development), provided the following conditions are satisfied:

(a) A planning decision must have been made on or after January 1, 1955, whereby permission for new development was refused or granted subject to conditions;

(b) The land in question must have an unexpended balance of established development value;

(c) The claimant's interest in the land must have been depreciated in value as a result of the decision;

(d) Compensation must not be excluded. Compensation is excluded, for example, in respect of the refusal of planning permission for any development which consists of or includes the making of a material change in the use of any building or other land, or relates to the display of advertisements, or where

50 Town and Country Planning Act 1971, s. 169.
51 Unless the application is of the sort which has to be referred to the Secretary of State: see s. 35 of the Act.

the reason, or one of the reasons, for refusal is that the development would be premature, for example, because of deficiency
in water supplies or sewerage services.[52]

Compensation is also excluded in respect of conditions as to the
number, or disposition, of buildings on land; the dimensions, design,
structure, external appearance or material of buildings; the layout of
land—including parking facilities; the use of buildings or land; the
location, design or construction of means of access to a highway or
the working of minerals.[53]

(iii) *Compensation for revocation or modification of planning per-*
mission

When the local planning authority make a revocation order[54]
revoking or modifying a permission, compensation will be payable.
This will cover the depreciation in the value of the land and expenditure
incurred in carrying out work rendered abortive by the revocation.[55]

Registration of compensation

Where the amount of compensation exceeds £20, the Secretary of
State may notify the county borough, or county district council, of the
details, and the authority must register the notice in the register of local
land charges.[56]

Repayment of compensation

No provision is made for the repayment of compensation paid for
restrictions on Eighth Schedule development. The Act contains provisions for the repayment of compensation in other cases.[57] It should
be noted that the person liable to pay is the person who carried out
the subsequent permitted development who may, of course, be a
different person from the one who received the compensation.

Local land charge search

A local land charge search should reveal the details of any compensation payments.[58] If a compensation payment has not been
entered on the register, the purchaser of the relevant land will not be
required to make any repayment.[59]

The inquiries of the local authority will reveal whether a right to
compensation has arisen which has not yet been registered.

[52] s. 147 (1).
[53] s. 147 (2).
[54] s. 45. See *ante*, p. 50.
[55] s. 164.
[56] s. 158. See *Ministry of Housing and Local Government* v. *Sharp* [1970] 2 Q.B. 223.
[57] ss. 159–161.
[58] s. 158, *supra*.
[59] *Stock* v. *Wanstead and Woodford B.C.* [1962] 2 Q.B. 479; *Ministry of Housing and Local Government* v. *Sharp, supra*.

F. Adverse Planning Decisions

Purchase notice

If planning permission is refused, or granted subject to conditions, so that the land is:

- (a) incapable of reasonably beneficial use in its *existing state*[60]; and
- (b) it cannot be rendered capable of *reasonably* beneficial use by any form of development which the authority or the Secretary of State is willing to sanction,

then the owner[61] of the land may serve a *purchase notice* on the authority requiring them to purchase his interest in the land.[62] The authority must then within three months serve a notice stating whether they, or another authority or statutory undertaker, are willing to comply with the purchase notice; or that they are not willing to comply, giving their reasons therefor. In the latter case the notice must be forwarded to the Secretary of State who may either confirm the notice, refuse it, or grant the permission applied for, or permission for any other development which will enable a reasonably beneficial use of the land to be made.[63]

Blight notice

Where land is, *inter alia*:

- (1) allocated by a development plan (including structure and local plans) for the purposes of any functions of a government department, local authority, etc.;
- (2) indicated in a development plan for construction or improvemen of a highway;
- (3) authorised by a special enactment to be compulsorily purchased;

and the owner[64] of the land has made reasonable endeavours to sell and has been unable to sell except at a price substantially lower than that at which it might reasonably have been expected to sell if it had not been affected as mentioned above, then the owner may serve a *blight notice* on the appropriate authority requiring the authority to purchase the land.[65]

If the authority object to the notice, they may serve a counter-notice. The claimant may then require the objection to be referred to the Lands Tribunal. Where no counter-notice is served, or where one

---

[60] See *R. v. Minister of Housing and Local Government, ex p. Chichester R.D.C.* [1960] 1 W.L.R. 587.
[61] s. 290; and see *London Corpn. v. Cusack-Smith* [1955] A.C. 337.
[62] s. 180.
[63] s. 182.
[64] A blight notice may only be served by a *resident* owner-occupier, any owner-occupier if the net annual value for rating of the property does not exceed £750, or the owner-occupier of an agricultural unit: s. 193. And see *Essex C.C. v. Essex Inc. Congregational Church Union* [1963] A.C. 808.
[65] s. 193.

has been served but has been withdrawn, or where on a reference to the Lands Tribunal the objection is not upheld, the authority is deemed to be authorised to acquire compulsorily and to have served a notice to treat.[66]

---

[66] Town and Country Planning Act 1971, s. 196.

CHAPTER 4

INFORMAL CONTRACTS FOR THE SALE OF LAND

A CONTRACT for the sale of land may be either (1) open, or (2) formal, or (3) part open and part formal. An *open contract* is one in which the parties have left its terms and conditions to be implied by the general law. A *formal contract* is one in which the terms and conditions, by which the parties are to be bound, are expressly set forth. For example, if the parties merely agree as to the property sold and the price, the contract is entirely an open contract. If, on the other hand, the parties also agree the date for taking possession and completion of the purchase, then the contract is only part open.

It is proposed in this chapter to deal with open contracts for the sale of land as follows:

(1) open contracts *made otherwise than by correspondence*;

(2) open contracts *made by correspondence*;

(3) the advantages and disadvantages of open contracts.

Formal contracts for the sale of land will be dealt with in the next chapter.

I. OPEN CONTRACTS FOR THE SALE OF LAND MADE OTHERWISE THAN BY CORRESPONDENCE

In any open contract for the sale of land made otherwise than by correspondence, the following are the more important terms and conditions implied:

(1) The vendor must make a good title to the property sold, free from incumbrances.[1]

(2) The vendor must, at his own expense, deliver to the purchaser and verify an *abstract of title* commencing with a *good root of title*.[2]

An *abstract of title* is an epitome of the documents (commencing with the root of title) and facts which constitute the vendor's title.[3]

A good *root of title* is a document which effects a dealing with the whole legal and equitable estate and interest in the property sold. It describes the property, and there is nothing in it which casts any doubt on the title.[4]

---

[1] See *post*, p. 119.
[2] *Re Cox and Neve's Contract* [1891] 2 Ch. 109, 118. See *post*, p. 119. For the vendor's obligations in the case of registered land, see *post*, p. 93.
[3] See *post*, p. 119.
[4] See *post*, p. 121.

The length of title which the vendor must show depends upon the tenure of the property sold and the estate or interest which the vendor has agreed to grant to the purchaser. Thus, the property may be freehold or leasehold and the purchaser may have agreed to acquire the fee simple, a term of years, or some other interest, and, where the property is leasehold, the whole lease or only a sub-lease. The title to be shown in each case is regulated by the following statutory and other provisions:

(i) Under an open contract for sale of freehold the abstract of title must commence with a good root of title *at least* fifteen years old.[5]

Often, of course, there will not have been any dealing with the land in that period,[6] and the root will be considerably older than fifteen years.

A purchaser will not be affected with notice of any matter or thing which he would have discovered if he had investigated or inquired into the title back beyond such root of title unless he actually makes such investigation or inquiries.[7]

(ii) The title to be shown when a person has agreed to acquire a leasehold interest under an open contract is provided for by section 44 of the Law of Property Act 1925. The contract may be one for the grant of a lease by a freeholder; for the grant of a sub-lease (or underlease) by a lessee; or of a sub-sub-lease (*i.e.* a sub-lease carved out of a sub-lease) by a sub-lessee; or for the assignment of an existing lease or sub-lease or sub-sub-lease, etc. The section provides for all these cases, and its effect may be stated in the form of rules, thus:

(a) Under an open contract by a freeholder to grant a lease, the lessee cannot demand any proof whatsoever of the freehold title.[8]

(b) Under an open contract by a lessee to grant a sub-lease, the sub-lessee is entitled to production of the lease itself, however old it may be, and to see the title under which the lease has been held for the past fifteen years if the lease is so old, otherwise the title to the lease since its commencement. But the sub-lessee *cannot demand any proof whatsoever of the title to the freehold, i.e.* the freehold reversion.[9]

(c) Under an open contract by a sub-lessee to grant a sub-sublease, the sub-sub-lessee is entitled to production of the sublease itself, however old it may be, and to see the title under

---

5 Law of Property Act 1969, s. 23. Before 1970 the period was 30 years under the Law of Property Act 1925, s. 44 (1); 40 years under the Vendor and Purchaser Act 1874; and before that Act it was 60 years. For advowsons, property held under a grant from the Crown, and reversionary interests, a longer title is required.
6 But the average change-over in ordinary suburban property is probably once in every 7 to 10 years.
7 Law of Property Act 1925, s. 44 (8).
8 Law of Property Act 1925, s. 44 (2), replacing Vendor and Purchaser Act 1874, s. 2.
9 Law of Property Act 1925, s. 44 (2). See *Gosling* v. *Woolf* [1893] 1 Q.B. 39; *Becker* v. *Partridge* [1966] 2 Q.B. 155.

which the sub-lease has been held for the past fifteen years if the sub-lease is so old, otherwise the title to the sub-lease since its commencement.   But the sub-sub-lessee *cannot demand any proof whatsoever of the title to the freehold reversion or the leasehold reversion, i.e.* the lease out of which the sub-lease was carved.[10]

(To sum up rules (b) and (c): under an open contract, an intending lessee can call for no title at all, while an intending sub-lessee, sub-sub-lessee, etc., can call for his *immediate landlord's title,* and nothing more. In other words, an intending tenant can call for production of the lease under which his immediate landlord is himself the tenant and for an abstract showing dealings with such lease for at least (where possible) the past fifteen years.)

(d)   Under an open contract to *assign* an existing lease, or sub-lease, the assignee is always entitled to production of the lease or sub-lease, which he has agreed to acquire, however old it may be, and to see the title under which the lease or sub-lease has been held for the past fifteen years, if it is so old, otherwise the title to the lease or sub-lease since its commencement.   But the assignee *cannot demand proof of the freehold reversion or any leasehold reversion.*[11]

The above rules may be illustrated thus:

A, a freeholder, agrees to grant a lease to B for ninety-nine years; B cannot demand proof of A's freehold title.

B then agrees to assign his lease to C.   C is entitled to see the lease itself, however old, but cannot demand proof of A's title, for that is the freehold reversion.

C then agrees to assign the lease to D.   D is entitled to see the lease itself, however old, and the assignment thereof from B to C, but D cannot demand proof of A's title, for that is the freehold reversion.

D then agrees to assign the lease to E.   E is entitled to see the lease itself, however old, and the assignment thereof from C to D, for this is the title under which D is holding.   If the assignment from C to D is less than fifteen years old, E can also call for the assignment from B to C, because such assignment constituted the title to the lease during part of the past fifteen years.   But E cannot demand proof of A's title, for that is the freehold reversion.

E then agrees to grant a sub-lease to F for thirty-five years.   F is entitled to see the original lease for ninety-nine years, however old it may be, and the assignment thereof from D to E.   But he cannot call for any earlier assignment unless the assignment to E was made less than fifteen years ago, in which case F may call for any assignment

---

[10] Law of Property Act 1925, s. 44 (2) (4), replacing Conveyancing Act 1881, s. 13.
[11] Law of Property Act 1925, s. 44 (2) (3), replacing Conveyancing Act 1881, s. 3 (1); and see *Frend* v. *Buckley* (1870) L.R. 5 Q.B. 213; *Williams* v. *Spargo* [1893] W.N. 100.

under which the property was held during any part of the past fifteen years. In any case, F cannot demand proof of A's title, for that is the freehold reversion.

Lastly, F agrees to assign his sub-lease to G. G is entitled to see the sub-lease itself, however old, but he cannot demand production of the original lease (or the assignments thereof) because that is the leasehold reversion, and he cannot demand proof of A's title, for that is the freehold reversion.

Before 1926, in all those cases where a person acquiring a leasehold interest had no right to examine the titles to the freehold and leasehold reversions, he was nevertheless affected with constructive notice of everything which he would have discovered if he had, in fact, examined them. This was known as the rule in *Patman* v. *Harland*.[12] It is very important to notice that the law on this point was reversed as regards contracts made on or after January 1, 1926.[13] Consequently, although such a person is still precluded from examining the titles to the freehold and leasehold reversions, he will no longer have constructive notice of what he would have discovered if the titles had, in fact, been examined.[14]

(3) On the assignment of a lease, the purchaser must assume, unless the contrary appears, that the lease was duly granted; and, on production of the receipt for payment of the last instalment of rent due, must assume, unless the contrary appears,[15] that the rent has been paid and that the covenants and provisions of the lease have been duly observed and performed up to the date of actual completion.[16]

On the assignment of an underlease, the purchaser must assume, unless the contrary appears, that the underleases *and all superior leases* were duly granted; and, on production of the receipt for payment of the last instalment of rent due under the underlease, must assume, unless the contrary appears,[15] that the rent reserved by the underlease *and all superior leases* has been paid and that the covenants and obligations contained in the underlease *and all superior leases* have been duly observed and performed up to the date of actual completion.[17]

(4) The vendor must prove the identity of the property sold with that described in the documents abstracted.[18]

---

[12] (1881) 17 Ch.D. 353.

[13] See Law of Property Act 1925, s. 44 (5). This provision does not apply if notice is obtained *aliunde, i.e.* from some cause other than the non-inspection of title deeds, such as registration or actual notice. The reduction in the statutory length of title by the Law of Property Act 1969 (*ante*) increases the risk of the purchaser not being able to discover a registered land charge; see Megarry and Wade, *The Law of Real Property* (3rd ed.), pp. 1036–1037; (1969) 32 M.L.R. 482 *et seq.*

[14] As to the position when the land is registered, see *White* v. *Bijou Mansions Ltd.* [1937] Ch. 610, and *post*, p. 181.

[15] *Re Highett and Bird's Contract* [1903] 1 Ch. 287; *Re Taunton etc. Building Society and Robert's Contract* [1912] 2 Ch. 381; *cf. Lockhart's Ltd.* v. *Bernard Rosen and Co.* [1922] 1 Ch. 433.

[16] Law of Property Act 1925, s. 45 (2); see *post*, p. 100.

[17] *Ibid.* subs. (3).

[18] See *post*, p. 94.

(5) Recitals, statements, and descriptions of facts, matters and parties contained in deeds, instruments, Acts of Parliament, or statutory declarations twenty years old at the date of the contract must, unless and except so far as they are proved to be inaccurate, be taken to be sufficient evidence of the truth of such facts, matters, and descriptions.[19]

(6) On a sale of any property in lots, a purchaser of two or more lots, held wholly or partly under the same title, shall not have a right to more than one abstract of the common title, except at his own expense.[20]

(7) The provisions of the Law of Property Act 1925, s. 45 (1),[21] concerning the purchaser's right to inquire into the title prior to the root of title, are somewhat complicated. The important effect of the section is as follows: the purchaser cannot require production of any abstract or copy of any deed, will, or other document, dated or made before the root of title, even though it creates a power (*other than a power of attorney*) which was subsequently exercised by one of the abstracted documents; nor may he require information of, or make any requisition concerning, any such deed, etc., or the prior title generally. Further, the purchaser must assume that all such deeds, etc., were duly executed by the proper parties, and that all abstracted recitals of such deeds, etc., are correct, unless the contrary appears.

So far, we have seen that a purchaser must assume that there was no flaw in any document prior to the root of title, and that all abstracted recitals of prior documents are correct, unless the contrary appears. To this, however, the section provides three exceptions. Even though the documents in question were executed before the root of title, the purchaser is entitled to production of or a copy of an abstract of:

(a) any power of attorney under which any abstracted document was executed [22];

(b) any document which created any interest, power or obligation, subject to which the property or any part of it was disposed of by an abstracted document. This, however, does not apply if such interest, power or obligation is shown to have ceased to exist, because then the purchaser is not concerned with it; and

(c) any document creating any limitation or trust by reference to which the property or any part of it was disposed of by an abstracted document.

It should be noted that if the purchaser discovers a flaw in the earlier title by any means whatsoever, there is nothing in this section to prevent him from resisting specific performance on the ground that the vendor's title is bad.[23]

---

[19] Law of Property Act 1925, s. 45 (6). And see *post*, p. 224.
[20] *Ibid.* subs. (5).
[21] Replacing and amending Conveyancing Act 1881, s. 3 (3).
[22] See *Re Copelin's Contract* [1937] 4 All E.R. 447.
[23] *Re Scott and Alvarez's Contract* [1895] 2 Ch. 603; and see *post*, pp. 92, 93.

(8) It will generally be necessary to obtain the deeds relating to the property sold, for three entirely separate purposes, as follows:

    (a) to enable the vendor to make his abstract;

    (b) to enable the purchaser to verify that abstract; and

    (c) to enable the vendor to hand over the deeds on completion of the purchase.

The following rules show upon whom the expense of obtaining the deeds in each of these cases will fall:

    (a) The vendor must pay the cost of obtaining all deeds necessary to enable him to *prepare the abstract* [24];

    (b) The purchaser must pay the cost of production of all deeds and other documents, Acts of Parliament, wills, probates, certificates, declarations, etc., which he may require to enable him to *verify* the abstract, unless such deeds and other documents, etc., are in the possession of the vendor or (since 1925) the vendor's mortgagee or trustee [25];

    (c) The vendor must pay the cost of obtaining the deeds, etc., for the purpose of *handing them over* to the purchaser on completion. [26]

(9) The vendor must pay the cost of stamping all documents of title which are insufficiently stamped. [27]

(10) The purchase must be completed as soon as the vendor shall have shown a good title. The vendor must do this within a reasonable time. The purchaser then prepares a conveyance at his own expense, and sends or takes it to the vendor for execution. At the same time he should tender the purchase-money. The vendor then executes the conveyance at his own expense, and gives possession of the property to the purchaser. The conveyance must be effectual to vest the whole estate contracted for, legal and equitable, in the purchaser; and it must contain or imply covenants for title. If, in order to make a good title, it is necessary for the vendor to procure the joinder of other parties to the conveyance, then the vendor must, at his own expense, procure the joinder of such parties.

If the vendor has agreed to convey the legal estate, and the legal estate is outstanding, the vendor must bear the expense of getting it in. [28]

(11) On completion, the vendor must hand over to the purchaser all documents of title relating solely to the land purchased, but he is entitled to retain:

    (i) any documents which relate to *other land* retained by him. If

---

[24] *Re Johnson and Tustin* (1885) 30 Ch.D. 42.
[25] Law of Property Act 1925, s. 45 (4).
[26] *Re Duthy and Jesson's Contract* [1898] 1 Ch. 419.
[27] For stamping, see *post*, pp. 213 *et seq.*
[28] Law of Property Act 1925, s. 42 (3); and see *post*, p. 87.

the documents relate to other property which is not land, such as a policy of insurance, he is not entitled to retain them [29.]

(ii) a trust instrument or other instrument creating a trust which is still subsisting; or

(iii) an instrument relating to the appointment or discharge of a trustee of a subsisting trust.[30]

If the vendor retains any document of title, he must give to the purchaser the statutory acknowledgment of the purchaser's right to production and delivery of copies and, unless he is a trustee or mortgagee, the statutory undertaking for safe custody.[31]

(12) Any act necessary to be done by either party to carry out the contract, such as the delivery of the abstract, delivery of the requisitions, or the preparation of the conveyance, must be done within a reasonable time.[32] In case of unreasonable delay by either party to do any act necessary to carry out the contract, the other party may serve a notice on the party in default requiring him to do such act within a reasonable time, specified in the notice, and stating an intention to terminate the contract if the notice is not complied with. If such notice is not complied with, the party in default will not be able to obtain specific performance of the contract and may be sued for breach of contract.[33]

(13) The vendor, until completion, may retain possession of the property, and will occupy the position of a trustee of the property for the purchaser,[34] and must pay all rates and outgoings up to the time fixed for completion. The purchaser bears accidental losses and takes the advantage of all additions or improvements.[35]

II. OPEN CONTRACTS FOR THE SALE OF LAND MADE BY CORRESPONDENCE

Before January 1, 1926, the same terms and conditions were implied in open contracts made by correspondence as in open contracts made otherwise than by correspondence.[36] In 1926, however, the Lord Chancellor, pursuant to the power for that purpose conferred upon him by section 46 of the Law of Property Act 1925, published the Statutory Form of Conditions of Sale 1925, which are to apply to contracts for the sale of land made by correspondence,[37] subject to any modifications, stipulations or intention to the contrary expressed in the

---

[29] *Re Williams and the Duchess of Newcastle's Contract* [1897] 2 Ch. 144.
[30] Law of Property Act 1925, s. 45 (9). See *Clayton* v. *Clayton* [1930] 2 Ch. 12; *Lewis* v. *Plunket* [1937] Ch. 306.
[31] *Ibid.* subs. (8); and see *post*, p. 238.
[32] *Compton* v. *Bagley* [1892] 1 Ch. 313.
[33] *Compton* v. *Bagley* [1892] 1 Ch. 313, 321; *Stickney* v. *Keeble* [1915] A.C. 386, 418.
[34] The trusteeship of the vendor is, however, of a qualified nature. See *post*, p. 189.
[35] See *post*, p. 190.
[36] See *ante*, pp. 59 *et seq.*
[37] For the difficulties surrounding the meaning of "correspondence," *e.g.* where an oral offer is accepted by letter, see Farrand, *Contract and Conveyance*, p. 68.

correspondence. These conditions may also by express reference be made to apply to *any* contract for sale of land. The conditions are as follows [38]:

1. Date fixed for completion [39]

The date for completion shall, unless otherwise agreed, be the first day after the expiration of seven weeks from the time when the contract is made, or if that day is a Sunday, Christmas Day, Good Friday or Bank Holiday, the next following working day.

2. Place for completion [40]

Completion shall take place at the office of the vendor's solicitors, or, if the vendor so requires, at the office of the solicitors of his mortgagees.

3. Possession and apportionment of outgoings [41]

(1) Provided that the purchaser has paid the purchase-money, or, where a deposit is paid, the balance, he shall, *as from the date fixed for completion* (but subject to the execution of any conveyance which ought to be executed by him [42]), be entitled to be let into possession, or into receipt of rents and profits. *From that date*, he must pay all outgoings. Up to that date, all current rents, rates, taxes and other outgoings shall (if necessary) be apportioned, and the balance shall be paid by or allowed to the purchaser on actual completion. For this purpose the purchaser shall be liable to pay to the vendor a proportionate part of the current rents accrued in respect of the property up to the date fixed for completion; provided that all rates shall be apportioned, so far as practicable, according to the period for which they are intended to provide, and not as running from the dates when the same are made or allowed.

(2) Where as respects any rate the date fixed for completion falls between the expiration of the period for which the last rate was made and the making of a new rate, the new rate shall, for the purposes of this condition, be deemed to have been made at the same rate in the pound as that at which the last rate was made, and shall be calculated from day to day.

4. Interest on purchase-money [43]

(1) If from any cause whatever (save as hereinafter mentioned) the

---

[38] Some of the conditions are not set out verbatim here, but in a modified form, in an attempt to make them more intelligible to the student.
[39] See further, *post*, p. 108.
[40] See further, *post*, p. 111.
[41] See further, *post*, pp. 104, 107.
[42] For execution of the conveyance by the purchaser, see *post*, p. 208.
[43] See further, *post*, p. 105.

completion of the purchase is delayed beyond the date fixed for completion, the purchase-money, or where a deposit is paid, the balance thereof, shall bear interest at the rate of £5 per cent. per annum, from the date fixed for the completion to the day of actual payment thereof.

(2) Provided that, if delay in completion arises from any other cause than the purchaser's own act or default, the purchaser may:

    (a) at his own risk, deposit the purchase-money, or where a deposit is paid, the balance thereof, at any bank in England or Wales, in his own name or otherwise; and

    (b) give notice in writing forthwith of such deposit to the vendor or his solicitors,

and in that case the vendor shall be bound to accept the interest, if any, allowed thereon, as from the date of such deposit, in lieu of the interest accruing after the date of the deposit, which would otherwise be payable to him under this condition.

(3) No interest shall become payable by the purchaser if delay in completion is attributable to:

    (a) a refusal by the vendor to deduce title in accordance with the contract, or to give an authority to inspect the register kept under the Land Registration Act 1925,[44] or to convey; or

    (b) any other wilful act or default of the vendor or his Settled Land Act trustees.

(4) The vendor shall, as from the date when interest becomes payable under this condition, have the option (to be exercised by notice in writing) of taking an apportioned part of the rents and profits, less apportioned outgoings, up to the date of actual completion, in lieu of the interest otherwise payable under this condition; and, if the said option is exercised, the same payments, allowances and apportionments shall be made as if the date fixed for completion had been the date of actual completion.

The said option shall not be exercisable in any case in which subclause (2) of this clause applies.

5. Delivery of abstract [45]

(1) The vendor shall deliver to the purchaser or his solicitor:

    (a) an abstract of the title to the property sold; or

    (b) in the case of land registered with an absolute or good leasehold title, the particulars and information which ought to be furnished in lieu of an abstract, with a written authority to inspect the register,

and in either case, within fourteen days from the date when the contract was made.

(2) Where land is registered with a possessory or qualified title, the

[44] For authority to inspect the register, see *post*, p. 93.
[45] See further, *post*, p. 101.

abstract (if any) shall only relate to estates, rights and interests, subsisting or capable of taking effect prior to the date of first registration,
or excluded from the effect of first registration, and dealings therewith,
and subject as aforesaid, the foregoing provisions relating to absolute
or good leasehold titles shall apply.[46]

6. Requisitions [47]

(1) The purchaser shall, within fourteen days after the actual
delivery of the abstract, or of the said particulars and information,
whether or not delivered within the time prescribed, send to the
solicitors of the vendor a statement in writing of all the objections
and requisitions (if any) to or on:

   (a)   the title or evidence of title;
   (b)   the abstract or the said particulars and information;
   (c)   the contract, as respects matters not hereby specifically provided
      for,

and subject thereto the title shall be deemed accepted.

(2) All objections and requisitions not included in any statement
sent within the time aforesaid, and not going to the root of the title,
shall be deemed waived.

(3) An abstract or the said particulars and information, though
in fact imperfect, shall be deemed perfect, except for the purpose of any
objections or requisitions which could not have been taken or made
on the information therein contained.

(4) An answer to any objection or requisition shall be replied to,
in writing, within seven days after delivery thereof and, if not so
replied to, shall be considered satisfactory.

7. Power to rescind [48]

(1) If the purchaser shall take or make any objection or requisition,
which the vendor is unable to remove or comply with, and the purchaser
shall not withdraw such objection or requisition within ten days after
being required, in writing, so to do, the vendor may, by notice in
writing delivered to the purchaser or his solicitor and notwithstanding
any intermediate negotiations, rescind the contract.

(2) This condition does not apply so as to prevent the enforcement
by a purchaser of any right conferred on him by section 42 of the Law
of Property Act 1925.[49]

(3) If the contract is so rescinded, the vendor shall, within one
week after default is made in complying with the requirement to withdraw the objection or requisition, repay to the purchaser his deposit
money (if any), but without interest, and the purchaser shall return

---

[46] See further as to proof of title to registered land, *post*, pp. 93 *et seq.*
[47] See further, *post*, p. 101.
[48] See further, *post*, p. 102.
[49] For s. 42, see *ante*, p. 64, and *post*, pp. 86, 87.

fortwith all abstracts and papers in his possession belonging to the vendor, and shall not make any claim on the vendor for costs, compensation, or otherwise.

8. Preparation of conveyance [50]

(1) The conveyance, or other instrument of transfer to the purchaser, shall be prepared by the purchaser and at his own expense, and the draft thereof shall be delivered at the office of the solicitors of the vendor at least ten days before the date fixed for completion, for perusal and approval of the vendor and other necessary parties (if any).

(2) The engrossment of such conveyance or transfer, for execution by the vendor and other necessary parties (if any), shall be left at the office of the vendor's solicitors within four days after the draft has been returned approved on behalf of the vendor and other necessary conveying parties (if any).

(3) Delivery of a draft or of an engrossment shall not prejudice any outstanding requisitions.

9. Power for vendor to resell after notice [51]

(1) If the purchaser shall neglect or fail to perform his part of the contract, the vendor may give to the purchaser, or to his solicitor, at least twenty-one days' notice in writing, specifying the breach, and requiring the purchaser to make good the default before the expiration of the notice.

(2) If the purchaser does not comply with the terms of the said notice:

(a) the deposit money, if any, shall, unless the court otherwise directs, be forfeited to the vendor, or, in the case of settled land, to his Settled Land Act trustees;

(b) the vendor may resell the property without previously tendering a conveyance or instrument of transfer to the purchaser;

and the following provisions shall apply.

(3) Any resale may be made, by auction or private contract, at such time, subject to such conditions, and in such manner generally, as the vendor may think proper, and the defaulting purchaser shall have no right to any part of the purchase-money thereby arising.

III. Advantages and Disadvantages of an Open Contract

The question must now be asked whether a sale of land under an open contract is advantageous or not to the purchaser or the vendor. It is an advantage to the *purchaser* in that he thereby becomes entitled to proof of the title back to a good root of title at least fifteen years old.[52]

---

[50] See further, *post*, p. 104.
[51] See further, *post*, p. 111.
[52] The longer the statutory length of title, the more advantageous it is for the purchaser. Before the Law of Property Act 1969 (when the statutory length of title was 30 years) it was quite common for this to be cut down by the terms of a formal contract. Now the statutory period is shorter, the advantage is less.

If, under a formal contract, he agrees to accept a shorter title, he will be deemed to have notice of all matters and things which he would have discovered if he had examined the title for the full statutory period. For example, A, in 1914, conveyed his land to B, and the conveyance contained restrictive covenants as to the use of the land. In 1920, B sold this land to C. In 1936, C agreed to sell this land to W, subject to a condition that the title should commence with the conveyance of 1920. W is bound by the restrictive covenants in the deed of 1914, on the ground that he has "constructive notice" of them, because, if he had refused to accept the shorter title, he would have discovered such covenants.[53] It is now no disadvantage to the purchaser to buy leaseholds on open contract, because he is no longer affected by constructive notice of matters and things affecting the freehold reversion.[54]

The *disadvantage* of an open contract to a purchaser is that, as he has entered into a contract without proper legal advice, the usual searches and inquiries [55] will not have been made.

On the other hand, it is generally disadvantageous to the *vendor* to enter into an open contract, unless made by correspondence.[56] He will be called upon to show the full statutory title. There will be no time fixed within which requisitions and objections are to be made, or for completion. There will be no provisions to confer on the vendor a right to rescind or to regulate the payment of interest on the purchase-money or the payment of compensation for misdescriptions. Therefore the vendor will generally prefer to enter into a formal contract containing conditions which are favourable to him in connection with the above and other similar matters.

---

[53] *Re Nisbet and Pott's Contract* [1906] 1 Ch. 386. 30 years was then the statutory length of title; see *ante*, p. 60.
[54] See *ante*, p. 62.
[55] See *ante*, pp. 34 *et seq.*
[56] See *ante*, pp. 65 *et seq.*

CHAPTER 5

FORMAL CONTRACTS FOR SALE OF LAND

Generally

A formal contract for the sale of land is traditionally divided into two parts:

(1) the particulars of sale, which describe the property, its nature, area, benefits, defects and any charges and liabilities to which it is subject; and

(2) the conditions of sale, which set forth the terms by which the parties are to be bound.

The proper office of the particulars is to describe the subject-matter of the contract; that of the conditions to state the terms on which it is sold.[1]

The layout and printing of the modern standard forms of contract and conditions of sale[2] do not make this traditional distinction as clear as it formerly was. Nevertheless the distinction may still be of some significance.[3]

A contract for the sale of registered land will usually be in the same form as one for unregistered land. Any special considerations with regard to registered land will be mentioned in the discussion which follows.

I. PARTICULARS OF SALE

Contents

The particulars should contain some or all, according to the circumstances, of the following:

(1) A physical description of the property, stating its character, area, situation, and its boundaries.

(2) A statement as to the tenure of the property,[4] whether freehold or leasehold; and if leasehold, short particulars of the terms of the lease, for example, the term and the rent.

(3) A statement as to the rights appurtenant to the property, for example, easements of which the property has, or is to have, the benefit.

---

[1] *Per* Malins V.-C. in *Torrance* v. *Bolton* (1872) L.R. 14 Eq. 124; and see *Blaiberg* v. *Keeves* [1906] 2 Ch. 175, 184.

[2] See *post*, p. 84.

[3] See Farrand, *Contract and Conveyance*, p. 38.

[4] As to the presumption that a sale is a sale of the fee simple free from incumbrances, see *post*, p. 76.

(4)　A statement as to the incumbrances, for example, easements, mortgages or restrictive covenants, to which the property is already, or is to be made, subject.[5]

(5)　If the property is let, short particulars of the terms of the lease, especially the term and the rent.

Maps and plans, which are commonly used to describe the property to be sold, form part of the particulars and are subject to the same rules.[6]

The vendor's solicitor in framing the particulars will generally follow the description in the title deeds.　But, while the solicitor is not expected to act as a surveyor, he should inquire into the facts in order that he may be able to describe the property correctly.[7]　Part of the vendor's original holding may have been sold off, in which case the plan to the conveyance to the vendor will not give a correct description of the land to be sold.[8]　Or encroachments may have been made increasing or diminishing the extent of the land to be sold.　The Limitation Act 1939, and the doctrine of estoppel, may result in variations to the original boundaries.[9]　Where a house on a building estate is sold off, it is not uncommon for the plan to be adapted from the original plan of the estate submitted for planning permission by the developers.　But sometimes (indeed, quite often), the position of a house and its boundaries, as finally erected on the ground, bears little or no relation to the original plan.　Thus, a purchaser, if he is wise, will have a proper survey made and insist on the subsequent conveyance being made by reference to that survey and not the vendor's plan. If the purchaser does not do this, then it is possible he is inviting trouble in the way of a boundary dispute, either for himself, or his successors in title, in the future.[10]

There are three points of special importance to keep in mind when preparing particulars.　First, one of the vendor's obligations under an open contract is to prove the identity of the property described in the contract with that in the deeds, although, as we shall see, this obligation may be limited by the conditions of sale.[11]　Secondly, the property must be described correctly.　If there is a misdescription of the property in the particulars, there will be a breach of contract by the vendor.　We shall see in this case that, subject to the conditions of sale, the purchaser will have various remedies open to him, depending on the

---

[5] See (1952) 49 L.S.Gaz. 29.

[6] *Re Lindsay and Forder's Contract* (1895) 72 L.T. 832.

[7] *Gordon-Cumming* v. *Houldsworth* [1910] A.C. 537.

[8] *Wallington* v. *Townsend* [1939] Ch. 588.

[9] See *e.g. Bell* v. *Marsh* [1903] 1 Ch. 528; *Hopgood* v. *Brown* [1955] 1 W.L.R. 213.

[10] Many boundary disputes arise in the case of houses built before the last war. Few houses were then built with garages.　Now their owners want a garage either at the back or side of the house and often there will hardly be room, so an inch or so one way or the other may make all the difference.　As to parcels, see *post,* p. 230.

[11] *Post,* p. 94.

seriousness of the misdescription.[12] Thirdly, the vendor is under an obligation to disclose all latent defects of title [13] and some latent physical defects in the property.[14] Breach of the former obligation is a breach of contract, *i.e.* a breach of the implied terms of a contract for sale of land that the sale is a sale of the fee simple free from incumbrances.[15] Misdescription and non-disclosure will now be discussed in turn.

A. Misdescription

The matters stated in the particulars must be stated accurately. If the property is not correctly described, either physically or as to its character, tenure, etc., there will be a misdescription and a breach of contract by the vendor. The effect of a misdescription as regards the remedies available to the purchaser, or indeed, to the vendor himself, depends upon the seriousness of the misdescription and the provisions in the conditions of sale.[16]

Statement of fact

For there to be a misdescription, there must be a misstatement of fact. The distinction between a statement of fact and an opinion should be noted. This distinction is important in relation to misrepresentations [17]; and it is also relevant in the context of misdescription. A mistaken *opinion* will not as such amount to a misdescription. Thus such expressions as " highly desirable residence " are mere expressions of opinion: typical auctioneers' or estate agents' sales-talk.[18] But a representation of fact may be inherent in a statement of opinion,[19] and so give rise to misdescription.

The rule in Flight v. Booth

If the misdescription is substantial, *i.e.* the purchaser would not be getting *substantially* the same thing as he agreed to buy, the vendor will be unable to enforce the contract, irrespective of any condition of sale. This principle is sometimes called the rule in *Flight* v. *Booth*,[20] where it was said:

" Where the description, although not proceeding from fraud, is in a material and substantial point so far affecting the subject matter of the contract that it may reasonably be supposed, but for

12 *Post*, p. 74.
13 *Post*, p. 78.
14 *Post*, p. 80.
15 *Post*, p. 76.
16 For conditions of sale, see *post*, p. 95.
17 *Ante*, p. 35.
18 See *Watson* v. *Burton* [1957] 1 W.L.R. 19; *cf.* (1972) 122 New L.J. 468.
19 *Bissett* v. *Wilkinson* [1927] A.C. 177; *Brown* v. *Raphael* [1958] Ch. 636.
20 (1834) 1 Bing.N.C. 370.

the misdescription, the purchaser might never have entered the contract at all, in such a case the contract is voided altogether." [21]

In *Flight* v. *Booth*, the particulars stated that, under the terms of the lease which formed the subject-matter of the contract, no offensive trades might be carried out on the property. In fact, the restrictions in the lease were much wider, and prohibited many trades of a perfectly inoffensive character. The vendor was unable to enforce the contract by specific performance, and the purchaser was entitled to the return of his deposit. [22]

Rescission

In such circumstances, *i.e.* where there is a substantial misdescription, the purchaser may himself take the initiative by bringing proceedings for a declaration that he is entitled to rescind the contract and for the return of his deposit. [23] It should be noticed, however, that a less serious misdescription may be sufficient to enable the purchaser to resist specific performance in an action by the vendor than is required to enable him to succeed in a claim to rescind the contract. [24]

Compensation

If the purchaser still wants the property as it is, in spite of the misdescription, and whether the misdescription be substantial or not, he may be able to get an order for specific performance with compensation, *i.e.* with an abatement of the purchase price. [25] However, specific performance with abatement will not be granted where the deficiency, or difference between the property as described and as it is in fact, is not capable of estimation in money terms. [26]

Purchaser's remedies generally

The purchaser must act before completion, for rescission can only be obtained after completion if the vendor is guilty of fraud [27] or if the misdescription repeats a misrepresentation made before contract, [28] and compensation for misdescription can only be obtained after completion (unless the misdescription was not discoverable until after completion [29]), if there is an express provision to that effect. [30] In any event, specific performance is not available to the purchaser where it would cause

---

[21] *Per* Lord Tindal C.J. at p. 377.
[22] And see *Watson* v. *Burton* [1957] 1 W.L.R. 19.
[23] *Jacobs* v. *Revell* [1900] 2 Ch. 858; *Ridley* v. *Osler* [1939] 1 All E.R. 618.
[24] *Re Terry and White's Contract* (1886) 32 Ch.D. 14.
[25] *Rutherford* v. *Acton-Adams* [1915] A.C. 866.
[26] *Rudd* v. *Lascelles* [1900] 1 Ch. 815 (restrictive covenants).
[27] *Joliffe* v. *Baker* (1883) 11 Q.B.D. 255.
[28] *Ante*, p. 35. Although the purchaser may have a remedy under the covenants for title (as to which, see *post*, p. 225) if the misdescription is embodied in the conveyance.
[29] *Clayton* v. *Leech* (1889) 41 Ch.D. 103.
[30] *Joliffe* v. *Baker, supra*; *Palmer* v. *Johnson* (1884) 13 Q.B.D. 351. See *post*, p. 96.

hardship to the vendor [31] or if the purchaser knew of the misdescription when the contract was entered into.[32]

Vendor's remedies

Looking at the position from the point of view of the vendor, where the misdescription is trivial, the vendor will be able to enforce specific performance with abatement.[33] He will not be entitled to specific performance if the misdescription is substantial. Where the misdescription is to the prejudice of the *vendor*, as, for example, where the area is greater than that stated in the contract, the vendor cannot claim an increase in the price,[34] though the court might refuse to order specific performance against him on the ground of hardship.[35]

Whether or not the deficiency or the difference is substantial, is a matter of fact for the court to decide in each case.[36] Some examples appear below. It seems that the test to be applied is an objective one.[36]

The rights of the parties will, in most cases, be governed by the conditions of sale. These are discussed in a subsequent section.[37]

Cases of misdescription

Misdescription takes a variety of forms. For example:

(1) *Quantity*

This is a very common ground of misdescription. Subject to the conditions of sale, the purchaser will be able to rescind unless the extent of the misdescription is so small that he will get substantially what he contracted to buy, in which case he may claim an abatement for the deficiency. In *Watson* v. *Burton* [38] the property was stated in the particulars to amount to approximately 3,920 square yards but it was found to contain only 2,360 square yards. It was held that a misstatement to the extent of 40 per cent. was substantial and the vendor's action for specific performance was dismissed and judgment given for the purchaser on his counterclaim for rescission and return of deposit. But in *Re Fawcett and Holmes' Contract* [39] the difference was between 1,372 square yards and 1,033 square yards. Part of the original holding of 1,372 square yards had been sold off, but this had been overlooked. However, this was held to be a case for compensation.

Each case will depend on the surrounding circumstances. If the

---

31 *Thomas* v. *Dering* (1837) 1 Keen 729, 746.
32 *Castle* v. *Wilkinson* (1870) L.R. 5 Ch.App. 534.
33 *Re Belcham and Gawley's Contract* [1930] 1 Ch. 56.
34 See *Re Lindsay and Forder's Contract* (1895) 72 L.T. 832.
35 *Manser* v. *Back* (1848) 6 Hare 443.
36 *Watson* v. *Burton* [1957] 1 W.L.R. 19, 25.
37 *Post*, p. 95.
38 [1957] 1 W.L.R. 19.
39 (1889) 42 Ch.D. 150.

amount of the deficiency is only small, but has, for example, the effect
of turning a piece of land with river frontage into a non-riparian
holding, the misdescription is substantial.[40]

(2) *Character of property*

In auction particulars (but not usually in particulars in a contract
for sale by private treaty) the property may be described in effusive
terms, such as " highly desirable residence." Such an expression is
clearly auctioneer's sales-talk, but it may not be so easy to draw the
line where other expressions are used. " Valuable business premises," [41] applied to business premises which could not be used for a
number of inoffensive trades, was not a fair description, and the
purchaser was held entitled to rescind and recover the deposit paid.[42]

Where the particulars of sale of an hotel stated that it was let to
" a most desirable tenant," when the tenant was, in fact, in arrears
with rent and on the verge of bankruptcy, the purchaser was held
entitled to refuse to complete.[43]

(3) *Tenure*

The particulars should not deal with title, other than to describe the
land by its correct tenure. So, for instance, where the land is leasehold,
the particulars should state whether it is held under a lease or an
underlease.[44] The vendor is assumed to be selling the unincumbered
fee simple, unless the contrary is stated.[45] It is a material misdescription, entitling the purchaser to rescind, to describe leasehold as freehold,
or an underlease as a lease.[46]

If the tenure is leasehold, short particulars of the lease should be
given, for example, as to the length of the term, the rent, and any
unusual covenants.[47]

It is a misdescription to describe as " registered land " land registered
only with possessory title.[48]

(4) *Tenanted properties*

Where the property to be sold is let, the particulars should state the

---

[40] *Arnold* v. *Arnold* (1880) 14 Ch.D. 270. For conditions of sale, see *post*, p. 95.
[41] Note the difference between a general description and a description of planning
use; see *London Investment etc. Co.* v. *Ember Estates* (1950) 1 P. & C.R. 188;
post, p. 77.
[42] *Hunt (Charles) Ltd.* v. *Palmer* [1931] 2 Ch. 287; and see *Flight* v. *Booth, supra.*
Note that where the purchaser claims the return of the deposit, the relief he seeks
in the claim or summons is that he is entitled to give a good receipt to the person
holding the deposit.
[43] *Smith* v. *Land and House Property Corpn.* (1884) 28 Ch.D. 7.
[44] *Re Russ and Brown's Contract* [1943] Ch. 34. And see *Re Thompson and
Cottrell's Contract* [1943] Ch. 97; *Becker* v. *Partridge* [1966] 2 Q.B. 155.
[45] *Hughes* v. *Parker* (1841) 8 M. & W. 244; *Re Ossemsley Estate Ltd.* [1937] 3 All E.R.
774, 778; *Timmins* v. *Moreland Street Property Co. Ltd.* [1958] Ch. 110, 132.
[46] *Nash* v. *Wooderson* (1885) 52 L.T. 459.
[47] *Molyneux* v. *Hawtrey* [1903] 2 K.B. 487.
[48] *Re Brine and Davies' Contract* [1935] Ch. 388.

essential terms of the lease, for example, the length of the term, the rent, etc.[49] In one case [50] the particulars of sale described the property as " late in the occupation of A at the rent of £290." In fact A had occupied the property for a year at a rent of £290, but for the previous quarter he had paid a rent of £1 and thus paid £291 for a tenancy of a year and a quarter. At the end of that time he had vacated the property, and another person agreed to pay a rent of £225 a year for it. This second person subsequently, however, paid £22 to be released from his agreement. Against the background of these facts, the court held the particulars of sale to contain a substantial misdescription entitling the purchaser to rescind. In another case, where four houses were described as " freehold decontrolled tenancies," and two of the rooms in the houses were in fact still controlled under the Rent Acts, the purchaser was held entitled to rescind.[51] Again, there was a mis-description where the particulars of sale stated the rent of controlled premises to be 28s. 3d. a week, but failed to mention that a notice of disrepair had been served which would reduce the rent to 15s. 7d. until the repairs were carried out.[52] On the other hand, where the property was sold subject to and with the benefit of weekly tenancies of two floors at £1 5s. 0d. and £1 1s. 6d. a week and it turned out that the maximum recoverable rents were 14s. 6d. and 13s. 6d. a week, it was held that there was no representation that the stated rents were legally recoverable.[53]

Where thirteen houses were described as being let under six leases, when in fact they were let under thirteen leases but the total amount of rents was the same, the misdescription was held to be material and the purchaser was entitled to rescind.[54]

(5) *Town and Country Planning*

The use to which the property may be put under the Town and Country Planning Acts, if described at all, must be correctly described. There is no implied warranty as to the fitness or suitability for any particular purpose of the property agreed to be sold.[55] But if the property is described as a dwelling-house, or building land, or office premises, then it would seem (although the matter is somewhat uncertain) that a purchaser could rescind if the use were not the authorised use under the Town and Country Planning Acts.[56] Thus, the description of land as suitable for building purposes, when, in fact,

49 For conditions of sale, see *post*, p. 101.
50 *Dimmock* v. *Hallett* (1866) 2 Ch.App. 21.
51 *Ridley* v. *Osler* [1939] 1 All E.R. 618.
52 *Re Englefield Holdings and Sinclair's Contract* [1962] 1 W.L.R. 1119.
53 *Schlisselman* v. *Rubin* [1951] W.N. 530; *cf. Gilchester Properties* v. *Gomm* [1948] 1 All E.R. 493; *ante*, p. 36.
54 *Lee* v. *Rayson* [1917] 1 Ch. 613.
55 See *Edler* v. *Auerbach* [1950] 1 K.B. 359.
56 See *Emmet on Title* (15th ed.), p. 111.

D*

it is zoned for amenity [57]; or, for business purposes when it is zoned for residential,[58] will enable the purchaser to rescind.

B. Non-Disclosure

Generally

In addition to the obligation not to mislead the purchaser by mis-description, the vendor is also bound to disclose all facts which might influence the purchaser, and which are not apparent to a person making a reasonably careful inspection of the property. It is sometimes said that a contract for the sale of land is one *uberrimae fidei*. But this is not so, as the general rule is that the vendor is not bound to disclose *all* facts to a prospective purchaser—in effect, the rule is *caveat emptor*.[59] But there are some matters the vendor is bound to disclose and it is probably better to treat the contract for the sale of land as *sui generis*. The vendor is bound to disclose all material *latent defects in the title*. He is also bound to disclose any *latent defect in the property* itself, if the defect is such that the property is of no use for the purpose for which the purchaser requires it and the vendor knows of that purpose.

We have already seen that the vendor must not make misrepresentations as to the property nor must he misdescribe it. *Misrepresentations* are made before the contract to induce the purchaser to enter into the contract. *Non-disclosure* is a form of misrepresentation in so far as it occurs before and may induce the purchaser to enter into the contract. Indeed, in some cases, even silence may amount to a misrepresentation, particularly where what is held back makes what has been stated untrue.[60] A *misdescription* occurs in the contract itself and causes a breach of contract. A misrepresentation may, of course, be repeated in the particulars and thus become part of the contract. Non-disclosure of defects of title also causes a breach of contract, being a breach of the implied (or express) term that the vendor is selling the fee simple free from incumbrances.[61]

Defects in title

As the vendor knows the title and the purchaser does not, it is the duty of the vendor to disclose all defects of title. Unless the contract provides to the contrary, the agreement for the sale of freehold land is an agreement to sell an estate in fee simple free from incumbrances.[61] Accordingly, the vendor must disclose all incumbrances, such as mortgages and leases, affecting the property.[62] Even if the purchaser

[57] *Spiller* v. *Bolton* (1947) 149 E.G. 450.
[58] *Smith and Olley* v. *Townsend* (1949) 1 P. & C.R. 28; (1950) 14 Conv.(N.S.) 308; *cf. London Investments etc.* v. *Ember Estates* (1950) 1 P. & C.R. 188. And see *post*, p. 98 for conditions of sale.
[59] *Terrene Ltd.* v. *Nelson* [1937] 3 All E.R. 937.
[60] See Cheshire and Fifoot, *The Law of Contract* (7th ed.), p. 238.
[61] *Hughes* v. *Parker* (1841) 8 M. & W. 244. See *ante*, p. 76.
[62] *Carlish* v. *Salt* [1906] 1 Ch. 335; *Re Ossemsley Estates Ltd.* [1937] 3 All E.R. 774.

has agreed to accept a particular title offered, as, for instance, where the conditions of sale require the purchaser to accept as correct a particular fact or state of affairs, the vendor will not be able to force the property on him unless he has made full disclosure to the purchaser.[63] Accordingly, where the purchaser had agreed to accept a title shorter than the statutory length of title,[64] the vendor was bound to disclose the fact that the deed forming the stipulated root of title was a voluntary one.[65] If, in the case of registered land, the title is possessory, this must be disclosed.[66] Restrictive covenants[67] and unusual and onerous covenants in a lease[68] must be disclosed. In the case of registered land, rights which are overriding interests must be disclosed, if, were the land unregistered, they would be defects which should be disclosed.

Other matters which have been held to amount to defects of title are: the service of a notice of disrepair resulting in a reduction of rents[69]; the receipt of notice to repair under a covenant in a lease[70]; the exclusion of minerals[71]; and the right of a third party to overhang part of the property agreed to be sold.[72]

Planning matters

There is no implied warranty that the existing use of the land agreed to be sold is the permitted use[73]; and the permitted use does not, it seems, have to be disclosed.[74] But it has been held that a vendor is bound to disclose the fact that the property was erected under a temporary planning permission and would have to be pulled down in two years,[75] and therefore it is sometimes suggested that, if the existing use is not the permitted use, that is a defect of title which must be disclosed.[76]

---

[63] *Re Haedicke and Lipski's Contract* [1901] 2 Ch. 666; *Becker* v. *Partridge* [1966] 2 Q.B. 155.

[64] See *ante*, p. 60.

[65] *Re Marsh and Earl Granville* (1882) 24 Ch.D. 11.

[66] *Re Brine and Davies Contract* [1935] Ch. 388.

[67] *Nottingham Patent Brick and Tile Co. Ltd.* v. *Butler* (1886) 16 Q.B.D. 778.

[68] *Re White and Smith's Contract* [1896] 1 Ch. 637; *Molyneux* v. *Hawtrey* [1903] 2 K.B. 487; *Allen* v. *Smith* [1924] 2 Ch. 308; *Becker* v. *Partridge* [1966] 2 Q.B. 155.

[69] *Re Englefield Holdings Ltd. and Sinclair's Contract* [1962] 1 W.L.R. 1119.

[70] *Beyfus* v. *Lodge* [1925] Ch. 350.

[71] *Bellamy* v. *Debenham* [1891] 1 Ch. 412. But the vendor need not disclose, *e.g.* the rights of the National Coal Board to all coal under the Coal Industry Nationalisation Act 1946.

[72] *Pemsel and Wilson* v. *Tucker* [1907] 2 Ch. 191; *cf. Greenhalgh* v. *Brindley* [1901] 2 Ch. 324 (where land to be sold enjoyed right of light by licence only of adjoining owner).

[73] See *Mitchell* v. *Beacon Estates (Finsbury Park) Ltd.* (1949) 1 P. & C.R. 32; (1950) 14 Conv.(N.S.) 308.

[74] See Farrand, *Contract and Conveyance*, p. 54; and *ante*, p. 77.

[75] *Sidney* v. *Buddery* (1949) 1 P. & C.R. 34; (1950) 14 Conv.(N.S.) 380.

[76] On the difficult question as to what planning matters are incumbrances or defects in title, see (1964) 28 Conv.(N.S.) 109–114. For conditions on planning matters, see *post*, p. 98.

We have seen [77] that although in *Re Forsey and Hollebone's Contract* it was suggested that there was no need to disclose any matter registered as a local land charge, the practice is to treat such matters, for example, an enforcement notice, as defects of title and disclose them.

Latent easements

The vendor is bound to disclose *latent*, but not patent, easements. A latent easement is one not discoverable by a reasonably careful inspection of the property, such as an underground culvert or drain,[78] or a right of way.[79]

Fraudulent concealment

The vendor must not, of course, physically conceal defects, for example, by papering over or in-filling. Such conduct will amount to fraud, entitling the purchaser to rescind and to damages. The preliminary inquiries will generally ask questions as to dry rot, woodworm, etc.,[80] and in the course of negotiations between the parties, the vendor may make representations as to the state of the property in this respect thus giving rise to liability for misrepresentation.

The Law of Property Act 1925 provides that any person disposing of property or any interest therein for money or money's worth, or his solicitor or agent, who conceals any instrument or incumbrance material to the title, is liable, *inter alia*, to an action for damages by the purchaser or the person deriving title under him.[81]

Purchaser's remedies

If the purchaser is aware of the defect not disclosed by the vendor, he will be bound to take the property as it is. But if the vendor has expressly agreed to give a particular title, he cannot avoid liability on the ground that the purchaser had notice of the defect.[82]

The purchaser's remedies in cases where he is unaware of the defect depend, as in the case of misdescription,[83] on how serious the defect is. In the absence of any condition to the contrary (and we shall see [84] that there usually are conditions of sale dealing with non-disclosure, etc.), if the non-disclosure is of a substantial defect the purchaser will be able to resist specific performance, or, if he wishes to take the

---

[77] *Ante,* p. 39.
[78] *Re Brewer and Hankin's Contract* (1899) 80 L.T. 127; *Re Puckett and Smith's Contract* [1902] 2 Ch. 258; *Shepherd* v. *Croft* [1911] 1 Ch. 521; *Re Belcham and Gawley's Contract* [1930] 1 Ch. 63.
[79] *Ashburner* v. *Sewell* [1891] 3 Ch. 405; *Yandle* v. *Sutton* [1922] 2 Ch. 199.
[80] *Ante,* p. 37.
[81] s. 183; see *District Bank Ltd.* v. *Luigi Grill Ltd.* [1943] Ch. 78.
[82] *Cato* v. *Thompson* (1882) 9 Q.B.D. 616; *Re Gloag and Miller's Contract* (1883) 23 Ch.D. 320.
[83] *Ante,* p. 74.
[84] *Post,* p. 95.

initiative himself, he may claim rescission,[85] or specific performance with a reduction in the price.[86] In *Re Puckett and Smith's Contract*,[87] for example, land was sold for building purposes. Unknown to the vendor, there was an underground culvert running across the land a short distance from the surface. This would not have been revealed by a reasonably careful examination of the property. It was held that the culvert made the property substantially different from what the purchaser had agreed to buy; and the purchaser was not bound to complete. But a different conclusion was reached in *Shepherd* v. *Croft*.[88] There the particulars of sale described the property as residential property also suitable for building development. There was, in fact, a drain crossing the property at a depth of about three feet. This was known to the vendor. It was held that the drain was a latent defect which the vendor should have disclosed, but, as the purchaser had bought the property *primarily for residence*, she was getting substantially what she had bargained for. Accordingly, specific performance was ordered against the purchaser subject to compensation for the defect.

The purchaser must pursue his remedies before completion. On completion, the term of the contract (express or implied) which provides that, in the absence of anything to the contrary, the vendor will convey an unincumbered fee simple estate,[89] merges in the conveyance.[90] Thereafter, the purchaser's remedy will be under the implied covenants for title.[91]

C. Defective Premises [92]

At common law, where there is a contract for the sale of a house to be erected, or in the course of erection, there is an implied term that the house will be fit for human habitation; and further, that the materials used are reasonably fit for the purpose for which they are required.[93] Where the house is partially built at the time of the contract, the implied warranty applies to all work, not merely that done after the date of the contract.[94] The implied warranty may be excluded by express terms, for example, where there are detailed specifications of

---

85 *Quaere* whether a more serious defect is required if the purchaser takes the initiative, see *ante*, p. 74, footnote 24.
86 It may be that where the purchaser seeks specific performance in a case where the court would not order it *against* him, he cannot claim compensation: *Rudd* v. *Lascelles* [1900] 1 Ch. 815.
87 [1902] 2 Ch. 258.
88 [1911] 1 Ch. 521. And see *Re Belcham and Gawley's Contract* [1930] 1 Ch. 63.
89 *Ante*, p. 76.
90 For merger, see *post*, p. 212.
91 *Post*, p. 225.
92 See generally (1964) 28 Conv.(N.S.) 276, 238, 478; (1968) 32 Conv.(N.S.) 21 (for the American position).
93 *Miller* v. *Cannon Hill Estates Ltd.* [1931] 2 K.B. 113; *Perry* v. *Sharon Development Co. Ltd.* [1937] 4 All E.R. 390.
94 *Jennings* v. *Taverner* [1955] 1 W.L.R. 932; *Hancock* v. *B.W. Brazier (Anerley) Ltd.* [1966] 1 W.L.R. 1317.

the work to be done and the materials to be used [95]; and the purchaser may lose his rights under the provisions of the contract by such a term as "on completion of the purchase and payment of the balance of the purchase money, the purchaser shall be deemed to be satisfied as to the quality and workmanship and materials." [96]

Where the house has already been completed at the date of the contract, there is no implied warranty of fitness for habitation.[97]

Although in most cases the vendor will be careful to exclude or limit his liability by the terms of the contract,[98] the purchaser may still have some remedy on the basis of a misrepresentation (or a collateral contract arising out of a misrepresentation) made by a salesman at the building site. For example, where the builder's representative told the purchaser that the house would be "just as good as the show house," it was held that the purchaser was entitled to damages for the misrepresentation when the house fell short of the standard of the show house.[99]

Until recently the general rule has been that a vendor is not liable in tort for a defective house.[1] Now, it seems, a builder-vendor will be liable for defects not detectable on a normal survey.[2]

Defective Premises Act

The state of the common law on defective premises was unsatisfactory. The matter was considered by the Law Commission and was the subject of its report on Civil Liability of Vendors and Lessors for Defective Premises, published in 1970.[3] The Law Commission acknowledged the improvement in the position of a purchaser brought about by the N.H.B.R.C. Scheme, which is discussed in the next section, but pointed out the limits of the scheme. It made certain recommendations and a draft Bill was appended to the Report. The Defective Premises Act 1972, which received the Royal Assent as this book was going to press, contains with modifications, the Law Commission's recommendations. The Act imposes on any person taking

---

[95] *Lynch* v. *Thorne* [1956] 1 W.L.R. 303; *cf. Hancock* v. *B. W. Brazier (Anerley) Ltd., supra*; (1972) 122 New L.J. 467.

[96] And see *Richards (A.) (Builders) Ltd.* v. *White* (1963) 107 S.J. 828 (notification of final inspection by local authority building surveyor to be conclusive evidence that the property has been satisfactorily completed); *cf. Billyack* v. *Leyland Construction Co. Ltd.* [1968] 1 W.L.R. 471.

[97] *Hoskins* v. *Woodham* [1938] 1 All E.R. 692 and the cases referred to above.

[98] The doctrine of fundamental breach might apply to make the exclusion ineffective; see generally Treitel, *The Law of Contract* (3rd ed.), pp. 181 *et seq.* And see *King* v. *Victor Parsons & Co.* [1972] 1 W.L.R. 801.

[99] *Birch* v. *Paramount Estates Ltd.* (1956) 168 E.G. 396.

[1] See *Cavalier* v. *Pope* [1906] A.C. 428; *Bottomley* v. *Bannister* [1932] 1 K.B. 458; *Otto* v. *Bolton* [1936] 2 K.B. 46. For various statutory and judicial inroads into the general rule, see (1964) 28 Conv.(N.S.) 289, 487; and see generally *Winfield and Jolowicz on Tort* (9th ed.), pp. 204 *et seq.*

[2] *Dutton* v. *Bognor Regis U.D.C.* [1972] 1 Q.B. 373.

[3] Law Com. Report No. 40 H.C.184. See (1970) 120 New L.J. 1187, 1211. For some criticisms, see (1971) 114 S.J. 961.

on work for or in connection with the provision of a dwelling (whether erection, conversion or enlargement) a duty to see that the work is done in a workmanlike, or, as the case may be, professional manner, with proper materials and so that the dwelling will be fit for habitation. It will not be possible to contract out of this duty, but the duty does not apply where, on the first sale or letting, the purchaser has the benefit of a scheme (approved by the Secretary of State) which provides cover for defects. The N.H.B.R.C. Scheme will presumably be such an approved scheme. The statutory duty is owed to the person (if any) ordering the work and *every person* who acquires an interest in the dwelling. The cause of action accrues, however, when the dwelling is completed or, if any rectifying work is done, when that is completed.

The Act comes into force on January 1, 1972.

N.H.B.R.C. Scheme [4]

Since 1937, the National House-Builders Registration Council (N.H.B.R.C.) have operated a scheme in an attempt to deal with the unsatisfactory common law position as to defective premises. The Council prepares and publishes model specifications laying down minimum standards of construction for dwellings and maintains a register of builders who are willing to submit their houses to the Council's Scheme. This involves regular inspection of the houses at all stages of construction and, after the house has been approved by the Council, the issue of a certificate of compliance with the Council's specification. As a condition of the issue of the certificate, the builder, by a separate contract with the purchaser, warrants that the house will be properly built, and undertakes to remedy defects arising from non-compliance with the specification, provided they are reported to him within two years of the issue of the certificate. The Council undertakes to indemnify the purchaser up to a specified limit[5] in the event of any loss occurring within ten years through the builder's failure to conform to the specification as a result, for example, of the builder's bankruptcy.

The N.H.B.R.C. Scheme certainly improves the position of the purchaser of a new house,[6] but, unfortunately, it has its limits. For instance, certain categories of properties are excluded from the Scheme[7]; the amount of the guarantee is limited; and it suffers from the inevitable weakness of a voluntary system.

---

[4] See generally, (1964) 28 Conv.(N.S.) 385; (1967) 117 New L.J. 1206, 1232, 1262; (1970) 120 New L.J. 471, 496; (1971) 121 New L.J. 144; (1972) 122 New L.J. 497. The relevant documents are to be obtained from the National House-Builders Registration Council, 58 Portland Place, London, W1N 4BU.

[5] £10,000, and there is a limit on total claims against any one builder (up to £250,000 depending on the circumstances).

[6] In 1970 the Council paid to over 1,000 people amounts ranging up to £5,800 (*sic*), in most of which situations the Act would not apply: see (1970) 120 New L.J. 1211.

[7] *e.g.* converted premises and where the purchaser is not going to live in the property himself.

Criminal proceedings

In appropriate circumstances, a vendor may be liable under the Trade Descriptions Act 1968, for example, where the vendor told the purchaser that the house was subject to the N.H.B.R.C. Scheme when it was not.[8]

II. CONDITIONS OF SALE

Generally

The formal contract may have been prepared for the purpose of a sale by auction or of a sale by private treaty. In either case, the terms of the contract, or *the conditions of sale* as they are called, are generally much the same, but they will necessarily differ in two respects: (1) certain conditions inserted when the sale is by auction are obviously inapplicable when the sale is by private treaty, for example, a condition as to withdrawing bids, or as to the vendor's right to bid; and (2) where the sale is by private treaty, certain conditions will often be inserted as a result of bargaining between the parties or their solicitors, for example, that the purchaser shall be allowed into possession before completion of the contract.

The conditions usually found in a contract are dealt with below. It is common nowadays for such conditions to be incorporated into the contract by reference to one or other of the two well-known sets of conditions, *i.e.* the Law Society's Conditions of Sale 1970 and the National Conditions of Sale, 18th edition, 1969. This saves setting out the conditions *in extenso*. Some local law societies have their own sets of conditions which may be merely modifications of the Law Society's Conditions. Some firms of solicitors have their own forms of conditions and sometimes a particular vendor, for example, a landowner, property developer or builder, may have special forms of conditions, but here again these are usually modifications of either the Law Society's or National Conditions.

We have seen [9] that, from the vendor's point of view, there are disadvantages in an open contract where the implied conditions are generally in favour of the purchaser. Accordingly, the vendor normally insists on conditions of a special nature (according to the circumstances) being inserted in the contract. The standard conditions of sale are based on the sort of conditions that have become commonplace over the years. The most recent editions of the Law Society's and National Conditions of Sale show even more similarity between them than their previous editions, and the present tendency is in this direction as judicial decisions on the conditions show the disadvantages of one and the advantages of another.[10]

---

[8] *Breed* v. *Cluett* [1970] 2 Q.B. 459.
[9] *Ante*, p. 70.
[10] For commentaries on the new Law Society's Conditions, see (1970) 67 L.S.Gaz. 741 and the Guide included with that number; (1971) 121 New L.J. 4, 28, 52, 87, 98, 122, 170, 335; (1972) 116 S.J. 3.

It has been accepted in the past that the National Conditions are slightly more favourable to the purchaser [11]; and this is probably still the case.[12]

General and Special Conditions

Conditions can be divided into two types—general and special. *General conditions* deal with the detailed machinery of a contract, such as the date and place of completion, the abstract and requisitions, and other matters which generally arise in every case. The use of standard conditions is clearly advantageous for this purpose, and it has established a certain uniformity of practice. But like any standard forms, they should be used with care, and the draftsman must always consider whether any of the standard conditions needs modification in view of any special circumstances. *Special conditions* deal with any matters not covered by the general conditions and refer specifically to those matters relevant to the particular contract in hand. They must be specifically dealt with by the vendor or his advisers; and expressly incorporated in the contract. Examples of special conditions are a condition requiring the purchaser to accept a shorter title than the statutory length of title [13]; or dealing with restrictive covenants affecting the land; or dealing with fixtures and fittings included in the sale.[14]

Preparation of Contract

The preparation of the conditions of sale is always a matter which requires care, since these conditions are inserted in order to restrict the ordinary rights of the purchaser who has not had any voice in their preparation. It is, therefore, essential that they should be clear and intelligible to a man of ordinary understanding; and that they should not be of such a nature as to mislead or deceive him.[15] Further, care should be taken that they are not too stringent, or they may deter prospective purchasers, although it is true to say that the vendor will generally be in the position where he can insist on whatever terms he likes. For example, on sales of houses on an estate, there will generally be a standard form of contract and conveyance, and the vendor will be unwilling to vary the standard terms or provisions.

The draft contract should be prepared by the vendor's solicitor as soon as he receives the title deeds. Where the property is in mortgage, an abstract of the vendor's title should be obtained from the mortgagees. Where the land is registered, the vendor's solicitor will only need to know the title number, and then he will be able to bespeak office copies of the entries on the register.[16]

---

11 See *e.g.* Farrand, *Contract and Conveyance,* p. 66.
12 The latest edition of the Law Society's Conditions is, it has been suggested, even more pro-vendor than previous editions: see (1971) 121 New L.J. 122.
13 *Post,* p. 92.
14 *Post,* p. 91.
15 *Re Banister, Broad* v. *Munton* (1879) 12 Ch.D. 131, 142, 143.
16 See *post,* p. 94.

It is the practice to submit the draft contract to the purchaser's solicitor in duplicate so that the purchaser's solicitor can retain one copy. A copy of any restrictive covenant affecting the property should be attached to the draft contract as a rider.[17] In the case of registered land, an office copy of the entries on the register [16] should accompany the draft contract.

The purchaser's solicitor will make any amendments he desires to the contract, and then return it approved to the vendor's solicitors. The approval is generally subject to satisfactory replies to the usual searches and inquiries. When the terms of the contract have been agreed, the vendor's solicitor will engross the contract, sending one copy to the purchaser for signature. If there are no major amendments, the draft contract may be used for the engrossment.[18] When the purchaser is satisfied with the preliminary inquiries and searches, contracts are exchanged.

Conditions Made Void by Statute

Certain conditions, some of which were at one time often met with in conditions of sale, have been made void by statute and now cannot be enforced against the purchaser, even though he has agreed to be bound by them. The following are the more important:

(1) A stipulation that a purchaser of a legal estate shall accept a title made with the concurrence of any person entitled to an equitable interest, if a title can be made free from the equitable interest under a trust for sale or under the Law of Property Act 1925 or under the Settled Land Act 1925, is void.[19] This means that if land is subject to a trust for sale, or is settled land, or is capable of being the subject of an *ad hoc* trust for sale or settlement,[20] the purchaser is always entitled to have his conveyance from the trustees for sale or tenant for life, and thereby take free from the equitable interests of the persons claiming under the trust for sale or settlement. It follows that any provision in the contract (inserted, perhaps, in an attempt to avoid the expense of a vesting deed or appointment of trustees necessary to give the vendor full overreaching powers) to the effect that the purchaser shall take his conveyance with the concurrence of the persons entitled to such equitable interest is void. Take a simple example. Land is vested in X upon trust for sale, the proceeds to be held upon trust for A for life, and after his death, for B. A stipulation in the contract to the effect that the purchaser of the freehold shall accept a conveyance from X (who, as a *sole* trustee for sale has no power of overreaching [21]) with the concurrence in the deed of A and B is void. The purchaser can insist upon a conveyance from X and another trustee

---

[17] A rider is an additional clause tacked on or annexed to a document.
[18] See *ante*, p. 3.
[19] Law of Property Act 1925, s. 42 (1).
[20] See Megarry and Wade (3rd ed.), pp. 152–154, 385 *et seq.*
[21] Unless X is a trust corporation.

appointed at the vendor's expense to give a valid discharge for the purchase-money.[22]

(2) A stipulation that a purchaser of a legal estate shall pay the cost of obtaining any necessary vesting order, or the appointment of new trustees, or the making of vesting instruments or conveyances on trust for sale, is void[23]; for example, on a sale by a tenant for life, the vendor cannot throw the expense of preparing the necessary vesting deed on to the purchaser.

(3) A stipulation that an outstanding legal estate shall be traced or got in by or at the expense of the purchaser, or that he shall not object to its remaining outstanding, is void.[24]

(4) A stipulation restricting the purchaser from employing his own solicitor, or that the conveyance shall be prepared by the vendor's solicitor, at the purchaser's expense, is void.[25] A purchaser is entitled to employ his own solicitor to act for him. There is, however, no objection to a provision that the vendor shall furnish a form of conveyance from which the purchaser's solicitor shall prepare a draft, and that the purchaser shall pay a *reasonable* fee therefor.[26]

(5) A stipulation that the purchaser shall not object to the title on the ground of the absence or insufficiency of stamps on any instrument executed after May 16, 1888, or that the purchaser shall assume the liability for the absence or insufficiency of such stamps, is void.[27] Such a stipulation is, however, valid as regards instruments executed on or before that date.

(6) A stipulation restricting or excluding any liability for any misrepresentation is void, except to the extent, if any, that, in any proceeding arising out of the contract, the court or arbitrator may allow reliance on it as being fair and reasonable in the circumstances of the case.[28]

The Usual Conditions of Sale

In the following pages we deal with the more important conditions of sale. Usually they are incorporated by reference, and they will only apply in so far as they are not inconsistent with any other conditions in the particular contract.[29]

(1) The auction

If there are conditions dealing with the auction,[30] these will usually

---

22 See *post*, p. 378.
23 Law of Property Act 1925, s. 42 (2).
24 *Ibid.* s. 42 (3).
25 *Ibid.* s. 48 (1).
26 *Ibid.* And see Costs of Leases Act 1958, s. 1.
27 Stamp Act 1891, s. 117.
28 Misrepresentation Act 1967, s. 3. See *ante*, p. 36.
29 Law Society's Conditions, Special Condition 1; National Conditions, Contract. On inconsistency, see *Re Debenham and Mercer's Contract* [1944] 1 All E.R. 364. For the difficulties which may be caused, *e.g.* by not completing a special condition as to completion, see *Smith* v. *Mansi* [1963] 1 W.L.R. 26; Farrand, *Contract and Conveyance*, pp. 31 and 67.
30 See Law Society's Conditions, Condition 20 (1); National Conditions, Condition 2

relate to the manner of conducting the sale.   They may fix a sum as the minimum advance which may be made at each bidding, for example, the bidding may have to go up in £100s.   They usually provide that the highest bidder shall be the purchaser; that the auctioneer shall have power to refuse any bid; that if any dispute arises respecting the bid, the auctioneer may either determine the dispute, or the property shall be put up again at the last undisputed bidding [31] and resold; and that no bid shall be retracted.   It is doubtful whether this last stipulation can be enforced.   The bid is a mere offer on the purchaser's part and, like any other offer, can be withdrawn at any time before acceptance. The acceptance of a bid does not take place until the fall of the auctioneer's hammer.[32]

If it is intended that the sale should be subject to a reserve price, this fact must be stated in the conditions.   For the Sale of Land by Auction Act 1867 provides that the particulars or conditions of sale by auction of any land must state whether such land will be sold without reserve, or subject to a reserve price, or whether the right for the vendor to bid is reserved; and that, if it is stated that the sale is to be without reserve, it shall not be lawful for the seller to employ any person to bid at the sale, or for the auctioneer knowingly to take any bidding from such person; but that when it is declared that the sale is subject to a right for the seller to bid, it shall be lawful for the seller, or any one person on his behalf, to bid at such auction in such manner as he may think proper.[33]   It will be noticed that if the vendor desires to bid, it is essential that he should expressly reserve this right in the particulars or conditions.   Hence, it has been held that, where the conditions merely state that the sale is subject to a reserve price, it is illegal for the vendor or his agent to bid, even in order to bring the bidding up to the reserve.[34]

The conditions also stipulate that the purchaser shall sign the contract.   A written memorandum is necessary to satisfy section 40 of the Law of Property Act 1925,[35] but it will be remembered that the auctioneer is the agent of the purchaser during the transaction of sale, and he can therefore bind the latter by signing the memorandum of sale on behalf of the purchaser, should the purchaser improperly refuse to do so.[36]

(2) The deposit

Nearly all contracts provide for the payment of a deposit by the purchaser.   The stipulations relating to the deposit may appear in the

---

[31] *Richards* v. *Phillips* [1969] 1 Ch. 39.
[32] *Payne* v. *Cave* (1789) 3 T.R. 148; *ante,* p. 8.
[33] Sale of Land by Auction Act 1867, ss. 5, 6.
[34] *Gilliat* v. *Gilliat* (1869) L.R. 9 Eq. 60.   For the memorandum on an auction sale, see *ante,* p. 11.
[35] *Ante,* p. 15.
[36] *Ante,* p. 11.

general conditions [37] (and so will usually be incorporated into the contract by reference) or amongst the special conditions.[38] The deposit is usually 10 per cent. of the purchase price.

Purpose of deposit

The payment of a deposit is a part payment of the purchase money, and will, of course, be allowed for on completing the purchase; but the object of requiring a deposit is chiefly to provide a sum which the vendor may retain if the purchaser fails to complete the purchase, and to give the vendor a security in respect of any loss which he may suffer by such failure.[39] The deposit may be retained by the vendor, even though the contract could not have been enforced by him by action owing to the absence of a memorandum in writing,[40] but not where there was actually no binding contract at all.[41] If the sale goes off due to the *vendor's* default, the deposit must be returned to the purchaser with interest.[42] Where the court refuses to grant specific performance of a contract, or, in any action for the return of a deposit, the court may, if it thinks fit, order the repayment of any deposit.[43] Where the vendor lawfully rescinds on account of the purchaser's default he is not entitled to sue for any outstanding part of the deposit.[44]

Capacity in which held

On a sale by auction, the deposit is usually paid to the auctioneer, who holds it as a *stakeholder* for both parties, and, until the contract is completed, he must not pay it over to the vendor without the consent of the purchaser. If the contract is completed, or the purchaser breaks the contract, the auctioneer is bound to pay the deposit to the vendor. But if the contract is broken by the vendor, the auctioneer must repay the deposit to the purchaser. The auctioneer is entitled to retain for his own benefit any interest he may receive in respect of the deposit while it is in his hands.

On the other hand, if the sale is by private treaty, the deposit is usually paid to the vendor's solicitor, who, in the absence of an

---

[37] See Law Society's Conditions, Condition 5 (1).
[38] Under the National Conditions the deposit is referred to in the memorandum of agreement.
[39] *Howe* v. *Smith* (1884) 27 Ch.D. 89, 95, 98, 101.
[40] *Monnickendam* v. *Leanse* (1923) 39 T.L.R. 445; and see *Low* v. *Fry* (1935) 152 L.T. 585 (where the vendor could sue on the cheque, under the Bills of Exchange Act 1882, apart from the contract). See further, conditions as to forfeiture of deposit, *post*, p. 112.
[41] *Chillingworth* v. *Esche* [1924] 1 Ch. 97 (where the agreement was subject to contract). The remedy is a quasi-contractual one, there being a total failure of consideration.
[42] *Soper* v. *Arnold* (1887) 37 Ch.D. 96, 100; *Jacobs* v. *Revell* [1900] 2 Ch. 858, 869.
[43] Law of Property Act 1925, s. 49 (2). The form of order is normally that one or other party is entitled to give a good receipt to the stakeholder: see *Smith* v. *Hamilton* [1951] Ch. 174. See *Charles Hunt Ltd.* v. *Palmer* [1931] 2 Ch. 287; *Finkielkraut* v. *Monahan* [1949] 2 All E.R. 234. Before 1926 the vendor could forfeit the deposit even though he was refused specific performance; see *Re Scott and Alvarez's Contract* [1895] 2 Ch. 603; *Beyfus* v. *Lodge* [1925] Ch. 350.
[44] *Lowe* v. *Hope* [1970] Ch. 94.

express provision to the contrary,[45] holds it as *agent* for the vendor. The solicitor, therefore, unlike the auctioneer, is not entitled to retain any interest received by use of the deposit, and he is bound to hand over the deposit with such interest to the vendor at request, and the purchaser has no claim against the solicitor for so handing it over.[46] It follows that if the deposit is to be paid to the vendor's solicitor, the purchaser should endeavour to procure a provision that the solicitor shall hold it as *stakeholder* for both parties.[47] The deposit will then be released to the vendor on the purchaser's instructions on completion.[48]

Where the vendor sells in a fiduciary capacity, for example, as personal representative or trustee, it is usual for the contract to provide for the deposit to be paid to the vendor's solicitors as agents for the vendor. Any money payable under the contract is trust money and should be under the control of the trustees. But as trustees can only be liable for wilful default, it is thought that they can safely authorise payment to the auctioneer, or estate agent, or the vendor's solicitor as stakeholder.[49]

An auctioneer is entitled to demand payment of the deposit in cash.[50] He may accept a cheque,[51] but he may not accept a bill or promissory note,[52] or an I.O.U.,[53] without the vendor's express authority.

(3) Exchange of contracts

The Law Society's Conditions, Condition 5 (2), provide that where exchange of contracts is effected by post, the contract shall be made when the last part is actually posted. This is a change from the previous edition, under which exchange was only effected at the time of actual delivery of the second part. The change restores the common law position. The National Conditions do not deal with the matter.[54]

(4) Fixtures, fittings, etc.

We have seen that [55] a sale of land will pass, without express mention, fixtures and timber. It is not always clear whether or not a chattel is a fixture, and the safer course is to deal with the matter

---

[45] See Law Society's Conditions, Condition 5 (1), which provides for the deposit to be paid to the vendor's solicitors as stakeholders; the National Conditions leave the matter to be dealt with specifically in the memorandum of agreement.
[46] *Mayson* v. *Clouet* [1924] A.C. 980.
[47] The Law Society's Condition 5 (1) provides for the deposit to be paid to the vendor's solicitors as stakeholders.
[48] For estate agents and deposits, see *ante*, p. 32.
[49] See Farrand, *Contract and Conveyance*, p. 246.
[50] *Johnston* v. *Boyes* [1899] 2 Ch. 73.
[51] *Farrer* v. *Lacy, Harland and Co.* (1883) 25 Ch.D. 636; (1886) 31 Ch.D. 42.
[52] *Williams* v. *Evans* (1866) L.R. 1. Q.B. 352.
[53] *Hodgens* v. *Keen* [1894] 2 I.L.R. 157.
[54] See *ante*, p. 15.
[55] *Ante*, p. 16.

expressly by a special condition. Accordingly, it is quite common for the contract to contain a special condition that certain fixtures and fittings are included in the sale, specifying the particular items in a schedule to the contract. The items may be included in the purchase price or an additional sum may be paid for them.

Where the sale includes chattels, the general conditions may contain a warranty by the vendor that he is the owner of the chattels, and that they are not subject to any hire, hire-purchase or credit-sale agreement.[56]

The conditions may also provide for a valuation of fixtures and fittings, timber or crops, where these are sold separately.

(5) Vendor's capacity

The contract will state in what capacity the vendor is selling, *i.e.* as beneficial owner, mortgagee, personal representative or trustee. The principal object of this provision is to inform the purchaser of the nature of the covenants for title to be given in the conveyance.[57]

The purchaser cannot refuse to complete if the vendor cannot convey in the capacity stated, but can convey in some other capacity, so long as the vendor has a good title which he can convey,[58] or the title is vested in some person whom he can compel to convey.[59]

One practical difficulty commonly encountered is the position where co-owners contract to sell. In such a case the co-owners (or not more than four of them if there are more than four) hold the legal estate on trust for sale for themselves as beneficial owners.[60] Where the vendors are the *only* beneficial owners, they can convey either as trustees or as beneficial owners. If the vendors contract to sell as trustees, the purchaser cannot insist on them conveying as beneficial owners. But if the contract is silent on the point, the purchaser may be able to insist on them conveying as beneficial owners.[61] We shall see [62] the difference between the covenants implied on a sale " as beneficial owners " and those covenants implied on a sale " as trustees "; and the purchaser's solicitors should hold out, in negotiating the contract, for the vendors to sell as beneficial owners.

(6) Title conditions

Length of title

It is usual to specify the root of title [63] in the *special* conditions, for

[56] Law Society's Conditions, Condition 20 (2); National Conditions, Condition 3.
[57] *Post*, p. 225.
[58] *Re Spencer and Hauser's Contract* [1928] Ch. 598 (contracted as trustees but could convey as personal representatives).
[59] *Re Bryant and Barningham's Contract* (1890) 44 Ch.D. 218 (trustee of strict settlement contracted to sell, but legal estate in tenant for life). See *post*, p. 119.
[60] Law of Property Act 1925, ss. 34, 36.
[61] See *Emmet on Title* (15th ed.), pp. 332, 333.
[62] *Post*, pp. 226, 228.
[63] *Post*, p. 121.

example, by a condition that the title shall commence with a particular deed. The vendor will sometimes wish to restrict the purchaser's right to call for the full statutory title,[64] as, for example, where the property is part of a settled estate and there has been no dealing for value with the property for many years. (This avoids having to provide a lengthy abstract of title.) Sometimes the vendor may wish to reduce the length of the title shown in order to avoid some document which would otherwise be revealed which contains a substantial or technical defect of title. In other cases, the full statutory length of title can be shown, but the vendor wishes the title to commence with a document which is not usually a good root of title.[63] In any event, the condition must not be framed in such a way as to mislead the purchaser. It must be clear and straightforward. The nature of the instrument with which the title is to commence must be properly and fully described. Thus, if the contract states that the title is to begin with " a conveyance " less than the statutory length of title, the purchaser is entitled to assume that the deed was made on an occasion on which the title would be investigated, and if the conveyance proves to be a voluntary one the purchaser can resist specific performance on the grounds that the condition was misleading.[65] An unsatisfactory document should not be put forward as the root unless its unsatisfactory nature is explained.[66]

Of course, if a purchaser is asked to accept a title less than the statutory length, or, as a root of title, a document which is not usually a good root, he will be put on notice that the title may be defective. The danger of accepting a title shorter than the statutory length is that the purchaser will be bound by interests which he would otherwise have discovered.[67] Where the land is in an area of compulsory registration, it will be important to consider how the acceptance of such a condition will affect the class of title which will be granted on registration.

Vendor must not hide defects in earlier title

The vendor must not, by restricting the length of title, endeavour to prevent the purchaser from discovering the defects in the earlier title. It is the duty of the vendor to disclose them, and if he fails to do so, the purchaser, on discovering the defects *aliunde*, can refuse to complete even though the contract contains an express condition that the purchaser shall make no objection to the prior title. In *Re Scott and Alvarez's Contract*,[68] for example, a purchaser bought property subject to a condition that he should not make any objection as to the intermediate title between a certain lease and an assignment

---

[64] *Ante*, p. 60.
[65] *Re Marsh and Earl Granville* (1882) 24 Ch.D. 11 (deed of gift).
[66] *Re Banister, Broad* v. *Munton* (1879) 12 Ch.D. 131.
[67] See Law of Property Act 1925, ss. 44 (8), 199 (1) (ii) (a).
[68] [1895] 2 Ch. 603.

of it but should assume that the assignment vested a good title in the assignees. It was afterwards discovered by the purchaser that there was a vital defect in the intermediate title, and that the assignees had *no title to the property*. It was held that, as the vendor could not give a good holding title, specific performance would be refused. Accordingly, whatever the terms of the condition, the purchaser can resist specific performance,[69] if he can show that the vendor has *no title at all*. But, if the vendor has a good holding title, the condition, depending on the wording used, may prevent any objection to a defect.[70]

Purchaser to assume certain facts

Sometimes, the condition requires the purchaser to assume certain facts. But the purchaser will not be bound if the facts to be assumed are, to the vendor's knowledge, not the true facts.[71] The proper course is for the vendor to disclose the defects and then provide that the purchaser shall raise no requisition or objection as to that particular defect.[72]

Possessory title

A possessory title can be forced on a purchaser even under an open contract, provided the possession has been for the statutory length of title.[73] Where a vendor agreed to show a title beginning with a particular document, which he did, but the intermediate title rested on a possessory title, the title was held by the court to be good.[74] Where, however, the contract provides that the vendor will prove twenty years uninterrupted possession, the purchaser cannot be forced to accept proof of possession for any lesser period.[75]

Registered land

The contract should state whether the title is freehold or leasehold, and whether absolute or less than absolute.[76] Under section 110 of the Land Registration Act 1925, the vendor is placed under certain statutory obligations to supply the purchaser with evidence of his title. The vendor, notwithstanding any stipulation to the contrary, must furnish the purchaser with an authority to inspect the register. Generally only the registered proprietor of the land or a charge thereon may inspect, but he may give authority for another to inspect.[77] He

---

[69] And he can claim for repayment of the deposit: Law of Property Act 1925, s. 49 (2); *post*, p. 204.
[70] *Re National Provincial Bank of England and Marsh* [1895] 1 Ch. 190.
[71] *Re Banister, supra*; *Nottingham Patent Brick and Tile Co.* v. *Butler* (1886) 16 Q.B.D. 778; *Wilson* v. *Thomas* [1958] 1 W.L.R. 422.
[72] *Re Sandbach and Edmondson's Contract* [1891] 1 Ch. 99.
[73] *Jacobs* v. *Revell* [1900] 2 Ch. 858.
[74] *Re Atkinson and Horsell's Contract* [1912] 2 Ch. 1.
[75] *George Wimpey and Co. Ltd.* v. *Sohn* [1967] Ch. 487.
[76] See *Re Brine and Davies' Contract* [1935] Ch. 388.
[77] Land Registration Act 1925, s. 112. Public inspection of the register is under consideration by the Law Commission; see the Law Commission's Published Working Paper (No. 32), 1970; (1970) 34 Conv.(N.S.) 369, 372.

must also, if required, furnish the purchaser with a copy of the subsisting entries on the register, and with any filed plan, plus copies or abstracts of any documents noted on the register in so far as they affect the land being sold. The cost of these copies and abstracts must be borne by the vendor, unless the purchase price does not exceed £1,000, in which case they are payable by the purchaser in the absence of any contrary stipulation. (In practice, vendors rarely insist on their rights in this respect.) In addition, the vendor must, subject to any stipulation to the contrary and at his own expense, furnish the purchaser with such copies, abstracts and other evidence as the purchaser would have been entitled to had the land not been registered, of any subsisting rights and interests appurtenant to the land, as to which the register is not conclusive. He must also, in the absence of any contrary stipulation, at his own expense furnish the purchaser with such copies, abstracts and other evidence of any matters excepted from the effect of registration, such as overriding interests,[78] as the purchaser would have been entitled to if the land were unregistered.

Notwithstanding any stipulation to the contrary, a vendor of registered land does not have to furnish the purchaser with any abstract or other written evidence or any copy or abstract of the land certificate or of any charge certificate,[79] apart from the copies, abstracts, and other evidence referred to above.

The vendor's obligation to supply copies of the subsisting entries on the register is, in practice, fulfilled by bespeaking office copies from the Registry. These office copies are admissible in evidence to the same extent as the originals.[80]

The Law Society's Conditions [81] modify the statutory obligations of the vendor by excluding the proviso that the purchaser must pay the cost of copies, etc., if the purchase price does not exceed £1,000 and by providing that any copies, etc. to be furnished by the vendor shall be office copies.[82]

(7) Identity

In the absence of an express condition to the contrary, the vendor is bound to furnish strict evidence of identity.[83] This may be difficult when, from the removal of landmarks, such as hedges or walls, it is impossible accurately to identify the component parts or " parcels " of the property sold with those mentioned in older deeds. The conditions therefore generally provide that the purchaser shall be satisfied on this point by a comparison of the description of the property in the particulars of sale with the title deeds, fortified, if he so requires and at

---

[78] For overriding interests, see *post*, p. 170.
[79] For certificates, see *post*, p. 174.
[80] Land Registration Act 1925, s. 113.
[81] Condition 7 (1) (*b*).
[82] The National Conditions do not deal with the point.
[83] See *ante*, p. 62.

his expense, by statutory declarations of the vendor or of other persons, evidencing long and undisputed possession of the property under those title deeds.[84] In the absence of an express condition to the contrary, the vendor is bound to furnish strict evidence of identity. A condition to the effect that the purchaser shall not be entitled to any evidence, except that afforded by the deeds themselves, amounts to a contract that the deeds do, in fact, show identity, and, if they do not, the purchaser is entitled to further proof.[85] Hence the provision in the conditions for giving the purchaser a *statutory declaration.*[86]

The condition further provides that the vendor shall not be required to define or show any title to boundaries, walls, fences, etc., or separately identify parts of the property held under different titles.

In the case of registered land the land is identified by reference to the title number and to the description in the property register. If only part of the land in the title is being sold, such part must be sufficiently described, if need be, by means of a plan.

(8) Misdescription

The general conditions usually deal specifically with misdescription.[87] The condition provides that any error, omission, or misstatement in the description of the property shall not annul the sale; and that only errors or misdescriptions materially affecting the description, or value of the property, shall be the subject of compensation. The condition also deals with errors, etc., in replies to any inquiry made in the course of negotiations. There is some uncertainty as to the validity of such a condition as regards misdescriptions originating in misrepresentations, in view of the provisions of section 3 of the Misrepresentation Act 1967.[88] If *both* rescission and compensation are excluded in any particular case, the exclusion may be ineffective; but if compensation is allowed, the condition might be considered fair and reasonable, and so effective.[89]

Rescission

Whatever the terms of the condition, the purchaser will not be compelled to complete the contract, unless he gets substantially what he has agreed to buy.[90] The conditions cannot override the effect of

84 Law Society's Conditions, Condition 12; National Conditions, Condition 12.
85 *Flower* v. *Hartopp* (1843) 6 Beav. 476; *Curling* v. *Austin* (1862) 2 D. & S. 129; *Re Bramwell's Contract* [1969] 1 W.L.R. 1659.
86 *i.e.* a statement made by the vendor or some other person under the Statutory Declarations Act 1835, the declarant being subject to penalties for any false statement which he makes.
87 Law Society's Conditions, Condition 13; National Conditions, Condition 17.
88 See *ante*, p. 36.
89 See (1970) 67 L.S.Gaz. 256, 287, 318.
90 *Lee* v. *Rayson* [1917] 1 Ch. 613.

the rule in *Flight* v. *Booth*.[91]   This is recognised by the Law Society's Conditions, for example, which provide that nothing in the conditions shall entitle the vendor to compel the purchaser to accept property which differs *substantially* from the property agreed to be sold.[92]

Compensation

The conditions may provide that no compensation shall be payable for trivial errors or misdescriptions,[93] and this is probably effective, subject to the application of section 3 of the Misrepresentation Act 1967.

If the condition tries to exclude compensation altogether, it will be ineffective where the defect is substantial and the vendor tries to compel the purchaser to complete.   In such a case, specific performance will only be awarded with an abatement of the price.[94]   If it is the purchaser seeking to enforce the contract, then the condition will be effective, if the vendor can convey substantially what he contracted to sell,[95] but not otherwise.

The condition, if worded to give compensation for errors in the description of the property, does not apply to misdescriptions of the title or defects of title.[96]   Still less will the condition be permitted to cover wilful omissions or misstatements.

If there is a condition that compensation shall be paid, it is advisable to stipulate that it shall apply only to errors of description pointed out *before* completion, otherwise the purchaser can take advantage of the condition even though the error is not discovered until after the conveyance has been executed.[97]

(9) Condition of property

There is usually a condition that the purchaser shall buy with full notice of the actual state and condition of the property, and shall take it as it is.[98]   Such a condition relates only to the physical quality of the land,[99] not to matters of title.[1]

This condition is particularly relevant to breach of covenants to repair.   A breach of covenant is a defect of title, and, ordinarily, the vendor will not be able to enforce the contract if he is in breach of covenant, even though the purchaser knows of the breach.[2]   But this

---

[91] *Ante*, p. 73.
[92] Condition 13 (4); *cf.* National Conditions (where the misdescription must be *material* to allow damages or compensation).
[93] See *e.g.* Law Society's Conditions, Condition 13 (1).
[94] *Jacobs* v. *Revell* [1900] 2 Ch. 858.
[95] *Re Terry and White's Contract* (1886) 32 Ch.D. 14.   See also *Cordingley* v. *Cheeseborough* (1862) 4 De G.F. & J. 379.
[96] *Re Beyfus and Masters* (1888) 39 Ch.D. 110.
[97] *Palmer* v. *Johnson* (1884) 13 Q.B.D. 351.
[98] Law Society's Conditions, Condition 4 (2) (*a*); National Conditions, Condition 12 (3).
[99] See *Butler* v. *Mountview Estates Ltd.* [1951] 2 K.B. 563.
[1] *Re Englefield Holdings Ltd. and Sinclair's Contract* [1962] 1 W.L.R. 1119.
[2] *Re Highett and Bird's Contract* [1903] 1 Ch. 287.

condition will enable the vendor to force the property on the purchaser, and to put the cost of repair on him.[3]

(10) Vacant possession

In the absence of contrary agreement, the vendor is bound to deliver vacant possession of the property to the purchaser on completion.[4] Vacant possession is not given if any person such as a tenant or licensee, or a trespasser has possession of the property.[5] Vacant possession does not merely mean the absence of persons in occupation of the premises, but applies also to the absence of objects on the premises.[6] Thus, if the vendor leaves rubbish on the premises, he does not give vacant possession.[7]

If premises are requisitioned by notice before completion, vacant possession is not given.[8] If premises are compulsorily acquired before completion, the purchaser can refuse to complete, unless, it seems, vacant possession could have been given at the date fixed for completion but actual completion is delayed by or at the request of the purchaser.[9]

The general conditions usually provide that vacant possession will be given on completion.[10]

(11) Local land charges and inquiries

One of the principal differences between the Law Society's Conditions and the National Conditions concerns planning and local authority matters. Condition 2 of the Law Society's Conditions places squarely on the purchaser the burden of finding out about these things. The property is sold subject to all matters registered with any local authority; and to all requirements, proposals, or requests of any such authority; and to all matters disclosed, or which might reasonably be expected to be disclosed, as a result of searches or inquiries, formal or informal, and whether personal or in writing, made by, or on behalf of, a purchaser, or which a prudent purchaser ought to make of any local authority.[11] Condition 2 (2) requires the vendor to give the purchaser notice in writing of any notice in respect of any closing, demolition or clearance order, or in respect of any proposed or

---

[3] *Lockhart's Ltd.* v. *Bernard Rosen and Co.* [1922] 1 Ch. 433; *Buller* v. *Mountview Estates Ltd., supra.*
[4] *Cook* v. *Taylor* [1942] Ch. 349.
[5] *Engell* v. *Fitch* (1869) L.R. 4 Q.B. 659; *Hissett* v. *Reading Roofing Co. Ltd.* [1969] 1 W.L.R. 1757.
[6] *Norwich Union Life Insurance Society* v. *Preston* [1957] 1 W.L.R. 813 (furniture).
[7] *Cumberland Consolidated Holdings* v. *Ireland* [1946] K.B. 264.
[8] *Cook* v. *Taylor, supra*; *James Macara Ltd.* v. *Barclay* [1945] K.B. 148.
[9] *Hillingdon Estates Co.* v. *Stonefield Estates Co.* [1952] Ch. 627.
[10] Law Society's Conditions, Condition 3 (1); National Conditions, Special Condition D.
[11] This condition replaces the former Condition 20. The former Condition 22 which placed certain obligations on the vendor with regard to planning matters is not repeated at all in the new edition. The former Condition 21 (which is also not repeated) provided for exchange of contracts before local searches (see *ante*, p. 34).

intended compulsory purchase received by the vendor before contract but subsequent to the commencement of negotiations between the parties. This is intended to cover the gap between the purchaser's searches and inquiries and exchange of contracts. If the vendor fails to give notice, the purchaser may rescind the contract. Under Condition 2 (4), the purchaser must indemnify the vendor against any liability in respect of compliance with any notice or order made by a local authority before or after the date of the contract. It has been suggested that this condition shows a shift of emphasis in favour of the vendor compared with the condition in the previous edition which it replaces.[12]

Certainly the National Conditions are better from the purchaser's point of view in this respect. If such matters have not been disclosed by the vendor, the purchaser may, if the Condition is specifically incorporated, serve a Condition 13 notice on the vendor, or his solicitor, requiring the matter to be cancelled or removed before completion. If the vendor cannot, or will not, do so, the purchaser can rescind. Condition 16 (3) and (4) requires the *vendor* to indemnify the purchaser against liability in respect of requirements of the local authority which have been entered in the register before contract and are not disclosed on the purchaser's search.

Condition 2 (3) of the Law Society's Conditions provides that the vendor shall not be liable for any misrepresentation, other than a dishonest one, if the purchaser obtained, or could have obtained, the true information from a local authority. It is uncertain whether this provision is invalid under section 3 of the Misrepresentation Act 1967.[13]

(12) Town and country planning

National Condition 15 entitles the purchaser to raise requisitions as to the authorised use of the property, and requires the vendor to give in reply all relevant information as may be in his possession.

Where the property is expressed to be sold on the footing of an authorised use which is specified in the special conditions, and, if, before completion, it appears that the specified use is not an authorised use, then the purchaser may, by notice, rescind. We have seen that the vendor is probably bound to disclose any charges, notices, etc., arising under the planning legislation.[14]

The Condition continues that the property is not, to the vendor's knowledge, subject to any charge, etc., other than those disclosed, and is sold subject thereto, but without prejudice to the purchaser's right to rescind, if the specified use is not an authorised use. Subject to the matters previously mentioned, the purchaser is deemed to buy with knowledge in all respects of the authorised use of the property.

---

12 (1971) 121 New L.J. 335; (1971) 121 New L.J. 122; *cf.* (1971) 121 New L.J. 170.
13 (1971) 121 New L.J. 6; (1971) 121 New L.J. 122. For s. 3, see *ante*, p. 36.
14 *Ante*, p. 79.

Such conditions are not altogether satisfactory. The condition as to planning matters in the previous edition of the Law Society's Conditions is not repeated in the new edition for this reason.[15]

(13) Easements, etc.

The conditions usually provide that the property is sold subject to all easements, quasi-easements, and other such rights, but without prejudice to the vendor's obligation to disclose latent easements.[16] This qualification is expressly recognised by the National Conditions. The new Law Society's Condition 4 refers to easements not already known to the purchaser or apparent on inspection which are known by the vendor to affect the same. Apparently, the intention of this condition is that the vendor should be obliged to disclose all burdens on the property, other than those disclosed in replies to local authority searches and inquiries.

Paragraph 2 (c) of the Law Society's Condition 4 has been the subject of some criticism; it is said to oust section 62 of the Law of Property Act 1925,[17] and allow a vendor to retain unspecified, almost limitless, rights over the property agreed to be sold in favour of his adjoining or neighbouring property.[18]

(14) Leases

On a sale of leaseholds, we have already seen [19] that, in the absence of any contrary agreement, the purchaser is entitled to see the lease, however old it may be. The purchaser is also entitled, it will be remembered, to proof of the title under which the lease has been held for the past fifteen years (if the lease is so old), but is not entitled to see the title to the reversion. The general conditions usually modify this latter restriction. Under the Law Society's Conditions, for example, if the lease is dated not more than fifteen years before the date of the contract, and was granted for a term exceeding twenty-one years, then the freehold title, and all other titles superior to the lease, are to be deduced for the period of not less than fifteen years prior to the date of the contract up to the date of the grant of the lease.[20] The conditions further provide that, in all cases, the immediate title to the term or interest sold shall commence with the lease or underlease granting it; and, in the case of an underlease, the purchaser shall be

---

[15] See (1971) 121 New L.J. 170; cf. (1971) 121 New L.J. 335.
[16] Law Society's Conditions, Condition 4; National Conditions, Condition 14. For the obligation to disclose latent easements, see *ante*, p. 80.
[17] *Post*, p. 233.
[18] See (1971) 121 New L.J. 28, 122, 171, 336. There is no such provision in the National Conditions. The condition in the previous edition, which dealt with severance of property, is omitted in the present edition.
[19] *Ante*, p. 60.
[20] Condition 8 (1) (a). The National Conditions do not deal with matters of title in this respect. For comment on Condition 8, see (1971) 121 New L.J. 30.

entitled to require the vendor to supply, in addition, an abstract or copy of the immediately superior lease.[21]

The conditions may provide for the lease or a copy to be made available to the purchaser before contract; and the purchaser shall therefore be deemed to have full notice of the contents of the lease.[22] But this does not protect the vendor against any misdescription.[23]

Sometimes, the last receipt for rent is made *conclusive* evidence that the covenants in the lease have been duly performed and observed.[24] There may have been breaches of a repairing covenant, of which the landlord is as yet unaware. We have seen [25] that the contract generally provides that the purchaser shall be deemed to buy with full notice of the actual state and condition of the property; and this will usually be sufficient to put the cost of repair on the purchaser.

The conditions may also provide that no objection shall be taken on account of the covenants in an underlease not corresponding with the covenants in any superior lease.[26] On the other hand, because it is not a defect in title that the covenants in the lease do not correspond (unless the underlessor puts the underlessee's holding in jeopardy), the conditions may therefore provide that objection *may* be made, if the discrepancy between the covenants is such as to give rise to forfeiture of any superior lease.[27]

We have already seen [28] that, very often, the terms of a lease require the landlord's consent to an assignment of the term. The general conditions usually provide that the vendor shall apply for the necessary licence to assign at his own expense; that the purchaser will supply such information and references, if any, as may reasonably be required of him; and that if, within a specific period, the licence is not granted, the vendor or either party may rescind.[29] If no time is specified for obtaining the licence, it must be obtained before the date fixed for completion; or, if no date is fixed, within a reasonable time.[30]

When land, which is held under one lease, is sold in lots, a special condition should provide that, if all the lots are not sold, the vendor will retain the lease and grant underleases to the respective purchasers of the lots which are sold; but, if all the lots are sold, the vendor will assign the lease to the purchaser of the lot for which the highest price was paid, and that purchaser shall thereupon grant underleases to the respective purchasers of the other lots.[31]

---

[21] Condition 8 (1) (*b*).
[22] See National Conditions, Condition 10 (2).
[23] See *ante*, pp. 76, 79.
[24] See *Re Highett and Bird's Contract* [1902] 2 Ch. 214; [1903] 1 Ch. 287; *cf*. Law of Property Act 1925, s. 45 (2) (3); *ante*, p. 62.
[25] *Ante*, p. 96.
[26] Law Society's Conditions, Condition 8 (2); National Conditions, Condition 10 (4).
[27] See Law Society's Conditions, Condition 8 (2).
[28] *Ante*, p. 14.
[29] Law Society's Conditions, Condition 8 (3); National Conditions, Condition 10 (5).
[30] See *ante*, p. 14. National Condition 10 (5) does not fix any time limit. Law Society Condition 8 (3) fixes three months.
[31] See *Re Judd and Poland and Skelcher's Contract* [1906] 1 Ch. 684.

(15) Tenanted properties

A statement that the property is subject to tenancies or underleases will not burden a purchaser with notice of the terms on which the tenants hold.[32] Consequently, the terms of any tenancies or underleases should be fully stated or particulars should be supplied to the purchaser. Alternatively, the conditions may provide that the tenancies and underleases can be inspected at the office of the vendor's solicitor before the sale; and that the purchaser is thereby deemed to have full notice of the contents.[33]

The conditions may also provide that the vendor shall be under no duty to represent or warrant the amount of the legally recoverable rent or other term of the tenancy nor that any legislation affecting the tenancy has been complied with.[34] In effect, this means that if the purchaser wants to obtain any warranties by the vendor on these matters, he must specifically mention them in his preliminary inquiries.[35]

(16) The abstract and requisitions

Delivery of abstract and requisitions [36]

The principal object of the general conditions is to deal with the machinery of conveyancing under the contract, *i.e.* the various steps to be taken thereunder and the time limits therefor. Accordingly, the conditions usually provide that the vendor shall deliver the abstract to the purchaser, or his solicitor, within a specified period, and that the purchaser shall send his requisitions or objections in respect of the title, and all matters appearing on the abstract, particulars or conditions of sale, within a further specified period.[37] These time limits are usually made of the essence of the contract, and so they should be carefully observed. In practice, a vendor will rarely object where requisitions are out of time; but this easy-going attitude may prejudice his position. For instance, he may find he has waived his right to enforce a strict observance of the time limits and thereby lost some remedy which might otherwise have been available to him.

A further time limit for observations on replies to requisitions may be included. It is also usually provided that in default of any requisitions or objections, the purchaser shall be deemed to have accepted the title.

Perfect abstract

It will be seen [38] that the general rule is that the abstract delivered

32 *Cabellero* v. *Henty* (1874) L.R. 9 Ch. 447.
33 Law Society's Conditions, Condition 3 (2); National Conditions, Condition 18.
34 Law Society's Conditions, Condition 3 (3). See *ante*, p. 77.
35 See (1971) 121 New L.J. 6.
36 As to the abstract and requisitions, see *post*, pp. 119 *et seq.*
37 Law Society's Conditions, Conditions 7, 10; National Conditions, Condition 8; Statutory Conditions, Conditions 5, 6; *ante*, pp. 67, 68.
38 *Post*, p. 119.

E

must be perfect, *i.e.* one which sets out truly and sufficiently every document forming a link in the vendor's title. The conditions may provide that an abstract shall be deemed perfect, even though it is in fact imperfect. But the purchaser will not be bound by such conditions, if the vendor has, in fact, no title at all.[39]

Rescission

The condition usually goes on to provide that, should the purchaser insist on any objection or requisition as to the title, particulars or conditions, which the vendor is unable, or unwilling, to remove, or comply with, then the vendor may, by notice in writing, rescind the contract, notwithstanding any intermediate negotiations or litigation in respect of the requisitions; and that the vendor shall thereupon return the purchaser his deposit, but without any interest, costs of investigating the title, or other compensation or payment whatsoever.[40] The words " any intermediate negotiation or litigation " are inserted to prevent the vendor losing his right to rescind by entering into correspondence with the purchaser[41] or commencing litigation with regard to the objection.[42] They will not enable the vendor to rescind after a judgment has been given against him.[43]

This power of rescinding the contract extends to requisitions or objections made in respect of matters arising subsequently to the delivery of the abstract, and which therefore do not appear on the original abstract.[44] It would seem that the unwillingness of the vendor to comply with requisitions must in any case be reasonable.[45] A refusal on grounds that, in the opinion of the court, are frivolous will disable the vendor from taking advantage of this condition.[46]

In *Selkirk* v. *Romar Investments Ltd.*,[47] the contract included the usual provision enabling the vendor to rescind if he was unable to comply with the purchaser's requisitions. There was a deficiency in the title offered. The root of title was a Crown grant (the property being in the Bahama Islands) in 1881 to Conception Canuta Kemp. This was followed by a conveyance in 1939 by one Maximo Edward Kemp, described in the recitals as the only son and heir-at-law of

---

[39] *Want* v. *Stallibrass* (1873) L.R. 8 Ex. 175; *Re Tanqueray-Willaume and Landau* (1882) 20 Ch.D. 465.
[40] Law Society's Conditions, Condition 18; National Conditions, Condition 9; Statutory Conditions, Condition 7. See generally *Selkirk* v. *Romar Investments Ltd.* [1963] 1 W.L.R. 1415.
[41] *Tanner* v. *Smith* (1840) 10 Sim. 410.
[42] *Proctor* v. *Pugh* [1921] 2 Ch. 256; and see *Re Spindler and Mear's Contract* [1901] 1 Ch. 908 (where the vendor was ordered to pay the costs of the action). Nor can he rescind where he has instituted proceedings for specific performance: *Public Trustee* v. *Pearlberg* [1940] 2 K.B. 1.
[43] *Re Arbib and Class' Contract* [1891] 1 Ch. 601.
[44] *Gray* v. *Fowler* (1871) L.R. 8 Ex. 249.
[45] *Re Jackson and Haden's Contract* [1906] 1 Ch. 412; *Re Weston and Thomas' Contract* [1907] 1 Ch. 244.
[46] *Quinion* v. *Horne* [1906] 1 Ch. 596.
[47] [1963] 1 W.L.R. 1415.

Conception Canuta Kemp deceased. Several questions arose on this: first, whether Mrs. Kemp died before or after June 22, 1914 (when the law as to the devolution of real estate on death had changed); secondly, whether she had died intestate; and thirdly, if she had died intestate, who was her heir-at-law. The purchaser's solicitors properly raised requisitions on these matters. The evidence called for was unobtainable; and the vendor's solicitors were unable to satisfy the purchaser's solicitors on the points raised, in spite of their obtaining three further affidavits dealing with the facts in question as far as possible. The vendor's solicitors then gave notice of rescission under the condition. The purchaser claimed (1) a declaration that the vendor was not entitled to rescind and (2) an order for specific performance. He contended that the vendor had not, before entering into the contract, made the deficiency known to him; and that that was a breach of the duty of frankness in matters of title which necessarily precluded the vendor from taking advantage of the right to rescission. This claim was rejected both at first instance and by the Privy Council. Their Lordships considered the nature of the equitable principle invoked in these cases. The vendor, in seeking to rescind, must not act arbitrarily, or capriciously, or unreasonably. Much less can he act in bad faith. He may not use the power of rescission to get out of the sale. Above all, he must not be guilty of " recklessness " in entering into his contract. " Reckless " in this context means an unacceptable indifference to the situation of a purchaser who is allowed to enter into a contract with the expectation of obtaining a title which the vendor has no reasonable anticipation of being able to deliver.[48] A vendor who has so acted is not allowed to call off the whole transaction by resorting to the contractual right of rescission.

If the purchaser has insisted on requisitions with which he knows the vendor cannot comply, the latter may at once rescind the contract, without giving him further time in which to waive his requisition.[49] The wording of the condition may,[50] or may not, allow the vendor to rescind the contract immediately. Both sets of standard conditions permit notice of rescission to be given if the purchaser does not withdraw the objection within ten days of being required to do so.[51] The vendor cannot, under colour of such a condition, rescind against a purchaser who is willing to waive his objections to the title and take the property without an abatement in price; but it is too late for the purchaser to withdraw his objection after the vendor has properly exercised his right to rescind.[52] Moreover, a vendor who fails to show any title whatever to the property cannot, by purporting to rescind under

[48] *Selkirk v. Romar Investments Ltd.* [1963] 1 W.L.R. 1415, 1422, 1423. See also *Re Jackson and Haden's Contract* [1906] 1 Ch. 412, 422; *Baines v. Tweddle* [1959] Ch. 679.
[49] *Duddell v. Simpson* (1866) L.R. 2 Ch.App. 102.
[50] See *Re Starr-Bowkett Building Society and Sibun's Contract* (1889) 42 Ch.D. 375.
[51] Law Society's Conditions, Condition 18 (1); National Conditions, Condition 9 (1).
[52] *Duddell v. Simpson, supra*; *Selkirk v. Romar Investments Ltd., supra*.

the conditions, escape his liability to recoup to the purchaser the expenses to which the latter has been put in investigating the title.[53]

In conclusion, the value of this condition to the vendor is that it enables him (if he has, in fact, a good title, and has duly performed his duties under the contract) to rescind upon any frivolous or untenable requisition; or upon one which would involve him in any unnecessary trouble or expense.[54]

(17) Preparation of conveyance

The general conditions usually provide for the preparation of the conveyance by the purchaser's solicitor and for the delivery of the draft conveyance to the vendor's solicitor for approval a specific number of days before the date fixed for completion and engrossment by the vendor.[55]

In the case of a lease, the lease is usually prepared by the vendor's solicitor.

The conditions may also provide for some of the provisions of the conveyance, such as an indemnity covenant in respect of restrictive covenants,[56] or covenants in a lease,[57] and an acknowledgment and undertaking.[58]

Both the Law Society's and the National Conditions [59] contain provisions against sub-sales. Such a provision was of particular importance while betterment levy lasted, but now that tax has been abolished there seems little point in preventing sub-sales.[60]

(18) Insurance

We shall see [61] that after contract the property agreed to be sold is at the risk of the purchaser. Generally, the purchaser effects his own insurance of the property from the time of contract. However, the general conditions usually provide for the rare (at least with regard to freeholds) case where the purchaser wishes to take over the vendor's insurance policy.[62]

(19) Occupation pending completion

A purchaser is entitled to possession, or, if the property is let, to receipt of the rents and profits, from the date fixed for completion. Often, the purchaser will want to take possession before completion, which

---

53 *Bowman* v. *Hyland* (1878) 8 Ch.D. 588; *Re Deighton and Harris' Contract* [1898] 1 Ch. 458; *Re Jackson and Haden's Contract, supra.*
54 *Re Merrett and Schuster* [1920] 2 Ch. 240; *Proctor* v. *Pugh* [1921] 2 Ch. 256.
55 Law Society's Conditions, Condition 11; National Conditions, Condition 19. See (1971) 121 New L.J. 52, 53. And see Statutory Conditions, Condition 8; *ante,* p. 69.
56 *Post,* p. 414.
57 *Post,* p. 269.
58 *Post,* p. 238.
59 Conditions 11 (4) and 4 (3) respectively.
60 See *post,* p. 195.
61 *Post,* p. 190.
62 Law Society's Conditions, Condition 6; National Conditions, Condition 21.

may, of course, be many weeks, indeed months, after contract.[63] The
general conditions usually provide for this possibility.[64] Before dealing
with the conditions, it should be mentioned that the taking of possession
may affect the purchaser's rights. For instance, it may lead to the
inference that he has waived any objections to the title.[65] Accordingly,
it is usual for the conditions to provide that a purchaser who takes
possession before completion shall not be deemed to have accepted
the vendor's title, or waived his right to raise requisitions or objections.[66]

The Law Society's Condition 14 provides, that, when the purchaser
of a dwelling-house takes up physical occupation before completion,
he shall be in occupation as the *licensee*, and not the tenant, of the
vendor; and shall pay and indemnify the vendor against all outgoings,
repairs and other expenses, in respect of the property.[67] From the
date of occupation, the purchaser is entitled to receive any rents from
any part of the property not occupied by him; and must pay the
vendor interest on the balance of the purchase-money at the rate (if
any) specified by the general or special conditions. On the request
of the vendor, at any time after the date fixed for completion, where
delay in completion is attributable to the default of the purchaser, or,
in the event of rescission or avoidance of the contract, the purchaser
must give up possession forthwith, in as good a state of repair as when
he went into possession. Entry into the property solely to do repairs
and decorations does not count as occupation for the purposes of the
condition. The condition does not apply if the purchaser is already
in possession as a tenant.[68]

National Condition 7 is in very similar terms.

(20) Interest on the purchase-money

The general conditions usually provide, that, if the purchase shall
not be completed on the date fixed for completion, then the purchaser
shall pay interest at a particular or specified rate on the balance of the
purchase-money from that date until the date of actual completion.[69]
The rate is commonly 2 per cent. above bank-rate.[70] In the absence of
such a condition, a purchaser is liable to pay interest [71] on his purchase-
money from the time when he took, or might safely have taken, possession of the property.[72]

---

[63] For instalment sales, see *post*, p. 196.
[64] Law Society's Conditions, Condition 14; National Conditions, Condition 7; and see Statutory Conditions, Condition 3 (1); *ante*, p. 66.
[65] See *Re Gloag and Miller's Contract* (1883) 23 Ch.D. 320; *post*, p. 135.
[66] Law Society's Conditions, Condition 14 (1); National Conditions, Condition 7 (3).
[67] For a comment on the condition, see (1971) 121 New L.J. 54.
[68] See the condition and *Joel* v. *Montgomery and Taylor* [1967] Ch. 272.
[69] Law Society's Conditions, Condition 16; National Conditions, Condition 6. See (1971) 121 New L.J. 87. For the Statutory Conditions, Condition 4, see *ante*, p. 66.
[70] Bank-rate is now (July 1, 1972) 6 per cent.
[71] At 4 per cent. per annum. See *Palmer* v. *Lark* [1945] Ch. 182.
[72] *Jones* v. *Mudd* (1827) 4 Russ. 118; *Re Keeble and Stilwell's Fletton Brick Co.* (1898) 78 L.T. 383.

Again, if there is no such condition and there is a delay in completion arising from the fault of the vendor, and the purchaser has not taken possession of the property, then the purchaser may elect whether he will pay interest on the purchase-money from the day fixed, charging the vendor with the rents and profits of the property, or whether he will waive his right to the rents and profits and pay no interest. But, if he has taken possession, then he must pay interest as from that date, even though there are no rents or profits.[73]

Where the above condition is inserted, it is now settled (after some uncertainty [74]) that the purchaser is bound by the condition even though he did not cause the delay. The mere existence of difficulties in the title, although justifying the purchaser in refusing to complete until they are removed, does not exempt him from the condition respecting payment of interest [75]; and in such a case he will only be entitled to the clear rents and profits actually received, without any claim for compensation. However, the purchaser may charge the vendor with an occupation rent, if the latter remains in actual occupation of the property.[76]

Vendor's wilful default

The condition as to interest will not be enforced by the court where there has been gross misconduct or wilful delay on the part of the vendor.[77] And this fact is usually expressly recognised by the condition.[78] What will amount to wilful default depends on the circumstances of each particular case. Thus it was held wilful for the vendor to go abroad two days before the date fixed for completion,[79] or to avoid being in a position to complete beyond the date fixed for completion.[80]

The Law Society's Conditions give the purchaser, in lieu of his other rights, the right to a sum equivalent to a fair rent for the property, where delay in completion is attributable to the vendor.[81]

Purchase-money deposited at bank

Where the condition merely provides that the purchaser shall pay interest on the purchase-money from the date fixed for completion, then it seems that the purchaser cannot discharge himself from his

---

[73] *Ballard* v. *Shutt* (1880) 15 Ch.D. 122; *Fletcher* v. *Lancashire etc., Pty. Co.* [1902] 1 Ch. 901.
[74] See *e.g. De Visme* v. *De Visme* (1849) 1 M. & G. 336, 347.
[75] *Williams* v. *Glenton* (1865) L.R. 1 Ch. 200; *Re Bayley-Worthington and Cohen's Contract* [1909] 1 Ch. 648.
[76] See *Sherwin* v. *Shakespear* (1854) 5 De M. & G. 517.
[77] *Esdaile* v. *Stephenson* (1822) 1 S. & S. 122.
[78] See Law Society's Condition 16 (2); National Condition 6 (2) (i).
[79] *Re Young and Harston's Contract* (1885) 31 Ch.D. 168; see also *Re Hetling and Merton's Contract* [1893] 3 Ch. 269; *Bennett* v. *Stone* [1903] 1 Ch. 509.
[80] *Re Wilson and Stevens' Contract* [1894] 3 Ch. 546; *Re Hewitt's Contract* [1963] 1 W.L.R. 1298.
[81] Condition 16 (4); see (1971) 121 New L.J. 87.

liability by depositing the purchase-money at a bank.[82] But if the conditions are silent on the subject of interest, perhaps the purchaser can discharge his liability by depositing the purchase-money at a bank, and giving notice of the deposit to the vendor.[83] Because of this uncertainty, it is desirable for the conditions to deal expressly with the matter, allowing the purchaser to deposit the balance of the purchase-money at some bank and requiring him to give notice of the deposit to the vendor. The vendor will then be bound to accept such interest as is actually produced from the deposit in lieu of the interest otherwise provided for under the condition.[84]

Option to take income instead of interest

We have seen above, that in the absence of any condition as to interest, the purchaser has the option to waive his right to the rents and profits and pay no interest. Conversely, the conditions usually provide that the vendor may elect, by notice to that effect, to take the income of the property instead of interest.[85] Such a condition only applies, of course, where, if he did not exercise the option, he would be entitled to interest. For example, the vendor cannot exercise the option where he is in default himself.[86]

Income tax on interest

If the purchaser is an individual, interest must now be paid gross, *i.e.* without deduction of tax.[87] But if the vendor is resident outside the United Kingdom or the purchaser is a company, not in a fiduciary or representative capacity, interest is payable under deduction of tax.

(21) Apportionment of receipts and outgoings

In the absence of any express condition on the matter, the vendor must discharge all outgoings until the date fixed for completion; or, if a good title has not been shown by then, until it is shown, and thereafter the purchaser is bound to discharge outgoings.[88] Conversely, the vendor is entitled to all rents and profits until that date; and the purchaser entitled thereafter.[89]

Except in the case of sums payable in advance and already due,[90] all rents and other periodical payments are to be considered as accruing from day to day, and are apportionable accordingly.[91]

[82] *Re Riley to Streatfield* (1887) 34 Ch.D. 386; *Pearlberg* v. *May* [1951] Ch. 699.
[83] *Bennett* v. *Stone* [1903] 1 Ch. 509, 524.
[84] See Law Society's Condition 16 (3); National Condition 6 (1) (ii).
[85] Law Society Condition 16 (1) (*b*); National Condition 6 (1) (i).
[86] *Re Hewitt's Contract* [1963] 1 W.L.R. 1298.
[87] Income and Corporation Taxes Act 1970, ss. 52–64.
[88] *Barsht* v. *Tagg* [1900] 1 Ch. 231, 234, 235; *Bennett* v. *Stone* [1903] 1 Ch. 509, 524.
[89] But where a tenant is in arrears with rent and pays such arrears or part of them to a vendor after the date when the purchaser becomes entitled to the receipts and further rent has become due, the vendor is not entitled to appropriate the payment to the arrears due before that date. *Plews* v. *Samuel* [1904] 1 Ch. 464.
[90] *Ellis* v. *Rowbotham* [1900] 1 Q.B. 740.
[91] Apportionment Act 1870, s. 2.

The general conditions usually provide that apportionment of the income and outgoings of the property shall be made as from the date fixed for completion and state the basis of the apportionment.[92] The apportionment is generally according to the relevant number of days [93] relative to the number of days in the year. So, for example, if leasehold property is being sold, and the rent is payable in advance, a proportion will have to be allowed for by the purchaser. If the rent is payable in arrears a proportion will have to be allowed to the purchaser. Any tax liability in respect of receipts and outgoings must also be apportioned between the parties.[94]

Rates will also have to be apportioned, save where the purchaser on account of his small income is entitled to rate rebate, in which case the vendor should claim repayment direct from the rating authority.[95]

(22) Completion

Date

The date for completion is usually specified in the special conditions. It may be, for example, four weeks after the date of the contract. Alternatively, provision may be made for it by the general conditions.[96] In the absence of such provision, the obligation is to complete within a reasonable time [97]; seven weeks would normally be held reasonable.

Conditional contract. In the case of a conditional contract, where no time limit is fixed for the fulfilment of the condition, the condition must be fulfilled, if at all, within a reasonable time.[98]

When time of the essence. At common law, the date fixed for completion was always regarded as " of the essence of the contract." This means that the party who was not ready to complete the contract on the date fixed for completion lost all his rights. In equity, however, time was not regarded as " of the essence of the contract," except in the cases mentioned below, and the court would therefore decree

---

[92] Law Society's Conditions, Condition 15 (2); National Conditions, Condition 5; Statutory Conditions, Condition 3; *ante*, p. 66.

[93] Note that the day of completion is generally calculated against the vendor, *e.g.* if the period of apportionment is March 26 to April 30 the number of days is 36 days.

[94] See Income and Corporation Taxes Act 1970, s. 86; *Emmet*, pp. 221, 222; *Simon's Taxes* (3rd ed.) A.4 109.

[95] See General Rate Act 1967, ss. 49, 50. For the refund of sums deposited or secured under the advance payments code contained in the Highways Act 1959 (*ante*, p. 37), see *Henshall* v. *Fogg* [1964] 1 W.L.R. 1127.

[96] The first working day after the expiration of five weeks from the date of the contract; Law Society's Conditions, Condition 15 (1); the first working day after the expiration of five weeks from the delivery of the abstract: National Conditions, Condition 4 (1); and see Statutory Conditions, Condition 1, *ante*, p. 66. If, though one or other of the standard sets of conditions is used, the contract provides that a date of completion is to be agreed, no date will be implied and the contract will become binding only when a date is agreed and inserted: *Gavaghan* v. *Edwards* [1961] 2 Q.B. 220.

[97] *Sanson* v. *Rhodes* (1840) 6 Bing.N.C. 261. And see *Johnson* v. *Humphrey* [1946] 1 All E.R. 460, 463; *Williams* v. *Greatrex* [1957] 1 W.L.R. 31.

[98] See *ante*, p. 14.

specific performance of the contract even though the time fixed for completion had passed. Since the Judicature Act 1873,[99] time is to be deemed to be of the essence of the contract at law only in cases in which it was formerly of the essence in equity. The result is that time is now of the essence of the contract only in the three following cases:

(1) When the contract expressly provides that time shall be deemed to be of the essence.[1]

(2) When the subject-matter of the sale is of such a nature that the parties must be taken to have intended time to be of the essence, for example, on the sale of a mining lease,[2] or of a public house.[3] If a contract for the sale of the property which is of such a nature that time is deemed to be of the essence of the contract expressly provides that completion shall take place " on or about " a certain date, this date is still to be considered of the essence of the contract, and if the purchaser fails to complete on that date or within a very short time thereafter, the vendor may rescind the contract and retain the deposit.[4] Time will not be of the essence of a contract for the sale of a dwelling-house unless expressly made so.[5]

(3) When one party delays unduly in performing his side of the contract the other party may serve on him a written notice specifying a date, reasonably distant, upon which the contract has to be completed. This date will then be of the essence of the contract.[6]

Where time is of the essence, default by either party will entitle the party not in default to exercise his rights of specific performance, rescission, or other rights as provided by the contract.[7] Where time is not of the essence, failure to complete in time merely gives rise to a claim for damages.[8] In most cases, no real damage is suffered; and the position is adequately covered by the condition dealing with the payment of interest.[9]

It should be noticed that specific performance can be sought as soon as the date for completion fixed by the contract has passed and before time has been made of the essence.[10] Proceedings for specific performance can even be commenced *before* the contractual date, but the

---

99 s. 25 (7); and see now Law of Property Act 1925, s. 41.
1 *Hudson* v. *Temple* (1860) L.J.Ch. 251; *Harold Wood Brick Co. Ltd.* v. *Ferris* [1935] 2 K.B. 198.
2 *Coslake* v. *Till* (1826) 1 Russ. 376.
3 *Powell* v. *Marshall Parkes & Co.* [1899] 1 Q.B. 710; *Harold Wood Brick Co. Ltd.* v. *Ferris, supra.*
4 *Lock* v. *Bell* [1931] 1 Ch. 35.
5 See *Smith* v. *Hamilton* [1951] Ch. 174, 179; *cf. Tilley* v. *Thomas* (1867) L.R. 3 Ch.App. 61.
6 *Stickney* v. *Keeble* [1915] A.C. 386.
7 *Post,* p. 111.
8 *Post,* p. 203.
9 *Phillips* v. *Lamdin* [1949] 2 K.B. 33.
10 *Marks* v. *Lilley* [1959] 1 W.L.R. 749; *Eva* v. *Morrow* (1966) 116 New L.J. 1657.

E*

court would not make any order before the contractual date has passed unless the defendant has already repudiated the contract.[11]

Making time of the essence. As mentioned above, the parties may make time of the essence by notice.[12] Such a notice is usually called a *notice to complete.*[13] It seems that before such a notice can be served a reasonable time must have elapsed since the date for completion fixed by the contract.[14] What is a reasonable time depends on all the circumstances of the case. In *Smith* v. *Hamilton*,[15] under a contract dated February 26, 1949, the completion date was fixed for April 4, 1949. The purchaser had difficulty in raising the purchase-money of £3,000, and it was suggested that a notice to complete, given fourteen days after the contractual date for completion would be premature. In most cases, however, a month would be sufficient.

The conditions of sale may permit a notice to complete to be given without allowing for the passage of a reasonable time from the contractual date.[16]

The time specified in the notice to complete must also be reasonable. What is reasonable again depends upon all the circumstances of the case. For instance, where the purchaser is in default, the amount of the purchase-money to be found; the likelihood of the purchaser being able to find it; and the stage reached in the transaction are all relevant considerations. In *Re Barr's Contract*,[17] under a contract dated January 19, 1956, the completion date was January 31, 1956. The purchase-price was £50,000. The vendors were well aware that the purchasers were relying on a sub-sale to provide the money necessary to complete. On February 1, 1956, completion not having taken place, the vendors served on the purchasers a notice to complete within twenty-eight days. It was held that the time of twenty-eight days was unreasonable in view of the fact that the negotiations for the sub-sale had broken down and accordingly the vendor's notice to complete was invalid.[18] In *Re Engall's Agreement*,[19] under a contract dated July 31, 1952, the completion date was September 30, 1952. The abstract had been delivered, and requisitions raised and replied to, but the purchasers had not submitted a draft conveyance by the completion date. Accordingly, notice to complete on or before November 5, 1952, was sent on October 21, 1952. The judge doubted whether the notice

---

[11] *Hasham* v. *Zenab* [1960] A.C. 316.
[12] For a form, see *post*, p. 412.
[13] *Purchasers* were given the right to serve a notice to complete by the 1959 National Conditions and by the new Law Society's Conditions.
[14] *Green* v. *Sevin* (1879) 13 Ch.D. 589. See generally on this point Farrand, *Contract and Conveyance*, pp. 219 *et seq.*; (1971) 45 A.L.J. 242.
[15] [1951] Ch. 174.
[16] See Law Society's Conditions, Condition 19 (2); National Conditions, Condition 22 (1). See (1971) 121 New L.J. 89.
[17] [1956] Ch. 551.
[18] And see *Ajit* v. *Sammy* [1967] 1 A.C. 255 (six days held reasonable where the purchaser had no money and no prospects of raising any).
[19] [1953] 1 W.L.R. 977.

to complete was long enough. He thought twenty-one days' notice would have been enough, provided it was after the draft conveyance had been agreed.

The conditions of sale, however, may provide for the period for completion in such a way as to make the reasonableness of the notice immaterial. An instance is where the condition provides that, upon service of the notice, the time specified shall be of the essence of the contract.[20]

Where time is made of the essence by notice, the party serving the notice, as well as the party on whom it is served, is bound by it. Thus in *Finkielkraut* v. *Monohan*,[21] where the vendor had served notice to complete, and on the date fixed for completion the purchaser was ready to complete but the vendor was not, the vendor was held to be in breach of contract and not entitled to specific performance. Hence the purchaser could rescind and reclaim his deposit.

Form of notice.[22] Under the 1953 edition of the Law Society's Conditions, the notice to complete under Condition 36 had to state expressly that the notice was made pursuant to that condition, and many a notice was ineffective for failure to observe that requirement. It seems that express reference to the new Condition 19 is not required, but, in practice, it is usual to refer to the particular Condition. The same would appear to apply to National Condition 22.[23]

It may be added that a notice, given under an express provision for notice to complete, which is bad for any reason, may operate as an effective common law notice.

Provision is made under the Law Society's Condition for agreed extensions of the period of a notice.[24]

Place of completion

The conditions generally provide for completion at the office of the vendor's solicitors or, if required by the vendor, at the office of the solicitors for the vendor's mortgagee.[25]

(23) Remedies on default

Vendor's remedies

The conditions dealing with notices to complete usually go on to

---

20 See Law Society's Conditions, Condition 19 (3); National Conditions, Condition 22 (2). *Cf.* previous editions of these Conditions and see *Re Barr's Contract* [1956] Ch. 551. *Cumberland Court (Brighton) Ltd.* v. *Taylor* [1964] Ch. 29.
21 [1949] 2 All E.R. 234.
22 For form, see Appendix, *post*, p. 412. For service of notice, see Law Society's Conditions, Condition 1 (2); National Conditions, Condition 22 (1).
23 *Cf.* the National Conditions, Condition 22—party serving notice must be ready and willing to fulfil his obligations—with the Law Society's Condition 19—ready, *able* and willing: see (1969) 119 New L.J. 1090.
24 Condition 19 (6).
25 Law Society's Conditions, Condition 15 (1); National Conditions, Condition 4 (2). And see Statutory Conditions, Condition 2; *ante*, p. 66.

deal with the consequences of default. Under the Law Society's Condition 19 (4), if the *purchaser* defaults, he must forthwith return all abstracts and other papers in his possession belonging to the vendor. In addition, he must, at his own expense, procure the cancellation of any entry relating to the contract in any register.[26] The vendor may without prejudice to any other rights or remedies available to him:

   (i) forfeit and retain, for his own benefit, the deposit paid by the purchaser; and
   (ii) resell the property.

If, on any such resale contracted within one year from the date fixed for completion, the vendor incurs a loss, the purchaser shall pay to the vendor as liquidated damages the amount of such loss, which shall include all costs and expenses reasonably incurred in any such resale or any attempted resale, subject to the vendor giving credit for any deposit paid; but any surplus shall be retained by the vendor.

National Condition 22 (3) provides, that, if the purchaser refuses or fails to complete in conformity with the notice, then his deposit be forfeit, and, if the vendor resells within six months of the expiration of the period of twenty-eight days of the notice, he shall be entitled (upon crediting the deposit) to recover from the purchaser the amount of any loss occasioned on the resale.[27]

Even in the absence of such a condition, the purchaser will lose his deposit if he improperly refuses to complete his contract,[28] and the vendor is entitled to resell.[29] If the purchaser repudiates the contract, the vendor, who exercises his rights under the condition, is not thereby precluded from suing the purchaser for damages for breach of contract[30]; but in assessing the amount of damages the deposit would have to be taken into account.[31] On the other hand, if the vendor rescinds the contract and forfeits the deposit, he is not entitled to damages in addition.[32]

The purpose of this condition is to enable the vendor to resell the property at once, instead of having to apply to the court for that purpose—as he might have to do if there were no condition on the subject. In practice, it is often arguable whether the purported exercise of his rights under the condition by the vendor is proper. He will therefore usually seek a declaration from the court that such exercise is proper, either in an action by him against the purchaser, or in his defence to proceedings for specific performance, or for the return of the deposit, by the purchaser against the vendor.[33]

---

26 *Ante*, p. 25.
27 And see Statutory Conditions, Condition 9; *ante*, p. 69.
28 *Hall* v. *Burnell* [1911] 2 Ch. 551.
29 *Essex* v. *Daniell* (1875) L.R. 10 C.P. 538.
30 *Harold Wood Brick Co. Ltd.* v. *Ferris* [1935] 2 K.B. 199.
31 *Shuttleworth* v. *Clews* [1910] 1 Ch. 176.
32 *Barber* v. *Wolfe* [1945] Ch. 187.
33 See generally the forms of proceedings in 34 Atkin's *Court Forms* (2nd ed.), pp. 301 *et seq.*

It should perhaps be mentioned again, that the vendor's right to resell on default will generally be without prejudice to the vendor's other rights. Often specific performance will be preferable for the vendor.[34]

Purchaser's remedies

The Law Society's Condition 19 goes on to set out the purchaser's remedies on the *vendor's* default. These are either:

(i) to enforce against the vendor, without further or other notice under the contract, such rights and remedies as may be available to the purchaser at law or in equity [35]; or

(ii) without prejudice to any right of the purchaser to damages, to give written notice to the vendor to repay the deposit forthwith.

On compliance with such a notice, the purchaser is no longer entitled to any right to specific performance of the contract; and he must return all abstracts and other papers in his possession belonging to the vendor.

National Condition 22 does not deal expressly with the purchaser's rights on default.

III. LEASEHOLD ENFRANCHISEMENT

Acquisition of freehold

The provisions of the Leasehold Reform Act 1967 in connection with the acquisition of the freehold and extension of the term are discussed elsewhere.[36]

The method of assessing the purchase-price in these cases is such as to produce a windfall for the tenant; and clearly, in most cases, he will purchase the freehold rather than take an extended lease. We shall briefly deal here with the *procedure* when a tenant desires to acquire the freehold. The general provisions on claims for an extension are much the same.

Tenant's desire notice

The first step is for the tenant to serve notice of his desire (a " desire notice " as it is called) on his landlord in the prescribed form.[37] Printed forms are available from law stationers. Copies of the notice must be served on any other persons known or believed to have interests superior to the claimant's tenancy.[38] Where the landlord

---

[34] See *post*, p. 201.
[35] See *post*, p. 201. For a comment on the Law Society's Condition 19, see (1971) 121 New L.J. 88, 89.
[36] *Post*, p. 277.
[37] See Leasehold Reform Act 1967, Sched. 3, Pt. II, para. 6; Leasehold Reform (Notices) Regulations 1967 and 1969. The inappropriate parts of the form should be deleted: see *Brynlea Property Investments Ltd.* v. *Ramsay* [1969] 2 Q.B. 253; *Lewis* v. *Harries* (1971) S.J. 508.
[38] Leasehold Reform Act 1967, Sched. 3, para. 8.

cannot be found, the Act empowers the High Court to make such order as it thinks fit in order to vest the property in the tenant.[39] The court may require the claimant to take further steps by way of advertisement or otherwise to trace the landlord. Provision is made for valuation of the freehold by a surveyor appointed by the President of the Lands Tribunal and payment of such sum into court. The court may order some person, usually the master or registrar, to execute the conveyance to the tenant.[40]

Effect of notice

The effect of a valid notice is to establish the relationship of vendor and purchaser between the landlord and tenant; and the contract should be duly protected by registration as an estate contract or, in the case of registered land, by notice or caution.[41] The rights and liabilities of the respective parties will pass to their estates on their death.[42] The tenant can assign his rights under the notice only with an assignment of his whole interest in the property.[43]

Action by landlord

Within two months of service on the landlord of the tenant's desire notice, the landlord should serve a notice in reply on the tenant in the prescribed form stating whether or not the landlord admits the tenant's right to the freehold. Until this period has passed the tenant cannot take any proceedings to enforce his rights.[44]

Usually the landlord will admit the tenant's right and the only dispute will be as to the price to be paid, in which case this will have to be decided by the Lands Tribunal.[45] Tenant's notices have also been contested on the ground that the property in respect of which the claim is made is not within the meaning of the Act.[46] Failure by the landlord to give a notice in reply does not, it seems, prevent him from subsequently denying the tenant's right.

At any time after receipt of the tenant's desire notice, the landlord may give notice to the tenant requiring a deposit equal to three times the annual rent, or £25 whichever is the greater[47]; or requiring him to deduce his title and furnish a statutory declaration as to his

[39] s. 27.
[40] See *Re Robertson's Application* [1969] 1 W.L.R. 109; *Re Frost's Application* [1970] 1 W.L.R. 1145.
[41] Leasehold Reform Act 1967, s. 5 (1) (5). For estate contracts, see *ante*, pp. 25–28.
[42] *Ibid*. s. 5 (1).
[43] *Ibid*. s. 5 (2).
[44] *Ibid*. Sched. 3, para. 7.
[45] Leasehold Reform Act 1967, s. 9; Housing Act 1969, s. 82. The decisions are regularly reported in the Estates Gazette.
[46] See *e.g. Wolf* v. *Crutchley* [1971] 1 W.L.R. 99; *Peck* v. *Anicar Properties Ltd.* [1971] 1 All E.R. 517.
[47] Leasehold Reform (Enfranchisement and Extension) Regulations 1967, Sched., Pt. 1, condition 1. The deposit must then be paid within 14 days of the notice.

occupation of the property.[48]   Neither of these notices amounts to an admission of the tenant's right to the freehold.

Deduction of title

The next stage which follows is for the tenant to give notice to the landlord requiring the landlord to deduce his title, or, in the case of registered land, requiring him to give authority to inspect the register and a copy of the entries on the register.   The landlord must comply with this notice within four weeks of receipt.[49]   Objections or requisitions must be made by the tenant within fourteen days of delivery of the abstract, etc., and the replies must also be given within fourteen days. Observations on replies must be made within seven days.[50]

Form of conveyance

At any time after he has given notice in reply to the tenant's desire notice, the landlord may give notice in writing to the tenant to state within four weeks the terms of the conveyance, i.e. restrictive covenants, easements, etc.[51]   The position is the same for the tenant who has a similar right once he is entitled to require his landlord to deduce title.[52]

Completion

Either party may give notice to complete after the expiration of one month after the price payable for the freehold has been fixed.   The effect of the notice to complete is to fix the completion day as the first working day after the expiration of four weeks from the giving of the notice.[53]

If either party then fails to complete, a default notice may be given by the party not in default requiring the default to be made good within two months.   If the tenant does not comply then, without prejudice to any other rights of the landlord under the Act or otherwise, the contract is discharged, save for the tenant's obligation to pay the landlord's costs; and the deposit is forfeited (but credit for the deposit must be given against any sums recovered against the tenant).   If it is the landlord who defaults, the contract is discharged, without prejudice to the tenant's rights under the Act or otherwise; and the latter is entitled to the deposit back and need not pay the landlord's costs.[54]

The tenant's solicitor must prepare the draft conveyance and deliver it to the office of the landlord's solicitors at least fourteen days before

---

48 *Ibid.* condition 2.   Title must then be deduced within 21 days.
49 *Ibid.* condition 3.
50 *Ibid.* condition 4.
51 As to the terms, see *post*, p. 279.
52 Leasehold Reform (Enfranchisement and Extension) Regulations 1967, Sched., Pt. 1, condition 5.
53 *Ibid.* condition 6.
54 *Ibid.* condition 10.

the date for completion. If the conveyance is to include fresh restrictive covenants, or if the tenant is going to mortgage the property contemporaneously with the conveyance, he must inform the landlord in sufficient time to allow him to give a priority notice.[55]

The Regulations provide for interest and apportionment.[56] The usual conveyancing procedure on approval and engrossment of the conveyance, execution and duplicates, etc., follows.[57]

Withdrawal by tenant

The tenant may, not more than one month after the price has been fixed, give written notice to the landlord that he is unable or unwilling to proceed. Thereupon his desire notice ceases to have effect. If he withdraws, the tenant must pay the landlord compensation for any interference resulting from the desire notice with the exercise by the landlord of his power to dispose of or deal with the property or any neighbouring property. The tenant cannot give a further desire notice for the following five years.[58]

IV. COMPULSORY PURCHASE

Compulsory purchase order

Well over fifty Acts confer powers of compulsory acquisition on local authorities, public undertakings, etc. It is beyond the scope of this book to deal with these powers.[59] We would only mention the Local Government Act 1933, Public Health Acts, the Highways Acts, the Housing Acts, and local Corporation Acts, as examples of such empowering legislation.

Most of these Acts require the local authority or other acquiring body to make a compulsory purchase order as the first step. The procedure is governed by the Acquisition of Land (Authorisation Procedure) Act 1946, the Housing Act 1957 or the local Act in the case of local authorities or by the empowering Act in the case of government departments and other statutory undertakings. The procedure generally gives a right to object to those affected which is followed by a local inquiry. We shall assume that the order is confirmed.

Purchase by agreement

In many cases the purchase may take place without the service of a notice to treat, *i.e.* the owner and the authority agree as to the sale.[60]

---

[55] *Ibid.* condition 9. For priority notices, see *post*, p. 160.
[56] *Ibid.* conditions 7 and 8.
[57] See *post*, pp. 206 *et seq.*
[58] Leasehold Reform Act 1967, s. 9 (3).
[59] See generally Cripps, *Compulsory Acquisition of Land* (11th ed.); *Encyclopaedia of Compulsory Purchase.*
[60] See Lands Clauses Consolidation Act 1845, s. 6; Compulsory Purchase Act 1965, s. 3; *Hooper* v. *Bourne* (1877) 3 Q.B.D. 258, 273; affd. (1880) 5 App.Cas. 1; *Kirby* v. *Harrogate School Board* [1896] 1 Ch. 437.

Notice to treat

Unless there is an agreement, the next step is for the acquiring authority to serve notice to treat on all persons having a legal or equitable interest in the land to be acquired.[61] This includes lessees (except tenants who have no greater interest than as tenant for a year or from year to year) and mortgagees.

The service of a notice to treat establishes a relationship between the owner of the land and the acquiring authority, analogous to that of vendor and purchaser.[62] The notice, however, does not constitute a contract for sale until the price has been agreed or otherwise fixed.[63] A notice to treat is only registrable as an estate contract (*i.e.* not as a local land charge) and that only when the price has been fixed.[64]

After the notice has been served, the purchase-money (or compensation) has to be agreed, and in default of agreement referred to the Lands Tribunal. The acquiring authority may enter on the land before the assessment of the amount payable with the consent of the owner; or, without consent, on payment into court of the value of the land, or, in certain cases, without payment.[65]

Conveyance

Once the purchase-money has been agreed or fixed, the owner of the land must, when required so to do by the acquiring authority, duly convey the land to the authority or as they direct.[66] The conveyance is generally taken in the same form as is used between an ordinary vendor and purchaser. If registered land is being acquired, the transfer must be made in Form 35 in the Schedule to the Land Registration Act 1925.[67]

If the owner refuses to convey, the acquiring authority may execute a deed poll and pay the purchase-money into court. The effect of the deed poll is to vest the property in the authority for all the estate and interest of the owner.[68]

There are special provisions for dealing with land subject to a mortgage, rentcharge, etc.[69]

General vesting declaration

There was previously a special procedure for expedited completion

---

[61] Lands Clauses Consolidation Act 1845, s. 18; Compulsory Purchase Act 1965, s. 5.
[62] *Post,* pp. 189 *et seq.*
[63] *Capital Investments Ltd.* v. *Wednesfield U.D.C.* [1965] Ch. 774.
[64] See Report of the Committee on Local Land Charges, 1952, Cmd. 8840, at pp. 11, 12.
[65] Lands Clauses Consolidation Act 1845, ss. 84, 85; Compulsory Purchase Act 1965, s. 11.
[66] Lands Clauses Consolidation Act 1845, s. 75; Compulsory Purchase Act 1965, s. 2, Sched. 1, para. 10 (1).
[67] Land Registration Rules 1925, rr. 121, 259.
[68] Lands Clauses Consolidation Act 1845, s. 77; Compulsory Purchase Act 1965, ss. 5, 9, Sched. 2, para. 2.
[69] Lands Clauses Consolidation Act 1845, ss. 108 *et seq.*; Compulsory Purchase Act 1965, ss. 14 *et seq.*

which the authority might use when acquiring land for planning purposes.[70]   Under this procedure, when the compulsory purchase order became operative, the Compulsory Purchase Act 1965 and the Land Compensation Act 1961, as modified, applied as if notice to treat had been served on interested persons, *i.e.* there was, in effect, a constructive notice to treat.

This has now been superseded by the general vesting declaration procedure.[71]   Where the procedure is to be used the notice which must be given by the authority that a compulsory purchase order has been made or confirmed or a subsequent notice must explain the procedure in the prescribed form [72] and invite owners of land covered by the C.P.O. to give information with respect to name, address and land also on a prescribed form. The G.V.D. will be executed not less than two months later. Notice in the prescribed form must then be given that the G.V.D. has been executed and that it will take effect on a specified date not less than twenty-eight days later. The effect of the declaration is to vest the legal estate in the land in the acquiring authority on the specified date.

---

[70] Town and Country Planning Act 1962, ss. 74 *et seq.*; repealed by Town and Country Planning Act 1971, Sched. 11.

[71] Town and Country Planning Act 1968, s. 30 and Scheds. 3 and 3A, as amended by the Land Commission (Dissolution) Act 1971, s. 6 (1).

[72] See Compulsory Purchase of Land (General Vesting Declaration) Regulations 1969. The notice must be registered as a local land charge: Town and Country Planning Act 1968, Sched. 3, para. 2 (3).

CHAPTER 6

INVESTIGATION OF TITLE

I. THE ABSTRACT OF TITLE

The vendor's obligation

As we have seen,[1] it is the duty of the vendor to show and make a good title to the property agreed to be sold. The vendor must, as it is said, perhaps somewhat imprecisely,[2] deduce his title. For the purpose of proving his title to the property the vendor must make, at his own expense,[3] and deliver to the purchaser, an abstract of title to the property agreed to be sold.

The meaning and nature of the abstract

An abstract is an epitome of the documents, events and facts, which constitute the vendor's title.

An abstract must be *perfect, i.e.* it must consist of connected summaries of the deeds, wills or other instruments, births, marriages and deaths, and other material events, which show that the vendor is able to convey, or able to *compel to be conveyed*, the estate or interest in the property agreed to be sold. It should be noted that it is not necessary that the vendor should show that he *himself* can convey the property; it is sufficient if he can show that the property is vested in some person whom he can *compel* to convey. For example, it is sufficient if A shows that he is a purchaser of the property from B under a contract that has not yet been completed, because A is then in a position, if he wishes, to compel B to convey direct to C (the purchaser from A).[4] Similarly, it is sufficient if the vendor is the controlling shareholder of a company which has the title to the property.[5] On the other hand, if the title is in some third party whose conveyance the vendor has no right, legal or equitable, to compel, then the purchaser can object to the title; and this is so even if the vendor offers to obtain the concurrence of such third party and the latter is willing to give it. Thus, in one case,[6] two persons sold land as trustees for sale. The abstract showed that the trust for sale did not arise until the death of a tenant for life who was still living. The land was therefore settled land; and the

---

[1] *Ante,* p. 59.
[2] See Farrand, *Contract and Conveyance,* pp. 110, 111.
[3] *Ante,* p. 59.
[4] For sub-sales, see *post,* p. 195. But see conditions, *ante,* p. 104.
[5] *Jones* v. *Lipman* [1962] 1 W.L.R. 832.
[6] *Re Bryant and Barningham's Contract* (1890) 44 Ch.D. 218.

power of sale was vested in the tenant for life and not the trustees. The vendors thereupon offered to procure a conveyance from the tenant for life, but the purchaser, who wanted to resile, refused to accept this. The court held that he was justified in his objection as he had no contract with the tenant for life and the trustees had no power to *compel* the concurrence of the tenant for life, although the latter was willing to give it. However, in another case,[7] where trustees, who had no power to sell under the trust deed, had entered into a contract to sell at the request of all the beneficiaries, it was held that the purchaser could not refuse to complete, because the trustees were acting as the authorised agents of the beneficiaries and could *compel* the beneficiaries to concur.

The vendor need not be able to convey at the date of the contract so long as he can do so before the purchaser purports to repudiate the contract.[8]

The form of the abstract

The traditional form of abstract is usually printed, typed or hand-written on brief-sized[9] paper; and the matter contained in it set out in a special form.[10] It is necessary to imagine that the sheet has been divided into five columns, comprising four margins and the main column, the latter being situated about the middle of the sheet. The various parts of each document, etc., are set out within the respective margins. The object of this method is to enable the conveyancer who is perusing the abstract to find easily any particular part of a document to which he may want to refer. The extreme left hand margin is used for the date and stamp of the document abstracted. It is also used for "marking" the abstract on verification.[11] The next margin is used for the nature of the document, *i.e.* conveyance, mortgage, etc., and the parties thereto; and it is within this margin that the principal operative parts of the document are set out. Recitals[12] and the habendum[13] are put in the third margin; and any trusts affecting the property in the fourth. The main column contains the heading to the abstract and the parcels (*i.e.* the description of the property[14]) in the document being abstracted. Specimen abstracts in the old and new forms are set out in the precedents at the back of the book.[10] Copies of any plans to the abstracted documents should be attached to the abstract.

If the abstract is very long, the first page may set out an epitome of

---

[7] *Re Baker and Selmon's Contract* [1907] 1 Ch. 238; and see *Re Spencer and Hauser's Contract* [1928] Ch. 598.

[8] *Re Hailes and Hutchinson's Contract* [1920] 1 Ch. 233; *Re Stone and Saville's Contract* [1963] 1 W.L.R. 163.

[9] *i.e.* having the measurements $16\frac{1}{2}$ inches by $13\frac{1}{2}$ inches.

[10] *Post*, pp. 409 *et seq.*

[11] *Post*, p. 124.

[12] *Post*, p. 223.

[13] *Post*, p. 235.

[14] *Post*, p. 230.

the documents abstracted, *i.e.* a list of the documents, their dates and nature and the parties thereto; and indicating the page of the abstract where the document is abstracted. In practice, the vendor often supplies the purchaser with the abstracts (or copies thereof) relating to earlier sales of the property which he has in his possession; and only has to prepare a fresh abstract of the conveyance to himself. In other words, the vendor does not always have to prepare a fresh abstract of the *whole* of the title deduced.

The preparation of a proper abstract is a true art and one which today is nearly dead. A quick glance at the abstracts in a bundle of documents of title of a property will show the gradual decline over the years in the standard of abstracting, not only in form but also in content. The earliest abstract is often a printed abstract showing the title of a settled estate; and this might be followed by several typed abstracts showing the original sale off of the property and the subsequent conveyances and dispositions, ending with an abstract of the conveyance to the vendor, which, not uncommonly, is handwritten (presumably because the typist is otherwise engaged). The early abstracts were in a special shorthand used in abstracting [15]; but the more recent ones are usually in longhand and often set out the documents *in extenso* rather than paraphrasing them.

Over the last decade, it has become common and acceptable for the abstract to be made up of photo-copies of the various documents together with an epitome of the documents by way of index.[16] This is generally satisfactory; and is certainly preferable to the poor abstracting of recent years, especially where the originals are typed; but not always, if old handwritten abstracts or conveyances are badly copied. It must also be remembered that colouring will have to be added to photo-copied plans; and any memoranda,[17] which are often indorsed on the inside of the back page of a conveyance, should not be overlooked.

The contents of the abstract

The abstract will begin with the root of title. Subject to any conditions on the matter,[18] the root must be a good one.

Root of title

A good root of title may be defined as a document which effects a dealing with the whole legal estate and equitable interest in the property sold, and wherein the property is described, and nothing appears to cast any doubt upon the title. If the document is deficient

---

[15] The precedent of an abstract at p. 410, *post,* is in the modern bastardised form of shorthand.
[16] See Farrand, *Contract and Conveyance,* pp. 109, 110. For form, see *post,* p. 410.
[17] See *post,* p. 213.
[18] See *ante,* pp. 91, 92.

in any of these particulars, the purchaser may require, in the absence of anything to the contrary in the contract, a good root of title.

The best roots of title are a *conveyance on sale* and a *legal mortgage.* In both cases the property will have been fully described and the earlier title examined at the time of the transaction. Since 1925, a legal mortgagee no longer obtains the fee simple; he obtains a long term of years or a charge by way of legal mortgage under the Law of Property Act 1925.[19] A legal mortgage made in the new form is, however, an acceptable root of title if sufficiently old, provided the mortgage contains recitals or statements showing that the mortgagor was entitled to the property in fee simple.[20] An *equitable* mortgage is not a good root of title. A *specific* devise of a testator who died before 1926 is a good root of title, but not a *general* devise because the devise contains no description of the property, and nothing appears to show that the testator was possessed of the property at the time of his death. An assent by personal representatives to a devise, whether specific or general, made by the personal representatives after 1925 and conforming with the requirements of section 36 of the Administration of Estates Act 1925 will constitute a good root of title.

A *voluntary* conveyance is a good root of title, if it complies with the above definition, and cannot be objected to if the conveyance was made at least fifteen years ago. It is not, however, so desirable as a conveyance on sale, because the title will not have been investigated at the time, and, therefore, if a voluntary conveyance less than fifteen years old is specified in the contract as the root of title, the nature of the conveyance must be clearly stated in the contract, otherwise the purchaser will be at liberty to rescind on the ground that he was misled.[21]

Title depending on Statutes of Limitation

A title depending without further proof upon adverse possession under the Statutes of Limitation [22] for twelve years or upwards is not a good title. Possibly the " squatter " obtained no title at all because, for example, the true owner was under disability during the period of adverse possession. Again, the " squatter," being merely a volunteer, takes subject to all equities.[23] Such a title, therefore, would be wholly unreliable. But if the vendor supplies a good root of title, and traces the title to a particular point, and from that point shows adverse possession in the vendor for a period sufficient to bar the rights of all persons then interested in the land, the purchaser must accept the title.[24]

---

[19] See *post*, p. 293.
[20] See *post*, p. 305.
[21] Unless the vendor is willing to prove his title back to a root of title at least 15 years old. See *ante*, p. 92.
[22] Now Limitation Act 1939.
[23] *Re Nisbet and Pott's Contract* [1906] 1 Ch. 386.
[24] *Re Atkinson and Horsell's Contract* [1912] 2 Ch. 1. See *ante*, p. 93.

Recital as root of title

In *Bolton* v. *London School Board*,[25] it was held that a deed twenty years old, containing a recital of seisin in fee simple, was a good root of title under an open contract. The court's reasoning was based on the provisions of the Vendor and Purchaser Act 1874 [26] that recitals contained in a deed twenty years old at the date of the contract shall, except so far as they are proved to be inaccurate, be taken to be sufficient evidence of the facts stated therein. But this decision is generally regarded as erroneous, and was dissented from in *Re Wallis and Grout's Contract*.[27] The Law of Property Act 1925 did not resolve the doubt thus created.

What the abstract should contain

After the document forming the root of title there should be abstracted every subsequent document (except as mentioned below), and a statement of every event such as a birth, a marriage or a death, which forms a link in the vendor's title. These matters should be abstracted in chronological order so as to show the devolution of the property from the root of title to the vendor. A legal mortgage must be abstracted even though the money has been repaid, in which case the vacating receipt must also be abstracted.[28]

Where the property agreed to be sold is part of a larger plot subject to a ground rent or a rentcharge, and there have been previous apportionments of the rent, then the duplicate conveyances of these earlier sales off (which should have been retained by the vendor) should be abstracted.[29]

The following matters, however, should *not* be abstracted:

(i) expired leases;

(ii) instruments (*i.e.* documents) relating to interests or powers which will be overreached [30] by the conveyances, for example, the instrument containing the trusts affecting the proceeds of land held upon trust for sale, or the trusts affecting settled land; and

(iii) equitable mortgages by deposit of deeds or agreement in writing if they have been discharged. This has been criticised, but it is well established and unlikely to be

---

[25] (1878) 7 Ch.D. 766.
[26] See now s. 45 of the Law of Property Act 1925; *ante*, p. 63.
[27] [1906] 2 Ch. 206. See Farrand, *Contract and Conveyance*, p. 81.
[28] For vacating receipts, see *post*, p. 335.
[29] See (1949) 46 L.S.Gaz. 131. The purchaser's solicitor should inquire as to any liability to collect apportioned rents; see (1960) 57 L.S.Gaz. 399. Where parts of land subject to a ground rent or rentcharge are sold off, and the rent is apportioned equitably (or informally, as it is sometimes called), *i.e.* without the concurrence of the rent owner, it is usual for the purchaser of the last part sold to covenant with the vendor to collect the informally apportioned rents and to be responsible for paying the whole rent.
[30] See Law of Property Act 1925, ss. 10, 27; Megarry and Wade (3rd ed.), p. 379.

disturbed.[31]   As already mentioned, a legal mortgage must
be abstracted, even though discharged;

(iv) the contents of a will need not generally [32] be abstracted,
save for the date, name and description of the testator and
the appointment of executors.   After 1925 a will operates
in equity.

It is usual to abstract certificates of official searches for land
charges.[33]

As already mentioned, the costs of preparing the abstract falls on
the vendor.[34]

Time for delivery of abstract

The time for the delivery of the abstract is generally specified in the
conditions.[35]

Verification of abstract

The vendor must verify the abstract by producing all the evidence
necessary to prove the statements it contains.   He produces (usually at
the office of his solicitor) for examination by the purchaser or his
solicitor all the abstracted deeds, and furnishes proof of all other
documents and facts on which the title depends, such as orders of the
court, births, marriages and deaths.   By the Law of Property Act
1925 [36] the purchaser, in the absence of agreement to the contrary,
must pay the cost of producing evidence not in the vendor's possession
or the possession of his mortgagee or trustee.   The vendor verifies the
abstracted deeds by producing the original documents.

In practice, the comparison of the abstract against the deeds is
delayed until completion.   On receipt of the abstract the purchaser's
solicitor peruses it and raises any requisitions necessary.   It is usual
to reserve the right to make such further requisitions as may be
necessary on inspection of the deeds.[37]

Proof of documents

Not only must the vendor produce the documents but he must also
prove them.   Production of the original is generally sufficient proof of
an abstracted document.   Technically, the vendor must also prove
due execution, but generally the purchaser's solicitor will be able to
rely on the statutory provisions or common law presumptions mentioned below.

---

[31] See (1963) 26 Conv.(N.S.) 455.
[32] Sometimes it will be necessary to ascertain the contents, *e.g.* to see if the will
created a trust for sale or strict settlement, where a subsequent assent is on the
trusts of the will; see *post*, p. 138.
[33] See Law Society's Digest, Opinion No. 90.
[34] *Re Johnson and Tustin* (1885) 30 Ch.D. 42.   See *ante*, pp. 59, 64.
[35] *Ante*, p. 101.
[36] s. 45 (4); *ante*, p. 64.
[37] *Post*, p. 134.

(i) Execution of documents

It is provided by section 4 of the Evidence Act 1938 that, in the absence of suspicious circumstances, deeds and documents twenty years old prove themselves, provided they come from proper custody, and possession had been held consistently with the provisions contained in the particular deeds. In practice, it is not usual for a purchaser to require evidence of the execution of the documents of title, even if such documents are not twenty years old, provided they are found in the proper custody.

(ii) Powers of attorney

If a deed has been executed under a power of attorney,[38] the purchaser can demand that the power of attorney be produced, and, if the power was created before 1883, proof that the power was not revoked by the donor's death or otherwise before it was exercised. But the Law of Property Act 1925 provided that such evidence was not necessary (1) where the power was given by an instrument executed after 1882 for valuable consideration and was expressed to be irrevocable [39]; and (2) where the power was given by an instrument executed after 1882, whether for valuable consideration or not, and expressing that the power should be irrevocable for a fixed term, not exceeding one year, and the power was acted on within that time.[40] In neither of the above cases was the donee of the power, or the purchaser, affected prejudicially by notice of an express revocation, or of the donor's death, disability or bankruptcy.

Unless the power related only to one transaction and was to be handed back to the donor on completion, every power of attorney to dispose of or deal with any interest in or charge upon land which was conferred by an instrument executed after 1925 was required by the Law of Property Act 1925 to be filed at the Central Office of the Supreme Court, and a purchaser might insist upon having the instrument creating the power (or a copy of it or the material portions of it) delivered to him free of expense, notwithstanding any stipulation to the contrary.[41] The Law of Property Act 1925 also provided that a power of attorney should be exercised in the name of the donor of the power, but an instrument executed in the name of the donee would be effective.[42]

The Powers of Attorney Act 1971 contains new provisions in relation to powers of attorney and delegation of trusts, giving effect to the recommendations of the Law Commission's Report on Powers of

[38] *i.e.* a document authorising one person to perform certain acts on behalf of another.
[39] s. 126.
[40] *Ibid.* s. 127.
[41] s. 125, as amended by the Law of Property (Amendment) Act 1926.
[42] *Ibid.* s. 123, re-enacting s. 46 of the Conveyancing Act 1881.

Attorney.[43]   The Act came into force on October 1, 1971.   Section 1 makes rules for the execution of powers of attorney.   An instrument creating a power of attorney made after the commencement of the Act must be signed and sealed by, or by the direction and in the presence of, the donor.   In the latter case, two other persons must be present as witnesses and must attest the instrument.

Section 2 abolishes the need to file or deposit powers of attorney or copies.   This does not affect any right to search for, inspect or copy, or obtain an office copy of, any instrument which had been filed or deposited before the commencement of the Act.   Section 3 deals with the proof of powers of attorney: it permits photographic copies certified in the manner prescribed by the Act to be used in addition to office copies which had been previously required.

Section 4 applies to powers of attorney given as security,[44] whenever created.   It provides that where a power is expressed to be irrevocable and is given to secure a proprietary interest of the donee or the performance of an obligation owed to the donee, then, so long as the donee has that interest or the obligation remains undischarged, the power shall be revoked—(i) by the donor without the consent of the donee; and (ii) by the death, incapacity or bankruptcy of the donor, or, if the donor is a body corporate, by its winding up or dissolution. A power to secure a proprietary interest may be given to the person entitled to the interest and any persons deriving title under him; and these persons shall be duly constituted donees of the power but without prejudice to any right to appoint substitutes given by the power.[45]

Section 5 deals with the protection of the *donee and third parties* where revocation has taken place without their knowledge.[46]   An attorney who acts in pursuance of a power at a time when it has, unknown to him, been revoked, does not incur any liability by reason of such revocation either to the appointor or to any other person.[47]   As regards *third parties,* it is provided that where a power has been revoked, and a person, without knowledge of the revocation, deals with the donee of the power, the transaction between them shall, in favour of that person, be as valid as if the power had then been in existence.[48] Where the power is expressed in the instrument creating it to be irrevocable and to be given by way of security, then, unless the person dealing with the donee knows that it was not in fact given by way of security, he is entitled to assume that the power is only capable of revocation by the donor acting with the consent of the donee. Accordingly, the third person is treated as having knowledge of the

[43] Law Com. No. 30, 1970, Cmnd. 4473; see (1970) 120 New L.J. 906.
[44] See *post*, p. 297.
[45] This replaces s. 128 of the Law of Property Act 1925.
[46] This replaces ss. 124–127 of the Law of Property Act 1925.
[47] Subs. (1).
[48] Subs. (2).

revocation only if he, in fact, knows that the power has been revoked in that manner.[49] Where the interest of the purchaser depends on whether a person dealing with the donee of a power had knowledge of the revocation of the power, it is to be conclusively presumed in favour of the purchaser that that person did not at the material time know of the revocation of the power if (a) the transaction between that person and the donee was completed within twelve months of the date on which the power came into operation; or (b) that person makes a statutory declaration, before or within three months after the completion of the purchase, that he did not at the material time know of the revocation of the power.[50] Section 5 applies whenever the power was created, but only to acts and transactions after the commencement of the Act.

Accordingly, today, a purchaser of unregistered land, who is to accept a title depending on a power of attorney, is concerned first to look at the *contents of the power,* including the extent of the authority conferred by it and its execution; and, secondly, to verify that the power is not *limited in time.* If he is the original purchaser, he must, of course, have no knowledge of the revocation or of any event which would revoke it; if he is a subsequent purchaser, he must see that the transaction was completed within twelve months of the power coming into operation, or, if not, that the proper statutory declaration, referred to above, has been made.[51]

As regards registered land, the above provisions equally apply. In addition, if any instrument executed by an attorney is delivered to the Registry, the registrar must be supplied with a copy and if the relevant transaction is not completed within twelve months of the date on which the power came into operation, evidence of non-revocation must be produced by statutory declaration.[52]

As to the execution of documents by an attorney, section 7 provides that the donee of a power may, if he thinks fit, execute any instrument or do anything in his own name rather than in the name of the donor, without prejudice to any statutory direction requiring an instrument to be executed in the name of an estate owner. The section applies whenever the power was created.[53]

Section 9 amends section 25 of the Trustee Act 1925 and allows trustees, personal representatives, tenants for life and statutory owners to delegate for a period not exceeding twelve months their trusts and duties by power of attorney, on certain conditions, even though they are not going out of the United Kingdom.[54]

---

[49] Subs. (3).
[50] Subs. (4).
[51] See (1971) 121 New L.J. 746, 748; (1971) 68 L.S.Gaz. 434, 437, 481, 482.
[52] See Land Registration (Powers of Attorney) Rules 1971, substituting a new r. 82 of the Land Registration Rules 1925; (see (1971) 121 New L.J. 764.
[53] This replaces s. 123 of the Law of Property Act 1925.
[54] *Cf. Green* v. *Whitehead* [1930] 1 Ch. 38; *post,* p. 138. See generally on the new provisions in this respect (1971) 121 New L.J. 766.

(iii) Copyhold assurances

These are proved by copies of the court roll signed by a steward.

(iv) Disentailing deeds

Disentailing deeds executed before 1926 are proved by certificates of enrolment.[55]

(v) Wills

Wills of realty are proved by production of probate or letters of administration with the will annexed, or office copies thereof. If the testator died before January 1, 1898 (when the Land Transfer Act 1897, came into force, before which probate as regards real property was unnecessary), by producing the will itself.

(vi) Enfranchisement of copyholds

Enfranchisement of copyholds is proved by production of the deed or award of enfranchisement.

(vii) Private Acts

Private Acts of Parliament are proved by production of a Queen's printer's copy.

(viii) Court orders

Orders of the court are proved by office copies.

(ix) Missing documents

If a document is missing, its destruction or loss must be proved by evidence of destruction or showing that proper searches have been made for it without result.[56]

Purchaser should examine all documents of which he knows

If the purchaser is informed of the existence of a document and is told that it does not affect the property agreed to be sold, he is not considered to have constructive notice of any equitable interest created by the document, but if the document is in the possession of the vendor he should ask for it to be produced, as it may have created a legal interest in the property.

Proof of facts

The vendor must also prove the facts (as distinct from the documents) stated in the abstract.

---

[55] If made after 1925, a disentailing deed does not require enrolment, and, therefore, the deed itself must be produced if it appears on the title at all, which ordinarily it would not, as it deals with an equitable interest only.

[56] This is one of the most common occasions for a statutory declaration. Many deeds were destroyed in enemy action during the 1939–45 war.

(i) Births, marriages and deaths

These, and matters of pedigree generally, are proved by the appropriate certificates where they are available. If, however, in the case of a death, the probate or letters of administration form a link in the title, such probate or letters of administration are sufficient evidence of the death concerned. In the absence of such evidence, in the case of death, if the persons who would be likely to have heard of the "deceased" have not heard of him for seven years, death may be presumed.[57] Entries in parish records, statements of deceased members of the family, entries in a family bible, and statutory declarations of living members of the family or others acquainted with the family, are all admissible as evidence. It should be pointed out that a statutory declaration of a living member of the family as to a matter of pedigree may become good evidence after his death, but it is not admissible evidence in litigation during his lifetime; and a statutory declaration of a stranger to the family is never admissible evidence in litigation. However, on a sale of land, such evidence is commonly accepted by conveyancers.

(ii) Bankruptcy

An adjudication in bankruptcy is proved by production of a copy of the *London Gazette* containing a notice thereof.[58] The appointment of a trustee in bankruptcy is proved by a certificate of the Department of Trade and Industry.[59] Any petition, order or certificate, made in bankruptcy proceedings is proved by the seal of any court having jurisdiction, by the signature of any judge having jurisdiction, or a certified copy.[60]

(iii) Assent before 1926

Before 1926, an assent might be implied a reasonable time (depending on the size and complexity of the estate) after the death.[31] Since 1925, assents in respect of legal estates in land must be in writing.[62]

(iv) Intestacies

Intestacies are proved by production of letters of administration.

(v) Negatives

It may be necessary to prove that certain events, which would have affected the title had they occurred, did not happen; for example,

---

[57] See *Re Watkins* [1953] 1 W.L.R. 1323.
[58] Bankruptcy Act 1914, s. 137 (2).
[59] *Ibid.* s. 143.
[60] *Ibid.* s. 139. For the registration of bankruptcy petitions and receiving orders, see *post*, p. 151.
[61] *Wise* v. *Whitburn* [1924] 1 Ch. 460.
[62] See *post*, p. 136.

that a previous owner of the land died without issue. Death without issue may be proved by statutory declaration of a person acquainted with the deceased. One of the most common negatives to be proved in the past was that there had been no severance of a joint tenancy. This difficulty is now dealt with by the Law of Property (Joint Tenants Act 1964.[63] The statutory provisions concerning non-revocation of power of attorney have been dealt with already.[64]

(vi) *Other matters affecting the title*

The happening of certain other events might or might not affect the title. The vendor must answer any questions as to whether an event which might have affected the title has occurred. If he replies it has not, the purchaser cannot require any further evidence—except possibly a statutory declaration by the vendor at the purchaser's expense. If he replies that the event happened, but did not affect the property sold, then the purchaser may require such evidence of this statement as is in the vendor's possession.

Presumptions

In some cases, the purchaser can be called upon to presume certain facts, for example:

(i) *Execution of deeds*

It will be presumed that the formalities necessary to the execution of a deed have been observed, and also that the deed was executed on the day of the date which it bears.[65]

(ii) *Alterations, etc., in deeds and wills*

There is also a presumption that alterations, erasures or inter-lineations in a *deed* were made *before* execution, whereas in the case of a *will* the presumption is that they were made *after* execution.

(iii) *Parties to the deed*

As to the parties to the deed, it is now provided by section 15 of the Law of Property Act 1925 that the persons expressed to be parties to any conveyance shall, until the contrary is proved, be presumed to be of full age at the date of the conveyance. This pro-vision is particularly important in view of the fact that an infant (or minor) cannot hold a legal estate in land after 1925.[66]

[63] *Post*, p. 143.
[64] *Ante*, p. 126.
[65] See *Gartside* v. *Silkstone, etc., Co.* (1882) 21 Ch.D. 762, and *ante*, p. 125.
[66] See Law of Property Act 1925, ss. 1 (6) and 19; Settled Land Act 1925, s. 27; and Family Law Reform Act 1969, s. 1.

(iv) Payment off of mortgage [67]

The purchaser may sometimes have to presume that a mortgage has been paid off. For example, in one case,[68] it was presumed that a mortgage debt had been paid off and the land reconveyed, although the reconveyance could not be produced. The vendor was able to prove that the land had been in the possession of himself and his predecessors in title for a very long period since the date of the mortgage; that the mortgage was not mentioned subsequently in the title deeds; and that he (the vendor) had been in possession of the title deeds for the last twenty-five years without any claim being made on him for principal and interest.

(v) Deaths

This has already been mentioned.[69]

(vi) Commorientes

Where two persons die together after 1925, and it is uncertain which of them survived the other, it is to be presumed, subject to any order of the court, that, for all purposes affecting the title to the property, the younger survived the elder.[70] This is a statutory presumption which may be rebutted by evidence, but the court has no discretion to displace the presumption merely on the ground that its operation might be unfair.[71] Further, evidence to show that two persons were killed together *instantly*, as, for example, in an air-raid, is not sufficient to prove that they died exactly *simultaneously*; the statutory presumption will, therefore apply.[71] No such presumption arises in the case of deaths occurring before 1926 [72] and there was, therefore, no way of settling the question in the absence of evidence of the order of deaths.

The presumption does not apply between husband and wife on the death intestate of the husband or the wife.[73]

II. REQUISITIONS

Examination of title

The conveyancer acting for the purchaser should call for proof of the vendor's title in accordance with the rules previously mentioned. He should note, for example, whether the abstract is complete, whether there are any defects in the form of the abstracted documents, and whether any equities or breaches of trust are disclosed, as, for example, where the abstract shows a conveyance from a trustee to himself without the beneficiaries being parties.

---

[67] See *post*, pp. 334 *et seq.*
[68] *Cooke* v. *Soltau* (1824) 2 S. & S. 154.
[69] *Ante*, p. 129.
[70] Law of Property Act 1925, s. 184.
[71] *Hickman* v. *Peacey* [1945] A.C. 304; *Re Rowland* [1963] Ch. 1.
[72] *Wing* v. *Angrave* (1860) 8 H.L.C. 183.
[73] Intestates' Estate Act 1952, s. 1 (4); *post*, p. 395.

Each conveyancer has his own method of examining the title [74] and many find it convenient, especially where the abstract is long or there are several abstracts, to prepare on rough paper an epitome or résumé of the title. This is best done under several column headings for date, stamp, nature of document, parties, property conveyed, incumbrances and remarks. For example:

Date	Stamp	Nature of document	Parties	Property Conveyed	Incum- brances	Remarks
1.10.1935	√	Con.	(1) Jn. Williams (2) Ric. Robertson	?	R.C.s	Identify property

This indicates a conveyance dated October 1, 1935, made between John Williams of the one part and Richard Robertson of the other part, the property conveyed being subject to restrictive covenants previously created. The stamp has been checked and was correct. There is only a verbal description of the property conveyed and the purchaser will want to confirm that the property conveyed by the conveyance included the property to be sold. The note might continue:

Date	Stamp	Nature of document	Parties	Property Conveyed	Incum- brances	Remarks
26.4.1960	√	L.C.Sch.	vs. Ric. Robertson	—	—	Clear
4.5.1960	√	Con.	(1) R. Robertson (2) Hen. Smith	√	Fresh R.C.s	√
4.5.1960	√	Mtge.	(1) Hen. Smith (2) National B.S.	√	—	√

This indicates a clear land charges search against Richard Robertson and a conveyance by him to Henry Smith. The stamp is correct. In this case the property conveyed is identifiable as the property agreed to be sold (because there was a plan to the 1960 conveyance). The conveyance is followed by a mortgage to the National Building Society.

The title shown in this example is satisfactory subject to:

    (1) the land charges search made against John Williams. If one was made before the 1935 conveyance it should be abstracted. If none was made the purchaser must search against that name;

    (2) the identification of the property conveyed by the 1935 conveyance;

    (3) the discharge of the current mortgage; and

    (4) a land charge search against Henry Smith.

The following are the principal steps that a conveyancer should take in examining the title:

    (1) He should check the root of title.[75] Is it a sufficient root of title, *i.e.* the root stipulated in the contract or, if none was stipulated, a good root?

---

[74] For a general scheme for perusal of an abstract, see *Emmet on Title* (15th ed.), pp. 147 *et seq.*

[75] *Ante*, p. 121.

(2) He should follow the devolution of the legal estate down to the vendor or to someone the vendor can compel to convey.[73] Can the title be deduced down to the vendor without a break? Did the persons, who, as shown in the abstract, transferred the property, have the power to transfer?

(3) He should check whether there are any defects in the form of the abstracted documents and that they were properly executed.[77]

(4) He should identify the property from the plans in the abstract.[78] There is usually no difficulty about this, but, in certain cases, it is not so easy. An instance is where the land has been developed. Here, it may be quite difficult to determine whether or not the property agreed to be sold is comprised in any earlier conveyance, especially where the land conveyed thereby was an undeveloped plot showing no points of identification.

(5) He should note all incumbrances, such as mortgages, easements and restrictive covenants affecting the land. If the purchaser wishes to develop the land, it should be considered how any incumbrances might affect development.[79]

(6) He should check the stamp on all deeds. The vendor must stamp all unstamped or insufficiently stamped deeds at his own expense.[80]

(7) He should check all results of land charge searches and consider whether any additional searches are required.

(8) Where the land is registered, he should note all charges, cautions, restrictions and matters noted on the title; and keep in mind the possibility of overriding interests, particularly the rights of persons in actual occupation.[81]

Requisitions on title

The purchaser, or his legal adviser, is entitled, subject to the provisions of the contract,[82] to put written requisitions and objections to the vendor with regard to any defect in the title that appears on the abstract, or is disclosed by examination of the deeds, or by the results of land charge searches. The vendor must then give a satisfactory answer to such requisitions in order to show a good title. In practice, requisitions are made on the title as it appears from the abstract before examination of the deeds. The latter is normally left until completion, the purchaser reserving the right to raise further requisitions, if need be, after such examination.

76 *Ante*, pp. 119, 123.
77 *Ante*, pp. 125, 130.
78 *Ante*, p. 94.
79 *Post*, pp. 140, 146.
80 *Ante*, p. 64.
81 *Post*, pp. 170, 171, 180 *et seq.*
82 See *ante*, pp. 92, 93, 101–104.

F

The purpose, nowadays, of requisitions is twofold:

(1) to raise inquiries as to the title shown by the abstract and by the verification thereof; and

(2) to raise inquiries as to other matters relating to the conveyance and the formalities on completion, for example, as to which deeds will be handed over on completion.

Technically, perhaps, requisitions should be limited to requisitions *on title*; but other matters are commonly raised, and, indeed, there may be a duty to do so if only to inquire whether the answers to preliminary inquiries would still be the same.[83]

Which requisitions should be put depends, of course, upon the particular title shown in the particular case; and also upon whether the sale is by open contract [84] or whether the purchaser's right to put requisitions is expressly restricted by the conditions of sale.[85]

Printed or standard forms of requisitions are generally used.[86] The same objections to the use of printed forms apply here as to preliminary inquiries.[87] The printed forms contain space for any special requisition arising in respect of the particular title.

The first requisition on the printed forms generally asks whether, if the preliminary inquiries were repeated, the answers would be the same. Subsequent common form requisitions deal with the various receipts to be produced by the vendor on completion,[88] which title deeds will be handed over on completion [89] and details of the completion.[90] We have seen that the right to raise further requisitions after examination of deeds and land charge searches have been made is generally reserved. The conditions will usually impose time limits on the making of requisitions, but these cannot exclude requisitions made thereafter which go to the root of the title.[91]

There are other common requisitions which are not usually printed. For example, where the land to be conveyed is part of a larger plot and the title deeds are to be retained by the vendor,[92] a requisition will be raised to remind the vendor's solicitor to endorse a memorandum of the conveyance to the purchaser on the retained deeds.[93] Again, where the property is subject to a mortgage, it is usual to ask the vendor's solicitor to confirm that the mortgage will be discharged on or before completion or that the usual undertaking will be given.[94]

[83] *Goody* v. *Baring* [1956] 1 W.L.R. 448, 456.
[84] *Ante*, p. 68.
[85] *Ante*, pp. 92, 93.
[86] See *e.g.* Form Conveyancing 28B obtainable from the Solicitors' Law Stationery Society Ltd.
[87] *Ante*, p. 36.
[88] See *post*, p. 210.
[89] See *post*, p. 211.
[90] See *post*, pp. 206, 210.
[91] *Ante*, pp. 101, 102.
[92] See *post*, p. 238.
[93] See *post*, p. 213.
[94] See *post*, p. 211.

Like preliminary inquiries, the requisitions are set out on the left-hand side of the page leaving room on the right for the replies. The requisitions should be sent in duplicate so that the vendor's solicitor can retain one copy. The vendor, or his solicitor, should attempt to answer proper requisitions fully; but answers to general inquiries are often worthless. Formerly, the requisitions often concluded with a general searching requisition as to the existence of any mortgages, writs of execution and other charges or incumbrances, etc. known to the vendor or his solicitor and not disclosed by the abstract. It was, however, held in *Re Ford and Hill* [95] that such a requisition was too searching and tended towards extra costs and delay, and need not be answered.

If the vendor's reply to a requisition on title is false, he is liable to be prosecuted,[96] and to an action for damages by the purchaser, or persons deriving title under him, for any loss sustained.[97] As the purchaser is already bound by the contract at this stage, there is no question of any liability for inducing him to enter into the contract; nor will there be any liability *in tort* for deceit or negligence, unless the falsehood relates to a matter which would have entitled the purchaser to rescind.[98]

In the absence of any conditions on the matter, requisitions must be delivered within a reasonable time. Generally, the conditions of sale will deal with the time for delivery of requisitions and replies thereto.[99] There will usually also be a condition giving the vendor the right to rescind the contract if the purchaser persists in any requisition with which the vendor is unable or unwilling to comply.[1]

Waiver of requisitions

A purchaser may waive, either expressly or impliedly, any objection or requisition which he has made. An acceptance of the title shown by the abstract is not a waiver of the right to require the verification of the abstract [2] or of any objection not disclosed by the abstract. A waiver may be implied from the fact that the purchaser has taken possession, unless he has done so with the consent of the vendor or under an express provision in the contract.[3] Waiver may also be implied from long delay in raising objections. Tender by the purchaser of a draft conveyance to the vendor,[4] or an attempt by the purchaser to resell the property,[5] may imply a waiver.

95 (1879) 10 Ch.D. 365.
96 Law of Property Act 1925, s. 183 (1).
97 *Ibid.* s. 183 (2); *ante*, p. 80.
98 See Farrand, *Contract and Conveyance*, p. 117; (1967) 117 New L.J. 1029.
99 *Ante*, p. 101.
 1 *Ante*, p. 102.
 2 *Southby* v. *Hutt* (1837) 2 My. & Cr. 207.
 3 But see *Margravine of Anspach* v. *Noel* (1816) 1 Madd. 310. And *ante*, p. 105.
 4 *Sweet* v. *Meredith* (1862) 8 Jur.(N.S.) 637.
 5 *Simpson* v. *Sadd* (1855) 24 L.J.Ch. 562.

III. The Vendor's Title

In this section we shall deal briefly with a number of points commonly arising in the investigation of title.

(i) Assents

After the payment of debts and death duties, it is the duty of the personal representatives to vest the deceased's property in the persons entitled under the will or intestacy, as the case may be. Before 1926, if the deceased left a will, this was effected, both as regards freeholds and leaseholds, by an assent which might be in writing or oral, or merely inferred from conduct. On the other hand, to pass the freeholds to the heir or leaseholds to the next-of-kin *on intestacy*, a conveyance under seal was essential.[6] The possibility of an assent being inferred from conduct where the deceased died testate caused great inconvenience in practice, because it was often very difficult to determine whether the executors had impliedly assented or not. If they had impliedly assented, the legal estate was in the devisee; but if they had not, it remained in them.[7]

This difficulty cannot arise after 1925 owing to section 36 of the Administration of Estates Act 1925 which provides for a uniform method of assent whether the deceased dies testate or intestate, before 1926 or after 1925. The legal estate in realty must now be conveyed by the personal representatives by deed to the person entitled under the will or intestacy; or, instead, it may be transferred by an assent in *writing*, signed by the personal representatives and naming the person in whose favour it is made.

An assent in writing is required even when the assent is to the same person or persons as the personal representative or representatives.[8]

Even after an assent in proper form has been made, the devisee or person entitled on intestacy is not wholly secure, for it is provided by the same section that a purchaser from the personal representatives will get a good title (except as against a previous purchaser) if he obtains from them a statement in writing that they have not previously assented, *unless* notice of a previous assent or conveyance has been indorsed on or annexed to the probate or letters of administration.[9] It follows that a person in whose favour an assent is made should take immediate steps to procure the indorsement or annexation of such notice.

The statement in writing by personal representatives referred to in the last paragraph gives useful protection to a purchaser of land from personal representatives. Section 36 (6) of the Administration of Estates Act 1925 provides that a purchaser of a legal estate for

---

[6] Land Transfer Act 1897, s. 3.
[7] See *Wise* v. *Whitburn* [1924] 1 Ch. 460.
[8] See *post*, p. 401.
[9] Administration of Estates Act 1925, s. 36 (5).

money or money's worth from personal representatives who takes his conveyance on the faith of a statement in writing by the personal representatives that they have not given or made a previous conveyance or assent in respect of the legal estate, will obtain a good title even though a previous conveyance or assent has been made, unless (i) the legal estate has previously been conveyed by the personal representatives or persons deriving title under them to a purchaser for money or money's worth; or (ii) notice of a previous conveyance or assent has been indorsed on the probate or letters of administration.

It follows that a purchaser from personal representatives should always obtain from them such statement in writing (in practice, the statement is by way of recital in the conveyance to the purchaser); and should also inspect the probate or letters of administration to ensure that no notice of a previous disposition has been indorsed thereon.

Section 36 (7) of the Administration of Estates Act contains a provision which is often found useful when title is being made through the devisee under a will or person entitled on an intestacy. It provides that an assent or conveyance made by a personal representative after 1925 (whether the testator or intestate died before or after the Act), in respect of a legal estate, shall, in favour of a purchaser, unless notice of a previous assent or conveyance affecting the legal estate has been placed on or annexed to the probate or letters of administration, be taken as sufficient evidence that the person in whose favour the assent or conveyance is given or made is the person entitled to have the legal estate conveyed to him and upon the proper trusts, if any, but shall not otherwise prejudicially affect the claim of any person rightfully entitled to the estate vested or conveyed or any charge thereon. But it was held in *Re Duce and Boots Cash Chemists (Southern) Ltd.'s Contract* [10] that if it appears from the assent or conveyance itself that it was not in fact made in favour of the person entitled to have the legal estate vested in him, the purchaser is not protected by this subsection; for example, if a house was devised to A subject to a trust to permit B to occupy the house rent free during B's life, a purchaser from A could not rely upon an assent in A's favour which recited the trust in favour of B and so showed that the house was settled land and that the assent should, therefore, have been made in favour of B as tenant for life, and not in favour of A.

For the further protection of purchasers from personal representatives, section 37 of the Administration of Estates Act provides that all conveyances of any interest in real or personal property, made by a person to whom probate or letters of administration have been granted, are valid, notwithstanding any subsequent revocation or variation of the grant. The purchaser, therefore, need not fear the possible revocation of letters of administration, for example, on the finding of a will, or

10 [1937] Ch. 642.

the possible revocation of probate, on the finding of a later will. The section makes statutory the law laid down in *Hewson* v. *Shelley*.[11]

An assent under hand, *i.e.* not under seal, does not attract stamp duty,[12] save when the assent is made to give effect to an appropriation under the statutory power involving an element of sale in the transaction.[13]

Where the will creates a trust, the assent to the trustees should create an *independent trust for sale, i.e.* it should be made to them upon trust for sale, etc., upon the trusts declared in the will. This is sometimes called the statutory form.[14] An assent to the trustees merely upon the *trust for sale under the will* or the *trust of a will* (without imposing an independent trust for sale) brings the will on to the title. In this case, the purchaser will have to see the terms of the will, to make sure that they do not inadvertently create a strict settlement,[15] in which case a vesting assent in favour of the tenant for life should have been made. In the case of a very simple will there is no harm in bringing the will onto the title. The form of assent on an independent trust for sale has the disadvantage that new trustees of *both* will and assent may be required; and this is sometimes overlooked.

(ii) Attorney

We have already considered the statutory provisions protecting the purchaser against revocation of the power.[16]

It must also be noted that one co-owner cannot give power of attorney to another co-owner except under section 25 of the Trustee Act 1925.[17]

(iii) Charities

Subject to certain exceptions mentioned below, no land which forms part of the permanent endowment of a charity, or which is held by or in trust for a charity, may be sold, leased, etc., without an order of the court or of the Charity Commissioners or the Secretary of State for Education and Science.[18] Any transaction entered into in respect of such land without the requisite consent is wholly void.[19] These restrictions do not apply to exempt charities, such as universities; certain transactions authorised by statute or a scheme, or to charities

---

[11] [1914] 2 Ch. 13.
[12] Administration of Estates Act 1925, s. 36 (11).
[13] *Jopling* v. *I.R.C.* [1940] 2 K.B. 282.
[14] See Law of Property Act 1925, Sched. 5, Form No. 9; Hallett's *Conveyancing Precedents*, pp. 109 *et seq.*
[15] *Post*, p. 351.
[16] *Ante*, p. 126.
[17] *Green* v. *Whitehead* [1930] 1 Ch. 38, 46; see *ante*, p. 127.
[18] Charities Act 1960, s. 29. See also Settled Land Act 1925, s. 29 for the powers of charity trustees generally.
[19] *Bishop of Bangor* v. *Parry* [1891] 2 Q.B. 277; *Milner* v. *Staffordshire Congregational Union (Incorporated) Trustees* [1956] Ch. 275.

subject to partial restraint. This latter class comprises charities exempted by order of the Charity Commissioners or the Secretary of State.[20] Two types of order are commonly made in respect of non-educational charities—" 1980 orders " and " non-occupation orders." The " 1980 " order relates to all the property of the charity held for its general purposes, or at any time occupied by it, but which does not form part of its permanent endowment; it exempts the charity from the requirement of consent for a specified period, i.e. until December 31, 1980 (and for this reason it is called a " 1980 " order). A " non-occupation " order is made in respect of specified property; and allows a sale without consent so long as it is not, and has not been, occupied for the purposes of the charity.

Many religious charities of all denominations have been exempted by regulations from the requirement of consent, if, during the three years preceding the transaction, the land has not been used otherwise than for one or more certain specified purposes, for example, as a place of worship, Sunday school, church hall, etc.[21]

The property may be vested in the charity trustee or trustees; or, in some cases, in the Official Custodian for Charities, when the powers of management will be in the trustee or trustees.[22]

The powers of charity trustees are generally speaking the powers of a tenant for life and the trustees of settled land.[23] It should be borne in mind that the trust deed may impose certain conditions on the exercise of the trustees' powers, such as the need for a resolution of some committee of the charity.

Evidence of the devolution of the trusteeship will be required. Section 35 of the Charities Act 1960, replacing earlier provisions, contains a useful provision which enables trustees to be appointed by a resolution of a meeting of the charity trustees plus a signed memorandum. This has the same effect as a deed of appointment of new trustees under section 40 of the Trustee Act 1925.

(iv) Companies

A purchaser must satisfy himself that a company has power to hold and dispose of land.[24] Usually the memorandum of association contains an express power to purchase, lease, etc., land. Even in the absence of express power, a trading company would have implied power to acquire and dispose of land if this were incidental to the objects of the company.[25]

20 Under ss. 29 (4), 45 (6) of the Charities Act 1960.
21 For such orders, see Tudor, *Charities* (6th ed.), pp. 703 *et seq.*
22 See further on the Official Custodian, Tudor, pp. 431 *et seq.*
23 Settled Land Act 1925, s. 29.
24 In the case of companies incorporated under the Companies Act 1948, express power to hold land in most cases was given by s. 14 of the 1948 Act. This section was repealed on the abolition of mortmain by the Charities Act 1960, s. 38, and was not replaced.
25 For the borrowing powers of companies, see *post*, p. 301.

When a company in liquidation sells land, the conveyancer must first ascertain the type of winding up. In the case of a *members' voluntary winding up*, the resolutions to wind up and appointing the liquidator and the statutory declaration of solvency[26] must be abstracted. In a *creditors' winding up*, copies of the resolutions passed at meetings of the company and of the creditors' appointment of the liquidator must be abstracted. In the case of *compulsory winding up*, the order of the court appointing the liquidator must be abstracted.

(v) Easements

The creation of an easement is dealt with in a subsequent chapter.[27] On investigation of title the purchaser is concerned to identify the easement and to confirm its effectiveness. The existence of an easement is a matter of title and must be considered in the same way as any other title to land. Often, of course, the easement will be created over land retained by the vendor and the title to the land to which the easement is appurtenant and the land over which the easement was granted will be the same. On other occasions the titles may be different, for example, in a case of a grant of mutual easements over a common driveway created between two adjoining properties where the space between the two properties is insufficient for there to be separate driveways.

The extent of the easement must be considered, particularly if the purchaser proposes some development on the land to be purchased. The extent of an easement depends on the construction of the grant; but it is not restricted to the exact mode of user originally enjoyed so long as there is no substantial change. The same applies where the easement has been acquired by prescription. For example, a mere increase in the amount of traffic using a right of way will not in itself be an excessive and improper exercise of the right. There seems to be a distinction between a change in *quantity*, which cannot necessarily be restrained, and a change of *quality* which can. But there is a stage when a change of quantity may become a change of quality.[28]

(vi) Equitable mortgages

It is not usual to abstract equitable charges made by individuals.[29] If the existence of such a charge comes to light, for example, because it has been registered,[30] the purchaser must insist on the discharge of the charge before completion or on an undertaking to discharge.[31]

---

[26] Under the Companies Act 1948, s. 283. The time limits for making the declaration and delivering it to the registrar must be observed.

[27] *Post*, p. 231. As to agreements and declarations as to mutual easements, see *post*, p. 415, clause 3.

[28] See *Jelbert* v. *Davis* [1968] 1 W.L.R. 589; *Woodhouse & Co. Ltd.* v. *Kirkland (Derby) Ltd.* [1970] 1 W.L.R. 1185.

[29] See *post*, p. 296.

[30] *Post*, p. 153.

[31] For the discharge of equitable mortgages, see *post*, p. 337.

Difficulty is sometimes caused where the charge affects other land. This is not uncommon in the case of a floating charge.[32] Floating charges in debentures are usually abstracted. However, if they are not, they will be revealed on a companies search.[33] When the charge affects other land, it is sufficient to accept a letter from the debenture holder (usually a bank) renouncing any claim to the property, as a sufficient discharge from the charge.[34]

(vii) Estate duty

On examining the abstract, the purchaser may discover a death proving a link in the title. It was formerly necessary for him to obtain proof that the death duties had been paid in those cases in which they were a charge upon the property. Estate duty is a charge on freeholds, but not leaseholds.[35] Such proof, however, is seldom necessary nowadays because, as regards deaths which occurred after 1925, the purchaser need only consider a charge for duties if it has been registered by the Inland Revenue Commissioners as a land charge, Class D (i)[36]; and it is not the general practice of the Commissioners to register such charges. Furthermore, by the joint effect of section 12 of the Customs and Inland Revenue Act 1889 and section 8 (2) of the Finance Act 1894, a purchaser (including a mortgagee) takes free from any charge for estate duty in respect of a death which occurred more than twelve years (and sometimes only six years) before the purchase (or mortgage). It follows that the purchaser is never concerned with death duties arising on a death which occurred at least twelve years ago (and sometimes only six years), and that after January 1, 1938 (when a death occurring before January 1, 1926, became outside the twelve-year limit), a purchaser can disregard the question of death duties except in the rare cases in which a charge has actually been registered.[37]

(viii) Flats and maisonettes

These cause peculiar difficulties in relation to the common parts of the block. If the flats are sold leasehold, there is no special difficulty as long as the easements over passages, stairs, etc. are properly considered; and the positive covenants, which are generally required to maintain the standards of the properties, are enforceable between landlord and tenant. It is not so easy to enforce these obligations if the properties are sold freehold, and, indeed, for many years mortgagees would rarely lend on such a security. Various schemes have been devised, including the formation of management companies, to provide

32 For floating charges, see *post*, p. 142.
33 *Post*, p. 163.
34 See *Emmet on Title* (15th ed.), pp. 142, 143.
35 Finance Act 1894, s. 9 (1).
36 See *post*, p. 155.
37 For gifts, see *post*, p. 142.

F*

for the maintenance of the properties; and these are generally satisfactory. Reference should be made elsewhere to the details of these schemes.[38]

(ix) Floating charges

If it appears from the abstract (for a debenture is usually abstracted) or from a company search, that the property agreed to be sold is subject to a floating charge [39] created by the vendor, then the purchaser must satisfy himself that the charge has not crystallised. Generally, he will be satisfied by a letter to this effect from some officer of the company, or the company's solicitor, and a clear result on his company search.[40]

Where a company is being wound up, a floating charge created by it within *twelve* months of the commencement of the winding up is, unless it is proved that the company immediately after the creation of the charge was solvent, invalid, except to the amount of any cash paid to the company.[41]   Where a company is in a poor financial state there is a temptation, especially for directors, to keep the company afloat by themselves lending money to it secured by a floating charge on the company's assets. The above provision as to the avoidance of floating charges helps to discourage this. Only the floating charge is invalidated. Any covenant to repay the money is still valid, for what it is worth. Solvent means able to pay its debts as they fall due.[42]

Further, any charge (floating or fixed) created by a company within *six* months of winding up, which, if it had been created by an individual within six months of the presentation of a bankruptcy petition on which he is adjudged bankrupt, would be deemed in his bankruptcy a fraudulent preference, is, in the event of the company being wound up, deemed to be a fraudulent preference and invalid.[43]

The lender on floating charges must therefore always take the risk of the charge being avoided under one or other of the above provisions. The charge must be protected by registration.[44]

(x) Gifts

Gifts may also be set aside if made to defeat creditors.[45]   A

---

[38] See George, *Sale of Flats* (3rd ed.). If the recommendations of some recent reports result in legislation, the need for some of these schemes will disappear; see Report of the Committee on Positive Covenants Affecting Land (the Wilberforce Committee) Cmnd. 2719 of 1965; Law Commission Report on Restrictive Covenants, Law Com. No. 11, 1967; Law Commission Working Paper (No. 36) on appurtenant rights, see (1971) 121 New L.J. 705.
[39] For floating charges generally, see Gower, *Modern Company Law* (3rd ed.), pp. 420 *et seq*; *Re Barleycorn Enterprises Ltd.* [1970] Ch. 465.
[40] See *Emmet on Title* (15th ed.), p. 298.
[41] Companies Act 1948, s. 322.
[42] See *Re Patrick and Lyon Ltd.* [1933] Ch. 786; *Re Yeovil Glove Co. Ltd.* [1965] Ch. 148.
[43] Companies Act 1948, s. 320; and see *Peat* v. *Gresham Trust Ltd.* [1934] A.C. 252.
[44] See *post*, pp. 163, 330.
[45] See *post*, p. 148.

further point in relation to estate duty on gifts must be mentioned. If land is given by X to A who sells it to B, estate duty is payable on X's death within seven years of the gift.[46] Previously, B, having notice of the potential liability to pay duty, was not protected against a claim for duty, not being a bona fide purchaser for value without notice.[47] This was changed as a result of the Finance Act 1957, s. 38, which, in effect, treats the purchase-money received by A as the gifted property and imposes the charge to duty on the proceeds of sale. But only a *purchaser* from the original donee is so protected.[48]

(xi) Joint owners

After 1925, there cannot be a *legal* tenancy in common. Whether the beneficial interests are joint or in common the legal estate is held on trust for sale for the persons beneficially entitled.[49] Those beneficially entitled, or the first four of them named in the conveyance, will be the trustees, in the absence of independent trustees being appointed.

On the death of one of two joint tenants, the beneficial interest of the deceased passes to the survivor.[50] It should be noted that a beneficial joint tenancy cannot be severed by will.

If the legal and beneficial interests become vested in the same person, the legal and equitable estates merge, the trust for sale can no longer subsist, and the survivor can sell as beneficial owner. The Law of Property (Amendment) Act 1926 provided that nothing in the Law of Property Act 1925 affected the right of a survivor of joint tenants who is solely and beneficially interested to deal with his legal estate as if it were not held on trust.[51] However, the purchaser could not tell whether the survivor was solely and beneficially interested in the absence of evidence of non-severance. We have already mentioned the difficulty of proving a negative.[52] Severance might well have occurred without the survivor's knowledge. In practice, it was often more convenient to appoint another trustee merely for the purposes of the sale.[53] By the Law of Property (Joint Tenants) Act 1964 it was provided that, in favour of a purchaser of a legal estate, the survivor of two or more joint tenants is deemed to be solely and beneficially interested if he conveys as beneficial owner or if the conveyance includes a statement that he is so interested. This protection does not apply, however, if, at any time before the date of the conveyance by the survivor (a) a memorandum of severance, signed by the joint tenants,

---

[46] See *post*, p. 348.
[47] See Finance Act 1894, ss. 8 (18), 9 (1).
[48] See further *Emmet on Title* (15th ed.), p. 1187; *Manning* v. *Turner* [1957] 1 W.L.R. 91.
[49] Law of Property Act 1925, ss. 34, 36.
[50] Administration of Estates Act 1925, ss. 1 (1), 3 (4).
[51] s. 7, Sched., amending Law of Property Act 1925, s. 36 (2).
[52] See *ante*, p. 129.
[53] See *Emmet on Title* (15th ed.), pp. 334, 335.

or one of them, that the joint tenancy has been severed, has been indorsed on or annexed to the conveyance by virtue of which the legal estate was vested in the joint tenants; or (b) a receiving order in bankruptcy or petition therefor has been registered under the Land Charges Act.[54]   The Act is deemed to have come into force on January 1, 1926.[55]   It does not apply to registered land.[56]

(xii) Leaseholds

We have already considered most of the matters which the purchaser must keep in mind when buying leaseholds, *i.e.* the need for consent to any assignment,[57] whether or not there has been any breach of any of the covenants in the lease.[58]   Inquiries will have been made as to whether or not the lease has been forfeited or whether any event has happened which could cause forfeiture.[59]   The possibility of surrender must be considered.[60]

(xiii) Mortgagee

We shall in a subsequent chapter deal with the mortgagee's power of sale.[61]   All that a purchaser is concerned to see is that the power of sale has *arisen*, *i.e.* that the mortgage money is due.   In the classical form of mortgage where there is a covenant for repayment after six months, the power of sale will arise at the end of that period.   In the case of an instalment mortgage if no such period is specified, the power of sale arises if one instalment is in arrears.[62]

(xiv) Mortgages [63]

Most houses are now acquired with the assistance of an advance on mortgage,[64] and, accordingly, mortgages commonly appear on the title.   The purchaser must check that earlier mortgages have been properly discharged.   Vacating receipts should be checked to see that the repayment has been made by the person entitled to the equity, otherwise the receipt may operate as a transfer.[65]   As we shall see,[66] it often happens that the receipt cannot be executed until several days after a sale; but it should be dated not later than the date of the conveyance on the sale to prevent the receipt operating as a transfer.

[54] s. 1.
[55] s. 2.
[56] s. 3.
[57] *Ante*, p. 100.
[58] *Ante*, p. 100.
[59] For relief from forfeiture, see *post*, pp. 263–267.
[60] See *Usher Brewery Ltd.* v. *P. S. King and Co. (Finance) Ltd.* (1969) 113 S.J. 815; *London and County (A. and D.) Ltd.* v. *Wilfred Sportsmen Ltd.* [1971] Ch. 764.
[61] *Post*, p. 316.
[62] The mortgagee's powers are restricted in the case of controlled and regulated mortgages, *i.e.* certain mortgages affecting property subject to controlled or regulated tenancies; see Fisher and Lightwood's *Law of Mortgage* (8th ed.), pp. 234 *et seq.*; *Nichols* v. *Walters* [1954] 1 W.L.R. 1.
[63] For equitable mortgages, see *ante*, p. 140; for floating charges, see *ante*, p. 142.
[64] See *post*, p. 338.
[65] *Post*, p. 336.
[66] *Post*, p. 212.

Where the vendor has created a mortgage, the purchaser must insist either on this being discharged before completion, or on an undertaking to discharge being given.[66] In such circumstances, there will be no need for the mortgagee to join in the conveyance.

In some cases, the validity of a mortgage must be carefully considered, such as when it is by or to a company,[67] or to a money-lender.[68]

(xv) Personal representatives

On an intestacy, the property of the deceased devolves on the administrators and is held by them upon trust for sale.[69] If the deceased died testate, his property devolves on his executors and they have wide statutory powers of dealing with the property.[70] The object of conferring these powers is to enable the personal representatives to raise money, if necessary, for the purpose of paying death duties and debts of the deceased and the costs of the administration.

Before the Land Transfer Act 1897, on a sale of freeholds by executors, the purchaser was not bound to inquire whether any debts remained unpaid until twenty years had elapsed after the testator's death; but after that time a presumption would arise that the debts had been paid and the purchaser could not safely complete without satisfying himself that the sale was for a proper purpose.[71] This time limit does not apply to a sale by an executor or administrator since the Land Transfer Act 1897. Since 1925, even notice that all debts, administration expenses and other liabilities have actually been paid does not invalidate a sale of either freeholds or leaseholds made by a personal representative whether the testator died before 1926 or after 1925.[72]

As regards the devolution of property in the case of a person who dies after 1925, all real estate, including leaseholds, to which he was entitled for any interest not ceasing on his death, devolves on his death on his personal representatives, and they are deemed in law to be his heirs and assigns within the meaning of all trusts and powers[73]; and, further, the personal representatives of a sole or last surviving trustee may exercise any power or trust which was capable of being exercised by such sole or surviving trustee.[74]

When there are two or more personal representatives, the question arises whether their powers are joint and several, or joint only, i.e. whether one can act alone or they must all act together. The position

---

[66] Post, p. 301.
[67] Post, p. 304.
[68] Administration of Estates Act 1925, s. 33, and see ante, pp. 136–138.
[70] Ibid. s. 39.
[71] Re Tanqueray-Willaume and Landau (1882) 20 Ch.D. 465. This did not apply to a sale of leaseholds by executors: Re Venn and Furze's Contract [1894] 2 Ch. 101; cf. Re Verrell's Contract [1903] 1 Ch. 65.
[72] Administration of Estates Act 1925, s. 36 (8) (12).
[73] Administration of Estates Act 1925, ss. 1, 3.
[74] Trustee Act 1925, s. 18.

differs according to whether the death occurred before 1926 or after 1925, and may be summarised as follows:

Deaths occurring before 1926

(a) The personal representatives had *joint and several* power over (i) pure personalty; (ii) leaseholds; and (iii) freeholds of which the deceased was the last surviving trustee or mortgagee.[75]

(b) Over freeholds (other than those of which the deceased was last surviving trustee or mortgagee) the personal representatives had (and still have) *joint* power only, except by order of the court.[76] In transactions taking place before 1912, it was necessary for all the executors named in the will to join, whether they proved the will or not, except those who had expressly renounced[77]; but in transactions taking place after 1911 it is sufficient to join only those who have actually proved the will.[78]

Deaths occurring after 1925

(a) The personal representatives have *joint and several* power over pure personalty only.

(b) Over all other property, *viz.* leaseholds and freeholds (including freeholds of which the deceased was last surviving trustee or mortgagee), they have joint power only, except by order of the court,[79] *i.e.* it is necessary to join all the executors who have actually proved the will.

After the payment of debts and death duties, it is the duty of the personal representatives to vest the deceased's property in the persons entitled under the will or intestacy, as the case may be. We have already dealt with assents.[80]

(xvi) Restrictive covenants [81]

If the purchaser is buying for development, it will be necessary to consider carefully the validity and extent of any restrictive covenants affecting the property. A very important point to note is that many old covenants are not in fact effective. A restrictive covenant is enforceable by a successor in title of the original covenantee only if it touches and concerns the land and the benefit of the covenant has (a) been properly annexed to the land intended to be benefited,[82] or (b) been properly assigned,[83] or (c) there was a proper scheme of development. It is unlikely that a building scheme will be found much before the beginning of this century in the absence of clear evidence

---

[75] Conveyancing Act 1881, s. 30.
[76] Land Transfer Act 1897, s. 2 (2).
[77] *Re Pawley and London and Provincial Bank* [1900] 1 Ch. 58.
[78] Conveyancing Act 1911, s. 12; Administration of Estates Act 1925 ss. 2 (2), 8.
[79] Administration of Estates Act 1925, s. 2 (2).
[80] *Ante*, p. 136.
[81] See further, *post*, p. 236.
[82] See *Marten* v. *Flight Refuelling Ltd.* [1962] Ch. 115.
[83] See *Russell* v. *Archdale* [1964] Ch. 38; (1968) 84 L.Q.R. 22.

of selling off in lots, although a more lenient view now seems to be taken by the courts.[84]   An unbroken chain of assignments can generally be discounted (because an express assignment of the benefit of the covenant is usually overlooked) and often proper words of annexation were not used.   Accordingly, it is likely that many old covenants are unenforceable; and, in many cases, it will be possible to obtain indemnity insurance against breach of covenant on counsel's opinion on the probable unenforceability of the covenants.   Alternatively, the purchaser (or the vendor before the sale) could apply to the court under section 84 (2) of the Law of Property Act 1925 for a declaration that the covenants are not enforceable.   A further alternative is to apply to the Lands Tribunal under section 84 (1) of the Law of Property Act 1925 as amended by the Law of Property Act 1969, s. 28, for the discharge or modification of the covenants.   The 1969 amendments have greatly improved this last procedure, in particular because planning matters can now be taken into account; and there is no doubt that many more applications will be made under this provision than has been the case in the past.[85]

(xvii) Settled land

The matters to be considered on a purchaser's investigation of title of settled land are discussed in detail in a subsequent chapter.[86]

(xviii) Spouse's rights

Matrimonial property is also dealt with in a later chapter.[87] Difficulties sometimes arise where the conveyance is taken in the husband's sole name, but the wife has contributed to the purchase, for example, by way of deposit, or by assisting towards the mortgage repayments, or by way of improvement.[88]   In such circumstances the husband holds upon an implied trust for sale for his wife and himself in shares according to their respective contributions.   Technically, on a sale the husband should appoint another trustee to act with himself, so that the purchaser can pay the purchase-money to two trustees and get a good discharge.[89]   But according to the paper title, i.e. the title deeds, the husband appears as sole owner; and it is demanding too much of the conveyancer to have to inquire as to the state of the husband's matrimonial affairs or whether his wife has contributed to the property.[90]   Accordingly, unless the purchaser has notice of the

---

[84] See *Re Dolphin's Conveyance* [1970] 1 Ch. 654.
[85] See (1969) 32 M.L.R. 489; (1970) 214 *Estates Gazette* 738, 1163; [1970] J.P.L. 424; Preston and Newsom, *Restrictive Covenants* (5th ed.), pp. 179 *et seq.*
[86] See *post*, p. 362.
[87] See *post*, p. 243.
[88] See *Pettitt* v. *Pettitt* [1970] A.C. 777; *Gissing* v. *Gissing* [1971] A.C. 886; see Matrimonial Proceedings and Property Act 1970, s. 37.
[89] See *Waller* v. *Waller* [1967] 1 W.L.R. 451.
[90] *National Provincial Bank Ltd.* v. *Ainsworth* [1965] A.C. 1175; *Caunce* v. *Caunce* [1969] 1 W.L.R. 286.

spouse's rights, he will probably get a good title by a conveyance from the husband himself.[91]   Where the vendor is himself in possession or occupation of the property to be sold, the purchaser will not be affected with notice of the equitable interest of any person who might be resident there and whose presence is consistent with the title offered.[92]

(xix) Trustees for sale

Sale by trustees for sale is dealt with in a subsequent chapter.[93] We have already mentioned sale by joint owners.[94]

(xx) Voluntary conveyances

By section 172 of the Law of Property Act 1925 a conveyance made with intent to defraud creditors is *voidable* at the instance of any person thereby prejudiced.   A voluntary conveyance will be presumed to be made with intent to defeat creditors if its effect is to deprive the grantor of the means of paying his debts.[95]   But a purchaser for value within ten years, unless the parties claiming under the settlement can in good faith without notice of the intent to defraud is not affected.[96]

Again, a voluntary settlement (this includes a conveyance) is voidable [97] by the trustee in bankruptcy of the settlor, if the settlor becomes bankrupt within two years of the making of the settlement; or even prove that, at the time of making it, the settlor could have paid his debts without employing the property settled, and that his whole interest therein passed from him.   But, as in the last case, it will be noticed that the settlement could not be upset against a purchaser for value who had no notice of an available act of bankruptcy.[98]

It follows, therefore, from what has been said above, that an intending purchaser need have no fear if he finds a voluntary conveyance on the title, unless he has notice, in the one case, of an intention to defraud the creditors, or, in the other, of an available act of bankruptcy.

IV.   NOTICE AND SEARCHES

A. Notice

Generally [99]

The purchaser will generally be bound by all *legal* estates and interests affecting the property, whether he has notice of them or not, provided that if such estates or interests are registrable, they are

---

[91] See (1970) 34 Conv.(N.S.) 240.
[92] *Caunce* v. *Caunce, supra;* for registered land, see (1969) 33 Conv.(N.S.) 240.
[93] See *post,* p. 376.
[94] *Ante,* pp. 143, 144.
[95] *Freeman* v. *Pope* (1870) L.R. 5 Ch.App. 538.
[96] Law of Property Act 1925, s. 172 (3); and see *Pearce* v. *Bulteel* [1916] 2 Ch. 544.
[97] Bankruptcy Act 1914, s. 42; *Re Carter and Kenderdine's Contract* [1897] 1 Ch. 776.
[98] *Re Hart, ex p. Green* [1912] 3 K.B. 6.   For registration of a bankruptcy petition or receiving order under the Land Charges Act 1925, see *post,* p. 151.
[99] See Megarry and Wade, *The Law of Real Property* (3rd ed.), pp. 121 *et seq.*

registered.[1] With regard to equitable interests adverse to the vendor's title, the purchaser is not bound by them if he obtains a legal estate from the vendor without notice, actual or constructive, of such interests.[2] He is bound if he has notice,[3] provided that if such interests are registrable, they are registered. Under a voluntary conveyance, for example, a person taking as donee under a gift is bound by both legal and equitable interests whether he has notice or not.

Actual notice

A purchaser with actual or express notice of an equitable interest before completion will be bound by it, subject to the effect of non-registration if the interest is registrable and to the doctrine of over-reaching. As we shall see, registration constitutes actual notice; but if a registrable interest is not registered, the purchaser will take free from it even if he has express notice of it.

It should be remembered that there are some equitable interests and rights, for example, restrictive covenants created before 1926, which are neither overreached nor registrable.

Constructive notice

A purchaser has constructive notice of any instrument or matter or act or thing which would have come to his knowledge if he had investigated the vendor's title to the land for the full statutory title. It must be remembered that, if a purchaser buys under conditions limiting his right to investigate the title, he is held to have constructive notice of all equitable interests (such as restrictive covenants) which he would have discovered if he had inquired into the vendor's title for the period during which the title is required to be shown by the law under an open contract. For a purchaser cannot avoid the consequences of receiving actual or constructive notice of equitable incumbrances by contracting not to investigate the title.[4] He will not, however, have notice of matters appearing on the title further back than the period fixed by statute, unless he actually investigates such prior title.

The purchaser will also have constructive notice of the rights of tenants and other persons, if any, in occupation of the property; accordingly, he should inspect the property.[5] A purchaser or mortgagee does not have constructive notice of a wife's right by virtue of her

---

[1] There is another exception, where the person entitled to the prior legal estate is postponed because of fraud or estoppel; *e.g.* as regards mortgages, *Northern Counties of England Fire Insurance Co.* v. *Whipp* (1884) 26 Ch.D. 482.

[2] Subject, where he takes under an overreaching conveyance, to his paying the purchase-moneys in accordance with the statutory provisions: see Law of Property Act 1925, s. 27.

[3] But not if the predecessor in title took free of the equitable interest: *Wilkes* v. *Spooner* [1911] 2 K.B. 473.

[4] *Re Cox and Neve's Contract* [1891] 2 Ch. 109; *Re Nisbet and Pott's Contract* [1906] 1 Ch. 386.

[5] *Post*, p. 186.

contribution to the purchase-price where her presence in the property is consistent with the title offered by her husband.[6]

Imputed notice

Notice to the purchaser's solicitor or other agent, *in the course of the transaction during which the agent was employed by the purchaser,* is notice to the purchaser.[7] In such a case, the purchaser is said to have imputed notice.

Registration as notice

Section 198 of the Law of Property Act 1925 provides that the registration of any instrument or matter under the provisions of the Land Charges Act 1925 shall be deemed to constitute actual notice of such instrument or matter.[8] Section 199 provides that a purchaser shall not be prejudicially affected by notice of any instrument or matter capable of registration under the Land Charges Act 1925 which is void or not enforceable as against him under that Act by reason of the non-registration thereof.[9]

B. Searches Generally

Searches to be Made

Before completion, the purchaser's solicitors must search in certain registers to discover the rights, if any, of third parties which are enforceable against the land. This is particularly important in the case of the land charges register. We have already seen that a search is often made to verify that the title has not been registered.[10] In this section we shall deal with (1) searches in the Land Charges Department of the Land Registry in London, (2) Yorkshire Deeds Registries searches and (3) company searches. We shall treat registered land separately.

(1) The Land Charges Department of the Land Registry in London

At this department, five registers are kept by the Registrar, namely:
    (i) a register of pending actions;
    (ii) a register of annuities;
    (iii) a register of writs and orders affecting land;
    (iv) a register of deeds of arrangement;
    (v) a register of land charges.

The search in each of these registers will be made against *the name* of the vendor (and sometimes some of his predecessors in title),[11] and cannot be made against the property in question. We shall now examine shortly the matters with which each of these registers is concerned.

---

[6] *Caunce* v. *Caunce* [1969] 1 W.L.R. 286.
[7] Law of Property Act 1925, ss. 199, 200. And see *Bailey* v. *Barnes* [1894] 1 Ch. 25; *Thorne* v. *Heard and Marsh* [1895] A.C. 495; *Jared* v. *Clements* [1903] 1 Ch. 428.
[8] For the Law of Property Act 1969, s. 24, see *ante,* p. 44; s. 25 (2), *post,* p. 160.
[9] See further, *post,* pp. 151 *et seq.*
[10] *Ante,* p. 44.
[11] See *post,* p. 160. Note, if the land is registered, no search is required.

(1) *The Register of pending actions*

A pending action (*lis pendens*) is any action, information or proceedings pending in court (including a petition in bankruptcy filed after 1925) relating to land (including leaseholds) or any interest in or charge on land.[12] A pending action must be re-registered every five years. If it is not registered, it will not bind a purchaser [13] of the land, unless he has *express notice* of it.[14] An unregistered bankruptcy petition, however, is binding against everyone except a bona fide purchaser for money or money's worth without notice of an available act of bankruptcy.[15]

If the issue in the action does not affect the title, the purchaser cannot generally refuse to complete.[16]

(2) *The Register of annuities*

Annuities found in this register are annuities (including rentcharges) for a life or lives or for a term of years or for any greater estate determinable on a life or lives which were created before 1926 (other than by a marriage settlement or a will), and were registered in this register before 1926. If not registered, such annuities will be void against a creditor or a purchaser [18] of any interest in the land charged therewith. If such annuities were created before 1926, but were not registered before 1926, they must be registered, after 1925, under Class E of the register of land charges and not in the register of annuities [17]; and if created after 1925, they must be registered in Class C of the register of land charges as " general equitable charges." [18] As no new annuities can be registered in the register of annuities, it will be seen that this register must eventually become extinct.[19]

(3) *The Register of writs and orders affecting land*

Writs and orders affecting land comprise (a) writs or orders affecting land issued or made by any court for the purpose of enforcing a judgment, statute or recognisance [20]; (b) any order appointing a receiver or sequestrator of land; and (c) any receiving order made in bankruptcy after 1925, whether it is known to affect the land or not.

---

[12] This does not include a share in the proceeds of sale of land: *Taylor* v. *Taylor* [1968] 1 W.L.R. 378; and see *Heywood* v. *B.D.C. Properties (No. 2)* [1964] 1 W.L.R. 267; [1964] 1 W.L.R. 971; but *cf. National Westminster Bank Ltd.* v. *Allen* [1971] 2 Q.B. 718.

[13] A " purchaser " means " any person (including a mortgagee or lessee) who, for valuable consideration, takes any interest in land or in a charge on land ": Land Charges Act 1925, s. 20 (8). See also the Land Charges Bill (1972).

[14] Land Charges Act 1925, s. 2; Land Charges Rules 1925, r. 1.

[15] Land Charges Act 1925, s. 3.

[16] *Bull* v. *Hutchens* (1863) 32 Beav. 615.

[17] See *post*, p. 156.

[18] See *post*, p. 153.

[19] See Land Charges Act 1925, s. 4.

[20] For charging orders under the Administration of Justice Act 1956, s. 35, see *Irani Finance Ltd.* v. *Singh* [1970] Ch. 59; *National Westminster Bank Ltd.* v. *Allen* [1971] 2 Q.B. 718; *ante*, p. 17.

The writ or order must be re-registered every five years, and if not registered will be void as against a purchaser [21] of the land. An unregistered receiving order in bankruptcy, however, is binding against everyone except a bona fide purchaser for money or money's worth without notice of an available act of bankruptcy.[22]

(4) *The Register of deeds of arrangement*

A deed of arrangement is a document, under hand or under seal, whereby a debtor compounds with his creditors or agrees to transfer property to trustees for the benefit of his creditors, and thereby becomes released from his obligations.[23] A deed of arrangement affecting land must be registered and re-registered every five years, and if not registered is void against a purchaser [21] of land which is comprised in or affected by the deed.

(5) *The Register of land charges* [24]

Land charges, as defined by section 10 of the Land Charges Act 1925,[24] are of six classes: A, B, C, D, E and F. We will deal with each in turn.

Class A land charges. Here will be registered statutory charges upon land made *pursuant to the application of some person.* These are rents, annuities, or principal moneys, the right to which arises by reason of an Act of Parliament, but which do not become a charge on the land until the necessary order has been made by the court. An example is the charge for compensation payable by a landlord to a tenant of an agricultural holding.[25] These Class A charges were first made registrable by the Land Charges Registration and Searches Act 1888 and are void against a purchaser [21] of land charged therewith or of any interest therein, unless they are registered before the completion of the purchase. A Class A charge does not, however, require registration if it was created before January 1, 1889, unless the charge has been transferred on or after January 1, 1889, and at least one year has elapsed since the date of such transfer.[26]

Class B land charges. These are, again, statutory charges similar to those registrable under Class A, but they arise *otherwise than pursuant to the application of any person*; this means that the Act of Parliament itself imposes them.

These charges do not include *local land charges*,[27] which are

---

21 For the meaning of " purchaser," see note 13, *ante,* p. 151.
22 Land Charges Act 1925, ss. 3, 6 and 7.
23 See Deeds of Arrangement Act 1914.
24 This legislation will shortly be consolidated by the Land Charges Bill (1972).
25 Agricultural Holdings Act 1948, ss. 72–74, 82. For further examples, see *Emmet on Title* (15th ed.), pp. 582, 583.
26 Land Charges Act 1925, ss. 13 and 14.
27 See *ante,* p. 39.

registrable in the registries kept by the local authorities and not in the Land Charges Department of the Land Registry. This exception is of importance because the majority of charges which arise under an Act of Parliament are local land charges. Class B charges were first made registrable by the Land Charges Act 1925 and are void against a purchaser [21] of the land charged therewith or of any interest therein, unless they are registered before the completion of the purchase. A Class B charge does not, however, require registration if it was created before January 1, 1926, unless the charge has been transferred on or after January 1, 1926, and at least one year has elapsed since the date of such transfer. [26]

A land charge of Class A (other than certain land improvement charges registered on or after January 1, 1970), [28] or of Class B, for securing money, when registered, takes effect as if it had been created by way of legal mortgage, but without prejudice to the priority of the charge. [29]

Class C land charges. This is the most important class of land charges, and comprises the following matters, none of which was registrable before 1926:

(i) PUISNE MORTGAGES. A puisne mortgage is any *legal* mortgage which is not protected by a deposit of documents relating to the legal estate affected. [30] This means that the mortgagee in question has not been given possession of the title deeds, generally because they have already been deposited with a prior mortgagee.

(ii) LIMITED OWNER'S CHARGES. A limited owner's charge is an equitable charge on settled property which arises by statute in favour of the tenant for life of such property if he has discharged some liability out of income which should have been discharged out of capital. For example, if the tenant for life pays estate duty out of his own pocket which should have been paid out of capital, he will have a charge under the Finance Act 1894, [31] on the settled property for the amount he has expended.

(iii) GENERAL EQUITABLE CHARGES. A general equitable charge is an equitable charge which is not secured by a deposit of documents relating to the legal estate affected, and is not included in any other class of land charge. [32] These comprise such charges as *equitable* mortgages on

[28] Land Charges Act 1925, s. 11A, added by the Law of Property Act 1969, s. 27.
[29] Land Charges Act 1925, s. 11.
[30] There may be several mortgages protected by deposit. Not all the documents need to be deposited to take the mortgage out of the class of puisne mortgages.
[31] See s. 9 (6).
[32] A charge on deposit and purchase-moneys is not a general equitable charge: *Georgiades* v. *Edward Wolfe and Co. Ltd.* [1965] Ch. 487; and see *Thomas* v. *Rose* [1968] 1 W.L.R. 1797.

the legal estate not protected by deposit of title deeds; the lien of a
vendor who has parted with the deeds to the purchaser; and an equitable
rentcharge. Annuities created after 1925 are also registrable in this
class.[33] The Land Charges Act 1925, however, expressly excludes from
registration charges arising, or affecting an interest arising, under a trust
for sale [34] or a settlement, for example, a mortgage by a tenant for life
of his *equitable life interest*. Such charges are protected by the giving
of written notice to the trustees of the settlement.[35]

(iv) ESTATE CONTRACTS. An estate contract is any contract by an
estate owner to convey or create a legal estate, including an option to
purchase or a right of pre-emption. Examples are: a contract for the
sale of land; a contract to grant or assign a lease; and a contract for a
mortgage.[36] This does not mean that, in order to be valid, every
contract between a vendor and purchaser must be registered.[37] The
vendor and purchaser are bound by the contract whether it is registered
or not; the object of registration is to protect the purchaser's rights
under the contract against other purchasers who may acquire a legal
estate from the vendor before completion of the purchase. It should
also be noticed that to be an " estate contract " it is not necessary that
the contract should be one to confer or create a legal estate in favour
of any particular person or persons. If, for example, there is a binding
contract between A and B under which A has the right to direct that a
defined part of B's land shall be sold to any person that A may name,
the contract is an estate contract and should be registered.[38] But a
contract dealing with property which is not identified or capable of
identification is never an estate contract.[38]

Any Class C land charge is void against a purchaser [39] of the land
charged or of any interest therein, unless it is registered before completion of the purchase. Class C land charges created before 1926 do
not require registration unless they have been transferred on or after
January 1, 1926, and at least one year has elapsed since the date of
such transfer. A puisne mortgage created before 1926 *may*, however, be
registered even *before* it is transferred. But it need not be; and if not
registered will be binding on purchasers who have notice of it, and,
possibly, also on those who have no notice if it was a legal mortgage

---

33 As to other annuities, see *ante*, p. 151 and *post*, p. 156.
34 See *Re Rayleigh Weir Stadium* [1954] 1 W.L.R. 786; *Taylor* v. *Taylor* [1968] 1
W.L.R. 378.
35 See Law of Property Act 1925, s. 137.
36 And see *Shiloh Spinners Ltd.* v. *Harding* [1972] Ch. 326 (rights of re-entry on
breach of covenant).
37 See *ante*, p. 26. A notice to treat (see *ante*, p. 117) is not registrable as an estate
contract until the price has been determined: *Capital Investments Ltd.* v. *Wednesfield
U.D.C.* [1965] Ch. 774.
38 *Turley* v. *Mackay* [1944] Ch. 37; and see *Sharp* v. *Coates* [1949] 1 K.B. 285;
Thomas v. *Rose* [1968] 1 W.L.R. 1797.
39 For the meaning of the word " purchaser," see note 13, *ante*, p. 151, and note
that as regards estate contracts " purchaser " here does not include a person who is
within the marriage consideration: see Land Charges Act 1925, s. 13 (2).

before 1926; the only object of registration would be automatically to affect purchasers with actual notice.[40]

A land charge created by a company registered under the Companies Act 1948 will be registered in the companies file in London [41]; and if such a charge was made before January 1, 1970, *for securing money* [42] further registration in the Land Charges Department of the Land Registry was unnecessary.[43] It followed that a purchaser buying from a company had to make this additional search in the Companies Register. The Law of Property Act 1969, s. 26, provides that charges of unregistered land (other than floating charges) created on or after January 1, 1970, and which are capable of registration as land charges must be registered under the Land Charges Act 1925 (as well as under the Companies Act).

Class D land charges. This class, like Class C, comprises charges which were not registrable before 1926.

(i) CHARGES FOR DEATH DUTIES. Here, the Inland Revenue Commissioners may register a charge against land for death duties in respect of a death which occurs after 1925—a privilege which, in practice, the Commissioners do not utilise.[44] If the charge is not registered, it is void against a purchaser of a legal estate in the land *for money or money's worth*.[45] No charge can be registered in respect of a death which occurred before 1926.

(ii) RESTRICTIVE COVENANTS. Restrictive covenants registrable in this class are covenants and agreements restrictive of the user of land entered into *after 1925*. Restrictive covenants entered into between lessor and lessee are *not* registrable here or elsewhere,[46] and it is therefore with covenants affecting the freehold interest that this provision is concerned. If a registrable restrictive covenant is not registered, it is void against a further purchaser of a legal estate in the land *for money or money's worth*.[47] The original covenantor is bound by the covenant whether it is registered or not. The object of the registration is to bind persons who thereafter acquire legal estates in the land from the covenantor. As in the case of death duties, restrictive covenants entered into before 1926 *cannot* be registered; and therefore a purchaser of the land takes subject to them, as he would have done before 1926, unless he is a bona fide purchaser for value of a legal estate without notice, actual or constructive.[48]

---

[40] See Land Charges Act 1925, s. 14 (2).
[41] Now removed from Bush House to City Road, E.C.1.
[42] *i.e.* a puisne mortgage or general equitable charge.
[43] Land Charges Act 1925, s. 10 (5); Companies Act 1948, s. 95.
[44] See *ante*, p. 141. For potential future liability for duty, see *ante*, p. 143.
[45] Land Charges Act 1925, s. 13 (2); Law of Property Act 1925, s. 17 (1).
[46] See *Dartstone* v. *Cleveland Petroleum Co.* [1969] 1 W.L.R. 1807.
[47] Land Charges Act 1925, s. 13 (2).
[48] Law of Property Act 1925, s. 2 (5).

(iii) EQUITABLE EASEMENTS. An equitable easement includes " any easement, right or privilege over or affecting land, being merely an equitable interest." [49] Examples are an easement informally granted under hand, and an easement for an estate other than equivalent to a fee simple absolute in possession or a term of years absolute. Equitable easements, like restrictive covenants, are registrable only if *created after 1925*, and if not registered they will be void against a purchaser of a legal estate *for money or money's worth*. If created before 1926, they will without registration bind all persons who acquire any interest in the land, except a bona fide purchaser for value of a legal estate without notice of them, actual or constructive.

Class E land charges. Under this class are annuities (as defined on p. 151, *ante*) which were *created before 1926*, but were not registered until after 1925; and, if not registered, they will not bind creditors or purchasers of any interest in the land charged therewith. It will be remembered that annuities created after 1925 are registrable as general equitable charges, and therefore no *new* annuities can be registered here. It follows that this class will in time become extinct.[50]

Class F land charges. This class comprises charges affecting land by virtue of the Matrimonial Homes Act 1967.[51] Where, at any time during the subsistence of the marriage, one spouse is entitled to occupy a dwelling-house by virtue of an estate or interest, then the other spouse's rights of occupation (*i.e.* if in occupation, a right not to be evicted, or if not in occupation, a right with the leave of the court to enter into and occupy the house [52]) are a charge on that estate or interest. Such charge has the same priority as if it were an equitable interest created at whichever is the latest of (1) the date when the estate or interest was acquired, (2) the date of the marriage and (3) the commencement of the Act, *i.e.* January 1, 1968.[53] A land charge of Class F is void against a purchaser of the land charged therewith or of any interest in such land, unless registered before completion of the purchase.[54] In the case of registered land the charge must be protected by notice or caution.[55]

The Act does not apply to a dwelling-house which has at no time

---

49 See *E. R. Ives Investments Ltd.* v. *High* [1967] 2 Q.B. 379; *Poster* v. *Slough Estates Ltd.* [1969] 1 Ch. 495; *Shiloh Spinners Ltd.* v. *Harding, supra.*
50 Land Charges Act 1925, ss. 4 (1), 5; and see *ante*, pp. 151 and 153.
51 See (1968) 32 Conv.(N.S.) 85; (1968) 31 M.L.R. 305.
52 Matrimonial Homes Act 1967, s. 1 (1); see also Land Charges (Matrimonial Homes) Rules 1967.
53 Matrimonial Homes Act 1967, s. 2. But if the spouse is not in occupation the rights of occupation do not arise at all unless a court order is made : see *Rutherford* v. *Rutherford* [1970] 1 W.L.R. 1479; (1971) 121 New L.J. 7. For the priority of an existing mortgagee when a Class F charge is registered, see Matrimonial Homes Act 1967, s. 2 (8).
54 Land Charges Act 1925, s. 13 (3), added by Matrimonial Homes Act 1967, Sched.
55 Matrimonial Homes Act 1967, s. 2 (7). See *post*, p. 180.

been the spouses' matrimonial home.[56] No registration is possible where a spouse is a co-owner of the legal estate, but it is provided that a wife[57] who has a mere equitable interest is not entitled to occupy the matrimonial home by virtue of that interest and accordingly she is not precluded from having rights of occupation under the Act.[58] Where a spouse is entitled by virtue of the Act to a charge on the estate or interest of the other spouse in each of *two or more* dwelling-houses, only one of the charges can be registered at any one time.[59]

The Act has caused some discussion as to the solicitor's duty in respect of advising registration.[60] The safest course is to advise registration as soon as the property is acquired. But, at this stage, when the parties cannot foresee matrimonial trouble, they may not be willing to follow this advice. In any event, registration should be effected as soon as the matrimonial troubles reach a stage where the property might be sold.[61]

A spouse who is not in occupation of the matrimonial home, and who is not entitled to be in occupation by virtue of an estate or interest, must obtain the leave of the court under the Act in order to acquire a right of occupation before registering a Class F land charge.[62]

A spouse's rights of occupation are lost if the other spouse loses his rights to occupy the property, for example, if an order for possession has been made against him.[63]

A spouse entitled to rights of occupation may make payments under a mortgage made by the other spouse, and such payments shall be as good as if made by the other spouse.[64]

Provision is made for the cancellation of registration on evidence of the death of either spouse,[65] or the termination of the marriage.[66]

A spouse entitled to rights of occupation may release her rights by writing, or agree in writing to postpone the priority of her charge.[67] This may happen, for example, if it is desired to raise a mortgage on the property, for clearly a mortgagee aware of the spouse's rights will insist on having priority.

[56] *Ibid.* s. 1 (8). See s. 1 (7) for the meaning of dwelling-house.
[57] Of course, it could also be a husband.
[58] *Ibid.* s. 1 (9), added by Matrimonial Proceedings and Property Act 1970, s. 38. This covers the case where the wife has a beneficial interest by virtue, *e.g.* of contributions to the purchase-price or to improvements (*ante*, p. 147). It does not apply where the wife is joint owner of the legal estate.
[59] *Ibid.* s. 3.
[60] See *e.g.* (1967) 111 S.J. 818, 819; (1968) 65 L.S.Gaz. 3.
[61] See *Miles* v. *Bull* [1969] 1 Q.B. 258; (No. 2) [1969] 3 All E.R. 1585.
[62] *Rutherford* v. *Rutherford, supra.*
[63] *Penn* v. *Dunn* [1970] 2 Q.B. 686.
[64] s. 1 (5).
[65] Unless there has been an order under s. 2 (2) continuing the charge beyond the death of the entitled spouse.
[66] ss. 2 (7), 6 (1), (3).
[67] s. 6 (2).

Where a contract is made for the sale of a house, or the grant of a lease thereof, the rights of occupation shall be deemed to have been released on the delivery to the purchaser or the lessee on completion of an application by the spouse entitled to the charge for cancellation of the registration of the charge, or the lodging of such an application at the Land Registry, whichever first occurs.[68]

Registration of land charges

Before considering searches for land charges, it is convenient to deal with the mode of registration of a land charge. Application for registration is made to the Land Charges Department of the Land Registry, which is situated at Kidbrooke in London, on the prescribed form [69] and with the appropriate fee. The applicant must specify on the form details of the estate owner, the register in which the charge is to be registered and short particulars of the instrument creating the charge. The function of the registrar is purely ministerial, and no investigation is made as to the validity of the application.[70] We have already mentioned the use of tactical registrations in the case of estate contracts.[71] Accuracy in the preparation of the form, particularly in the names of the estate owner, is important, and when (as will shortly happen) the alphabetical index is computerised, absolute accuracy about names in registering and searching will be essential.[72]

Exclusion of certain charges from Land Charges Act 1925

It is no longer necessary to register a land charge created by a conveyance of the land affected by the land charge where the conveyance leads to first registration of title.[73]

Method of search

A personal search may be made, or an application may be made for an official search.[74] An official search is essential for full protection for the purchaser. Where a purchaser has obtained an official certificate of the result of the search, any entry which is made in the register after the date of the certificate and before completion of the purchase, and is not made pursuant to a priority notice [75] entered on the register before the certificate is issued, does not affect the purchaser if the purchase is completed before the end of the fifteenth working day after the date of the certificate.[76] For this reason an official

---

[68] s. 4.
[69] L.C. 4 (or L.C. 19 for Class F land charges) obtainable from law stationers.
[70] See Land Charges Act 1925, s. 1 (6).
[71] See *ante*, p. 27.
[72] See (1969) 32 M.L.R. 123, note 22; (1971) 35 Conv.(N.S.) 155. And see *Oak Co-operative Building Society* v. *Blackburn, post*, p. 159.
[73] Land Registration and Land Charges Act 1971, s. 9.
[74] Land Charges Act 1925, ss. 16, 17.
[75] For priority notices, see *post*, p. 160.
[76] Law of Property (Amendment) Act 1926, s. 4 (2); Land Charges Rules 1972.

search is requisitioned by the purchaser immediately prior to completion. As a matter of convenience the certificate of the result of the search is stamped with the date when this priority ends.

Application for an official search is made on the prescribed form.[77] It is absolutely essential to enter the names against which search is to be made, and the proper description of the land,[78] correctly in the application form. In favour of a purchaser (this includes a lessee or mortgagee[79]) or intending purchaser, an official certificate of search is conclusive, affirmatively or negatively, as the case may be, as against persons interested under such registrable matters or documents.[80] But this protection only applies if the application for the search is made in the correct name. In *Oak Co-operative Building Society* v. *Blackburn*[81] one FRANCIS DAVID BLACKBURN was the owner of 34, Union Street, Southport. He carried on business as an estate agent under the name of Frank D. Blackburn or Frank David Blackburn or Frank Blackburn. He contracted to sell the property to Phyllis Cairns under some sort of instalment sale.[82] This agreement was subsequently registered as an estate contract against FRANK DAVID BLACKBURN. Mr. Blackburn applied to the building society for a mortgage. The building society applied for an official search against the name FRANCIS DAVIS BLACKBURN, giving the proper description of the property. The search was clear but the certificate of search bore the note " No subsisting entries clearly affecting but the following entries which may or may not relate thereto appear." Then followed the name " Blackburn, Francis David " and the address " 26, Crescent Road, Southport " and details of an earlier mortgage. The society made an advance. Mr. Blackburn defaulted and the society sought possession. Phyllis Cairns claimed that the society was bound by her estate contract. At first instance Ungoed-Thomas J. held that she was not protected by registration because it was not in the name of the estate owner. The Court of Appeal unanimously reversed this decision, deciding that registration in what may fairly be described as a version of the full names of the vendor is effective against someone who fails to search at all and also against someone who searches against the wrong name, as the society did in that case. If the search had been made against the correct name, the society would have taken free from the entry of the estate contract, a clear search being conclusive. Where, as here, the *entry* had been made against the wrong name and the *search* had been against the wrong name, the question was: which party was to suffer the loss? In the circumstances, since Mr. Blackburn ordinarily passed under the name " Frank " or " Frank David,"

[77] Form L.C. 11. This should be obtained by the student.
[78] See *Du Sautoy* v. *Symes* [1967] Ch. 1146.
[79] Land Charges Act 1925, s. 20 (8).
[80] *Ibid*. s. 17 (3).
[81] [1968] Ch. 730.
[82] For instalment sales, see *post*, p. 196.

and the building society had not searched against the correct name, it was decided that the registration of the estate contract was not a nullity against the society. Accordingly, the building society was deemed to have had actual notice of the estate contract by virtue of section 198 of the Law of Property Act 1925.[83] It may be noted that the Court of Appeal criticised personal searches as foolish and folly.[84] We have already seen [85] that only an official certificate is conclusive.

This difficulty about names does not arise in registered conveyancing, because the charges are protected by entry on the register.[86]

The search should be made against the vendor and any persons claiming under him. The abstract will generally disclose earlier searches,[87] in which case the search against the vendor will be the only one to be made. But if searches have not been made previously, the purchaser should search. The Law of Property Act 1969, s. 25, gives a right to compensation out of public funds to a purchaser who suffers loss because of the existence of a registered land charge of which he had no actual knowledge,[88] and which he could not have discovered when he bought, i.e. because it was registered against someone who was the estate owner before the root of title, assuming the root to be a good root at least fifteen years old.

On receipt of the application, the staff of the Department will duly make the necessary searches and issue the certificate of the search.[89]

Priority notice

Any person intending to make an application for the registration of a land charge may give priority notice at least fifteen working days before the registration is to take effect. The notice is entered in the register to which the intended application when made will relate and then, if the charge itself is registered within thirty working days after the notice was given, the registration will take effect from the moment of the creation of the charge. In reckoning the number of days under this section, Sunday and other days when the Registry is not open to the public are to be excluded.[90]

For example, let us take the case of a conveyance which imposes a restrictive covenant upon the purchaser. The vendor will register the priority notice at least fifteen days before completion, and then, within thirty working days after the date of the notice (not the date of completion), he will register the restrictive covenant as a land charge.

---

[83] The decision has been criticised: see (1968) 31 M.L.R. 705; (1968) 112 S.J. 450.
[84] [1968] Ch. 730, 743, 744.
[85] Ante, p. 159.
[86] See further (1969) 32 M.L.R. 121, 124. For protection of contracts for the sale of registered land, see ante, p. 27.
[87] See Emmet on Title (15th ed.), p. 144.
[88] For the purposes of this provision the question whether any person had actual knowledge is to be determined without regard to s. 198 of the Law of Property Act 1925: Law of Property Act 1969, s. 25 (2). See post, p. 161.
[89] Arrangements can be made for the results to be telephoned, etc.
[90] Law of Property (Amendment) Act 1926, s. 4, as amended by the Land Charges Rules 1972; and note the consolidating Land Charges Bill (1972).

Before such registration, we will imagine that the purchaser has mortgaged the land. The mortgagee will be bound by the restrictive covenant even though at the time of the mortgage it was not registered, because, a priority notice having been given, the registration dates back to the date of the creation of the charge, *i.e.* the date of completion.

Criticism of the system of registration of land charges

These criticisms will be familiar from the study of real property.[91] The register is a *names* register. The purchaser may not know the names of all the estate owners since 1926. The further away one gets from 1926, the greater the risk becomes. The reduction by the Law of Property Act 1969 of the statutory length of title [92] increased the risk that a purchaser will be bound by a land charge registered against the name of an estate owner whose identity is concealed behind the root of title.[93] The provisions for compensation for undisclosed land charges in section 25 of the Law of Property Act 1969 [94] help the purchaser to some extent. These provisions apply to certain transactions completed after January 1, 1970, namely: a sale or exchange; a mortgage; a grant of a sub-lease for a term of years derived out of a *leasehold* interest; any compulsory purchase; and a conveyance under the Leasehold Reform Act 1967.[95] The right to compensation does not apply to a grant of a term of years out of the *freehold*, or a mortgage of such a term by the lessee. The charge must have been registered against the name of an owner of an estate in the land who was not (as owner of any such estate) a party to any transaction, or concerned in any event, comprised in the relevant title [96] and the purchaser must have had no actual knowledge of the charge.[97] On the question whether the purchaser had actual knowledge, registration is irrelevant.[98] But the purchaser must have carried out the usual searches for whichever is the longer of (a) a period starting with a good root of title at least fifteen years old or (b) the period for which he stipulated.[99] The compensation is payable by the Chief Land Registrar after an action therefor in the High Court.[1] The Chief Land Registrar can make rules to provide, *inter alia*, for the making of appropriate registrations after a claim has been made to ensure that the undisclosed charge is disclosed in future searches.[2] Where compensation has been

[91] See *e.g.* Megarry and Wade, p. 1037; Law Commission Report on Land Charges Affecting Unregistered Land (Law Com. No. 18), 1969.
[92] See *ante,* p. 60.
[93] See (1966) 110 S.J. 179, 201.
[94] And see *ante,* p. 160.
[95] s. 25 (9).
[96] The intention is that compensation should be paid if the land charge is registered against a name which would not appear on a normal investigation of the title as a party to the transaction.
[97] s. 25 (1) (*b*) (*c*).
[98] s. 25 (2).
[99] s. 25 (10).
[1] s. 25 (6).
[2] s. 25 (7); Land Charges Rules 1970.

paid in a case where the purchaser would have had knowledge of the charge but for the fraud of any person, the Chief Land Registrar may recover the amount paid from that person.[3]

(2) The Yorkshire Deeds Registries [4]

If the land agreed to be sold is situated in Yorkshire, a search in the appropriate deeds registry may still be necessary. The Yorkshire Deeds Registries were established by the Yorkshire Registries Act 1884. There were three registries, one for the North Riding at Northallerton, one for the East Riding (including Kingston-upon-Hull) at Beverley, and one for the West Riding at Wakefield. The City of York was not subject to the Act. The Law of Property Act 1925, s. 11, provided that after 1925 it was only necessary to register an instrument operating to transfer a legal estate and a charge by way of legal mortgage. Priority was governed by the date of registration, not according to the dates of the deeds.[5] Registration constituted actual notice to all persons and for all purposes.[6] A purchaser was bound by all assurances which required registration, provided they were registered before completion of the purchase, but not otherwise. The search was made against the last purchaser for value and all persons claiming under him.

In addition to the deeds registry, the appropriate Registry maintained a land charges register. Puisne mortgages, general equitable charges, restrictive covenants, equitable easements, and estate contracts, had to be registered in the appropriate Yorkshire Registry; and such registration rendered registration at the Land Charges Department of the Land Registry unnecessary.[7]

The Law of Property Act 1969, s. 16, provided for the gradual closing down of the Yorkshire Deeds Registries as compulsory registration of title was applied to any part of the district of each registry. Registration of title became compulsory in Teesside in the North Riding on September 1, 1970; and in Leeds and Sheffield in the West Riding from October 1, 1970.[8] Accordingly, the North Riding Deeds Registry and the West Riding Deeds Registry began to close on those dates respectively. Thereafter no registrations in those registries of deeds or land charges were permitted. The registries were to remain open for two years for the purposes of the registration of instruments made before the relevant dates, for searches, and for the provision of copies and extracts of deeds registered. Land charges which would

---

[3] s. 25 (8). On these provisions generally, see (1969) 32 M.L.R. 483–485.
[4] Formerly, if land was situated in Middlesex, search in the Middlesex Deeds Register was necessary, but that register was closed for all purposes by the Middlesex Deeds Act 1940. For the historical background to the deeds registries, see Glasgow, *A Modern View of Conveyancing* (1969), Chap. 8.
[5] Yorkshire Registries Act 1884, s. 14.
[6] Law of Property Act 1925, s. 197.
[7] Land Charges Act 1925, s. 10 (6).
[8] Registration of Title (Teesside, Leeds and Sheffield) Order 1970.

previously have been registered in those registries became registrable in London. Provision is made by section 17 of the 1969 Act for registration of puisne mortgages registered in Yorkshire in a deeds registry in London as land charges. Section 121 of the Law of Property Act 1969 provides for indemnity to persons suffering loss from the closure of the deeds registries.

These searches are not required where the land is registered.

(3) The Companies Registry

Where the vendor is a company, the purchaser will need to search the file of the company at the Companies Registry in London,[9] for any specific charges affecting the land created before January 1, 1970, and for floating charges. Before the Law of Property Act 1969, registration in the Companies Registry was in lieu of registration under the Land Charges Act 1925.[10] Section 26 of the 1969 Act provides that charges of unregistered land (other than floating charges) capable of being registered as land charges created on or after January 1, 1970, must be registered at the Land Charges Department at Kidbrooke as well as under the Companies Act.

There is no machinery in relation to the Companies Register similar to official searches for land charges, and, therefore, the search must be made as late as possible before completion. It is usual to employ a firm of law agents specialising in this work to make the search. They will usually also report as to whether or not there has been a resolution by the company for winding up, a petition or order for winding up, the appointment of a receiver, whether or not the company has been struck off the register, and whether or not any floating charges have crystallised.[11] This search is not necessary when the land is registered.[12]

(4) Land Registry

We have seen [13] that a search is sometimes made to verify that the land has not been registered.

V. REGISTERED LAND

(1) Introductory

Land registration generally [14]

Attempts have been made from time to time to facilitate the transfer of land by a system of registration of title, *i.e.* to secure a public record of ownership of land and to enable the person whose name appears on

9 Now removed from Bush House, Strand, to City Road, E.C.1. For a note on the working of the Registry, see (1971) 115 S.J. 3.
10 Land Charges Act 1925, s. 10 (5).
11 See *ante*, p. 142.
12 Land Registration Act 1925, s. 60 (1). See *post*, pp. 298–300.
13 *Ante*, p. 44.
14 See Rouff and Roper, *Registered Conveyancing* (3rd ed.); Law Commission Working Papers Nos. 32 and 37; (1972) 88 L.Q.R. 93.

the register as proprietor to deal with the land as readily and cheaply
as he can deal with his stocks and shares. The first Land Transfer Act
was passed in 1875, but because under this Act registration was voluntary and most owners of land declined to incur the cost of registration,
the Land Transfer Act of 1897 amended and extended the Act of
1875 by providing that registration of title should be compulsory in
certain areas. These Acts are consolidated and in part amended by
the Land Registration Act 1925.[15]

Registration of title is now compulsory in most of the larger urban
areas of England and Wales; and it is intended that the whole country
shall be subject to compulsory registration by the end of 1977.[16]

Objects of land registration

The primary objects of land registration under the Land Registration Act 1925 are fourfold. First, it greatly facilitates and cheapens the
investigation of title [17]; secondly, it facilitates dealings with land which
is subject to settlements, trusts, and other equities; thirdly, it provides
simple methods of effecting transfers and charges; and fourthly, it gives,
to a greater or lesser degree, a State guarantee of title to purchasers
and mortgagees of the registered land.

When registered land is purchased or mortgaged, the purchaser or
mortgagee is relieved of the necessity of investigating the title in the
manner in which it is necessary to investigate title to unregistered land.
In some cases it will be necessary for him to investigate the title prior to
its registration, and he will have to inquire as to the existence of certain
third-party rights; but his investigation will consist mainly in an inspection of the register with the authority of the vendor or mortgagor.
There he will find that the vendor or mortgagor is the proprietor, and
he will discover most of the incumbrances and third-party rights to
which the land is subject.[18]

Because there is generally less work to do on a dealing with
registered land, the legal costs are less than those in unregistered
conveyancing. On first registration, however, the purchaser has the
ordinary costs of unregistered conveyancing plus the costs of his
application for registration.

We shall see that the only estates which can be registered are legal
estates (the fee simple absolute in possession and the term of years
absolute); and the registered proprietor must therefore always be an
estate owner.[19] The Act provides facilities for the protection of
persons with beneficial interests in registered land, and for the protection of assignees and mortgagees of such beneficial interests. Further,

---

[15] Further amendments were made by Acts in 1936, 1966 and 1971.
[16] See (1969) 32 M.L.R. 121, 122.
[17] The system is not perfect nor free of difficulties; see *e.g.* (1962) 26 Conv.(N.S.) 169;
(1966) 19 C.L.P. 26; (1968) 84 L.Q.R. 528.
[18] For overriding interests, see *post*, p. 170.
[19] The Land Registration Acts are conveyancing rather than property Acts; see
Farrand, *Contract and Conveyance*, p. 159.

the overreaching machinery which is available to vendors of unregistered land is available also to vendors of registered land.

The Land Registration Act 1925 and the Land Registration Rules 1925 made pursuant to that Act prescribe forms of transfer and charge which may be used on sales and mortgages of registered land. These forms are rather simpler and shorter than the forms necessary for dealing with unregistered land, and have the advantage, therefore, of saving time and expense.

Another advantage of a registered title is that the title is, in effect, guaranteed by the State. In some cases the guarantee is an absolute one, and in some cases it is subject to certain qualifications.[20] The guarantee takes the form of an indemnity to the persons injured by such matters as errors or omissions in the register, rectification of the register, loss or destruction of documents, etc. If a registered title turns out to be defective, the guarantee does not rectify the defect, but it provides an indemnity to the persons injured (with certain exceptions). The indemnity is met out of moneys provided by Parliament.[21] Thus, the ultimate responsibility falls on the State.

The registration of title must not be confused with the registration of third-party rights, for example, land charges, or with the registration of deeds affecting land in Yorkshire. We have already seen that a great many third-party rights are now registrable as land charges in respect of land wherever situated, and that the object of the registration of such rights is to give notice of their existence to persons dealing with the land affected. The registration of title, on the other hand, means that the estate owner of the land procures himself to be registered as proprietor of that land at the Land Registry, in much the same way as an owner of shares is registered in the books of the company as owner of the shares. After registration, the registered title of the proprietor is to a greater or lesser extent guaranteed by the State. All dealings with the legal estate in the land are recorded on the register in one of the various ways which we shall discuss, and an examination of the register at any time will reveal in whom the land is vested and (subject to certain important exceptions) to what third-party rights it is subject.

The registries

The headquarters of the Land Registry is situated in Lincoln's Inn Fields, London,[22] and all business relating to land registration is conducted under the control of the Chief Land Registrar. It is provided by sections 132–134 of the Land Registration Act 1925 that the Lord Chancellor may, with the concurrence of the Treasury, from time to

---

[20] See *post*, p. 172.
[21] See the Land Registration and Land Charges Act 1971, s. 1, which abolishes the insurance fund which had previously existed. For amounts of claims in recent years, see (1968) 84 L.Q.R. 528, 549; (1971) 35 Conv.(N.S.) 390.
[22] For the meaning of " H.M. Land Registry," see the Land Registration and Land Charges Act 1971, s. 12. It is understood that the title to the headquarters is not registered.

G

time establish district registries and appoint district registrars. Nine district land registries have been established in various parts of the country; and each area of compulsory registration is allotted to a particular district registry which is the only proper office for registrations relating to land in that area.[23]

Land registration rules

For regulating the mode in which the register is to be made and kept; the procedure on applications for registration; prescribing the forms to be observed; and for many other purposes concerning the registration of title, section 144 of the Land Registration Act 1925 contains provisions for the making of rules by the Lord Chancellor. Under this section rules have been made, and are known as the Land Registration Rules 1925.[24] Section 145 of the Act provides for fee orders.[25]

(2) Compulsory registration

The compulsory area originally consisted only of the administrative county of London.[26] By section 120 of the Land Registration Act 1925 registration could be made compulsory in any specified county or county borough by Orders in Council.[27] Many Orders have been made so that most of the larger urban areas are in compulsory areas [28]; and it is hoped that the whole country will be covered by compulsory registration by 1977.[29]

Until the suspension of voluntary registration by the Land Registration Act 1966,[30] voluntary registration was permitted whether the land was in a compulsory area or not (except in those cases in which registration is not permitted anyway).

In the case of unregistered land in a compulsory area, the following provisions apply by virtue of section 123 of the Land Registration Act 1925:

    (1) On a sale [31] of freeholds, the title must be registered within two months of the sale.

    (2) On a grant of a lease for a term of forty years or more, the

---

[23] For the areas and the district registries, see *Halsbury's Laws* (3rd ed.), Vol. 23, Supplement and Service.

[24] See also the Land Registration Rules 1956, 1964 and 1967 and Land Registration (Official Searches) Rules 1969, etc.

[25] See Land Registration Fee Orders 1970 and 1971.

[26] By Order in Council dated July 18, 1898, and subsequent supplementary orders; see Land Transfer Act 1897, s. 20.

[27] The previous procedures leading to extension of registration were abolished by the Land Registration Act 1966, s. 1 (1).

[28] For a current list, see *Halsbury's Laws* (3rd ed.), Vol. 23, Supplement and Service.

[29] See *ante*, p. 164.

[30] s. 1. There are some important exceptions, including lost deeds cases and larger building estates; see (1967) 31 Conv.(N.S.) 7. *Post*, p. 215.

[31] The registry do not take too restrictive a view of the word " sale," so that, *e.g.* a release by one joint owner to another as part of a settlement in divorce proceedings would be accepted; see further Ruoff and Roper, pp. 194–197.

leasehold title must be registered within two months of the grant of the lease.

(3) On a sale of an existing lease, the title must be registered within two months of the assignment, if at the time of the assignment the lease has forty or more years unexpired.

If the title is not registered within two months of the conveyance or lease or assignment (or within such longer time as the registrar or the court permits [32]), in accordance with the above provisions, the grant will be void as regards the legal estate; and will operate to give to the grantee a minor interest only.[33] In practice, the registry will accept a late application on payment of the proper fee (£1) and any reasonable explanation for delay.[32]

As regards registration of ordinary leaseholds, it may be useful to summarise the position as follows:

(1) If the lease has not more than twenty-one years to run, it cannot be registered, whether in a compulsory area or not.[34]

(2) On the assignment of a lease having at least forty years to run or the grant of a lease for forty years or more, the leaseholds, if in a compulsory area, must be registered.[35]

(3) A lease for a term of more that twenty-one years must be registered if the title of the superior estate out of which it is carved is already registered, whether in a compulsory area or not.[36]

(4) Leases under (1) above are protected as overriding interests.[37] Leases under (2) or (3) above are, of course, protected if registered; but if not registered they should be protected by notice entered against the reversionary title.[38]

(3) What interests in land may and may not be registered

Registrable interests

After 1925, the only interests in land in respect of which a proprietor can be registered are interests capable of existing as legal estates, *i.e.* a fee simple absolute in possession or (subject to certain qualifications) a term of years absolute.[39] All interests in the land other than that of the registered proprietor are either minor interests or overriding interests. We will explain minor interests and overriding interests below.

---

[32] Land Registration Act 1925, s. 123 (1).
[33] *Ibid.*; *post*, p. 214. See further as to the effect of non-registration, Farrand, *Contract and Conveyance*, p. 147; (1968) 32 Conv.(N.S.) 391.
[34] See *post*, p. 170.
[35] Land Registration Act 1925, s. 123; *supra*.
[36] See *post*, p. 168.
[37] *Post*, p. 170.
[38] *Post*, p. 180. The present position as to leases is clearly not satisfactory; (1961) 24 M.L.R. 135, 139, 140; Law Commission Working Paper No. 32, Part B.
[39] Land Registration Act 1925, s. 2.

But there are certain leaseholds of which the owner cannot be registered as proprietor. They are:

(1) Leaseholds held under a lease with twenty-one years or less unexpired [40];

(2) Leaseholds held under a lease containing an absolute prohibition against assignment *inter vivos* [41]; and

(3) Leaseholds held under a lease created for mortgage purposes so long as there is a subsisting right of redemption.[42]

Leases and assignments of terms of forty years or more *must* be registered if the land is in a compulsory area.[43]

If the title to the superior estate is registered, a lease for more than twenty-one years *must* be registered whether the land is in a compulsory area or not.[44] In all other cases, for example, a lease for a term of thirty years where the grantor's title is not registered, registration was optional. But voluntary registration was suspended by the Land Registration Act 1966.[45]

The Law Commission has proposed that all leases of over twenty-one years should be capable of substantive registration and the distinction between twenty-one and forty years leases should be abolished.[46]

Minor interests

The following definition of minor interests is contained in section 3 of the Land Registration Act 1925:

" Minor interests " mean the interests not capable of being disposed of or created by registered dispositions and capable of being overridden (whether or not a purchaser has notice thereof) by the proprietors unless protected as provided by this Act, and all rights and interests which are not registered or protected on the register and are not over-riding interests and include:

(a) in the case of land on trust for sale, all interests and powers which are under the Law of Property Act 1925 capable of being overridden by the trustees for sale, whether or not such interests and powers are so protected; and

(b) in the case of settled land, all interests and powers which are under the Settled Land Act 1925 and the Law of Property Act 1925 or either of them, capable of being overridden by the tenant for life or statutory owner, whether or not such interests and powers are so protected as aforesaid.

We must understand from this rather complicated definition, read

---

[40] *Ibid.* s. 8 (1). But see " Overriding interests," *post*, p. 170.
[41] *Ibid.* s. 8 (2).
[42] *Ibid.* s. 8 (3). As to the protection of mortgages, see *post*, pp. 180, 298.
[43] *Ibid.* s. 123.
[44] *Ibid.* ss. 18, 19 (2); see Ruoff and Roper, p. 474.
[45] See *ante*, p. 166.
[46] Law Commission's Published Working Paper (No. 32), 1970; see (1970) 34 Conv.(N.S.) 369.

with other parts of the Act to which we cannot refer in detail here,[47] that minor interests include (1) equitable interests which arise by a dealing with registered land which is carried out off the register, for example, where registered land is sold and conveyed just as if it were unregistered instead of by a registered transfer, and (2) the equitable interests of the persons beneficially interested in settled land or land held upon trust for sale. These interests can in general be protected by some entry on the register, for example, by a caution [48] against the title to the land which they affect; but the person entitled to the minor interest cannot be registered with a separate title as proprietor of such interest.

Since minor interests cannot be registered, by what means is an assignee of a minor interest to protect his interest and preserve his priority? It will be recalled that the assignee of an existing equitable interest in unregistered land protects his interest and preserves his priority by giving a written notice to the trustees.[49] If, however, the land is registered, the assignee of a minor interest therein protects his priority by lodging a " priority caution " or " inhibition " at the Land Registry, and his priority will date from the time when such caution or inhibition is lodged.[50] The caution or inhibition is not entered on the register, but is entered in a special index called the " Index of Minor Interests." The index will thus contain a record of all dealings with minor interests affecting the registered land in question, and will regulate the priority of the assignees of such interests. It is very important to notice that the Index of Minor Interests forms no part of the register itself. The register will reveal the proprietorship of, and the dealing affecting, the legal estate only; the Index of Minor Interests contains only dealings with the existing equitable interests in the registered land. It follows that a purchaser of a legal estate in the registered land from the proprietor is in no way concerned with the Index of Minor Interests; on a sale by the proprietor such minor interests are overreached, and attach to the proceeds of sale. Suppose, for instance, land, the title to which is registered, is vested in X and Y upon trust for sale, the proceeds to be held for A for life with remainder to B absolutely. B mortgages his equitable remainder (which is a minor interest) to C. C should at once lodge a priority caution, which will be entered in the Index of Minor Interests. X and Y then sell and transfer the land to P. P is not concerned with the entry of C's interest in the Index, and C's interest attaches to the proceeds of sale in the hands of X and Y.

---

[47] See *e.g.* Land Registration Act 1925, s. 101.
[48] See *post*, p. 181.
[49] *Dearle* v. *Hall* (1828) 2 Russ. 1, 48; Law of Property Act 1925, s. 137.
[50] Land Registration Act 1925, s. 102. An inhibition is applicable to an absolute assignment of the whole interest without any right of redemption, and a caution to other cases. On the Minor Interests Index generally, see the Law Commission's Working Paper No. 37, Pt. C.

Overriding interests

Overriding interests are defined by section 3 of the Land Registration Act 1925, the important part of the definition being as follows:

" ' Overriding interests ' mean all incumbrances, interests, rights, and powers not entered on the register but subject to which registered dispositions are by this Act to take effect. . . ."

These interests, then, are interests which are always binding on any person who acquires any interest in registered land, even though there is no reference whatever to them in any part of the register. What interests are overriding interests? The full list is given in section 70 of the Act, but it will be sufficient for us to set out here the most important:

    (a) rights of common, public rights, profits à prendre, rights of way, watercourses, rights of water and other easements not being equitable easements;

    (b)–(d) ....;

    (e) land tax,[51] or annuities payable for the redemption of or in lieu of tithe rentcharge [52];

    (f) rights acquired or in course of being acquired under the Limitation Act 1939;

    (g) the rights of every person in actual occupation of the land or in receipt of the rents and profits thereof, save where inquiry is made of such person and the rights are not disclosed;

    (h) all estates, rights, interests and powers excepted from the effect of registration;

    (i) rights under local land charges unless and until protected on the register as prescribed by rules;

    (j) rights of fishing and sporting;

    (k) leases for any term or interest not exceeding twenty-one years granted at a rent without taking a fine.[53]

All the above interests (overriding interests), whether noted on the register or not, will bind the purchaser of the registered land,[54] and though the registrar *may* enter notice of their existence on the register, he is not bound to do so [55] except in one case—he *must* enter notice of an easement created *by an instrument* and affecting the land at the time when it was first registered.[56] This does not apply, however, to an easement which arose other than by an instrument, for example, where the easement is a prescriptive right. If there are no overriding interests affecting the land, the registrar *may* make an entry on the register to that effect, but this will rarely happen [57]; and, in any

[51] Now abolished; see Finance Act 1963, Pt. V, Sched. 14.
[52] See Tithe Act 1936.
[53] *City Permanent Building Society* v. *Miller* [1952] Ch. 840. See Law Commission's Working Paper No. 32, Pt. B, III.
[54] Land Registration Act 1925, s. 70 (1).
[55] *Ibid*. s. 70 (3).
[56] *Ibid*. s. 70 (2); see *Re Dance's Way* [1962] Ch. 490.
[57] *Ibid*. s. 70 (1); Land Registration Rules 1925, r. 197.

event, it seems that such an entry can only be made where there has been a previous entry of the existence of an overriding interest and there is evidence that such interest has been discharged.[58]

It is necessary to say something more about class (g) mentioned above, namely the rights of persons in actual occupation. The right must be a recognised proprietary right capable of binding successors in title.[59] It may be legal or equitable. The most common instances are the right of a tenant in occupation under an unregistrable or unregistered lease; the right of a person in occupation under an agreement for a lease [60]; or the right of a tenant under an option to renew the lease or to purchase the reversion.[61] Other examples are the right of a vendor, under an unpaid vendor's lien, where he remains in occupation of the property as tenant under a sale-and-lease-back transaction [62]; and the right of a person in occupation who is entitled in equity to the property held by the proprietor.[63]

Physical presence on the land is required [64]; and the rights of a person who is in occupation are not overridden where the vendor is, or appears to be, also in occupation.[65]

(4) The register

Three parts

The register consists of three parts: (1) the Property Register, (2) the Proprietorship Register, and (3) the Charges Register.[66] A title number is allotted to every title which is entered on the register.[67] The contents of these various registers are as follows:

(1) *The Property Register* contains the description of the land and estate comprised in the title with a reference to the general map kept at the registry, or (more usually) to the filed plan of the land. In addition, there are such notes as have to be entered relating to the exclusion of mines and minerals, appurtenant easements, non-guaranteed easements,[68] agreements and declarations as to party walls and light and air, and covenants for the benefit of the land.[69]

[58] See *Re Dance's Way* [1962] Ch. 490, at pp. 510–511.
[59] See *National Provincial Bank Ltd.* v. *Ainsworth* [1965] A.C. 1175. For rights under the Matrimonial Homes Act 1967, see *ante*, p. 156. But where, *e.g.* a wife has contributed to the purchase of a house taken in her husband's sole name and she is in occupation, she may have an overriding interest, notwithstanding s. 74 of the Land Registration Act 1925 which provides that no person dealing with a registered estate shall be affected with notice of any trust; see (1969) 33 Conv.(N.S.) 254.
[60] See the " feeding the estoppel " cases, *post*, p. 303.
[61] *Webb* v. *Pollmount* [1966] Ch. 584. An option is in fact usually protected by notice under s. 49 of the Land Registration Act 1925; see *ante*, p. 29.
[62] See *London and Cheshire Insurance Co. Ltd.* v. *Laplagrene Property Co. Ltd.* [1971] Ch. 499. See *post*, pp. 193, 270.
[63] *Hodgson* v. *Marks* [1971] Ch. 892.
[64] See *Strand Securities* v. *Caswell* [1965] Ch. 958.
[65] *Hodgson* v. *Marks, supra.* See (1971) 35 Conv.(N.S.) 255; (1971) 121 New L.J. 784, 821. See also the Law Commission's Working Paper No. 37, Pt. B.
[66] See *post*, p. 172, note 74.
[67] Land Registration Rules 1925, r. 2.
[68] *i.e.* those where the title of the grantor is not registered or produced.
[69] See Land Registration Rules 1925, r. 3.

In the case of leaseholds, this register will contain, in addition to the descriptions of the property, particulars of the lease and the title number of the lessor's title, if registered.[70]

If any land is sold off or added, a reference will be made in this register and also indicated on the filed plan.

(2) *The Proprietorship Register* states whether the title is absolute, good leasehold, qualified, or possessory [71]; and contains the name, address and description of the proprietor of the land, and any cautions, inhibitions and restrictions affecting his right of disposing thereof.[72]

(3) *The Charges Register* contains charges and incumbrances affecting the land (including notices of leases and certain other notices of adverse interests), all dealings with registered charges and incumbrances, and such notes as have to be entered relating to covenants, conditions and other rights adversely affecting the land.[73]

The register is kept on a card index system, the three parts of the register in respect of a property being filed on a single card.[74]

Maps and Indexes

There are kept in the registry an " Index Map " showing the position and extent of every registered estate; a " Name Index " containing an up-to-date list of proprietors' names, and showing the registered numbers of the titles, charges or incumbrances of the persons named as proprietors; an " Application Book " containing a list of pending applications for registration; a " General Map " consisting of a series of maps based on the Ordnance Map; and a " Parcels Index " containing the reference numbers of the parcels shown on the General Map.[75]

The index of proprietors' names is open to the inspection of registered proprietors only; but if any person satisfies the registrar that he is interested generally (*e.g.* as the trustee in bankruptcy or executor or administrator of the proprietor) in the property of any proprietor he may inspect the index. The Index Map and Application Book, and the General Map and Parcels Index, are open to public inspection.[76]

Rectification of the register

Wide powers are given for rectification of the register, either by order of the court; or by the registrar (with an appeal to the court [77]) by section 82 of the Land Registration Act 1925 in the various cases

---

[70] Land Registration Rules 1925, r. 5.
[71] As to the difference between these various titles, see *post*, pp. 174 *et seq.*
[72] Land Registration Rules 1925, r. 6.
[73] *Ibid.* r. 7.
[74] For model registers and plans, see Ruoff, *Concise Land Registration Practice* (2nd ed.), Appendix A.
[75] *Ibid.* rr. 8, 9 and 10.
[76] *Ibid.* r. 12. See *Re Dance's Way* [1962] Ch. 490.
[77] And see Land Registration Rules 1925, rr. 298, 299.

enumerated in that section. In particular, the power to rectify can generally be exercised in a case where the wrong person has been registered as proprietor; or where an entry has been obtained by fraud or made under a mistake; or where by reason of some error or omission, rectification is just. But, unless in the particular case rectification is just, no rectification is permissible if it affects the title of a proprietor who is *in possession*, unless the disposition to him was void, or he was party or privy to the fraud, mistake or omission in respect of which rectification is sought.[78]

An example might be helpful. In the *Chowood Case*,[79] a Mrs. Lyall had acquired a possessory title by adverse possession (under the Limitation Act 1939) to a piece of land which was included in land in respect of which Chowood Ltd. was later registered with absolute title. At the time of the conveyance to Chowood which led to first registration, Mrs. Lyall was in possession, and Chowood therefore took subject to her overriding interest and to her proprietary right acquired by adverse possession. She successfully claimed rectification of the register.

In *Re 139 High Street, Deptford*, a Mr. Dobkins had been registered with absolute title as proprietor of a shop, 139 High Street, and an annexe thereto. Mr. Dobkins was in possession, and he did not know (nor did his vendor) that the annexe belonged to the British Transport Commission. The Commission successfully applied for rectification; and it was held that Dobkins had, on his application for registration, contributed to the mistake.

Provisions are contained in section 83 of the Land Registration Act 1925 [80] for indemnity of any person suffering loss by reason of any rectification of the register, or by any error or omission occurring in the register; but no indemnity can be claimed by a person who has himself caused or substantially contributed to the loss by his fraud or lack of proper care,[81] or who derived his title (otherwise than by a registered disposition for value) from such person.

No compensation was payable in the *Chowood Case*, because Chowood's title was all along subject to Mrs. Lyall's rights, and, accordingly, the company had suffered no loss by the rectification. After *Re 139 High Street, Deptford*, Mr. Dobkins successfully claimed compensation.

---

[78] Land Registration Act 1925, s. 82 (3); and see *Chowood* v. *Lyall* [1930] 2 Ch. 156; *Re Leighton's Conveyance* [1937] Ch. 149; *Re 139 High Street, Deptford* [1951] Ch. 884; *Claridge* v. *Tingey* [1967] 1 W.L.R. 134 (*sub nom. Re Sea View Gardens* [1966] 3 All E.R. 935).

[79] And see *Re Boyle's Claim* [1961] 1 W.L.R. 339.

[80] s. 83 (5), as amended by the Land Registration and Land Charges Act 1971, s. 3.

[81] The expression " lack of proper care " replaces the words " any act, neglect or default of his " introduced by the Land Registration Act 1966, s. 1 (4); see (1968) 84 L.Q.R. 528. The purpose of this change is to remove any doubt that a person suffering loss may be deprived of compensation if he has contributed to the loss by an innocent act; see (1971) 35 Conv.(N.S.) 394.

(5) Certificates

Land certificate

On completion of the registration of freehold or leasehold land, and if there is no registered charge, a land certificate is handed over to the applicant or, if he prefers, deposited in the Registry.[82] If there is a registered charge, the land certificate is kept in the Registry and a charge certificate issued to the chargee.[83]

A land certificate contains an office copy of the entries in the register and an office copy of the filed plan.[84] Sometimes, for example, when there are complicated drainage rights, the deed creating these rights may be included (or " sewn up " as it is technically known) in the certificate.

The land certificate replaces the title deeds as evidence of the owner's title to the land. If not already deposited in the Registry, it must be produced to the registrar on every entry in the register of a disposition by the registered proprietor; and a note of such entry officially indorsed thereon.[85] It is because the entries on the land certificate may not be up to date that a purchaser must inspect the register.[86]

Charge certificate

On the registration of a charge, a charge certificate is prepared and issued to the chargee. The land certificate must be deposited at the Registry until the charge is cancelled.[87] The charge certificate, like the land certificate, contains a copy of the entries on the register and a copy of the filed plan. The original charge is usually attached to the certificate. Sometimes, however, the original charge may be indorsed with a certificate of registration and returned to the mortgagee, a certified copy of the charge being retained in the Registry. In this case the original charge is treated for all purposes as the charge certificate.[88]

(6) What titles can be registered

Kinds of title

Freehold land may be registered with either (1) an absolute title, or (2) a qualified title, or (3) a possessory title; and leaseholds may be registered (except in those cases in which they cannot be registered at all [89]), not only with absolute, qualified or possessory title, but also with (4) a good leasehold title. We shall examine these various titles in turn.

---

[82] Land Registration Act 1925, s. 63.
[83] *Post*, p. 299.
[84] Land Registration Rules 1925, rr. 261, 264.
[85] Land Registration Act 1925, s. 64.
[86] *Ante*, p. 93.
[87] Land Registration Act 1925, s. 65.
[88] See Ruoff and Roper, pp. 29–30.
[89] See *ante*, p. 166.

Absolute title

The effect of first registration of freehold land with an absolute title is to confer on the person registered (who is called " the first registered proprietor ") the fee simple in possession in the land, subject:

(1) to the incumbrances and other entries, if any, appearing on the register; and

(2) to overriding interests, if any, affecting the land, unless the contrary is expressed on the register; and

(3) where the first registered proprietor is not entitled to the land for his own benefit, to any minor interest of which he has notice (for example, if trustees for sale are registered as proprietors, their estate is subject to the interests of the beneficiaries).

But the first registered proprietor takes free from all other estates and interests whatsoever, including estates and interests of the Crown.[90]

The effect of first registration of leaseholds with absolute title is to vest in the first registered proprietor the possession of the leasehold interests described, subject to the qualifications (1), (2) and (3) above mentioned in the case of freehold land, and subject also to all implied and express covenants, obligations and liabilities incident to such leaseholds, but free from all other estates and interests whatsoever, including estates and interests of the Crown.[91]

Qualified title

Where on examination it appears to the registrar that the title can be established only for a limited period, or subject to certain reservations, then an entry may be made on the register qualifying the title accordingly. A title of this nature is called a qualified title; and the registration has the same effect, in the case of freeholds, as registration of an absolute title, and in the case of leaseholds, as registration of an absolute or good leasehold title, as the case may be, save that it does not affect the enforcement of any estate, right or interest appearing by the registrar to be excepted.[92]

Possessory title

The registration of a person as first proprietor of freeholds or leaseholds with possessory title has the same effect as registration with an absolute title, but the registration does not affect or prejudice any estate, right or interest adverse to the title of the first registered proprietor and which is capable of arising at the time of his registration.[93] In other words, if the proprietor is registered with *absolute* title, the State guarantees that there is nothing adverse to the proprietor's title except such matters as appear on the register, and possibly overriding interests; whereas if the proprietor is registered with *possessory* title

[90] Land Registration Act 1925, s. 5. See *Re Suarez* [1924] 2 Ch. 19.
[91] *Ibid.* s. 9. See the Law Commission's Working Paper No. 32, Pt. C, I.
[92] Land Registration Act 1925, ss. 7, 12. A qualified title cannot be applied for. The application in the first instance will be for absolute or good leasehold title.
[93] *Ibid.* ss. 4, 6, 11. See *Re King* [1962] 1 W.L.R. 632.

only, the State gives no guarantee as regards any matters adverse to the
title and capable of arising at the time of first registration.

Good leasehold title

An absolute title cannot be registered in respect of leasehold land
until the title both of the leasehold *and the freehold*, and to any intermediate leasehold that may exist, is approved by the registrar; but a
person can be registered as proprietor of leasehold land with " good
leasehold " title, if the title to the leasehold is approved by the
registrar. First registration of leasehold land with a good leasehold
title has the same effect as registration with an absolute title, except
that it does not affect or prejudice the enforcement of any estate, right
or interest affecting, or in derogation of, the title of the lessor to grant
a lease.[94]

Examination of title by registrar

It should be noted that the registrar has a wide discretion [95] in
accepting or rejecting titles.[96] Few titles are rejected outright. Moreover, many titles with technical defects [97] are accepted without comment
by the registry.

Conversion into absolute or good leasehold title

It is clearly advisable that as many registered titles as possible
should be absolute or good leasehold, because it is only in respect of
such titles that the full benefit of the system of land registration
is obtained.[98] It is, accordingly, provided by section 77 of the Land
Registration Act 1925 that, subject to certain conditions, the registrar
in some cases *must*, and in other cases *may*, convert an existing
registered title into an absolute or good leasehold title. It is not
necessary for us to examine this section in detail; it will be sufficient
to enumerate the cases with which the section deals as follows:

(1) Where land was registered before 1926 with a possessory title,
the registrar *may*, if satisfied as to the title, register it at any
time as absolute or good leasehold, with or without the consent
of the proprietor.[99]

(2) On a transfer for value of land registered with qualified good
leasehold, or possessory title, the registrar *may*, if satisfied as
to the title, enter the title of the transferee as absolute or good
leasehold with or without the transferee's consent.[1]

[94] *Ibid.* ss. 8, 10.
[95] Sometimes called its " Nelson's eye."
[96] Land Registration Act 1925, s. 13 (c).
[97] Such as the absence of a written assent by the personal representatives in their own
favour as trustees before 1964; see *post*, p. 401.
[98] See *ante*, p. 175 and *supra*.
[99] Land Registration Act 1925, s. 77 (1).
[1] *Ibid.* s. 77 (2).

(3) Where land has been registered with possessory title, if freehold land, for fifteen years, or if leasehold land, for ten years, the registrar *must*, if satisfied that the proprietor is in possession, enter the title of the proprietor of the freehold land as absolute, and the proprietor of the leasehold land as good leasehold.[2]

(4) Where land has been registered with good leasehold title for at least ten years, the registrar *may*, if he is satisfied that the proprietor or successive proprietors has or have been in possession during such period, *at the request* of the proprietor enter his title as absolute.[3]

(7) Transfers of registered land

Effect of transfer

A registered transfer *for value* of freehold land, registered with an absolute title, confers on the transferee an estate in fee simple in the land or other legal estate expressed to be created subject (1) to the incumbrances, if any, appearing on the register; and (2) unless the contrary is expressed on the register, to overriding interests, if any [4]; but free from all other estates and interests, including those of the Crown.[5]

A registered transfer *for value* of freehold land registered with a qualified or possessory title has the same effect as if the title were absolute, save that, in the case of a qualified title, it does not affect the rights or interests appearing by the register to be excepted, and, in the case of a possessory title, does not affect any right or interest adverse to the title of the first registered proprietor and subsisting or capable of arising at the time of the registration of such proprietor.[6]

A registered transfer of freehold land made without valuable consideration is, so far as the transferee is concerned, subject to any minor interests [7] subject to which the transferor held the same, but in other respects has exactly the same effect as a transfer for value.[8]

Registered transfers of leasehold land have the same effect as registered transfers of freehold land, according as they were made with or without valuable consideration and the title registered was absolute, qualified or possessory; but instead of conferring an estate in fee simple, they are deemed to vest in the transferee the possession of the land transferred for all the leasehold estate described in the registered lease subject (1) to all implied and express covenants, obligations and liabilities incident to such estate; (2) to all incumbrances entered on the register; and (3) unless the contrary is expressed in the register, to overriding interests, if any.[9] Transfers of leasehold land registered with a good

---

[2] *Ibid.* s. 77 (3) (*b*).
[3] Land Registration Act 1925, s. 77 (4).
[4] As to overriding interests, see *ante*, pp. 170 *et seq.*
[5] Land Registration Act 1925, s. 20 (1).
[6] Land Registration Act 1925, s. 20 (2).
[7] As to minor interests, see *ante*, pp. 168 *et seq.*
[8] Land Registration Act 1925, s. 20 (3).
[9] *Ibid.* s. 23.

leasehold title do not affect or prejudice the enforcement of any estate, right or interest affecting, or in derogation of, the lessor's title to grant the lease.[10]

Unregistered transfer of registered land

Though a transfer of registered land should be, and generally is, effected by a registered transfer, an unregistered disposition is not wholly inoperative. It is provided by section 101 of the Land Registration Act 1925 that registered land may be dealt with by an unregistered assurance just as if it were unregistered land. Such unregistered assurance, however, will not be effective to transfer the legal estate, but will confer upon the grantee a minor interest only. This interest will, like any other minor interest, be overridden by a subsequent registered transfer for value, but it may be protected by notice, caution, or inhibition, as provided in the Act.[11]

If a transaction with registered land is made by a registered disposition, any instrument made by the proprietor off the register for carrying out the same transaction is void, so far as the transaction is effected by the registered disposition.[12] But this will not be so if the registrar issues a certificate to the effect that such unregistered disposition is necessary and useful owing, for example to lengthy recitals or personal covenants.[13]

(8) Death or bankruptcy of registered proprietor

Death of registered proprietor

On the death of a proprietor of any registered land or charge, his personal representative is entitled to be registered as proprietor, with the addition of the words " executor or executrix (or administrator or administratrix) of [name] deceased." To procure registration, the personal representative must produce to the registrar the probate or letters of administration.[14] It is not, however, necessary for the personal representative to apply for registration, because he can, without being registered, transfer any land or charge of which the deceased was registered proprietor, or dispose of it by way of assent.[15] On delivery at the registry of the transfer or assent made by a personal representative (and of the probate or letters of administration if the personal representative has not been registered as proprietor), the registrar must register the person named therein as proprietor.[16]

---

[10] *Ibid.* s. 23 (2). For the implied covenants on a transfer of registered leaseholds, see *ibid.* s. 24.
[11] See *ante*, p. 169.
[12] Land Registration Act 1925, s. 39.
[13] Land Registration Rules 1925, r. 96.
[14] Land Registration Act 1925, s. 41; Rules, r. 168.
[15] Rules, r. 170.
[16] *Ibid.*

Bankruptcy of registered proprietor

On the bankruptcy of a proprietor of any registered land or charge, his trustee in bankruptcy, when appointed, may be registered as proprietor, and, in the meantime, the official receiver may be registered as proprietor on production of an office copy of the order adjudging the proprietor bankrupt and a certificate signed by the official receiver that any registered land or charge is part of the property of the bankrupt.[17] On the death of a proprietor registered as official receiver or trustee in bankruptcy, his personal representatives cannot be registered, but steps must be taken to register his successor in office.[18]

As soon as practicable after registration of a petition in bankruptcy as a pending action under the Land Charges Act 1925 [19] the registrar must register a notice (called a *creditor's notice*) against the title of the proprietor of any registered land or charge affected, and such notice will operate to protect the rights of all creditors of such proprietor.[20] As soon as practicable after registration of a receiving order in bankruptcy under the Land Charges Act 1925,[21] the registrar must enter an inhibition (called a *bankruptcy inhibition*) against the title of the proprietor of any registered land or charge affected.[22] The effect of the inhibition is to prevent any dealing with the registered land or charge until the inhibition is vacated except the registration of the official receiver or the trustee in bankruptcy as proprietor.[23]

(9) Settled land and land held upon trust for sale

Settled land

Settled land is registered in the name of the tenant for life or statutory owner, and the beneficial interests arising under the settlement take effect as minor interests only.[24]

In order to protect the interests of the beneficiaries, restrictions are entered on the register to prevent any dealings with the land which would prejudice the beneficiaries. Examples are (i) to prevent a disposition under which capital money arises (unless the money is paid in accordance with the Settled Land Act 1925); and (ii) to prevent any disposition of the land which is not authorised by that Act, except with the leave of the registrar.[25] If settled land was registered before 1926 in the name of a proprietor who, after 1925, would not be the person entitled to apply for registration, the person entitled to be registered must apply for registration and is entitled to be registered without the necessity of any transfer.[26] Thus, if before 1926 trustees

---

[17] *Ibid.* rr. 174–177.
[18] *Ibid.* r. 173.
[19] See *ante*, p. 151.
[20] Land Registration Act 1925, s. 61 (1).
[21] See *ante*, p. 151.
[22] Land Registration Act 1925, s. 61 (3).
[23] *Ibid.* s. 61 (4).
[24] Land Registration Act 1925, s. 86 (1). As to " minor interests," see *ante*, p. 168.
[25] *Ibid.* s. 86 (2) (3). Rules, rr. 56–58, 99–101, 104, 170.
[26] Land Registration Act 1925, s. 92.

of settled land were registered as proprietors under the Land Transfer Act 1897, the tenant for life became entitled, after the Land Registration Act 1925 came into force, to be registered as proprietor in the place of the trustee.

Where land is held on trust for sale, express or implied or imposed by statute, the trustees for sale will be registered as proprietor of the land.[27]

(10) Notices, cautions, inhibitions and restrictions

Notices

Any lessee or other person entitled to, or interested in, a lease or any agreement for a lease of registered land, where the term granted is not an overriding interest,[28] may apply for registration of notice of the lease or agreement. On the entry of such notice, the registered proprietor of the land and every person deriving title under him (except proprietors of incumbrances registered prior to the registration of the notice) are deemed to be affected with notice of the lease or agreement as being an incumbrance on the land. If the lease is binding on the proprietor of the land, as it normally would be, such notice can be registered without his concurrence; but if it is not binding on him, the notice cannot be registered except with his concurrence or under an order of the court.[29]

No notice can be registered in respect of a lease which is an overriding interest, because transferees are bound by such leases in every case; and, for the same reason, it is not necessary to register notice of a leasehold interest which is itself registered under a separate title because here the lease will automatically be noted against the registered title of the lessor. Notice, however, of all other leases should be registered, for otherwise they may be extinguished on a transfer of the registered land for value. However, if the lessee is in possession, he has an overriding interest as a person " in actual occupation," [30] and a transferee will therefore take subject to his interest whether registered or not.

Provision is also made for registration of notices of certain other rights, interests and claims, such as rentcharges; the severance of any mines from the surface; land charges until registered as registered charges; and restrictive covenants affecting registered freehold land.[31]

As regards a restrictive covenant, the notice takes the place of registration of the covenant as a land charge.[32] When notice of a restrictive covenant has been entered on the register, the proprietor of the land and those deriving title under him are deemed to have notice

---

[27] *Ibid.* s. 94.
[28] See *ante*, p. 170.
[29] Land Registration Act 1925, s. 48.
[30] *Ante*, p. 171.
[31] Land Registration Act 1925, ss. 49, 50. For mortgages, see *post*, p. 299.
[32] *Ibid.* s. 50 (1).

of the covenant and are, therefore, bound by it.[33]   Thus, a lessee of registered land is bound by a restrictive covenant notice of which has been entered on the register against the freehold title, although he had no express notice of the covenant when the lease was granted; and this is so even though the lessee was not entitled to inspect the register relating to the freehold title, because he had agreed to take the lease under an open contract.[34]

Cautions

The effect of a caution is to entitle the person lodging it to notice of any proposed dealing with the land. It may be lodged either against the first registration of unregistered land or against dealings with land already on the register.

Cautions against first registration.   A caution against first registration of unregistered land may be lodged by any person having or claiming such an interest in the land as entitles him to object to any disposition thereof being made without his consent.[35]   The person lodging the caution is entitled to notice of any application for registration of the land.   The notice will require the cautioner to appear and oppose the registration if he thinks fit, within a certain time (usually fourteen days), and the land cannot be registered until that time has expired or the cautioner has entered an appearance, whichever may first happen.[36]   The person applying for registration is thus prevented from obtaining registration and effecting a registered disposition of the land without the knowledge of the person claiming the interest which entitled him to object to any dealing.   Any person may lodge the caution who claims to be interested in the land, for example, as beneficial owner, or as tenant for life, or as a purchaser under an existing contract for sale, or as plaintiff in a pending action concerning the land.[37]

Cautions against dealings.   Any person interested under an unregistered instrument or as a judgment creditor, or otherwise, in any land or charge registered in the name of any other person may lodge a caution against dealings with such land by the person registered as proprietor.[38]   The effect of the caution is that no dealing by the proprietor can be registered or protected by the register, until notice has been served by the registrar on the cautioner warning him that his caution will cease to have effect after expiration of a certain period, usually fourteen days.[39]   If before the expiration of this period the cautioner appears before the registrar, the registrar may delay the registration of any dealings with the land or charge, or the making

---

[33] *Ibid.* s. 50 (2).
[34] *White* v. *Bijou Mansions Ltd.* [1937] Ch. 610.
[35] Land Registration Act 1925, s. 53 (1); *Elias* v. *Mitchell* [1972] 2 W.L.R. 740.
[36] *Ibid.* s. 53 (3).
[37] See Form 14, Sched. to the Land Registration Rules 1925.
[38] Land Registration Act 1925, s. 55 (1).
[39] See Land Registration Rules 1925, r. 218, para. (2).

of any entry on the register for such period as he thinks just, but if the cautioner does not appear, the caution ceases on the expiration of the period unless the registrar otherwise orders.[40]

Inhibitions

An inhibition is an order or entry forbidding for a time, or until the occurrence of an event named in the order or entry, or generally until further order or entry, any dealing with any registered land or registered charge. It may be granted by the court, or, subject to an appeal to the court, by the registrar, on the application of any person interested.[41] For example, an inhibition is entered in the event of a receiving order in bankruptcy being registered under the Land Charges Act 1925, against the proprietor of any registered land [42]; but as a general rule, inhibitions are placed on the register only in cases of great emergency, where no other means are available to prevent fraud or injustice.

Restrictions

A restriction is an entry on the register, *made on the application of the registered proprietor himself,* that no transaction to which the application relates shall be effected unless the following things, or such of them as the proprietor may determine, are done, namely:

(1) unless notice of application for the transaction is sent by post to a named address; or

(2) unless the consent of some person or persons named by the proprietor is given to the transaction; or

(3) unless some other matter or thing is done which may be required by the applicant and approved by the registrar.[43]

If the registrar is satisfied as to the right of the applicant to give the directions, he must enter the restrictions on the register, and no transaction may then be effected except in conformity with the restrictions.[44] Restrictions can only be entered subject to the approval of the registrar, and can at any time be withdrawn or modified at the instance of any person appearing by the register to be interested in such directions. Restrictions may also be set aside by order of the court.[45]

Unlike a caution or an inhibition, a restriction is a friendly and not a hostile proceeding, and it is therefore preferable to either of the others in cases where the concurrence of the registered proprietor can be obtained. The following restrictions are commonly encountered:

(1) joint proprietors' restriction,[46] unless the applicant states on

---

[40] Land Registration Act 1925, s. 55 (1) (2). See *Re White Rose Cottage* [1965] Ch. 940; *Parkash* v. *Irani Finance Ltd.* [1970] Ch. 101; *post,* p. 300.
[41] Land Registration Act 1925, s. 57.
[42] *Ibid.* s. 61 (3); and see *ante,* p. 151.
[43] Land Registration Act 1925, s. 58 (1).
[44] *Ibid.* s. 58 (2).
[45] *Ibid.* s. 58 (4).
[46] Land Registration Act 1925, s. 58 (3); Rules, r. 213; Form 62.

the application form that the survivor can give a valid receipt for capital money[47];

(2) company restriction, which is entered automatically, under which no charge by the company is to be registered unless a certificate has been furnished that the charge does not contravene the provisions of the memorandum and articles; and

(3) local authority restrictions under which no disposition is to be registered unless made in accordance with the Act under which the land was acquired.[48]

(11) Investigation of title

Absolute title

From the above, it will be seen that on a sale by a proprietor of land registered with an absolute title, the investigation of title by the purchaser involves no more than an inspection of the register and consideration of any appurtenant rights or interests and overriding interests.[49] As to incumbrances, if any, the purchaser will ascertain these from the charges register, and if the register does not show to whom the incumbrance belongs, the vendor must, before completion, either furnish an abstract of the title to the incumbrance or procure its cancellation on the register. The purchaser should require the vendor to give him authority to inspect the register, and the register should be searched immediately before completion.[50] An official search can be obtained.[51] If the search shows that any caution affects the land, it must be warned,[52] and completion delayed until the notice to the cautioner has expired or the caution is withdrawn. If a restriction or inhibition is found, the transfer must be made in accordance therewith.[53] If the search is satisfactory, the purchaser can safely complete on having the land certificate and instrument of transfer handed to him or lodged in the registry.

Possessory title

On a sale of land registered with a possessory title, the purchaser will require the same evidence of title as in the case of land registered with absolute title, and, in addition, he must investigate the title prior to first registration, and all estates and interests arising thereout, in the same manner as if the land were not registered.

Qualified title

On a sale of land with qualified title, the purchaser will require the

---

[47] Or rather strikes out the inappropriate alternatives in the relevant para. of the form; see *post*, p. 216.
[48] For a convenient table of restrictions, see Ruoff and Roper, pp. 813 *et seq.*
[49] For the protection of the purchaser under the registered system, see (1969) 32 M.L.R. 121. See also *Re Evans' Contract* [1970] 1 W.L.R. 583.
[50] *Ante*, p. 174.
[51] *Post*, p. 184.
[52] *Ante*, p. 181.
[53] As to cautions, restrictions, inhibitions, see *ante*, pp. 180 *et seq.*

same evidence of title as in the case of land registered with an absolute title, and also such evidence as to any estate right or interest excluded from the effect of registration (*i.e.* by reason of which the title is " qualified " and not absolute) as the purchaser would be entitled to if the land were unregistered.

Official searches

Any person authorised to inspect the entries in the register relating to any title, charge or incumbrance, may apply to the registrar in writing, signed by himself or his solicitor, to make an official search and to issue a certificate of the result. If a purchaser of registered land has obtained an official certificate of the result of a search, he will not be affected by any entry made in the register after the date of the certificate and before his application for registration is made, provided his application is made in proper form, and is accompanied by the land certificate, and is delivered at the registry before the office is opened or deemed to be opened on the sixteenth day after the date of the delivery of the application for search.[54] Apart from this search no searches are necessary on a sale of registered land, except for local charges.

Prior to first registration

Where unregistered land, in a district where registration is compulsory, is purchased, the title will be investigated by the purchaser in the same manner as if it were not intended that the purchaser should be registered. It might be advisable for the purchaser, as soon as the contract is executed, to lodge a caution against first registration,[55] so as to avoid the risk of losing his lien for his deposit on the vendor selling to another person who has no notice of the contract. The conveyance may be in the ordinary form.[56] The index map and application book should be inspected at the registry for the purpose of ascertaining that the land has not been already registered and that no application for registration is pending; and inquiry should be made whether any caution against first registration has been lodged.[57] The sale can then safely be completed, and application for first registration should be made.[58]

(12) Land registration generally

The State guarantee

The system of registration of title established by the Land Registration Act 1925, does not, as do some other systems,[59] provide for " indefeasible " titles in the sense that the titles are entirely conclusive

---

[54] Land Registration Rules 1925, r. 292; Land Registration (Official Searches) Rules 1969.
[55] See *ante*, p. 181.
[56] *Post*, p. 221.
[57] *Ante*, p. 44.
[58] *Post*, p. 214.
[59] See Ruoff, *An Englishman Looks at the Torrens System* (1957).

and incontravertible. However, in most systems of registration a title obtained by fraud can be set aside, unless an innocent purchaser has been registered. But the English system does allow registered titles to be upset more easily than elsewhere. A reason for this, it has been suggested, is that in this country the law relating to registered land is merely an appendage to the law of the land generally, not an entirely separate code.[60] We have already seen [61] how rectification of the register is allowed in certain circumstances under the 1925 Act, even against the registered proprietor in possession. Indeed, it has been conclusively shown how restrictive judicial interpretation has eroded the special protection given to the registered proprietor in possession against whom the register is rectified.[62] The State guarantee is therefore not so much in that the register is indefeasible, but that, if the register is rectified, compensation will be paid to the person who suffers. But we have also seen [63] that there are circumstances in which compensation will not be paid. The Land Registration Act 1966 took away the right to compensation in other cases, but the Land Registration and Land Charges Act 1971 has restored the position to a great extent.[64] The experience of other systems has shown us that indefeasibility cannot be attained. The English system is at present deficient in so far as there can be rectification without compensation. Rectification and compensation should be complementary.[65]

The mirror principle

The mirror principle involves the proposition that the register is a mirror which reflects accurately and completely and beyond all argument the current facts that are material to a man's title. In a perfect system the register would disclose all rights and interests, whether adverse or beneficial. But this would be quite impracticable, both from the point of view of the length of the documentation that would be needed,[66] and the extent of the investigation that would be involved. Moreover, there are certain rights which might not be revealed, however careful the investigation. An example is the right of a person who has acquired, or is in the course of acquiring, a title by adverse possession under the Limitation Act 1939. Such a right is an overriding interest, which, as we have seen,[67] is enforceable against the proprietor of registered land even though it does not appear on the register. Overriding interests have been called the Achilles' heel

---

[60] See (1954) 18 Conv.(N.S.) 130, 132. The Land Registration Acts are conveyancing rather than property statutes; see *ante*, p. 164, note 19.
[61] *Ante*, p. 173.
[62] (1968) 84 L.Q.R. 528.
[63] *Ante*, p. 173.
[64] *Ante*, p. 173, note 81.
[65] See generally, Farrand, *Contract and Conveyance*, pp. 186 *et seq.*; (1969) 32 M.L.R. 121, 138–141; (1972) 88 L.Q.R. 126 *et seq.*
[66] See (1961) 24 M.L.R. 135.
[67] See *ante*, p. 170.

of land registration.[68] They are the cause of the most serious criticism of the registration system.[69] However, to be fair, it must be conceded that the same problem exists in unregistered conveyancing in that such interests are matters which are not generally disclosed on title deeds or in abstracts.[70]

VI. INSPECTION OF THE PROPERTY

Rights of persons in possession

The purchaser should inspect the property and inquire as to the rights of the persons, if any, who are in possession of the property, for he has constructive notice of such rights, provided that, if they are registrable, they are registered. Occupation of the property by a tenant is notice to the purchaser of the interest of the tenant [71] and his rights under his tenancy, but not of any rights not apparent from the lease, such as a right to rectification or rescission of his lease.[72]

Registered land

The need to inspect the property and make inquiries of persons in possession is greater in the case of registered land. Overriding interests, to which the proprietor takes subject, include the rights of every person in actual occupation of the land or in receipt of the rents and profits thereof, save where inquiry is made of such and the rights are not disclosed.[73] An option to purchase the freehold reversion granted to a tenant under a document separate from the lease was held binding on a purchaser, even though the tenant had failed to protect the option by a caution and his rights did not arise from his occupation of the land as a tenant.[74] If the land had been unregistered, and the option had not been registered as a Class C (iv) land charge,[75] the purchaser would have taken free from the option. An unpaid vendor's lien [76] is an overriding interest where the vendor remains in occupation under a sale and lease-back transaction,[77] even though the vendor is in occupation as tenant.[78] And where the owner executed a voluntary transfer

[68] See Glasgow, *A Modern View of Conveyancing* (1969), p. 247.
[69] See generally Farrand, pp. 163 *et seq.*; Ruoff and Roper, *Registered Conveyancing* (3rd ed.) pp. 99–101; (1972) 88 L.Q.R. 103 *et seq.*
[70] *National Provincial Bank Ltd.* v. *Hastings Car Mart Ltd.* [1964] Ch. 9, 15; [1963] 2 W.L.R. 1015, 1019, 1020.
[71] See *National Provincial Bank Ltd.* v. *Hastings Car Mart Ltd.* [1964] Ch. 665; *National Provincial Bank Ltd.* v. *Ainsworth* [1965] A.C. 1175; and *Hunt* v. *Luck* [1902] 1 Ch. 428. But not of the landlord: *Hunt* v. *Luck, supra.* And see (1971) 121 New L.J. 77; (1972) 122 New L.J. 530.
[72] *Smith* v. *Jones* [1954] 1 W.L.R. 1089. See also (1970) 34 Conv.(N.S.) 305.
[73] Land Registration Act 1925, s. 70 (1) (*g*); see *ante*, p. 171.
[74] *Webb* v. *Pollmount* [1966] Ch. 584. Such an option is collateral to the lease: see *ante*, p. 30.
[75] *Ante*, p. 29.
[76] For the unpaid vendor's lien, see *post*, p. 193.
[77] For sale and lease-back, see *post*, p. 270.
[78] *London and Cheshire Insurance Co. Ltd.* v. *Laplagrene Property Co. Ltd.* [1971] Ch. 499 (where it was conceded and therefore not decided, that the lien was an overriding interest).

of her house on terms that she should retain the beneficial interest therein and she remained in actual occupation, a subsequent purchaser of the land and his mortgagee took subject to her overriding interest.[79]

VII. INVESTIGATION OF TITLE BY MORTGAGEE

Generally

Investigation of title by, or on behalf of, a mortgagee is carried out in a similar way to investigation of title on behalf of a purchaser.[80] There will not usually be a preliminary contract for the advance, and, accordingly, the lender will be able to withdraw from the transaction if he so wishes. If there is an unqualified preliminary agreement, it cannot be specifically enforced at the suit of the borrower[81] whose only remedy is therefore in damages.

Those advising the lender must consider what will happen if the worst comes to the worst and the lender has to sell the property. Accordingly, the lender may demand better proof of title than the borrower was entitled to. The solicitor for a purchaser who is raising the purchase-money by mortgage advance must therefore carefully consider the likely effect on the chances of getting the advance if he accepts a " barring out " clause, *i.e.* that the purchaser shall accept a certain title without objection[82] in the contract between the borrower and his vendor.

The usual inquiries and searches will be made. A solicitor acting for a mortgagee should not rely on the searches made by the mortgagor in the absence of specific authority to do so.[83] In practice, the purchaser's solicitor proceeds in the usual way as if there were to be no mortgage.

A number of special matters for the mortgagee's consideration, such as tenancies before the mortgage, are discussed in the chapter on mortgages.[84]

The form and content of mortgage deeds is dealt with in a subsequent chapter.[85]

The mortgagee's costs of investigating the title and of the preparation and execution of the mortgage deed are payable by the mortgagor.[86]

VIII. INVESTIGATION OF TITLE TO LEASEHOLDS

Generally

This is carried out in the usual way for investigating title, and in the

---

[79] *Hodgson* v. *Marks* [1971] Ch. 892.
[80] See (1971) 115 S.J. 315.
[81] *South African Territories* v. *Wallington* [1898] A.C. 309. But a contract for debentures is specifically enforceable: Companies Act 1948, s. 92.
[82] *Ante*, p. 92.
[83] For land charge search for bankruptcy only, see (1954) 61 L.S.Gaz. 770.
[84] *Post*, p. 303.
[85] Chap. 12.
[86] *Wales* v. *Carr* [1902] 1 Ch. 860.

discussion which has gone before, we have dealt with such matters as the title the purchaser can call for,[87] consent to assignment [88] and **breach of covenant.**[89] **We** would only mention here the necessity for the purchaser's solicitor to consider carefully the covenants in the lease, and, in particular, how a right to assign, etc. with permission not to be unreasonably withheld can be practically nullified by a user covenant restricting the use of the premises to a particular type of business.[90]

---

[87] *Ante,* pp. 60, 99.
[88] *Ante,* p. 100.
[89] *Ante,* p. 100.   And see p. 144.
[90] *Sykes* v. *Midland Bank Executor and Trustee Co. Ltd.* [1969] 2 Q.B. 518; affd. [1971] 1 Q.B. 113.   See (1969) 119 New L.J. 454.

CHAPTER 7

EFFECT OF CONTRACT PENDING COMPLETION

I. THE POSITION OF THE PARTIES GENERALLY

Vendor becomes trustee for the purchaser

The moment you have a valid contract for sale, the vendor becomes in equity a trustee for the purchaser of the property sold; and the beneficial ownership passes to the purchaser. Accordingly, the vendor is bound to take reasonable precautions to preserve the property; and the purchaser is entitled to all benefits which may accrue to the property, while the vendor must bear the losses. But the vendor's trusteeship is of a special nature, for he himself also has a beneficial interest in the property. He has a right to retain possession of the property until the purchase-money is paid and the right to take the rents and profits until that time. Furthermore, he has a lien on the property for the purchase-money.[1]

Until completion of the purchase, the vendor must exercise the same care over the property agreed to be sold as a trustee must over property subject to a trust. He must therefore take proper precautions to prevent injury to the property[2] by trespassers, *e.g.* vandals[3]; or by burst pipes and the like, although, as we shall see,[4] the purchaser will usually effect his own insurance of the property on signing the contract. If injury or damage is done to the property, the vendor must pay compensation to the purchaser.[5] The vendor should not do anything himself to despoil the property, such as removing a door[6] or fixtures.[7] Nor may he leave rubbish on the property at completion.[8] There is no obligation on the vendor to keep buildings in *repair*, but he must take reasonable steps to prevent deterioration[9]; at least, where the purchaser is in default, up to the date fixed for completion.[10] Unlike a trustee, a vendor is not generally entitled to an indemnity for the cost of preserving the property.[11]

---

[1] *Lysaght* v. *Edwards* (1876) 2 Ch.D. 499, 506–510, *per* Jessel M.R.; *Clarke* v. *Ramuz* [1891] 2 Q.B. 456. For the vendor's lien, see *post*, p. 193.
[2] See (1971) 68 L.S.Gaz. 224, 225.
[3] Note the new summary procedure for possession aimed at " squatters " in Ord. 113 of the Rules of the Supreme Court; Ord. 26 of the County Court Rules; (1971) 121 New L.J. 518.
[4] *Post*, p. 191.
[5] *Clarke* v. *Ramuz, supra.*
[6] *Phillips* v. *Lamdin* [1949] 2 K.B. 33.
[7] See fixtures, *ante*, p. 16.
[8] *Cumberland Consolidated Holdings Ltd.* v. *Ireland* [1946] K.B. 264. For the obligation to give vacant possession, see *ante*, p. 97.
[9] *Phillips* v. *Silvester* (1872) 8 Ch.App. 173.
[10] *Golden Bread Co.* v. *Hemmings* [1922] 1 Ch. 162.
[11] *Re Watford Corporation and Ware's Contract* [1943] Ch. 83 (vendor paid contributions under War Damage Act 1941).

Where appropriate, the vendor must also manage the property in the same way as a trustee. For example, he may continue to run a business which has been agreed to be sold [12]; or, in the case of tenanted property, re-let it if it becomes vacant pending completion.[13] So long as he acts reasonably, he is entitled to be indemnified against any loss incurred in carrying on a business after the contractual date for completion.[14]

The vendor is only a trustee of the property agreed to be sold, not also, for example, of any compensation paid to the vendor on the derequisitioning of the property [15] or for dilapidations.[16] On paying of the purchase-money, the vendor becomes a trustee in the full sense for the purchaser.[17]

Purchaser entitled to benefits and must suffer losses

From the date of the contract until completion, the purchaser is entitled to all benefits which may accrue to the property purchased, such as an increase in value,[18] and, conversely, must suffer all losses not attributable to the default of the vendor, should the property deteriorate in value. As it is said, the risk passes to the purchaser upon the making of the contract. So the purchaser must complete even if the property agreed to be sold becomes subject to a compulsory acquisition between contract and completion.[19]

Insurance

If, before completion, the house is burnt down, the purchaser must nevertheless complete the purchase and pay the full purchase-price.[20] The purchaser may, however, have the benefit of the vendor's insurance. Section 47 of the Law of Property Act 1925 provides that if the property has been insured by the vendor, then the vendor is to hold the policy on behalf of the purchaser; and the policy is to be handed to the purchaser on completion. But the section is to take effect subject to any stipulation to the contrary contained in the contract, and

---

[12] *Golden Bread Co.* v. *Hemmings, supra.*

[13] *Earl of Egmont* v. *Smith* (1877) 6 Ch.D. 469. Although it may be necessary for him to seek the purchaser's views on the matter first: *Abdullah* v. *Shah* [1959] A.C. 124; and see *Raffety* v. *Schofield* [1897] 1 Ch. 937.

[14] *Golden Bread Co.* v. *Hemmings, supra.* And see Farrand, *Contract and Conveyance*, pp. 204–207.

[15] *Re Hamilton-Snowball's Conveyance* [1959] Ch. 308. And see *Rayner* v. *Preston* (1881) 18 Ch.D. 1 (insurance policy moneys).

[16] *Re Lyne-Stephens and Scott-Miller's Contract* [1920] 1 Ch. 472.

[17] *Bridges* v. *Mees* [1957] Ch. 475.

[18] Even though it occurs through the vendor's expenditure: *Monro* v. *Taylor* (1848) 8 Hare 60.

[19] *Hillingdon Estates Co.* v. *Stonefield Estates* [1952] Ch. 627.

[20] *Paine* v. *Meller* (1801) 6 Ves. 349; *Rayner* v. *Preston, supra.* And at common law he was not entitled to the benefit of any insurance policy effected by the vendor in his name alone, for he was a third party as regards such contract: *Castellain* v. *Preston* (1883) 11 Q.B.D. 380; but see now s. 47 of the Law of Property Act 1925, *supra.* Nor was the vendor entitled to the policy-moneys because a contract of fire insurance is a contract of *indemnity*, and if the vendor received the purchase-moneys he had lost nothing.

to *any requisite consents of the insurers,* and to payment by the purchaser of the proportionate part of the premium from the date of the contract. In practice, most fire insurance policies permit assignment and expressly provide that a purchaser shall be entitled to the benefits of the policy on notification of his interest. In other words, to have the benefit of the section, in the absence of anything to the contrary in the contract, the purchaser has merely to notify the insurers of his interest. However, most purchasers prefer to effect a new policy in their own names,[21] in which case the vendor should maintain his insurance until completion.

The standard conditions of sale provide that, if so required by the purchaser, the vendor will consent to or obtain, at the purchaser's expense, an indorsement of notice of the purchaser's interest in the policy, and the purchaser shall pay to the vendor on completion a proportionate part of the premium. Subject thereto the vendor shall not be bound to maintain any such policy.[22] The combination of these conditions and the provisions of section 47 of the Law of Property Act 1925 is recognised to be not very satisfactory.[23]

In the case of leaseholds, there is often a covenant in the lease that the tenant will insure with a certain insurance office (the landlord thereby obtaining a commission). This will generally be the only occasion when the purchaser will find it convenient to take over the vendor's insurance. If the vendor has failed to insure pursuant to such a covenant, he will be in breach of covenant and of the contract (which is to assign a valid lease) and the purchaser could not be compelled to complete.

It is the duty of the purchaser's solicitor to draw his client's attention to the fact that the risk passes to the purchaser on execution of the contract. It seems to be generally accepted that a solicitor has implied authority to effect insurance cover on the purchaser's behalf.[24]

II. THE EFFECT OF THE DEATH OF EITHER PARTY

Death of vendor

If the vendor dies before completion, the contract must be carried out by his personal representatives.[25]

---

21 If the purchaser takes over the vendor's insurance but fails to notify the insurers of his interest he may, it has been suggested, be entitled to the policy-moneys under the Fires Prevention (Metropolis) Act 1774, s. 83 (which is not confined to the Metropolitan area). This has been doubted and in practice the Act is not generally relied upon.

22 Law Society's Conditions, Condition 6; National Conditions, Condition 21.

23 See *e.g.* (1971) 121 New L.J. 30; (1971) 68 L.S.Gaz. 224.

24 *Grover & Grover Ltd.* v. *Mathews* [1910] 2 K.B. 401.

25 Administration of Estates Act 1925, ss. 1–2. See generally Fry, *Specific Performance* (6th ed.), pp. 93 *et seq.* If the vendor was a tenant for life, or a person having the powers of a tenant for life, the contract can be enforced by or against his successors in title for the time being, and such person is empowered to make any proper disposition to complete his predecessor's contracts: Settled Land Act 1925, ss. 63, 90.

Conversion

Whenever there is a specifically enforceable contract to sell realty, the realty is treated as part of the vendor's personalty from the moment the contract is made. Accordingly, if the deceased vendor left his realty to X and his personalty to Y, the purchase-money in respect of land which the deceased had contracted to sell will go to Y,[26] unless the will was made or confirmed by codicil made after the contract, in which case the testator will be taken to have been aware of the contract and intended the devisee to take the purchase-money.[27]

Death of purchaser

If the purchaser dies before completion, his personal representatives can sue and be sued upon the contract for sale.[28] The doctrine of conversion also applies in the purchaser's case, *i.e.* his interest will be treated as realty. For example, if the deceased purchaser by his will gave his realty to X and his personalty to Y, X will be entitled to the deceased's interest under the contract.[29] By virtue of section 35 of the Administration of Estates Act 1925 X would have to pay the purchase-money, unless the testator has signified a contrary intention by his will, deed or other document.[30] The vendor is entitled to payment from the personal representatives, and is not concerned as to where the eventual burden of the payment falls.

Options

Whether an option can be enforced between successors in title to the original parties has already been discussed.[31] The doctrine of conversion applies also to an option to purchase land.[32]

III. The Effect of the Bankruptcy of Either Party

Bankruptcy of vendor

If the vendor becomes bankrupt before completion, his trustee in bankruptcy can enforce the contract against the purchaser,[33] and, conversely, the purchaser can enforce the contract against the trustee in bankruptcy,[34] unless the latter disclaims.[35] The trustee cannot, however, disclaim the *contract* unless he disclaims the *land*.[36] The

---

[26] *Fletcher* v. *Ashburner* (1779) 1 Bro.Ch. 497.

[27] A specific gift of land is also adeemed by notice to treat by a local authority or other undertaking on compulsory acquisition once the price is agreed: *Harding* v. *Metropolitan Ry.* (1872) L.R. 7 Ch. 154.

[28] See generally Snell's *Equity* (26th ed.), p. 520.

[29] See generally Parry, *The Law of Succession* (6th ed.), pp. 100–101.

[30] See generally Snell, p. 357.

[31] See *ante*, p. 30.

[32] See *ante*, p. 31; *Re Birmingham* [1959] Ch. 523.

[33] Unless time is of the essence and at the date for completion the trustee has not been appointed: *Powell* v. *Marshal, Parkes & Co.* [1899] 1 Q.B. 710.

[34] *Pearce* v. *Bastable's Trustee* [1901] 2 Ch. 122.

[35] Under the Bankruptcy Act 1914, s. 54.

[36] *Re Bastable* [1901] 2 K.B. 518; Bankruptcy Act 1914, s. 54 (6).

result is that, in practice, the trustee will not disclaim, because the disclaimer will have the effect of destroying the trustee's right both to the land and the purchase-money. The disclaimer would not affect the equitable interest of the purchaser in the property under the contract; and it seems, therefore, that the purchaser could obtain a vesting order from the court relating to the legal estate, without the obligation of paying the purchase-money.

Bankruptcy of purchaser

If the purchaser becomes bankrupt before completion, his trustee in bankruptcy can enforce the contract against the vendor [37]; and the vendor can enforce the contract against the trustee,[38] unless the trustee disclaims.[39] If the trustee disclaims, the vendor can keep the deposit and prove in the purchaser's bankruptcy for any damage suffered by reason of the disclaimer.[40]

Disclaimer

A disclaimer must be made within one year of the trustee's appointment. If, however, within a month of his appointment, the trustee still has no knowledge of the property, then disclaimer may be made within a year of his acquiring the knowledge. The period may be cut down to twenty-eight days by written notice by the other party. The twenty-eight days may, however, be extended by the court.[41]

IV. LIENS OF VENDOR AND PURCHASER

Vendor's lien

From the moment of the contract, and even though the purchaser has been allowed to take possession or the conveyance has been made,[42] the vendor has an equitable lien, in the nature of an equitable charge, on the land for the amount of any purchase-money remaining unpaid.[43]

The vendor may enforce his lien by an application to the court either for a declaration of the lien [44] and an order for a resale; or for an order that possession be restored to him; or for any other remedy available to a chargee.[45] On a resale, any surplus of price belongs to the purchaser; and, if the land be resold at a lower price, the vendor can claim the difference from the purchaser.

[37] *Re Nathan, ex p. Stapleton* (1879) 10 Ch.D. 586, 590.
[38] See *Jennings' Trustee* v. *King* [1952] Ch. 899.
[39] *Holloway* v. *York* (1877) 25 W.R. 627.
[40] *Re Parnell, ex p. Barrett* (1875) L.R. 10 Ch. 512.
[41] Bankruptcy Act 1914, s. 54.
[42] For the vendor's lien when the purchase-money is paid by instalment, see *Nives* v. *Nives* (1880) 15 Ch.D. 649.
[43] *Mackreth* v. *Symmons* (1808) 15 Ves. 329; *Re Birmingham* [1959] Ch. 523; *London and Cheshire Insurance Co. Ltd.* v. *Laplagrene Property Co.* [1971] Ch. 499; see generally Snell's *Equity* (26th ed.), pp. 490–492.
[44] For declaration as a remedy, see *post*, p. 205.
[45] *Re Stucley* [1906] 1 Ch. 67. For chargee's remedies, see *post*, pp. 316 *et seq.*

The lien may be renounced or excluded by the terms of the agreement between the parties, but the mere fact that a receipt for the purchase-money is given does not constitute renunciation.[46] The lien may be lost by the vendor taking other security on the property, or by operation of the Statutes of Limitation.[47] The vendor's lien has recently become of topical interest in the context of the vendor leaving the bulk of the purchase-moneys outstanding on mortgage. If the mortgage is avoided for any reason, for example, in the case of a company purchaser for failure to register as a company charge,[48] the vendor may be able to rely on his lien for the balance of the purchase-money due to him. But if it appears from the circumstances that the vendor intended to rely upon the mortgage only, and not upon the lien, then the lien will be gone.[49] And where an equitable mortgage is created by deposit of the deeds, which implies a contract that the mortgagee may retain the deeds until he is paid, this implied contract is part and parcel of the mortgage. It is not a separate lien. It has no independent existence apart from the mortgage, so that if the mortgage is avoided, the right to retention of the deeds is lost too.[49]

If the lien is to bind third parties, it must be registered as a general equitable charge under the Land Charges Act 1925[50]; or, in the case of registered land, protected by notice,[51] unless, in either case, the vendor has the title deeds. In the case of registered land, the vendor's lien will also be an overriding interest, provided, that is, the vendor is in actual occupation; and this will be so even where the vendor is a tenant under a lease-back arrangement.[52]

Purchaser's lien

Until the actual conveyance to him, the purchaser has an equitable lien on the land to be purchased for any money paid to the vendor by way of deposit or otherwise, and also, it seems, for his expenses incurred in pursuance of the contract.[53] So, for example, an intended lessee has a lien for money expended on the property in the event of the lease not being granted.[54] The purchaser's lien is enforceable in the same manner as the vendor's lien for unpaid purchase-money. Similarly, the lien should be registered as a land charge; and it may be lost through failure to register in the same way.[55]

---

[46] See *London and Cheshire Insurance Co. Ltd.* v. *Laplagrene, supra.*
[47] *Re Stucley, supra.*
[48] *Post,* p. 330. See *Capital Finance Co. Ltd.* v. *Stokes* [1969] 1 Ch. 261.
[49] *Capital Finance Co. Ltd.* v. *Stokes, supra.* But see (1970) 33 M.L.R. 131.
[50] *Ante,* p. 153.
[51] *Ante,* p. 180.
[52] *London and Cheshire Insurance Co. Ltd.* v. *Laplagrene, supra.* See *ante,* p. 171. For lease-back transactions, see *post,* p. 270.
[53] *Rose* v. *Watson* (1864) 10 H.L.C. 671, 684.
[54] *Re Furneaux and Aird's Contract* [1906] W.N. 215; *cf. Brewer Street Investments* v. *Barclays Woollen Co.* [1954] 1 Q.B. 428 (where there was no contract).
[55] *Supra.*

V. SUB-SALES

The purchaser may assign the benefit of the contract to a third party, in the absence of any provision in the contract to the contrary.[56] The benefit of the contract is a legal chose in action within section 136 of the Law of Property Act 1925, so that, if there is an absolute assignment of the benefit of the contract by the purchaser in writing under the hand of the assignor, the assignee can sue the vendor in his own name.[57] The purchaser cannot, however, transfer his *obligations* under the contract, except with the consent of the vendor, *i.e.* there is a novation.[58] In practice, the original purchaser does not drop out of the picture. There is not usually any assignment of the benefit of the contract, but a separate contract between the purchaser and the sub-purchaser. The conveyance is then by the vendor to the sub-purchaser by the direction of the purchaser; and the original purchase-price is paid to the vendor; and the balance, where the sub-sale is at an increased price, paid to the purchaser.

Sub-sales are quite commonly encountered in connection with development property; and the period between contract and sub-sale may often be many years. The advantage to the purchaser in not taking a conveyance but in relying merely on the contract is a stamp duty saving, no stamp being paid on the contract. On the conveyance under the sub-sale, the duty is reckoned on the purchase-price under the sub-sale, whether it be more or less than the original price.[59] It is, of course, paid by the sub-purchaser.

While betterment levy existed,[60] it was common practice to provide by the contract that the vendor should not be bound to convey to any person other than the original purchaser. The reason for such a condition was the risk to the vendor of liability for levy in respect of a purchase-price in excess of that actually received by him, for example, where the sub-sale was at an enhanced price.

Both sets of standard conditions of sale provide that the vendor shall not be required to convey to any person other than the purchaser,[61] with a qualification in the case of the National Conditions that the vendor may be required to convey to a sub-purchaser if he is satisfied that he will not be liable for betterment levy. As betterment levy has now been abolished, there would seem to be nothing in the National Conditions to prevent sub-sales.

---

[56] *Earl of Egmont* v. *Smith* (1877) 6 Ch.D. 469, 474. In the case of leaseholds the original purchaser must join in to guarantee the performance of the covenants: *Curtis Moffat Ltd.* v. *Wheeler* [1929] 2 Ch. 224.

[57] For assignment generally, see Treitel, *The Law of Contract* (3rd ed.), Chap. 6.

[58] *Tollhurst* v. *Associated Portland Cement Manufacturing (1900) Ltd.* [1902] 2 K.B. 660, 668; affd. [1902] A.C. 414.

[59] Stamp Act 1891, s. 58 (4) (5); *Maples* v. *I.R.C.* [1914] 3 K.B. 303; *Fitch Lovell* v. *I.R.C.* [1962] 1 W.L.R. 1325.

[60] See now Land Commission (Dissolution) Act 1971; *ante*, p. 104.

[61] Law Society's Conditions, Condition 11 (4); National Conditions, Condition 4 (3).

Disposition by vendor

The vendor cannot dispose of the property agreed to be sold except subject to the contract [62]; and if he attempts to do so, he may be prevented by injunction.

The grantor of an option cannot dispose of the property subject to the option free from the option if it has been duly registered or protected. [63]

VI. INSTALMENT SALES

When used [64]

In the case of poorer quality property, such as that in an area scheduled for redevelopment in the near future, it may only be possible to sell the property if the bulk of the purchase-money is to be left on mortgage by the vendor or is to be paid by instalments. The safer method from the vendor's point of view is to take a mortgage (the so-called "mortgage back" system). But if the purchaser-mortgagor defaults in repayments, the vendor-mortgagee may now have some difficulty in exercising his remedies. [65]

Where a substantial part of the purchase-money has been paid by way of deposit, the vendor may agree to accept the balance by instalments, and either rely on his lien for the payment of such instalments, [66] or require them to be secured by a mortgage of the property. Such a mortgage may be so drafted that no moneys will be payable under the mortgage and the vendor will not exercise his rights thereunder unless the purchaser-mortgagor defaults in payment of the instalments of the purchase-money.

Rental purchase

The alternative to a mortgage is for a contract for sale providing for payment of the purchase-money by instalments. Unless the bulk of the purchase-money has been paid by way of deposit, completion should be delayed until the whole of the purchase-money has been paid. To protect the purchaser, the contract should be registered as an estate contract. [67]

Such arrangements can be made on a genuine sale of property. But this method has also been used as a way of avoiding the effects of the Rent Act. Rather than let so that the Rent Act will apply, the property is sold on the instalment basis. [68] It is thought, however, that the court would apply the Rent Act where the contract was not

[62] That is, assuming the contract for sale to have been duly registered or, in the case of registered land, protected (see *ante*, p. 25).
[63] See *Gardner* v. *Coutts & Co.* [1968] 1 W.L.R. 173.
[64] See (1971) 121 New L.J. 427, 487.
[65] See *post*, p. 323.
[66] See *ante*, p. 193.
[67] See *ante*, p. 25.
[68] And see "Deferred purchase," *post*, p. 197.

bona fide,[69] for example, where part of the moneys payable is attributable to rent or payment for use and occupation.

The form of rental purchase agreements varies and they tend to be an amalgam of contract, lease and mortgage.[70] The agreement usually provides that the purchaser may take possession as licensee and that he shall insure and repair the premises. The agreement may also provide that, on default by the purchaser in payment of any instalment, the vendor may on notice re-enter and repossess the property. Conditions commonly provide for the forfeiture of all instalments paid to date.

Whether such a condition could be enforced by the court will depend on the circumstances.[71] If only a few instalments have been paid, the condition may take effect. But if, for example, 90 per cent. of the purchase-money has been paid, it is doubtful whether the court will allow the vendor to retain this amount.[72] Accordingly, it is safer to provide for forfeiture of the deposit plus a sum equal to the interest at a specified rate on the balance of the purchase-money for the period during which the purchaser was in occupation.[72]

Deferred purchase

This is a contract for the purchase of a lease of a house with the intention of avoiding the Rent Act. Rather than let the property, the landlord agrees to grant a ninety-nine years lease at a premium or assign an existing term, the purchaser to take possession forthwith but completion to be delayed for a specified period, for example, two years. The contract provides for a high rate of interest, say, 20 per cent. or more per annum, on the purchase-money. In practice the matter is never completed and the purchaser pays interest on the purchase-money by weekly payments as long as he occupies the property.[73]

Again, such an arrangement might be held to be within the Rent Act.[69]

VII. STAMP DUTY ON CONTRACT

Contract under hand

There was formerly a fixed duty of 6d. on a contract for the sale of land for more than £5. In the case of a formal contract consisting of two parts, a 6d. postage stamp would be affixed to each part, and each party would sign one part over the stamp. Some informal contracts, for example, those made up of correspondence, were not in practice stamped. In the case of other informal contracts, the

---

69 *Hopwood* v. *Hough* [1944] L.J.N.C.C.R. 80; and see generally the Report of the Committee on the Rent Acts (the Francis Committee) (1971, Cmnd. 4609), Chap. 15.
70 For a form, see (1971) 121 New L.J. 435.
71 *Stockloser* v. *Johnson* [1954] 1 Q.B. 476.
72 *Mayson* v. *Clouet* [1924] A.C. 980.
73 See Report of the Committee on the Rent Acts (1971, Cmnd. 4609), Chap. 15; *The Sunday Times*, July 26, 1970.

parties usually appreciated the need for a stamp. This 6d. stamp duty was abolished as from August 1, 1970, by the Finance Act 1970.[74]

Contract under seal

A contract under seal must be stamped 50p (10s.).[75]

Ad valorem duty

Where property (subject to certain exceptions) vests in the purchaser by virtue of the contract, no other method of transfer being required, the contract must be stamped *ad valorem*, *i.e.* on a sliding scale according to the value of the property.[76] If a formal transfer is afterwards made, no further duty will be payable, the document effecting the transfer being stamped with a denoting stamp.[77]

Ad valorem stamping of the contract most commonly occurs on a sale of a business. Stamp duty can be saved on such an occasion by apportioning the purchase-price between the various assets. Stamp duty is not payable in respect of cash, money in the bank on current account, or those assets which pass by mere delivery.[78] Part of the purchase-money should be apportioned to these assets, and not uncommonly a greater value is attributed to them than their true value, thus reducing the balance of the purchase-money in respect of which duty is payable.[79]

Ad valorem duty on the purchase of goodwill can be paid either on the contract or the assignment of the goodwill. Before the abolition of the 6d. duty (see above) it was usual to stamp the contract 6d. and not to have an express transfer of goodwill, thus saving *ad valorem* duty on the value of the goodwill. The vendor could not object to this course.[80]

VIII. VENDOR AND PURCHASER SUMMONS

In the event of any dispute between the vendor and the purchaser in respect of any requisition or other matter arising out of or connected with the contract, either party may apply to the court by originating summons; and the court may make such order as may appear just, and direct how and by whom the costs are to be paid.[81] Such a summons is generally known as a vendor and purchaser summons. The

---

[74] s. 32 and Sched. 7, para. 1 (2) (*a*).
[75] Stamp Act 1891, s. 15; Decimal Currency Act 1967.
[76] But the contract was deemed properly stamped, if stamped 6d. or 10s., for the purpose of proceedings to enforce specific performance or to recover damages.
[77] Stamp Act 1891, s. 59.
[78] Unless the transfer purports to assign such assets, in which case duty will be payable.
[79] But if undervalued the Commissioners can assess the transfer of the undervalued items as on a voluntary disposition thereof: Finance (1909–10) Act 1910, s. 74 (5).
[80] See generally Pinson, *Revenue Law* (5th ed.), Chap. 38; (1949) 93 S.J. 348; (1953) 17 Conv.(N.S.) 4.
[81] Law of Property Act 1925, s. 49, re-enacting and extending the Vendor and Purchaser Act 1874, s. 9.

advantage of the summons is that it enables the parties to settle difficulties arising on the title by a summary and comparatively inexpensive means.

A vendor and purchaser summons is not available to decide questions of construction affecting the rights of third parties. It is available for construction of the contract,[82] though not for questions affecting the *validity* or *existence* of the contract, nor where questions of fraud are involved [83] (in these cases proceedings should be commenced by writ). Generally, it may be said that the summons is available for the determination of isolated points of dispute between the parties, such as whether the vendor has shown a good title [84], the right of either party to rescind [85]; whether the vendor is bound to answer a particular requisition [86] or the right of the purchaser to recover his deposit.[87]

---

[82] See *Re Wallis and Barnard* [1899] 2 Ch. 515; *Re Nichols and Van Joel's Contract* [1910] 1 Ch. 43; *Wilson* v. *Thomas* [1958] 1 W.L.R. 422; *Re Bramwell's Contract* [1969] 1 W.L.R. 1659.
[83] *Re Sandbach and Edmondson's Contract* [1891] 1 Ch. 99.
[84] *Re Brine and Davies Contract* [1935] Ch. 388.
[85] *Re Jackson and Woodburn's Contract* (1887) 37 Ch.D. 44.
[86] *Re Evans' Contract* [1970] 1 W.L.R. 583.
[87] *Re Hargreaves and Thomson's Contract* (1886) 32 Ch.D. 454; *Re Stone and Saville's Contract* [1963] 1 W.L.R. 163. And see 34 *Atkin's Court Forms* (2nd ed.), pp. 298–300, 317, 318, 321.

CHAPTER 8

REMEDIES

Mistake and misrepresentation

Before dealing with the various remedies available where there is a dispute in relation to a contract for the sale of land, we shall say a brief word about mistake and misrepresentation.

Sometimes the parties enter into a contract under some misunderstanding. Both parties may be mistaken on the same point, or they may be mistaken on different points, or only one party may be under a misapprehension. The general rule at common law is that mistake does not vitiate the contract.[1] But there are exceptions, for example, if both parties are mistaken as to the existence of the subject-matter,[2] or the price.[3] On the other hand, where a purchaser mistakenly thought the sale included more land than in fact it did, there being no misrepresentation to induce such belief, he was bound by his bid.[4]

The plea of *non est factum* (mistakenly signed documents) can only rarely be established by persons of full capacity.[5]

Equity generally followed the common law rules as to mistake,[6] but, as specific performance was a purely discretionary remedy, it might set the contract aside or allow specific performance on terms. So today the courts may take account of mistake. For example, where both parties thought the property agreed to be sold was subject to a statutory tenancy and the price was fixed on that basis, whereas the tenant had left the property without asserting his rights, thus giving the purchaser an unexpected bargain, the court refused the purchaser specific performance and ordered rescission of the contract on condition that the vendor entered into a fresh contract to sell the property to the purchaser at a proper vacant possession price.[7]

We have already seen [8] how the court may order rectification where the written contract does not correctly express the parties' previous agreement. And even where the mistake is unilateral, the court may intervene by giving the party who is not mistaken the choice of submitting to rectification or suffering rescission.[9]

---

[1] See generally Treitel, *The Law of Contract* (3rd ed.), Chap. 22.
[2] *Cooper* v. *Phibbs* (1867) L.R. 2 H.L. 149; *cf. Bligh* v. *Martin* [1968] 1 W.L.R. 804.
[3] *Webster* v. *Cecil* (1861) 30 Beav. 62.
[4] *Tamplin* v. *James* (1880) 15 Ch.D. 215.
[5] *Saunders* v. *Anglia Building Society* [1971] A.C. 1004.
[6] See *e.g. Tamplin* v. *James, supra.*
[7] *Grist* v. *Bailey* [1966] Ch. 532.
[8] *Ante*, p. 25.
[9] *Paget* v. *Marshall* (1884) 28 Ch.D. 255.

We have already mentioned the remedies for misrepresentation,[10] and would only repeat here the rights of the innocent party to claim damages or rescission for *negligent* misrepresentation, even after completion, subject to the power of the court to award damages in lieu of rescission.[11]

Specific performance

The principal remedy for breach of a contract for the sale of land is specific performance.[12] This is, of course, in the discretion of the court; but as damages are not generally an adequate remedy (land usually being a unique commodity) specific performance will be ordered at the suit of either party to the contract almost as a matter of course.

Specific performance can sometimes be obtained when there is no right to recover damages at law, for example, when an oral contract has been partly performed by the plaintiff.[13]

As a rule, the plaintiff, in an action for specific performance, must show that there is a binding contract between himself and the defendant[14] and a reasonable apprehension that the defendant will not perform it. It is not necessary to prove an *actual breach* of the contract. We have already seen,[15] for example, how a writ for specific performance may be issued before the date for completion.[16]

The defendant to the action will in most cases only be the other party to the contract. However, a judgment may be obtained against a transferee of the property who is not a party, for instance where the transferee is a pure volunteer, or took with notice of the prior contract,[17] or takes only an equitable title.[18]

The absence of a memorandum is a good defence to an action for *damages*, but not to an action for specific performance where there has been a sufficient act of part performance.[19] Apart from this, any defence which would be a good defence to an action for damages at common law will be a good defence to an action for specific performance, for example, that there was no consideration for the contract. Further, because the remedy for specific performance is purely discretionary, the order may be refused on certain grounds which would

10 See *ante*, p. 35.
11 Misrepresentation Act 1967, ss. 1, 2.
12 See generally Snell's *Principles of Equity* (26th ed.), pp. 639 *et seq.*
13 See *ante*, p. 22.
14 *See ante*, pp. 8 *et seq.*
15 *Ante*, p. 109.
16 *Marks* v. *Lilley* [1959] 1 W.L.R. 749; *Hasham* v. *Zenab* [1960] A.C. 316.
17 *Greaves* v. *Tofield* (1880) 14 Ch.D. 563, 572.
18 *Flinn* v. *Pountain* (1889) 58 L.J.Ch. 389. See Snell, p. 643; and note *Jones* v. *Lipman* [1962] 1 W.L.R. 832.
19 See *ante*, p. 22.

constitute no defence to an action for damages, for example, unreasonable delay in commencing proceedings [20]; lack of mutuality [21]; misleading conditions in the contract [22]; and mistake or hardship. [23]

The plaintiff must be ready, willing and able to perform his part of the contract, if he is to succeed.

Summary judgment

A special procedure is provided by the Rules of the Supreme Court [24] whereby the plaintiff may apply for summary judgment in an action for specific performance where there is no defence. [25] The action is commenced by writ. The plaintiff then applies by summons, supported by an affidavit as to the facts, and stating that in the deponent's belief there is no defence. The summons must set out or have attached to it minutes (*i.e.* the terms) of the judgment sought by the plaintiff. If the contract was in writing, and there is clearly no defence, an order may be made by a master or, in appropriate cases, district registrar. If there is any reasonable defence, leave will be given to the defendant to defend, and the action will then proceed in the usual way with statement of claim, defence, etc.

Greenwood v. Turner *motion*

Another special procedure available to a vendor in a specific performance action, where the purchaser is already in possession, is the so-called *Greenwood* v. *Turner* [26] motion. An application to the court is made by motion, supported by affidavit, after issue of the writ, for an order that either the balance of the purchase-money be paid into court within a stated time or the purchaser give up possession. [27]

Effect of order for specific performance

The usual order in a vendor's action declares that the contract ought to be specifically performed; orders accounts and inquiries as to interest due on the balance of the purchase-money and rents (if any) received from the property, payment of the certified balance and costs, and the execution of the conveyance and delivery of the deeds. The judgment in a purchaser's action is in much the same form. If the vendor fails to execute the conveyance, the purchaser may apply for an order

---

[20] *i.e.* laches: *Levy* v. *Stogdon* [1898] 1 Ch. 478; see now the Limitation Act 1939, ss. 2 (7), 29. See also *Williams* v. *Greatrex* [1957] 1 W.L.R. 31.

[21] *Elliott and H. Elliott (Builders) Ltd.* v. *Pierson* [1948] Ch. 452 (vendor had no title); *Flight* v. *Bolland* (1828) 4 Russ. 298 (specific performance never granted to an infant).

[22] See *e.g. Re Marsh and Earl Granville* (1882) 24 Ch.D. 11; *ante,* p. 92. The deposit may now be recovered under Law of Property Act 1925, s. 49 (2).

[23] *Malins* v. *Freeman* (1837) 2 Keen 25; but *cf. Tamplin* v. *James* (1880) 15 Ch.D. 215; *Van Praagh* v. *Everidge* [1902] 2 Ch. 266.

[24] Ord. 86.

[25] *Horton* v. *Kurzke* [1971] 1 W.L.R. 769.

[26] [1891] 2 Ch. 144.

[27] See *Maskell* v. *Ivory* [1970] Ch. 502.

appointing some person, usually the master or registrar, to convey in the vendor's name. If a purchaser fails to comply with the order, the vendor is entitled to an order for rescission and forfeiture of the deposit,[28] but not to damages.

If the vendor claims specific performance, he cannot, while the action continues, claim to forfeit the deposit, for by bringing an action for specific performance he has elected to treat the contract as being still on foot.[29] In practice, the vendor will also claim damages for breach of contract or rescission as alternative heads of relief.

Damages

If the vendor breaks the contract, the general rule is that the purchaser is entitled to recover, by way of damages, the loss which naturally follows from the breach, or may be considered to have been contemplated by the parties when the contract was made as the probable result of the breach.[30] This will comprise:

(1) return of the deposit, and, unless otherwise agreed, interest thereon;

(2) interest on the purchase-money, if it has been lying idle to the knowledge of the vendor;

(3) the expenses incurred in investigating the title; and

(4) general damages for loss of the bargain, including, for example, the cost of lodgings.[31]

If, however, the vendor breaks the contract by reason of the fact that his title is defective and he therefore cannot complete, the purchaser is entitled to recover as damages only the losses mentioned under (1), (2) and (3) above, and *not* general damages for loss of bargain. This is known as the rule in *Flureau* v. *Thornhill*[32] (approved by the House of Lords in *Bain* v. *Fothergill*[33]). The rule applies to an action for damages for breach of contract, even where the vendor knew at the time of the contract that he could not make a title, but in that case the purchaser may be able to obtain general damages in an action for fraud.[34]

It should be carefully noted that if the land sold is subject to a mortgage which the vendor is unable to pay off, this inability is not a defect in the vendor's title which will enable him to take advantage of the rule in *Flureau* v. *Thornhill*. In such a case, if the vendor fails

28 See *Hall* v. *Burnell* [1911] 2 Ch. 551.
29 *Public Trustee* v. *Pearlberg* [1940] 2 K.B. 1.
30 *Hadley* v. *Baxendale* (1854) 9 Ex. 354; *Diamond* v. *Campbell-Jones* [1961] Ch. 22; *Cottrill* v. *Steyning and Littlehampton B.S.* [1966] 1 W.L.R. 735; *Lloyd* v. *Stanbury* [1971] 1 W.L.R. 535; 115 S.J. 582.
31 See *Beard* v. *Porter* [1948] 1 K.B. 321.
32 (1776) 2 W.Bl. 1078.
33 (1874) L.R. 7 H.L. 158; and see *Engell* v. *Fitch* (1869) L.R. 4 Q.B. 659; *Day* v. *Singleton* [1899] 2 Ch. 320; *Jones* v. *Gardiner* [1902] 1 Ch. 191; *Braybrooks* v. *Whaley* [1919] 1 K.B. 435; and *J.W. Cafés* v. *Brownlow Trust* [1950] 1 All E.R. 894.
34 *Bain* v. *Fothergill, supra.*

to pay off the mortgage and complete, he will be liable for general damages.[35]

If the purchaser breaks his contract, the vendor is entitled to recover as damages the difference between the purchase-price and the lower price received on a resale effected within a reasonable time. If the vendor elects not to sue for damages (as, of course, he will if he has suffered none), he can apparently retain any deposit that has been paid, but if he sues, such deposit must be set off against the damages claimed.[36] The above, however, is subject, after 1925, to the power of the court to order the repayment of any deposit either where the court refuses to grant specific performance of a contract or in any action for the return of a deposit.[37]

Rescission

Either party may rescind,[38] either under a specific provision in the contract[39] or as an equitable remedy, as an alternative to damages. Rescission under the terms of the contract is merely the exercise of a contractual right, as to which the court has no discretion. Rescission as an equitable remedy depends on the court's discretion and so may be granted subject to certain terms or conditions. Rescission as an equitable remedy is appropriate for breach of contract, misrepresentation,[40] misdescription and non-disclosure.[41]

Rescission means cancelling the contract and restoring the parties to their original positions.[42] The plaintiff cannot claim both rescission *and* damages.[43] A purchaser may, however, claim to recover his deposit,[44] or any part-payment or instalments, and the costs of investigating title, etc. In practice, a claim for damages for breach of contract will be sought as an alternative to rescission.

A deposit is a sum paid by a purchaser to a vendor as a guarantee that he will perform his part of the contract,[45] so that, if the purchaser defaults, the vendor will be entitled to forfeit the deposit in addition to rescission, unless the court exercises its discretion to order the return of the deposit.[46] If it is the vendor who defaults, for example, by purporting to repudiate the contract, then the purchaser may claim the return of his deposit, in addition to rescission.

---

[35] *Re Daniel* [1917] 2 Ch. 405; and see *Thomas* v. *Kensington* [1942] 2 K.B. 181.
[36] *Howe* v. *Smith* (1884) 27 Ch.D. 89; *Shuttleworth* v. *Clews* [1910] 1 Ch. 176.
[37] Law of Property Act 1925, s. 49 (2); see *Finkielkraut* v. *Monahan* [1949] 2 All E.R. 234; *Smith* v. *Hamilton* [1951] Ch. 174.
[38] For the different meanings of rescission, see (1955) 19 Conv.(N.S.) 116; (1970) 120 New L.J. 437.
[39] See *ante*, p. 102.
[40] See *ante*, p. 35.
[41] See *ante*, pp. 73 *et seq.*
[42] Accordingly, it is not available if this cannot be done.
[43] *Barber* v. *Wolfe* [1945] Ch. 187.
[44] But not the unpaid balance of a deposit: *Lowe* v. *Hope* [1969] 3 W.L.R. 582.
[45] See *ante*, p. 89.
[46] See *ante*, p. 89.

Declaration

Where either party has exercised his rights under the contract, such as to resell and claim any loss on resale or to rescind, he may wish to have it confirmed that he was entitled to do so. Accordingly, he will seek a declaration that the deposit has been effectively forfeited or the contract effectively rescinded.[47]

---

[47] For rights under conditions of sale, see *ante*, pp. 111–113.

CHAPTER 9

COMPLETION

I. MEANING OF COMPLETION

Date for completion

If, when the investigation of the title is concluded, the vendor has shown a good title according to the contract, the purchaser is bound to accept the title and complete the contract accordingly. We have seen what, in the absence of an express provision, the date for completion will be, but a date for completion is generally expressly specified. Except, however, in those cases where time is of the essence of the contract, the parties are not obliged to complete on the date fixed for completion, and reasonable delay will not entitle either to rescind. The object of fixing a date for completion is to specify a day upon which the parties will endeavour to complete and to provide a day as from which the outgoings will be apportioned and interest become payable in the event of actual completion being delayed.[1]

What amounts to completion

Completion of the contract on the part of the vendor consists (1) in conveying with a good title the property agreed to be sold, and (2) delivering up actual possession or enjoyment.[2] On the purchaser's part, it lies (1) in accepting such title, (2) in preparing and tendering a conveyance for the vendor's execution, (3) accepting such conveyance, (4) taking possession, and (5) paying the price.

Acceptance of title

The purchaser's acceptance of the title is not a formal act or notice. It takes place when the vendor's last answer to the purchaser's requisitions is received without objection.[3] But this acceptance is merely an acceptance of the title put forward by the vendor, and does not preclude the purchaser from raising objections to the title on account of defects subsequently discovered from other sources, such as searches.[4]

II. PREPARATION AND EXECUTION OF CONVEYANCE

Preparation of conveyance [5]

After having examined the abstract with the title deeds (although

---

[1] See generally, *ante*, pp. 108–111.
[2] As to the vendor's obligation to give vacant possession, see *ante*, p. 97.
[3] *Re Highett and Bird's Contract* [1902] 2 Ch. 214.
[4] As to searches, see *ante*, p. 150.
[5] For forms of conveyance and transfer of registered land, see *post*, Chap. 10.

this may be left to the actual completion [6]), and having obtained satisfactory replies to his requisitions, the purchaser's solicitor prepares a draft conveyance [7] and submits it to the vendor's solicitor for his approval.[8] The vendor's solicitor is not entitled to object to the form of the conveyance and is only entitled to amend it so far as is necessary to prevent prejudice to his client.[9] In the case of an estate development, the contract may provide that the conveyance shall be in the form of a standard conveyance prepared on behalf of the vendor for which the purchaser shall pay a nominal fee.[10] When the draft has been approved, it will be engrossed by the purchaser, *i.e.* it will be printed or typed out in fair copy. The engrossment will then be executed by the purchaser in appropriate cases, for example, where the purchaser covenants with the vendor,[11] and it is then delivered to the vendor for execution and handing over to the purchaser on completion.

Execution of conveyances

The conveyance will sometimes be executed at the time of actual completion, but, more commonly, it will be previously executed by the vendor.

The conveyance must be signed,[12] sealed and delivered by the vendor. As to signature, a witness is not essential, except in the case of a registered transfer, where a witness other than the executing party's spouse is required,[13] but it is the invariable practice to have one or two witnesses to facilitate proof of due execution. A purchaser is entitled to have, at his own cost, the execution of the conveyance attested by some person appointed by him, who may be his solicitor or another [14]; but such attestation is unusual. The purchaser is not entitled to require that the conveyance to him be executed in his presence or in that of his solicitor.[14] Sealing was formerly a solemn ceremony with the use of wax and seals. Little remains of these formalities today. Nowadays on engrossment the purchaser's solicitor will stick a small red disk representing a seal onto the deed and the signing of the deed will in effect operate as a sealing.[15]

---

6 See *post*, p. 210.
7 The costs of preparing the conveyance are the purchaser's; see *ante*, p. 104. For the use of a transfer where the transaction leads to first registration, see *post*, p. 243.
8 For conditions as to preparation of conveyance, see *ante*, p. 104.
9 Law Society's Digest, Opinion 1356.
10 See Law of Property Act 1925, s. 48; *ante*, p. 87.
11 *e.g.* restrictive covenants or a covenant for indemnity; see *post*, p. 208.
12 Law of Property Act 1925, s. 73. See further as to the method of execution, *post*, p. 413.
13 Land Registration Rules 1925, Sched., Forms 19 *et seq.*
14 Law of Property Act 1925, s. 75.
15 Strictly perhaps the vendor should either touch the wafer or disk or he should sign the deed with the intention of executing the document as a deed: *Stromdale & Ball Ltd.* v. *Burden* [1952] Ch. 223. But it will often be impossible to prove either of these requirements and either may be presumed. If, as often happens, the disk subsequently falls off, the court would probably assume that there had once been one attached: *cf.* Farrand, *Contract and Conveyance,* p. 415.

Where the vendor is a company, section 74 of the Law of Property Act 1925 provides that, in favour of a purchaser, a deed is deemed to have been duly executed if the company's seal is affixed thereto in the presence of and attested by its clerk, secretary or other permanent officer or his deputy, and a member of the board of directors, council or other governing body of the corporation; and where the seal purporting to be the seal of the corporation has been affixed to a deed, attested by persons purporting to be persons holding such offices, the deed is deemed to have been executed in accordance with the requirements of the section and to have taken effect accordingly.[16]   This mode of execution is in addition to, not in substitution for, any other legal mode of execution.   Execution imports not only sealing the document, but also delivering it as an executed document, so in the case of a company, if the deed is to take effect as an escrow, this intention must be clearly shown.[17]

Where the execution is by a person acting for the vendor under a power of attorney, the purchaser should satisfy himself that the power has not been revoked.[18]   If the instrument executed by the attorney is a registered transfer, a copy of the power of attorney will have been delivered to the Registrar.[19]

The conveyance should be executed by the purchaser where it contains covenants by him, for example, if the deed imposes restrictive covenants or reserves a rentcharge.[20]   But non-execution will not prevent the vendor and his successors in title enforcing their rights [21] after the purchaser has accepted the benefit of the conveyance.[22] Execution by a purchaser is not required in order to give effect to a reservation in the conveyance.[23]

Execution in duplicate

In some cases, the conveyance will be engrossed in duplicate. Where, for example, the vendor reserves a rentcharge, the contract may provide for a conveyance and duplicate conveyance, and, in such a case, both conveyances will be signed by the parties.

Effect of execution

A deed operates from the time it is delivered.   If there are a number of parties to a deed, it will operate as soon as one party executes it so far as it concerns that party.   Thus, where a conveyance

---

[16] See *Beesly* v. *Hallwood Estates* [1961] Ch. 105; *D'Silva* v. *Lister House Development Ltd.* [1970] Ch. 17.
[17] *D'Silva* v. *Lister House Development Ltd., supra.*   For escrows, see *post*, p. 209.
[18] See *ante*, pp. 125–127.
[19] See *ante*, p. 127.
[20] But in the latter case covenants are implied on the part of the grantee even though he does not execute the deed: Law of Property Act 1925, s. 77.
[21] *May* v. *Belville* [1905] 2 Ch. 605, 612.
[22] *Naas* v. *Westminster Bank Ltd.* [1940] A.C. 366.
[23] Law of Property Act 1925, s. 65.   See *post*, p. 235.

is to be executed by both vendor and purchaser, and it is executed only by the vendor, the legal estate nevertheless passes to the purchaser. But a deed does not take effect if it is delivered in escrow [24] or is conditional on the execution of the other party or parties.[25]

Delivery

Delivery may be actual, as where the deed is actually handed over, or virtual, where the deed has been completely executed but it has not yet been handed over to the other party. " Delivery " is used in the old legal sense, namely, an act done so as to evince an intention to be bound. If, for example, prior to actual completion, the party executing the deed executes the deed declaring that he delivers it as his act and deed [26] (or some other similar expression) and hands it to his solicitor, then the deed has been delivered.[27] Thus delivery may be unqualified, but it may also be subject to a condition (see below).

The sealing of a deed by a company prima facie imports delivery.[28]

Delivery in escrow

Delivery will usually be subject to a condition, expressed or implied, that it is not to take effect until the condition has been fulfilled. In the case of a conveyance, it is probably implied that the conveyance is not to take effect until payment. But a deed cannot be delivered as an escrow if it is subject to an overriding power to recall it.[29]

The deed may be delivered to the agent of the party who executed it; to a third party; or to the other party to the deed.[30]

In the case of leases, where it is the usual practice to have both a lease and a counterpart lease, it is readily to be inferred that delivery of the counterpart is a condition of the escrow.[31]

Where a deed has been delivered as an escrow, it cannot be recalled pending performance of the condition on which it was delivered. Accordingly, where a lease had been executed by a company as an escrow, the condition being the usual one, mentioned above, that there should be a counterpart, and the tenant had executed the counterpart, the company could not recall the lease.[31]

Once the condition is fulfilled, the execution relates back to actual delivery, although the usual practice is to date the conveyance with the actual date of completion.

---

[24] For escrows, see *infra.*
[25] *Naas* v. *Westminster Bank Ltd., supra.*
[26] *Xenos* v. *Wickham* (1867) L.R. 2 H.L. 296.
[27] *Vincent* v. *Premo Enterprises Ltd.* [1969] 2 Q.B. 609.
[28] *Beesly* v. *Hallwood Estates Ltd., supra; cf. Windsor Refrigerator Co. Ltd.* v. *Branch Nominees Ltd.* [1961] Ch. 88; revsd. (on another point) 375.
[29] *Windsor Refrigerator Co. Ltd.* v. *Branch Nominees Ltd., supra.*
[30] *Thompson* v. *McCullogh* [1947] K.B. 447.
[31] *Beesly* v. *Hallwood Estates Ltd., supra; D'Silva* v. *Lister House Development Ltd., supra.* See generally Farrand, pp. 419 *et seq.*; (1967) 117 New L.J. 1287; (1970) 34 Conv.(N.S.) 145.

Purchaser mortgaging

Where, as will usually be the case, the purchaser is raising the purchase-money by mortgage of the property, the same conveyancing process
of submitting and approving the draft mortgage, etc., will have
meanwhile been going on between the purchaser-mortgagor and the
mortgagee.

III. ACTUAL COMPLETION

Place of completion

Completion usually takes place at the office of the vendor's
solicitors, or the office of the solicitors of the vendor's mortgagee.[32] The
conveyance, if it has not already been executed by the vendor and
delivered to his solicitor as an escrow, is then executed there. The
conveyance and the title deeds are handed over in exchange for the
purchase-money.

If the title deeds have not been previously examined by the purchaser's solicitor, they will be examined immediately before completion.
The abstract should be " marked " as examined.[33] The purchaser's
solicitor will also examine the conveyance, which will then be dated, if
this has not been done before. Sometimes completion is effected by
post.

Completion statement

Some days prior to the day of completion, the vendor's solicitor
will have sent the purchaser's solicitor a completion statement. This
is a short statement showing the amount the vendor requires on completion. It will show the balance of the purchase price due to the
vendor, after deducting the deposit and taking account of any apportionments required. If the property agreed to be sold is let, an apportionment of rent may be necessary, and, in most cases, rates will have to
be apportioned.[34] Sometimes, the purchaser will have agreed to buy
some carpets or curtains or other fittings. If the purchaser has gone
into possession before completion, interest on the balance of the
purchase-money may be due to the vendor,[35] and interest may also be
due if there is a delay in completion due to the purchaser's fault.[36]

Receipts for outgoings will be produced at completion to support
the completion statement.

Payment of purchase-money

The purchaser must take care that he pays the balance of the
purchase-money to such person or persons only as are entitled to

[32] See Law Society's Conditions, Condition 15; National Conditions, Condition 4 (2);
   Statutory Conditions, Condition 2; see *ante*, p. 111.
[33] See the form of abstract, *post*, p. 409.
[34] See *ante*, p. 107.
[35] See *ante*, p. 105.
[36] See *ante*, p. 105. For form, see *post*, p. 411.

receive it, and give a good discharge for it. Where the purchaser has notice of any incumbrance on the property sold, he must pay the amounts due to the incumbrancers direct; and the surplus, if any, of the purchase-money he should pay to the vendor. If the vendor's solicitor produces a duly executed deed containing a receipt clause,[37] the deed is sufficient authority for the purchaser to pay the money to the solicitor,[38] even if the vendor is a trustee.[39]

The vendor is only bound to accept bank-notes or coins,[40] and he may refuse to take a cheque or any other negotiable security.[41] In practice, bank drafts are always accepted without special arrangements. Where a solicitor is authorised to receive purchase-money, he is not at liberty to accept payment otherwise than in cash or notes without express authority from his client.[42]

Where the deposit is in the hands of a stakeholder other than the vendor's solicitor, a letter from the purchaser releasing the deposit is needed for handing over to the vendor so that he can obtain the money from the stakeholder. Where the purchaser is mortgaging the property, the purchase-money or the appropriate part will be paid by the mortgagee.

Rights of purchaser to title deeds

On paying the purchase-money, the purchaser is entitled to the title deeds relating to the property sold. In certain circumstances, for example, where the deeds relate to other property of the vendor, the vendor is entitled to retain the deeds,[43] giving an acknowledgment and undertaking in respect thereof in the conveyance.[44]

When deeds are handed over, the purchaser should sign a duplicate schedule of deeds as receipt therefor, one copy for retention by the vendor and one for the purchaser. Where the purchaser is mortgaging the property, the mortgagee's solicitor gives the receipt and the purchaser hands over the duly executed mortgage.

If the purchaser is taking over the vendor's insurance, the policies should be handed over. And if the property is let, the vendor should hand over authorities to the tenants to pay their rent to the purchaser.

Finally, in a case where a land charge registration has to be discharged, a duly signed application for vacation of the entry should be handed over to the purchaser.

Undertaking to discharge mortgage [45]

Where, as will usually be the case, the vendor's mortgage is to be

---

37 See *post*, p. 225.
38 Law of Property Act 1925, s. 69.
39 Trustee Act 1925, s. 23 (3).
40 Coinage Act 1971, ss. 2, 3.
41 *Johnston* v. *Boyes* [1899] 2 Ch. 73.
42 *Pope* v. *Westacott* [1894] 1 Q.B. 272.
43 Law of Property Act 1925, s. 45 (9). See *ante*, p. 64.
44 See *post*, p. 238.
45 For discharge of mortgage generally, see *post*, pp. 333 *et seq.*

discharged out of the purchase-money, it will often not be possible for
the vendor to deliver the discharged mortgage with the remainder of the
title deeds on completion. For example, where the mortgagee is a
building society, it may take some days to have the vacating receipt
executed. Accordingly, it is now common practice for completion to
take place upon the undertaking of the vendor's solicitor to discharge
the mortgage and to forward the discharged mortgage to the purchaser's
solicitor within a specified period.[46]

Merger of contract in conveyance

After the execution of the conveyance, any action arising from the
agreement between the parties must be founded on the conveyance.
The contract, it is said, merges in the conveyance. This rule is subject
to two qualifications. First, where the conveyance does not carry out
the agreement between the parties, rectification may be available.[47]
Secondly, merger only takes place to the extent that the conveyance
covers the same ground as the contract. There is no merger if the
conveyance was intended to cover only a portion of the ground
covered by the contract.[48]

Some examples may make this clearer. For instance, if the vendor
fails to prove his title in accordance with the contract, for example, if
subsequently to the conveyance it appears that the vendor had
previously conveyed away part of the land to be sold, then the purchaser has no remedy on the contract, but must rely, so far as he is able,
on the covenants for title implied by the conveyance.[49] On the other
hand, if the vendor contracted to complete the house in a proper and
workmanlike manner, the execution of the conveyance does not merge
the contract on this point in the absence of express provision in the
conveyance.[50] Similarly, there was no merger where the contract contained a special condition that vacant possession would be given on
completion, and the purchaser was unable to get vacant possession
after completion because part of the property was occupied by a
protected tenant.[51]

A *collateral* agreement, whether or not contained in the contract, may
therefore be enforced after completion though not included in the
conveyance. For instance, an agreement to construct a road, not on the

---

[46] For the form of undertaking recommended by the Council of the Law Society,
see Precedent, *post*, p. 437. For the risk of liability under such undertaking,
see Fisher and Lightwood's *Law of Mortgage* (8th ed.), p. 495; (1971) 115
S.J. 684.
[47] See *ante*, p. 25.
[48] *Palmer* v. *Johnson* (1884) 13 Q.B.D. 351; *Eagon* v. *Dent* [1965] 3 All E.R. 334;
Hissett v. *Reading Roofing Co. Ltd.* [1969] 1 W.L.R. 1757.
[49] See *post*, p. 226.
[50] *Lawrence* v. *Cassell* [1935] 2 K.B. 83; *Hancock* v. *B. W. Brazier (Anerley) Ltd.*
[1966] 1 W.L.R. 1317. See further *ante*, p. 81. For the N.H.B.R.C. agreement,
see *ante*, p. 83.
[51] *Hissett* v. *Reading Roofing Co. Ltd.*, *supra*.

property conveyed, but giving access thereto, was held enforceable after completion.[52]

Neither of the standard conditions of sale deals specifically with merger.[53]

In the case of registered land, any merger depends on both execution and registration.[54]

The purchaser may sue on a misrepresentation after completion.[55]

IV. MATTERS SUBSEQUENT TO COMPLETION

Indorsements

After completion, it may be necessary to indorse a memorandum of the conveyance on some other document, for example, on a conveyance where only part of the land comprised therein was being sold, or on the probate where the vendors were executors.[56]

Notice of assignments

Where leaseholds are assigned, the terms of the lease may require notice of the assignment to be given to the lessor.[57]

Notice will also be required on the assignment of choses in action if the assignment is to take effect as a legal assignment,[58] or to obtain priority.[59]

Stamping

The conveyance must be duly stamped by the purchaser within thirty days of execution.[60] The effect of failure to stamp a deed or document which requires stamping is not, generally, to invalidate it, but to render it inadmissible in evidence until it has been duly stamped.[61] A penalty is payable on late stamping.[62] The stamp duty varies according to the amount of the consideration, *i.e.* the duty is *ad valorem*. If the consideration does not exceed £10,000 and the conveyance contains the appropriate certificate of value,[63] no duty is payable; and, similarly, if the consideration does not exceed £15,000, the duty is at a reduced rate.[64]

Even if there is no duty payable in respect of the conveyance, the

---

52 *Jameson* v. *Kinmel Bay Land Co. Ltd.* (1931) 47 T.L.R. 593.
53 *Cf.* 1953 edition of Law Society's Conditions, Condition 33, considered in *Hissett* v. *Reading Roofing Co. Ltd.*, *supra.*
54 *Knight Sugar Co.* v. *The Alberta Railway & Irrigation Co.* [1938] 1 All E.R. 266 (P.C.); and see *Lever Finance* v. *Needleman's Trustee* [1956] Ch. 365.
55 See *ante*, p. 201.
56 For indorsement on probate, see *ante*, p. 137.
57 See *post*, p. 425 and p. 261 for covenants against assignment.
58 Law of Property Act 1925, s. 136.
59 *Dearle* v. *Hall* (1828) 3 Russ. 1, 48; Law of Property Act 1925, s. 137.
60 Stamp Act 1891, s. 15 (2).
61 *Ibid.* s. 14 (4).
62 *Ibid.* s. 15.
63 See *post*, p. 239.
64 Finance Bill 1972.

conveyance must still be produced to the Inland Revenue Commissioners to be stamped with a stamp denoting it has been so produced (the " P.D." stamp).[65] Failure to produce leads to a fine and the inadmissibility of the document in evidence. The purchaser is also required to furnish certain particulars as to the property and consideration to the Commissioners.[66] The original purpose of this was to facilitate the valuation of the land for land value tax, a tax which was abolished in 1934. The information was required for the purposes of betterment levy, which has also been abolished.[67] The particulars are still required, however, for use by the Inland Revenue Valuation Office in valuing land for estate duty and stamp duty purposes, and in advising government departments and local authorities who are acquiring or disposing of land.

We have already mentioned the special stamping considerations on the sale of a business [68] and on a sub-sale.[69] Two further points require to be made. On a gift, the conveyance is stamped *ad valorem* [70] and must be adjudicated,[71] but no " P.D." stamp is required. A certificate of value may be included in appropriate cases so that no duty or only a reduced rate of duty will be paid. Where, as commonly happens, a building plot is conveyed and at the same time there is a separate building agreement, duty is only payable on the consideration under the building agreement if the vendor of the land and the builder are the same persons and the contracts are interdependent.[72]

Mortgage duty has been abolished as from August 1, 1971.[73]

V. REGISTRATION OF TITLE

(1) First registration

If the property conveyed is in an area of compulsory registration of title, then application for registration must be made within two months of the date of the conveyance. Similarly, an assignment on sale of a term having not less than forty years to run, or a lease for not less than forty years, leads to registration.[74]

If, as will often be the case, the transaction has been completed by an advance on mortgage, the application may, and usually will, be made by the mortgagee.[75] The documentation is generally prepared by the purchaser's solicitor.

[65] Finance Act 1931, s. 28.
[66] *Ibid*. Sched. 2.
[67] *Ante*, p. 195.
[68] *Ante*, p. 198.
[69] *Ante*, p. 195.
[70] It is chargeable with the same duty as if it were a conveyance on sale, with the substitution of the value of the property for the amount of the consideration.
[71] Finance (1909–10) Act 1910, s. 74.
[72] *Kimbers & Co.* v. *I.R.C.* [1936] 1 K.B. 132. See Monroe, *The Law of Stamp Duties* (4th ed.), pp. 57, 58.
[73] Finance Act 1971, s. 64.
[74] See *ante*, p. 166.
[75] Land Registration Rules 1925, rr. 72, 73; *post*, p. 297.

We have already dealt with the occasions when registration is compulsory,[76] and we saw that failure to register in such circumstances means that the purchaser or tenant does not obtain a legal estate.[77]

Until the Land Registration Act 1966 voluntary registration was possible even where the property lay outside the area of compulsory registration. This was useful in those cases where there was some technical defect in the title to which the Registrar would not take objection [78]; voluntary registration would clear the defect. However, voluntary registration was suspended by the 1966 Act,[79] save in the following cases:

(1) where the applicant's deeds have been destroyed by enemy action during the Second World War or as a result of some national disaster, such as widespread floods;

(2) where it can be proved that the entire set of title deeds to the property has been lost by the owner's solicitors or destroyed whilst in the solicitor's proper custody;

(3) where there is a developing building estate containing twenty or more houses or plots, or a purpose-built flat development of comparable size, and the applicant or his solicitor can give the requisite certificates and undertakings as to the development;

(4) where the applicant is a local authority or development corporation and the land is going to be sold or leased directly or indirectly for housing development.[80]

As already noted, if the registration is compulsory, then the application for registration must be made within two months of the conveyance. If the application is not received by the Registry within this period, an order for an extension of time must be sought under section 123 of the Land Registration Act 1925. The application should be made in a covering letter accompanying the application and a fee of £1 is payable for such an order.[81] An explanation for the delay must be given, such as pressure of work, documents temporarily mislaid, etc. However, where the delay in applying is more than a year, then one or other of the special forms of application appropriate to the circumstances (for use not following a recent purchase) must be used. Such forms incorporate matters to be certified by the applicant's solicitor not contained in the usual forms.

Any person entitled to apply for first registration may lodge a priority notice, reserving priority for a specified application intended to be subsequently made. If the application itself is then made within fourteen days of the lodgment of the priority notice, the application

76 *Ante*, p. 166.
77 Land Registration Act 1925, s. 123. See Farrand, *Contract and Conveyance*, p. 147; (1968) 32 Conv.(N.S.) 391.
78 As to the acceptability of title to the Registry, see *post*, p. 176.
79 So that the Registry could press ahead with the extension of compulsory registration.
80 See (1967) 31 Conv.(N.S.) 7.
81 Land Registration Fee Order 1970, Sched., para. X.

is dealt with in priority to any other application affecting the same land.[82]   This procedure is rarely used.

The application for first registration must be made on the appropriate prescribed form of application delivered at the proper office of the Land Registry.[83]   The proper office is the appropriate District Land Registry for the area.[84]   The application is usually sent by post.   There are now more than twenty prescribed application forms for differing sets of circumstances, depending on the title sought and whether the applicant is a company or individual.[85]   Some local authorities and other public bodies have their own forms.

The application form must be duly completed and signed in the firm name of the solicitor applying.   Rubber stamp signatures are not permitted, save in exceptional cases.   Care should be taken in completing the form.   Special points to note in addition to signatures are:

    (1)   The applicant's name and address.   The address must be one within the United Kingdom.   For this purpose the Channel Isles, the Isle of Man and Eire are not included.   Several addresses, for example, the applicant's usual address and the addresses of his bank and solicitors, may be given.

    (2)   There is a paragraph in the certificate incorporated in the application form stating that (a) the applicant is solely entitled, or (b), in the case of joint owners, stating that the survivor can give a valid receipt for capital money, etc., or (c), in the case of trustees, tenants for life, etc., that the applicant is estate owner within the meaning of section 4 of the Land Registration Act 1925.   The inappropriate parts of this paragraph should be deleted.

    (3)   The date of the application must not ante-date the deed leading to first registration.

The application must be accompanied by a list in triplicate of all documents delivered,[86] and all the deeds and documents relating to the applicant's title that are in his possession or under his control, including contracts, requisitions, counsel's opinions, etc.[87]   A certified copy of the conveyance to the applicant, or other document inducing registration, and of any accompanying charge is required.[88]   It is also helpful to the Registry to include a certified copy of any other relevant documents, such as a recent deed of grant of mutual easements, a copy of which will be filed in the Registry or " sewn up " in the certificate.[89]

The application must be accompanied by the appropriate fee which

---

[82] Land Registration Rules 1925, r. 71.
[83] *Ibid.* r. 19.
[84] *Ante,* p. 166.
[85] Forms are obtainable from law stationers, *e.g.* Form 1B (freehold for purchaser other than corporate body on recent purchase).
[86] Rules, r. 20 (iv).   Printed form A13 is available for this.
[87] *Ibid.* r. 21 (2).
[88] *Ibid.* rr. 20 (ii), 21, 92, 139.
[89] See *ante,* p. 174.

varies according to the value of the property.[90] No fee is payable in respect of a mortgage by an applicant for first registration which accompanies the application.[91]

On receipt of the application in the Registry, the application will be entered under a title number in the record of pending applications [92] and the list of pending applications.[93] If a caution against first registration has been entered, notice will be given by the Registry to the cautioner.[94]

The application must contain sufficient particulars of the land, by plan or otherwise, to enable the property to be fully identified on the Ordnance Map or the Land Registry General Map.[95] The first stage of the registration process is the mapping, *i.e.* the preparation of the plan to be filed in the certificate. As soon as possible after the receipt of the application, a preliminary identification of the land is made on the index map.[96] The land is usually registered with " general boundaries." Except where there is a note in the property register that the boundaries have been fixed, the filed plan or general map is deemed to indicate only the general boundaries of the registered land in the title. A survey of the land is only made if it cannot otherwise be fully identified; for example, a survey is sometimes required where part of the first floor of one property is situate over the site of the adjoining property. A survey and even the Ordnance Map sometimes reveal that the conveyance plan is inaccurate, in which case it will have to be rectified and initialled by the parties.[97]

The next stage is the examination of title. We have already noted [98] that the Registry will generally not take technical points on the title (and this was why voluntary registration was so useful to cure technically defective titles). If the value of the property does not exceed £700, the Registry may rely on the form of certificate by a solicitor incorporated in the application form [99] and a very cursory examination.[1] Furthermore, the Act provides that, if the Registrar, on examining any title, is of opinion that the title is open to objection but that nevertheless it is a title the holding under which will not be disturbed, he may approve it.[2] The Registry may therefore (and in

---

[90] See Land Registration Fee Order 1970.
[91] *Ibid.*, Abatement 1.
[92] Land Registration Rules, rr. 24, 83 (commonly called the " Day List ").
[93] *Ibid.* r. 10. See *Strand Securities Ltd.* v. *Caswell* [1965] Ch. 958, 968.
[94] See *ante*, p. 181.
[95] Rules, r. 20 (iii).
[96] See *Lee* v. *Barrey* [1957] Ch. 251.
[97] The incidence of faulty plans is one in eight: see (1969) 32 M.L.R. 127.
[98] *Ante*, p. 176.
[99] The certificate states, amongst other things, that the solicitors acted for the applicant on the purchase and investigated the title for a period of not less than 15 years and that the conveyance to the purchaser validly conveyed the estate and interest purported to be conveyed. A selection of these application forms should be obtained by the student.
[1] Land Registration Rules 1925, r. 29.
[2] Land Registration Act 1925, s. 13, proviso (*c*).

practice do) ignore mere technical defects in title. The Registry will examine the documents accompanying the application; and a draft of the entries on the register is prepared. The usual entries relate to the mortgage of the property and any adverse easements and restrictive covenants affecting the property (these appear in the Charges Register [3]), and appurtenant easements, exceptions of mines and minerals and provisions as to party walls and light and air (which appear in the Property Register). Requisitions may be raised by the Registry. These generally relate to the solicitor's failure to complete the documentation properly, such as not certifying the copy deed inducing registration or failing to complete the blanks in the accompanying charge, rather than matters of substance. The Registry may make further searches and inquiries.

An application is rarely rejected outright. The title may have to be put right by some confirmatory deed, just as in unregistered conveyancing. The most common example of rejection of the title occurs where absolute leasehold title is sought, but the reversionary title has not or cannot be supplied (as is necessary).

The deed inducing registration, *i.e.* the conveyance, assignment or lease to the applicant, and, in the case of leaseholds, the lease (if not the deed inducing registration and if it is available) are marked with the " first registration " stamp.[4] This prevents any fraudulent dealing by the proprietor with the deeds.

Before any registration with absolute or good leasehold title is completed, it may be advertised,[5] but this is rarely done.

The final stage of the registration process is the preparation of the register and the land certificate (and, where appropriate, the charge certificate).

If there is no charge, the land certificate is issued to the proprietor. The documents accompanying the application for registration, except those required to be retained in the Registry, such as the certified copy of the deed inducing registration, are returned to the applicant. The old title deeds are not necessarily obsolete. Thus, the proprietor of leasehold land must retain the original lease, if he had it, and pre-1926 deeds containing restrictive covenants must also be retained. Furthermore, positive covenants are not usually referred to on the register and any deeds containing these will have to be retained.

The certificate of title
We have already dealt with the form of the certificate.[6]

Dealings prior to first registration
A person who has the right to apply for first registration may deal

---

[3] In the case of leaseholds the covenants in the lease do not appear in the register.
[4] *Ibid.* s. 16.
[5] Land Registration Rules 1925, rr. 31, 32, 33.
[6] *Ante*, p. 174.

with the land before he is himself registered as proprietor,[7] for example, by transfer on a sub-sale. In this case, the transferee will be deemed to be the applicant for first registration.[8]

Title shown procedure

This procedure is concerned with the first registration of houses on building estates. It is an attempt to avoid the repeated examination of title to numerous plots of a building estate as they are sold off, when the title in each case will be exactly the same. The initiative must be taken by the developer or his solicitor who should write to the appropriate Registry describing the location and nature of the estate and how it is to be sold off.

The procedure can only be used in the following circumstances:

    (1) the estate must be within an area of compulsory registration;

    (2) the vendor's title must be derived from a single conveyance or lease;

    (3) the estate must comprise not less than fifty houses;

    (4) it must be intended to sell off the properties within a reasonably short period of time;

    (5) the estate must consist of regularly shaped plots in a symmetrical pattern;

    (6) a standard form of conveyance or lease must be adopted;

    (7) the developer must be prepared to give the Registry the fullest degree of assistance in investigating the title, mapping, etc.

If the Registrar is prepared to consider the developer's request, the title will be examined, and once he is satisfied as to this and other matters, such as plans, etc., he will issue a letter stating that he has investigated the title and that, without further production of title, he will be prepared to register a purchaser from the developer with absolute title on the production of certain documents, such as a normal application form, a certificate of search in the Land Charges Department against a specified person or persons, a release by the debenture holder together with the appropriate fee.

The contracts for the sales off of the parts of the estate must then contain a condition to the effect that the vendor's title has already been deduced to and accepted by the Registrar (as evidenced by his letter, a copy of which should be attached to the contract) and that no further investigation of title is to be made beyond an inspection of the letter and of any deeds containing restrictive covenants or other incumbrances to which the letter refers. The contract must also provide for the use of the standard form of transfer.[9]

---

[7] Land Registration Act 1925, s. 37 (3); Rules, r. 72 (1).

[8] *Post*, p. 243.

[9] See further Ruoff and Roper (3rd ed.), pp. 263 *et seq.*

(2) Registered dealings

Application for registration

The application must be made on the prescribed form appropriate to the nature of the dealing.[10] It must be accompanied by the land or charge certificate, as appropriate; the transfer or other dealing with a certified copy thereof; the certificate of the result of an official search of the register [11]; and the proper fee. The registration is then completed in the Registry by the appropriate modification to the register. For example, in the case of a transfer of the whole, no new covenants, etc., being created, by the deletion of the transferor's name in the Proprietorship Register and the addition of the transferee's name and address and a reference to the application number and price in the remarks column of that register.[12]

---

[10] For example, Form A4 for a dealing with the whole of the land; **Form A5 for a** dealing with part of the land. These are obtainable from law stationers.
[11] See *ante*, p. 184.
[12] See *post*, p. 242.

CHAPTER 10

CONVEYANCES AND TRANSFERS

I. UNREGISTERED LAND: CONVEYANCES

WE have seen [1] that, if he is satisfied with the vendor's title, the purchaser or his solicitor [2] draws up a draft conveyance and submits it to the vendor or his solicitor for his approval. When the draft is approved, it is engrossed (that is, a fair copy is made) and it will then be ready for execution by the parties.

It is proposed to deal with conveyances of unregistered land by discussing their contents separately. The reader is advised, when reading the following, to study simultaneously Forms 6 to 9 in the Appendix: if each part of the deed is thus noted as it is discussed, the subject will be rendered much more easy to understand.

A. Commencement

Until 1926 a deed nearly always began with the words " This Indenture made the (date)." But deeds are now described according to the nature of the transaction intended to be effected and a deed may be described simply as a deed or, for example, as a conveyance, vesting deed, settlement, mortgage, charge, lease or otherwise, whichever is the most fitting word.[3]

B. Date

The date is not, strictly speaking, part of the deed, nor is it necessary. A deed takes effect from the date on which it is delivered, not from the date inserted in it, so that if there is no date in it, or if it has a false date (differing from the date of delivery) or an impossible date (such as February 30), the deed is valid and it takes effect from the date of delivery, oral evidence being admitted to prove the actual date of delivery.[4] Nevertheless, the date appearing in the deed is presumed to be the date of delivery unless it appears to the contrary.

C. Parties [5]

The parties to the conveyance should, in general, comprise, besides the

---

[1] See *ante*, p. 207.
[2] But see Law of Property Act 1925, s. 48 (1); *ante*, p. 87.
[3] Law of Property Act 1925, s. 57.
[4] *Goddard's Case* (1584) 2 Co.Rep. 4b.
[5] Capacity of the parties is not dealt with here as such: for this, see Gibson's *Conveyancing* (20th ed.), Chap. 2. Nor is the Law of Property Act 1925, s. 56, dealt with: for this, see Farrand, *Contract and Conveyance*, pp. 277–278.

vendor and the purchaser, every person whose consent or concurrence is necessary to make a conveyance of the estate or interest contracted to be sold and also all persons who enter into any of the covenants contained in the deed. But there is, of course, no necessity to join persons whose rights will be overreached by the conveyance. For example, on a sale of settled land or land held on trust for sale, the purchaser takes free from the beneficial interests, provided the purchase-money is paid to at least two trustees or a trust corporation or (in the case of settled land) into court. The powers of sale of a tenant for life or statutory owner under a strict settlement and of trustees for sale are dealt with in a later chapter.[6] The following points should also be noted.

Personal representatives

On an intestacy, administrators hold the deceased's property on trust for sale.[7] Moreover, personal representatives have wide statutory powers of dealing with the deceased's property.[8] The object of conferring these powers is to enable the personal representatives to raise money, if necessary, for the purpose of paying estate duty, the debts of the deceased and the costs of the administration. When there are two or more personal representatives, the question arises whether one can act alone or they must all act together. The position where the death occurred after 1925 is that the personal representatives have joint and several power over pure personalty, that is, one of them can act alone, but in the case of other property (that is, freeholds and leaseholds), where there are two or more personal representatives a conveyance (which includes, for example, mortgages and leases[9]) cannot generally be made without the concurrence therein of all such representatives or an order of the court.[10]

Mortgages

The mortgagee's power of sale is discussed in a later chapter.[11] A mortgagor can sell the land. The purchaser will in such cases usually covenant to pay the principal and interest and indemnify the vendor against any liability under the mortgage. Again, the mortgagor and the mortgagee may together sell the land, the mortgagee releasing the land from the mortgage in return for some or all of the purchase-price.

---

[6] See *post*, pp. 361 *et seq.*, 376 *et seq.*

[7] Administration of Estates Act 1925, s. 33. And see *ante*, pp 145, 146.

[8] *Ibid.* s. 39.

[9] *Ibid.* s. 55 (1) (iii).

[10] *Ibid.* ss. 2, 3. See *Harrison* v. *Wells* [1967] 1 Q.B. 263. Note that a sole personal representative, acting as such, has power to give valid receipts for proceeds of sale or other capital money: see Law of Property Act 1925, s. 27 (2) as amended by Law of Property (Amendment) Act 1926, Sched.; Settled Land Act 1925, s. 18 (1). For Administration of Estates Act 1925, ss. 36 and 37, see *ante*, pp. 136 *et seq.*

[11] See *post*, pp. 316 *et seq.*

D. Recitals

Recitals are of two kinds, namely, narrative and introductory. Narrative recitals set out the facts and instruments necessary to show the vendor's title: for example, a conveyance often recites that the vendor is seised of the property concerned in fee simple, if such be the case. Introductory recitals explain the motive or purpose of the deed containing them: for example, a conveyance often recites that the vendor has agreed to sell and the purchaser to buy the property concerned at the agreed price. These two examples of recitals commonly appear together in a conveyance, as in Form No. 6 in the Appendix.

Opinions vary as to the extent to which recitals should be used. In the simplest form of deed no recitals need be used, although recitals are, from the purchaser's point of view at any rate, advisable because of estoppel (discussed below) and are often useful for other purposes. At least there is no doubt that the modern tendency is to have short recitals, if they are used, instead of the unnecessarily long ones which prevailed in the past; and, whereas recitals were not usually numbered in the past, the modern and convenient practice is to set them out in numbered paragraphs, save that the two common recitals in the form mentioned above are often run together.

Some of the cases where, and reasons why, recitals may be useful are as follows:

(1) Estoppel

Recitals in a deed estop all persons on whose behalf they are made, and persons claiming under them, from disputing their accuracy. Thus, if a conveyance recites that the vendor is seised in fee simple, he will be estopped from denying that he was so seised at the date of the deed.[12] But in order that a recital may operate by estoppel, it must be precise and unambiguous: thus, if the recital states that the vendor is " seised or otherwise well and sufficiently entitled " to the property, this will not amount to an estoppel.[13] Because of estoppel, it is always best to insert at least some such recital as that appearing in Form No. 6 in the Appendix.

(2) Recitals in abstracts

A purchaser must assume, unless the contrary appears or one of three stated exceptions applies, that recitals contained in abstracted instruments of any document forming part of the title prior to the root are correct.[14]

(3) Recitals in instruments twenty years old

Recitals contained in deeds or instruments twenty years old at the

---

[12] See *Cumberland Court (Brighton) Ltd.* v. *Taylor* [1964] Ch. 29.
[13] *Heath* v. *Crealock* (1874) L.R. 10 Ch. 22.
[14] Law of Property Act 1925, s. 45 (1). *Ante*, p. 63.

date of the contract are, unless they are proved to be inaccurate, to be taken to be sufficient evidence of the truth of the matters they state.[15] By virtue of this and the last-mentioned provision, recitals may be inserted in order to be used on later sales of the property, though from a realistic point of view these two provisions are likely to prove useful more because of good fortune than because of a predetermined design. In any event, the provisions afford help to purchasers when perusing, and vendors when showing, title.

Nevertheless, in inserting recitals, care should be exercised to avoid any conflict with the operative part of the deed. If the operative part is clear and precise, nothing contained in the recitals will control it, but if the recitals are clear and precise and the operative part is ambiguous, the recitals will be held to explain and limit the meaning of the operative part.[16]

Finally, sometimes, in order to save the necessity of long recitals, a deed may be expressed to be supplemental to a previous instrument, in which case the later instrument will be read and have effect as if it contained a full recital of the previous instrument.[17]

E. Operative Part
The operative part of a conveyance consists of the following:

(1) Testatum
The testatum commences the operative part, taking the form, " NOW THIS DEED WITNESSETH . . . ."

(2) Consideration
A deed does not require any consideration to support it. However, if there is consideration it is advisable to express it in the conveyance, for the following reasons:

(a) Under the Stamp Act 1891,[18] a penalty of £10 is imposed on any person who, with intent to defraud, does not fully and truly set forth all the facts and circumstances affecting the liability of the instrument to or the amount of *ad valorem* duty chargeable.

(b) The statement of the consideration is followed by the receipt clause, the advantages of which are discussed below.

(c) If the consideration is stated in the deed, it is evidence that the deed is not voluntary, and since a voluntary deed has certain disadvantages the statement of the consideration is advisable. It is true that extrinsic evidence may be admissible to prove the true consideration,[19] but it is clearly advisable to state the correct consideration

---

[15] *Ibid.* s. 45 (6).
[16] See *Jenner* v. *Jenner* (1866) L.R. 1 Eq. 361.
[17] Law of Property Act 1925, s. 58.
[18] s. 5.
[19] *Turner* v. *Forwood* [1951] 1 All E.R. 746.

in the deed. Two examples of the disadvantages to which voluntary deeds are subject are as follows. A voluntary conveyance made with intent to defraud creditors is voidable at the instance of anyone thereby prejudiced [20]; and a voluntary disposition of land made with intent to defraud a subsequent purchaser is voidable at the instance of that purchaser. [21]

(3) Receipt clause

The receipt clause is usually placed in brackets after the statement of the consideration, taking some such form as " the receipt whereof the vendor hereby acknowledges." A receipt clause should be inserted, for a receipt for consideration money in the body of a deed is a sufficient discharge for the same to the person paying it, without any further receipt being indorsed on the deed. [22] Further, a receipt for consideration in the body of the deed or indorsed thereon is, in favour of a subsequent purchaser without notice that the consideration was not in fact paid, sufficient evidence of the payment thereof. [23] Finally, the production by a solicitor of a deed having in the body thereof or indorsed thereon a receipt for the consideration, the deed being executed, or the indorsed receipt being signed, by the person entitled to give a receipt, is sufficient authority for the payment of the purchase-money to the solicitor, without (as was formerly necessary) the solicitor producing any separate authority. [24]

(4) Vendor's covenants for title

Introduction [25]

In early grants of land, the vendor would warrant that he was giving a good title to the purchaser, who could compel him to grant a plot of land equal in value if the warranty was unjustified. As the feudal system declined, warranties died out but covenants were given instead, the remedy for their breach being damages. The covenants became standardised and the Conveyancing Act 1881 made it unnecessary to write them out at length in a conveyance by providing that the standardised covenants, which were set out in the Act, were to be imported if certain short phrases (for example, " as beneficial owner ") were used to describe the capacity in which the vendor conveyed. These provisions are now contained in the Law of Property Act 1925. [26] The remedy for breach of the covenants is still damages.

[20] Law of Property Act 1925, s. 172. See *ante*, p. 148.
[21] *Ibid*. s. 173.
[22] *Ibid*. s. 67.
[23] *Ibid*. s. 68. And see *London and Cheshire Insurance Co. Ltd.* v. *Laplagrene Property Co. Ltd.* [1971] Ch. 499.
[24] Law of Property Act 1925, s. 69.
[25] See, further, Farrand, *Contract and Conveyance*, pp. 302–303; Simpson, *An Introduction to the History of Land Law*, pp. 109–110.
[26] s. 76 and Sched. 2.

" As beneficial owner "

By section 76 (1) of the Law of Property Act 1925 certain covenants are implied in a conveyance for valuable consideration executed after 1881, by a person who conveys and is expressed to convey " as beneficial owner "—for example, " the Vendor as beneficial owner hereby conveys . . . ." These implied covenants are:

(i) That the vendor has power to convey the interest he has agreed to sell. This covenant will be broken if, for example, the vendor has a lesser estate than the estate he purports to convey or he has already conveyed the property or part of it elsewhere. The latter situation quite commonly occurs in building developments because of poor mapping.[27] The remedy on the covenants is generally the only remedy available to the purchaser after completion.

(ii) That the purchaser should have quiet enjoyment of the property conveyed.[28] A breach of this covenant will usually amount to a breach of the covenant for power to convey, but its insertion is advantageous because an action on the covenant for quiet enjoyment is not barred until twelve years after the interference, whereas an action on the covenant for power to convey is barred after twelve years from the execution of the conveyance.[29]

(iii) That the property conveyed is free from incumbrances, except those subject to which the conveyance is expressed to be made. This covenant will be broken if, for example, the land is subject to a mortgage.

(iv) That, by way of further assurance, the vendor will do all other acts and things necessary to perfect the purchaser's title, at the purchaser's expense. This covenant will be broken if, for example, the vendor refuses to discharge an outstanding mortgage at the purchaser's request.[30]

In an assignment of leasehold property [31] for valuable consideration executed after 1881 by a person who conveys and is expressed to convey " as beneficial owner," there are implied, in addition to the above four covenants, covenants:

(v) That the lease is valid and subsisting at the date of the assignment.

(vi) That the rent has been paid and the lessee's covenants have been observed up to the date of the assignment.

The above covenants are only implied in a conveyance for valuable consideration, so that the expression " beneficial owner " will imply no covenants in a voluntary conveyance.

When a person, as beneficial owner, directs another to convey, he is

---

27 See as to boundary disputes, *ante,* p. 72.
28 See the discussions on the landlord's covenant, *post,* p. 267: the same principles generally apply here.
29 See *post,* p. 229.
30 See further (1970) 34 Conv.(N.S.) 178.
31 See *post,* p. 268.

to be deemed to have entered into the above covenants.[32] This will operate, for example, in the case of a sub-sale.

Burden of covenants and qualified covenants

Unlike the benefit (as to which, see below), the burden of the implied covenants does not run with the land. Only the covenantor is liable in damages for a breach of any of the above covenants. Further, even his liability is not absolute but qualified. This means that he is liable only for a breach of any of the covenants due to his own acts or omissions or to those of someone claiming under him or in trust for him, or someone through whom he derived his title *otherwise* than by purchase for value, or someone claiming under such last-named person.[33]

For example, A grants a legal easement over his land to B and later conveys his land " as beneficial owner " to C. Subsequently, C conveys the land " as beneficial owner " to D. If B disturbs D's quiet enjoyment by exercising his easement, D cannot sue C on the implied covenant for quiet enjoyment, for C is not responsible for A's acts or omissions because he purchased from A for value. But D can sue A, because the benefit of the covenants between A and C runs with the land: this is discussed shortly. Suppose that in this example C had acquired the land from A otherwise than for value (as by way of gift from A): D could sue C, because C's covenants would cover the acts or omissions of A (C having derived title from A otherwise than by purchase for value): in this case, on the other hand, D could not sue A, for when A gave the land to C he would not have given any covenant (or any effective covenant[34]) to C.[35]

Benefit of covenants

The benefit of the implied covenants runs with the land, so that they are enforceable, not only by the person or persons with whom they are entered into but also by every person in whom the covenantee's estate or interest or any part thereof is from time to time vested.[36] The effect of this is discussed in the above example.

By way of mortgage

Where a conveyance is by way of mortgage the mortgagor will convey " as beneficial owner," and he will thereby imply virtually the same covenants as the above,[37] save that they are in such a case absolute,[37] not qualified, so that the mortgagor undertakes liability for everybody's acts or omissions.

---

[32] Law of Property Act 1925, s. 76 (2).
[33] See the leading case of *David* v. *Sabin* [1893] 1 Ch. 523.
[34] See *ante*, p. 226.
[35] See further, Megarry and Wade, pp. 612–613; and Farrand, *Contract and Conveyance*, pp. 304–306.
[36] Law of Property Act 1925, s. 76 (6).
[37] Law of Property Act 1925, s. 76 (1) (C) and (D). See (1964) 28 Conv.(N.S.) 205.

Other covenants

Besides the covenants implied by the words " as beneficial owner," there are less extensive ones. In a conveyance by way of settlement, if the settlor conveys and is expressed to convey " as settlor," he will thereby imply a covenant for further assurance only.[38] Though this is the case whether or not the settlement is for value, the settlor covenants only for himself and persons deriving title under him. If someone conveys and is expressed to convey as trustee, mortgagee, personal representative, committee, receiver, or under an order of the court, he will imply merely a covenant that he has not himself effected any incumbrance[39]; though again the disposition need not be for value for the covenant to arise. When a tenant for life sells under his statutory powers, he conveys " as trustee," and thereby implies a covenant that he has not himself incumbered. Beneficial joint tenants or tenants in common who hold the legal estate as joint tenants on trust for themselves may convey " as trustees " or " as beneficial owners ": which is to be the case should appear in the contract.

" Conveys and is expressed to convey " [40]

The covenants are implied if a person " conveys and is expressed to convey " as beneficial owner, trustee and so forth. The better view is that the vendor's true capacity is of no consequence, so that, for example, a person who is actually a trustee can, by conveying " as beneficial owner " imply the more extensive covenants,[41] though there are opposing opinions to the effect that the covenants are implied only if a person in fact has the capacity in which he is expressed to convey.[42] Because there is this doubt, a purchaser who wishes to obtain the more extensive covenants from, say, a trustee, might either procure that the " beneficial owner " covenants are set out expressly in the conveyance or (much less drastically but just as effectively) have inserted in the conveyance a clause which specifically incorporates into the conveyance the covenants in the Second Schedule, Part I, to the Law of Property Act 1925 (which contains the " beneficial owner " covenants[43]). These devices avoid using the words " as beneficial owner " in the conveyance.

Express limitation or variation

If a conveyance is expressly made subject to an incumbrance or other defect, no breach of the covenants for title can arise in respect

---

[38] Law of Property Act 1925, s. 76 (1) (E).
[39] *Ibid.* s. 76 (1) (F).
[40] See generally, Farrand, *Contract and Conveyance*, pp. 314–315; Megarry and Wade, p. 610; (1942) 7 Conv.(N.S.) 3; (1953) 17 Conv.(N.S.) 407; (1968) 32 Conv.(N S.) 123.
[41] See *e.g. David* v. *Sabin* [1893] 1 Ch. 523; *Parker* v. *Judkin* [1931] 1 Ch. 475.
[42] See *Fay* v. *Miller, Wilkins and Co.* [1941] Ch. 360; *Pilkington* v. *Wood* [1953] Ch. 770.
[43] See (1968) 32 Conv.(N.S.) 123; Farrand, *Contract and Conveyance*, p. 315.

of such incumbrance or defect. But in the absence of such express words limiting or varying the effect of the implied covenants, they will be literally construed. Thus, the implied covenants extend to incumbrances or other defects of which the purchaser knew at the time of the conveyance, even those apparent on the face of the conveyance, unless the conveyance is expressly made subject to them.[44]

Limitation period

The time for bringing an action on the covenants for title is limited to twelve years from the date when the cause of such action arose.[45] In the case of the covenant for power to convey, the cause of action arises immediately on the execution of the conveyance[46] and is therefore barred in twelve years from that date. In the case of the covenant for quiet enjoyment, the cause of action does not arise, and so time does not begin to run, until there has been an actual interference with that enjoyment.[47] It has been held[48] that the covenant for freedom from incumbrances is broken on the execution of the conveyance, but the better view seems to be that this is wrong and that the cause of action only arises when there is an actual interference with enjoyment.[49] The covenant for further assurance is broken, and time begins to run, when there has been a request to execute a document or do something else to perfect the title and it has been refused.[50] The two additional covenants implied in the case of leasehold property[51] will be broken on the execution of the conveyance, as will the covenant implied by one who conveys as trustee, mortgagee, personal representative, committee, receiver, or under an order of the court, that he has not personally effected any incumbrance.

(5) Words of conveyance

The words of conveyance are those which operate to pass the relevant estate or interest in the property from the vendor to the purchaser. The words " the Vendor hereby grants " are sufficient, but the word " grant " is not essential.[52] It is equally sufficient, and the most common practice, to use the words " the Vendor [as beneficial owner, or as the case may be] hereby conveys." But any words will

---

[44] See *G. W. Ry.* v. *Fisher* [1905] 1 Ch. 316; *Page* v. *Midland Ry.* [1894] 1 Ch. 11; (1970) 34 Conv.(N.S.) at pp. 194–196. The court, however, can rectify the conveyance by inserting a proviso limiting or varying the effect of the covenants to the extent necessary to give effect to the true agreement of the parties as expressed in the contract: *Butler* v. *Mountview Estates Ltd.* [1951] 2 K.B. 563.
[45] Limitation Act 1939, s. 2 (3). See (1970) 34 Conv.(N.S.) at pp. 193–194. Damages are assessed as at the date of the conveyance save in the case of breach of the covenant for quiet enjoyment: see (1970) *Estates Gazette Digest* 902.
[46] See *Spoor* v. *Green* (1874) L.R. 9 Ex. 99 at p. 110.
[47] See *Spoor* v. *Green, supra.* at p. 111.
[48] *Turner* v. *Moon* [1901] 2 Ch. 825.
[49] See *Nottidge* v. *Dering* [1909] 2 Ch. 647, affirmed [1910] Ch. 297.
[50] See *Jones* v. *King* (1815) 4 M. & S. 188.
[51] See *ante*, p. 226.
[52] Law of Property Act 1925, s. 51 (2).

J

suffice if the intention to transfer the relevant estate or interest is clear. For example, where the grantor assented by a document under seal in circumstances where a conveyance, and not an assent, was appropriate, it was held that the legal estate was nevertheless transferred to the grantee, this being the manifest intention of the document.[53]

F. Parcels

The parcels consist of a description of the property, commonly commencing " ALL THAT . . . ." If the parcels are lengthy, they may be set out in a schedule to the deed. The description should, if appropriate, be the same as in the earlier title deeds, so as to prevent any question as to the identity of the property conveyed with that described in such earlier deeds. However, if the old description is insufficient to identify the property to be conveyed with certainty, because, for example, of a change in the nature of the property (such as rebuilding) or of the surroundings (such as new roads or the renaming of old roads), a new description should be framed and both the old description and the new one should be referred to in the conveyance, in order to show subsequent purchasers the identity of the land being sold. Indeed, even in the absence of some such apparent change, the purchaser is well advised to inspect the property to see that the description is correct.[54]

Alternatively, the property is often described by reference to a plan drawn on or annexed to the deed. The purchaser cannot insist on a plan if a sufficient description and identification can be given without one,[55] but the vendor can be compelled to convey by reference to a plan if the property cannot be identified without one.[56]

Often the parcels set out a description in words and also refer to a plan drawn on or annexed to the deed. Here, it should be made clear which is to override the other in the event of their failure to correspond. In one case,[57] after describing the property the deed continued " all of which said premises are more particularly described in the plan endorsed on these presents and are delineated and coloured red in such plan." It was held that the plan prevailed. But if the plan is drawn on or annexed to the deed " for the purpose of facilitating identification only " [58] or " by way of identification, and not of limitation," the description in words prevails.

Certain presumptions may aid in the construction of the parcels. There is a presumption that the owner of land abutting on a road is the

---

[53] *Re Stirrup's Contract* [1961] 1 W.L.R. 449.
[54] See *Hopgood* v. *Brown* [1955] 1 W.L.R. 213; *Willson* v. *Greene* [1971] 1 W.L.R. 635. And see *ante*, p. 72.
[55] *Re Sharman and Meade's Contract* [1936] Ch. 755.
[56] *Re Sparrow and James' Contract* [1910] 2 Ch. 60.
[57] *Eastwood* v. *Ashton* [1915] A.C. 900.
[58] *Hopgood* v. *Brown* [1955] 1 W.L.R. 213, *per* Jenkins L.J. at p. 228; and see *Willson* v. *Greene, supra.*

owner of the soil up to the middle line,[59] and that the owner of land abutting on a non-tidal river is the owner of the bed of the river up to the middle line: and when either of them conveys his land it is presumed, if the parcels are not to the contrary, that he intends to convey, not merely the land as set out in the plan or described in the parcels, but also his half of the soil of the road [60] or bed of the river.[61] Where one piece of land is separated from another by a hedge and an artificial ditch, the hedge and ditch are presumed to belong to the owner of the land which is on the same side of the ditch as the hedge,[62] though the presumption will be rebutted by a different delineation in the title deeds.[63]

It should be mentioned that a conveyance of land is deemed to include and operates to convey, with the land, all fixtures even though they are not expressly referred to in the deed.[64]

As for party walls, the reader is referred to Precedent 8 in the Appendix.[65]

G. General Words

This requires some introduction. In drafting a conveyance it may be necessary to consider the rights (if any) which each party is to have over the land of the other, in cases where the vendor retains other land, or the rights (if any) which the purchaser may exercise over a third party's land. The following situations may arise.

(1) The land conveyed may be subject to some right, such as a right of way, created in the past, and the conveyance should be made expressly subject to such a right. This matter is dealt with under the heading " Habendum," which follows shortly.[66]

(2) The vendor may wish to except something (such as minerals) from the conveyance or to reserve to himself a new right over the land conveyed (such as a right of way). This should be done by way of express exception, reservation or regrant. This topic is dealt with later under the heading " Exceptions and Reservations." [67]

(3) There may be certain rights already appurtenant to the land, such as a right of way previously created. Such rights pass automatically at common law by the conveyance of the land to which they are annexed, though it is usual to set out the rights in the conveyance after the parcels, and to introduce them by the words " TOGETHER WITH . . . ." [68]

---

59 *Re White's Charities* [1898] 1 Ch. 659. For the surface, see Highways Act 1959, s. 226.
60 *Berridge and Another* v. *Ward* (1861) 10 C.B.(N.S.) 400.
61 *Micklethwait* v. *Newlay Bridge Co.* (1886) 33 Ch.D. 133.
62 See *Marshall* v. *Taylor* [1895] 1 Ch. 641.
63 *Davey* v. *Harrow Corporation* [1958] 1 Q.B. 60.
64 Law of Property Act 1925, s. 62 (1). See *ante*, p. 16.
65 *Post*, p. 415 and note 47.
66 See *post*, pp. 235–236.
67 See *post*, pp. 234–235.
68 For parcels, see *ante*, pp. 230–231.

(4) The vendor may grant to the purchaser rights over land retained by the vendor. For example, he may grant him a right of way over the vendor's retained land. Such rights will again be introduced by the words "TOGETHER WITH" and will follow the parcels. If the land has the benefit of already existing rights and new rights are also to be granted, it might be more convenient to set out the different sets of rights in schedules.

(5) New rights may arise *impliedly* in favour of the conveyed land over land retained by the vendor. This brings us to the "general words."

Formerly, conveyances contained after the parcels what were known as the "general words," which commenced with the phrase "together with" and purported to convey to the purchaser all rights and easements, *profits à prendre*, and other rights appurtenant to the property, or at any time enjoyed with it, or reputed to form part of it. Rights which are already appurtenant pass automatically at common law by the conveyance, as we have seen, and in such cases the general words were never strictly necessary; but they were added to show an express intention that such rights should be included in the grant and nowadays any rights already appurtenant to the land are usually set out or referred to in the conveyance, as we have seen.

But it might happen that the vendor was retaining other land belonging to him and adjoining the land sold. Any rights which the vendor had been exercising over the land retained for the benefit of the land sold could not exist as easements, because a man could not have an easement over his own land. Such rights were known as quasi-easements, and on a sale of the portion of the vendor's land benefited by them they became full easements which could be exercised over the portion the vendor kept, in so far as they were continuous and apparent, were necessary to the reasonable enjoyment of the land sold, and were prior to and at the time of the grant used by the vendor for the benefit of the portion sold. This is known as the rule in *Wheeldon* v. *Burrows* [69] and is based on the principle that "a grantor shall not derogate from his own grant." For example, if X owned a plot of land and he customarily crossed part of it to gain access to the part where he resided, on a sale of the latter part the purchaser would be able to exercise as an easement the right of way over the retained part which had until then been a quasi-easement. Although this rule operated by virtue of the conveyance without reference to the right concerned, the general words would leave no doubt as to the passing of all such rights, and they were often so widely framed that they would probably also pass rights which were neither continuous nor apparent and which were not strictly necessary for the reasonable enjoyment of the land sold.

[69] (1879) 12 Ch.D. 31. See (1967) 83 L.Q.R. 240.

The general words have, since 1861, been altogether omitted. Section 62 (1) of the Law of Property Act 1925 [70] provides that " a conveyance of land shall be deemed to include and shall by virtue of this Act operate to convey, with the land, all buildings, erections, fixtures, commons, hedges, ditches, fences, ways, waters, watercourses, liberties, privileges, easements, rights, and advantages whatsoever, appertaining or reputed to appertain to the land, or any part thereof, or, at the time of conveyance, demised, occupied, or enjoyed with, or reputed or known as part or parcel of or appurtenant to the land or any part thereof." The provision has a wide effect, converting quasi-easements into full easements even though they are not continuous and apparent [71] or necessary to the reasonable enjoyment of the land sold [72] within the rule in *Wheeldon* v. *Burrows*. A reference in the conveyance to easements and other rights falling within section 62 (1) is therefore unnecessary, except when it is desired that any of them shall *not* pass by the conveyance, the section applying only if and so far as a contrary intention is not expressed in the conveyance, and having effect subject to the terms of the conveyance and the provisions therein contained. [73]

Section 62 applies to conveyances [74] of land, not to contracts, but *Wheeldon* v. *Burrows* does apply to contracts. [75] Thus, if the contract is silent as to the rights which the purchaser is to have over other land retained by the vendor, [76] the rule in *Wheeldon* v. *Burrows* applies to the contract, and the purchaser is not entitled to the more extensive rights enumerated in section 62; in the conveyance, the vendor can include a phrase cutting down the effect of section 62. [77] It must often happen in practice that the implied general words will not have been properly qualified and the purchaser will thus acquire more than he is entitled to under his contract. In such cases, where the mistake is a mutual one, the court has jurisdiction to rectify the conveyance so as to give effect to the real intention of the parties as expressed or implied in the contract, [78] though the scope of rectification is limited because, for example, it depends on the court's discretion. The moral is that, when a vendor is selling part of his land and keeping part, it should be made certain in the contract exactly what is to be the position as regards any quasi-easements, and the position as there stated should be properly reflected in the conveyance.

---

[70] See also s. 62 (2); s. 62 reproduces Conveyancing Act 1881, s. 6.
[71] See *Ward* v. *Kirkland* [1967] Ch. 194.
[72] See *Goldberg* v. *Edwards* [1950] Ch. 247.
[73] s. 62 (4).
[74] See Law of Property Act 1925, s. 205 (1) (ii) for definition.
[75] *Borman* v. *Griffith* [1930] 1 Ch. 493.
[76] But see *ante*, p. 232.
[77] See *Re A Contract Between Peck and the School Board for London* [1893] 2 Ch. 315.
[78] *Clark* v. *Barnes* [1929] 2 Ch. 368.

H. " All the Estate " Clause

It was formerly usual for the general words to be followed by the " all the estate " clause, which transferred all the vendor's estate and interest in the property. It was, however, useless, and now it is always omitted, for, if and so far as a contrary intention is not expressed in the conveyance, " every conveyance is effectual to pass all the estate, right, title, interest, claim and demand which the conveying parties respectively have, in, to, or on the property conveyed, or expressed or intended so to be, or which they respectively have power to convey in, to, or on the same." [79]

I. Exceptions and Reservations

The vendor may except or reserve rights and benefits to himself. Where the vendor expressly excepts from the effect of the grant something which is already in existence at the time of the grant, this is an exception. For example, the vendor may exclude mines and minerals from the conveyance. Where the vendor expressly reserves to himself something entirely new, this is a reservation. For example, the vendor may reserve to himself a rentcharge. Finally, the vendor may take a regrant from the purchaser of some right. For example, he might take a regrant to himself of an easement over the land conveyed. Often the word " reservation " is used to include a regrant (as of an easement) but strictly speaking it is only applicable to a rent (including a rentcharge). [80]

Exceptions and reservations can, and always could, be created even though the purchaser does not execute the conveyance. In the case of a regrant, the conveyance had, before 1926, to be executed by the purchaser in order to create a legal right, such as a legal easement. The conveyance would then operate to convey the land to the purchaser and, by reason of the purchaser's execution, as an immediate regrant of a legal easement to the vendor. If the purchaser did not execute the conveyance, the reservation would give to the vendor an equitable easement only. [81] Alternatively, the vendor could convey to the purchaser in fee simple to the use that the vendor should have, say, an easement over the land and subject thereto to the use of the purchaser in fee simple. By virtue of the Statute of Uses 1535, and section 62 of the Conveyancing Act 1881 such a conveyance would operate to vest in the vendor a legal easement even though the conveyance was not executed by the purchaser.

After 1925 the position is more simple. A conveyance to uses is no longer possible owing to the repeal of the Statute of Uses and section 62 of the Conveyancing Act 1881. [82] Moreover, it is now

---

[79] Law of Property Act 1925, s. 63.
[80] See Farrand, *Contract and Conveyance*, pp. 343–344.
[81] *May* v. *Belleville* [1905] 2 Ch. 605.
[82] Law of Property Act 1925, s. 207 and Sched. 7.

provided,[83] in effect, that in conveyances made after 1925, a mere reservation [84] in the conveyance of a legal estate (for example, of a legal easement) in favour of the vendor or any other person will operate to vest in the vendor or such other person the legal estate reserved, and it is not necessary for the purchaser to execute the conveyance or to make any regrant.

Exceptions and reservations should be distinguished from already existing rights in or over the land, such as easements previously created over the land. Exceptions and reservations are introduced by the words " EXCEPT AND RESERVING . . ." and follow the parcels and the reference to any already subsisting appurtenant rights and any newly created rights for the benefit of the land. Already existing rights over the land are introduced by the words " SUBJECT TO . . ." and come after the habendum, a discussion of which follows.

J. Habendum [85]

The habendum, which commences with the words " TO HOLD . . . ," defines the estate conveyed to the purchaser.

Before 1882, if it was intended to grant an estate in fee simple, it was necessary to convey the property to the grantee " and his heirs." To create an estate tail, it was necessary to convey the land to the grantee " and the heirs of his body," though the words " of his body " were not indispensable, provided similar words of procreation (such as " of his flesh ") were employed after the word " heirs." To create a life estate, appropriate words of limitation, such as " for life " could be used; in addition, if words inappropriate to a fee simple or an estate tail were used, a life estate arose.

The Conveyancing Act 1881 provided that, in regard to deeds executed after 1881, it was sufficient, in the limitation of a fee simple, to use the words " in fee simple " without the word " heirs " and in the limitation of an estate tail to use the words " in tail " without such words as " heirs of his body." The old words of limitation could still be used, but the enactment did not permit any other terms than those just mentioned to be substituted for the old words. Therefore, for example, if land was conveyed to A " in fee," he took a life estate only.[86]

In a deed executed after 1925, a fee simple estate can be conveyed without employing words of limitation for " a conveyance of freehold land to any person without words of limitation, or any equivalent expression, shall pass to the grantee the fee simple or other the

[83] *Ibid.* s. 65 (1). See *Johnstone* v. *Holdway* [1963] 1 Q.B. 601; *Cordell* v. *Second Clanfield Properties* [1969] 2 Ch. 9; (1971) 35 Conv.(N.S.) 324.
[84] This presumably means regrants as well as reservations in the strict sense (*i.e.* of rent).
[85] For words of limitation, see Megarry and Wade, pp. 50–67.
[86] *Re Ethel and Mitchell and Butler's Contract* [1901] 1 Ch. 945. The court might, however, rectify the words of limitation if there was a mistake: see *Banks* v. *Ripley* [1940] Ch. 719.

whole interest which the grantor had power to convey in such land, unless a contrary intention appears in the conveyance." [87] But it is still desirable and customary to use the words " in fee simple," so as to avoid uncertainty. Strict words of limitation are still necessary to create an entailed interest,[88] which is now necessarily equitable [89]; and some such words as " for life " must be employed to create a life interest, which is also now always equitable.[89]

As has been mentioned, if the conveyance is to take effect subject to existing incumbrances, this should be expressly stated after the habendum. The reason for this is that unless the property is expressly conveyed subject to them, the vendor will be liable on his implied covenants for title in the event of such incumbrances being enforced against the purchaser, and this is so even though the purchaser at the time of the conveyance was aware of such incumbrances and though they are apparent on the face of the conveyance.[90]

K. Restrictive Covenants [91]

The purchaser or, less commonly, the vendor, sometimes enters into covenants with the other party to the conveyance. The conditions of sale in the contract will provide for the covenants, if any, to be inserted in the conveyance.

Positive covenants, for example that the purchaser is to erect buildings on the property purchased by him, are, both at law and in equity, binding on the covenantor only and subsequent purchasers are not bound.[92] The inconvenience of this rule is especially pronounced where flats are concerned, for each owner relies on the others keeping their flats in repair, and in such cases the tendency is to let on long leases, for the relationship of landlord and tenant will make the burden of the covenants run.[93]

The covenants most frequently inserted in freehold conveyances are those restricting the purchaser from using the land in certain ways, and in particular from building or carrying on trade or business upon it: our main concern is with such negative, or restrictive, covenants. The covenantor will be liable under the covenant and the covenantee will be able to enforce it against him because there is privity of contract between them. The main question, however, is how far, first, the burden and, second, the benefit of the covenant can run with the land so as to be enforceable against and by successors in title.

---

[87] Law of Property Act 1925, s. 60 (1). This provision is useful if the habendum is accidentally omitted.
[88] *Ibid.* s. 130 (1).
[89] *Ibid.* s. 1.
[90] See *ante*, pp. 228–229.
[91] For discharge and modification of restrictive covenants, see Law of Property Act 1925, s. 84, as amended by Law of Property Act 1969, s. 28.
[92] *Austerberry* v. *Oldham Corporation* (1885) 29 Ch.D. 750.
[93] See *post*, pp. 268–269. For avoiding the rule that the burden of positive covenants does not run with the land, see Farrand, *Contract and Conveyance*, pp. 397–401. The benefit of positive covenants can run with the land.

Burden

Restrictive covenants may be enforced by injunction against persons claiming under the covenantor, under the doctrine of equity enunciated in *Tulk* v. *Moxhay*,[94] provided:

    (a) the covenant was entered into for the benefit of other land in the same neighbourhood as the burdened land[95];

    (b) the covenant is restrictive, not positive[96];

    (c) the wording shows that the covenantor and his successors, and not merely the covenantor himself, are to be bound: this will be deemed by statute[97] if the covenant is made after 1925, unless a contrary intention is indicated[98];

    (d) the covenant is registered as a land charge[99] if made after 1925[1] or, if made before 1926, the person against whom it is sought to enforce the covenant is not a bona fide purchaser for value of a legal estate without notice, actual or constructive, of the covenant and does not claim through such a person.[2]

Benefit

The benefit of a restrictive covenant can run with the land, provided:

    (a) the covenant touches and concerns land of the covenantee and is capable of benefiting it[3];

    (b) the benefit of the covenant has been transferred to the person seeking to enforce it by one of the following methods. First, a restrictive covenant may be so worded that the benefit of the covenant is annexed to the property intended to be benefited, in which case it will pass as incident thereto upon any subsequent conveyance.[4] But there is no annexation unless the covenant is capable of benefiting the whole of the land intended to be benefited. If it can only benefit part of the land, the court will not sever the covenant and regard it as attached to that part of the land which it can benefit[5] unless the covenant was expressly entered into for the benefit of any part of the land, when it will be annexed to each part of the property capable of benefiting[6]; it is thus wise expressly to annex the covenant to each part of the benefited land. A typical phrase of annexation appears

---

94 (1848) 2 Ph. 774. See generally (1971) 87 L.Q.R. 539.
95 *Formby* v. *Barker* [1903] 2 Ch. 539.
96 *Haywood* v. *Brunswick Permanent Benefit Building Society* (1881) 8 Q.B.D. 403.
97 Law of Property Act 1925, s. 79.
98 *Ibid.* s. 79; and see *Re Royal Pavilion, Ramsgate* [1961] Ch. 581.
99 Class D (ii).
1 Land Charges Act 1925, ss. 10 (1), 13 (2); Law of Property Act 1925, s. 198 (1).
2 See *Wilkes* v. *Spooner* [1911] 2 K.B. 473 and *Re Nisbet and Potts' Contract* [1906] 1 Ch. 386.
3 *Re Union of London and Smith's Bank Ltd.'s Conveyance* [1933] Ch. 611.
4 *Rogers* v. *Hosegood* [1900] 2 Ch. 388. And see (1972) 36 Conv.(N.S.) 20.
5 *Re Ballard's Conveyance* [1937] Ch. 473.
6 *Marquess of Zetland* v. *Driver* [1939] Ch. 1. And see *Drake* v. *Gray* [1936] Ch. 451; *Russell* v. *Archdale* [1964] Ch. 38; *Re Jeff's Transfer (No. 2)* [1966] 1 W.L.R. 841.

in Precedent 8 in the Appendix.[7]   Secondly, the benefit of the
covenant may be expressly assigned if there has been a failure to
annex it.[8]   Finally, there may be a building scheme, which exists
where a common vendor lays out land in lots, which he sells subject
to restrictive covenants, each purchaser taking on the understanding
that the covenants are to benefit each of the other lots.[9]

L.   A Note on Appurtenant and Adverse Rights

It will be seen that the various appurtenant and adverse rights affecting
the land conveyed may make the conveyance somewhat complicated.
Thus, the first clause of a conveyance may take the following pattern:
operative part; parcels; already appurtenant rights; newly created
rights for the benefit of the land; exceptions and reservations; habendum; already existing adverse rights; reference to newly created adverse
restrictive covenants (which will be set out in a later clause).   Precedent
7 in the Appendix should clarify the position as will Precedent 8.

M.   Acknowledgment and Undertaking

Although the vendor should usually hand over to the purchaser all the
documents of title concerning the land conveyed, it frequently happens
that a vendor is entitled to retain documents.   For example, when the
vendor retains any part of the land to which any documents of title
relate, he is entitled to retain such documents, and he may retain
a document which creates a trust which is still subsisting or an instrument relating to the appointment or discharge of a trustee of a subsisting
trust.[10]

Formerly, if any of the title-deeds were retained by the vendor, he
covenanted that he, his heirs or assigns, would produce the title-deeds
in question to the purchaser, or to any person lawfully claiming under
him, whenever reasonably requested so to do, and would, in the
meantime, keep the deeds safe, unless prevented by fire or other
inevitable accident.   The Conveyancing Act 1881 [11] provided for these
covenants to be substituted by an acknowledgment by the vendor of
the purchaser's right to production of the title-deeds and an undertaking for their safe custody.   The relevant provisions are now
contained in the Law of Property Act 1925.[12]   This statutory acknowledgment and undertaking is now adopted in place of the old covenant
for production and safe custody.

The *acknowledgment* imposes, by virtue of the Law of Property
Act 1925 [13]:

---

[7] *Post*, p. 414.
[8] See *Re Union of London and Smith's Bank Ltd.'s Conveyance* [1933] Ch. 611;
   Stilwell v. *Blackman* [1968] Ch. 508.
[9] See *Elliston* v. *Reacher* [1908] 2 Ch. 374; *Re Dolphin's Conveyance* [1970] Ch. 654;
   Brunner v. *Greenslade* [1971] Ch. 993.   For forms, see Preston and Newsom,
   Restrictive Covenants Affecting Freehold Land (5th ed.).
[10] Law of Property Act 1925, s. 45 (9); *ante*, pp. 64–65.
[11] s. 9.
[12] s. 64.   For a form, see Precedent 8 in the Appendix: *post*, pp. 414–416.
[13] s. 64 (4).

(i) an obligation to produce the documents or any of them at all reasonable times for the purpose of inspection, and of comparison with abstracts or copies thereof;

(ii) an obligation to produce the documents or any of them for proving or supporting the title of the person entitled to request production, as at a trial;

(iii) an obligation to deliver true copies or extracts of or from the documents or any of them.

The *undertaking* imposes, by virtue of the Law of Property Act 1925,[14] an obligation to keep the documents safe, whole, uncancelled, and undefaced, unless prevented from so doing by fire or other inevitable accident.

If the vendor is a trustee, personal representative, or mortgagee, he merely gives an acknowledgment of the purchaser's right to production, and not an undertaking for safe custody.[15]

Both the acknowledgment and the undertaking bind the person giving them so long only as the documents are in his possession, but the obligations run with the possession of the documents and so bind all persons who have possession of the documents from time to time, so long as such possession is retained.[16] The obligations imposed by the acknowledgment can be enforced by the person to whom it is given and all persons claiming any estate or interest under him, except a lessee at a rent [17]: it seems that the same is the case in relation to the undertaking, though this is not expressed. In other words, the burden of the acknowledgment and undertaking runs with the deeds, and the benefit runs with the land.

N. Certificate of Value: Stamp Duty

The conveyance must be duly stamped. The *ad valorem* duty charged on conveyances or transfers on sale is at the rate of 50p per £50 of the consideration. However, duty is payable at progressively reduced rates if the consideration is less than £15,000 or £10,000, whichever the case may be, and there is included in the conveyance a certificate of value, that is, a statement certifying that the transaction effected by the instrument does not form part of a larger transaction or series of transactions in respect of which the amount or value, or aggregate amount or value, of consideration exceeds £10,000 or £15,000, as the case may be.[18] Hence, the presence of such a certificate in conveyances where the consideration is £15,000 or below.

[14] s. 64 (9).
[15] This is the custom of conveyancers.
[16] Law of Property Act 1925, s. 64 (2) (9).
[17] *Ibid.* s. 64 (3).
[18] See Stamp Act 1891, Sched. 1; Finance Act 1958, s. 34; Finance Act 1967, s. 27; Finance Act 1970, s. 32 and Sched. 7; Finance Bill 1972. See generally, Pinson, *Revenue Law* (5th ed.), Chap. 32. For a form, see *post*, p. 413.

O. Execution: Testimonium

The conveyance is concluded by a testimonium, which sets forth that the several parties to the deed have duly set thereto their respective hands and seals. Execution of the conveyance has been dealt with previously.[19]

II. REGISTERED LAND: TRANSFERS

Form of transfer

As in the case of unregistered land, once the purchaser's solicitor has seen that the vendor's title is in order,[20] he will prepare a transfer. The forms contained in the schedule to the Land Registration Rules 1925 must be used in all matters to which they refer, or are capable of being applied or adapted, with such alterations and additions, if any, as are necessary or desired and the Registrar allows.[21] Instruments for which no form is provided in the schedule or to which the scheduled forms cannot conveniently be adapted, must be in such form as the Registrar directs or allows, the scheduled forms being followed as far as possible.[22] The scheduled forms deal with a wide range, covering, for example, the transfer of freehold and leasehold land respectively, forms concerned with settled land and forms concerned with charges. The reader should refer to them and to Precedent 10 in the Appendix to this book.[23]

As regards the transfer of freehold land, the following brief points should be noted. It will be convenient to mention them in the same order as they are dealt with under the heading of " Unregistered land: Conveyances." [24]

(1) There is no commencement to a registered land transfer corresponding with that of a conveyance of unregistered land. There is, however, a prescribed heading to the scheduled forms.[25]

(2) The comments on date and parties made in connection with conveyances of unregistered land generally relate also to transfers.

(3) Recitals are unusual in transfers of registered land, though they may sometimes be inserted.[26]

(4) As for the operative part, the relevant scheduled forms [27] contain no testatum. The consideration will be stated and, although there is no receipt clause in the relevant scheduled

---

[19] *Ante,* pp. 207–209. For a form of testimonium, see *post,* p. 413.
[20] See *ante,* p. 207.
[21] Land Registration Rules 1925, r. 74.
[22] *Ibid.* r. 75.
[23] See *post,* p. 417.
[24] See *ante,* pp. 221 *et seq.*
[25] See Form 19; and *post,* p. 417.
[26] See Farrand, *Contract and Conveyance,* pp. 290–291.
[27] Forms 19 and 20.

forms, the printed transfer forms which can be bought do contain such a clause; it is wise to have a receipt clause, as in the case of conveyances of unregistered land; the advantages have already been stated.[28] For the purpose of introducing the vendor's covenants for title implied under section 76 of the Law of Property Act 1925[29] a person may, in a registered transfer, be expressed to transfer as beneficial owner, as settlor, and so forth as in the case of unregistered land, but no reference to covenants implied under section 76 is to be entered in the register.[30] Any covenant implied by virtue of section 76 in a transfer takes effect as though it was expressly made subject to all charges and other interests appearing or protected on the register at the time of the execution of the transfer and affecting the covenantor's title and to any overriding interests of which the purchaser has notice and subject to which it would have taken effect had the land been unregistered.[31] Finally, the word of conveyance contained in the scheduled forms is " transfers " rather than " conveys."

(5) The parcels in a transfer of all the land contained in a registered title reads, in the relevant scheduled form,[32] " the land comprised in the title above referred to " (there being, at the top of the form, a reference to the district, title number and property), so that the description in the property register is imported. In a transfer of part of the land in a title, the parcels reads " the land shown and edged with red on the accompanying plan and known as . . . being part of the land comprised in the title above referred to ": if it is desired that a particular verbal description be entered on the register, the words " and described in the Schedule hereto " can be inserted between the short description and " being part . . ." [33]

(6) The general words implied in conveyances under the Law of Property Act 1925 apply, so far as applicable thereto, to dispositions of a registered estate.[34] New rights, such as easements, can be created in favour of the land, as in conveyances of unregistered land. Rights which are already appurtenant to the land pass without special mention and adverse rights also need not be mentioned because they will either appear on the register or be overriding interests.

---

28 See *ante,* p. 225.
29 See *ante,* pp. 225–229.
30 Land Registration Rules 1925, r. 76.
31 *Ibid.* r. 77.
32 Form 19.
33 Form 20. Where sufficient particulars to enable the land to be fully identified on the General Map, Ordnance Map, or Filed Plan, can be furnished without the special plan, such particulars may be introduced into the form instead of the reference to a plan (note to Form 20), though usually a special plan is needed.
34 Land Registration Act 1925, s. 19 (3): and see *ibid.* s. 20 (1) (see *post,* pp. 242–243). See *ante,* pp. 231–233.

(7) The "all the estate" clause implied by the Law of Property Act 1925 [35] will also be implied in a transfer of registered land.[36]

(8) The comments on exceptions and reservations made in respect of conveyances of unregistered land apply here also.[37]

(9) There is no habendum in the scheduled forms of transfer.[38]

(10) A proprietor may in a registered disposition generally impose, so far as the law permits, any obligation by covenant with respect to the building on or other user of the registered land or any part thereof,[39] so that the comments concerning restrictive covenants made in connection with unregistered land are relevant to registered land.[40]

(11) There is no acknowledgment and undertaking in the scheduled forms,[41] for they are generally unnecessary.[42]

(12) A certificate of value, when appropriate, will be included in a transfer.

(13) A transfer will be executed in the same way as a conveyance and the scheduled forms [41] include an attestation clause.[43]

Registration of transferee

The instrument of transfer must be produced to the Registrar and must be accompanied by the land certificate.[44] The application for registration must be made under the appropriate application cover.[45] The transaction is completed by the Registrar entering on the register the name of the transferee as proprietor of the land transferred.[46]

Effect of registered transfer

In the case of a freehold estate registered with an absolute title, a disposition of the registered land, or of a legal estate therein, for valuable consideration, when registered, confers on the transferee or grantee an estate in fee simple or other legal estate expressed to be created, together with all rights, privileges and appurtenances belonging or appurtenant thereto, including the appropriate rights and interests which would, under the Law of Property Act 1925 have been transferred if the land had not been registered, subject to any incumbrances and other entries appearing on the register and, unless the contrary is

---

[35] See *ante*, p. 234.
[36] See Land Registration Act 1925, s. 20 (1).
[37] See further Farrand, *Contract and Conveyance*, pp. 348–349.
[38] See Forms 19 and 20.
[39] Land Registration Act 1925, s. 40 (1).
[40] A notice of the covenant should be entered in the charges register of the land subjected to it; in the case of registered land, such notice takes the place of . registration as a land charge: Land Registration Act 1925, s. 50; Land Registration Rules 1925, r. 212.
[41] See Forms 19 and 20.
[42] See Farrand, *Contract and Conveyance*, pp. 411–412 for exceptions.
[43] And see Land Registration Act 1925, s. 38 (1).
[44] Land Registration Act 1925, s. 64.
[45] See *ante*, p. 220.
[46] Land Registration Act 1925, s. 19 (1).

expressed on the register, to any overriding interests affecting the estate transferred or created, but free from all other estates and interests.[47]

Rule 72 [48]

Where a person who has the right to apply for registration as first proprietor desires to deal with the land in a way permitted by the Land Registration Act 1925 before he is himself registered as proprietor, he may do so in the manner which would apply if he were in fact the registered proprietor: in the case of a transfer, the transferee is deemed to be the applicant for first registration: and a dealing made in such a way, when completed by registration, has the same effect as if the person making it were registered as proprietor.[49] This provision is useful in cases where registration is to be effected after the land has been conveyed, for it permits the use of a transfer as if the land were already registered, instead of a conveyance.[50]

Rectification of register and indemnity

This has been dealt with in a previous section.[51]

III. HUSBAND AND WIFE

Land may be conveyed or transferred to co-owners, rather than to a single purchaser. In such a case, the co-owners generally [52] hold the legal estate as joint tenants on trust for sale for themselves as beneficial joint tenants or tenants in common.[53] The most common instance in practice arises where a husband and wife purchase property and this will now be briefly discussed.[54] Usually the spouses will have the land conveyed or transferred to themselves as beneficial joint tenants. In such a case, the instrument may simply convey or transfer the land to the purchasers " as beneficial joint tenants," when a statutory trust for sale will arise,[53] or the trust for sale may be set out expressly.[55] Which method is adopted seems in many cases to be largely a matter of taste.

Where the trust for sale is created expressly, a clause which is often inserted is one giving the trustees the same powers of dealing with the land as an absolute beneficial owner. Such a clause extends the

---

[47] Land Registration Act 1925, s. 20 (1). For the effect of a transfer for valuable consideration of freehold land registered with a qualified or possessory title, or a transfer of freehold land made without valuable consideration, see *ante*, p. 177.
[48] For unregistered dealings with registered land, see Land Registration Act 1925, Pt. IX; *ante*, p. 178.
[49] Land Registration Act 1925, s. 37; Land Registration Rules 1925, r. 72. See *ante*, p. 218.
[50] See further, Hallett, *Conveyancing Precedents*, pp. 1107–1109.
[51] See *ante*, p. 172.
[52] If there are more than four, the four first named who are able and willing to act will be the trustees: Trustee Act 1925, s. 34; see *ante*, p. 143.
[53] Law of Property Act 1925, ss. 34–36; see *ante*, p. 143.
[54] See generally Hallett's *Conveyancing Precedents*, pp. 298–303; 1296–1298; Farrand, *Contract and Conveyance*, pp. 369–379.
[55] See Precedent 9 in the Appendix.

powers which the trustees would otherwise have. **Trustees for sale have**, in relation to land, **all the powers of a tenant for life and the trustees of a settlement under the Settled Land Act 1925.**[56] There are certain limits on these statutory powers. For example, land may be leased for a term which must not (save in the case of a building, mining or forestry lease) exceed fifty years.[57] Where the conveyance states that the purchasers are to have the powers of an absolute beneficial owner, such limits will not operate.[58]

Where the spouses are beneficial joint tenants, upon the death of one of them the other becomes entitled to his or her interest in the property, because of the *ius accrescendi*.[59] The position where a dispute arises as to the sale or retention of the property is discussed later.[60]

In a book on the elements of conveyancing it is not appropriate to deal at length with the difficult questions which can arise—as on a break-down of the marriage—with regard to the ownership of matrimonial property where the conveyance is not clear as to the spouses' respective interests. It seems that " the beneficial ownership of the property in question must depend upon the agreement of the parties determined at the time of its acquisition. If the property in question is land there must be some lease or conveyance which shows how it was acquired. If that document declares not merely in whom the legal title is to vest but in whom the beneficial title is to vest that necessarily concludes the question of title as between the spouses for all time and, in the absence of fraud or mistake at the time of the transaction, the parties cannot go behind it at any time thereafter even on death or the break-up of the marriage." [61] If the conveyance does not state " in whom the beneficial title is to vest," as where the conveyance is taken in the name of one spouse only, difficult questions can arise, as the reader is doubtless aware.[62] These difficulties at least serve to emphasise the desirability, where the spouses agree to such a course, of making them beneficial joint tenants.

---

[56] Law of Property Act 1925, s. 28 (1); *post*, p. 378.
[57] Settled Land Act 1925, s. 41; *post*, p. 364.
[58] In the case of registered land, a clause giving the purchasers the powers of an absolute beneficial owner is unnecessary: see Ruoff and Roper, *Registered Conveyancing* (3rd ed.), p. 406; see Land Registration Act 1925, ss. 18, 25.
[59] See generally, Megarry and Wade, Chap. 7.
[60] *Post*, pp. 376–377.
[61] *Pettit* v. *Pettit* [1970] A.C. 777 at p. 813, *per* Lord Upjohn.
[62] See *Pettit* v. *Pettit* [1970] A.C. 777; *Gissing* v. *Gissing* [1971] A.C. 886; Matrimonial Proceedings and Property Act 1970, s. 37; (1969) 32 M.L.R. 570; (1970) 34 Conv.(N.S.) 156, 349; (1969) 85 L.Q.R. 330; (1970) 86 L.Q.R. 98.

CHAPTER 11

LEASES

I. AGREEMENTS FOR LEASES AND LEASES

Introduction

When a fee simple estate is sold, it is usual for the parties to enter into a contract and then to execute a conveyance. But when land is let, although this may equally be accomplished by entering into an agreement for a lease and then executing the lease itself, in most cases it is achieved *either* by executing a lease *or* by entering into an agreement for a lease. The reason why an agreement alone is often sufficient will appear later.[1]

It is convenient to deal with agreements for leases and then with the form of actual leases.

Agreements for leases

(1) *The requirement of writing*

An agreement for a lease for however short a term is an agreement for the disposition [2] of land within section 40 of the Law of Property Act 1925, and accordingly is unenforceable by action unless some memorandum or note in writing has been signed by the party to be charged or by some other person lawfully authorised by him.[3] The absence of written evidence is fatal to an action for damages for breach of the agreement, but specific performance may be obtained even in the absence of such written evidence, if there has been a sufficient act of part performance on the part of the plaintiff, who may be the landlord or the tenant.[4] For example, the act of a tenant in taking possession or of a landlord in giving up possession under a parol or unsigned agreement is a sufficient act of part performance for the court to decree specific performance of the agreement against the landlord in the first case [5] or the tenant in the second case.[6] However, payment of rent is in itself not a sufficient act of part performance.[7]

(2) *Formal and open agreements for leases*

Agreements for leases may be either formal or open. A formal

---

[1] See *post*, p. 248.
[2] Law of Property Act 1925, s. 205 (1) (ii).
[3] Where the negotiations are subject to contract for the grant of a lease there is no contract, even though there may be correspondence or other documentation as to the agreement, until the exchange of the lease and the counterpart: *D'Silva* v. *Lister House Development Ltd.* [1971] Ch. 17; see *ante*, p. 24.
[4] See *ante*, pp. 15 *et seq*. for s. 40 and part performance.
[5] *Pain* v. *Coombs* (1857) 1 De G. and J. 34: *Kingswood Estate Co. Ltd.* v. *Anderson* [1963] 2 Q.B. 169.
[6] *Kine* v. *Balfe* (1813) 2 Ball and B. 343 (Irish case). See also *Rawlinson* v. *Ames* [1925] Ch. 96.
[7] *Chaproniére* v. *Lambert* [1917] 2 Ch. 356.

agreement will specify the various covenants and conditions which it is intended to insert expressly in the lease itself, whereas an open agreement will either make no provisions as to such covenants and conditions or will provide that the lease shall contain the " usual covenants and conditions."

As a rule, formal agreements are neither usual nor desirable in the case of ordinary occupation leases. Where the lease is to take effect at once, and is to contain only the ordinary covenants, there is no point in having a formal preliminary agreement, which will specify precisely all the covenants and clauses which are to be inserted in the lease, and which will be immediately followed by a formal lease: there is thus unnecessary repetition. Consequently, such agreements are seldom entered into, except in cases where the intended tenant has to fulfil certain conditions before he becomes entitled to require a lease or where the parties intend to rely on a mere agreement and do not contemplate the immediate (or even any) execution of a formal lease.[8]

As we have seen, an open agreement will either provide expressly that the lease itself shall contain the " usual covenants and conditions " or it will be silent as to the covenants and conditions to be inserted in the lease. In such latter case, the law implies a term in the agreement to the effect that the lease shall contain the " usual covenants and conditions." In either case, it is necessary to consider what covenants and conditions come within the meaning of the word " usual," and which are therefore to be expressly inserted in the lease made pursuant to the agreement. Briefly, the more important ones are as follows. There will be covenants by the tenant to pay rent, to pay tenant's rates and taxes,[9] to keep and deliver up the premises in repair and to allow the landlord to enter and view the state of repair. There will be a covenant by the landlord for quiet enjoyment, which will be in the usual qualified form.[10] Finally, there will be a condition of re-entry for non-payment of rent, but not in any other event[11]; it follows that if it is desired that the lease should contain a condition of re-entry in the event of, for instance, failure to repair or bankruptcy, the agreement should make express provision to that effect.

On the other hand, examples of covenants which are not " usual " are a covenant not to assign without consent[12] and a covenant against using the premises for trade.[13]

The question of what title is to be shown under a contract for the grant of a lease has been dealt with in a previous chapter.[14]

(3) *Registration as a land charge*

If an agreement for a lease, whether formal or open, is entered into

[8] See *ante*, p. 245, and *post*, p. 248.
[9] See *post*, p. 257.
[10] *Hampshire* v. *Wickens* (1878) 7 Ch.D. 555.
[11] See *Re Anderton and Milner's Contract* (1890) 45 Ch.D. 476.
[12] *De Soysa* v. *De Pless Pol* [1912] A.C. 194.
[13] *Propert* v. *Parker* (1832) 3 My. and K. 280.
[14] See *ante*, pp. 60 *et seq.*; pp. 99, 100.

after 1925, it requires registration as an estate contract,[15] and if it is not registered it will not bind a purchaser of a legal estate for money or money's worth even if he had notice of the agreement.[16]

The form of a lease

(1) *Formalities*

Certain formalities must be complied with if it is desired to create a term of years absolute, which is, of course, a legal estate.[17] Briefly, a lease is void for the purpose of creating a legal estate unless made by deed. However, an exception exists in the case of a lease taking effect in possession for a term not exceeding three years (whether or not the tenant is given power to extend the term) at the best rent which can be reasonably obtained without taking a fine, and such an excepted lease may be made in writing or even verbally.[18]

(2) *Leases not fulfilling the above requirements*

As for cases where the above formalities have not been complied with, the position has developed as follows. If a tenant entered into possession and paid a yearly rent under a lease not fulfilling such formalities, the common law regarded him as a tenant from year to year on the terms of the void lease so far as they were not inconsistent with a yearly tenancy.[19] In equity,[20] however, a lease which was void at law because not under seal would be treated as an agreement of which specific performance would be granted, provided it was in writing or, if verbal, there had been an available act of part performance. Indeed, even if no decree of specific performance had been obtained, the parties were regarded in equity as having the same rights and liabilities between themselves as would have existed if a formal lease had been executed, for equity regards that as done which ought to be done. The common law courts too treated a lease not under seal as an agreement for a lease if it was in writing, but the only remedy at law was damages, not specific performance.

Thus, the remedies in equity were much more potent than those at law. However, it was enacted by the Judicature Act 1873 [21] that in any case where the rules of law and equity were in conflict, the equitable rule should prevail. Consequently, in *Walsh* v. *Lonsdale*,[22] in 1882, where the tenant was in possession under an agreement in writing to grant a lease for seven years instead of under a lease by

---

[15] Class C (iv) land charge; see *ante*, pp. 25 *et seq.*
[16] Land Charges Act 1925, ss. 10, 13 (2); Law of Property Act 1925, s. 198 (1).
[17] Under Law of Property Act 1925, s. 1 (1).
[18] See Statute of Frauds 1677, ss. 1 and 2; Real Property Act 1845, s. 3; Law of Property Act 1925, ss. 52–54.
[19] See *Doe* d. *Rigge* v. *Bell* (1793) 5 T.R. 471; *Clayton* v. *Blakey* (1798) 8 T.R. 3.
[20] *Parker* v. *Taswell* (1858) 2 De G. and J. 559; *Zimbler* v. *Abrahams* [1903] 1 K.B. 577.
[21] s. 25 (11).
[22] (1882) 21 Ch.D. 9.

deed as required by statute,[23] it was held that he should be treated
in every court as being an actual tenant for seven years, holding under
the terms of the written agreement, upon which terms he would have
held if a lease had been granted to him under seal.

As has often been said, the doctrine of *Walsh* v. *Lonsdale* leads to
the aphorism that " a contract for a lease is as good as a lease." It
is for this reason that, as we have said,[24] in many cases an actual lease
is never executed and the parties rely solely on the agreement for a
lease. Though the aphorism is substantially true, it is necessary to
keep in mind certain respects in which an agreement differs from a
lease.[25] For example, whereas a lease, being a legal estate, binds
everyone, a tenant's interest under an agreement for a lease is merely
equitable, and does not bind a purchaser of a legal estate for money or
money's worth unless it is registered as an estate contract.[26] In order
to gain protection, the tenant under an agreement should register his
interest.[26]

(3) *Summary*

The present position as to the form of a lease may be summarised
thus:

(i) a lease, to create a legal estate, must be under seal, except a
lease taking effect in possession for three years or less at the best rent
reasonably obtainable without taking a fine, and such an excepted
lease may be made in writing or even verbally;

(ii) if there is an agreement for a lease, then, provided it is in
writing or there has been an available act of part performance, the
parties will be treated as if there were a proper lease (subject to the
shortcomings mentioned above);

(iii) any unsealed lease which by law is required to be under seal
will be treated as an agreement for a lease: the position is then as in
(ii) above.

II. IMPLIED TERMS

A. Implied, Usual and Express Covenants

We now come to the contents of the lease, or tenancy agreement,
particularly the covenants, which set out the rights and duties of the
parties. There are certain *implied* covenants, which are deemed to be
incorporated in a lease or tenancy agreement, except to the extent that
express provision is made to the contrary: these implied covenants are
dealt with shortly. Again, as we have seen,[27] an open *agreement* may

---

[23] Real Property Act 1845, s. 3.
[24] See *ante*, p. 245.
[25] See Megarry and Wade, *The Law of Real Property* (3rd ed.), pp. 632–635.
[26] *Ante*, p. 246. Where the contract was made before 1926, the old doctrine of notice
    applies.
[27] *Ante*, p. 246.

provide that the lease made pursuant to such agreement shall contain the " *usual* covenants and conditions," or it may be silent as to what covenants and conditions are to be inserted in the lease when it is made, when the law implies a term in the agreement to the effect that the lease shall contain the " *usual* covenants and conditions ": these have been discussed above. Finally, there are certain *express* covenants which the parties may undertake and which are often inserted in leases when there is no preceding contract, or in tenancy agreements when the parties are to depend on the agreement without executing an actual lease. Some of the express covenants will relate to matters which the implied or the usual covenants would otherwise cover, and some will relate to further matters. Express covenants are discussed later.

B. Implied Obligations

The following are implied obligations, that is, those which will be implied in the lease or tenancy agreement, save to the extent that express provision is made to the contrary.

Obligations upon the tenant

These are:

(1) *To pay rent*

There is a common law obligation to pay for the use and occupation of land. It is, however, usual and wise to insert in the lease an express covenant to pay rent, for then the landlord has a right to rent against the tenant for the duration of the term, even after he has assigned the lease. Otherwise the tenant's obligation ceases when he assigns his interest to another.

(2) *To pay tenant's rates and taxes* [28]

(3) *To keep in repair*

This obligation arises in so far as a tenant is liable for waste. It is necessary to distinguish voluntary waste, which consists of positive acts of destruction, from permissive waste, which consists of negative neglect to repair or maintain. It is also necessary to differentiate various types of tenancy. A tenant for a term of years is liable in respect of both types of waste, so that he must keep the property in the same state of repair as at the commencement of the term,[29] though in such types of lease there will usually be an express covenant to repair. A yearly tenant must not commit voluntary waste and is bound to use the property in a tenant-like manner.[30] It has been stated [31] that a yearly tenant must keep the property " wind-and-water-tight," which would make him liable for some permissive waste, but the position is

---

[28] See *post,* p. 257.
[29] See *Davies* v. *Davies* (1888) 38 Ch.D. 499.
[30] *Marsden* v. *Edward Heyes Ltd.* [1927] 2 K.B. 1.
[31] See *Wedd* v. *Porter* [1916] 2 K.B. 91.

not clear.[32] Finally, a weekly tenant (and, it seems, a monthly or quarterly tenant) is not bound to repair, but he must use the property in a tenant-like manner: for example, he must clean the windows and mend the electric light when it fuses, but apart from such matters the tenant is not liable for disrepair caused by fair wear and tear.[32]

(4) *To permit the landlord to enter and view the condition of the property*

This implied obligation only arises where the landlord is by express covenant[33] or impliedly[34] bound to repair, or in some cases by virtue of statute,[35] but he will usually make an express reservation of the right to enter in the event of non-payment of rent or breach of any of the tenant's covenants or his bankruptcy.[36]

Obligations upon the landlord

These are:

(1) *Covenant for quiet enjoyment*

In the absence of an express covenant for quiet enjoyment, a covenant for quiet enjoyment will be implied by any words sufficient to constitute the relationship of landlord and tenant,[37] and a breach entitles the tenant to damages from the landlord. The covenant will be broken if the tenant's enjoyment of the property is interrupted, as where the landlord persistently knocks on the tenant's door and uses threats in an attempt to induce him to leave.[38] The implied covenant is limited to breaches occurring during the continuance of the landlord's interest, so that if the tenant is disturbed by a person who has a title paramount to that of the landlord he cannot sue.[39] The advantage of the express covenant[40] (which, if inserted, excludes any implied covenant) is that the landlord's liability does not end when his interest does but lasts for the duration of the term.[41]

(2) *Non-derogation from grant*

The landlord must not derogate from his grant. For instance, if a landlord lets property to a timber merchant and erects buildings on his neighbouring land which stop air reaching timber to dry it, the tenant can sue him for damages.[42]

(3) *Repair*

The landlord is under no implied obligation to repair and he does

---

[32] See *Warren* v. *Keen* [1954] 1 Q.B. 15, at p. 20.

[33] *Saner* v. *Bilton* (1878) 7 Ch.D. 815.

[34] *Mint* v. *Good* [1951] 1 K.B. 517.

[35] See *e.g.* Agricultural Holdings Act 1948, s. 17; Housing Act 1961, s. 32.

[36] See *post*, p. 263.

[37] *Budd Scott* v. *Daniell* [1902] K.B. 351; *Markham* v. *Paget* [1908] 1 Ch. 697.

[38] *Kenny* v. *Preen* [1963] 1 Q.B. 499.

[39] *Adams* v. *Gibney* (1830) 6 Bing. 656; *Baynes and Co.* v. *Lloyd and Sons* [1895] 2 Q.B. 610.

[40] See *post*, p. 267.

[41] *Evans* v. *Vaughan* (1825) 4 B. and C. 261. For the covenant for quiet enjoyment, see further Woodfall, *Landlord and Tenant* (27th ed.), Vol. 1, pp. 562–576; *Megarry and Wade*, pp. 681–683; Gibson's *Conveyancing* (20th ed.), pp. 408–409, 462–465.

[42] See *Aldin* v. *Latimer Clarke, Muirhead and Co.* [1894] 2 Ch. 437.

not impliedly covenant that the premises are fit for the purpose for which they are required. The general rule is that the tenant must take the property as he finds it. To this, however, there are certain exceptions,[43] for example:

(a) Where the premises consist of a furnished house or flat (but not an unfurnished house or flat[44]), there is an implied condition in the lease that, at the commencement of the tenancy, the house is habitable.[45] The landlord is liable on the condition only if the house or flat is uninhabitable at the commencement of the tenancy, and is under no liability only because it becomes uninhabitable at some later time.[46]

(b) Under the Housing Act 1957,[47] in a letting of a house at a rent not exceeding certain specified amounts,[48] there is (notwithstanding any contrary agreement) an implied condition that the house is fit for human habitation at the commencement of the tenancy and an implied undertaking by the landlord to keep it so during the tenancy.[49] However, the landlord will not be liable for a breach of this undertaking unless he has notice of the defect, whether patent or latent.[50] Moreover, the condition and undertaking are not implied when a house is let for a term of not less than three years upon the terms that it be put by the tenant into a condition reasonably fit for human habitation and the lease is not determinable at the option of either party before the expiration of three years.

(c) Under the Housing Act 1961,[51] in a lease of a dwelling-house granted after October 24, 1961, for a term of less then seven years, there is implied a covenant by the landlord to keep in repair the structure and exterior[52] and to keep in repair and proper working order the installations for the supply of water, gas and electricity and for sanitation and space or water heating. Such implied covenant is not to be construed as requiring the landlord to carry out repairs for which the tenant is liable by virtue of his duty to use the premises in a tenant-like manner; or to rebuild or reinstate the premises in the case of destruction or damage by fire, tempest, flood or other inevitable accident; or to keep in repair anything which the tenant is

---

[43] See also Offices, Shops and Railway Premises Act 1963, s. 42; Occupiers' Liability Act 1957. And see Defective Premises Act 1972.

[44] *Cruse* v. *Mount* [1933] Ch. 278.

[45] *Smith* v. *Marrable* (1843) 11 M. and W. 5.

[46] *Sarson* v. *Roberts* [1895] 2 Q.B. 395.

[47] s. 6. And see Housing Act 1969, s. 71.

[48] *i.e.* not exceeding £80 a year if it is in the County of London or £52 elsewhere: these figures are £40 and £26 respectively where the contract of letting was made before July 6, 1957. " Rent " means the actual rent paid even though that rent is inclusive of rates: *Rousou* v. *Photi* [1940] 2 K.B. 379.

[49] There is no such obligation if it is not capable of being made fit for human habitation at a reasonable cost: *Buswell* v. *Goodwin* [1971] 1 W.L.R. 92.

[50] *Morgan* v. *Liverpool Corporation* [1927] 2 K.B. 131; *McCarrick* v. *Liverpool Corporation* [1947] A.C. 219.

[51] ss. 32, 33. See (1962) 26 Conv.(N.S.) 187.

[52] See *Brown* v. *Liverpool Corporation* [1969] 3 All E.R. 1345.

entitled to remove from the dwelling-house. Any covenant or agreement purporting to exclude or limit the landlord's obligations is void, though the county court may, with the consent of the parties concerned, authorise a provision excluding or modifying the implied obligation, if such provision is reasonable.

III. EXPRESS CONTENTS OF LEASES

It is convenient, as in the case of conveyances, to go through the clauses of a simple lease one by one. (See Form 18 in the Appendix.)

A. Premises

The Premises begin with the words " THIS LEASE made the
day of   between   ." As for the date, see the comments on conveyances.[53]

After the date come the parties.[54] A tenant in fee simple may grant a lease for any length of time. The powers of a tenant for life and statutory owners under the Settled Land Act 1925 are discussed in a later chapter.[55] Trustees for sale have, in relation to land, all the powers of a tenant for life and the trustees of a settlement under the Settled Land Act 1925 though such powers must be exercised by the trustees for sale with such consents (if any) as would have been required on a sale under the trust for sale.[56] Personal representatives have, for the purposes of administration, all the powers conferred by law on trustees holding land on trust for sale.[57] Thus, trustees for sale and personal representatives have basically the same power to lease as exists under the Settled Land Act 1925. A tenant for years can sub-let for a period shorter than the term vested in him, though regard must be had to any covenant not to sub-let.[58] The powers of leasing of mortgagors and mortgagees are discussed in a later chapter.[59]

A simple form of lease does not require any recitals, though they are sometimes of help. For example, if a tenant sub-lets, the fact that he has obtained the head landlord's consent as required by the head lease may be recited in the sub-lease.

If there are no recitals, the description of the parties is immediately followed by the Operative Part, which begins by setting out the consideration for the lease. The consideration consists usually in the rent to be paid and the covenants to be observed by the tenant. But

---

53 *Ante*, p. 221.
54 For capacity of minors, people with mental disorder, married women, corporations, etc., see Gibson's *Conveyancing*, pp. 391 *et seq*. A person cannot grant a lease to himself: see *Rye* v. *Rye* [1962] A.C. 496; (1962) 78 L.Q.R. 175.
55 *Post*, p. 364.
56 Law of Property Act 1925, s. 28. And see *post*, pp. 377, 378.
57 Administration of Estates Act 1925, s. 39.
58 See *post*, p. 261.
59 *Post*, p. 314.

it may consist of any benefit conferred on the landlord by the tenant, and it often consists, besides the rent and covenants, in the payment of a premium or the execution of repairs or improvements on the property demised. Next come the words of demise by which the term is created. The word " demise " is the best for expressing the fact that the landlord leases the property, and is the only word which need be employed for that purpose, but any words showing a clear intention to lease will have the same effect.[60]

Next come the Parcels. The general rules to be observed in framing parcels were discussed in the chapter on Conveyances and Transfers [61] and need not be repeated here.

It should be noted that, since a lease is " a conveyance " within section 62 of the Law of Property Act 1925,[62] the general words [63] are implied in a lease in the same way as they are implied in a conveyance on sale. This is so even though the lease was under hand only, being, for example, a lease for a term of one year [64] but the section does not apply to an agreement for a lease exceeding a term of three years.[65]

After the parcels come any licences, exceptions or reservations (save that of the rent) which may be agreed upon. These vary with the circumstances of each particular case. For example, the tenant of a flat may be granted the use of a coal cellar.

B. Habendum

Certainty of term

The habendum in a lease differs from that in a grant of freehold in that technical words of limitation were never necessary in the former to make out the extent of the interest granted. The habendum should name the tenant himself and set out with certainty when the term is to begin and when it is to end, for a lease for an uncertain period is void.[66] The term may begin at a past, present or future date.[67]

" Interesse termini "

Formerly, a tenant had no estate until he entered into possession: until then he had merely an *interesse termini*, an interest which he could grant to another, but no estate. The doctrine of *interesse termini* was abolished by the Law of Property Act 1925.[68] Any term, whether

---

[60] In the case of a *tenancy agreement*, the wording is usually " The Landlord lets and the Tenant takes " or " The Landlord agrees to let and the Tenant to take."

[61] See *ante*, pp. 230–231.

[62] Law of Property Act 1925, s. 205 (1) (ii).

[63] See *ante*, p. 231.

[64] *Wright* v. *Macadam* [1949] 2 K.B. 744.

[65] *Borman* v. *Griffith* [1930] 1 Ch. 493.

[66] *Lace* v. *Chantler* [1944] K.B. 368, which is of general application. The Validation of War-time Leases Act 1944 validates the type of lease actually concerned in the case: see *post*, p. 255.

[67] See *Ladyman* v. *Wirral Estates Ltd.* [1968] 2 All E.R. 197.

[68] s. 149 (1) (2).

created before or after January 1, 1926, now takes effect from the date fixed for its commencement without the need for actual entry.

Reversionary leases

Before 1926 a lease could be granted one year to commence in any year in the future without any limit as to the period of time between the two dates. These leases were called reversionary leases, and must not be confused with leases of the reversion, discussed below. But the Law of Property Act 1925 [69] makes void a term at a rent or granted in consideration of a fine created after 1925 to take effect more than twenty-one years from the date of the instrument purporting to create it. This provision applies also to a contract to create such a term,[70] but it does not apply to any term taking effect in equity under a settlement or created out of an equitable interest under a settlement, or under an equitable power for mortgage, indemnity or other like purposes.

Leases of the reversion

It has always been possible for a landlord to make a lease of his reversion. For example, if A, a freeholder, leases his land to B for twenty-one years from January 1969, he can, while B's lease is still subsisting, grant a lease of the same land to C for fifty years from January 1970. C is then B's landlord, and when B's lease expires, C can take possession of the land. If A leases his land to C for seven years, that is, for a shorter period than B's lease, C will not, of course, be entitled to possession of the land, but his lease will operate as an assignment to him of the reversion for a term of seven years, and for that period he will be in the position of B's landlord, entitled to the rent under B's lease and to enforce all the covenants contained in such lease. Nothing in the Law of Property Act 1925 affects the rule of law that a legal term may be created to take effect in reversion expectant on a longer term, which rule is confirmed by the Act.[71]

Duration must be fixed

The rule that the maximum [72] duration of a lease must be fixed has led to several statutory qualifications to common law concepts.

(a) Leases "for the duration of the war"

It was held by the Court of Appeal in the Second World War that

---

[69] s. 149 (3).
[70] See *ante*, p. 29.
[71] s. 149 (5).
[72] Although the maximum duration must be fixed, the lease may end prematurely, as by forfeiture. Moreover, the requirement that the maximum duration of a term of years has to be ascertained before the term takes effect has no direct applicability to periodic tenancies: *Re Midland Railway Co.'s Agreement* [1971] Ch. 725.

a lease " for the duration of the war " was void because the duration of the term was not fixed.[73] The decision affected a great number of leases granted during the war and as a result the Validation of Wartime Leases Act 1944 was passed. The Act converted leases for the duration of the war into leases for ten years, determinable by the landlord or the tenant by one month's notice given after the end of the war. It should be noted that the Act is of limited scope, relating as it did to the Second World War alone and not affecting other leases of uncertain duration.

(b) *Leases for a life or lives or until marriage*

It was formerly possible to create a lease at a rent for a life or lives or for a term of years determinable with life or lives or on the marriage of the tenant. This is no longer possible after 1925. The effect of the Law of Property Act 1925 [74] is to convert any such lease, whether made before or after the Act came into force, into a lease for a term of ninety years if such lease was granted at a rent or in consideration of a fine. The lease can be determined after the death or marriage, as the case may be, by one month's written notice served by either party. Such notice must be made to expire on one of the quarter days applicable to the tenancy, or, if there are no quarter days specially applicable to the tenancy, on one of the usual quarter days.

The provision does not, however, apply to any term taking effect in equity under a settlement or created out of an equitable interest under a settlement for mortgage, indemnity, or other like purpose.

(c) *Perpetually renewable leases*

Another form of lease sometimes encountered before January 1, 1926, was a perpetually renewable lease. Such a lease was for a fixed term, and gave to the tenant and the persons claiming under him, but not to the landlord, the right to renew the lease at the end of the term for a like period, and so on indefinitely. By the Law of Property Act 1922,[75] all perpetually renewable leaseholds existing on January 1, 1926, became on that date terms of 2,000 years calculated as from the date upon which the existing term commenced, and all perpetually renewable leaseholds created after 1925 take effect as terms of 2,000 years calculated from the date upon which the lease is to commence.

Sometimes it was provided in a perpetually renewable lease that on each renewal the tenant should pay a fine to the reversioner. Such fines cease to be payable after 1925 and instead the tenant must, during the continuance of the 2,000 years term, pay an additional annual rent.

---

[73] *Lace* v. *Chantler* [1944] K.B. 368: see *supra*, note 66.
[74] s. 149 (6).
[75] s. 145 and Sched. 15. See *Parkus* v. *Greenwood* [1950] Ch. 644; *cf. Northchurch Estates Ltd.* v. *Daniels* [1947] Ch. 117; *Re Hopkins' Lease* [1972] 1 W.L.R. 372.

The 2,000 year term may be determined by the tenant or persons claiming under him on any date on which the perpetually renewable term would have expired if it had not been converted by the Act, and had not been renewed. The determination is effected by written notice given at least ten days before such date to the person entitled to the reversion. The person entitled to the reversion has no power to determine the term at the dates of renewal.

C. Reddendum

Then follows the Reddendum, which specifies the rent which the tenant is (to use the common form) to " yield and pay," and the days on which it is to be paid. The reservation of rent ought to be certain as to the amount and the time when payable. A rent is sufficiently certain if it can be calculated with certainty at the time when it becomes payable.[76] In practice if the term of the lease is for more than a few years, there will be provision for rent review at the end of a specified period, for example, every five or seven years. Alternatively, the rent may be tied to some fluctuating standard, such as the price of gold, or the retail prices index.[77]

Rent cannot be reserved to a stranger.[78] The Reddendum should not state to whom the rent is to be paid, for if the rent is reserved generally the law will carry it to the owner of the reversion for the time being,[79] whilst an incomplete or mistaken reservation may give rise to difficulties.

The lease should contain a stipulation, in the event of the term being put an end to by the landlord's re-entry, for payment by the tenant of a proportionate part of the rent for the fraction of the current period by which rent is payable (such as a quarter) up to the day of such re-entry.

D. Covenants

We shall now discuss the more important of the express covenants often inserted in leases.

(1) Covenant to pay rent

Although there is a common law obligation to pay reasonable remuneration for use and occupation,[80] it is usual to insert an express covenant to pay the rent, on the days and in the manner previously mentioned in the reddendum. The reason for the insertion of an express covenant has been mentioned earlier.[80]

---

[76] See *Greater London Council* v. *Connolly* [1970] 2 Q.B. 100.
[77] For forms, see 11 *Encyclopaedia of Forms and Precedents* (4th ed.), pp. 299 *et seq.*
[78] See *Oates* v. *Frith* (1615) Hob. 130.
[79] See *Whitlock's Case* (1609) 8 Co.Rep. 69b.
[80] See *ante*, p. 249.

(2) Covenant to pay taxes

The object of the covenant for payment of rates and taxes is to throw upon the landlord or the tenant certain burdens which would, in the absence of agreement, have to be borne by the other party. Such covenants can take a number of forms and the subject is complex. The reader is referred to Precedent 18 in the Appendix [81] and to standard works on the law of landlord and tenant.[82]

(3) Covenant to repair

Express covenants to repair vary considerably though in a long lease the tenant will commonly covenant to carry out all the repairs, while in a short lease the landlord will commonly covenant to carry out repairs to the structure and the exterior of the demised property.

Tenant's covenant to repair

In some cases, especially in a tenancy agreement, the tenant will undertake obligations in wide, general terms—for example, simply to " keep in repair." In other cases, he may enter into particular detailed covenants relating to such matters as the painting of the property.

The meaning of a covenant depends on the particular wording employed, but a number of words and phrases have been considered in various cases. If the tenant covenants to " repair " or to " repair and keep in repair," he is only bound, by keeping the premises in as nearly as possible the same condition as when they were demised, to take care that they do not suffer more than the operation of time and nature would effect, and he is not bound to rebuild the premises.[83] However, the word " repair " may connote the renewal or replacement of a *subsidiary* part of the premises, as distinct from reconstruction of the entirety.[84]

A covenant to " put " the premises into repair binds the tenant, if they are out of repair, to put them into a better condition than existed when he took them.[85]

Landlord's covenant to repair

It will be recalled that the landlord may be bound to repair in certain cases because of the obligations which the law implies.[86] Apart from this, the liability for repairs imposed on the landlord will depend on negotiation between the parties, as in the case of the tenant's repairs.[87]

---

[81] See *post*, p. 424.
[82] See Woodfall, *Landlord and Tenant* (27th ed.), Vol. 1, Chap. 12.
[83] *Gutteridge* v. *Munyard* (1834) 7 C. and P. 129; *Lister* v. *Lane* [1893] 2 Q.B. 212.
[84] *Lurcott* v. *Wakeley* [1911] 1 K.B. 905. And see *Brew Brothers Ltd.* v. *Snax (Ross) Ltd.* [1970] 1 Q.B. 612.
[85] *Belcher and Green* v. *M'Intosh* (1839) 2 Moo. and Rob. 186.
[86] *Ante*, pp. 250–252.
[87] See *Davstone Estates Ltd.'s Leases* [1969] 2 Ch. 378.

Landlord's remedies for breach of tenant's covenant

The landlord can sue the tenant for damages for breach of the covenant to repair, though he will be able to exercise his right of re-entry if, as is usual, there is a forfeiture clause in the lease.[88]   At common law, a landlord could commence an action against the tenant for damages for breach of the covenant or an action to enforce a proviso for re-entry as soon as the covenant was broken.   In connection with the latter, the tenant has the advantage of section 146 of the Law of Property Act 1925 [89] which requires the landlord to serve a notice on the tenant and entitles the tenant to claim relief: this is discussed later.[90]   Again, the tenant may have the advantage of the provisions of the Leasehold Property (Repairs) Act 1938 [91] which applies both to actions for damages and to actions for re-entry and which concerns tenancies for terms of years certain of seven years or more, with at least three years unexpired, save for tenancies of agricultural holdings.   In such cases, the landlord may not commence an action for damages or seek to enforce a forfeiture clause for breach of the covenant to repair unless he has served on the tenant, at least one month previously, " such a notice as is specified in section 146 (1) of the Law of Property Act 1925," [90] and such notice must state that the tenant may serve a counter-notice.   After the service of such a notice, the tenant may within twenty-eight days serve on the landlord a counter-notice stating that he claims the benefit of the Act of 1938. If this counter-notice is served, the landlord may not proceed to enforce his right of re-entry or his right to damages either by action or otherwise without leave of the court.   Such leave will only be given if the landlord proves one of a number of particular grounds, such as that the immediate remedying of the breach in question is requisite for preventing substantial diminution in the value of his reversion, or that the breach can be immediately remedied at an expense that is relatively small in comparison with the much greater expense that would probably be occasioned by postponement of the necessary work.

Measure of damages

Formerly the measure of damages for breach of the tenant's covenant to repair differed according to whether the breach was committed and action was brought during the continuance of the term or at the end of it.   In the former case the measure of damages was the extent of the damage to the reversion, that is, the difference between the value of the reversion with the premises in their actual state of repair and its value with the premises in their proper state of repair.[92]

---

88 See *post,* p. 263.
89 See also Landlord and Tenant Act 1927, s. 18 (2); Recorded Delivery Service Act 1962, s. 1 (1). See *post,* p. 265.
90 See *post,* pp. 263–267.
91 As amended by the Landlord and Tenant Act 1954.
92 *Ebbetts* v. *Conquest* [1895] 2 Ch. 377; *Conquest* v. *Ebbetts* [1896] A.C. 490.

In the latter case, the measure of damages was the actual amount which it would cost to put the premises in proper repair, and in this case the landlord could claim damages even if he had suffered none, as where on the expiration of the lease or soon afterwards the premises were to be pulled down and rebuilt.[93] Now, however, the measure of damages cannot exceed the extent of the damage to the reversion, whenever the breach was committed; and, in particular, the landlord can recover no damages if, on the expiration of the lease or shortly after, the premises are to be pulled down or reconstructed so as to render the repairs covered by the covenant valueless.[94]

Internal decorative repairs

If a tenant is liable to carry out *internal decorative repairs* he may in certain circumstances be relieved of his liability. If a notice has been served on a tenant requiring him to effect such repairs, he may apply to the court, and if, having regard to all the circumstances, including in particular the length of the tenant's term or interest remaining unexpired, the court is satisfied that the notice is unreasonable, it may relieve the tenant wholly or partly from liability to effect such repairs.[95] But this provision does not apply [96]:

(a) where the liability is under an express covenant to put the property (as distinct from keeping it) in decorative repair and the covenant has never been performed;

(b) to repairs necessary or proper for sanitary purposes or preservation of the structure;

(c) to any statutory liability to keep a house reasonably fit for human habitation;

(d) to any covenant or stipulation to yield up the premises in a specified state of repair at the end of the term.

Tenant's remedies for breach of landlord's covenant to repair

If the landlord does not execute repairs in accordance with his covenant, the tenant can sue for damages: he is not entitled to withhold rent [97] or to leave the property [98] merely because the landlord has not observed his covenant to repair. The tenant cannot usually sue unless he gives the landlord prior notice of the disrepair.[99]

---

[93] *Joyner* v. *Weeks* [1891] 2 Q.B. 31.
[94] Landlord and Tenant Act 1927, s. 18. The cost of the repairs will usually be a sound indication of the extent of the damage to the reversion: *Jones* v. *Herxheimer* [1950] 2 K.B. 106; *Smiley* v. *Townshend* [1950] 2 K.B. 311. Section 18 is limited to an action for damages for breach of a covenant *to repair*: see *Moss' Empires Ltd.* v. *Olympia (Liverpool) Ltd.* [1939] A.C. 544; *Eyre* v. *Rea* [1947] K.B. 567.
[95] Law of Property Act 1925, s. 147.
[96] *Ibid.* s. 147 (2).
[97] *Hart* v. *Rogers* [1916] 1 K.B. 646.
[98] *Surplice* v. *Farnsworth* (1844) 7 M. and G. 576.
[99] *Makin* v. *Watkinson* (1870) L.R. 6 Ex. 25.

(4) Covenant to insure

The tenant often covenants that he will insure the premises in the joint names of the landlord and of the tenant, or in the name of one of the two, and that he will, if required, produce the insurance policy and the receipts for premiums. It is also common and advisable to stipulate that he will, in case of fire, lay out the insurance moneys in rebuilding or repairing the premises, for the landlord might, in the absence of such a provision, be unable to procure that they are used in such manner [1]; by this means the landlord obtains a security that the premises will be rebuilt.

If the covenant stipulates that the insurance shall be effected in the joint names of the landlord and the tenant, it is broken if the insurance is effected in the name of the tenant only,[2] but not if it is effected in the name of the landlord only.[3] If the covenant provides that the tenant shall insure with a specified company or with one to be approved by the landlord, the landlord has an absolute right to withhold his approval of an alternative office, without giving any reasons.[4]

If the property is uninsured for any length of time, there is a breach of covenant, even if the time is only a short one and even if there is in fact no fire.[5]

(5) Covenant restrictive of user

Where the premises, or part of them, consist of a dwelling-house, it is usual to insert a covenant that the tenant will not use the house for purposes of trade or business, or otherwise than as a private dwelling-house, without the consent in writing of the landlord. It is advisable to insert a general restriction against carrying on trade or business, rather than a restriction to the effect that particular kinds of trade or business are not to be carried on without consent or one restraining " offensive " trades only. The reason is that such explicit clauses often give rise to disputes, whereas a general prohibition allows the landlord to exercise his judgment upon each application made to him for his consent and his rights under the covenant will not be limited by any consideration as to the nature of the trade or business proposed to be carried on. It should be noted that the word " business " is more extensive than the word " trade ": thus, to keep a school is a business [6] but to keep a private lunatic asylum is not a trade.[7]

---

[1] But see *Mumford Hotels Ltd.* v. *Wheler* [1964] Ch. 117. See also *Re King, Robinson* v. *Gray* [1963] Ch. 459.

[2] *Doe* d. *Muston* v. *Gladwin* (1845) 6 Q.B. 953.

[3] *Havens* v. *Middleton* (1853) 10 Ha. 641.

[4] *Tredegar* v. *Harwood* [1929] A.C. 72.

[5] *Penniall* v. *Harborne* (1848) 11 Q.B. 368.

[6] *Doe* d. *Bish* v. *Keeling* (1813) 1 M. and S. 95.

[7] *Doe* d. *Wetherell* v. *Bird* (1834) 2 A. & E. 161. " Every trade is a business, but every business is not a trade " (*per* Lord Denman C.J., at p. 166).

(6) Covenant not to assign or underlet

A covenant often inserted in leases is a covenant against assignment or sub-letting or parting with possession of the premises or any part thereof without the consent in writing of the landlord. The covenant against assignment should, if intended to prohibit underletting, be expressly worded to that effect, for a covenant merely not to assign does not prevent the tenant from granting an underlease of part of the term,[8] although an underlease of the whole term amounts to an assignment.[9]

The lease may contain a covenant by the tenant in unqualified terms not to assign or sublet or part with possession. This amounts to an absolute prohibition and the landlord need not consent to such an act.[10] But it is more usual for the covenant to be qualified so as to prohibit such acts without the landlord's consent. In this latter case, the covenant is subject to certain statutory provisions:

(a) The lease sometimes provides that a fine shall be paid to the landlord in respect of his consent to assign or underlet. Such a provision is unobjectionable and enables the landlord to refuse his consent unless the fine is paid. However, in the absence of such express provision, it is enacted that a lease, whenever made, containing a covenant not to assign or underlet without consent, shall be deemed to contain a proviso to the effect that no fine shall be payable in respect of the consent.[11] The provision does not make the payment of a fine illegal and if, therefore, the landlord demands a fine when he is not entitled to do so, and the tenant pays it without protest, the tenant cannot recover the sum paid.[12] But if, in a case where the landlord is not entitled to demand a fine, he gives his consent subject to the payment of a fine, the tenant is entitled to treat the consent as unconditional and to assign or underlet there and then,[13] or he may apply to the court for a declaration that he is entitled forthwith to assign or underlet.[14]

(b) A qualified covenant may be simply in the terms " without the landlord's consent " or it may go further and state " such consent not to be unreasonably withheld." In any event, in leases, whenever made, containing a covenant not to assign or underlet without consent, such a covenant is deemed to be subject to a proviso that such consent is not to be unreasonably withheld.[15] It has been held that the refusal will be unreasonable unless it is made in respect of the intended

8 *Crusoe* d. *Blencowe* v. *Bugby* (1771) 3 Wils. 234.
9 *Beardman* v. *Wilson* (1868) L.R. 4 C.P. 57.
10 See *F. W. Woolworth and Co. Ltd.* v. *Lambert* [1937] Ch. 37, *per* Romer L.J., at pp. 58–59.
11 Law of Property Act 1925, s. 144.
12 *Andrew* v. *Bridgman* [1908] 1 K.B. 596.
13 *Ibid.*
14 *West* v. *Gwynne* [1911] 2 Ch. 1.
15 Landlord and Tenant Act 1927, s. 19 (1). Leases of agricultural holdings are excluded from the provision: s. 19 (4).

K

user of the premises by, or the personality of, the proposed assignee or underlessee,[16] but this has been doubted [17] and it is best considered as a guideline and not as a strict principle. The parties to a lease cannot restrict the ambit of this provision by an express stipulation as to what should be deemed to be reasonable.[18] What is unreasonable is a question of fact, though examples can be given.[19] Thus, it has been held that if a landlord refuses consent to the grant of an under-lease unless the underlessee covenants to pay to him the rent reserved by the head lease, the refusal is unreasonable.[20] Under the Race Relations Act 1965,[21] the landlord's consent is treated as being unreasonably withheld if it is withheld on the ground of colour, race or ethnic or national origins.

If the tenant fails to ask for the landlord's consent before he assigns or sub-lets, he is guilty of a breach of covenant, and this is so even though the landlord's refusal to consent would in fact be unreasonable.[22] If the tenant does ask for the landlord's consent and the landlord unreasonably refuses it, the tenant cannot recover damages [23] (though he can if the landlord is bound by an express covenant not to decline his consent unreasonably [24]) but he can at once assign or underlet without any consent [23] or can apply to the court for a declaration that he is entitled to do so.[25] Since it is often difficult to feel sure that the landlord's refusal is unreasonable, an assignee or sub-lessee would generally hesitate to proceed in the absence of such a declaration.

(c) It is enacted [26] that in the case of a building lease [27] for more than forty years, containing a covenant against assigning, underletting or parting with possession without licence or consent, such covenant shall, notwithstanding any express provision to the contrary, be deemed to be subject to a proviso to the effect that in the case of any assignment, underletting or parting with possession effected more than seven years before the end of the term, no consent or licence shall be required, if notice in writing of the transaction is given to the landlord within six months after the transaction is effected.

Finally, it should be noted that the covenant not to assign, sub-let

---

[16] *Houlder Bros. and Co. Ltd.* v. *Gibbs* [1925] Ch. 575.
[17] *Tredegar* v. *Harwood* [1929] A.C. 72. And see *Pimms Ltd.* v. *Tallow Chandlers* [1964] 2 Q.B. 547; and (1969) New L.J. 7.
[18] *Re Smith's Lease, Smith* v. *Richards* [1951] 1 All E.R. 346.
[19] See Megarry and Wade, pp. 699–700.
[20] *Balfour* v. *Kensington Gardens Mansions Ltd.* (1932) 49 T.L.R. 29.
[21] s. 5.
[22] *Barrow* v. *Isaacs* [1891] 1 Q.B. 417; *Eastern Telegraph Co.* v. *Dent* [1899] 1 Q.B. 835.
[23] *Treloar* v. *Bigge* (1874) L.R. 9 Ex. 151.
[24] *Ideal Film Renting Co. Ltd.* v. *Neilsen* [1921] 1 Ch. 575.
[25] *Young* v. *Ashley Gardens Properties Ltd.* [1903] 2 Ch. 112 (consent given but subject to unreasonable condition).
[26] Landlord and Tenant Act 1927, s. 19 (1).
[27] This is a lease where the tenant covenants to build on the demised land. Leases of agricultural holdings and mining leases are excluded from this provision.

or part with possession does not apply to an involuntary alienation by operation of law. Thus, no breach occurs on the lease being taken in execution,[28] or on the bankruptcy of the tenant when the term will become vested in his trustee in bankruptcy.[29] Nor does a bequest of the term amount to a breach of the covenant.[30]

E. Proviso for Re-entry and Forfeiture

There are several ways in which a lease may terminate, such as by effluxion of time or by notice to quit. These are important, but they are more appropriately dealt with in works on real property [31] or landlord and tenant [32] than in a book on the elements of conveyancing. However, one means by which a lease may terminate, namely, forfeiture, which is very important to the conveyancer, will be dealt with here.

The proviso for re-entry is to the effect that whenever any part of the rent shall have been in arrear for, usually, twenty-one days, whether the same shall have been formally demanded or not, or whenever the tenant shall commit a breach of any of his covenants or become bankrupt, the landlord may re-enter upon the premises, and that thereupon the term granted shall absolutely determine. The proviso should state that the re-entry for non-payment of rent may be made whether the rent has been legally demanded or not, for this wording enables the landlord to re-enter without any formal demand for rent.[33]

It is important to note that unless the right to forfeit and re-enter is expressly reserved in the lease, no such right exists and the landlord must rely solely upon his remedy in damages for breach of the covenants and sometimes an injunction, and distress for recovery of the rent.

The landlord may exercise his right by taking actual physical possession, but this is neither usual nor wise because if he employs force he might commit a criminal offence,[34] and it is provided that where any premises are let as a dwelling on a lease which is subject to a right of re-entry or forfeiture, it is not lawful to enforce that right otherwise than by proceedings in court while any person is lawfully residing in the premises or part of them.[35] It is therefore, usual to

---

[28] *Doe* d. *Mitchinson* v. *Carter* (1798) 8 T.R. 57; and see (1799) 8 T.R. 300.
[29] *Re Riggs, ex p. Lovell* [1901] 2 K.B. 16. Contrast *Re Wright, ex p. Landau* v. *The Trustee* [1949] Ch. 729.
[30] *Fox* v. *Swann* (1655) Sty. 482; *cf.* (1963) 27 Conv.(N.S.) 159.
[31] See *e.g.* Megarry and Wade, pp. 658–680.
[32] See *e.g.* Woodfall, *Landlord and Tenant* (27th ed.), Vol. 1, Chap. 17.
[33] *Doe* d. *Harris* v. *Masters* (1824) 2 B. & C. 490. It is true that by the Common Law Procedure Act 1852, s. 210, the landlord is absolved from making a formal demand even though he does not expressly exclude such a need, but this only applies if there is half a year's rent in arrear and no sufficient distress can be found upon the premises.
[34] Forcible Entry Acts 1381–1623. These are largely superseded by the Rent Act 1965, s. 31, below.
[35] Rent Act 1965, s. 31.

enforce the right of re-entry and forfeiture by taking legal proceedings.[36] At common law the landlord was entitled to take advantage of the proviso for re-entry as soon as the event in respect of which it was exercisable occurred. This would often inflict great hardship on a tenant who was ready and willing to make amends by paying all arrears of rent or compensating the landlord for breach of covenant, as the case might be. If the forfeiture arose by reason of non-payment of rent, equity from early times granted relief to the tenant, but such relief was not generally granted against forfeiture for breach of other covenants.[37] The tenant's right to relief against forfeiture is now regulated by statute, and consequently the position at common law and the relief formerly granted in equity are, generally speaking, no longer of any practical importance.[38] The tenant's present position differs according to the nature of the breach which gives rise to the forfeiture, and the various cases will now be dealt with.

Forfeiture for non-payment of rent

The landlord's right to forfeit for non-payment of rent arises immediately the rent is in arrear for the number of days specified in the proviso for forfeiture contained in the lease, and the landlord, if excused by the lease or by statute[39] from making a formal demand for the rent, is entitled to re-enter at once or commence proceedings for possession. But if the tenant, at any time before the trial, tenders to the landlord all the rent and arrears, together with costs, all further proceedings are to cease[40]; however, this relief is limited because it only operates if at least one half year's rent is in arrear.[41] A more important provision is that the tenant may apply to the court for relief against the forfeiture after it has been effected.[42] If the re-entry is made pursuant to the court's judgment, the claim for relief must be made within six months of the re-entry,[42] but if it is made by the landlord without bringing court proceedings there is no time limit for making the claim for relief[43] (save that relief will not be given in respect of stale claims). If the tenant applies for relief within the appropriate time, the court may grant relief, thus putting the tenant in to his former position, if he pays all arrears of rent and costs and it is equitable that he should be relieved.

---

[36] When such proceedings are taken, the re-entry is effected by the service, and not merely by the issue, of the writ; *Canas Property Co. Ltd.* v. *K. L. Television Services Ltd.* [1970] 2 Q.B. 433.

[37] *Hill* v. *Barclay* (1811) 18 Ves. 56; *Barrow* v. *Isaacs* [1891] 1 Q.B. 417.

[38] But see *e.g. Thatcher* v. *C. H. Pearce and Sons (Contractors) Ltd.* [1968] 1 W.L.R. 748; below, note 43.

[39] See *ante*, note 33. If he is not so excused, he must make a formal demand.

[40] Common Law Procedure Act 1852, s. 212.

[41] *Standard Pattern Co. Ltd.* v. *Ivey* [1962] Ch. 432.

[42] Common Law Procedure Act 1852, ss. 210–212.

[43] This is because in such cases the equitable rules apply and not the Act: *Thatcher* v. *C. H. Pearce and Sons (Contractors) Ltd., supra.*

Forfeiture for breach of covenants other than for payment of rent

Except in certain cases[44] a landlord cannot exercise immediately a right of re-entry for breach of a covenant other than the covenant for payment of rent. Under section 146 of the Law of Property Act 1925, before proceeding to enforce the right of re-entry by action or otherwise, the landlord must first serve on the tenant a notice which:

(a) specifies the breach complained of; and
(b) requires the tenant to remedy the breach if it is capable of remedy[45]; and
(c) requires the tenant to make compensation in money for the breach.[46]

After the service of the notice, the landlord must wait a reasonable time to enable the tenant to comply with the notice. If the notice is not complied with, the landlord may proceed, by action or otherwise, to enforce the right of re-entry, but the tenant may, in the landlord's action, if any, or in an action brought by himself, apply to the court for relief, and the court has a discretion to grant the tenant relief.[47] It should be noted that if the landlord has entered, it is too late for the tenant to obtain relief[48]; he has not got six months in which to apply for relief as in the case of forfeiture for non-payment of rent.

A landlord seeking to enforce a right of re-entry for breach of a covenant to repair must not only serve the notice discussed above but must prove that the tenant had knowledge of the service of the notice and that a time reasonably sufficient to enable the repairs to be executed has elapsed since knowledge of such service came to the tenant. If the notice was sent by registered post, the tenant is to be deemed, unless the contrary is proved, to have had knowledge of the service of the notice as from the time when the letter would have been delivered in the ordinary course of post[49]: sending by recorded delivery will have the same effect.[50]

Forfeiture on bankruptcy of tenant, or his interest being taken in execution

The forfeiture clause in the lease will generally extend to the bankruptcy[51] of the tenant or his interest being taken in execution.

---

44 Law of Property Act 1925, s. 146 (8): in the two cases set out in subsection (8), the first of which is now unimportant and the second of which is specialised, the landlord need not serve any notice and the court cannot grant the tenant relief.
45 If the breach is incapable of remedy, the notice is sufficient even though it does not require it to be remedied: see *Rugby School (Governors)* v. *Tannahill* [1935] 1 K.B. 87; *Hoffman* v. *Fineberg* [1949] Ch. 245; *Egerton* v. *Esplanade Hotels (London)* [1947] 2 All E.R. 88; *Glass* v. *Kencakes Ltd*. [1966] 1 Q.B. 611.
46 The notice is not invalidated merely because no such compensation is demanded: *Lock* v. *Pearce* [1893] 2 Ch. 271; *Rugby School (Governors)* v. *Tannahill, supra*.
47 See *Westminster (Duke of)* v. *Swinton* [1948] 1 K.B. 524.
48 *Rogers* v. *Rice* [1892] 2 Ch. 170.
49 Landlord and Tenant Act 1927, s. 18 (2). See also Leasehold Property (Repairs) Act 1938; *ante*, p. 258.
50 Recorded Delivery Service Act 1962, s. 1 (1).
51 If the tenant is a company, bankruptcy includes liquidation: Law of Property Act 1925, s. 205 (1) (i).

There are special provisions contained in section 146 of the Law of Property Act 1925 regulating the landlord's position in these events.[52] These provisions may be summarised as follows:

(1) Section 146 does not apply to a condition for forfeiture on the tenant's bankruptcy or on taking in execution of his interest if contained in a lease of:

(a) agricultural or pastoral land;
(b) mines or minerals;
(c) a public-house or beershop;
(d) a furnished dwelling-house; or
(e) property with respect to which the personal qualifications of the tenant are of importance for the preservation of the value or character of the property, or on the ground of neighbourhood to the landlord, or to any person holding under him.

In the above cases, therefore, the landlord can forfeit the lease on the tenant's bankruptcy or the taking in execution of his interest, and the landlord need not serve any notice and the court has no power to grant the tenant relief.

(2) Apart from the above cases, if the landlord wishes to enforce his right of re-entry within one year of the bankruptcy or taking in execution, and the tenant's interest has not been sold before the expiration of that year, the landlord must serve the section 146 notice and the court can grant the tenant relief.

(3) If the landlord desires to re-enter after the end of one year, he can re-enter without the service of the notice and the court cannot grant relief, provided the lessee's interest has not been sold before the expiration of the year.

(4) If the tenant's interest is sold within one year from the bankruptcy or taking in execution, section 146 applies and the landlord cannot re-enter without first serving a notice and the court can grant relief.

Underleases

Since the existence of an underlease necessarily depends on the continued existence of the lease out of which it was granted, it follows that the forfeiture of the lease operates as a forfeiture of the underlease. However, it is provided [53] that where a head landlord is proceeding by action or otherwise to enforce a right of re-entry, whether on the ground of non-payment of rent or otherwise, the court may, on an application by a sub-tenant either in the head landlord's action (if any) or in an action brought by himself, make an order vesting the property in the sub-tenant upon such conditions as the court thinks fit, but in no case is a sub-tenant entitled to require a lease to be granted to him

---

[52] Law of Property Act 1925, s. 146 (9) (10).
[53] Law of Property Act 1925, s. 146 (4), as amended by Law of Property (Amendment) Act 1929, s. 1. Relief is available to a mortgagee.

for a term longer than he had under his original sub-lease. The court has power to grant such relief even in those cases where relief could not have been granted to the tenant himself, as where the tenant of agricultural property has become bankrupt.[54] A person in adverse possession cannot apply for relief.[55]

Waiver

The landlord's right to forfeit the lease may be waived, either expressly or impliedly. An implied waiver occurs if the landlord, knowing of his right to forfeit, does something showing an intention to treat the lease as still subsisting, as by accepting rent becoming due after the breach giving rise to the right of re-entry.[56] In the case of a continuing breach, such as the breach of a covenant to keep in repair, the waiver extends only to the landlord's right down to the date of the act of waiver, and after such act the covenant continues to be broken and the landlord is nevertheless entitled to forfeit the lease.[57] A waiver is deemed to extend merely to the breach to which it specially relates and not to operate as a general waiver of the benefit of the covenant concerned, unless a contrary intention appears.[58]

F. Landlord's Covenant for Quiet Enjoyment

The proviso for re-entry is followed by a covenant on the part of the landlord that the tenant shall, provided that he pays the rent and observes the covenants mentioned in the lease, peaceably enjoy the premises without any interruption by the landlord or any person lawfully claiming under him. The implied covenant for quiet enjoyment, and the advantage of inserting an express one, have been mentioned earlier.[59]

G. Testimonium

The deed concludes with the ordinary Testimonium, and should, if there is no counterpart, be executed by both the landlord and the tenant: but it is more usual to have a counterpart, in which case the lease is signed by the landlord, and the counterpart by the tenant. Both instruments should be properly attested.

IV. Assignments

The tenant may assign the residue of the term or the landlord may assign his reversion.

---

54 See *supra.*
55 *Tickner* v. *Buzzacott* [1965] Ch. 426.
56 *Doe* d. *Gatehouse* v. *Rees* (1838) 4 Bing.N.C. 384.
57 See *Segal Securities Ltd.* v. *Thoseby* [1963] 1 Q.B. 887.
58 Law of Property Act 1925, s. 148. See also *ibid.* s. 143.
59 *Ante,* p. 250.

Assignment of the lease

The tenant may, during the currency of the lease, assign the residue of the term to a purchaser. This may occur in the case of a relatively short lease, such as a seven-year lease of a shop, or in the case of a long lease, such as a 999-year lease of a dwelling-house. In the latter type of case, which arises frequently in practice, the purchase price is likely to be the same as if the property were freehold and the rent will be a low ground rent. Contracts to assign leaseholds have already been discussed.[60] The assignment itself, which actually transfers the legal estate to the purchaser, is essentially similar to a conveyance of freehold land. The following points should be borne in mind:

(1) *Deed*

The assignment must be made by deed,[61] however short the term of the lease and even if it was created orally.

(2) *Landlord's consent*

If the lease requires the landlord's consent to an assignment,[62] this should be obtained and the fact should be recited.

(3) *" Beneficial owner "*

The vendor will assign (not convey) the property to the purchaser, and he will often do so " as beneficial owner." [63] The habendum will state that the purchaser is to hold the property for the residue of the term created by the lease and subject to the rent and covenants therein stated.

(4) *Tenant's liability*

The tenant continues to be liable, even after the assignment and indeed until the lease terminates, to the landlord under his covenants, such as to pay rent. Thus, if the assignee breaks a covenant, the landlord may sue the original tenant.[64] Alternatively, the landlord may be able to sue the assignee himself, under the rules discussed below, though he cannot recover damages twice. If the landlord does recover from the original tenant, the latter will be able to sue the assignee under his covenant for indemnity, mentioned below.

(5) *Assignee's liability*

The assignee will be bound to the landlord to observe those covenants in the lease which " touch and concern the land," [65] such

[60] *Ante*, pp. 15 *et seq.*; 99–100.
[61] Law of Property Act 1925, s. 52.
[62] See *ante*, p. 261.
[63] For covenants for title, see the discussion in Chap. 10: *ante*, pp. 225–229.
[64] Law of Property Act 1925, s. 79.
[65] *Spencer's Case* (1583) 5 Co.Rep. 16.

as the covenant to pay the rent or to repair, but not those covenants which do not touch and concern the land. If the landlord chooses to sue the tenant rather than the assignee for a breach of covenant (as to which, see the above comments), the assignee will usually be liable to indemnify the tenant. This latter liability may arise expressly, but in any event an assignee for valuable consideration impliedly covenants that he, or the persons deriving title under him, will, from the date of the assignment, pay the rent, observe the tenant's covenants and indemnify the assignor against all claims on account of any omission to pay the rent or any breach of any of the covenants.[66]

(6) Landlord's liability

The assignee will be able to enforce against the landlord the latter's covenants which touch and concern the land,[65] such as the covenant for quiet enjoyment, but not those which do not touch and concern the land.

(7) Forms

The Schedule to the Land Registration Rules 1925 prescribes certain forms for the transfer of leasehold land.[67]

Assignment of the reversion

If the landlord assigns his reversion, the assignee can sue the tenant in respect of those covenants which have " reference to the subject-matter " of the lease,[68] that is, touch and concern the land. Only the assignee and not the assignor can bring an action, even where the breach occurred while the assignor held the reversion.[69] Again, on an assignment of the reversion the assignee is bound by the landlord's covenants which have " reference to the subject-matter " of the lease.[70]

V. TAXATION

Income tax [71]

A landlord is liable to tax under Schedule A on the annual profits arising in respect of rents from leases or agreements for leases of land in the United Kingdom [72]; the chargeable profits are ascertained by

---

[66] Law of Property Act 1925, s. 77 (1) (C) and Sched. 2, Pt. IX. See also ibid. s. 77 (1) (D) and Sched. 2, Pt. X; Land Registration Act 1925, s. 24.

[67] See Forms 32–34. And see ante, pp. 166–168 for leases in the case of registered land generally.

[68] Law of Property Act 1925, s. 141.

[69] Re King, Robinson v. Gray [1963] Ch. 459. And see London and County (A. and D.) Ltd. v. Wilfred Sportsman, Ltd. [1971] Ch. 764; Arlesford Trading Co. Ltd. v. Servansingh [1971] 1 W.L.R. 1080.

[70] Law of Property Act 1925, s. 142.

[71] See Pinson, Revenue Law (5th ed.), Chap. 6.

[72] Income and Corporation Taxes Act 1970, s. 67. In the case of furnished lettings, rent may be taxable under Case VI of Sched. D instead of Sched. A.

deducting from the rents such items as payments made by the landlord for repairs.[73] There are special provisions dealing with taxation of premiums, for they do not fall within the provision just mentioned. Where the payment of a premium is required under a lease not exceeding fifty years, the landlord is treated as becoming entitled when the lease is granted to an amount by way of rent (in addition to any actual rent) equal to the amount of the premium reduced by 1/50th of that amount for each complete period of twelve months (other than the first) comprised in the duration of the lease.[74] Thus, in the case of a short term more of the premium is chargeable than in the case of a long term, and if the term is fifty-one years no premium is chargeable.[75]

Where land is sold on the terms that it shall be reconveyed to the vendor, the vendor is chargeable to tax under Case VI of Schedule D on any amount by which the price at which the land is sold exceeds the price at which it is to be reconveyed.[76] Further, where the terms of the sale provide for the grant of a lease-back to the vendor, the foregoing provision applies as if the grant of the lease were a reconveyance of the land at a price equal to the sum of the amount of the premium (if any) and the value at the date of the sale of the right to receive a conveyance of the reversion immediately after the lease begins to run.[77] But this latter provision does not apply if the lease is granted, and begins to run, within one month after the sale.[78] The conveyance with a lease-back is a popular means of furnishing finance to develop land; it will be seen from the above that it should be ensured that the lease-back is granted and takes effect within one month of the sale.[79]

Stamp duty [80]

Duty is charged under the heading "Lease or Tack" in the First Schedule to the Stamp Act 1891.[81] The duty varies with a number of factors, such as the amount of the rent and the length of the term.

VI. SPECIAL CASES

It will be noticed from the discussion so far in this chapter that different statutes, such as the Housing Act 1961 and the Leasehold Property (Repairs) Act 1938, have imposed various rules which alter or add to many of the common law rules relating to leases. We now

---

[73] See Income and Corporation Taxes Act 1970, ss. 72–77.
[74] *Ibid.* s. 80 (1).
[75] Note, however, *ibid.* s. 84.
[76] *Ibid.* s. 82 (1).
[77] *Ibid.* s. 82 (3).
[78] *Ibid.* s. 82 (3), proviso. And see Finance Bill (1972).
[79] See (1971) 68 L.S.Gaz. 346; (1971) 115 S.J. 87; (1972) 122 New L.J. 429.
[80] See Pinson (5th ed.), Chap. 35.
[81] As amended: F.A. 1963, ss. 55, 56; F.A. 1970, s. 32; Finance Bill (1972).

come to a number of statutes whereby the legislature imposes fundamental schemes which radically alter the common law in connection
with different types of property. The subjects vary according to the
kind of property concerned, but relate to such matters as security
of tenure, control of rent and compensation for improvements.

A. Unfurnished Premises

The legislation known as the Rent Acts is now consolidated by the
Rent Act 1968 which controls the rents and gives security of tenure in
respect of tenancies of unfurnished dwellings.   It is essential to know
what is meant by " protected," " statutory," " controlled " or " regulated " tenancies.   These terms will be briefly defined before the main
provisions of the Act are discussed.[82]

Protected tenancies

A protected tenancy is a contractual tenancy which falls within the
provisions of the Act.[83]   It is a tenancy where:
(a) The property is a dwelling-house, which may be a house or
part of one, let as a separate dwelling.[84]   If a house (in the popular
sense) comprises a number of separate flats, each flat may be a separate
dwelling-house within the Act.   The dwelling must be let, so that
property held under a licence is excluded.   The Act excludes certain
types of property from protection, such as a dwelling-house which
consists of or comprises premises licensed to sell liquor for consumption
on the premises.[85]   Sometimes property is used partly for living accommodation and partly for business purposes, such as a shop with a flat
above.   In such cases, the Rent Act may apply or Part II of the
Landlord and Tenant Act 1954 [86] may apply.[87]   Again, a tenancy
is not protected at any time when the interest of the landlord under the
tenancy belongs to the Crown [88] or to bodies such as the council of a
county or county borough.[89]
(b) The dwelling-house has or had on " the appropriate day " a
rateable value not exceeding, if it is in Greater London, £400 or, if it is
elsewhere, £200.[90]   " The appropriate day " means March 23, 1965,

---

[82] This subject is so complex that only a brief outline, which is by no means complete
or exhaustive, can be given here.   See Woodfall, *Landlord and Tenant* (27th ed.),
Vol. 2, Chap. 23, and generally the Report of the Committee on the Rent Acts
(the Francis Committee) 1971 Cmnd. 4609.
[83] *i.e.* the Rent Act 1968: all references in this heading (" Unfurnished Premises ")
are to that Act, unless otherwise stated.
[84] s. 1 (1).
[85] s. 9 (2).
[86] See *post*, pp. 281–287.
[87] Broadly speaking, if the tenancy would be controlled on the assumption that the
Rent Act applied, that Act will apply, but if it would be regulated on the
assumption that the Rent Act applied, Pt. II of the Landlord and Tenant Act
1954, will apply.   See s. 9 of the Rent Act 1968; Woodfall, Vol. 2, p. 1445; and
Hill and Redman, *Law of Landlord and Tenant* (15th ed.), p. 905.
[88] s. 4.
[89] s. 5.
[90] s. 1 (1) (a).

or, if no rateable value was then shown in the valuation list, the date on which such a value is or was first shown in the valuation list.[91] This provision will cover most tenancies.

(c) The rent payable is at least two-thirds of the rateable value, being the rateable value on the "appropriate day," as above.[92] In this connection it should be noted that if the dwelling-house is let at a rent which includes payments in respect of board, attendance or use of furniture, the Act does not apply.[93] For this purpose, there is no bona fide letting at a rent which includes payments for attendance or furniture unless the amount of rent fairly attributable to attendance or furniture forms a substantial part of the whole rent,[94] which is a question of fact.[95] The importance of these provisions is that, in order to take the tenancy out of the protection afforded in respect of tenancies of unfurnished premises and bring it within the less stringent rules applicable to tenancies of furnished premises,[96] the landlord must do more than put a few poor sticks of furniture in the premises.

If any one of the above tests is not fulfilled, the tenancy is not a protected one within the Rent Act 1968.

Statutory tenancies

Despite the determination of a contractual, protected tenancy, the tenant is nevertheless entitled, by virtue of the Act, to remain in possession of the premises. In such cases, so long as he occupies the dwelling-house as his residence, he is the statutory tenant.[97] Thus, for example, if the landlord of premises held under a periodic tenancy which is protected by the Act gives the tenant notice to quit, the tenant is entitled to stay in possession, and he must observe, and is entitled to the benefit of, the terms of the determined contractual tenancy, so far as they are consistent with the provisions of the Act.[98]

A statutory tenant has a mere personal right to stay in possession and does not have a proprietary interest, so that, for example, he cannot assign anything to anyone else.[99] But a statutory tenant can be changed by an agreement in writing between himself (" the outgoing tenant ") and an " incoming tenant," when the latter will be deemed to be the statutory tenant.[1]

Controlled tenancies

A protected tenancy falling within the requirements mentioned

---

[91] s. 6 (3).
[92] s. 2 (1) (a).
[93] s. 2 (1) (b).
[94] s. 2 (3).
[95] See *Maclay* v. *Dixon* (1944) 170 L.T. 49.
[96] See *post*, p. 275.
[97] s. 3 (1) (a).
[98] s. 12 (1).
[99] *Keeves* v. *Dean* [1924] 1 K.B. 685.
[1] s. 14. For the position when the statutory tenant dies, see *post*, p. 275.

above will be either controlled or regulated. Similarly, a statutory tenancy which follows the previous contractual, protected tenancy will be either controlled or regulated.

A protected or statutory tenancy is controlled if:

(a) The rateable value of the dwelling-house on November 7, 1956, did not exceed, if it was in the metropolitan police district or the City of London, £40, or, if it was elsewhere, £30.[2]

(b) The premises were not erected after August 29, 1954, and are not separate and self-contained premises produced by conversion after that date of other premises.[3]

(c) The tenancy is not, or, in the case of a statutory tenancy, the preceding contractual tenancy was not, one granted for a term of years certain exceeding twenty-one years.[4]

(d) The tenancy or, in the case of a statutory tenancy, the preceding contractual tenancy, was created by a lease or agreement coming into operation before July 6, 1957, or the tenancy is granted to a person who was the tenant of premises under a controlled tenancy and those premises and the premises comprised in the protected tenancy in question are the same, or one of those premises consists of, or includes part of, the other premises.[5]

Regulated tenancies

A regulated tenancy is a protected or statutory tenancy which is not a controlled tenancy,[6] so that if a protected or statutory tenancy does not fulfil any one of the tests of a controlled tenancy it will be a regulated tenancy.

Security of tenure

We have seen that, despite the determination of a contractual, protected tenancy, the tenant is allowed to remain in possession as a statutory tenant. In order to regain possession, the landlord must obtain an order of the court, which cannot make an order for possession of a dwelling-house which is let on a protected tenancy or subject to a statutory tenancy unless the court considers it reasonable to make such an order *and* either

(a) the court is satisfied that suitable alternative accommodation is available for the tenant; or

(b) one of a number of specified grounds exists—for example, that any rent lawfully due from the tenant has not been paid, or that the tenant has been convicted of using the dwelling-house for immoral or illegal purposes, or, in certain circumstances, that the dwelling-house

---

[2] s. 7 and Sched. 2, para. 1 (*a*).
[3] Unless certain conditions are fulfilled. S. 7 and Sched. 2, paras. 1 (*b*) and 3.
[4] ss. 7, 113 and Sched. 2, para. 1 (*c*).
[5] s. 7 and Sched. 2, paras. 1 (*d*) and 4.
[6] s. 7 (2).

is reasonably required by the landlord for his occupation as a residence.[7]
These grounds are basically the same whether the tenancy is regulated
or controlled, but in the case of a regulated tenancy there are four
special cases where possession can be recovered and where the reasonableness of the order is irrelevant—for example, where an owner-
occupier requires the house for himself and certain conditions are
fulfilled.[8]

Unless the case falls within one of the four special grounds just
mentioned, the court may adjourn the proceedings for possession, stay
or suspend the execution of an order for possession or postpone the
date of possession, subject to such conditions as it thinks fit.[9] For
example, where possession is sought on the ground of non-payment of
rent, an order will usually be suspended on terms that the tenant
continues to pay the current rent plus so much a week off the arrears.[10]

Rent control

Different systems of rent control operate, depending on whether
the tenancy is controlled or regulated.

(a) *Controlled tenancies* [11]

The rent recoverable cannot exceed " the rent limit," which is
calculated from three factors:

(i) the gross value of the dwelling shown in the valuation list on
November 7, 1956, or on the first subsequent date on which a gross
value was shown in the valuation list, multiplied by " the appropriate
factor," which will be greater the more onerous is the landlord's
responsibility for repairs, but which cannot exceed seven-thirds;

(ii) the rates paid by the landlord;

(iii) the amount which represents a reasonable charge for any
services for the tenant provided by the landlord or for any furniture
which the tenant is entitled to use.[12]

This rent limit can be increased in certain cases, as where the landlord spends money on improving the dwelling.[13]

(b) *Regulated tenancies* [14]

Here, the Act provides for the registration of rents. If no rent is
registered, the rent limit is as follows. If, not more than three years
before the regulated tenancy began, the dwelling-house was subject to
another regulated tenancy, the rent limit is the rent payable under that

---

[7] s. 10, Sched. 3, Pt. I.
[8] s. 10. Sched. 3, Pt. II.
[9] s. 11.
[10] See County Court Practice 1972, Form 138, p. 698.
[11] Pt. V of the Act.
[12] ss. 52, 67, Scheds. 4, 8 and 9.
[13] s. 56.
[14] Pts. III and IV of the Act.

other tenancy or, if there was more than one, the last of them; in any other case, the rent limit is the rent payable under the terms of the lease or agreement creating the tenancy, as varied, if the tenancy began before December 8, 1965, by any agreement made before that date.[15] The landlord, or the tenant, or both jointly, may apply to a rent officer to register a rent as a fair rent.[16] Where a rent is registered, the rent limit is the rent registered.[17] Where a rent has been registered, no application by the tenant alone or by the landlord alone for the registration of a different rent can be made within the next three years except on the ground that there has been a change in the condition of the dwelling-house (including improvement), the terms of the tenancy or any other circumstances, so that the registered rent is no longer a fair one.[18]

Death of tenant

There are special rules relating to the succession to a tenancy on the death of a protected or statutory tenant. Briefly, if he leaves a widow who was residing with him, she will become a statutory tenant; otherwise, a member of his family who was residing with him will become a statutory tenant. On the death of such " first successor " a similar succession takes place, but thereafter there is no succession.[19]

B. Furnished Premises

Part VI of the Rent Act 1968 applies to contracts whereby one person grants to another the right to occupy a dwelling as a residence in consideration for a rent which includes payment for the use of furniture or for services.[20] The requirements as to rateable value are the same as in the case of protected tenancies.[21] The protection afforded in the case of such " Part VI contracts " is as follows:

Control of rents

The landlord or the tenant may refer the contract to a rent tribunal,[22] which may approve the rent or reduce it or, if the cost of providing any services has increased, increase it.[23] The local authority keeps a register of rents as approved, reduced or increased by the tribunal.[24] The landlord or the tenant may refer the case to the tribunal for reconsideration of the registered rent on the ground of change of

---

[15] s. 20 (3).
[16] Pts. III and IV of the Act and Scheds. 5, 6 and 7.
[17] s. 20 (2).
[18] s. 44 (3).
[19] Sched. 1.
[20] s. 70. And see *ante*, p. 272. All references in this heading (" Furnished Premises ") are to the Rent Act 1968, unless otherwise stated. See also *ante*, p. 271, note 82.
[21] s. 71. See *ante*, p. 271.
[22] s. 72.
[23] s. 73.
[24] s. 74.

circumstances, and the tribunal may approve, reduce or increase the rent.[25] The registered rent forms the rent limit.[26]

Security of tenure

First, if, after a Part VI contract has been referred to a tribunal, a notice to quit is served before six months have expired from the tribunal's decision, the notice will not take effect until the six months has expired: the tribunal may substitute a shorter period for the six months.[27] Secondly, if a notice to quit has been served and the contract has been referred to the tribunal (whether before or after the service of the notice to quit) and the period at the end of which the notice is to take effect has not expired, the tenant may apply to the tribunal to extend such period.[28] The tenant may, by making successive applications, be able to remain in the premises indefinitely. However, he cannot make such an application if the tribunal has substituted a shorter period for the initial six months' protection [29]; and the landlord may apply to the tribunal to reduce the period which must expire before the notice to quit will become effective under the above provisions if, for example, the tenant does not comply with the terms of the contract.[30]

Since the above scheme of security of tenure only relates to cases where a notice to quit is appropriate, it can be circumvented by creating a fixed term rather than a periodic tenancy.[31]

C. Long Tenancies of Dwellings

A special kind of protection is afforded to certain tenants by Part I of the Landlord and Tenant Act 1954. This applies to a tenancy:

(a) which is a long tenancy, that is, a tenancy granted for a term of years certain exceeding twenty-one years [32];

(b) which is at a low rent, that is, where the rent is less than two-thirds of the rateable value of the property, the rateable value being that which would for the purposes of the Rent Act 1968 be taken as its rateable value on the appropriate day.[33] If this requirement is fulfilled, the tenancy is, of course, one which falls outside the protection of the Rent Act 1968 [34];

(c) where " the qualifying condition " is fulfilled, that is, the

---

[25] s. 75.
[26] s. 76.
[27] s. 77.
[28] s. 78.
[29] s. 78 (1) (c).
[30] s. 80.
[31] When the term expires, the landlord should not accept rent, for this might bring into being a periodic tenancy.
[32] Landlord and Tenant Act 1954, s. 2 (1) (4). All the references in this heading (" Long Tenancies of Dwellings ") are to this Act, unless otherwise stated.
[33] s. 2 (1) (5). *Ante*, p. 271.
[34] See *ante*, p. 272.

circumstances are such that on the tenancy ending the tenant would, if the tenancy had not been one at a low rent, be entitled to retain possession by virtue of the Rent Act.[35] This means, for example, that the property must be a dwelling-house (that is, a house or part of one) let as a separate dwelling.[36]

Protection

It is provided that a tenancy within the above provisions shall not come to an end on the term date (that is, the date of expiry of the term[37]) except by being terminated under the Act, and if not then so terminated shall continue until so terminated.[38] The landlord can terminate the tenancy by following a specified procedure which includes giving a notice (complying with certain conditions) which either:

(a) contains proposals for a statutory tenancy within the Rent Act; or

(b) contains notice that, if the tenant is not willing to give up possession, the landlord proposes to apply to the court for possession on one or more of certain grounds (which include grounds corresponding to some of those on which possession can be obtained under the Rent Act) and states the ground or grounds on which he proposes to apply.[39]

Tenants holding under long leases are now more likely to seek to avail themselves of the provisions of the Leasehold Reform Act 1967 if that Act applies to their lease. This subject is discussed next.

D. Leasehold Enfranchisement

The Leasehold Reform Act 1967 provides for a system of leasehold enfranchisement whereby a tenant may, if certain requirements are fulfilled, acquire the freehold. Instead, he may acquire an extended lease of the property concerned.

Requirements to be fulfilled

In order to be able to take advantage of the Act, the following requirements must be fulfilled:

(1) The claimant must be a tenant of a leasehold house.[40] " House " includes any building designed or adapted for living in and reasonably so called. Where a building is divided horizontally, the flats into which it is divided are not separate " houses," though the building as a whole may be, and where a building is divided vertically

---

[35] s. 2 (1).
[36] See *ante*, " Unfurnished Premises."
[37] s. 2 (6).
[38] s. 3.
[39] ss. 4, 12.
[40] s. 1 (1). All references in this heading (" Leasehold Enfranchisement ") are to the Leasehold Reform Act 1967 unless otherwise stated.

(into terraced houses) the building as a whole is not a "house" though any of the units into which it is divided may be.[41]

(2) The tenancy must be a long tenancy, which means a tenancy granted for a term of years certain exceeding twenty-one years.[42]

(3) The tenancy must be at a low rent, which will be the case when the yearly rate of rent payable under the tenancy is less than two-thirds of the rateable value of the property on the "appropriate day," which is usually March 23, 1965,[43] or, if later, the first day of the term.[44]

(4) The rateable value of the house and premises [45] must not be more than £200 or, if it is in Greater London, than £400, on the appropriate day, which again is usually March 23, 1965.[46]

(5) At the relevant time (that is, at the time when the tenant gives notice of his desire to have the freehold or an extended lease [47]), the claimant must have been tenant of the house under a long tenancy at a low rent, and occupying it as his residence, for the last five years or for periods amounting to five years in the last ten years.[48]

Death of tenant

Where the tenant of a house dies while occupying it as his residence, and on his death a member of his family [49] resident in the house becomes (for example, by will) tenant of it under the same tenancy, then the latter is treated as having been the tenant, and occupying the house as his residence, during any period when:

(a) he was resident in the house as his only or main place of residence; and

(b) the deceased was, as tenant, occupying the house as his residence.[50]

Exercise of tenant's rights

If the above requirements are fulfilled, the tenant may give to the landlord written notice of his desire to have the freehold or an extended lease,[51] whichever he prefers, and he may do this whenever he wishes.

If he gives notice of his desire to have the freehold, the landlord is bound to make, and the tenant to accept, a grant of "the house and premises" for an estate in fee simple absolute, subject to the tenancy and to tenant's incumbrances,[52] but otherwise free from incumbrances.[53]

---

[41] s. 2. See *Lake* v. *Bennett* [1970] 1 Q.B. 663; *Peck* v. *Anicar Properties Ltd.* [1971] 1 All E.R. 517.

[42] s. 1 (1) (*a*); s. 3.

[43] s. 4 (1) (*a*).

[44] s. 1 (1) (*a*); s. 4.

[45] See *post*, p. 279.

[46] s. 1 (1) (*a*); s. 1 (4).

[47] See *post*.

[48] s. 1 (1) (*b*).   And see s. 1 (2) (3).

[49] This includes, *e.g.* the deceased's wife, husband, son, daughter, father or mother: s. 7 (7).

[50] s. 7.

[51] ss. 8 (1), 14 (1).

[52] *e.g.* sub-tenancies.

[53] s. 8 (1).

In the phrase " the house and premises," the reference to premises is generally to be taken as referring to any garage, outhouse, garden, yard and appurtenances which at the relevant time [54] are let to the tenant with the house and are occupied with and used for the purposes of the house.[55] The price payable for the house and premises on a conveyance is the amount which at the relevant time [56] the house and premises, if sold in the open market by a willing seller, might be expected to realise on certain assumptions,[57] the object being that the landlord be paid for the land on which the house stands.[58]

On ascertaining the amount payable as the price for the house and premises, but not more than one month after the amount payable has been determined,[59] the tenant may give written notice to the landlord that he is unable or unwilling to acquire the house and premises at the price he must pay, and thereupon the notice of his desire to have the freehold ceases to have effect and any further notice to the same effect will be void if given within the following five years.[60]

The conveyance must not generally be framed so as to exclude or restrict the general words implied in conveyances under section 62, or the all-estate clause implied under section 63, of the Law of Property Act 1925,[61] unless the tenant consents to the exclusion or restriction; but the landlord is not bound to convey to the tenant any better title than that which he has or could require to be vested in him, nor to enter into any covenant for title other than such covenant [62] as is implied in the case of a person conveying and expressed to convey as trustee or mortgagee.[63]

The *procedure* applicable when a tenant desires to acquire the freehold is dealt with more fully elsewhere.[64]

Where the tenant gives notice of his desire to have an extended lease, the landlord is generally bound to grant, and the tenant to accept, in substitution for the existing tenancy a new tenancy of the house and premises [65] for a term expiring fifty years after the term date (that is, the date of expiry [66]) of the existing tenancy.[67] The new

---

[54] " Relevant time " means the time when a claimant gives notice of his desire to have the freehold or an extended lease: s. 37 (1) (d).
[55] s. 2 (3).
[56] See note 54 above.
[57] s. 9; and see Housing Act 1969, s. 82.
[58] In cases falling within the Act, the idea is that " the land belongs in equity to the landowner and the house belongs in equity to the occupying leaseholder ": White Paper on Leasehold Reform in England and Wales (Cmnd. 2916) para. 4.
[59] In default of agreement, the Lands Tribunal determines the price payable for the house and premises: s. 21 (1) (a).
[60] s. 9 (3). A notice of his desire to have an extended lease will not be void.
[61] See ante, pp. 233, 234.
[62] See Law of Property Act 1925, s. 76 (1) (F), and ante, p. 228.
[63] s. 10 (1). There are detailed provisions in the Act dealing with the conveyance as regards such matters as rights of support, rights of way and restrictive covenants (s. 10), rentcharges (s. 11) and mortgages on the landlord's estate (ss. 12, 13).
[64] Ante, pp. 113 et seq.
[65] See s. 2 (3); supra.
[66] s. 37 (1) (g).
[67] s. 14 (1).

tenancy is generally to be on the same terms as the existing one, but with such modifications as may be required or appropriate to take account of such matters as the omission from the new tenancy of property comprised in the existing tenancy.[68] The new tenancy must provide that as from the date of expiry of the original tenancy [69] the rent payable for the house and premises shall be, briefly, " a ground rent in the sense that it shall represent the letting value of the site (without including anything for the value of buildings on the site)." [70]

Where a tenancy of a house and premises has been extended, then, generally speaking, the right of the tenant to acquire the freehold is not exercisable unless notice of his desire to have the freehold is given not later than the original term date [71] of the tenancy, and there is no further right to an extension of the tenancy.[72]

Landlord's overriding rights

The Act provides for three overriding rights of the landlord:

(1) Where a tenancy has been extended, or the tenant has a right to an extended lease and gives notice of his desire to have one, the landlord may, at any time not earlier than twelve months before the original term date [71] of the tenancy, apply to the county court [73] for an order that he may resume possession of the property on the ground that for purposes of redevelopment he proposes to demolish or reconstruct the house and premises.[74] If the court is satisfied that the landlord has established this ground, the court will by order declare that the landlord is entitled to obtain possession of the house and premises and the tenant is entitled to be paid compensation by the landlord,[75] the compensation being the amount which the tenancy would realise in the open market, at the date when the order for possession becomes final, upon certain assumptions.[76]

(2) Where the tenant has a right to acquire the freehold or an extended lease and has given notice of his desire to have it, the landlord may, at any time before effect is given to the notice, apply to the county court [73] for an order that he may resume possession of the property on the ground that it is or will be reasonably required by him for occupation as the only or main residence of himself or of an adult member of his family.[77] The landlord cannot apply if, *inter alia*, his interest was purchased or created after February 18,

---

[68] s. 15 (1).
[69] Until such date, the rent will be at the original rate.
[70] s. 15 (2).
[71] *i.e.* the date of expiry of the term without an extension: s. 37 (1) (g).
[72] s. 16.
[73] s. 20 (1).
[74] s. 17 (1) (4).
[75] s. 17 (2).
[76] s. 17 (3); Sched. 2 (which contains detailed provisions).
[77] s. 18 (1); an adult member of the family is defined in s. 18 (3).

1966.[78] If the court is satisfied that the landlord has established this ground, the court will [79] by order declare that he is entitled to obtain possession of the house and premises and the tenant is entitled to be paid compensation, the measure being as in (1) above, by the landlord.[80]

(3) Where an area is occupied under tenancies held from one landlord, he may have powers of management which would disappear when enfranchisement takes place if the Act did not provide otherwise. The Secretary of State for the Environment, on an application made within two years of January 1, 1968,[81] may grant a certificate that, in order to maintain adequate standards of appearance and amenity and regulate redevelopment in the area in the event of tenants acquiring the landlord's interest in their house and premises, it was in the Secretary of State's opinion likely to be in the general interest that the landlord should retain powers of management; the High Court may then, on an application made within one year of the giving of the certificate, approve a scheme giving the landlord such powers and rights as are contemplated by this provision.[82]

E. Business Premises

A tenant of business premises often spends money on improving the premises by effecting alterations and extensions and also often establishes a goodwill in connection with the business. On the expiration of the tenancy the landlord would, because of these two factors, be able to let the premises at an increased rent either to the existing tenant or to a new one, and so he would profit at the expense of the existing tenant, if it were not for the legislation which is designed to protect business tenants.

Under Part I of the Landlord and Tenant Act 1927 a tenant of business premises was entitled, on the expiration of his lease, to compensation from the landlord for improvements effected on the premises and for goodwill, or, in some cases, to the grant of a new lease of the same premises.

Compensation for goodwill did not succeed and was abolished by the Landlord and Tenant Act 1954.[83] Security of tenure is now provided for by Part II of the Act of 1954, as amended by Part I of the Law of Property Act 1969. Alternatively, the tenant may be entitled to compensation for disturbance in some cases. The provisions of the Act of 1927 concerning compensation for improvements still apply, with some amendment.

---

[78] s. 18 (2).
[79] But not if greater hardship would be caused by making the order than by refusing to make it: proviso to s. 18 (4).
[80] s. 18 (4) (5); Sched. 2.
[81] See s. 41 (4); Leasehold Reform Act 1967 Commencement Order 1967 (S.I. 1967 No. 1836).
[82] s. 19.
[83] s. 45.

(1) Security of tenure

Tenancies to which Part II of the Act of 1954 applies

For this purpose, " tenancy " includes a tenancy created by lease or underlease, by an agreement for a lease or underlease or by a tenancy agreement.[84] Tenancies at will are not within the Act.[85] Nor are licences[86]: a licence, rather than a lease, can therefore avoid the effect of the Act.[87] The property comprised in the tenancy must be or include " premises which are occupied by the tenant and are so occupied for the purposes of a business carried on by him or for those and other purposes." [88] " Business " includes " a trade, profession or employment and includes any activity carried on by a body of persons, whether corporate or unincorporate." [89] " Activity " is wide and covers, for example, a members' lawn tennis club.[90] The word " premises " is also wide and it has been held that it can include land with no buildings on it, such as gallops used to train racehorses.[91] More obvious examples of cases falling within the provisions are shops and factories.

Part II of the Act thus affects many tenancies. However, the following tenancies are specifically excluded from its effect[92]:

(a) tenancies of agricultural holdings, which are subject to separate legislation[93];

(b) tenancies created by mining leases;

(c) tenancies where the property is let under a tenancy which either is a controlled tenancy within the Rent Act or would be such a tenancy if it were not a tenancy at a low rent[94];

(d) tenancies of premises licensed for the sale of intoxicating liquor for consumption on the premises except, for example, restaurants, where a substantial proportion of the business consists of transactions other than the sale of intoxicating liquor;

(e) certain tenancies granted by reason of the tenant being the holder of an office, appointment or employment;

(f) tenancies granted for a term certain not exceeding six months, unless the tenancy contains provision for renewing the term or for extending it beyond six months from its beginning, or unless the tenant and any predecessor who carried on the tenant's business have been in occupation for a period which exceeds twelve months.[95]

---

[84] s. 69 (1). Sections referred to in this heading (" Business Premises ") are all to the Landlord and Tenant Act 1954 unless otherwise stated.

[85] *Wheeler* v. *Mercer* [1957] A.C. 416; *Manfield and Sons Ltd.* v. *Botchin* [1970] 2 Q.B. 612.

[86] For licences, see generally Megarry and Wade, pp. 775–783.

[87] See *Shell-Mex and B.P. Ltd.* v. *Manchester Garages Ltd.* [1971] 1 W.L.R. 612.

[88] s. 23 (1).

[89] s. 23 (2). See *e.g. Abernethie* v. *A. M. & J. Kleiman Ltd.* [1970] 1 Q.B. 10.

[90] *Addiscombe Garden Estates Ltd.* v. *Crabbe* [1958] 1 Q.B. 513.

[91] *Bracey* v. *Read* [1963] Ch. 88.

[92] s. 43.

[93] See *post*, p. 287.

[94] See *ante*, pp. 271 *et seq.*

[95] See Law of Property Act 1969, s. 12.

The machinery providing for security of tenure

A tenancy to which Part II of the Act of 1954 applies will not come to an end " unless terminated in accordance with the provisions of this Part of this Act." [96] The effect of this provision is that after expiry by effluxion of time a tenancy will carry on and—for example, in the case of a periodic tenancy—the landlord cannot serve an effective notice to quit. The tenancy will not come to an end unless it is terminated:

(a) by a common law notice to quit given by the *tenant* [97]—for example, in the case of a periodic tenancy. But the notice to quit is ineffective if it is given before the tenant has been in occupation in right of the tenancy for one month. [98]

(b) by surrender, [97] unless the instrument of surrender was executed before, or was executed in pursuance of an agreement made before, the tenant had been in occupation in right of the tenancy for one month [99];

(c) by forfeiture, or the forfeiture of a superior tenancy [97];

(d) by a renewal of the tenancy by written agreement [1]; or

(e) in accordance with the special provisions of the Act, which provides for three further possible ways of termination, as follows:

(i) *Termination by the tenant.* A tenant may terminate the tenancy by the usual common law notice to quit, as we have seen. Moreover, in the case of a tenancy granted for a term of years certain he may terminate it by giving to the landlord, not later than three months before the date on which, apart from the Act, the tenancy would end by effluxion of time, a notice in writing that he does not desire the tenancy to be continued [2]; and a tenancy granted for a term of years certain which is continuing by virtue of the Act [2] may be brought to an end on any quarter day by not less than three months' notice in writing given by the tenant to the landlord. [3]

(ii) *Termination by the landlord.* The landlord may terminate the tenancy by notice to the tenant not more than twelve nor less than six months before the date it specifies for termination, which must not be earlier than the date on which, apart from the Act, the tenancy could have been brought to an end by notice to quit given by the landlord or would have come to an end by effluxion of time. [4] If the tenant, within two months after the landlord's notice, notifies the

---

[96] s. 24 (1). See *Weinbergs Weatherproofs* v. *Radcliffe Paper Mill Co.* [1958] Ch. 437; *Bowes-Lyon* v. *Green* [1963] A.C. 420.
[97] s. 24 (2).
[98] Law of Property Act 1969, s. 4 (1) (*a*).
[99] *Ibid.* s. 4 (1) (*b*).
[1] s. 28.
[2] *i.e.* under s. 24 (1), *supra.*
[3] s. 27.
[4] s. 25.

landlord in writing that he will not be willing to give up possession,[5] he may apply to the court for a new tenancy not less than two nor more than four months after the giving of the landlord's notice.[6]

(iii) *The tenant's request for a new tenancy.* Alternatively, so long as the tenancy is one granted for a term of years certain exceeding one year or granted for a term of years certain and thereafter from year to year,[7] the tenant may himself set in motion the machinery for a new tenancy by serving on the landlord [8] a notice requesting a new tenancy beginning with such date, not more than twelve nor less than six months after the making of the request, as is specified therein: such date must not be earlier than the date on which, apart from the Act, the current tenancy would come to an end by effluxion of time or could be brought to an end by notice to quit given by the tenant.[9] Again, the tenant may then apply to the court for a new tenancy not less than two nor more than four months after the making of the request.[10]

THE LANDLORD'S OPPOSITION TO A NEW TENANCY.   The landlord may oppose the tenant's application for a new tenancy in either situation (ii) or (iii) above.   Where the tenant's application to the court follows the landlord's notice to terminate, the grounds of opposition must be stated in the landlord's notice [11]; and where the tenant's application to the court follows his request for a new tenancy, the landlord's grounds of opposition must be stated by him by a notice given within two months of the tenant's request.[12]   The grounds of opposition are,[13] briefly:

(a) the tenant's failure to comply with his obligations as respects the repair and maintenance of the holding;

(b) the tenant's persistent delay in paying rent which has become due;

(c) other substantial breaches by the tenant of his obligations under the tenancy;

(d) that the landlord has offered and is willing to provide reasonable alternative business accommodation for the tenant;

(e) where the current tenancy was created by subletting part only of the property comprised in a superior tenancy, that the aggregate of the rents obtainable on separate lettings would be substantially less than the rent obtainable on a letting of the property as a whole, and

---

[5] s. 25 (5).
[6] s. 29 (2) (3).
[7] s. 26 (1).
[8] See *Stylo Shoes* v. *Prices Tailors* [1960] Ch. 396.
[9] s. 26 (2).
[10] s. 29 (3).   See *Kammins Ballrooms Co. Ltd.* v. *Zenith Investments (Torquay) Ltd.* [1971] A.C. 850.
[11] s. 25 (6); s. 30 (1).
[12] s. 26 (6); s. 30 (1).
[13] s. 30.

that on the termination of the current tenancy the landlord requires possession for the purpose of letting or otherwise disposing of the property as a whole;

(f) that on the termination of the current tenancy the landlord intends [14] to demolish or reconstruct the premises [15];

(g) that on the termination of the current tenancy the landlord intends [14] to occupy the holding for the purposes, or partly for the purposes, of a business to be carried on by him therein, or as his residence.[16]

THE NEW TENANCY. Unless the landlord satisfies the court on one or more of the above grounds of opposition, the court must grant a new tenancy. The *property* comprised in the new tenancy will generally be that comprised in the current tenancy.[17] The *duration* of the new tenancy will be such as is agreed between the landlord and tenant, or, in default of such agreement, such as may be determined by the court to be reasonable, being, if it is a tenancy for a term of years certain, a tenancy for a term not exceeding fourteen years.[18] The *rent* will be such as may be agreed between the landlord and tenant, or as, in default of such agreement, may be determined by the court to be that at which the holding might reasonably be expected to be let in the open market by a willing landlord, disregarding such things as goodwill built up by the tenant or certain improvements carried out by him.[19] The other terms of the tenancy will be such as may be agreed between the landlord and the tenant or as, in default of such agreement, may be determined by the court, having regard to the terms of the current tenancy and to all relevant circumstances.[20]

Avoidance of the provisions relating to security of tenure

The Act of 1954 provides that any agreement relating to a business tenancy (whether contained in the instrument creating the tenancy or not) is void in so far as it purports to preclude the tenant from making an application or request for a new tenancy or provides for the termination or the surrender of the tenancy in the event of his making such an application or request or for the imposition of any penalty or disability on the tenant in that event.[21]

The Law of Property Act 1969 [22] now makes an exception to the

---

[14] The landlord's object must have " moved out of the zone of contemplation—out of the sphere of the tentative, the provisional and exploratory—into the valley of decision " (*per* Asquith L.J. in *Cunliffe* v. *Goodman* [1950] 2 K.B. 237 at p. 254. See *e.g. Reohorn* v. *Barry Corporation* [1956] 1 W.L.R. 845; *Gregson* v. *Cyril Lord Ltd.* [1963] 1 W.L.R. 41.

[15] Note s. 31A, added by Law of Property Act 1969, s. 7.

[16] For the availability of this ground of opposition, see s. 30 (2). Note also s. 30 (3), added by Law of Property Act 1969, s. 6.

[17] s. 23 (3); s. 32 (1); and see s. 31A, added by Law of Property Act 1969, s. 7.

[18] s. 33.

[19] s. 34, amended by Law of Property Act 1969, s. 1. And see Law of Property Act 1969, s. 2.

[20] s. 35.

[21] s. 38 (1).

[22] s. 5, which adds a new subs. (4) to s. 38 of the Act of 1954.

provision just mentioned.   If the persons who will be the landlord and
the tenant in relation to a tenancy to be granted for a term of years
certain, which will be a tenancy within Part II of the Act of 1954,
jointly apply to the court, it may authorise an agreement excluding
in relation to that tenancy the provisions of the sections [23] of the Act
relating to the continuation of tenancies; and on the joint application of
the landlord and the tenant under a tenancy falling within Part II, the
court may authorise an agreement for the surrender of the tenancy on
such date or in such circumstances as may be specified in the agreement and on such terms (if any) as may be so specified.

In the absence of the parties agreeing, the new provision cannot
be used.   But it may be that the effect of the provision of the Act
of 1954 prohibiting contracting out can be avoided—for example, by
providing in the lease for a considerable rise in the rent in the later
years of the term and giving the tenant the right to terminate the lease
before this operates.[24]   However, such attempts may in fact fall within
the above provision of the Act of 1954 and accordingly caution is
advised.

(2) Compensation for disturbance

Where, on an application for a new tenancy in the above circumstances, the court is precluded from making an order for the grant of a
new tenancy by reason of any of the last three grounds of opposition
mentioned above (that is, grounds (e), (f) and (g)), the tenant is
entitled on quitting to recover compensation for disturbance from the
landlord.[25]   The compensation recoverable is the rateable value of
the holding; or if, during the whole of the fourteen years immediately
preceding the termination of the current tenancy, the holding has been
occupied for the purposes of a business carried on by the tenant and
any predecessors of his in such business, the compensation is twice the
rateable value.[26]

The right to compensation may be excluded or modified by agreement [27]; except that where, during the five years immediately preceding
the date on which the tenant is to quit the holding, the premises have
been occupied for the purposes of the same business carried on by
the occupier or succeeding occupiers, any agreement which purports
to exclude or reduce compensation is void.[28]

(3) Compensation for improvements

Under Part I of the Landlord and Tenant Act 1927 [29] the tenant

---

[23] *i.e.* ss. 24–28.
[24] See Hallett's *Conveyancing Precedents*, p. 399, for other suggestions.
[25] s. 37 (1), amended by Law of Property Act 1969, s. 11.
[26] s. 37 (2) (3).
[27] s. 38 (3).
[28] s. 38 (2).
[29] As amended by Pt. III of the Landlord and Tenant Act 1954.

of a holding to which it applies [30] is entitled at the termination of the tenancy, on quitting his holding, to be paid by his landlord compensation in respect of any improvement made by him or his predecessors in title (not being a trade or other fixture which the tenant is by law entitled to remove) which at the termination of the tenancy adds to the letting value of the holding.[31]

In order to become entitled to compensation on quitting, the tenant must observe a certain procedure. This involves serving on the landlord, when the tenant proposes to make the improvement, a notice of his intention to make such improvement, to which the landlord may make objection, and observing certain time limits in making his claim.[32]

In the absence of agreement between the parties, the amount of the compensation is determined by the court.[33] It cannot exceed the net addition to the value of the holding as a whole which results directly from the improvement; or the reasonable cost of carrying out the improvement at the termination of the tenancy, subject to a deduction of an amount equal to the cost (if any) of putting the works constituting the improvement into repair, except so far as such cost is covered by the tenant's liability under any covenant or agreement as to the repair of the premises.[34]

Contracting out of Part I of the Act of 1927 is generally prohibited.[35]

F. Agricultural Holdings

The Agriculture Act 1947 lays down certain standards of good husbandry and good estate management, but this subject does not directly concern us here.[36] The main statute is the Agricultural Holdings Act 1948, and this deals with security of tenure; compensation to the tenant for disturbance and for improvements, and to the landlord for deterioration; and the control of rents. These will be dealt with in turn, but first it is necessary to define the holdings to which the Act of 1948 applies.

The definition of agricultural holdings

An agricultural holding is " the aggregate of the *agricultural land* comprised in a *contract of tenancy,* not being a contract under which the said land is let to the tenant during his continuance in any office,

---

[30] Pt. I applies to premises held under a lease, other than a mining lease, and used wholly or partly for carrying on any trade or business, and not being agricultural holdings: Act of 1927, s. 17 (1); and see s. 17 (2) (3) (4).

[31] Act of 1927, s. 1.

[32] See the Act of 1927, s. 3; the Act of 1954, s. 47.

[33] Act of 1927, ss. 1 (3), 21; Act of 1954, s. 63 (2).

[34] Act of 1927, s. 1 (1), proviso: and see s. 1 (2).

[35] Except in the case of certain contracts made before December 10, 1953. See Act of 1927, s. 9; Act of 1954, s. 49.

[36] See Woodfall, *Landlord and Tenant,* Vol. 2, pp. 1229–1230.

appointment or employment held under the landlord." [37] " Contract of tenancy " means " a letting of land, or agreement for letting land, *for a term of years or from year to year*." [38] Where land is let by an agreement made on or after March 1, 1948, to a person for use as agricultural land for an interest less than a tenancy from year to year, or a person is granted a licence to occupy land for use as agricultural land, and the circumstances are such that if his interest were a tenancy from year to year he would in respect of that land be the tenant of an agricultural holding, then the agreement takes effect as if it were an agreement for the letting of the land for a tenancy from year to year,[39] so as to bring such an agreement within the Act.[40] However, expressly excluded from the effect of this provision are a letting or grant approved by the Minister of Agriculture, Fisheries and Food before the agreement was entered into and an agreement for the letting of land, or the granting of a licence to occupy it, made in contemplation of the use of the land only for grazing or mowing during some specified period of the year.[41]

" Agricultural land " means " land used for agriculture which is so used for the purposes of a trade or business." [42] " Agriculture " includes, *inter alia*, horticulture, fruit growing, dairy farming and livestock breeding and keeping, and the use of land as grazing land, meadow land, market gardens and nursery grounds.[43]

(1) Security of tenure

The scheme for security of tenure is as follows. First, the tenancy may not terminate in the normal way when the term is over but may be extended by the Act; secondly, the tenancy cannot be terminated unless a proper notice to quit complying with the Act is given; thirdly, even where such a notice is prima facie valid, the tenant may in many cases prevent it from operating by serving a counter-notice. The provisions are as follows.

Statutory extension of tenancies

As stated above, some tenancies for less than from year to year and some licences are converted by the Act into tenancies from year to year. It is also provided that a tenancy of an agricultural holding for a term of two years or upwards shall, instead of terminating on the expiration of the term for which it was granted, continue, as from the

[37] s. 1 (1). All references in this heading (" Agricultural Holdings ") are to the Agricultural Holdings Act 1948, unless otherwise stated.
[38] s. 94 (1).
[39] s. 2 (1). See *Verrall* v. *Farnes* [1966] 1 W.L.R. 1254.
[40] It has been held that a letting for one year comes within this provision: *Bernays* v. *Prosser* [1963] 2 Q.B. 592.
[41] s. 2 (1) and proviso. A " specified period of the year " may be as long as 364 days (*Reid* v. *Dawson* [1955] 1 Q.B. 214) but cannot be a full year (see *Rutherford* v. *Maurer* [1962] 1 Q.B. 16).
[42] s. 1 (2).
[43] s. 94 (1). And see *Rutherford* v. *Maurer* [1962] 1 Q.B. 16.

expiration of that term, as a tenancy from year to year, unless, not less than one year nor more than two years before the date fixed for the expiration of the term, a written notice has been given by either party to the other of his intention to terminate the tenancy.[44] Such a notice is deemed to be a notice to quit within the Act,[45] so that the provisions of the Act relating to a counter-notice [46] apply to it.

In the case of a tenancy for a term which exceeds one year but is less than two years, the protection of the Act does not operate and a notice to terminate is not necessary,[47] for the tenancy is not " for a term of two years or upwards," [48] nor is it a letting " for an interest less than a tenancy from year to year." [49] Thus, if the tenant only wants the tenancy for a short time and the landlord wishes to be able to recover possession, the grant of a lease for, say, eighteen months is advisable, for it will expire by effluxion of time without the necessity of a notice to quit.[50]

Proper notice to quit is required

The Act provides that a notice to quit an agricultural holding shall, notwithstanding any provision to the contrary in the contract of tenancy of the holding, be invalid if it purports to terminate the tenancy before the expiration of twelve months from the end of the then current year of tenancy.[51] There are certain exceptions [52] to the provision— for example, where a receiving order in bankruptcy is made against the tenant.

Counter-notice by the tenant

Even where the landlord has served a notice to quit in accordance with the foregoing provisions, the Act provides that if the tenant, not later than one month from the giving up of the notice to quit, serves on the landlord a counter-notice in writing requiring that section 24 (1) shall apply to the notice to quit, then the notice to quit will not have effect unless the Agricultural Land Tribunal consents to its operation.[53] There are, however, seven cases [54] where the tenant is not entitled to serve a counter-notice and where the landlord's notice to quit will be effective. In order to be able to invoke any of the seven cases the landlord must state in his notice to quit which one he wishes

---

[44] s. 3 (1).   S. 3 has effect notwithstanding any agreement to the contrary: s. 3 (4).
[45] s. 3 (2).
[46] See *post.*
[47] *Gladstone* v. *Bower* [1960] 2 Q.B. 384.
[48] Within s. 3 (1).
[49] Within s. 2 (1).
[50] For a form, see Hallett's *Conveyancing Precedents,* pp. 576–577.
[51] s. 23 (1).   This provision applies to a notice to quit given by the tenant, not merely to one by the landlord: *Flather* v. *Hood* (1928) 44 T.L.R. 698.   It should be noted that a notice to quit given before the tenancy commences is ineffective: *Lower* v. *Sorrell* [1963] 1 Q.B. 959.
[52] s. 23 (1), proviso.
[53] s. 24 (1).
[54] s. 24 (2).

to take advantage of.[54] Examples of the seven cases are where the interest of the landlord in the holding has been materially prejudiced by the tenant's breach of a term of the tenancy; where the tenant is bankrupt or has compounded with his creditors; and where the tenant *with whom the contract of tenancy was made* has died within three months before the date of the giving of the notice to quit. With regard to the last-mentioned case, the words italicised may cause problems. For example, if the original tenant dies and the tenancy devolves on someone else, upon the latter's death a counter-notice is not precluded because the contract of tenancy was not made with that person.[55] The draftsman should usually ensure that the tenancy is one from year to year and not for a fixed term. The landlord will be able to recover possession on the tenant's death, whereas in the case of a tenancy for a fixed term, if the tenant died during the term, the term would carry on vested in the successor to the deceased tenant.[56]

Assuming none of the seven cases to apply, the notice to quit will be ineffective on the tenant's counter-notice unless the Agricultural Land Tribunal consents to the operation of the notice to quit. The Tribunal can give its consent in five cases[57]—for example, where the carrying out of the purpose for which the landlord proposes to terminate the tenancy is desirable in the interests of good husbandry.

(2) Compensation [58]

For disturbance

Where the tenancy terminates by reason of a notice to quit given by the landlord and in consequence the tenant quits the holding, then compensation for disturbance is payable by the landlord to the tenant.[59] This is so even if the notice was not valid.[60] Compensation is not payable in certain of the seven cases where a tenant's counter-notice cannot be given.[61] The amount of compensation payable is the amount of the loss or expense which is unavoidably incurred by the tenant in connection with the sale or removal of his household goods, implements of husbandry, fixtures, farm produce or farm stock.[62] Alternatively, the tenant may recover as compensation an amount equal to one year's rent, without proof of any such loss or expense.[62] In no case is the tenant entitled to compensation in excess of two years' rent of the holding.[62] With certain exceptions,[63] the tenant is

[55] *Costagliola* v. *Bunting* [1958] 1 W.L.R. 580. See also *Clarke* v. *Hall* [1961] 2 Q.B. 331; and *Lewis (Jenkin R.) and Son Ltd.* v. *Kerman* [1971] Ch. 477.
[56] See Hallett's *Conveyancing Precedents*, p. 400.
[57] s. 25 (1); Agriculture Act 1958, s. 3. Note the proviso to s. 25 (1).
[58] Generally, a tenant or landlord is entitled to compensation in accordance with the provisions of the Act and not otherwise, and is so entitled notwithstanding any agreement to the contrary: s. 65.
[59] s. 34 (1).
[60] *Kestell* v. *Langmaid* [1950] 1 K.B. 233.
[61] Proviso to s. 34 (1).
[62] s. 34 (2).
[63] See Agriculture (Miscellaneous Provisions) Act 1968, s. 10.

entitled, in addition to the above, to " a sum to assist in the reorganisation of the tenant's affairs," equal to four times the annual rent.[64]

For improvements

The tenant is entitled [65] on the termination of the tenancy, on quitting the holding, to obtain from his landlord compensation for improvements begun on or after March 1, 1948, which are known as " new improvements." [66]

For deterioration

The landlord is entitled to recover from the tenant, on the tenant's quitting the holding on the termination of the tenancy, compensation in respect of dilapidation or deterioration of, or damage to, the holding caused by the tenant's failure to farm in accordance with the rules of good husbandry, the amount of compensation being the cost, as at the date of the tenant's quitting the holding, of making good the dilapidation, deterioration or damage.[67]

(3) Control of rents

The landlord or the tenant may by notice in writing served on the other party demand a reference to arbitration of the question what rent should be payable, and the arbitrator is then to determine what rent should be properly payable, being the rent at which the holding might reasonably be expected to be let in the open market by a willing landlord to a willing tenant, disregarding such matters as improvements executed by the tenant.[68] A reference may not be made more often than every three years.[69] It is also provided that where the landlord has carried out certain improvements he can increase the rent by an amount equal to the increase in the rental value of the holding attributable to the carrying out of the improvement.[70]

---

[64] Agriculture (Miscellaneous Provisions) Act 1968, s. 9.
[65] s. 47.
[66] s. 46: " old improvements," begun before that date, are governed by ss. 35-45. See also s. 56.
[67] ss. 57, 58.
[68] s. 8.
[69] s. 8 (3).
[70] s. 9.

CHAPTER 12

MORTGAGES

I. FORM [1]

A. Mortgages of Land before 1926

Mortgages of freeholds

A legal mortgage of freeholds before 1926 consisted usually of a conveyance of the fee simple with a proviso for reconveyance when the debt secured by the mortgage was paid off. This form of mortgage had become common in the sixteenth century. An earlier form of mortgage by way of a lease of the mortgaged property remained as an alternative form of mortgage, but this had become obsolete in the nineteenth century.

Equity of redemption

As the usual form of mortgage was therefore a conveyance of the mortgagor's whole estate, any subsequent mortgage was necessarily equitable being an assignment of the mortgagor's equity of redemption.[2] The equity of redemption was an estate or interest created by the Courts of Equity at the end of the sixteenth century and later recognised by the Courts of Common Law. Even though the mortgagor had conveyed the land to the mortgagee, he was in equity still considered to be the owner of the land subject to the mortgage; and this position was recognised by the mortgagor's right to the land, called the equity of redemption.

Mortgages of leaseholds

A legal mortgage of leaseholds before 1926 was made either by an assignment of the whole term with a proviso for re-assignment when the debt was paid off; or else by a sub-demise for a term, one or more days less than the whole term, with a proviso for cesser on redemption, *i.e.* that the term would cease when the debt was paid off. Where the mortgage was made by way of assignment, the mortgagee became liable for the rent and covenants under the lease. The usual practice, therefore, was to make the mortgage by sub-demise to avoid that effect. A mortgage of leaseholds in either form was originally liable to destruction by forfeiture of the mortgaged term for breach of covenant. Relief against forfeiture was later given.[3]

---

[1] See generally Megarry and Wade, *The Law of Real Property* (3rd ed.), Chap. 14; Fisher and Lightwood's *Law of Mortgage* (8th ed., 1969), Pt. 1.
[2] For the meaning of the equity of redemption, see Megarry and Wade, p. 884.
[3] See *ante*, p. 266.

Equitable mortgages

We have already seen that a second or subsequent mortgage of freeholds was necessarily equitable. Equitable mortgages by the owners of legal estates in land were also created by an agreement for a mortgage, either by an agreement in writing satisfying the statutory requirements[4] or one constituted by an act of part performance, *i.e.* by a deposit of title deeds.[5] Mortgages of equitable rights in land were made by way of assignment with a proviso for re-assignment on payment off of the debt.

Equitable charges

An equitable charge of land was created when land was expressly or constructively made liable, or specifically appropriated, to the discharge of a debt or some other obligation.

B. Mortgages of Land after 1925

Mortgages of freeholds

After 1925 a legal mortgage of freeholds can be created only in one of two ways, either by a grant of a long term of years to the mortgagee, usually, but not necessarily, 3,000 years, subject to a proviso for cesser[6] on redemption, or by a charge by deed expressed to be by way of legal mortgage.[7] A mortgage cannot be made by conveyance after 1925. A purported conveyance of a fee simple by way of mortgage operates as a demise for 3,000 years.[8]

Mortgages of leaseholds

A legal mortgage of leaseholds after 1925 is made either by way of sub-demise, the sub-term being usually ten days less than the head-term, with a proviso for cesser on redemption; or, by a charge by deed expressed to be by way of legal mortgage.[9] A mortgage cannot be made by assignment after 1925. A purported assignment by way of mortgage operates as a sub-demise.[10]

Legal charge

A charge by deed expressed to be by way of legal mortgage—commonly known as a legal charge—gives the mortgagee (chargee) the same protection, powers and remedies as if a term of 3,000 years

---

[4] *i.e.* of s. 4 of the Statute of Frauds 1677 (see now Law of Property Act 1925, s. 40; *ante*, pp. 15 *et seq.*).
[5] See *post*, p. 296.
[6] For the meaning of a proviso for cesser, see *post*, p. 311.
[7] Law of Property Act 1925, s. 85 (1). For forms, see *post*, pp. 426 *et seq.*
[8] *Ibid.* s. 85 (2).
[9] *Ibid.* s. 86 (1). For form of mortgage by sub-demise, see *post*, p. 431.
[10] *Ibid.* s. 86 (2). See *Grangeside Properties Ltd.* v. *Collingwoods Securities Ltd.* [1964] 1 W.L.R. 139.

L

had been created in his favour.[11]   A legal charge does not, however, create an actual, or even a notional, term in the chargee.[12]

The Law of Property Act 1925, therefore, offered alternative forms of mortgage. It may be noticed that the mortgage by demise was nothing new. As regards freeholds, the Act merely reintroduced a method that had existed long before; and, as regards leaseholds, mortgage by sub-demise was the usual form of mortgage of leaseholds at that time. The legal charge was a novelty. It is, perhaps, to be regretted that it was found desirable to incorporate into a legal charge, by the reference to the protection, powers and remedies of the mortgagee by demise or sub-demise, the nature and effect of such mortgages. All that a mortgagee is really concerned about is that he has the appropriate remedies in the event of default by the mortgagor. It would have been preferable to have made the legal charge a statutory charge only, but to have attached to it the appropriate remedies for the mortgagee.[13]

Advantages of legal charge

A legal charge is now the more common form of mortgage. It has some advantages over a mortgage by demise or sub-demise. These are :

(1) It is, perhaps, more intelligible to the mortgagor. (Solicitors have some difficulty in explaining to their clients, where there is a mortgage by demise, why their clients are leasing their property to the building society for 3,000 years.) A legal charge merely charges the property.

(2) It is more convenient where the mortgagor is mortgaging both freeholds and leaseholds together, *i.e.* where what is sometimes called a combined or mixed mortgage is required. A legal charge merely charges both types of property. The alternative would either be for a mortgage containing one clause for a demise of the freeholds and another clause for a sub-demise of the leaseholds, or separate mortgages altogether.

(3) We have seen [14] that many leases contain a covenant by the tenant not to sub-let, assign, etc. A mortgage by sub-demise of leaseholds would fall within the scope of such a covenant, and would, therefore, be absolutely prohibited or require the landlord's consent according to the terms of the covenant. A legal charge, which, we have seen,[15] does not create a sub-term, is not within the terms of such a covenant (though, usually, charges are also prohibited).[16]

---

[11] *Ibid.* s. 87 (1).
[12] See *Cumberland Court (Brighton) Ltd.* v. *Taylor* [1964] Ch. 29; *cf. Ushers' Brewery Ltd.* v. *P. S. King & Co. (Finance) Ltd.* (1969) 113 S.J. 815.
[13] As to the mortgagee's remedies, see *post,* pp. 316 *et seq.*
[14] *Ante,* p. 261.
[15] *Supra.*
[16] *Grand Junction Co. Ltd.* v. *Bates* [1954] 2 Q.B. 160, 168.

Disadvantages

There is said to be one disadvantage in using a legal charge. The statutory form of legal charge [17] does not contain a proviso for redemption, *i.e.* the equivalent of the proviso for cesser in a mortgage by demise. As we shall see,[18] the effect of the proviso is to fix the date upon which, if the mortgagor defaults, the mortgagee's remedies *qua* mortgagee [19] arise. The absence of a proviso for redemption is said to affect prejudicially the chargee in the exercise of his remedies. However, the better view is that, in the absence of such a proviso, the remedies of the chargee arise on the mortgagor's default in repaying at the date fixed in the covenant for repayment.[20] In any case, it is quite common to include an express proviso for redemption in a legal charge.[21]

Second and subsequent mortgages

Whichever form of mortgage is used, the mortgagor retains a legal estate; and second and subsequent legal mortgages may be made in the same form as the first and prior legal mortgage.[22] When made by demise, each successive mortgage is for a term usually one day longer than the term of the previous mortgage.

Statutory mortgage

A special form of legal charge, known as the statutory mortgage, is provided by the Law of Property Act 1925,[23] re-enacting provisions in the Conveyancing Act 1881. One or other, according to the circumstances, of the statutory forms [24] must be used; and a covenant for repayment by the mortgagor and for discharge on repayment by the mortgagee are implied.[25] Although quite commonly used before 1925, the statutory mortgage is rarely used today.[26]

Equitable mortgages

An equitable mortgage of land is generally used to secure a temporary loan or bank overdraft. Such a mortgage had in the past two minor advantages over a legal mortgage. These were:

(1) An equitable mortgage under hand only attracted a lower rate of stamp duty. But, as mentioned below, most equitable mortgages are in any event made under seal. And where an equitable mortgage was under hand only, if the terms of the document gave the mortgagee

---

17 See Law of Property Act 1925, Sched. V, Form 1.
18 *Post*, p. 311.
19 As compared to his purely contractual remedy under the covenant for repayment.
20 See Cheshire, *Modern Real Property* (11th ed.), p. 632.
21 See Precedent 19, *post*, p. 427.
22 See *post*, p. 327.
23 s. 117.
24 See *ibid.* Sched. IV, Forms 1–4.
25 s. 117 (2).
26 Most mortgages are to building societies, which prefer their own forms.

the powers and advantages of a legal mortgagee, the mortgage fell outside the definition of an equitable mortgage under the Stamp Act 1891.[27] Mortgage stamp duty has now been abolished.[28]

(2) An equitable mortgage does not usually appear on the title to the property. But few people today would be particularly embarrassed if, on a sale of their property, the purchaser were to learn that they had raised the purchase-money by mortgage, or had subsequently mortgaged the property to raise money.

Accordingly, the only advantage today of an equitable mortgage is its informality. Equitable mortgages are sometimes created by a mere deposit of deeds without anything further, where, for example, the parties do not obtain legal advice. But, as we shall see,[29] an equitable mortgage should be by deed if the mortgagee is to have his full remedies; and if a deed has to be prepared, one might just as well have a proper legal mortgage.

An equitable mortgage of land may be created by an agreement for a mortgage satisfying the requirements of section 40 of the Law of Property Act 1925[30]; or, as we have seen,[31] by a deposit of title deeds as security for a loan with or without an accompanying memorandum of deposit. Formal agreements for a mortgage are rarely encountered. An exception is the case where a vendor agrees to leave part of the purchase-money outstanding secured on the property to be sold. Here, the contract may include a special condition to this effect.[32] Informal written agreements for a mortgage are rarer still. The much more common form of equitable mortgage is that created by the deposit of the title deeds of the property. Such a deposit, where it is intended to be a security for the loan, operates as an act of part performance.[33] Where the parties have had legal advice, the deposit is generally accompanied by some document setting out the terms of the loan. The question may then arise whether the mortgage is constituted by the deposit or the accompanying document.[34]

The accompanying document should be under seal, thus giving the mortgagee the statutory power of sale, etc.[35] Where the memorandum accompanies a deposit, it should refer to the deposit and state that it was made with the intent that the property should be equitably charged with the repayment of the moneys advanced. The memorandum will usually contain an *undertaking* by the mortgagor *to execute a legal charge* when required to do so by the mortgagee. The power of sale implied in a memorandum under seal only extends to the equitable

---

[27] s. 86 (2), s. 86 (1) (*e*); and see *United Realization Co.* v. *I.R.C.* [1899] 1 Q.B. 361.
[28] Finance Act 1971, s. 64.
[29] *Post.*
[30] *Ante,* p. 15.
[31] *Ante,* p. 293.
[32] See *e.g. Capital Finance Co. Ltd.* v. *Stokes* [1969] 1 Ch. 261.
[33] *Russel* v. *Russel* (1783) 1 Bro.C.C. 269. For part performance, see *ante,* p. 22.
[34] See *Re White Rose Cottage* [1965] Ch. 940.
[35] *Post,* pp. 316 *et seq.* For form, see *post,* p. 433.

interest. It is therefore necessary to extend the equitable mortgagee's power of sale by the devices of a *declaration of trust* and, in addition or alternatively, a *power of attorney.* The purpose of a trust of the legal estate is to enable the mortgagee on exercising the power of sale to vest the legal estate in the mortgaged property in himself.[36] It consists of a declaration by the mortgagor that he holds the mortgaged property in trust for the mortgagee and makes the statutory power of appointing new trustees [37] exercisable by the mortgagee. On default by the mortgagor, the mortgagee may appoint himself or any other as trustee, and the legal estate in the mortgaged property will then vest in the new trustee.[38]

Additional protection for the mortgagee is given if the mortgagor irrevocably appoints the mortgagee, and anyone deriving title under him, as the attorney of the mortgagor. On default, the mortgagee can then convey the legal estate in the mortgaged property. A conveyance under such a power is not an exercise of the power of sale, and, accordingly, the purchaser will take the property subject to subsequent incumbrances as well as prior incumbrances.[34]

Equitable charges

Equitable charges are created in the same way as they were before 1926.[39] In such situations the charge will generally operate as an equitable mortgage,[40] unless the document creating the charge is a will or settlement.[41]

C. Mortgages of Registered Land

(1) First registration

Where a transaction leads to registration,[42] it may be completed in the usual form for unregistered land and any mortgage may be in such form. Alternatively, the registered land forms of mortgage referred to below may be used. Where, as will often be the case, the transaction has been completed by an advance on mortgage, the application is generally made by or on behalf of the lender,[43] for the lender will not want to part with the deeds to allow an application by the borrower; and until an application has been made for registration of the land, no mortgage thereof can be accepted for registration.[44] The mortgage so made is registered or protected in the same way as where the land is already registered (see below). The application for

---

[36] See *London and County Banking Co.* v. *Goddard* [1897] 1 Ch. 642.
[37] Trustee Act 1925, s. 36.
[38] *Ibid.* s. 40.
[39] *Ante,* p. 293.
[40] *Cradock* v. *Scottish Provident Association* (1893) 69 L.T. 380; affd. (1894) 70 L.T. 718; *London County and Westminster Bank* v. *Tompkins* [1918] 1 K.B. 515.
[41] See *Re Owen* [1894] 3 Ch. 220; *Re Lloyd* [1903] 1 Ch. 385.
[42] See *ante,* p. 166.
[43] Land Registration Rules 1925, r. 73 (2).
[44] *Ibid.* r. 72 (3).

the registration of the land will cover the mortgage. The existence of the mortgage (this includes debentures creating a fixed or floating charge in the case of a company [45]) must be declared on the application form; and the original mortgage—in the case of a printed form of mortgage it should be made certain that all the blanks have been duly completed—and a certified copy thereof must be included in the documents accompanying the application. No fee is payable in respect of a mortgage by an applicant for first registration which accompanies the application.[46]

(2) Forms of mortgage of registered land

A proprietor of registered land may, subject to any entry on the register,[47] create a mortgage of the land in any one of three ways. He may:

1. Charge the land by a registered charge [48];
2. Mortgage the land as if it were not registered [49];
3. Create a lien on the land by deposit of the land certificate.[50]

Registered charge

It seems that only a legal mortgage may be the subject of substantive registration as a registered charge.[51] Provided the charge is made by deed, no special form is required. But the land comprised in the charge must be described either by reference to the register or sufficiently enough to enable it to be identified without reference to any other document; and the deed must not refer to any prior interests or charges except such as are overriding interests or are entered on the register.[52]

The charge may be made by way of legal mortgage or contain a demise or sub-demise. Subject to any provision to the contrary contained in the charge, it will take effect as a charge by way of legal mortgage.[53]

Subject to any entry to the contrary on the register, a covenant is implied by the proprietor of the land at the date of the charge to pay principal and interest, if any, at the appointed time, and, in default, to pay interest half-yearly. A covenant is also implied in the case of leaseholds to pay the rent and perform and observe the covenants and conditions of the lease, and to indemnify the proprietor of the charge and persons claiming under him against the covenants, etc.[54] Express

---

[45] A company charge must be registered at the Companies Registry before it is lodged for registration: see Land Registration Rules 1925, r. 145 (2).
[46] Land Registration Fee Order 1970, Abatement 1.
[47] Such as a restriction; see *ante*, p. 180.
[48] Land Registration Act 1925, s. 25.
[49] *Ibid*. s. 106.
[50] *Ibid*. s. 66.
[51] *Re White Rose Cottage* [1965] Ch. 940.
[52] Land Registration Act 1925, s. 25 (2). For form, see *post*, p. 432.
[53] *Ibid*. s. 27 (1) (2).
[54] *Ibid*. s. 28.

covenants are, in practice, generally added to the statutory form of registered charge because the implied covenants do not extend to the other common covenants found in mortgages, for example, as to insurance and repairs.[55]

Application for registration is made under the appropriate application cover, and the charge is completed by the registrar entering on the Charges Register the person in whose favour the charge is made and particulars of the charge.[56] A charge certificate is issued to the chargee,[57] and the land certificate must be deposited at the registry until the charge is cancelled.[58]

A second legal mortgage may be made by way of registered charge. Subject to any entry to the contrary on the register, registered charges on the same land rank according to the order of *registration*, and not the order of *creation*.[59]

Subject to any entry on the register to the contrary, the registered proprietor of a registered charge has all the powers of a legal mortgagee of unregistered land.[60] So, he may exercise the statutory powers of sale, etc.[61] If he enters into possession and acquires a title under the Limitation Act 1939, he may procure himself to be registered as proprietor of the land (subject to persons entered in the register as prior incumbrancers), and he will be in the same position as a purchaser on a sale made in exercise of the mortgagee's statutory power of sale.[62]

Mortgages off the register

Subject to any entry to the contrary on the register, a registered proprietor may mortgage the land by deed or otherwise, in any manner in which a mortgage may be created on unregistered land, provided the land is described in the mortgage in such a way as is sufficient to enable the registrar to identify it without reference to any other document.[63] A legal mortgage may be protected by a caution in a specially prescribed form called a mortgage caution.[64] This procedure is obsolescent. Alternatively, the mortgage may be protected either:

(1) by ordinary caution[65]; or
(2) by notice as a land charge,[66] where the mortgage is registrable as a land charge.[67]

---

[55] See *post*, p. 427.
[56] *Ibid.* s. 26.
[57] Land Registration Rules 1925, r. 262.
[58] Land Registration Act 1925, s. 65.
[59] *Ibid.* s. 29.
[60] *Ibid.* s. 34 (1); *Lever Finance Ltd.* v. *Needleman's Property Trustee* [1956] Ch. 375.
[61] See *post*, p. 316.
[62] Land Registration Act 1925, s. 34 (2). For the effect of a foreclosure order or sale, see *ibid.* s. 34 (3) (4) (5).
[63] *Ibid.* s. 106 (1).
[64] *Ibid.* s. 106 (2). *Barclays Bank Ltd.* v. *Taylor* [1972] 2 W.L.R. 1038.
[65] *Ibid.* s. 54. As to the nature of cautionable interests, see (1971) 35 Conv.(N.S.) 21.
[66] *Ibid.* ss. 49, 64.
[67] See *post*, p. 329.

Until so protected, the mortgage will take effect only in equity and will be capable of being overridden as a minor interest.[68]

A caution gives protection to the mortgagee in that it gives notice of his interest. Before any subsequent dealing is registered, he is entitled to notice and to be heard.[69] Where a mortgage is protected by notice, this means that every subsequent proprietor or incumbrancer is deemed to be affected with notice of the mortgage.[70] A prior mortgage so protected has priority over subsequent mortgages.[71] But where a prior mortgage has not been protected by notice there is nothing in the Land Registration Act or Rules to indicate the order of priority between such mortgage and any subsequent mortgage nor whether actual notice is relevant.[72]

Deposit of certificate

The registered proprietor of any registered land or charge may, subject to any overriding interest, and to any estates, interests, charges or rights registered or protected on the register at the date of the deposit, create a lien on the land or charge, by deposit of the land or charge certificate. Such a lien is equivalent to a lien created by a deposit of title deeds or of a mortgage of unregistered land [73] by an owner entitled beneficially to the land or the mortgage respectively.[74]

The deposit is generally accompanied by a memorandum under seal, thus giving the depositee the statutory power of sale, etc. As in the case of an equitable mortgage of unregistered land, the question may arise as to whether the mortgage is created by the deposit or the memorandum.[75]

The security may be protected by notice of a deposit given to the registry [76] and noted on the register [77] or by notice as a land charge.[78]

Where the depositor is a transferee the land certificate must first be sent to the registry for the registration of the transfer before it can be deposited. A notice of *intended* deposit should be given in this case.[79]

D. Mortgages of Other Property

Chattel mortgages

Legal mortgages of personal chattels are made by way of bill of

---

[68] Land Registration Act 1925, ss. 101 (2), 106 (4).
[69] *Ibid.* s. 55; Rules, rr. 218 and 220. And see *Re White Rose Cottage* [1965] Ch. 940, 949, 950; *Parkash* v. *Irani Finance Ltd.* [1970] Ch. 101.
[70] *Ibid.* s. 52.
[71] *Re White Rose Cottage, supra.* See (1966) 19 *Current Legal Problems* 26.
[72] See *Re White Rose Cottage* [1964] Ch. 483, 492; and generally (1971) 35 Conv.(N.S.) 100, 168.
[73] In the case of a charge the transaction would be an equitable sub-charge.
[74] Land Registration Act 1925, s. 66.
[75] *Re White Rose Cottage* [1965] Ch. 940. See *ante,* p. 296.
[76] Land Registration Rules 1925, r. 239. Notice is given on printed form 85A.
[77] The notice operates as a caution under s. 54 of the Act: r. 239 (4); see *ante,* p. 181. No notice may be entered while another such notice is on the register: r. 243.
[78] *Re White Rose Cottage, supra.*
[79] Land Registration Rules 1925, r. 240.

sale. In view of the technical and specialised nature of bills of sale, this topic is not dealt with in this book, and reference should be made to the subject elsewhere.[80]

Mortgages of shares and other choses in action

A legal mortgage of shares is made by a transfer of the shares to the mortgagee, subject to an agreement for their retransfer on repayment of the loan. Such a transfer makes the mortgagee a shareholder with the rights and liabilities of such a person, so more commonly a mortgage of shares is an equitable mortgage made by a deposit of the share certificates with the mortgagee, which does not. The deposit may be accompanied by a memorandum of deposit setting out the terms of the loan and sometimes also by a form of transfer of the shares executed by the mortgagor in blank, *i.e.* leaving the name of the transferee blank.[81]

Mortgages of other choses of action, such as a policy of insurance[82] or a beneficial interest in a trust fund, are made by assignment, which may be either a legal assignment satisfying the requirements of section 136 of the Law of Property Act 1925,[83] or an equitable assignment.[84] A mortgage of equitable rights must either be in writing signed by the mortgagor or his agent, authorised in writing, or made by will.[85]

E. Debentures

Company borrowing powers

If there is no power to borrow, the security will be void and the loan may not be recoverable. Generally, there is an express power to borrow in the memorandum; but, in the absence of express power, power to borrow will be implied in the case of an ordinary trading or commercial company. The power to borrow is limited to borrowing for legitimate purposes.[86]

A mortgage by a company may take the usual form of mortgage by an individual, *i.e.* a *fixed* charge over *specified* property. But, usually, there is also, as further security, a *general* charge over the rest of the company's assets, both present and future.

[80] See Fisher and Lightwood's *Law of Mortgage*, Chap. 4. It should be noted, however, that the Bills of Sale Acts do not apply where the hirer is a company. There has been an increase in chattel mortgages in recent years between company borrowers and finance house lenders; see (1971) 121 New L.J. 291, 299. Also a bill of sale may be made inadvertently as in the sham hire-purchase cases; see (1960) 23 M.L.R. 399, 516.
[81] See Fisher and Lightwood, pp. 99 *et seq.*
[82] See *post,* p. 339.
[83] See Snell, *Equity* (26th ed.), pp. 79 *et seq.* For legal mortgages of insurance policies, see also Policies of Assurance Act 1867.
[84] Snell, *ubi supra,* pp. 83 *et seq.*
[85] Law of Property Act 1925, s. 53 (1) (c). Notices of the assignment must be given to the insurance company, trustees of the trust fund, etc.; see generally Fisher and Lightwood, Chap. 6.
[86] *Re Introductions Ltd.* [1970] Ch. 199; *cf. Charterbridge Corpn. Ltd.* v. *Lloyds Bank Ltd.* [1970] Ch. 62.

L*

Floating charge

A floating charge is an equitable charge on some or all of the present and future property of the company. Under a floating charge the company can continue to use its assets in the ordinary course of business. The charge remains floating and the property liquid until some default is made or steps taken to enforce the security, whereupon the floating charge *crystallises*.[87]

Debentures

All mortgages by a company are technically debentures,[88] but a typical debenture is one of a series issued by a large public or private company to raise capital for expansion. Such debentures are like shares and are transferable in the same way on a register maintained by the company.[89]

Debentures, though complete in themselves, are usually further secured by a covering trust deed. The use of a trust deed separates the debenture holders from the security holders, the latter being the debenture trustees (generally a trust corporation). This means that the company has to deal only with the trustees rather than many individual debenture holders, and, if there is a fixed charge of the company's realty, the legal estate will be conveniently vested in the trustees. The trustees can watch over the interests of the debenture holders and usually have a special expertise in this type of work. The trust deed generally sets out the terms of the loan, providing for payment of capital and interest; sets out various charges, fixed and floating, over the company's assets; and states the events on which the floating charge is to crystallise, etc. The lender's principal remedy is the appointment of a receiver,[90] and the deed will contain provisions dealing with the powers and duties of the receiver.

A debenture generally provides that no mortgage or charge ranking *pari passu* with, or in priority to, the debenture shall be created by the company. If this restriction is duly noted in the register,[91] no subsequent charge will obtain priority. Generally, the trust deed provides that all debentures in the same series shall rank *pari passu* (the *pari passu* clause). In addition the deed may be so worded that it is to be security also for further advances and further issues of debentures to rank *pari passu* with the original issue (" open-end debentures ").[92]

We have already dealt with the provisions in the Companies Act 1948, for avoiding certain floating charges.[93]

[87] See generally Gower, *Modern Company Law* (3rd ed.), Chap. 19.
[88] See Companies Act 1948, s. 455.
[89] See *post*, p. 340.
[90] See *post*, p. 323.
[91] For registration of charges, see *post*, p. 330.
[92] On the form of debentures, see Fisher and Lightwood, Chap. 7.
[93] *Ante*, p. 142.

II. THE CONTENTS OF A MORTGAGE

The date

Most mortgages today are made to secure an advance by a building society to the mortgagor to assist him to purchase a house which is the mortgaged property.[94] The conveyance to the mortgagor and the mortgage are in such circumstances generally dated the same date and executed simultaneously. Nevertheless, the conveyance and the mortgage are separate transactions and the conveyance must precede the mortgage by a short period of time.[95] It not uncommonly happens that a purchaser after contract but before completion will purport to grant a lease of the property he has agreed to purchase. Such a grant creates a tenancy by *estoppel, i.e.* the " lessor " is estopped from repudiating the tenancy and the " tenant " is estopped from denying its existence. On the completion of the sale the estoppel is " fed " by the legal estate acquired by the purchaser on the conveyance and the tenancy becomes a legal tenancy. As the conveyance precedes the mortgage, the lease is binding on the mortgagee even if, as will usually be the case, the terms of the mortgage prevent the mortgagor from leasing.[96]

The position is similar in the case of registered land, save that the mortgagee is bound not only where there has been a purported grant, but also where the " tenant " has taken possession under *an agreement* for a lease.[97]

Parties

The mortgagor and the mortgagee should be described as the borrower and the lender respectively. These descriptions avoid confusion and transposition.

In certain cases, such as where the borrower is a woman or a private limited company, the lender will insist on additional security by requiring a surety or guarantor to join in to covenant payment of the mortgage debt.

Other forms of *collateral security* are sometimes taken by the mortgagee. Collateral security may be taken from the borrower himself on some other property besides the property which is the principal security. A common example of this type is where the borrower as part of the mortgage transaction has effected an endowment insurance and mortgages the insurance policy as collateral security. When the borrower has substantial income tax or surtax liability, a mortgage linked with an endowment policy or other

---

[94] See *post*, p. 338.
[95] *Church of England B.S.* v. *Piskor* [1954] Ch. 553; *Capital Finance Co. Ltd.* v. *Stokes* [1969] 1 Ch. 261. See generally (1960) 80 L.Q.R. 370.
[96] See *post*, p. 314.
[97] In this case the tenant's interest is an overriding interest. See Land Registration Act 1925, ss. 20 (1), 70 (1) (g); *Grace Rymer Investments Ltd.* v. *Waite* [1958] Ch. 831.

insurance is advantageous. The borrower gets tax relief on the mortgage payments and on the insurance premiums, and the insurance moneys payable at the end of the term of the policy should be sufficient to pay off the mortgage and leave the borrower with a reasonable balance.

Some lenders require further protection by requiring the borrower to effect a *mortgage protection policy*; and even where it is not required by the lender the borrower will be wise to effect such a policy. This is usually a policy on the life of the borrower providing for the payment of the amount due to the lender in the event of the borrower's death before the mortgage has been repaid.[98]

Mortgage by co-owners

Co-owners, or those of them who are the trustees for sale of the property,[99] can mortgage as such trustees.[1] Where the same persons are both the trustees and the beneficiaries, they can mortgage by virtue of their beneficial ownership.[2]

Mortgage to several mortgagees

Where a legal mortgage is made to several persons, the legal estate vests in the mortgagees, or the first four named, as joint tenants upon trust for sale.[99] In mortgages to several mortgagees made after 1881, the mortgage moneys are, as between the mortgagees and the mortgagor, and as between the mortgagees and purchaser, deemed to be moneys belonging to the mortgagees on a joint account.[3]

Trustees

Trustees have statutory powers of mortgaging under section 16 of the Trustee Act 1925 and section 28 of the Law of Property Act 1925 and will generally be given express power under the trust deed.[4]

Trustees have power to lend on mortgage, subject to the provisions of the Trustee Act 1925 and the Trustee Investments Act 1961, or under an express power.[5]

Limited owners

Mortgages by other limited owners are dealt with elsewhere.[6]

Moneylenders

In the past decade there has been a marked increase in lending,

---

[98] Note Building Societies Act 1962, s. 33.
[99] See *ante*, p. 143.
[1] See *post*, p. 378.
[2] For a mortgage by husband and wife co-owners, see *post*, p. 430.
[3] Law of Property Act 1925, ss. 111, 113 (I) (*a*). See *post*, pp. 309, 310.
[4] And see *post*, p. 378.
[5] See generally *Lewin on Trusts* (16th ed.), pp. 314 *et seq.*, 370.
[6] *i.e.* tenants for life, *post*, p. 364; personal representatives, *ante*, p. 145; companies, *ante*, p. 301. See generally, Fisher and Lightwood, Chap. 11.

mostly on second mortgages,[7] by self-styled finance companies or banks. In fact, a good many of these mortgagees are moneylenders, and therefore subject to the requirements as to licensing and the formalities of the loan contract of the Moneylenders Acts 1900–27. Various devices have been used to avoid the Acts,[8] and there are exceptions, for bona fide banks, etc.,[9] the scope of which are somewhat uncertain. There is no doubt that the moneylending legislation needs a thorough overhaul.[10]

If the formalities of the loan contract[11] are not observed, the security will be void.[12] The effect of the Act, which was intended to protect borrowers from the pressures of lenders, is, in many cases nowadays, to allow the borrower to raise unmeritorious defences to claims by lenders and to avoid liability.[13] The moral for those advising lenders is to take extreme care that the proper formalities have been observed, and for those advising borrowers to consider carefully the transaction and the terms in case a claim to avoid liability can be raised.

But a moneylender whose security is void may, in appropriate cases, be able to rely on a lien by way of subrogation.[14]

Recitals

The borrower's title and the agreement for the loan should be recited. The tendency in some modern conveyancing forms is, as we have seen,[15] to omit recitals. The use of recitals has previously been mentioned.[16] Full recitals in a mortgage make the mortgage a better root of title.[17] The recitals may also operate by way of estoppel for the benefit of the lender.[18]

Covenant for repayment

This usually consists of a covenant by the borrower which refers to, and acknowledges receipt of, the sum lent, and undertakes that, in consideration thereof, the borrower will on a specified day (usually

---

[7] See *post*, p. 327.
[8] See the Report of the Committee on the Enforcement of Judgment Debts (the Payne Committee), 1969, Cmnd. 3909, para. 1358.
[9] See *e.g. Premor Ltd.* v. *Shaw Brothers* [1964] 1 W.L.R. 978; *U.D.T. Ltd.* v. *Kirkwood* [1966] 2 Q.B. 431; and Companies Act 1967, s. 123.
[10] See, generally, the Report of the Committee on Consumer Credit (the Crowther Report), 1971, Cmnd. 4596.
[11] Moneylenders Act 1927, s. 6.
[12] And see *Spector* v. *Ageda* [1971] 3 W.L.R. 498; 121 New L.J. 621 (loan to pay off illegal loan void).
[13] See the Crowther Report, paras. 6.11.2–4. But probably the borrower cannot recover payments made; see *Cook* v. *Greendon Investments* (1969) 113 S.J. 35.
[14] (1972) 122 New L.J. 431.
[15] *Ante*, p. 223.
[16] See *ante*, p. 223.
[17] It has been suggested that without recitals a mortgage is not a good root of title; see Williams, *Contract of Sale of Land*, p. 31, note (r).
[18] *District Bank Ltd.* v. *Webb* [1958] 1 W.L.R. 148.

six months from the date of the deed) pay to the mortgagee the same sum, with interest in the meantime at a given rate per cent.[19]

This covenant makes the mortgagee a specialty creditor of the mortgagor—a position which he would not hold otherwise, since the implied contract for repayment arising out of the loan [20] raises a simple contract debt only. The express covenant is, therefore, an advantage to the lender, because an action on the covenant only becomes barred after twelve years, rather than six years.[21]

If no date for repayment is fixed, the debt is repayable on demand.[22]

Covenant for payment of interest

The covenant to repay the principal debt is followed by a covenant by the mortgagor that if the principal sum lent, or any part of it, shall remain unpaid after the day fixed for repayment, then the mortgagor shall, so long as it remains unpaid, pay interest on it at a specified rate. In addition, the covenant should also name the days on which such interest is to be paid, these being usually arranged so as to secure half-yearly or quarterly payments.[23]

The covenant should provide for the payment of interest after as well as before judgment.[24] The reason for this is that a security merges in another security of a higher nature. Thus, a mortgage debt merges in a judgment, subject to any provision to the contrary contained in the mortgage; and interest on the judgment will only be at the rate of 4 per cent. per annum, although the rate of interest in the mortgage will usually be much higher. The provision mentioned to pay interest " as well after as before judgment " is a contrary intention sufficient to prevent merger and enable the lender to obtain the mortgage rate of interest even after judgment.[25]

Reduction of interest on punctual payment

Here, too, should be inserted any proviso which may have been agreed upon for reduction of the rate of interest on punctual [26] payment of the sums secured by the last-mentioned covenant. The covenant for payment of interest at a higher rate, followed by a proviso for reducing that rate, is a circuitous method of imposing a penalty on the mortgagor if he does not pay his interest regularly. This object cannot be effected directly, owing to the doctrine of equity which

---

[19] For a form, see *post*, p. 427. Personal liability under the covenant may be negatived where *e.g.* the mortgagors are trustees or personal representatives, or limited to interest only, where the mortgagor is a tenant for life.

[20] *Cf. Cityland and Property (Holdings) Ltd.* v. *Dabrah* [1968] Ch. 166.

[21] Limitation Act 1939, ss. 2, 23; and see *Sutton* v. *Sutton* (1882) 22 Ch.D. 511.

[22] *Lloyds Bank Ltd.* v. *Margolis* [1954] 1 W.L.R. 644.

[23] For a form, see *post*, p. 427.

[24] For a form, see *post*, p. 427.

[25] See Fisher and Lightwood, pp. 530–532.

[26] *i.e.* on the exact date fixed for payment: *Hanley Theatre of Varieties* v. *Broadbent* [1898] 1 Ch. 348.

treats a proviso that the rate of interest shall be increased in default of punctual payment as a penalty against which relief will be granted.[27]

Rate of interest allowed

There is no restriction on the rate of interest, save in the case of moneylenders where a rate of interest exceeding 48 per cent. will be presumed excessive.[28] But some other provision in the mortgage affecting interest, such as where interest is added to the principal to make a single sum payable by instalments, the whole of which may be due on default of payment of even a single instalment, may be void, in which case interest at a lower rate will be fixed by the court.[29]

If no rate is fixed by the parties, it may be fixed by the court.[30]

Option mortgage scheme

The Housing Subsidies Act 1967, Pt. II, gives to those borrowing for house purchase or improvement from certain qualifying lenders, such as building societies, insurance companies, etc., a right to opt to receive Exchequer subsidy by way of credit towards their mortgage repayments. The purpose of the scheme is to put those with small incomes who do not get any real tax relief advantage on their mortgage in the same position as those who do have the advantages of tax relief.[31] The scheme results, in effect, in a reduction by two per cent. of the interest rate.[32]

Capitalisation of interest

There is no objection to interest in arrear itself carrying interest if the parties choose to make a bargain to that effect.[33] But it must then be kept in mind that an exercise of the power of sale on the ground that interest is two months in arrears will not be available.[34] A capitalisation clause, *i.e.* a clause that interest in arrear shall itself carry interest, will not operate if the mortgagee is in possession of tenanted property and receives sufficient rent to pay interest before the period of capitalisation has expired.[35]

Variation of interest

If the mortgage is likely to remain on foot for a long time, it will be wise to provide for variation in the interest rate. It may be that some upper limit must be fixed (otherwise the provision might be a

---

[27] *Strode* v. *Parker* (1694) 2 Vern. 316; *Wallingford* v. *Mutual Society* (1880) 5 App.Cas. 685.
[28] Moneylenders Act 1927, s. 10 (1).
[29] *Cityland and Property (Holdings) Ltd.* v. *Dabrah, supra.*
[30] *Re Drax* [1903] 1 Ch. 781; *Mendl* v. *Smith* (1943) 169 L.T. 153.
[31] See *post,* p. 339.
[32] See further Fisher and Lightwood, Chap. 36.
[33] *Clarkson* v. *Henderson* (1880) 14 Ch.D. 348.
[34] *Davy* v. *Turner* (1970) 114 S.J. 884.
[35] *Wrigley* v. *Gill* [1906] 1 Ch. 165.

penalty) and in practice the rate is generally geared to a specified percentage above the current bank rate or the going rate for mortgages generally.

Repayment by instalments

Many mortgages today provide for repayment by instalments. There are two principal types of instalment mortgage—*flat rate* and *fixed instalment*. *Flat rate* mortgages take the form of repayment by specified instalments, comprised partly of principal and partly of interest, over a specified period. The amount of the instalments remains the same throughout the mortgage term, although the proportion of each instalment which is allocated to principal or interest varies, the amount allocated to principal increasing throughout the period. Under *fixed instalment* mortgages a fixed amount of principal is repaid each year together with interest on the balance for the time being outstanding.[36]

Instalment mortgages may take the usual form of a covenant to repay at a fixed date, but with a proviso that the lender will accept repayment by specified instalments so long as they are punctually paid. This is the form of drafting to be preferred because on a sale by the mortgagee, a purchaser will not be concerned to see if default has been made so long as the specified period has passed.[37] Alternatively, there may be a *direct* covenant for repayment by instalment (*i.e.* neither the traditional six months' period, nor any other period, for the payment is specified) with a proviso that the whole debt shall be immediately repayable on default.[38]

In those cases where the interest element is added to the principal to form one sum, provision should be made for a *pro rata* discount on either early repayment or the exercise by the mortgagee of his powers. In *Cityland and Property (Holdings) Ltd.* v. *Dabrah*[39] the loan was £2,900 but the mortgage provided for repayment of £4,553 by monthly instalments over six years with interest. The whole of the outstanding balance became due on default. The borrower defaulted after several payments and the lender claimed possession. The borrower claimed that the " premium," *i.e.* the difference between the £2,900 and the £4,553, was unreasonable as it was equal to 57 *per cent.* of the loan and represented interest at 19 *per cent.* It was held that the premium was an unreasonable collateral advantage and the lender was only entitled to £2,900 with interest at 7 *per cent.*[40]

---

[36] For endowment mortgages, see *post*, p. 339. *Standing mortgages* are those where there is no provision for regular repayment of principal, which is left outstanding until the end of the term, only interest being payable meanwhile.
[37] See *post*, p. 318.
[38] For forms, see *post*, p. 430.
[39] [1968] Ch. 166.
[40] See further the Payne Committee Report (*ante*, p. 305, note 8), para. 1355, where there is an example of a loan of £1,000 repayable with " agreed charges " of £500, so that if the borrower defaulted on the first payment, interest would be at 600 *per cent*, and if he defaulted after five payments, at 100 *per cent*.

A covenant for repayment by instalment should be subject to the proviso that, notwithstanding payments have been duly made, the lender may call the money in.[41] In the absence of such a provision, it may be that the money cannot be called in, if, that is, the borrower is not in default. The ability to call the loan in is useful to force repayment, and, in the absence of a variation of interest clause, may be used as a lever to raise the interest rate, *i.e.* the lender may threaten to call the loan in unless the borrower agrees to pay the higher rate. It is also useful as a means of preventing the mortgagor transferring the equity. The mortgagor cannot be prevented from selling his property subject to the mortgage, but the threat of calling the money in may induce him not to do so without appropriate terms being imposed by the lender.

Covenant not to call in the loan

The mortgage sometimes provides that, so long as there is no default by the borrower, the lender will not call in the loan. In the absence of such a provision, the loan may be called in at any time after the date for repayment; or, in the case of an instalment mortgage with direct covenant,[42] and subject to what was said above, at any time.

Postponement of redemption

Where there is a covenant by the lender not to call in the loan, there is often a proviso that the borrower shall not be entitled to redeem for a specified period. Such a provision is effective as long as it is not a " clog on the equity of redemption." [43] The mere length of time of the postponement is not in itself an objection to the enforceability of the provision. The nature of the interest mortgaged is relevant. If a short term is mortgaged, and the postponement is for the whole or nearly the whole of the term, the provision may be bad.[44] But long postponements will be possible for freeholds and long leaseholds.[45]

Joint account clause

Where the mortgage money was advanced by two or more persons jointly, it was formerly necessary to insert in the mortgage deed a declaration that it belonged to them on a joint account in equity as well as at law; and that, consequently, the survivor should remain entitled in equity, as well as at law, to the sums secured by the mortgage deed. The reason for this was that the Courts of Equity

---

[41] See *post*, p. 431.
[42] *Ante*, p. 308.
[43] See Megarry and Wade (3rd ed.), pp. 932–934.
[44] *Fairclough* v. *Swan Brewery Co. Ltd.* [1912] A.C. 565.
[45] See *Knightsbridge Estates Trust Ltd.* v. *Byrne* [1938] Ch. 741; [1939] Ch. 441 (C.A.); [1940] A.C. 613 (H.L.) (postponement of 40 years). Debentures may be irredeemable: Companies Act 1948, s. 89. And see Agricultural Credits Act 1932, s. 2.

assumed, in the absence of a distinct statement to the contrary, that where two or more people lent money jointly it could not have been their intention that the right to it should belong exclusively to the survivor, but that, although they took a joint security, each meant to lend his own money, and to take back his own; and, consequently, they were deemed tenants in common in equity. Therefore, on the death of one, the survivor could not, on payment off of the mortgage, give a discharge of the mortgage debt without the concurrence of the personal representatives of the deceased mortgagee. In cases where the mortgagees were trustees of money, this difficulty could be avoided by stating that the mortgagees were trustees, because the presumption that they were tenants in common in equity would not then arise. But it was not desirable to state in the mortgage deed that the money lent was trust money, for that would have the disadvantage of affecting every person dealing with the property with notice of the trust and would incorporate the title relating to the trust into the title of the mortgagor.[46] This is not now so important as before, since a person dealing in good faith after 1925 with either mortgagor or mortgagee is not concerned with any trusts affecting the mortgage money or the income of it, whether he has notice of the trust or not.[47]

Since the Conveyancing Act 1881 the joint account clause is never strictly necessary, because that Act provided that where the mortgage money is expressed to be advanced by, or owing to, two or more persons, out of money belonging to them on a joint account, or where the mortgage is made to them jointly and not in shares, then the mortgage money for the time being due to those persons on mortgage is deemed to be and remain money belonging to those persons on a joint account as between them and the mortgagor; and the receipt in writing of the survivors or last survivor of them, or of the personal representatives of the last survivor, is a complete discharge for all money for the time being due, notwithstanding any notice to the payer of a severance of the joint account.[48] In mortgages to trustees and others advancing money on a joint account, the usual practice, since this Act, has been to state in the deed that the mortgagees advance the money " out of moneys belonging to them on a joint account " but these words, though usual, are not strictly necessary.

The demise or charge

After the covenant for repayment follows the demise or charge.[49] Absolute covenants for title are implied where the mortgagor demises or charges as beneficial owner.[50]

The demise or charge must be of specific realty. Future-acquired

---

[46] *Re Blaiberg and Abraham's Contract* [1899] 2 Ch. 341.
[47] Law of Property Act 1925, s. 113. And note *ibid*. s. 112.
[48] *Ibid*. ss. 111, 113 (1) (*a*).
[49] For forms, see *post*, pp. 427 and 431.
[50] Law of Property Act 1925, s. 76. See *ante*, pp. 226, 227; (1964) Conv.(N.S.) 205.

property may be equitably charged [51] and general words are sufficient for this.[52] In a legal charge the actual words " charged by way of legal mortgage " may be necessary.[53]

After the operative part come the parcels, which are described in the usual way.[54] These are followed, in the case of a mortgage by demise, by the habendum which usually limits the mortgagee's estate, if the mortgaged property is freehold, for a term of 3,000 years, and if the property is leasehold, for the residue of the term created by the lease except the last ten days thereof.[55]

Proviso for redemption

After the demise follows the proviso for cesser, *i.e.* a provision that if the mortgagor shall on a specified day pay to the mortgagee the mortgage debt, then the mortgage term will cease. In the case of a legal charge, there may be included a similar proviso that on payment on the specified date the mortgagee will discharge the security.[56] In either case, the specified date should be the same date as that stated in the covenant for repayment,[57] *i.e.* usually six months from the date of the mortgage. The proviso for cesser and the proviso for discharge are not essential, since in the former case the term ceases while in the latter case the charge is discharged by payment.[58] They are inserted in order to fix a date as from which the mortgagee's rights *qua* mortgagee are exercisable.[59]

Collateral advantages

We have already seen that the right to redeem can properly be postponed.[60]

Sometimes, the mortgagor will enter into covenants whereby the mortgagee is to receive some benefit in addition to payment of principal and interest. An example is a covenant by a mortgagor, who is a publican, to purchase all his beer from the mortgagee, who is a brewer. In preparing any such covenants, the draftsman must bear in mind the equitable rule that any provision which is unfair or unconscionable, or is in the nature of a penalty clogging the equity of redemption, or inconsistent with or repugnant to the right to redeem, will be held void by the court.[61] This applies to a provision enabling

[51] A debenture is an example of this.
[52] See *Syrett* v. *Egerton* [1957] 1 W.L.R. 1130; *Barker* v. *Barker* [1952] P. 184.
[53] *Cf. Cityland and Property (Holdings) Ltd.* v. *Dabrah* [1968] Ch. 166; *Sopher* v. *Mercer* (1967) C.L.Y. 2543. A legal charge is defined as a *charge* by deed *expressed to be by way of legal mortgage*; see *ante*, p. 293.
[54] See *ante*, p. 230.
[55] See *ante*, p. 293.
[56] See *ante*, p. 295.
[57] See *ante*, p. 305.
[58] See *post*, pp. 334, 335.
[59] See *ante*, p. 295.
[60] *Ante*, p. 309.
[61] *Kreglinger* v *New Patagonia Meat and Cold Storage Co. Ltd.* [1914] A.C. 25; *Cityland and Property (Holdings) Ltd.* v. *Dabrah, supra.*

the mortgagee to make himself absolute owner of the property by the exercise of an option to purchase, though a right of pre-emption given to the mortgagee is valid [62]; and to any provision preventing the mortgagor from freely employing or disposing of the mortgaged property after redemption.[63] A provision limiting the mortgagor's use of the property during the continuance of the mortgage only may be valid.[64] But if the right to redeem is postponed, the postponement and the restriction, which might by themselves be valid, may together be unenforceable.[65]

The perpetuity rule does not apply to mortgages and, therefore, provisions in a mortgage for repayment by instalments over a long period or for postponement of the right to redeem for a long period are not void as infringing that rule.[66]

Covenants by mortgagor

After the proviso for redemption follow the borrower's covenants. If the mortgaged property is subject to restrictive covenants, and also in the case of mortgaged leaseholds, the borrower will covenant to observe and perform the various covenants affecting the property. The usual covenants by the borrower relate to insurance, repair, town and country planning matters, letting, etc.[67]

Insurance

The mortgage will usually contain a covenant by the mortgagor to insure all buildings and fixtures on the property; to keep them, so long as the mortgage lasts, insured for a specified amount; and to apply all moneys which may be received under such insurance or *any other* insurance [68] in repairing any part of the premises, or fixtures which may be destroyed by fire, or, if the lender so requires, in discharge of the mortgage debt.

The mortgagor's covenant to insure was formerly followed by a proviso that, in default of his keeping the premises insured, the mortgagee might do so, and add all money thus expended to the principal sum lent. But this has been unnecessary since the Conveyancing Act 1881, which conferred upon the mortgagee the statutory power to insure. By the Law of Property Act 1925 [69] a mortgagee,[70] if the deed has been executed after December 31, 1881, and no contrary

---

[62] *Salt* v. *Marquis of Northampton* [1892] A.C. 1; *Samuel* v. *Jarrah Timber and Wood Paving Corp. Ltd.* [1904] A.C. 323; *Lewis* v. *Frank Love Ltd.* [1961] 1 W.L.R. 261. For options and rights of pre-emption, see *ante*, p. 28.
[63] *Noakes and Co. Ltd.* v. *Rice* [1902] A.C. 24; *Bradley* v. *Carritt* [1903] A.C. 253.
[64] *Biggs* v. *Hoddinott* [1898] 2 Ch. 307. See Megarry and Wade, pp. 931 *et seq.*
[65] *Esso Petroleum Co. Ltd.* v. *Harper's Garage (Stourport) Ltd.* [1968] A.C. 269; *Texaco Ltd.* v. *Mulberry Filling Station Ltd.* [1972] 1 W.L.R. 814.
[66] *Knightsbridge Estates Trust Ltd.* v. *Byrne* [1940] A.C. 613.
[67] For form, see *post*, p. 427.
[68] See *Halifax Building Society* v. *Keighley* [1931] 2 K.B. 248.
[69] s. 101 (1) (ii), replacing Conveyancing Act 1881, s. 19.
[70] A registered chargee has the same powers; see *ante*, p. 299.

intention has been expressed therein, has power, at any time after the date of the mortgage deed, to insure any part of the mortgaged property for an amount not exceeding that specified in the deed, or if no amount has been specified in the deed, then for an amount no greater than two-thirds of the sum which would be required to restore the property were it totally destroyed.[71] The premiums paid for any such insurance are to be charged on the mortgaged property, in addition to the mortgage money, and to carry interest at the same rate as the mortgage money.[72] All money received under any insurance of mortgaged property effected under the Act, or by the mortgagor under an obligation in the mortgage deed, is to be laid out, if the mortgagee so requires, in making good the loss or damage on account of which the money is received, and subject to this, and to any special covenant to the contrary, it is to be applied in discharge of the mortgage debt.[73]

Though an express covenant by the mortgagor to insure is not essential, it has certain advantages over the statutory power. First, it may increase the amount in which the mortgagee may insure under his statutory power; secondly, it may enable the mortgagee to sue the mortgagor personally for premiums paid instead of merely adding them to the mortgage debt; and thirdly, as the mortgagee has a statutory power of sale on breach of any covenant by the mortgagor at any time after the mortgage debt becomes due, it affords a guarantee that a proper insurance will be maintained.

Building society mortgages generally provide for the society to insure and to recoup the premium from the borrower.

Repair

There is no statutory or other obligation on the borrower to repair the premises in the absence of express provision in the deed. The mortgagee is entitled to have the mortgaged property preserved from deterioration as a security and so, for example, if the borrower left the premises vacant, the lender could take steps to keep out vandals. But, in the absence of express provision to keep in repair, the lender will be in difficulty. So an express provision is usually inserted which permits the lender to see to the repairs if the borrower defaults. In addition, there is usually a further covenant by the borrower to pay the costs of any repairs incurred.

Covenant against letting

The mortgage usually contains a covenant by the borrower not to assign or part with possession of the property, and, where the lender is a building society, to occupy the premises personally.

[71] s. 108 (1) and (2).
[72] s. 101 (1) (ii).
[73] Law of Property Act 1925, s. 108 (3) (4).

Power to grant leases

Before the Conveyancing Act 1881 it was necessary to insert in the mortgage deed express provisions concerning leases of the mortgaged property.   In the absence of such, the mortgagor could not make a lease binding on the mortgagee; and, conversely, the mortgagee could not make a lease which was binding on the mortgagor.   This inconvenience was remedied by the 1881 Act, s. 18, which is now replaced by section 99 of the Law of Property Act 1925.   Now a mortgagor [74] in possession (so long as no receiver has been appointed) and a mortgagee [75] in possession (or before taking possession if a receiver has been appointed and is acting) has a statutory power of making, in the case of mortgages after 1925, agricultural or occupation leases for any term not exceeding fifty years and building leases for any term not exceeding 999 years.   If a receiver has been appointed, the mortgagee may by writing delegate his power of leasing to the receiver.[76]

Exclusion and restrictions of power

In practice, the mortgagor's leasing powers are generally excluded or restricted by the mortgage deed.   The statutory powers apply only if and so far as a contrary intention is not expressed in the mortgage or otherwise in writing.[77]   But the statutory powers cannot be modified or excluded in a mortgage of agricultural land,[78] nor so as to prevent the carrying out of an order of the court for a tenancy of business premises.[79]   If there were no limitation on the mortgagor's powers, he could create leases or tenancies, which, besides being binding on the mortgagee, might be protected tenancies under the Rent Act.[80] This would reduce the mortgagee's security, because, if he had to sell the property with a sitting tenant, he would not get as good a price for it.   Since the Leasehold Reform Act 1967 [81] it has become all the more important to exclude the mortgagor's leasing powers, as the tenant has the right, subject to certain conditions, to acquire the freehold at a low price, again reducing the security.   Accordingly, if the mortgagor's statutory power of leasing is not excluded altogether, it should be restricted by requiring the consent of the mortgagee to the lease.   The mortgagee can then control the type of person who becomes tenant. Where there is a provision that the *statutory power* of leasing shall not be exercised without the mortgagee's consent and the mortgagor leases

---

[74] The expression " mortgagor " in ss. 99 and 100 does not include an encumbrancer deriving title under the original mortgagor: s. 99 (18); s. 100 (12).
[75] A registered chargee has the same powers; see *ante*, p. 299.
[76] Law of Property Act 1925, s. 99 (19).
[77] Law of Property Act 1925, s. 99 (13).
[78] Agricultural Holdings Act 1948, Sched. 7, para. 2; See *Pawson* v. *Revell* [1958] 2 Q.B. 360; *Rhodes* v. *Dalby* [1971] 1 W.L.R. 1325.
[79] Landlord and Tenant Act 1954, s. 36 (4).
[80] *Ante*, p. 271.   For tenancies by estoppel, see *ante*, p. 303.
[81] *Ante*, p. 277.

without reference to his statutory powers (*i.e.* under his common law powers), such a lease is outside the statute and therefore no breach of the terms of the mortgage.[82] It is quite clear that a mortgagor can grant a tenancy binding *on himself* whatever the limitations in the mortgage. After the *Iron Trades* case,[82] it became common to include in the mortgage not only limitations on the statutory power of leasing but also on the mortgagor's " common law " power of leasing. However, it is not thought that such extension is really necessary to protect the mortgagee.[83]

If the mortgage permits the mortgagor to exercise the statutory leasing powers with the consent of the mortgagee, the tenant who claims that his tenancy is binding on the mortgagee carries the onus of proving consent.[84] If the mortgage provides that the lessee shall not be concerned to inquire as to whether consent to the lease to him has been given, the mortgagee may be estopped from denying that the lease was made with his consent.[85]

A tenancy may become binding on the mortgagee even where the statutory powers are excluded, or, where consent is required, he has not given consent. This will happen where the mortgagee approbates the tenancy by accepting the tenant as his own, in which case a new tenancy is created binding on the mortgagee.[86] Receipt of the rent by a receiver appointed by the mortgagee does not create a new tenancy between the tenant and the mortgagee, since the receiver is the agent of the mortgagor.[87]

Extension of statutory powers

The statutory powers of leasing are only exercisable by a mortgagee in possession. Accordingly, the mortgage may provide for the powers to be exercisable by the mortgagee without going into possession. The statutory powers are also very restricted, in particular as to the length of the term and the fact that no premium may be taken; and in many circumstances, such as when disposing of a building estate or block of flats or offices, a long lease at a premium is the obvious way of disposition. Hence the statutory power should be extended to enable

---

[82] *Iron Trades Employers' Insurance Association Ltd.* v. *Union Land and House Investors Ltd.* [1937] Ch. 313.
[83] Restrictions on the mortgagor's leasing powers operate as a means of avoiding the effect of Pt. II of the Landlord and Tenant Act 1954 (security of tenure of business premises). The scheme is for the would-be landlord to charge the property to a " friendly " chargee. The charge will restrict the mortgagor's leasing powers. The mortgagor will then lease to the tenant. This lease is not binding on the chargee so the tenant can be got rid of by the mortgagor defaulting and the " friendly " mortgagee exercising his powers. See *Precedents for The Conveyancer,* 5-2. For a scheme by way of lease and mortgage to avoid capital gains tax, see (1970) 120 New L.J. 936; *cf. Thompson* v. *Salah* [1972] 1 All E.R. 530.
[84] *Taylor* v. *Ellis* [1960] Ch. 368.
[85] *Lever Finance Ltd.* v. *Needleman's Property Trustee* [1956] Ch. 375.
[86] *Stroud Building Society* v. *Delamont* [1960] 1 W.L.R. 431; *Chatsworth Properties Ltd.* v. *Effiom* [1971] 1 W.L.R. 144.
[87] See *post,* p. 324.

the mortgagee (in practice a receiver to whom the mortgagee has delegated his powers[88]) to grant leases at ground rents taking a premium.[89]

The lease

Under the statutory power the lease must take effect in possession
not later than twelve months after its date.[90]   The length of the term
has already been mentioned.[91]   It may be convenient to extend the
mortgagee's leasing power to any length of term.[92]   The best rent must
be reserved and no fine taken.[93]   Again, the mortgagee's power should
be modified in this respect.[92]   The lease must contain a covenant by the
lessee for payment of rent and a condition of re-entry on the rent not
being paid within a time therein specified not exceeding thirty days.[94]
A counterpart of the lease must be executed by the lessee and delivered
to the lessor.   The execution of the lease by the lessor is, in favour
of the lessee and all persons deriving title under him, sufficient evidence
of the execution and delivery by the lessee.[95]   In the case of a lease
by a mortgagor, the mortgagor must, within one month after making
the lease, deliver to the mortgagee, or, if more than one, the first
mortgagee, a counterpart of the lease duly executed by the lessee, but
the lessee himself is not concerned to see that this has been complied
with.[96]   Failure to deliver a counterpart to the mortgagee does not
invalidate the lease, although it will cause the statutory power of sale
to become immediately exercisable.[97]   The provisions of section 99
referring to a lease extend and apply, so far as circumstances admit,
to any letting, and to an agreement whether in writing or not for
leasing or letting.[98]

If a lease fails to comply with the above provisions, if it was made
in good faith and the lessee has entered into possession thereunder,
it takes effect in equity as a contract for the grant, at the request of the
lessee, of a valid lease of like effect as the invalid lease.[99]

Modification of statutory power of sale

Sale is the mortgagee's principal remedy nowadays.   Foreclosure
was the traditional remedy, but this became rare earlier in this century,[1]

---

[88] See Law of Property Act 1925, s. 99 (19).
[89] For a form, see Fisher and Lightwood, p. 619 (supplement).
[90] Law of Property Act 1925, s. 99 (5).
[91] *Ante*, p. 314.
[92] See *ante*, p. 315.
[93] Law of Property Act 1925, s. 99 (6).   A lump sum for rent in advance is a fine
for this purpose: *Hughes* v. *Waite* [1957] 1 W.L.R. 713; *Grace Rymer Investments
Ltd.* v. *Waite* [1958] Ch. 831.
[94] Law of Property Act 1925, s. 99 (7); See *Pawson* v. *Revell* [1958] 2 Q.B. 360.
[95] *Ibid.* s. 99 (8).
[96] *Ibid.* s. 99 (11); see *Public Trustee* v. *Lawrence* [1912] 1 Ch. 789; *Rhodes* v. *Dalby*
[1971] 1 W.L.R. 1325.
[97] *Public Trustee* v. *Lawrence, supra.*
[98] Law of Property Act 1925, s. 99 (17); see *Pawson* v. *Revell, supra.*
[99] Law of Property Act 1925, s. 152 (1); see *Pawson* v. *Revell, supra.*
[1] Institutional lenders do not wish to have the mortgaged property vested in themselves.

although it now appears to be reviving,[2] and the new restrictions on possession [3] may make it more popular. There is nothing which can be done in the mortgage deed to make foreclosure easier, save perhaps to shorten the legal date for redemption.[4] Foreclosure is a slow and cumbersome process [5] and the court is often reluctant to make an order if there is a good " equity " in the property, i.e. the value of the property exceeds the mortgage debt; otherwise the mortgagee gets a windfall. In such a case, the court will usually order a sale of the property.[6] Even after an order absolute the foreclosure can be reopened.[7]

Because of the difficulties surrounding foreclosure, it became the almost universal custom to insert in the mortgage deed an express power for the mortgagee to sell the property, and thus realise his security. As between the mortgagee and the mortgagor, this power was not to be exercised until there had been some default on the part of the mortgagor; but since a purchaser could not be expected to go into the question whether the power to sell had arisen, it was generally provided that, as regards the safety and protection of a purchaser, no sale purporting to be made in exercise of the power should be invalidated by the fact that the mortgagee ought not to have sold.

So far back as the year 1860, an Act, known as Lord Cranworth's Act, was passed which provided that a power of sale by the mortgagee, with its ancillary provisions, should be deemed to be contained in every mortgage deed executed after the passing of the Act, subject to anything to the contrary contained in the deed. But the power of sale which the Act gave to mortgagees was so framed as to be less advantageous to them than that usually inserted in mortgage deeds by conveyancers, and, consequently, the statutory power was seldom relied upon.

The Conveyancing Act 1881 [8] repealed the enactment previously mentioned, and conferred on mortgagees whose mortgages were made by deed after 1881, statutory power of sale and other powers. These provisions reappear without substantial alteration in the Law of Property Act 1925 [9] and the express power of sale formerly inserted by conveyancers is now properly omitted. Though a legal mortgage only conveys a term of years to the mortgagee, he has power on a sale to convey the fee simple or other the whole interest of the mortgagor in the property.[10]

[2] See Report of the Committee on the Enforcement of Judgment Debts, para. 1360.
[3] See post, p. 323.
[4] See ante, p. 311.
[5] See Megarry and Wade (3rd ed.), pp. 899–902.
[6] Under s. 91 of the Law of Property Act 1925.
[7] Lancashire and Yorkshire Reversionary Interest Co., Ltd. v. Crowe (1970) 114 S.J. 435.
[8] s. 19.
[9] Law of Property Act 1925, s. 101.
[10] Ibid. ss. 88, 89; post, p. 321.

The statutory power of sale is implied in every mortgage made by deed after 1881, except so far as its application appears by the mortgage deed to be limited or excluded.[11]

When power of sale arises

Section 101 of the Law of Property Act 1925 provides that the mortgagee shall have power, *when the mortgage money has become due*, to sell, or to concur with any other person in selling, the mortgaged property, or any part thereof, either subject to prior charges or not, and either together or in lots, by public auction or private contract, subject to such conditions as he thinks fit, with power to vary any contract for sale and to buy-in at an auction, or to rescind any contract for sale and to resell, without being responsible for any loss occasioned thereby.[12] It should be noted that once the mortgagee has entered into a contract to sell in exercise of his statutory power, the mortgagor cannot prevent the sale from proceeding by tendering the mortgage money to the mortgagee.[13]

The mortgage money becomes due immediately after the date fixed for repayment, or, in the case of an instalment mortgage where there is no such date, as soon as an instalment has become due and is unpaid.[14] If the mortgage money is payable on demand, notice must usually be given.[15] The statutory power can be modified,[16] and often in such a way that the money becomes due on an earlier date than that provided by the section (for example, the date of the mortgage).

When power of sale exercisable

It is provided by section 103 of the Law of Property Act 1925 that, as between the mortgagee and the mortgagor, the former is not to *exercise* the power of sale conferred by the Act unless and until:

    (i) notice requiring payment of the mortgage money has been served on the mortgagor, or one of several mortgagors, and default has been made in payment of the mortgage money for three calendar months after such service[17]; or

    (ii) some interest under the mortgage is in arrear and unpaid for two calendar months after becoming due[18]; or

    (iii) there has been a breach of some provision contained in the mortgage deed, or in the Act, and on the part of the mortgagor,

---

[11] *Ibid.* s. 101 (3) (4).
[12] For registered charges, see Land Registration Act 1925, s. 34 (1); *ante*, p. 299; *Lever Finance Ltd.* v. *Needleman's Property Trustee* [1956] Ch. 375. For restrictions on the power of sale under controlled and regulated mortgages, see Rent Act 1968, ss. 94 *et seq.*
[13] *Waring* v. *London and Manchester Assurance Co. Ltd.* [1935] Ch. 310; *Property and Bloodstock Ltd.* v. *Emerton* [1968] Ch. 94.
[14] *Payne* v. *Cardiff R.D.C.* [1932] 1 K.B. 241.
[15] *Lloyds Bank Ltd.* v. *Margolis* [1954] 1 W.L.R. 644.
[16] Law of Property Act 1925, s. 101 (3) (4).
[17] *Barker* v. *Illingworth* [1908] 2 Ch. 20. The notice is usually to pay at the end of three months or, if the statutory period has been modified, other period specified.
[18] For the effect of a capitalisation clause on this, see *ante*, p. 307.

or of some person concurring in making the mortgage, to be observed or performed, other than and besides a covenant for payment of the mortgage money and interest thereon.[19]

Notice, where required, should be given to subsequent incumbrancers, of whom the mortgagee has notice, as well as to the mortgagor,[20] and, since registration is equivalent to notice, the mortgagee should search in the case of unregistered land in the Land Charges Department of the Land Registry, and in the case of registered land in the appropriate District Registry, to see if any subsequent mortgages have been registered.

These restrictions on the exercise of the statutory power are commonly modified by express exclusion or reduction in the time limits specified.[21]

The distinction between the power *arising* and becoming *exercisable* is important in relation to a purchaser, who need only satisfy himself that the power has arisen. Accordingly, in the case of an instalment mortgage where there is no specified date for repayment,[22] proof of non-payment is technically required.

Protection of purchaser

Where a sale is made in professed exercise of the power of sale conferred by the Act, the title of the purchaser is not impeachable on the ground that no cause had arisen to authorise the sale; or that due notice had not been given; or, where the mortgage is made after 1925, that the leave of the court, when required, was not obtained; or that the power was otherwise improperly or irregularly exercised. Further, the purchaser is not, either before or after conveyance, concerned to see or inquire whether the power is being properly and regularly exercised; but any person damnified by an unauthorised, or improper, or irregular exercise of the power is to have his remedy in damages against the person exercising the power.[23] But this protection is afforded only to a purchaser who acts in good faith, and consequently if the purchaser in fact knew that the exercise of the power was improper or irregular, he should not complete.[24] A conveyance on sale by a mortgagee made after 1925 is deemed to have been made in exercise of this statutory power unless the contrary appears.[25]

Where the statutory or express power for a mortgagee either to sell or appoint a receiver is made exercisable by reason of the mortgagor committing an act of bankruptcy or being adjudged bankrupt, then that power may not, if the mortgage deed was executed after 1925,

---

[19] *e.g.* failure to fulfil requirements of statutory leasing power: *Public Trustee* v. *Lawrence* [1912] 1 Ch. 789.
[20] *Hoole* v. *Smith* (1881) 17 Ch.D. 434; and see Law of Property Act 1925, s. 205.
[21] For form, see *post*, p. 428.
[22] See *ante*, p. 308.
[23] Law of Property Act 1925, s. 104 (2).
[24] See *Selwyn* v. *Garfit* (1888) 38 Ch.D. 273; *Born* v. *Turner* [1900] 2 Ch. 211.
[25] Law of Property Act 1925, s. 104 (3).

be exercised *only* on account of the act of bankruptcy or adjudication, without the leave of the court.[26]   As mentioned above, a purchaser is not concerned to see that an order of the court has been obtained.

Of course, as between mortgagor and mortgagee, the mortgagee must exercise the power of sale with reasonable care to obtain a proper price,[27] and if he acts in time the mortgagor may be able to stop the sale.   Otherwise his remedy will be one for accounts and inquiries against the mortgagee.

Extension of power of sale

The power of sale may usefully be extended to permit sale subject to a rentcharge or " sale " by way of long lease at a premium and subsequent sale of the reversion [28] or sale by instalments.

Sale under equitable mortgages

The statutory power of sale applies only if the mortgage is by deed.[29]   For this reason, an equitable mortgage by deposit should always be accompanied by a memorandum under seal.[30]

Notices

Any notice required to be served on the mortgagor must be in writing.   It is sufficient, however, if the notice is addressed to the mortgagor simply as " mortgagor " without mentioning his name; or generally to the persons interested, without any name, and notwithstanding that any person to be affected by the notice is absent, under disability, unborn or unascertained.   The notice will be sufficiently served if it is left at the mortgagor's last-known place of abode or business in the United Kingdom; or is affixed or left for him on the land or on any house or building, comprised in the mortgage; or is sent by registered post or recorded delivery, if not returned through the post as undelivered.[31]   If the mortgagee is dead, his executors or administrators can not only sell the property but can also convey the legal estate in it, whatever its tenure may be.[32]

It will not be often that the mortgagee has to give notice requiring payment of the mortgage money, because interest will usually be two months in arrears.[33]   But, in practice, a notice requiring payment will often be given, because in most cases the borrower is given ample opportunity of remedying his default.

---

[26] Law of Property Act 1925, s. 110.
[27] See *Cuckmere Brick Co. Ltd.* v. *Mutual Finance Ltd.* [1971] Ch. 949; (1971) 121 New L.J. 54, 540.   And see Fisher and Lightwood, pp. 310, 314.   For building societies, see Building Societies Act 1962, s. 36.
[28] See Fisher and Lightwood, p. 619, supplement.
[29] *Ante*, p. 317.
[30] *Ante*, p. 296.
[31] Law of Property Act 1925, s. 196; Recorded Delivery Service Act 1962, s. 1.
[32] *Ibid.* s. 106.
[33] See *ante*, p. 318.

The form of conveyance

The statutory power of sale (in the case of mortgages made after 1911) includes power to impose restrictive covenants or conditions on the unsold part of the mortgaged property, or on the purchaser and any property sold; and to sell the mortgaged property, or any part thereof, or any mines or minerals, apart from the surface:

    (i) with or without a grant or reservation of rights for building or other purposes in relation to the property remaining in mortgage or the property sold;

    (ii) with or without an exception or reservation of mines or minerals in or under the mortgaged property and with or without a grant or reservation of powers of working, easements, etc., for or connected with mining purposes in relation to the property sold or retained; and

    (iii) with or without covenants by the purchaser to expend money on the land sold.[34]

We have already seen that it is usual to extend the statutory power to permit sale subject to a rentcharge, sale by instalments, etc.[35]

The conveyance will recite the mortgage and the agreement for sale and the mortgagee will convey or assign, as appropriate, as mortgagee.[36]

Where only part of the mortgaged land is sold, mutual easements, provisions as to party-walls and an acknowledgment for production[37] may be included.

The effect of the conveyance, etc.

On a sale by a legal mortgagee of freeholds, the conveyance will vest in the purchaser the legal estate in fee simple, subject to all estates, interests, and rights which have priority to the mortgage, but free from all estates, interests and rights to which the mortgage has priority. The mortgagee's term or charge and all subsequent mortgage terms or charges will merge or be extinguished as respects the land conveyed.[38]

On a sale by a legal mortgagee of leaseholds, the conveyance will operate to convey to the purchaser not only the mortgage term, but also the leasehold reversion of the mortgagor. The purchaser will take subject to all estates, interests, and rights which have priority to the mortgage, but free from all estates, interests, and rights to which the mortgage has priority. The mortgagee's term or charge and all subsequent terms or charges will merge in the leasehold reversion and be extinguished.[39]

A transfer of registered land under the power of sale operates to

[34] Law of Property Act 1925, s. 101 (2), replacing Conveyancing Act 1911, s. 4.
[35] *Ante*, p. 320.
[36] For the implied covenants for title, see *ante*, p. 228. For a form of conveyance by a mortgagee, see *post*, p. 418.
[37] See *ante*, p. 238.
[38] Law of Property Act 1925, ss. 88, 104.
[39] *Ibid.* ss. 89, 104.

transfer the registered estate and any mortgage term, express or implied, merges therein.[40]

The mortgagee, his executors, administrators, or assigns are not to be responsible for any involuntary loss incurred on the exercise of the power of sale nor with any trust matter connected therewith [41]; and his or their receipt in writing is to be a sufficient discharge for any money arising under the power of sale, and a person paying the same to him or them is not to be concerned to inquire whether any money remains due under the mortgage.[42]

An equitable mortgagee can only convey his equitable interest, unless the accompanying memorandum includes a power of attorney or declaration of trust, in which case the fee simple can be conveyed or the term of years assigned.[43]

Application of proceeds of sale

The money arising from the sale, after discharging or providing for any prior incumbrances to which the sale is not made subject, or after payment into court of a sum to meet any prior incumbrance,[44] is to be applied by the mortgagee:

First, in payment of his costs and expenses of sale;

Secondly, in discharge of the mortgage debt;

and the residue is to be paid to the person formerly entitled to the mortgaged property, or *authorised to give receipts for the proceeds of sale thereof*: words which include subsequent incumbrancers.[45]

Right to possession

It is no good having a power of sale unless the mortgagee can sell with vacant possession. The mortgagor will not usually give up possession voluntarily and an application to the court by the mortgagee for an order for possession will normally be required. Taking active physical possession without a court order is unwise,[46] unless the mortgagor has abandoned the premises, and even then some mortgagees, such as building societies, as a matter of course seek a possession order before entry.

Mortgagor in possession. After the execution of the mortgage, the mortgagor is usually allowed to retain possession of the mortgaged property, until he defaults in payment of interest or instalments when

---

[40] Land Registration Act 1925, s. 34 (5).
[41] Law of Property Act 1925, s. 106.
[42] *Ibid.* s. 107.
[43] See *ante*, p. 297; *Re White Rose Cottage* [1965] Ch. 940.
[44] Law of Property Act 1925, s. 50; Trustee Act 1925, s. 63.
[45] *Ibid.* s. 105, replacing Conveyancing Act 1881, s. 21 (3); *Re Thomson's Mortgage Trusts* [1920] 1 Ch. 508; and see *Young* v. *Clarey* [1948] Ch. 191; *Matthews (C. & M.) Ltd.* v. *Marsden Building Society* [1951] Ch. 758; Fisher and Lightwood, pp. 314 *et seq.*
[46] Because this may give rise to liability to prosecution under the Forcible Entry Acts 1381–1623.

the mortgagee will want to exercise his remedies. The mortgage sometimes expressly provides that the mortgagor shall be entitled to retain possession; and, in the case of instalment mortgages, there is sometimes a provision that the mortgagee shall not take possession until default. Such a provision may even be implied.[47] The mortgagor's right to possession may also be secured by an attornment clause or by his becoming tenant to the mortgagee. The nature and purpose of an attornment clause is discussed subsequently.[48] The mortgagor may become tenant to the mortgagee by virtue of a provision in the mortgage qualifying the mortgagee's prima facie right to possession.[49] In the absence of attornment or tenancy, the precise nature of the relations between mortgagor and mortgagee is a matter of debate. The mortgagor is sometimes called a tenant at will to the mortgagee, or tenant *by*, as distinguished from tenant *at*, sufferance.[50]

Mortgagee's right to possession.[51] Whatever the nature of the relationship may be in the absence of attornment or tenancy or any provision to the contrary in the mortgage a legal mortgagee is prima facie entitled to possession immediately after the execution of the mortgage.[47] As Harman L.J. vividly put it, the mortgagee is entitled to go into possession " before the ink is dry on the mortgage." [52] The mortgagee's right to possession does not depend upon any default by the mortgagor. Previously, the mortgagee was entitled to an order for possession as a matter of course. The Administration of Justice Act 1970 now gives the court [53] powers to adjourn proceedings for possession, to stay or suspend an order for possession, or postpone the date for delivery of possession, where there is a reasonable chance of the mortgagor making good his default.[54]

Appointment of receiver

The mortgagee has power, when he has become entitled to exercise his power of sale,[55] to appoint a receiver of the income of the mortgaged property, or any part thereof, by writing under his hand. The mortgagee may appoint a receiver, even though the mortgagee has taken possession of the mortgaged land.[56] Provisions relating to the appointment,[57] powers, remunerations and duties of a receiver are to be found

---

[47] *Birmingham Citizens' Permanent Building Society* v. *Caunt* [1962] Ch. 883, 890.
[48] *Post*, p. 325.
[49] *Wilkinson* v. *Hall* (1837) 3 Bing.N.C. 508.
[50] See further Fisher and Lightwood, p. 278.
[51] See generally (1961) 25 Conv.(N.S.) 278; (1969) 22 C.L.P. 129; (1970) 120 New L.J. 808, 829; Payne Committee Report, Pt. IX. For the right of an equitable mortgagee to possession, see Megarry and Wade, p. 917.
[52] *Four-maids Ltd.* v. *Dudley Marshall (Properties) Ltd.* [1957] Ch. 317, 320.
[53] Now often the county court, see Administration of Justice Act 1970, s. 37.
[54] Administration of Justice Act 1970, s. 36; see (1970) 120 New L.J. 829.
[55] Law of Property Act 1925, s. 101 (1) (iii); see *ante*, p. 318. A registered chargee has the same power: see *ante*, p. 299.
[56] *Refuge Assurance Co. Ltd.* v. *Pearlberg* [1938] 1 Ch. 687.
[57] A corporate body may not be appointed receiver of a company: *Portman Building Society* v. *Gallwey* [1955] 1 W.L.R. 96.

in section 109 of the Law of Property Act 1925.[58]   The receiver is to
be deemed to be the agent of the *mortgagor,* who alone is to be
responsible for his acts and defaults, unless the mortgage deed otherwise provides.   The receiver is to demand (and, if necessary, to recover
by action or otherwise), all the income of the property, and he has
power to give effectual receipts for such income, and a person paying
money to him is not to be concerned to inquire whether any case has
happened to authorise the receiver to act.   He may exercise the
mortgagee's powers of leasing and accepting surrenders of leases, if
these powers have been delegated to him in writing by the mortgagee;
and, if so directed in writing by the mortgagee, he must insure against
fire to the extent to which the mortgagee might have insured.

The receiver is to apply money received by him as follows:
  (i) in discharging rents, taxes, rates and other outgoings;
 (ii) in keeping down annual sums or other payments and interest
       on all principal sums having priority to the mortgage;
(iii) in payment of his own commission and of fire, life, or other
       insurance premiums payable under the mortgage deed or the
       Act, and the cost of repairs directed in writing by the
       mortgagee [59];
 (iv) in payment of interest accruing due under the mortgage in
       respect whereof he is receiver;
  (v) in or towards the discharge of the principal money if so
       directed in writing by the mortgagee [60];
and he must pay the balance to the mortgagor, or other person, who,
but for the possession of the receiver, would have been entitled.

The mortgagee will usually prefer a sale.   But there are occasions,
where the property is let and thus producing an income, when the
appointment of a receiver is useful.   For example, the lender may not
want to call in the loan, because the interest rate is advantageous.   Or,
where an immediate sale will not raise enough to pay off the mortgage
and the borrower has no other means, the lender may prefer to appoint
a receiver, if the property is sufficient to keep down the mortgage
interest.

The appointment of a receiver is one of the principal remedies of
debenture holders.[61]

A mortgagee should never take possession of the mortgaged property
himself because a high standard of business vigilance is then imposed
on him.[62]   If he appoints a receiver, who is, as we have seen, the agent
of the *mortgagor,* the mortgagee is protected.

---

[58] Replacing s. 4 of the Conveyancing Act 1881; see generally Fisher and Lightwood,
   Ch. 17.
[59] See *White* v. *Metcalfe* [1903] 2 Ch. 567.
[60] Law of Property Act 1925, s. 109 (8).
[61] See *ante,* p. 302.   For the effect of the appointment in these circumstances, see
   Gower, *Modern Company Law,* pp. 434 *et seq.*
[62] *White* v. *City of London Brewery Co.* (1889) 42 Ch.D. 237.

The statutory provisions in connection with receivers are somewhat limited. In particular, the rate of commission for the receiver is much too low, and in debentures especially it is usual to set out in detail provisions as to the powers, duties and rights of the receiver.

The appointment may be made under hand only but in practice it is usually made under seal.[63]

The receiver should give notice of his appointment to the tenants of the property.[64]

Power to consolidate

In the case of mortgages made after 1881, a mortgagor may redeem any one mortgage without paying any money due on any separate mortgage made by him, or by any person through whom he claims, on other property: but this applies only if, and so far as, a contrary intention is not expressed in the mortgage deeds or one of them.[65] If, therefore, it is desired that the mortgagee's right of consolidation shall be preserved, a clause must be inserted in the mortgage deed declaring that section 93 of the Law of Property Act 1925 shall not apply to the security.[66] It is desirable to insert this clause if the mortgage is, or is likely to become, one of a series of mortgage transactions between the same parties and it is in practice inserted as a matter of course.[67]

Further advances

A mortgage sometimes provides that the property is to be security for any further advances made by the lender, for example, where the mortgage is to secure a current account. Or the mortgage may expressly require the lender to make further advances, for example, where the mortgage is to assist the development of a property and the further advances are to be made at various stages of building. The right of a mortgagee to tack further advances to his original security so as to gain priority over intermediate mortgages is preserved by the Law of Property Act 1925 subject to certain conditions.[68]

Attornment clause

If the mortgagor is in actual occupation of the mortgaged property, the mortgage deed may contain a clause in which the mortgagor declares himself to be tenant to the mortgagee in respect of all the mortgaged premises, and agrees to pay a yearly rent accordingly.[69]

---

[63] For a form of appointment, see Fisher and Lightwood, p. 651.
[64] For a form of notice, see Fisher and Lightwood, p. 653.
[65] Law of Property Act 1925, s. 93, replacing Conveyancing Act 1881, s. 17.
[66] For a form, see *post*, p. 428.
[67] See further Megarry and Wade, pp. 920–926; for registered land practice, see Ruoff and Roper, (3rd ed.), pp. 549–552.
[68] Law of Property Act 1925, s. 94. See Megarry and Wade, pp. 972 *et seq.*: and *McCarthy and Stone Ltd.* v. *Julian S. Hodge and Co. Ltd.* [1971] 1 W.L.R. 1547.
[69] See (1966) 30 Conv.(N.S.) 30; (1969) 22 C.L.P. 129; Fisher and Lightwood, p. 32. For form, see *post*, p. 429.

M

The clause, however, is often omitted nowadays. Formerly, the rent was fixed at an amount equivalent to the annual interest, so that if the interest was in arrear, the mortgagee could distrain for the arrears in the position of a landlord destraining for arrears of rent. Latterly the rent has become nominal.

The inclusion of the attornment clause or an express power of distress, however, rendered the instrument a bill of sale within the Bills of Sale Act 1878, and it therefore required registration under that Act, and, if not registered, a distress would be illegal.[70] A mortgagor would naturally object to registration of his mortgage as a bill of sale, and consequently the clause ceased to be inserted for its original purpose. It has been held, however, that, notwithstanding the Bills of Sale Act 1878, the attornment clause is still valid for the purpose of creating the relation of landlord and tenant between the mortgagee and the mortgagor even though the mortgage was not registered as a bill of sale,[71] and it therefore enables the mortgagee, if he wishes to recover possession, to do so summarily by proceedings before the justices under section 1 of the Small Tenements Recovery Act 1838.[72] But mortgagees, save for local authority mortgagees, seldom avail themselves of this procedure.

Another reason for the insertion of the clause was to enable the mortgagee to obtain summary judgment in a possession action in the High Court, which he could do in the position of a landlord suing his tenant for possession, but not as mortgagee. But the clause is no longer necessary for this purpose, because summary judgment is available to a mortgagee independently of attornment.[73] It should also be remembered that every action in which there is a claim for payment of principal or interest secured by a mortgage of land, or for possession, must now be assigned to the Chancery Division.[74] The proceedings may and usually will be commenced by originating summons, but a writ may still be employed.

The reservation of rent in an attornment clause would, if standing alone, create a yearly tenancy between the mortgagor and the mortgagee which could not be put an end to without a half a year's notice.[75] In order to obviate this, the attornment clause is generally followed by a proviso enabling the mortgagee to enter upon the premises at any time, without notice, and thus to determine the tenancy created by the clause.[76]

---

[70] *Re Willis, ex p. Kennedy* (1888) 21 Q.B.D. 384.

[71] *Mumford* v. *Collier* (1890) 25 Q.B.D. 279; *Kemp* v. *Lester* [1896] 2 Q.B. 162.

[72] *Dudley and District Benefit Building Society* v. *Gordon* [1929] 2 K.B. 105.

[73] R.S.C., Ord. 88.

[74] *Ibid.* For possession actions in the county court, see Administration of Justice Act 1970, s. 37: *ante*, p. 323.

[75] See *Hinckley and Country Building Society* v. *Henny* [1953] 1 W.L.R. 352; *Regent Oil Co. Ltd.* v. *J. A. Gregory (Hatch End) Ltd.* [1966] Ch. 402.

[76] The bringing of proceedings to recover possession will determine the tenancy, because this has the same effect as re-entry and taking possession: *Woolwich Equitable Building Society* v. *Preston* [1938] Ch. 129.

An attornment by the mortgagor to a second mortgagee is valid even though he has attorned tenant to the first mortgagee.[77]

III. SECOND MORTGAGES

Use

Second and subsequent mortgages were common in the past but had become fairly unusual in this century until the 1960s. This renaissance was a result of a combination of a change in the hire-purchase laws in the Hire-Purchase Acts of 1964 and 1965, which caused finance houses to seek further outlets, and the tax relief advantages of mortgages and other loans, which induced many people to borrow to pay for purchases rather than pay cash, together with rising house prices. The continued inflation of property values [78] has resulted in good " equities " on properties subject to a first mortgage, i.e. the difference between the mortgage debt and the value of the property, sufficient to support a further advance.[79] We have already seen [80] the importance of the money-lending legislation in this context.

Form

Accordingly, it is possible to have several mortgages on the same property. Sometimes, the second mortgage may be a further charge in favour of the first mortgagee, but the second mortgagee may be and often is a different lender, for example, the first mortgagee may be a building society and the second mortgagee a finance company.

We have already mentioned the form of such mortgages.[81] The mortgage will usually recite any prior mortgage, the state of the mortgage debt, i.e. how much principal and interest (if any) is still due (this will give the lender a remedy under the covenants for title [82]), and the agreement for the loan. The charge or demise will be subject to the prior mortgage. It is vital to make the power of sale exercisable on any default under the prior mortgage, and to include a power for the mortgagee to settle with prior mortgagees and to redeem their securities, and a charge of the costs of so doing on the mortgaged property.

As the first mortgagee will generally have the title deeds, a subsequent mortgage should be registered as a puisne mortgage.[83] Notice of the mortgage should be given to the first mortgagee. The purpose of this notice is to prevent the first mortgagee making further advances to the mortgagor ranking in priority to the second mortgage. Registration

---

[77] *Re Kitchin, ex p. Punnett* (1880) 16 Ch.D. 226.
[78] This is due, to some extent at least, to the general availability of mortgages; see e.g. (1971) 115 S.J. 677.
[79] See generally the Crowther Report, paras. 2.4. 48–53; 6.4. 22–25.
[80] *Ante*, pp. 304, 305.
[81] *Ante*, p. 295.
[82] *Ante*, p. 227.
[83] *Post*, p. 329.

as a land charge is not in itself sufficient for this purpose.[84]   Notice also ensures that the second mortgagee is paid the balance of any surplus proceeds of sale on a sale by the prior mortgagee and that the title deeds are handed over to him on discharge of the prior mortgage. Registration as a land charge is not in itself sufficient for the latter purpose.[85]

A second mortgagee has all the remedies of a first mortgagee, but generally he will not be able to exercise them while the first mortgagee is exercising the same remedies.

Disadvantages

The disadvantages of second mortgages are stated to be the risk of tacking[86] and consolidation,[87] the absence of the title deeds and the fact that the first mortgagee may sell.   But the risks are small if the mortgage is registered and notice of it duly given and there is a sufficient equity in the property.[88]

IV.   SUB-MORTGAGES

Generally

A sub-mortgage is a mortgage of a mortgage: sometimes a mortgagee wishes to receive only part of his money and is unwilling to disturb his original investment.   In such a case, instead of calling in his mortgage, the mortgagee can create a sub-mortgage, *i.e.* a mortgage of the mortgage debt and security.   Alternatively, he may wish to raise money on the security of the mortgage.

Form

A sub-mortgage of £1,000 of a mortgage of £2,000 consists in substance of a covenant to pay £1,000 and interest and a transfer of the mortgage for £2,000, subject to redemption on payment of £1,000 and interest.   The deed recites the original mortgage, the fact that the debt is still due, and the agreement by the sub-mortgagee for a loan to the mortgagee.   Where the original mortgage is a legal charge, the original mortgagee has no estate for a term of years out of which to create a sub-term.   In this case, the sub-mortgage will consist of an assignment of the mortgage debt to the sub-mortgagee, to hold to the said sub-mortgagee " subject to the proviso for redemption hereinafter contained," *i.e.* to re-transfer on payment of the amount lent and interest, and a transfer of the benefit of the original mortgage, subject

[84] See Law of Property Act 1925, s. 94 (2), as amended by the Law of Property (Amendment) Act 1926, s. 7, Sched.
[85] See Law of Property Act 1925, s. 96 (2), added by the Law of Property (Amendment) Act 1926, Sched.
[86] *Ante*, p. 325.
[87] See *ante*, p. 325.
[88] See Fisher and Lightwood, Chap. 10.

also to the proviso for redemption. Alternatively, advantage may be taken of section 114 of the Law of Property Act 1925, and the benefit of the mortgage transferred,[89] subject to redemption on payment of principal and interest. Where the original mortgage is by demise, a legal sub-mortgage consists of an assignment of the mortgage debt and either a sub-demise or legal charge of the property comprised in the original mortgage. Where the original mortgage is a sub-demise of leaseholds either a sub-sub-demise or legal charge may be used.[90]

Effect of sub-mortgage

The effect of a sub-mortgage is to put the sub-mortgagee in the position of a transferee of the principal mortgage.[91] The sub-mortgagee can exercise the statutory power of sale conferred by the original mortgage, as well as that conferred by the sub-mortgage.[92] He has, then, two distinct powers of sale. The power of sale contained in the sub-mortgage is only to be exercised if the sub-mortgagor makes default; the sale passes the benefit of the debt, but the land is sold subject to the mortgagor's equity of redemption. The power of sale contained in the original mortgage is only to be exercised if the original mortgagor makes default, but, if exercised, it passes the land to the purchaser free from all equity of redemption. In the first case, the purchaser from the sub-mortgagee purchases the mortgage debt and the security; in the second case he purchases the land itself. The sub-mortgagee should give notice to the mortgagor of the sub-mortgage.[93]

Sub-charges of registered charge

The proprietor of a registered charge may charge the mortgage debt in the same manner as a proprietor of the land may charge the land.[94] The sub-charge must be completed by registration.[95]

V. REGISTRATION OF CHARGES

Puisne mortgages

In the case of registered land, if a legal mortgagee does not obtain the title deeds, he should register his mortgage as a land charge of Class C (i) (a puisne mortgage).[96] We have already mentioned the procedure for application for registration.[97]

Equitable mortgages

An equitable mortgage accompanied by title deeds is expressly

---

89 *Post*, p. 331.
90 See generally Fisher and Lightwood, Chap. 14.
91 *Post*, pp. 331, 332.
92 Law of Property Act 1925, ss. 88, 89, 205 (xvi).
93 *Bateman* v. *Hunt* [1904] 2 K.B. 530.
94 Land Registration Act 1925, s. 36.
95 Land Registration Rules 1925, rr. 163, 164, 166.
96 See *ante*, p. 153.
97 See *ante*, p. 158.

excluded from Class C (iii) land charges, *i.e.* general equitable charges. It seems that such a mortgage is registrable as an estate contract (land charge Class C (iv)),[98] but it is not the practice of conveyancers to register a protected equitable mortgage as an estate contract unless there is an *express* agreement to create a legal mortgage. Equitable mortgages not accompanied by title deeds are registrable as general equitable charges.

Company charges

Those mortgages made by a company which are registrable as land charges must be so registered. Registration under the Companies Act 1948 is no longer sufficient for a land charge in place of registration under the Land Charges Act 1925. Charges by companies of unregistered land (other than floating charges) created after January 1, 1970, which are capable of registration as land charges, should be registered under the Land Charges Act 1925, as well as under the Companies Act 1948.[99]

Most mortgages and charges made by companies are registrable under the Companies Act 1948.[1] Particulars of a new charge created by a company and the charge itself must be sent to the Registrar so that they are received by him within twenty-two days of registration.[2] On registration, the Registrar issues a certificate, which is conclusive that all the required particulars as to registration have been complied with.[3] Failure to register makes the charge void as against other creditors (even though they have notice of the charge) and against the liquidator. The charge remains good against the company itself. If the charge is void, anything ancillary to it, such as a vendor's lien, is also void.[4]

Where a vendor leaves part of the purchase-money outstanding on a mortgage on the property, registration should be made under section 95 of the Companies Act 1948 and not under section 97, which applies where a company acquires property already subject to a charge.[5]

If a floating charge contains a provision that no mortgage or charge ranking *pari passu* or in priority to the debenture shall be created by the company,[6] this restriction should be noted in the registration of the charge. Where this is done, a subsequent mortgagee will have notice of the restriction.[7]

---

[98] (1962) 26 Conv.(N.S.) 446–449; *cf.* (1941) 7 C.L.J. 252.
[99] Law of Property Act 1969, s. 26. For registered land, see *ante*, p. 298.
[1] ss. 95 *et seq.* On the weaknesses of the registration system, see Gower, *Modern Company Law* (3rd ed.), pp. 427 *et seq.*
[2] For extension of the time, see Companies Act 1948, s. 101.
[3] See *Re Nye (C. L.) Ltd.* [1971] Ch. 442.
[4] *Re Molton Finance Co. Ltd.* [1968] Ch. 325; *Capital Finance Co. Ltd.* v. *Stokes* [1969] 1 Ch. 261; but see (1970) 33 M.L.R. 131.
[5] *Capital Finance Co. Ltd.* v. *Stokes, supra.*
[6] See *ante*, p. 302.
[7] *Wilson* v. *Kelland* [1910] 2 Ch. 306.

Registered charges

We have already dealt with first registration of mortgages and protection of mortgages of registered land.[8]

VI. TRANSFER OF MORTGAGES

Concurrence of mortgagor

As a rule, it is not necessary for the mortgagor to join in a transfer of the mortgage, as the mortgagee has power to assign the mortgage debt and interest and the security without the concurrence of the mortgagor. But if a mortgagee has taken possession, he cannot give it up without the permission of the mortgagor,[9] and if he transfers the mortgage without the concurrence of the mortgagor, he remains liable for his own acts and defaults done or made while he is in possession, and becomes liable, after the transfer, for the acts and defaults of the transferee, unless he transfers under the direction of the court.[10] Moreover, it is always advisable, if the mortgagor is willing to concur, to make him a party to a transfer of the mortgage, because, by joining in the transfer deed, he becomes bound by the recital in the transfer deed as to the state of the debt. If he is not a party, inquiry should be made of him before completion as to the state of accounts between him and the mortgagee (because part of the mortgage debt might have been paid off); and notice of the transfer should be given to him; for, if he is not a party and has no notice of the transfer, he might set off against the claim of the transferee not only all moneys paid by him towards the discharge of the mortgage debt before the assignment but also moneys so paid after the assignment but before he had notice of it.

Form of transfer

On the transfer of a mortgage before 1926, a mere transfer of the benefit of the mortgage was not sufficient to pass the legal estate to the transferee,[11] and it was therefore necessary that the deed of transfer should contain an express conveyance of the mortgaged property, as well as an assignment of the mortgage debt. This inconvenience was removed by section 114 of the Law of Property Act 1925, which provides that a deed executed by a mortgagee after 1925, purporting to transfer his mortgage or the benefit thereof, whenever the mortgage was made, shall operate, unless the contrary intention is therein expressed, to transfer to the transferee:

    (i) the right to recover the money, or the unpaid part thereof, and interest;

---

[8] *Ante*, pp. 297 *et seq.*
[9] *Prytherch* v. *Williams* (1889) 42 Ch.D. 590.
[10] *Hall* v. *Heward* (1886) 32 Ch.D. 430.
[11] This did not apply to statutory mortgages. For statutory mortgages, see *ante*, p. 295.

(ii) the benefit of all securities for the same;

(iii) the benefit of all covenants and powers; and

(iv) all the mortgagee's estate or interest in the mortgaged property, subject to the right of redemption then subsisting.[12]

Where the mortgagor is a party to the transfer, the mortgagee conveys and transfers by direction of the mortgagor directing " as beneficial owner "; and the full covenants for title are thereby implied on the part of the mortgagor.[13] Whether the mortgagor is a party or not, the mortgagee transfers the benefit of the mortgage " as mortgagee " so as to imply a covenant that he has not incumbered.[14]

When both mortgagee and transferee are clients of the same solicitor, it is possible to make the transfer by deed indorsed on the original mortgage deed. Brevity may also be obtained by making the transfer supplemental to the mortgage, in which case the transfer is read as if it were indorsed on the mortgage deed or contained a full recital thereof.

When the mortgage is vested in trustees, and the fact of their being trustees does not appear on the title, and the mortgage has to be transferred upon an appointment of new trustees, it was formerly necessary to frame the transfer so as " to keep the trusts off the title," for if they were disclosed, the instrument declaring the trust became a title deed to the mortgaged property. This was done by reciting that the mortgage debt belonged in equity to the transferees on a joint account and that the transferors had agreed, at the request of the transferees, to make a transfer of the mortgage debt and securities. The transfer was then expressed to be made in pursuance of the said agreement and " in consideration of the premises," and the mortgage was transferred to the transferees. But now, by section 113 of the Law of Property Act 1925, it is provided that a person dealing in good faith after 1925 with a mortgagee, or with the mortgagor if the mortgage has been discharged, shall not be concerned with any trust at any time affecting the mortgage money or the income thereof, whether or not he has notice of the trust.[15]

A transfer of a mortgage of leaseholds follows the same general form as the transfer of a mortgage of freeholds.

Transfer of equitable mortgages

Where there is an agreement or memorandum, the transfer is made in the usual way under section 114 of the Law of Property Act 1925 by a deed transferring the benefit of the mortgage. If there were merely a deposit of deeds, the transfer would be effected by delivery

---

[12] For transfer by indorsed receipt, see *post*, p. 336. For transfer in lieu of discharge, see *post*, p. 335.

[13] Law of Property Act 1925, s. 76 (2), Sched. 2.

[14] *Ibid.* s. 76 (1) (*f*). See Farrand, *Contract and Conveyance*, p. 312. For a form, see *post*, p. 434.

[15] See *ante*, p. 310.

of the deeds to the transferee, with or without a memorandum as to the transfer.[16]

Transfer of registered charge

The charge may be transferred in the prescribed manner,[17] and the transfer is completed by registration of the transferee as proprietor of the charge. A transfer of a sub-charge[18] is effected in the same manner.

Transfer of sub-mortgages

Whether the sub-mortgage is by demise or legal charge, the transfer is effected by a transfer of the benefit of the sub-mortgage under section 114 of the Law of Property Act 1925.

Notice of transfer

Notice of the transfer should be given to the mortgagor, if he was not party to the transfer, by the transferee. After such notice the mortgagor will only get a good discharge from the mortgage by paying the transferee.[19]

Transfer after mortgagee's death

Where the mortgagee dies after 1925, the mortgaged property vests in his personal representatives under the Administration of Estates Act 1925 and can be transferred by them. But whether the property is freehold or leasehold, the transfer must be executed by all the executors who have proved the will, or all the administrators if the mortgagee died intestate.[20] The benefit of the mortgage is usually vested in a beneficiary by transfer rather than assent. An assent will transfer the *estate or interest*, but a transfer under section 114 is necessary for the *debt*.[21]

VII. TERMINATION OF MORTGAGES

The method by which, on repayment of the mortgage money,[22] the estate or interest of the mortgagee is determined differs according to the method by which the estate or interest was created; and also according

---

16 See *Re Richardson* (1885) 30 Ch.D. 396; *Brocklesby* v. *Temperance Building Society* [1895] A.C. 173.
17 Land Registration Act 1925, s. 33; Rules 1925, r. 153 (the prescribed form is Form 54).
18 See *ante*, p. 329.
19 *Dixon* v. *Winch* [1900] 1 Ch. 736; *Turner* v. *Smith* [1901] 1 Ch. 213.
20 Administration of Estates Act 1925, ss. 1–3; and see *ante*, p. 222.
21 See Hallett's *Conveyancing Precedents*, p. 698.
22 Notice to redeem is usually necessary: see *Cromwell Property Investment Co. Ltd.* v. *Western and Toovey* [1934] Ch. 322. Actual repayment is necessary for discharge; see *Keller (Samuel) Holdings Ltd.* v. *Martins Bank Ltd.* [1971] 1 W.L.R. 43. For discharge by statute (under the Housing Acts, Rent Acts, etc.), see Fisher and Lightwood, Chap. 33.

to whether the mortgage terminated before 1926 or after 1925. We shall deal first with the position before 1926, and secondly with the position after 1925.

A. Termination of Mortgages before 1926

Legal mortgages

When the mortgage money was paid off before 1926, the mortgagee of freeholds was bound to reconvey by deed the legal estate in fee simple to the mortgagor.[23] If the mortgaged property consisted of leaseholds the mortgagee, if the mortgage was by assignment, reassigned and released; if the mortgage was by sub-lease the mortgagee, even if the sub-lease was a second or later mortgage,[24] surrendered and released to the mortgagor the property comprised in the mortgage.[25]

Equitable mortgages

If the mortgage was equitable only, no reconveyance was necessary, and the property was discharged from the debt by a receipt for the mortgage money and interest.

Building society mortgages

No reconveyance was necessary on payment off of a building society mortgage owing to section 42 of the Building Societies Act 1874, which provided that a receipt under the seal of the society, countersigned by the secretary or manager, indorsed or annexed to the mortgage, should be sufficient to vacate the security and revest the estate in the person for the time being entitled to the equity of redemption without any reconveyance.[26] Building society mortgages are still vacated by a receipt indorsed.[27]

B. Termination of Mortgages after 1925

Satisfied terms

It is provided by section 116 of the Law of Property Act 1925 [28] that, after the money secured by a mortgage has been discharged, the term will become a satisfied term and will cease. It follows, therefore, that if the mortgage was secured by a term of years granted to the mortgagee, no reconveyance of any kind is necessary, and that

---

[23] If there was no reconveyance, but the mortgagor remained in possession, the mortgagee's legal estate would, under the Statutes of Limitation, be extinguished at the end of 13 years from the time of the money being repaid to him, because after repayment the mortgagor was treated for the purposes of the statute as a tenant at will; see *Sands to Thompson* (1883) 22 Ch.D. 614.

[24] *Re Moore and Hulme's Contract* [1912] 2 Ch. 105.

[25] In the rare case of freehold mortgages by demise, no surrender was necessary as the term ceased on repayment by virtue of the Satisfied Terms Act 1845.

[26] Similar provisions were contained in the Friendly Societies Acts 1875 and 1896.

[27] Building Societies Act 1962, s. 37; see *post*, p. 337.

[28] See also s. 5.

the term will automatically cease the moment the mortgage money is paid. In practice, a receipt for the money will be required, not for the purpose of vacating the mortgage, but to evidence the repayment.

Vacating receipt

Whenever a mortgage was made, whether of leaseholds or freeholds, section 115 of the Law of Property Act 1925 provides that a receipt indorsed on, written at the foot of or annexed to the mortgage deed after 1925 will be sufficient to vacate the mortgage without any reconveyance, surrender or release; and if the mortgage was by demise or sub-demise, the receipt will generally operate to merge the mortgage term in the immediate reversion, and in other cases it will operate as a reconveyance to the person entitled to the equity of redemption. To be operative, the receipt must state the name of the person who repays the money, and must be executed by the chargee by way of legal mortgage, or the person in whom the mortgaged property is vested and who is legally entitled to give a receipt.[29] It is not necessary for the receipt to be under seal.[30] In a receipt given under the section covenants " as mortgagee " are implied.[31]

Some mortgagors may prefer a more elaborate discharge of their mortgages than a mere receipt indorsed, and it is accordingly provided by section 115 of the Law of Property Act 1925 that its provisions are not to affect the right of any person to require a reassignment, surrender, release or transfer to be executed in lieu of a receipt. This provision apparently applies to mortgagors however the mortgage was created, and whether by a long term of years or otherwise, but, since a mortgage by a long term of years ceases automatically on repayment, and in other cases the receipt indorsed is a simple and effective method of vacating the security, it is seldom in practice that a more elaborate form of discharge is insisted upon.

Where only part of the mortgage money is repaid, a statutory receipt is not applicable, as section 115 of the Law of Property Act 1925 refers to a receipt for *all money thereby secured.* If no part of the security is to be discharged, a simple receipt will suffice. If part of the land is discharged, a release and surrender should be used.[32]

Mortgagor can compel transfer

Before the Conveyancing Act 1881 [33] it was the duty of the mortgagee on being paid off to reconvey to the mortgagor, and he could

29 For a form, see *post,* p. 435. This section has no application to a charge or incumbrance registered under the Land Registration Act 1925; see *post,* p. 337.
30 *Simpson* v. *Geoghegan* [1934] W.N. 232. For building societies, see *post,* p. 337.
31 s. 115 (6).
32 For undertakings to discharge a mortgage, see *ante,* p. 211.
33 s. 15, as amended by Conveyancing Act 1882, s. 12.

not be forced to convey to any other person unless the words " or as the mortgagor, his heirs, or assigns shall direct " were added at the end of the proviso for redemption.[34] But the mortgagor and any subsequent incumbrancer, on paying off the mortgagee, may now require him to transfer the mortgage to any third person notwithstanding any stipulation to the contrary.[35] But this power of the mortgagor to compel a transfer can only be exercised on payment to the mortgagee of the same sum as he would be entitled to on redemption; and the power is not exercisable at all if the mortgagee is or has been in possession of the mortgaged property.[36]

Receipt operating as transfer

As stated above, a receipt indorsed will generally operate either to merge the mortgage term in the immediate reversion or as a reconveyance to the person entitled to the equity of redemption. But where, by the receipt, the money appears to have been paid by a person who is not entitled to the immediate equity of redemption, the receipt will operate to *transfer the mortgage* to the person paying the money,[37] and this is so even though the receipt does not expressly state that the person paying the money was not entitled to the immediate equity of redemption.[38] For this reason, it is important that the receipt is dated the same date as, and not after, any conveyance contemporaneous with its discharge.[39] To this, however, there are three exceptions; three cases, that is, in which, although the person paying the money is not the person apparently entitled to the immediate equity of redemption, the receipt will nevertheless operate as a discharge and not a transfer to him. These are as follows [40]:

(i) where it is expressly provided that the receipt shall not operate as a transfer [41];

(ii) where the mortgage is paid off out of capital money or other money in the hands of a personal representative or trustee applicable for the discharge of the mortgage, and the receipt does not expressly provide that it shall act as a transfer; or

(iii) where the money is paid by the mortgagor himself, and there is an intervening mortgagee. Here, the person with the intervening mortgage is the person with the immediate equity of redemption; but nevertheless the receipt will operate as a discharge.[42]

---

[34] For the proviso for redemption, see *ante*, p. 311.
[35] Law of Property Act 1925, s. 95.
[36] *Ibid.* subs. (3).
[37] Law of Property Act 1925, s. 115 (2) (3).
[38] *Simpson* v. *Geoghegan, supra.*
[39] See (1971) 68 L.S.Gaz. 175.
[40] Law of Property Act 1925, s. 115 (2).
[41] See *Pyke* v. *Peters* [1943] K.B. 242; *Cumberland Court (Brighton) Ltd.* v. *Taylor* [1964] Ch. 29.
[42] See *Parkash* v. *Irani Finance Ltd.* [1970] Ch. 101.

Building society receipts

A building society mortgage may be discharged either under section 115 of the Law of Property Act 1925 [43] or under section 37 of the Building Societies Act 1962. The principal difference between the two forms is that under the Law of Property Act, but not under the Building Societies Act, the receipt must state the name of the person who pays the money. Consequently, a statutory receipt under the Building Societies Act cannot operate as a transfer. Subsection (4) (which allows the mortgagor to require a reassignment, etc.) and subsection (7) (which, if the appropriate references are made, allows only one receipt where there is a mortgage and further charge or several deeds) of section 115 of the Law of Property Act do not apply to a statutory receipt in the Building Societies Act form.

Discharge of registered charge

A registered charge is discharged by notification on the register.[44] The prescribed form (Form 53) of discharge should be used,[45] but a statutory receipt under the Law of Property Act 1925, the Building Societies Act 1962 and the Small Dwellings Acquisition Acts 1899 to 1923 will be accepted. Application for cancellation should then be made to the appropriate District Land Registry under the appropriate application cover accompanied by the form of discharge or other proof of satisfaction and by the relevant charge certificate.[46] The entry of the charge on the register will be cancelled, as also will the charge certificate, if all the land to which it relates is discharged from the charge. Mortgages in unregistered form are discharged by statutory receipt in the usual way. In other cases the discharge should be in Form 53, save where a mortgage existing at the time of first registration has been noted on the register, when Form 53 is not applicable. Cautions may be withdrawn,[47] and a notice of deposit will be withdrawn on a written request or consent signed by the person entitled to the lien.[48]

Discharge of equitable mortgages

Statutory receipt is inapplicable. If the mortgaged property has been assigned, the mortgage is discharged by reassignment. In other cases a simple receipt or mere cancellation of any document or redelivery of deeds suffices. If only part of equitably mortgaged property is to be discharged, a letter from the mortgagee stating that he has no charge on the property released is normally acceptable.[49]

---

[43] See subs. (9). The receipt must be under seal.
[44] The Law of Property Act 1925, s. 115, does not apply: subs. (10).
[45] See *post*, p. 436.
[46] Land Registration Rules 1925, rr. 151, 152.
[47] *Ibid.* r. 68; in Form 16.
[48] *Ibid.* r. 246; Form 86.
[49] But see (1962) 26 Conv.(N.S.) 449–453.

Reassignment of life policies

A statutory receipt may be used to reassign a life policy which is the subject of a formal mortgage, and even a simple receipt is acceptable. However, the printed forms of mortgages of policies used by those who accept such security usually provide for reassignment. Notice of discharge should be given to the insurance company. An equitable mortgage of a policy may be discharged by redelivery and cancellation of any memorandum.

Discharge of sub-mortgages

A legal sub-mortgage is usually discharged by statutory receipt. An informal sub-mortgage is discharged by redelivery and cancellation of any memorandum. Notice of discharge should be given to the mortgagor under the principal mortgage.

Mortgagor's right to return of title deeds

On payment off of the mortgage, the mortgagor is entitled to have the deeds returned to him by the mortgagee.[50] If the rights of the *mortgagee* have become statute-barred, the mortgagor is entitled to demand the deeds from the mortgagee without repayment of the mortgage money.[51]

VIII. USE OF MORTGAGES

Generally

The economic role of mortgages has changed over the past century. The traditional mortgage (which is well described in many nineteenth-century novels) was by a landowner of his estate to raise capital for development or living expenses. The typical mortgage today is by the owner of a dwelling-house of that house to a building society.

The basic principles of the law of mortgages have not changed, however, and have shown themselves capable of dealing with the changed position of mortgagors and mortgagees.[52] The general trend has been to protect the mortgagor; and all the more so now that the usual mortgagor is a person giving his home as security.[53]

Mortgages of land now play an important part in the consumer credit field (the outstanding mortgage debt in 1969 was nearly £11,000 millions, which is by far the largest credit debt).[54] Mortgages also play an important part in property development.

House purchase

Even if the purchaser could pay cash for his house, it will generally

[50] *Rourke* v. *Robinson* [1911] 1 Ch. 480.
[51] *Lewis* v. *Plunket* [1937] Ch. 306.
[52] See *e.g. Cityland and Property (Holdings) Ltd.* v. *Dabrah* [1968] Ch. 166.
[53] See *e.g.* Administration of Justice Act 1970, s. 36.
[54] See Crowther Report, paras. 1. 1. 5–6, Table 2. 11, and generally.

be more advantageous for him to raise the purchase-money by an advance on mortgage. The reason for this is that the interest payable under the mortgage is deducted in estimating a person's total income for tax purposes. The higher the purchaser's income, the greater the tax relief obtainable. The bigger the loan, the bigger the relief. The effective rate of interest payable under the mortgage is therefore reduced. The purchaser will be able either to invest any free cash (which otherwise he would have spent in the purchase of the house) or use this for other purposes.[55]

Consumer credit

This advantage of tax relief, to some extent at least, also explains the great increase in second mortgages in the past decade.[56] There was a ready market for money-lending to persons wanting to obtain loans for new cars, yachts, or consumer goods, who were prepared to mortgage their houses, whether by way of first or second mortgage, for this purpose. Tax relief was available on the interest payable under the mortgage, but not on hire-purchase interest.

Restrictions on tax relief

The 1969 Finance Act made major changes in the law allowing interest as a deduction in calculating a person's taxable income. The general rule was that such deduction was no longer allowed, except in certain specified cases.[57] The principal exceptions were the purchase of a house or land and the improvement of a house or land.[58] In the usual case of a mortgage to enable the purchaser of a dwelling-house to raise the purchase-money, relief continued to be allowed in respect of the interest paid under the mortgage or any collateral mortgage but the 1972 Finance Bill restores the right to relief as it existed before 1969, subject to the disallowance of the first £35 where the loan was not for the purchase or improvement of a house, etc.

Endowment mortgages

Under this type of mortgage the principal is left outstanding until the end of the mortgage term when the principal is paid off in a single sum from the proceeds of an endowment policy taken out by the mortgagor on his own life and for a term equal to the mortgage term. The mortgagor is entitled to tax relief on his policy premiums[59] and

---

[55] It was this advantage, enjoyed by a mortgagor who paid tax at the standard rate, which led to the option mortgage scheme (as to this, see *ante*, p. 307).

[56] See *ante*, p. 327.

[57] Finance Act 1969, ss. 19 *et seq.*, now replaced by the Income and Corporation Taxes Act 1970, ss. 57 *et seq.* For building society mortgage interest, see I.C.T.A. 1970, s. 343. Tax relief on overdraft interest is only available for three years after the loan: I.C.T.A. 1970, s. 57 (1).

[58] Income and Corporation Taxes Act 1970, s. 57.

[59] Income and Corporation Taxes Act 1970, s. 19.

his mortgage interest and if, as is usually the case, the policy is a "with profits" one, there should be a substantial surplus over the principal at the end of the term.[60]

Investment property

Mortgages also play a part in investment in real estate. An entrepreneur who pays cash for his properties is going to be restricted in expansion by lack of capital. He should really make use of the policy of high gearing, *i.e.* he should maximise the mortgage potential of his properties. Buying properties with the aid of a mortgage will give the purchaser more ready cash for deposits on other properties. The mortgage interest can be offset against profits. If the value of the property increases, the owner will probably be able to raise more money on the security of the property for further acquisitions.

Large profits have been made out of the purchase of blocks of offices and flats with little outlay by the owners. For example, a block of shops and offices was acquired in 1962 for £72,000. A mortgage for £55,000 was arranged, so the purchaser's actual cash outlay was £17,000. The cost of the mortgage and maintenance of the property was £4,398 and the rents were £5,480, so the block showed a net return of £1,082 or 6·4 per cent. on the purchaser's cash outlay of £17,000. That in itself is not a particularly attractive investment. But over the years the rents were increased and in 1965 the gross rental was £9,026. The same year the block was revalued at £115,000. A new mortgage for £76,000 was obtained, the original mortgage was paid off, and £21,000 cash was released. The original cash investment of £17,000 was therefore recovered in four years and the purchaser had a further £4,000 in hand. Moreover, he had an equity in the block amounting to £39,000.[61]

Debentures

Large public companies generally raise funds for expansion or development by the issue of debentures or debenture stock.[62] Often these are quoted securities and they are a popular form of investment for pension funds, insurance companies, and other institutional investors. Provision is usually made for repayment on a specified date and interest is paid on the debentures at a fixed rate. Capital acquired by the issue of debentures is called loan capital. Loan capital has advantages both from the point of view of the holders of the equity share capital [63] and the company; and loan capital has to some extent

---

[60] See generally *e.g.* (1971) 219 *Estates Gazette* 1112.
[61] See the "Insight" article in *The Sunday Times*, November 8, 1970.
[62] See *ante*, p. 301.
[63] As it introduces an element of "gearing," *supra*, into the capital structure of the company. If the gross profits of the company increase and the liability for interest is fixed, the proportion of the profits available for stockholders increases.

superseded preference share capital, since the dividends payable on preference shares are not deductible for corporation tax purposes, whereas interest on loan capital is usually deductible.[64]

IX. Obtaining the Mortgage

Assisting the purchaser with his mortgage arrangements is now one of the tasks of a solicitor acting for a purchaser.[65] In some cases, of course, the purchaser will be able to arrange a mortgage on his own, but in many cases the solicitor will be able to help, if only by assisting the purchaser to complete a mortgage application form. In some cases, because of the circumstances, for example, the age of the property or of the purchaser, a building society advance may not be available, in which case the solicitor will often be able to assist by arranging a private mortgage or putting the purchaser in touch with the local authority or some insurance or mortgage company or broker. If the purchaser is selling his own house a *bridging loan* from a bank (*i.e.* a temporary loan to be repaid out of the proceeds of sale) may be obtainable, once contracts for the sale of the purchaser's house have been exchanged.

Contracts should not be exchanged until the purchaser has an effective offer of an advance. In the past, contracts were sometimes made subject to finance,[66] but this practice seems to have died out with the increase of building society mortgages.

[64] For sale and lease-back as a manner of raising capital, see *ante*, p. 270. For the importance of pension funds in property investment, see (1971) 219 E.G. 939.
[65] See Moeran, *Practical Conveyancing*, pp. 18 *et seq.*
[66] *Ante*, p. 14, note 64.

Chapter 13

SETTLEMENTS: GENERAL CONSIDERATIONS

I. Settlements of Land [1]

There are two ways of settling land, that is, of creating successive interests in land. First, there is the strict settlement, often referred to simply as a settlement. Secondly, there is the trust for sale.

Strict settlements

The strict settlement was created as a means of tying up land in a family indefinitely, as where land was granted to a person for life, with remainder to his first son in tail, the settlement containing complicated provisions for the benefit of the life-tenant's wife and younger children. Formerly when land was settled there was no one who could deal with it freely by way of sale, mortgage, lease and so on, with the serious consequence that there was no means of dealing with the land for the purpose of raising money for its cultivation, improvement or repair. Accordingly, express powers were often conferred by the settlement on the tenant for life. Thus, he was sometimes enabled to sell the fee simple estate in all or part of the land, the purchase-money being handed to trustees and the beneficial interests of himself and others under the settlement being overreached, thus becoming attached to the money instead of the land. Nevertheless, many settlements did not contain such powers, with the result that in the early part of the nineteenth century great quantities of settled land were in a state of deterioration for want of cultivation and repair.

It was the legislature which rectified this state of affairs by giving certain statutory powers of dealing with settled land in the course of the nineteenth century. The most important statute was the Settled Land Act 1882, which had the object of rendering settled land alienable, and this was done by giving to the tenant for life statutory powers of dealing with the land, as by sale, mortgage or lease. If he sold the land, a purchaser took free from the trusts of the settlement, which were overreached. These powers were given not only to a tenant for life proper but also to others, such as a tenant in tail.

Trusts for sale

Trusts for sale began to become popular in the second half of the

[1] See Megarry and Wade, *The Law of Real Property* (3rd ed.), pp. 287–303; Thompson, *English Landed Society in the Nineteenth Century.*

342

nineteenth century. Whereas the object of the strict settlement was to tie up land indefinitely in the eldest male branch of the family, the trust for sale was a convenient means of providing for investments, which could be changed at opportune moments, with no idea of keeping property tied up, and this was so even though the trustees usually had power to postpone sale, so that the original property might in fact be retained for some time; further, the beneficial interests of trusts for sale, which were often created on marriage, would usually be for the husband for life, then for the wife for life, then for the issue of the marriage, so that there was no leaning in favour of an eldest son. Because the trust for sale placed no emphasis on the wish to retain a particular piece of land, and because of its resultant flexibility, it was especially useful for providing for the investment of funds made in business, and hence was sometimes called a " trader's settlement."

In the case of a trust for sale, the land (or other property) is vested in trustees, who hold it upon trust to sell it and invest the purchase money. The property until sale and the investments after sale are to be held on trust for certain people.

The 1925 legislation

The Settled Land Act 1925 repealed the Act of 1882, but retained its basic scheme subject to certain important amendments. For instance, whereas before 1926 the legal fee simple estate was vested in trustees for the beneficiaries or else the beneficiaries themselves had successive legal estates, such as life estates or entails, after 1925 the legal fee simple is vested in the tenant for life, or, in some cases, the statutory owner [2] on trust for the beneficiaries including the tenant for life himself: legal life estates and entails can, of course, no longer exist.[3] Again, certain amendments were made to trusts for sale by the legislation of 1925. Thus, for example, the Law of Property Act 1925 imposes trusts for sale in certain cases where they had not operated before 1926, as in the case of co-ownership of land.[4]

Differences

Strict settlements differ from trusts for sale in the following important respects. First, the legal estate in settled land is vested in the tenant for life or statutory owner, whereas the legal estate in land settled upon trust for sale is vested in the trustees. Secondly, the powers of dealing with settled land belong to the tenant for life or statutory owner, whereas the powers of dealing with land upon trust for sale belong to the trustees. Finally, strict settlements are regulated by

[2] See *post,* p. 355.
[3] Law of Property Act 1925, s. 1.
[4] Law of Property Act 1925, ss. 34–36.

the Settled Land Act 1925, whereas trusts for sale are excluded from its operation [5] and fall within the Law of Property Act 1925.

Comparative advantages [6]

Land can now be settled, therefore, either by strict settlement or by trust for sale. Which method is chosen will depend on the circumstances. The principal advantage of a strict settlement is that the tenant for life controls the property and this may well be desirable in the case of a large landed estate. However, this situation is less likely to arise now than it was in and before the nineteenth century. The advantages of the trust for sale over the strict settlement have brought about the result that a strict settlement will in general only be encountered nowadays in two situations. The first is where the settlement was created in or before the early part of this century and is still subsisting. The second is where it is a new settlement but has been created inadvertently, as in the case of a testator leaving his house to his wife for her life and then to his children; the complicated procedure of the Settled Land Act, which is entirely unsuitable, is thus invoked, and a cheaper, simpler and more appropriate course would be in such a case to devise the house upon trust for sale. Nevertheless, because of the two situations just mentioned, strict settlements are still encountered by the conveyancer and it is necessary to understand the operation of such settlements.

The main advantages of a trust for sale are as follows:

(a) Nowadays a settlor is more likely to wish to provide benefits for his children equally than to constitute his eldest son the main beneficiary and his younger children lesser beneficiaries. The trust for sale is more appropriate in the former case, for concurrent interests can be given to all the children. It is true that joint tenants for life sometimes exist but the idea behind strict settlements is to invest one person with power to deal with the land; and where those entitled for life are entitled as tenants in common (as opposed to joint tenants) a trust for sale arises anyhow.[7]

(b) If it is desired to control future dealings with the land, a trust for sale is more appropriate. In the case of a strict settlement, it is not possible to create fetters on the tenant for life's exercise of his powers such as his power of sale.[8] But in the case of a trust for sale a stipulation that some person or persons must first consent to a sale may be imposed. Thus, if the consent of the beneficiaries is made necessary before a sale can be made, the settlor ensures that the beneficiaries

[5] Settled Land Act 1925, s. 1 (7), which was added by Law of Property (Amendment) Act 1926.
[6] See (1938) 85 L.J. Newspaper, 355; 54 L.Q.R. 576; (1944) 8 Conv.(N.S.) 147; [1957] C.L.P. 152; [1962] C.L.P. 194; Megarry and Wade, pp. 392–393; Hanbury's *Modern Equity* (9th ed.), pp. 523–527.
[7] Settled Land Act 1925, s. 36.
[8] Settled Land Act 1925, s. 106; see *post*, p. 365.

can decide whether to retain the property as land or to convert it (actually, as well as notionally) into money. It may even be that land held subject to a trust for sale can be rendered inalienable, as where the trustees are only to sell with the concurrence of a person who can only benefit under the trust if the land is not sold when the beneficiary entitled for life dies.[9]

(c) The trust for sale can be used to create a discretionary trust. A discretionary trust can exist under a strict settlement, but this is unlikely. The discretionary trust has become increasingly popular during this century, as an alternative to the traditional fixed trust where property is settled on trust for successive life beneficiaries. Discretionary trusts are discussed shortly. It is true that, where the property settled is personalty, the trust for sale is sometimes dispensed with and there is a straightforward discretionary trust, but if the property settled is land there will be a trust for sale, the rents and profits until sale and the proceeds of sale being subjected to the discretionary trust.

(d) A trust for sale can be used to settle personalty, such as shares in a company, or land, or both together, whereas a strict settlement relates only to land. Since the trend is to settle personalty rather than land nowadays, this is an important consideration.

II. TRUSTS OF PERSONALTY

Hitherto we have dealt mainly with settlements of land. Settlements are now more commonly made of personalty, such as cash or shares in companies. In this case, the strict settlement is of course irrelevant, for that only applies to land. There are various ways of settling personalty. For example, there may be a trust for sale, as where the fund consists of residuary estate settled by a will (which may include both land and personalty) combined with a fixed trust for successive life beneficiaries or alternatively with a discretionary trust. Again, as where shares are settled *inter vivos*, the trust for sale may be dispensed with, and there may be a straightforward fixed trust for successive life beneficiaries or alternatively a straightforward discretionary trust.

III. DISCRETIONARY TRUSTS AND PROTECTIVE TRUSTS [10]

Many trusts, at any rate if they comprise substantial assets, are now created as discretionary trusts. Here, the trustees hold the property on trust to exercise their discretion in paying the income of the fund or appointing the capital of the fund in favour of such of the discretionary objects (the beneficiaries) as they decide. The trustees may be bound

---

[9] See *Re Inns* [1947] Ch. 576 at p. 582. It should be borne in mind that if any requisite consent cannot be obtained, any person interested may apply to the court, which has power to render needless such consent, as where consent is refused: Law of Property Act 1925, s. 30; *Re Beale's S.T.* [1932] 2 Ch. 15.

[10] See (1957) 21 Conv.(N.S.) 55, 110, 323; Hanbury's *Modern Equity* (9th ed.), Chap. 10; Snell's *Principles of Equity* (26th ed.), pp. 147–152; and *post*, pp. 372 and 381.

to pay or appoint, but have a discretion as to which of the beneficiaries is or are to benefit; here the trustees must exercise their discretion in favour of one or some of the beneficiaries. Or the trustees may be empowered to pay or appoint to whom, if any, of the beneficiaries they may choose, and to accumulate any income not distributed; here, they need not benefit anyone.[11] In either case no particular beneficiary is entitled to any interest in any income or capital but only has a hope of receiving it, and this is the principal feature of the discretionary trust.

The main attraction of the discretionary trust lies in the considerable fiscal advantages, which will be discussed shortly.[12] Another attraction is the flexibility of such a trust. Under a fixed trust the beneficiary or beneficiaries are generally entitled for life and, of course, their circumstances can change considerably during that time. There may be times when income from the trust merely increases their surtax liability. Under a discretionary trust the trustees can pay income when and to whom it is needed. It follows that the extravagance of any beneficiary can be curbed simply by the trustees deciding not to give him anything out of the settled funds. A further advantage is that if a beneficiary becomes bankrupt the trust assets are not put in jeopardy, for nothing can be claimed by his trustee in bankruptcy. This aspect requires a little introduction. If a beneficiary under a fixed trust becomes bankrupt, his interest will, in the normal course of events, pass to his trustee in bankruptcy. The draftsman should seek to avoid this by providing for the determination of his interest on his bankruptcy. Equally, the settlor may wish to restrain a beneficiary from alienating his interest by providing for its determination upon an attempt to alienate.

The first point to note is that a *condition* prohibiting alienation or a *condition* that the beneficiary's interest is to cease on bankruptcy is void.[13] But if an interest is given *until* alienation is attempted or *until* bankruptcy, the limitation is valid and the interest will determine if the beneficiary attempts to alienate or becomes bankrupt, and so in the latter case the claim of his trustee in bankruptcy is defeated.[14] The distinction is artificial, depending on the language used. The draftsman should take care to use such words as " until," when the determinable limitation will be valid, and not to use such words as " on condition that." [15] Moreover, even if the correct words are used, it is important to note that a person cannot settle *his own* property on himself until he becomes bankrupt (as where he gives himself an interest for

---

[11] See *Gartside* v. *I.R.C.* [1968] A.C. 553; *Sainsbury* v. *I.R.C.* [1970] Ch. 712.

[12] See *post*, pp. 348–349.

[13] See *Brandon* v. *Robinson* (1811) 18 Ves. 429; *Rochford* v. *Hackman* (1852) 9 Hare 475.

[14] See *Brandon* v. *Robinson, supra*; *Rochford* v. *Hackman, supra*; *Ex p. Cooke* (1803) 8 Ves. 353.

[15] See Megarry and Wade, pp. 75–78.

life or until he becomes bankrupt), for such a disposition would be a fraud on the bankruptcy law,[16] and on his bankruptcy his interest would pass to his trustee in bankruptcy.[17] But this last rule only applies to bankruptcy, and there is no objection to a person settling his own property on himself for life and making his life interest determinable if he attempts to alienate.[18] Nevertheless, because that rule applies in the case of bankruptcy, it reduces the attraction of using the device of a determinable interest where a settlor settles his own property on himself for life, though such a device is useful where the settlor settles property on someone else.

The above is the position where the settlement adopts fixed trusts, such as successive life interests. But if there is instead a discretionary trust, if a beneficiary purports to assign his interest or becomes bankrupt the assignee or trustee in bankruptcy is entitled to nothing from the trust, for the beneficiary himself was entitled to nothing, and this is so even if the beneficiary was himself the settlor.[19] But if the trustees actually pay money to a beneficiary, it seems that his assignee or trustee in bankruptcy is entitled to such money.[20]

Alternatively, a protective trust[21] may be created. This consists of a determinable fixed trust where the principal beneficiary's life interest is determinable if he attempts to alienate or becomes bankrupt or something else happens to deprive him of the income of the fund, when a discretionary trust comes into being, in favour of the principal beneficiary and, usually, his wife and issue. Under section 33 of the Trustee Act 1925, where income is directed to be held on protective trusts for the benefit of any person for the period of his life or for any less period, then the protective trusts set out in that section are imported; this is the usual practice, though it is possible to set out the protective trusts expressly. However, it is expressly provided that nothing in section 33 operates to validate any trust which would, if contained in the instrument creating the trust, be liable to be set aside[22]: hence, the statutory protective trusts should not be invoked where a person settles *his own* property on himself, for on his bankruptcy his interest would vest in his trustee in bankruptcy.[23] Protective trusts are not so common nowadays, the modern trust being more likely to be a straightforward discretionary trust without the prior determinable life interest.

There are thus considerable advantages inherent in the discretionary trust, but there is the disadvantage that the settlor bestows control of the property and the right to decide whom to benefit on the trustees;

[16] *Higinbotham* v. *Holme* (1811) 19 Ves. 87.
[17] *Re Burroughs-Fowler* [1916] 2 Ch. 251.
[18] *Brooke* v. *Pearson* (1859) 27 Beav. 181.
[19] See *Holmes* v. *Penney* (1856) 3 K. & J. 90.
[20] *Re Coleman* (1888) 39 Ch.D. 443. See, however, *Re Ashby* [1892] 1 Q.B. 872.
[21] For series of protective trusts, see (1958) 74 L.Q.R. 182.
[22] Trustee Act 1925. s. 33 (3).
[23] See *supra*, notes 16 and 17.

and, though he may indicate his hopes as to the mode of operation of the trust and though such hopes will usually be followed in practice, the trustees may ignore the settlor's wishes if they choose to do so.

IV. TAXATION

Before the various forms of settlement are considered further in the next two chapters, some aspects of the element of taxation will be briefly discussed. This is a very important topic, especially in the case of large settlements, and is one with which the draftsman must be familiar if he is to save tax for the beneficiaries. Some examples of the tax implications are as follows.[24]

Estate duty [25]

One way of saving estate duty is for a person to give away his property in his lifetime, so that it cannot pass on his death. The gift may be outright or by way of settlement, but duty will be chargeable if certain conditions are not fulfilled.[26] The more important of these conditions are as follows. Assuming the property is being settled, if duty is to be avoided the settlor must transfer the property to the trustees at least seven years before he dies, though if he dies in the fifth, sixth or seventh year from the transfer the amount of duty payable decreases progressively.[27] Again, the settlor must be entirely excluded from the property settled and from any benefit by contract or otherwise. For example, if the settlor is a trustee and is entitled to remuneration for his services, he is not excluded from benefit.[28] Thus, the draftsman should ensure that the settlor cannot possibly receive any benefit, for example by expressly providing that no power (such as a power of appointment) can be exercised in the settlor's favour and by providing that the settlor is to receive no remuneration as a trustee.

The above comments relate to estate duty on the death of the *settlor*. We shall now consider duty on the deaths of the *beneficiaries* under the trust.[29] Briefly, if at any time during the seven years before his death the deceased was entitled to a beneficial interest in possession in settled property, there is a passing on his death; thus, for example, if the deceased was entitled at the date of his death to the income of the whole trust fund, the whole fund passes on his death and is dutiable;

---

24 It will be appreciated that only a bare outline of some of the points involved can be given here.

25 See Pinson, *Revenue Law* (5th ed.), Chaps. 22 and 23.

26 Finance Act 1894, s. 2 (1) (c).

27 In the case of a gift made for charitable or public purposes, the settlor need only survive one year for all duty to be avoided.

28 *Oakes* v. *Commissioner of Stamp Duties of New South Wales* [1954] A.C. 57.

29 Finance Act 1894, s. 2 (1) (b), as substituted by Finance Act 1969, s. 36; s. 2 (1) (b) (iv) rarely applies; s. 2 (1) (b) (ii) is omitted from the discussion in an attempt to keep the text brief yet clear.

if at the date of death he was entitled to half the income, a " slice " equal to half the property in the trust fund passes.[30]

It will be noticed that if the settlor gives successive life interests in the whole fund, on each successive death the whole fund falls to be charged to duty. That was the position before 1969 and still is. Before 1969, the discretionary trust was used to avoid this situation. Whether or not the trustees had to distribute income or had power to accumulate,[31] no particular beneficiary had any interest in the trust fund, so that when an individual beneficiary died there was no passing for estate duty purposes. This was one of the principal attractions of the discretionary trust, though there was a passing [32] if the trust ended on a death, as where the last of the beneficiaries died.

In respect of deaths after April 15, 1969, there is a new mode of charging duty in the case of discretionary trusts, and such mode applies to the death of any beneficiary.[33] Briefly, where the deceased was immediately before his death eligible to benefit as a result of the discretion and he has so benefited at any time during the period of seven years before his death, duty is payable on his death. The property passing is that part of the trust fund which bears to the whole fund the same proportion as the income of the fund paid to the deceased during the seven years before his death bears to the whole of the income of the fund arising in that period.[34] This provision has to some extent curbed the attractive features of the discretionary trust, but it still has considerable fiscal advantages over a fixed trust if it is carefully administered.[35]

Income tax and surtax

Just as one of the objects of settling property *inter vivos* may be to take it out of the settlor's estate for estate duty purposes, another object may be to prevent the income of the property being subjected to income tax and surtax in his hands by giving the income to beneficiaries (such as his children) under the settlement. But in certain circumstances the income is nevertheless treated as that of the settlor.[36] For example, if a settlement is revocable, the income of the fund is treated as the settlor's. This occurs, *inter alia*, if any person has power to revoke the settlement and thereupon the settlor or his or her spouse may become entitled to any property in the trust fund or any income thereof.[37] Because this provision is wide-ranging, it is advisable to provide expressly that no power or discretion conferred

---

[30] Finance Act 1969, s. 37 (1) (*b*).
[31] See *Gartside* v. *I.R.C.* [1968] A.C. 553; *Sainsbury* v. *I.R.C.* [1970] Ch. 712.
[32] Under Finance Act 1894, s. 1: see *e.g. Scott and Coutts and Co.* v. *I.R.C.* [1937] A.C. 174; *Burrell and Kinnaird* v. *Att.-Gen.* [1937] A.C. 286.
[33] Finance Act 1969, s. 36; the substituted s. 2 (1) (*b*) (iii).
[34] Finance Act 1969, s. 37 (3).
[35] See Potter and Monroe, *Tax Planning* (6th ed.), pp. 153 *et seq.*
[36] See Pinson, *Revenue Law* (5th ed.), Chap. 10.
[37] Income and Corporation Taxes Act 1970, s. 445.

on the trustees by the settlement or by law shall ever be exercisable for the benefit of the settlor or any spouse of the settlor or shall operate so as to permit any payment to the settlor or any spouse of the settlor.

CHAPTER 14

STRICT SETTLEMENTS

THIS chapter contains a brief discussion of those provisions of the Settled Land Act 1925 which are likely to be of concern to the conveyancer today, such as the tenant for life's power to sell, but it does not deal with such matters as the trusts of a strict settlement.[1] The reasons for this latter omission are, first, that the ordinary practitioner is today unlikely, for reasons mentioned above,[2] to have to draft the trusts of a strict settlement and, secondly, that where he comes across an already existing strict settlement, the beneficial interests do not generally concern him.[3]

I. MEANING OF "SETTLEMENT"

"Settlement"

A settlement exists in each of the following situations[4]:

(a) Where land stands limited in trust for any persons by way of succession. This is the most common case. An example is where land stands limited to A for life, with remainder to B for life, with remainder to C absolutely.

(b) Where land stands limited in trust for any person in possession for an entailed interest whether or not capable of being barred or defeated. For example, if A is tenant in tail in possession he can deal with the fee simple as tenant for life and so overreach his equitable interest and the equitable interests of all other persons interested in the entail: by then barring the entail, he would become entitled to the purchase-money absolutely. Alternatively, he could bar the entail first and then sell the land as beneficial owner.

(c) Where land stands limited in trust for any person in possession for an estate in fee simple or for a term of years absolute subject to an executory disposition over. An example is where land is held by A and B on trust for C in fee simple but for D in fee simple if D marries.

(d) Where land stands limited in trust for any person in possession for a base or determinable fee or any corresponding interest in leasehold land. Thus, if land is held upon trust for A for life, with

---

[1] For the typical trusts of a strict settlement, resettlements, compound settlements, *ad hoc* settlements and *ad hoc* trusts for sale, see Megarry and Wade, *The Law of Real Property* (3rd ed.), pp. 303 *et seq.*: none of these topics is dealt with here. For registered land, see *ante*, p. 179.
[2] See *ante*, pp. 344, 345.
[3] See *post*, pp. 362, 363.
[4] Settled Land Act 1925, s. 1 (1). The situation in s. 1 (1) (iv) cannot exist since 1949: Married Women (Restraint upon Anticipation) Act 1949.

remainder to B in tail, and B disentails without the consent of A as
protector, and so creates a base fee, on A's death B could sell the
fee simple as tenant for life and so overreach his own equitable interest
and the equitable interest of the remainderman, or he could enlarge
the base fee into a fee simple and sell as beneficial owner.

It will be noticed that in cases (b) to (d) above the land is in fact
" limited in trust for any persons by way of succession " within (a)
above: nevertheless the Act assigns separate headings to these three
cases, though unnecessarily.

(e) Where land stands limited in trust for a minor in possession
for an estate in fee simple or for a term of years absolute. After 1925
a legal estate cannot be vested in a minor.[5] Where a minor is
entitled to land the land is thereby settled land, but the minor is not
a tenant for life or a person with the powers of a tenant for life under
the Act. In such a case the powers of a tenant for life are usually
vested in the trustees of the settlement, who in such circumstances are
called the statutory owner.[6]

(f) Where land stands limited in trust for any person for an estate
in fee simple or for a term of years absolute contingently on the
happening of any event. An example is where land is held upon
trust for A if and when he marries. In the meantime there is a
settlement and the statutory owner[6] can deal with the land. A, being
only contingently entitled, does not have the powers of a tenant for
life.[7]

(g) Where land stands charged whether voluntarily or in consideration of marriage or by way of family arrangement, with the payment of
any rentcharge for the life of any person, or any less period, or of any
periodical sums for the benefit of any persons. For example, the land
might be subject to a jointure rentcharge which secures an annuity to
the wife of the tenant for life for her life if he dies before her. When
land is subject to a rentcharge of the kind just defined, a person
beneficially entitled to the land for an estate in fee simple or for a
term of years absolute subject to the charge has the powers of a
tenant for life.[8] When the land is sold the interest of the rentchargee
will be overreached. However, the person who has the powers of a
tenant for life in such cases need not treat the land as settled land and
sell as tenant for life but may sell the land as absolute owner subject
to the rentcharge, which will continue to attach to the land in the
purchaser's hands.[9] This convenient provision avoids the necessity
of appointing trustees, executing a vesting instrument and so forth
for the purpose of a sale under the Settled Land Act, in a case where

[5] Law of Property Act 1925, s. 1 (6). And see Family Law Reform Act 1969, s. 1.
[6] See *post*, p. 355.
[7] See S.L.A. 1925, s. 20. The Settled Land Act is referred to as " S.L.A." for the
rest of this chapter.
[8] S.L.A. 1925, s. 20 (1) (ix).
[9] Law of Property (Amendment) Act 1926, s. 1.

the purchaser is willing to purchase subject to the charge. It should be noted that not every rentcharge on land gives rise to a settlement under this paragraph: it is only when the rentcharge is created voluntarily or in consideration of marriage or by way of family arrangement. In any other case, as where a rentcharge is created for money or money's worth, its existence will not result in a settlement. In such a case the owner of the land can sell subject to the rentcharge but cannot overreach it by selling as a tenant for life.[10]

" Settled land "

Land which is the subject of a settlement is called settled land.[11] Thus, for example, land limited for persons in succession or land held in trust for a minor is settled land, provided always that there is no trust for sale, trusts for sale being excluded from the provisions of the Settled Land Act 1925.[12] Settled land may comprise either settled freeholds or settled leaseholds: in the latter case, which is less common than the former, the tenant for life can sell the lease under his statutory power of sale but he cannot sell the freehold reversion.

Duration of the settlement

Once land has become settled land, the settlement will continue to subsist and the land will remain settled land so long as any limitation, charge or power of charging under the settlement subsists or is capable of being exercised or, even in the absence of these, so long as the person who, if of full age, would be entitled as beneficial owner to have the land vested in him for a legal estate is a minor[13] and, in either case, so long as the land is not held on trust for sale.[14]

II.   MEANING OF " TENANT FOR LIFE " AND " STATUTORY OWNER "

" Tenant for life "

Under section 19 of the Settled Land Act 1925, a person of full age who is beneficially entitled under a settlement to possession of settled land for his life, as where land stands limited in trust for A for life, with remainder to B in tail, is the tenant for life of that land. This raises no difficulty.

In addition, the expression " tenant for life " includes anyone (except a statutory owner) who has the powers of a tenant for life under the Act.[15] Such persons are enumerated in section 20, which provides that each of the following persons who is of full age shall,

---

[10] Unless he first creates an *ad hoc* trust for sale or settlement: see *ante*, p. 351, n. (1).
[11] S.L.A. 1925, s. 2.
[12] S.L.A. 1925, s. 1 (7) (added by Law of Property (Amendment) Act 1926, Sched.).
[13] S.L.A. 1925, s. 3.
[14] Law of Property (Amendment) Act 1926, Sched. See *supra*.
[15] S.L.A. 1925, s. 117 (1) (xxviii).

when his estate or interest is in possession, have the powers of a tenant for life [16]:

   (a) A tenant in tail.

   (b) A person entitled to land for an estate in fee simple or for a term of years absolute subject to an executory limitation over, as where land is held by trustees for A in fee simple but for B in fee simple if B marries.

   (c) A person entitled to a base fee [17] or a determinable fee (as where land is granted to A in fee simple until Westminster Abbey falls down).

   (d) A tenant for years determinable on life, not holding merely under a lease at a rent. This provision applies only where the term in question takes effect under a settlement, as where land is demised to A for fifty years or until his earlier death. It has already been seen [18] that if a lease at a rent is granted to A for a term of years determinable on his death he will get a term of ninety years.[19]

   (e) A tenant for the life of another, that is, a tenant *pur autre vie*.

   (f) A tenant for his own or any other life, or for years determinable on life, whose estate is liable to cease in any event during that life, or is subject to a trust for accumulation of income. For example, if land is limited to A for life, but his enjoyment of the land is suspended during a trust for accumulation of income, A has the powers of a tenant for life, notwithstanding the trust for accumulation.[20]

   (g) A tenant by the curtesy.[21]

   (h) A person entitled to the income of land under a trust or direction for payment thereof to him during his own or any other life, or until sale of the land, or until forfeiture, cesser or determination of his interest by any means, unless the land is subject to an immediate binding trust for sale. This provides for the case where a person is entitled to the income of land, as opposed to the enjoyment of the land itself: such a person has the powers of a tenant for life. However, this provision does not apply to a person who is entitled only to a defined *part* of the income [22] and not the whole or to a discretionary beneficiary [23]: such persons cannot exercise the powers of a tenant for life.

---

[16] The situation in s. 20 (1) (x) cannot exist now: Married Women (Restraint upon Anticipation) Act 1949.
[17] See *ante*, p. 352.
[18] *Ante*, p. 255.
[19] See further *Re Hazle's Settled Estates* (1885) 29 Ch.D. 78; *Re Catling* [1931] 2 Ch. 359.
[20] See *Re Beauchamp* [1914] 1 Ch. 676; *Re Musgrave* [1916] 2 Ch. 417.
[21] For the rare cases where curtesy still exists, see Megarry and Wade, pp. 327–328; 522 *et seq.*
[22] *Re Frewen* [1926] Ch. 580.
[23] *Re Gallenga Will Trusts* [1938] 1 All E.R. 106.

(i) A person beneficially entitled to land for an estate in fee simple or for a term of years absolute subject to any estates, interests, charges, or powers of charging, subsisting or capable of being exercised under a settlement. For example, if A is entitled to land in fee simple subject to a voluntary rentcharge, so that the land is settled,[24] A can deal with the land as tenant for life and so overreach the rentcharge, or, alternatively, he can sell the land subject to the rentcharge.[24]

" Statutory owner "

In all the above cases the person in question has all the powers of a tenant for life and can therefore deal with the land, as by sale or lease. Because such persons are included in the expression " tenant for life," [25] that expression has a wide ambit. Nevertheless, there are certain cases where there is neither a tenant for life (in the narrower sense) within section 19 nor a person with the powers of a tenant for life within section 20. The Act refers to two basic situations where this arises and in such cases the statutory owner has the statutory powers. The two basic situations are as follows:

(i) *Minority of tenant for life*

Where an infant is beneficially entitled in possession to land for an estate in fee simple or for a term of years absolute or would if of full age be a tenant for life or have the powers of a tenant for life, the statutory powers will be exercisable during the minority by a personal representative, if the land is vested in one, or by the trustees of the settlement.[26] Those with the statutory powers are in such a case called the " statutory owner." [27]

(ii) *Lack of tenant for life* [28]

It is, as we have seen, possible that under a settlement there is no tenant for life within section 19 and no person having the powers of a tenant for life within section 20—for example, where land is held upon trust to pay two-thirds of the income thereof to X for life, with a direction to accumulate the other one-third,[29] or where the land is held under a discretionary trust.[30] In such cases the powers of a tenant for

---

[24] See *ante*, p. 352.
[25] Where there are two or more persons of full age who are beneficially entitled under a settlement to possession of settled land as joint tenants, they together constitute the tenant for life and will exercise the statutory powers jointly (S.L.A. 1925, s. 19). But where those entitled are entitled as tenants in common, a trust for sale arises (S.L.A. 1925. s. 36) and so the land is no longer settled land (S.L.A. 1925, s. 1 (7), *ante*, p. 353.
[26] S.L.A. 1925, s. 26.
[27] S.L.A. 1925, s. 117 (1) (xxvi).
[28] For the position where the tenant for life is of unsound mind, see L.P.A. 1925, s. 22 (1), as amended by the Mental Health Act 1959, Sched. 8; for a bankrupt tenant for life, see S.L.A. 1925, ss. 24 and 103.
[29] *Re Frewen* [1926] Ch. 580. See *ante*, p. 354.
[30] *Re Gallenga Will Trusts* [1938] 1 All E.R. 106. See *ante*, p. 354.

life are exercisable by any person of full age on whom such powers are
by the settlement expressed to be conferred or, in the absence (which
is often the case) of such express provision, by the trustees of the
settlement.[31] While such person or the trustees are exercising the
powers of a tenant for life in these circumstances, they are again
called the statutory owner.[27]

III.   THE " TRUSTEES OF THE SETTLEMENT "

The following persons are trustees of the settlement [32]:

   (i) The persons, if any, appointed by the settlement to be trustees
with power to sell the settled land. In fact, the trustees will
be unable to exercise such power because any power conferred
on the trustees or other persons is to be exercisable by the
tenant for life or statutory owner and not by the trustees or
other persons.[33]   But the purported conferring of such power
will constitute such persons the trustees of the settlement.
Thus, if a settlement expressly confers on A and B a power
to sell the settled land and also appoints C and D to be Settled
Land Act trustees, A and B will be the trustees of the settlement and the appointment of C and D will be ineffectual.

  (ii) If there are no persons within (i), the persons, if any, who are
by the settlement declared to be trustees for the purposes of
the Settled Land Act. Since (i) is seldom applicable, and since
trustees are nearly always expressly appointed for the purposes
of the Act, the trustees will usually be found under (ii).

 (iii) If there are no persons within (i) or (ii), the persons, if any,
appointed by the settlement to be trustees with power of or
upon trust for sale of any *other* land comprised in the same
settlement and subject to the same limitations.

 (iv) If there are no persons within (i) to (iii), the persons, if any,
who are under the settlement trustees with *future* power of
sale or under a *future* trust for sale of the settled land.

  (v) If there are no persons within (i) to (iv), the persons, if any,
appointed by deed to be trustees of the settlement by all the
persons who are together able to dispose of the whole equitable
interest in the land.

Where a settlement is created by will, and there are no trustees of
such settlement under (i) to (v) above, the testator's personal representatives are, until other trustees are appointed, trustees of the
settlement.[32] In the case of a referential settlement, where land is
settled upon the same trusts as other land previously settled, if no
trustees of the second settlement are expressly appointed under (ii)

---

[31] S.L.A. 1925, s. 23.
[32] S.L.A. 1925, s. 30.
[33] S.L.A. 1925, s. 108; see *post*, p. 365.

above, the trustees of the first settlement will also be the trustees of the second settlement.[34]   In any case where there are no trustees of the settlement under any of the above provisions, the tenant for life, or statutory owner, or any other person having an estate or interest in the settled land, may apply to the court for the appointment of trustees.[35]

Deed of declaration

Where persons have been appointed trustees of a settlement, they or their successors in office remain such trustees as long as the settlement subsists.[36]   The provisions of the Trustee Act 1925, relating to the appointment of new trustees and to the discharge and retirement of trustees [37] apply to Settled Land Act Trustees.[38]   Wherever a new Settled Land Act trustee is appointed, or one is discharged, a " deed of declaration " must be executed supplemental to the last or only principal vesting instrument,[39] containing a declaration that the persons therein named are now, by reason of the appointment or discharge, the trustees of the settlement and a memorandum of their names and addresses must be indorsed on such principal vesting instrument.[40] This deed of declaration with the memorandum indorsed on the vesting instrument is all that a purchaser from the tenant for life need concern himself with in regard to the appointments and discharges of trustees made after 1925: the purchaser cannot demand to see the instrument whereby the appointment or discharge is effected, and is bound and entitled to rely on the statements contained in the deed of declaration.[41]   Every deed of declaration must, if the trustee was appointed or discharged by the court, be executed by such person as the court may direct, and in any other case must be executed by:

(i) the person, if any, with power under the settlement to appoint new trustees;

(ii) the persons named in the deed of declaration as the trustees of the settlement; and

(iii) any trustee who is discharged or retires.[42]

The duties [43] of the trustees will appear in the course of this chapter.   They include giving consent to the exercise of certain statutory powers [44] and receiving notice of the tenant for life's intention

---

[34] S.L.A. 1925, s. 32; and see s. 91.
[35] S.L.A. 1925, s. 34.
[36] S.L.A. 1925, s. 33.
[37] See *post*, pp. 373 *et seq.*
[38] Trustee Act 1925, s. 64.
[39] See *post*, p. 360.
[40] S.L.A. 1925, s. 35 (1) and see Trustee Act 1925, s. 35.
[41] S.L.A. 1925, s. 110 (2) (*d*).
[42] S.L.A. 1925, s. 35 (2).
[43] See Megarry and Wade, pp 365, 366.
[44] See *post*, p. 366.

N

to exercise certain other powers,[45] acting as statutory owner in certain cases [46] and holding capital money.[47]

IV. CREATION OF SETTLEMENTS [48]

Position of tenant for life

Before 1926 a settlement was created either by vesting the legal estate in fee simple in trustees on trust for the beneficiaries (such as to X and Y on trust for A for life and then on trust for B for life) or by conveying successive legal interests direct to the beneficiaries (such as to A for life and then to B in tail). Since 1925 legal life estates and legal remainders cannot exist,[49] so that the beneficial interests under a settlement must now be equitable and the legal estate (the fee simple or term of years) must be vested in some person on the appropriate trusts for the beneficiaries.

Therefore, under the Settled Land Act, the legal estate is vested in the tenant for life, or statutory owner, on trust for those beneficially entitled under the settlement. Thus, the tenant for life has two capacities. First, he is the estate owner in whom is vested the legal estate, usually in fee simple, and also the statutory powers of dealing with the settled land. Secondly, he is entitled to his own limited interest beneficially. Thus, if land is settled on A for life with remainder to B in tail with remainder to C in fee simple, the legal fee simple estate will be conveyed to A, who will hold it on trust for himself for life with remainder to B in tail with remainder to C in fee simple (all these being equitable interests). As beneficial owner of the life interest, A can deal with it as he wishes. Thus, he might sell it and keep the proceeds, give it away or settle it. A can deal with the legal fee simple estate under his statutory powers.[50] If he sells the legal fee simple estate, the proceeds will be paid to the trustees of the settlement, who will hold them on trust for A for life with remainder to B in tail with remainder to C absolutely, that is, the beneficial interests will be overreached. In other words, when A deals with the legal estate he does so in his capacity of a trustee, but when he deals with his beneficial life interest he does so as absolute owner thereof.

Two documents

Before 1926, settlements were generally created by one document, which would convey the legal estate to trustees on the desired trusts or to the beneficiaries for successive legal interests, setting out all the

---

[45] See *post*, p. 365.
[46] See *ante*, pp. 355–356.
[47] See *post*, pp. 363, 366.
[48] For transitional provisions relating to settlements made before 1926, see Law of Property Act 1925, Sched. 1, and S.L.A. 1925, Sched. 2.
[49] Law of Property Act 1925, s. 1.
[50] See *post*, pp. 361 *et seq.*

trusts. This was inconvenient, for when the tenant for life sold the land the settlement formed a link in the title and had to be investigated by the purchaser.[51] This was laborious to the purchaser and troublesome to the beneficiaries, whose private beneficial interests could be seen by the purchaser.

Since 1925 this difficulty is removed by the Settled Land Act 1925 whereby every settlement of land must be made by two documents, and if it is not so made it will not operate to transfer or create a legal estate.[52] The general scheme is that one instrument, called a vesting deed or vesting assent, conveys the legal estate in fee simple to the tenant for life or statutory owner to be held by him on the trusts which are set out in the other instrument, called the trust instrument, which will also appoint the trustees of the settlement. A purchaser of the settled land must investigate the vesting deed or assent, but he cannot, except in certain cases,[53] examine the trust instrument. Thus the trusts are kept off the title and the purchaser's task in examining the title to settled land is now much easier.

If, after 1925, an attempt is made to create a settlement by one document alone, the legal estate remains in the settlor and the one document will operate as the trust instrument. The tenant for life can in such a case call on the trustees to execute a vesting deed in his favour and so put the settlement in order.[54] In fact, no vesting deed need be made until the tenant for life or statutory owner demands it, and there is no necessity for them so to demand until it is desired to make a disposition of the settled land, but then the Act makes a vesting deed necessary by providing, in effect, that any purported disposition of the settled land *inter vivos* by any person (other than a personal representative)[55] before a vesting instrument has been executed shall not operate to pass a legal estate but shall operate only as a contract[56] for value to carry out the transaction after the necessary vesting deed has been executed.[57] Even when, in such circumstances in the case of a settlement *inter vivos*[58] a vesting deed has been executed the position is not as straightforward as if the settlement had been properly made in the first place, for a purchaser has to make the same laborious inquiries as a purchaser did before 1926.[59]

The different vesting instruments[60] and the trust instrument will now be considered.

51 See *post*, p. 362.
52 S.L.A. 1925, s. 4 (1).
53 See *post*, pp. 362, 363, and *post*, note 59.
54 S.L.A. 1925, s. 9.
55 There are other exceptions to the operation of s. 13; see Megarry and Wade, pp. 311–312; *Re Alefounder's W.T.* [1927] 1 Ch. 360.
56 Such contract requires registration as an estate contract.
57 S.L.A. 1925, s. 13.
58 For settlements by will, see *post*, p. 360.
59 S.L.A. 1925, s. 110 (2); and see *post*, p. 363.
60 For vesting orders, see S.L.A. 1925, s. 12.

Principal vesting deed

When a settlement is made *inter vivos* after 1925, the vesting deed (called a principal vesting deed) conveys the legal estate in fee simple (or a legal term of years) to the tenant for life or statutory owner, but if such legal estate is already vested in such person (as where A settles his own land on himself for life with remainders over) it is sufficient if the vesting deed declares that the land is vested in him for that estate.[61] Every principal vesting deed must contain the following [62]:

(a) a description of the settled land;

(b) a statement that the settled land is vested in the person or persons to whom it is conveyed or in whom it is declared to be vested upon the trusts from time to time affecting the settled land;

(c) the names of the trustees of the settlement;

(d) any powers conferred by the trust instrument which are additional to the statutory powers [63];

(e) the name of any person for the time being entitled under the trust instrument to appoint new trustees of the settlement.

Subsidiary vesting deed

While a settlement is in existence, additional land may be acquired and become subject to the trusts of the settlement, as where capital money [64] is used to purchase additional land. In such a case the land acquired will not be mentioned in the original vesting deed and so a separate one, called a " subsidiary vesting deed," must be executed to convey the additional land to the tenant for life or statutory owner.[65] This must contain [66]:

(a) particulars of the last or only principal vesting deed or vesting assent affecting land subject to the settlement;

(b) a statement that the land conveyed is to be held upon and subject to the same trusts and powers as the land comprised in such last or only deed or assent;

(c) the names of the trustees of the settlement;

(d) the name of any person for the time being entitled to appoint new trustees of the settlement.

Vesting assent

When a settlement is created by a will coming into effect after 1925, the will constitutes the trust instrument.[67] The legal estate vests in

[61] S.L.A. 1925, s. 4 (2).
[62] S.L.A. 1925, s. 5.
[63] See *post*, pp. 361 *et seq.* for the statutory powers.
[64] See *post*, p. 366.
[65] S.L.A. 1925, s. 10 (1).
[66] S.L.A. 1925, s. 10 (2). No reference to the trust instrument or any additional powers thereby conferred is necessary.
[67] S.L.A. 1925, s. 6.

the deceased's personal representatives, who hold the land on trust, if and when required so to do, to convey it to the tenant for life or statutory owner.[67] Rather than do this by a vesting deed, they can use a vesting assent in writing, which must however contain the same matters as a principal vesting deed.[68]

Trust instrument

This is usually a deed or will.[69] It must[70]:
 (a) declare the trusts affecting the settled land;
 (b) appoint the trustees of the settlement;
 (c) contain the power, if any, to appoint new trustees;
 (d) set out any powers intended to be conferred by the settlement in extension of those conferred by the Act;
 (e) bear any *ad valorem* stamp duty which may be payable in respect of the settlement.

Contrast between vesting instrument and trust instrument

It will be seen that the trust instrument actually appoints the trustees, confers any additional powers and confers the power to appoint new trustees. The principal vesting deed or vesting assent merely says what the trust instrument has done in these matters, thus giving the purchaser (who will investigate the vesting instrument) the information he needs about the trust instrument. The trusts themselves are set out in the trust instrument and are thus kept off the legal title, because a purchaser from the tenant for life does not examine the trust instrument.

V. Powers of Tenant for Life and Statutory Owner

We have seen[71] that the tenant for life can deal with his own beneficial interest as he chooses; such dealings do not affect the other beneficiaries under the settlement. Again, we have seen[71] that, as trustee, the tenant for life can also deal with the legal estate under the statutory powers; in exercising these powers, he is subject to certain restrictions and in such cases his dealings bind the other beneficiaries under the settlement. The more important of these statutory powers will now be briefly examined, though the power of sale will be discussed at greater length, for that is the power which above all shows the machinery of the Act in operation.[72] It should be remembered that the statutory owner has the same powers as the tenant for life.[73]

---

[68] S.L.A. 1925, s. 8 (4). The slight advantage of a vesting assent is that it does not need a deed stamp.
[69] See S.L.A. 1925, s. 1 (1).
[70] S.L.A. 1925, s. 4 (3).
[71] *Ante*, p. 358.
[72] For other powers (*e.g.* to exchange, to dispose of principal mansion house), see Megarry and Wade, pp. 338–358.
[73] *Ante*, p. 355.

A. Power of Sale

The Power

The tenant for life may sell the settled land, or any part thereof.[74] A sale must generally be made for the best consideration in money that can reasonably be obtained,[75] and may be made by auction or private contract.[76]

Purchaser's investigation of title

A purchaser from a tenant for life or statutory owner must require the same proof of title as if he was purchasing from a beneficial owner —that is, a perfect abstract commencing with a good root of title.[77] In order to show title in the tenant for life, it was, as we have seen,[78] formerly necessary to abstract the settlement itself, so that the purchaser could satisfy himself that the land was comprised in the settlement, that the vendor was the tenant for life and that the persons stated to be the trustees of the settlement were properly constituted as such and therefore the proper persons to receive the purchase-money. But since 1925, as we have seen,[78] a settlement must be created by two documents.   The trust instrument is not to appear on the title and should not be abstracted at all; only the vesting instrument will be abstracted and will constitute the link in the title between the settlor and the tenant for life.   The purchaser is not, with certain exceptions mentioned below, bound or entitled to call for production of the trust instrument or any information concerning it and he is bound and entitled, if the last or only principal vesting instrument contains the statements and particulars required by the Act, to assume that:

    (a) the person in whom the land is thereby vested or declared to be vested is the tenant for life or statutory owner and has all the powers of a tenant for life under the Act;

    (b) the persons thereby stated to be the trustees of the settlement or their successors appearing to be duly appointed, are the properly constituted trustees of the settlement;

    (c) the statements and particulars required by the Act contained in the vesting instrument were correct at the date thereof;

    (d) the statements contained in any deed executed in accordance with the Act declaring who are the trustees of the settlement are correct;

    (e) the statements contained in any deed of discharge,[79] executed in accordance with the Act, are correct.

Because of the above principles, it is sometimes said that the

---

[74] S.L.A. 1925, s. 38 (i).
[75] S.L.A. 1925, s. 39 (1).
[76] S.L.A. 1925, s. 39 (6).
[77] See *ante*, p. 119.
[78] See *ante*, p. 359.
[79] See *post*, p. 369.

vesting instrument is a curtain, behind which the trusts are concealed and behind which a purchaser cannot look.[80] There are, however, certain exceptional cases where a purchaser from a tenant for life or statutory owner is concerned, and entitled, to examine the trust instrument in order to verify the accuracy of the *first* vesting deed or assent in the following particulars:

(i) the land disposed of is comprised in the settlement;

(ii) the person in whom the land is vested or declared to be vested by the vesting deed or assent is the person in whom it ought to be vested as tenant for life or statutory owner;

(iii) the persons stated in the vesting deed or assent to be trustees of the settlement are the properly constituted trustees of the settlement.

Of these exceptional cases[81] where a purchaser may examine the trust instrument, the two most important ones are (a) where the settlement was created before 1926 and (b) where an instrument *inter vivos* intended to create a settlement is executed after 1925 but does not comply with the requirements of the Act with respect to the method of effecting it.[82]

Payment of purchase-money

Capital money payable in respect of a transaction by a tenant for life or statutory owner, such as the proceeds of a sale, is not, of course, payable to him for his own benefit but must be paid to the trustees of the settlement, who must number at least two or be a trust corporation, or into court (at the tenant for life's option)[83]; otherwise the conveyance to the purchaser will not take effect under the Act.[84] This does not mean that the conveyance will be void, for it will pass the legal estate to the purchaser; but the equitable interests will not be overreached and so the purchaser will hold the legal estate subject to the equitable interests under the settlement and will not be able to pass a good title to a later purchaser. Therefore, the purchaser should be very careful to pay the purchase-money in the proper way.

Effect of conveyance by tenant for life or statutory owner

Such a conveyance operates to pass to the purchaser the legal estate or other less interest which it purports to convey and such estate will vest in the purchaser free and discharged from certain interests but subject to others. For example, the purchaser will take free from the beneficial interests under the settlement, which will be overreached (that is, become attached to the purchase-money) so long

---

[80] See Megarry and Wade, pp. 314–316.
[81] S.L.A. 1925, s. 110 (2).
[82] See *ante*, p. 359.
[83] S.L.A. 1925, s. 75 (1).
[84] S.L.A. 1925, s. 18 (1).

as the above requirements as to the payment of the purchase-money are fulfilled. On the other hand, the purchaser will take subject, for example, to a legal mortgage made by the tenant for life for securing money actually raised at the date of the conveyance.[85]

B. Power to Grant Leases

A tenant for life can grant leases[86] of the settled land, or of part thereof, for any term not exceeding:
  (i) 999 years in the case of a building lease or a forestry lease;
  (ii) 100 years in the case of a mining lease;
  (iii) 50 years in the case of any other lease.
Leases granted under the Act must:
  (a) be by deed (with the exception of certain leases not exceeding three years: see below);
  (b) be made to take effect in possession not later than twelve months after its date, or in reversion after an existing lease having not more than seven years to run at the date of the new lease;
  (c) reserve the best rent that can reasonably be obtained;
  (d) contain a covenant by the lessee for payment of the rent and a condition of re-entry on the rent not being paid within a time therein specified not exceeding thirty days.

A lease at the best rent that can be reasonably obtained without fine, and whereby the lessee is not exempted from punishment for waste may be made where the term does not exceed twenty-one years, notwithstanding that no notice[87] is given to the trustees of the settlement or that there are no trustees of the settlement: and such a lease may be made by writing under hand where the term does not exceed three years from the date of the writing.

The tenant for life is usually[88] entitled to all the rent payable under a lease of the settled land as income of the land; but any fine received on the grant of a lease is deemed to be capital money arising under the Act.

C. Power to Mortgage

A tenant for life can mortgage the settled land to raise money for a number of specified purposes[89]—for example, to pay for an improvement authorised by the Act or the settlement or to extinguish manorial incidents. The money raised by the tenant for life by mortgage should be paid to the trustees of the settlement as capital money and applied by them for the purpose for which it was raised.

[85] See S.L.A. 1925, s. 72. For a full treatment, see Megarry and Wade, pp. 380–385.
[86] See S.L.A. 1925, ss. 41–48; *Re Morgan's Lease* [1972] Ch. 1.
[87] For notices, see *post*, p. 365.
[88] There is an exception in the case of mining leases: see S.L.A. 1925, s. 47.
[89] S.L.A. 1925, s. 71.

D. General Considerations

Enlargement, restriction and release of powers of a tenant for life

The powers of dealing with the settled land conferred by the Act are very wide, but the settlor may by the settlement expressly confer additional powers or enlarge the powers already conferred by the Act. But the settlor cannot confer powers on any person, such as the trustees of the settlement, other than the tenant for life or statutory owner, and if he purports to do so, such powers become exercisable by the tenant for life or statutory owner just as if they were additional powers conferred on him.[90]

Although the powers of a tenant for life or statutory owner may be enlarged by the settlement, any provision in a settlement purporting or attempting or tending to forbid or prevent a tenant for life or statutory owner from exercising any statutory power is void and, notwithstanding anything in the settlement, his exercise of any statutory power is not to occasion a forfeiture.[91] Thus, if A devises a house to B for life with a gift over to C if B ceases to live there, B is the tenant for life under a settlement. If B merely leaves the house to live elsewhere, the gift over to C will take effect and B will lose his interest.[92] But if B leaves the house because of some exercise of his statutory powers, such as a sale, he will not lose his interest, because to hold otherwise would tend to prevent the exercise of his statutory powers; in such a case he would continue to enjoy his life interest in the proceeds of sale.[93] In such cases the tenant for life would be well advised to sell before he leaves the property.

Again, a tenant for life cannot release or assign or validly contract not to exercise his powers; such a contract is void.[94] But a statutory owner can release his powers,[95] in which case the trustees of the settlement will have the powers of a tenant for life.[96]

Notices and consents to be given before exercise of statutory powers

Before exercising his more important powers, including those of sale, mortgaging or leasing (except where the lease does not exceed twenty-one years at the best rent[97]), the tenant for life or statutory owner must give a month's *notice* by registered post[98] of his intention to carry out the particular transaction to each of the trustees and

90 S.L.A. 1925, ss. 108, 109.
91 S.L.A. 1925, s. 106.
92 *Re Haynes* (1887) 37 Ch.D. 306.
93 *Re Paget's S.E.* (1885) 30 Ch.D. 161. See generally Megarry and Wade, pp. 360–362.
94 S.L.A. 1925, s. 104.
95 *Re Craven's S.E.* [1926] Ch. 985.
96 S.L.A. 1925, s. 23 (1) (b). See *ante*, pp. 355–356.
97 See *ante*, p. 364.
98 Or recorded delivery: Recorded Delivery Service Act 1962, s. 1, Sched.

N*

their solicitor if known.[99]   However, a person dealing in good faith with the tenant for life is not concerned to inquire whether such notice has been given,[1] so that his title is not affected by any lack of such notice.

The *consent* of the trustees of the settlement or an order of the court is necessary for the exercise of certain of the tenant for life's powers, such as to sell the principal mansion house in certain cases.[2]

Capital money

Money arising through the exercise of the powers given by the Settled Land Act 1925, such as money arising from a sale of the settled land, is called " capital money." [3]   It must be paid to the trustees of the settlement and invested according to the direction of the tenant for life or in default thereof according to the trustees' discretion, or alternatively it must be paid into court and invested under its direction.[4]   The investments are those authorised by the Settled Land Act 1925.   Such investments include trustee investments within the Trustee Investments Act 1961, authorised improvements,[5] and purchase of land in fee simple or of leasehold land held for sixty years or more unexpired at the time of purchase.[6]   The capital money while remaining uninvested and the investments thereof devolve as land and go to the same persons successively in the same manner as land from which the money arises would, if not disposed of, have devolved, and the income of the investments is applied as the income of the land would have been applicable if it had not been sold.[7]

Improvements

The tenant for life may effect improvements on the settled land which are authorised by the Settled Land Act 1925 and these may be paid for out of capital money.   However, in some cases the tenant for life must repay the cost of the improvements from income.   This depends on whether the improvement effected falls within Parts I, II or III of the Third Schedule to the Act, the position being briefly as follows:

> (i) Part I specifies twenty-five improvements which are such as permanently to benefit the settled land, such as drainage, bridges, irrigation, roads or cottages for labourers.   The tenant

---

[99] S.L.A. 1925, s. 101.   Except in the case of mortgages the notice may be a general one, *i.e.* a notice to the effect that a tenant for life intends, *e.g.* to sell from time to time without specifying any particular sale contemplated.

[1] S.L.A. 1925, s. 101 (5).

[2] S.L.A. 1925, s. 65.

[3] S.L.A. 1925, s. 117 (1) (ii).   Some receipts are of an income, rather than a capital, nature, *e.g.* rent (usually): see *ante*, p. 364.

[4] S.L.A. 1925, s. 75.

[5] See *post*.

[6] S.L.A. 1925, s. 73.

[7] S.L.A. 1925, s. 75.

for life cannot be required to repay the cost of these out of income.

(ii) Part II specifies six improvements which may or may not be of permanent benefit to the settled land, such as houses for land agents or managers, offices and workshops and certain structural additions or alterations to buildings. Here, the trustees or the court *may* require the money to be repaid by instalments out of the income of the land.

(iii) Part III specifies three types of improvement of a less permanent character, such as heating apparatus for buildings or the installation of artificial light. Here, the trustees or the court *must* require the money to be repaid by instalments out of the income of the land.[8]

VI. CHANGE OF OWNERSHIP

We have discussed the position where the tenant for life or statutory owner sells the settled land under his statutory power. Here we shall briefly examine the position where the ownership of the land changes while the settlement subsists.

Death of tenant for life

When the tenant for life dies the settlement may nevertheless continue to subsist, as where the land is settled on A for life with remainder to B for life with remainder to C in fee simple and A dies; or the settlement may come to an end, as when B dies in the foregoing example. The effect is different in either case:

(i) If the settlement does not come to an end on the tenant for life's death, the legal estate in the settled land will usually vest in the trustees of the settlement as his *special* personal representatives,[9] whereas his other property will vest in his *general* personal representatives, such as the executors he appoints by his will. The general personal representatives, having paid the deceased's debts and estate duty, must assent in favour of the beneficiaries, thus vesting the property concerned in the proper beneficiary: this will be done by *simple* (or ordinary) assent.[10] Equally, it is the duty of the special personal representatives, having received a special grant of probate or letters of administration, to provide for the payment of estate duty and then, by *vesting* deed or assent, to transfer the legal estate to the next tenant for life or statutory owner. If such transfer is made by deed, it is a principal vesting deed.[11] If the transfer is made by

---

[8] See generally S.L.A. 1925, ss. 83, 84, Sched. 3. The money needed to effect authorised improvements may, if desired, be raised by mortgaging the settled land: S.L.A. 1925, s. 71, and *ante*, p. 364.

[9] Administration of Estates Act 1925, s. 22 (1); Judicature Act 1925, s. 162, as amended by Administration of Justice Act 1928, s. 9.

[10] See *post*, p. 400.

[11] See *ante*, p. 360.

vesting assent, it must contain the same statements and particulars as are required by the Settled Land Act 1925, to be inserted in a principal vesting deed.[12] The special personal representatives may deal with the settled land and the general personal representatives may deal with the deceased's other property without the concurrence of each other.[13]

(ii) Where the settlement comes to an end on the tenant for life's death, the land passes to his general personal representatives and no special grant will be made to the trustees of the settlement as special personal representatives.[14] When the general personal representatives have completed their duties of administration they must vest the land in the person who has become entitled by a simple (not a vesting) assent in writing.[15] For example, if land is settled on A for life with remainder to B in fee simple, on A's death his general personal representatives will transfer the land to B by simple assent. Again, if land is settled on A for life with remainder to X and Y upon trust to sell and hold the proceeds upon certain limitations, on A's death the settlement comes to an end and X and Y can require A's personal representatives to vest the land in them (by a simple assent) on trust for sale. The assent in such cases need not contain the statements and particulars required in a principal vesting deed.

Minor attaining majority

We have seen [16] that where a minor is beneficially entitled in possession to land for an estate in fee simple or for a term of years absolute or would if of full age be a tenant for life or have the powers of a tenant for life, the statutory powers will be exercisable during the minority by a personal representative, if the land is vested in one, or by the trustees of the settlement. When the minor reaches full age, he may require the person or persons in whom the land is vested to convey it to him, and this will be done by a vesting deed or vesting assent containing all the proper statements and particulars.[17]

Tenant for life surrendering or forfeiting his interest

This requires some introduction. If the tenant for life assigns his beneficial life interest, the statutory powers do not thereby pass to the assignee but remain exercisable by the tenant for life (unless the assignment is in favour of the next remainderman, as to which see below), and this is so whether the assignment is by way of sale or by operation of law, as in the case of the tenant for life's bankruptcy.[18] But the position of an assignee for value (which includes an assignment

---

[12] S.L.A. 1925, ss. 7 and 8; see *ante*, p. 360.
[13] Administration of Estates Act 1925, s. 24.
[14] *Re Bridgett and Hayes' Contract* [1928] Ch. 163.
[15] S.L.A. 1925, ss. 7 and 8. See *post*, p. 400.
[16] See *ante*, p. 355.
[17] S.L.A. 1925, ss. 7 (2), 8 (4).
[18] S.L.A. 1925, s. 104.

by operation of the law of bankruptcy [19]) is protected because his rights will attach to the land before it is sold and to the money or securities for the time being representing it after it is sold. Again, if the assignment so provides or if it takes effect by operation of the law of bankruptcy, and notice of the assignment is given to the trustees of the settlement, no investment or application of capital money affected can be made without the assignee's *consent* except an investment in authorised trustee securities. Again, unless the assignment otherwise provides, *notice* of an intended transaction by the tenant for life by way of exercise of his statutory powers must be given to the assignee, though a purchaser is not concerned to see or inquire whether such notice has been given.[20]

There is one exception to the rule that a tenant for life does not lose his powers by reason of an assignment of his beneficial life interest, and this is where the life interest is surrendered to the person next entitled under the settlement with intent to extinguish the life interest. In such a case the tenant for life will lose his powers and they will become exercisable as if he were dead.[21] For example, if land is settled on A for life with remainder to B for life with remainder to C in fee simple, and A surrenders his life interest to B, A will lose his statutory powers which will become exercisable by B. A must forthwith convey the land to B as the next tenant for life.[22] This he will do by a vesting deed.[23]

A tenant for life may lose his life interest and his statutory powers for other reasons than surrender—for example, forfeiture. For example, if land is settled on A for life but the settlement limits his interest so as to be forfeited if he changes his name, with a gift over to B for life, with remainder over, then on A's changing his name his interest in the settled land ceases and he loses his statutory powers. Here again, A must forthwith convey the land by a vesting deed to B, the next tenant for life.[24]

VII. DEED OF DISCHARGE

When a settlement of land has come to an end, there is nothing in the vesting deed to record the fact, and therefore some document is necessary to enable the person who has become wholly entitled to deal with the land as absolute owner without disclosing the contents of the trust instrument. Accordingly, when a person has become entitled to settled land free from the equitable interests, the trustees are bound to execute a deed of discharge declaring that they are discharged

[19] S.L.A. 1925, s. 104 (10).
[20] S.L.A. 1925, s. 104. For assignments before 1926, see that section.
[21] S.L.A. 1925, s. 105.
[22] S.L.A. 1925, s. 7 (4).
[23] S.L.A. 1925, s. 8 (4) (*a*).
[24] S.L.A. 1925, ss. 7 (4), 8 (4) (*a*).

from the trusts of the land.[25]   This frees the land from the provisions of the Settled Land Act 1925 and a purchaser of a legal estate is bound and entitled to assume that the land has ceased to be settled.[26]

[25] S.L.A. 1925, s. 17. No deed of discharge is necessary in certain cases.
[26] S.L.A. 1925, ss. 17 (3), 110 (2) (*e*).

Chapter 15

TRUSTS FOR SALE

I. Form of Trust for Sale

To create a settlement of land upon trust for sale [1] two documents are used, namely, the conveyance on trust for sale and the settlement. The conveyance conveys the land to the trustees upon trust to sell the land. The settlement sets out the trusts of the proceeds of sale and the rents and profits until sale. By means of using these two documents, the settlement is prevented from becoming one of the documents of title to the land, and the trusts, which will be overreached on a sale, are kept off the title. [2]

To create a settlement of pure personalty, the property must similarly be transferred to the trustees by the appropriate form of transfer. Thus, if the property consists of shares in companies, it must be transferred to the trustees by a proper form of transfer and the necessary entries must be made in the books of the companies. The trusts will be set out in a separate settlement. In other cases, the property—for example, silver plate—may be transferred to the trustees by a transfer contained in the settlement itself.

In addition to setting out the trusts, the settlement usually confers various powers upon the trustees, which will be dealt with later.

II. The Trusts

The beneficial interests created by a trust for sale vary according to the wishes of the individual settlor. The traditional trust for sale was that created upon marriage, where the husband or his family, or the wife or her family, would settle property for the benefit of the spouses and their future issue. Taking the example of a settlement of land by the husband upon trust for sale, the trustees would be directed to hold the proceeds of sale, and the rents and profits until sale, and the investments representing them, after the solemnisation of the marriage, upon trust to pay the income of the trust fund to the husband for life and after his death to the wife for life. Then they would be directed to hold the trust fund and its income in trust for such of the issue of the marriage in such shares as the husband and wife should by

---

[1] *i.e.* an " immediate binding trust for sale " within s. 205 (1) (xxix) of the Law of Property Act 1925. See Megarry and Wade, *The Law of Real Property* (3rd ed.), pp. 366–370; Hanbury's *Modern Equity* (9th ed.), pp. 514–518.

[2] Where registered land is held on trust for sale, express or implied, the trustees for sale will be registered as proprietors of the land: Land Registration Act 1925, s. 94.

deed jointly appoint [3] or, in default thereof, as the survivor of them should by deed or will appoint. In default of any appointment, the trustees would be directed to hold the trust fund and its income in trust for the children or child of the marriage who being male should attain twenty-one or being female should attain that age or marry under that age, if more than one in equal shares. The ultimate trust would be that if there should be no child of the marriage who should attain a vested interest, the trustees should hold the trust fund and its income from and after the wife's death in trust for the husband absolutely.

It is still, of course, perfectly possible to create fixed trusts, such as the one just outlined. Another example would be a settlement created by a will in favour of the testator's wife for life with remainder to his children in equal shares. Nowadays, however, fixed trusts are less popular, in the case of large funds at any rate, as we have seen.[4]

A typical modern settlement, which is nowadays more likely to be of pure personalty than of land and which may well dispense with the trust for sale, will simply provide for the trust fund to be held on discretionary trusts. It will further direct that any land that may be or become subject to the settlement shall be held on trust for sale and will provide that the proceeds of sale and the rents and profits until sale shall be held on the same discretionary trusts as the rest of the trust fund. Discretionary trusts are discussed in an earlier chapter [5] and later in this chapter.[6]

III.   Appointment, Disclaimer and Retirement of Trustees

Appointment of original trustees for sale

The settlement will name the initial trustees. The number cannot generally be greater than four in the case of land held on trust for sale,[7] though it may be in the case of settled pure personalty. If more than four persons are named as trustees, the four first named who are able and willing to act will be the trustees.[7] At least two trustees should be appointed and kept up in order that they may give valid receipts for purchase-moneys.[8]

Disclaimer

A person who is appointed a trustee is under no obligation to accept the trusteeship but may disclaim the office of trustee, and if he does so it will amount to a disclaimer of the legal estate in the trust

---

[3] For defective execution of powers and frauds on powers, see Snell's *Principles of Equity* (26th ed.), pp. 601–604; 619–624.

[4] *Ante*, pp. 345–349.

[5] *Ante*, pp. 345–349.

[6] *Post*, pp. 381–382.

[7] Trustee Act 1925, s. 34. For exceptions, see s. 34 (3).

[8] See *post*, p. 378.

property.[9] This means that he declines from the beginning to under-take the trust. This is unlike retirement,[10] which means that the trustee, having undertaken the trust, wishes later to be discharged from his duties. If a trustee wishes to disclaim, he must do so before taking any part in the administration of the trust; otherwise, he will be deemed to have accepted the trusteeship, and if a trustee accepts the post he cannot disclaim.[11] A trustee may not disclaim part only of the trusts but must disclaim all or none, and if he attempts to disclaim part only his disclaimer will have no effect.[12] A disclaimer may be in any form—by deed, in writing, verbal or even inferred from conduct—but in practice it is usually effected by deed. If one of two or more trustees disclaims, the trust property will vest in the other trustee or trustees,[13] and if all the trustees disclaim or a sole trustee disclaims, the trust property will remain vested in the settlor or, if he is dead, will vest in his personal representatives.[14] It is clearly advisable for the settlor to consult his prospective trustees before he appoints them.

Appointment of new trustees [15]

An express power of appointing a new trustee or new trustees may be conferred on some person or persons by the instrument creating the settlement, but because ample powers are now conferred by statute [16] an express power is often omitted, though the settlor may expressly reserve to himself the power to appoint new trustees during his lifetime. Statutory provision is made both as to the person or persons who are to make the appointment and the circumstances in which the appointment may be made.

A new trustee or new trustees can be appointed *to fill a vacancy* arising where a trustee dies, remains out of the United Kingdom for more than twelve months, desires to be discharged from the trust, refuses or is unfit to act (as by bankruptcy) or is incapable of acting (as by old age), is an infant or is removed under a power contained in the instrument creating the trust. The person or persons to make the appointment are the person or persons nominated for the purpose by the instrument creating the trust or, if there is no such person able and willing to act, the surviving or continuing trustees or trustee or the personal representatives of the last surviving or continuing trustee.[17]

An *additional* trustee or trustees may be appointed where there are not more than three trustees, none of whom is a trust corporation,

---

9 *Re Birchall* (1889) 40 Ch.D. 436.
10 See *post*, p. 375.
11 *Re Sharman's W.T.* [1942] Ch. 311.
12 *Re Lord and Fullerton's Contract* [1896] 1 Ch. 228.
13 *Adams* v. *Taunton* (1820) 5 Madd. 435.
14 *Mallot* v. *Wilson* [1903] 2 Ch. 494.
15 For appointment by the court, see Snell, pp. 213–215.
16 Trustee Act 1925, s. 36.
17 Trustee Act 1925, s. 36 (1) (2).

but not so as to increase the total number of trustees beyond four. The person or persons to make the appointment are the person or persons nominated for the purpose by the instrument creating the trust or, if there is no such person able and willing to act, the trustee or trustees for the time being.[18] It is not obligatory to appoint an additional trustee except when the settlement or a statute[19] so provides. This provision merely confers a power to do so where an additional trustee is desired.

When new trustees are appointed to fill a vacancy, any number of trustees may be appointed, so that the number of trustees may be increased,[20] save that in the case of a trust for sale of land (or a strict settlement of land) the number cannot generally be increased beyond four.[21] If the appointment is of additional trustees, as opposed to the appointment of trustees to fill vacancies, the total number may never be increased beyond four.[18]

It is not obligatory (save as stated below) to appoint more than one new trustee where only one was originally appointed, or to fill up the original number of trustees where more than two trustees were originally appointed. But a trustee will not be discharged from his trust unless there will be either a trust corporation or at least two individuals to act as trustees (except where only one trustee was originally appointed and a sole trustee when appointed will be able to give valid receipts for capital money, which will occur if the trust property is pure personalty[22]). Nothing in the Trustee Act authorises the appointment of a sole trustee, not being a trust corporation, where the trustee, when appointed, would not be able to give valid receipts for capital money.[23] For example, if three trustees are appointed and one dies and one becomes incapable of acting, if the trust is of land the remaining trustee should appoint at least one more trustee to act with him, so as to enable the trustees to give valid receipts; and if the remaining trustee wishes to retire he will have to appoint either two more new trustees or a trust corporation in his place, otherwise he will not be discharged from the trust.

The appointment of trustees under the above provisions may be made in writing but in practice a deed is nearly always employed. When the appointment is made, it is also necessary to vest the trust property in the new trustees jointly with the old ones. This can be done by the execution of appropriate transfers, but a more simple method is permitted provided the trustees are appointed by deed, for if a deed appointing new trustees contains a declaration (called a vesting declaration) to the effect that the trust property shall vest in

---

[18] Trustee Act 1925, s. 36 (6).
[19] See *e.g.* Law of Property Act 1925, s. 27.
[20] Trustee Act 1925, s. 37 (1).
[21] See *ante*, p. 372. For exceptions, see Trustee Act 1925, s. 34 (3).
[22] See Trustee Act 1925, s. 14.
[23] Trustee Act 1925, s. 37.

the persons who by virtue of the deed of appointment become or are the trustees, the deed operates, without any conveyance or assignment, to vest the trust property in the new and the old trustees together as joint tenants.   Further, in appointments of new trustees by deed after 1925, the vesting declaration is implied in the deed of appointment unless the deed contains an express provision to the contrary.[24]   Therefore, since 1925, the deed appointing the trustees will also automatically operate to vest the trust property in the new trustees jointly with the old ones.   But there are certain kinds of property to which these provisions do not apply.   They are [25] :

(a) land held by the trustees upon mortgage to secure trust money;
(b) leaseholds which contain a covenant not to assign or underlet without consent, unless such consent has been obtained or unless the vesting declaration would not operate as a breach of covenant or give rise to a forfeiture; and
(c) any share, stock, annuity or property which is only transferable in books kept by a company or other body, or in manner directed by or under an Act of Parliament.

In these cases the property must be passed to the new trustees in the appropriate way.

Retirement of trustees

If a new trustee is being appointed at the same time as a trustee retires,[26] the retirement will be effected by the same instrument as that appointing the new trustee.   The deed will be made between the continuing trustees, the retiring trustee and the new trustee.   It will recite the desire of the retiring trustee to retire and that the continuing trustees and the retiring trustee desire to appoint the new trustee in his place.   The deed will proceed to make the appointment of the new trustee, and will be executed by all parties.   A vesting declaration will (since 1925) be implied in the deed and will operate to vest the trust property in the continuing trustees jointly with the new trustee, except as regards the three types of property mentioned above.[27]

Where a trustee wishes to be discharged without a new trustee being appointed in his place, he may retire if the retirement is made by deed, in which he declares his desire to be discharged and his co-trustees and any person empowered to appoint new trustees consent to the discharge and to the vesting in the co-trustees alone of the trust property, and if after the retirement there will be either a trust corporation or at least two individuals to act as trustees.[28]   A vesting declaration will be implied in the deed (if made after 1925) and will

[24] Trustee Act 1925, s. 40. For a form of appointment, see *post*, p. 440.
[25] Trustee Act 1925, s. 40 (4).
[26] See *ante*, p. 373.
[27] Trustee Act 1925, s. 40.
[28] Trustee Act 1925, s. 39.

operate to vest the trust property in the continuing trustees alone, except as regards the three types of property mentioned above.[29]

If the Public Trustee is appointed to be a trustee, the other trustees may retire by deed even though the Public Trustee thereby remains to act alone, and they need not obtain any consents to their retirement.[30]

Removal

A trustee can be removed if there is a power to do so in the instrument creating the trust, or in accordance with the statutory provisions mentioned above [31] (for example, where he remains out of the United Kingdom for more than twelve months), or by the court for the beneficiaries' welfare.[32]

IV. SALE BY TRUSTEES

Power to postpone sale

When land is held upon trust for sale the trustees have power to postpone the sale, unless a contrary intention appears in the settlement.[33] Further, the trustees are not liable if they postpone the sale for an indefinite period unless the settlement contains an express direction to the contrary, and a purchaser of a legal estate is not concerned with any directions respecting the postponement of a sale.[33] If one or more of the trustees desires to sell but the others do not so desire, the court may compel the latter to join in the sale because the trust for sale imposes a duty to sell and prevails unless the trustees are unanimous in exercising the power to postpone the sale; the duty to sell may be enforced at the instance of even one trustee but the power to postpone can only be exercised by all of them.[34]

The last-mentioned rule is subject to the further provision that the trustees must consult the beneficiaries and, so far as consistent with the general interest of the trust, give effect to the wishes of the majority according to the value of their interests.[35] But this provision only applies to statutory trusts for sale or those which evince an intention that it should apply,[36] so that most expressly created trusts for sale do not fall within its ambit. The provision is of especial concern where a statutory trust for sale arises by virtue of the co-ownership of land.[37] In such cases, the trustees and the beneficiaries are often the same persons, holding the legal estate as joint tenants on trust for themselves as joint tenants or tenants in common. Because of the

[29] Trustee Act 1925, s. 40.
[30] Public Trustee Act 1906, s. 5 (2).
[31] See *ante*, p. 373.
[32] See *Letterstedt* v. *Broers* (1884) 9 App.Cas. 371.
[33] Law of Property Act 1925, s. 25.
[34] *Re Mayo* [1943] Ch. 302. See Megarry and Wade, p. 373; Snell, pp. 247–248.
[35] Law of Property Act 1925, s. 26 (3), as amended by Law of Property (Amendment) Act 1926, Sched.
[36] Law of Property (Amendment) Act 1926, Sched.
[37] Law of Property Act 1925, ss. 34–36.

provision just mentioned, the majority according to the value may compel a postponement of sale even if the minority wish to exercise the trust for sale, so that the rule that the duty to sell can be imposed on a majority is qualified.

A further principle is that the court, in deciding whether or not to order a sale [38] in case of disagreement, will take into account any contract or other relevant factor. For example, a co-owner will not be able to compel a sale if he has contracted not to sell without the consent of the others.[39] Again, if a house is purchased by a husband and wife as the matrimonial home, an order for sale will not be made while the marriage subsists, though if the marriage ends in divorce the court will order a sale at the instance of one of the spouses.[40]

Consents to sale

We have seen [41] that the trustees may be required by the settlement to obtain the consent of a person or persons before they sell the land subject to the trust, and the purchaser must then consider how far he is concerned to see whether such consents have been obtained. If the trustees are directed to obtain the consent of more than two persons, it is sufficient so far as the purchaser is concerned if he sees that the consent of any two is obtained, and if any person whose consent is required is a minor or under disability the purchaser need not see that his consent is obtained.[42] However, this merely protects the purchaser. The trustees will nevertheless commit a breach of trust if they sell without fulfilling their duty to obtain the requisite consents, and if a minor's or mental patient's consent is required the trustees must obtain the consent of the parent or guardian or receiver.[43]

Mode of sale

Trustees for sale may sell all or any part of the property, either subject to prior charges or not, and either together or in lots, by public auction or by private contract, subject to any such conditions respecting title or evidence of title or other matters as the trustees think fit, with power to vary any contract for sale, and to buy in at any auction, or to rescind any contract for sale and to resell, without being answerable for any loss.[44] They may sell any part of the land, whether the division is horizontal, vertical or made in any other way.[45]

If the trustees make depreciatory conditions of sale, not strictly

---

[38] See Law of Property Act 1925, s. 30.
[39] *Re Buchanan-Wollaston's Conveyance* [1939] Ch. 738.
[40] *Jones* v. *Challenger* [1961] 1 Q.B. 176; *Jackson* v. *Jackson* [1971] 1 W.L.R. 59.
[41] See *ante*, p. 344.
[42] Law of Property Act 1925, s. 26 (1) (2).
[43] Law of Property Act 1925, s. 26 (2), as amended by Mental Health Act 1959, s. 149. and Sched. 7.
[44] Trustee Act 1925, s. 12 (1).
[45] Trustee Act 1925, s. 12 (2).

necessary having regard to the state of the title, they will be liable to
the beneficiaries to make good any loss thereby caused to the trust
estate.   However, it is provided that no sale can be impeached by a
beneficiary on the ground that the conditions of sale were unnecessarily
depreciatory, *unless it also appears* that the consideration for the sale
was thereby rendered inadequate; and no sale can, after the execution
of the conveyance, be impeached as against the purchaser on the
ground that any of the conditions subject to which the sale was made
may have been unnecessarily depreciatory, *unless it appears* that the
purchaser was acting in collusion with the trustees at the time when the
contract for sale was made; and no purchaser is at liberty to object
to the title on the aforesaid grounds.[46]

Overreaching

A purchaser of a legal estate from trustees for sale is not concerned
with the equitable interests of the beneficiaries, which are overreached
provided he pays the purchase-money to at least two trustees or a trust
corporation.[47]

V.   POWERS OF TRUSTEES

Some of the more important powers of trustees for sale are as follows.

Powers of investment

The trustees have, in relation to land and to the proceeds of sale,
all the powers of a tenant for life and the trustees of a settlement under
the Settled Land Act 1925,[48] and so, for example, they may lease or
mortgage the land held by them.   If they hold land, they may
purchase other land with the proceeds of sale,[49] unless they are no
longer trustees for sale of land because they have sold all the land
subject to the trust.[50]   In addition, trustees for sale have the wide
powers of investment conferred by the Trustee Investments Act 1961.[51]
Nevertheless, it is common to confer on the trustees an express power
of investment which is wider than the statutory power.   For example,
the trustees may be empowered to invest in such investments as may
seem fit to them [52] or they may be expressly given the same powers
of investment as if they were absolutely and beneficially entitled to the
trust property.

It may be that the trustees will wish to buy a house as a dwelling
for the beneficiaries.   If the trust instrument merely gives them power

---

[46] Trustee Act 1925, s. 13.
[47] Law of Property Act 1925, ss. 2, 27.
[48] Law of Property Act 1925, s. 28 (1).
[49] Settled Land Act 1925, s. 73 (1) (xi); *Re Weldsted's W.T.* [1949] Ch. 296.
[50] *Re Wakeman* [1945] Ch. 177.
[51] See Snell, pp. 224–235.
[52] See *Re Harari's S.T.* [1949] 1 All E.R. 430.   See *post*, pp. 438–439.

to invest in land, they will not have power to fulfil that wish.[53] The trust instrument should expressly confer upon the trustees the power to purchase a house as a dwelling for the beneficiaries.

Maintenance and advancement

It is desirable that the trustees should have power of advancing to a beneficiary a portion of the share of the trust capital to which he is or may become entitled and also of maintaining an infant beneficiary out of the income of his share. Formerly it was necessary to insert express powers for these purposes in the settlement, but now powers of advancement and maintenance are implied by statute. Sometimes it is desired expressly to extend or restrict the statutory powers, but generally they are suitable.

(1) *Statutory power of maintenance*

In the case of an instrument which comes into operation after 1925, section 31 of the Trustee Act 1925 provides that where property is held by trustees in trust for any person for any interest, whether vested or contingent, then, subject to any prior interests or charges affecting that property, the trustees may at their sole discretion apply the whole or such part of the income of that property towards the maintenance, education or benefit of an infant beneficiary as may in all the circumstances be reasonable. If on attaining the age of eighteen years [54] the beneficiary has not a vested interest in the income of the property, the trustees must pay the income of the property, and of any accretion thereto under the following provision, to the beneficiary until he either attains a vested interest therein or dies, or until failure of his interest.

During the minority of a beneficiary, the trustees must accumulate such income as is not applied for maintenance. If the beneficiary's interest in the income during his minority or until his marriage was vested, or if on attaining his majority or marrying under that age he becomes absolutely entitled to the property from which the income arose, he is entitled to such accumulations on attaining his majority or marrying earlier. Otherwise, the trustees must hold the accumulations as an accretion to the capital of the property from which they arose.[55]

The statutory power to apply income for maintenance applies in the case of a contingent interest only if the limitation or trust carries the intermediate income of the property.[56] Section 31 applies only if and so far as a contrary intention is not expressed in the trust instrument.[57]

---

[53] *Re Power* [1947] Ch. 572.
[54] Family Law Reform Act 1969, s. 1.
[55] Trustee Act 1925, s. 31 (2).
[56] *Ibid.* s. 31 (3). See Snell, pp. 288, 392–397.
[57] Trustee Act 1925, s. 69 (2); *Re Turner's Will Trusts* [1937] Ch. 15; and see *Re Erskine's S.T.* [1971] 1 W.L.R. 162. For form, see *post*, p. 438.

(2) *Statutory power of advancement*

In the case of a settlement made after 1925, section 32 of the Trustee Act 1925 confers a power of advancement where the trust property consists of money or securities or of property held upon trust for sale. Trustees have an absolute discretion to pay any capital money for the advancement or benefit of any person entitled to the capital or any share of it, whether absolutely or contingently, whether his interest is subject to a gift over on the occurrence of any event, whether he is entitled in possession or in remainder or reversion, and whether or not his interest is liable to be defeated by the exercise of a power of appointment or diminished by the increase of the class to which he belongs. The power is very wide. Thus, it has been held that the word "benefit" is the widest possible word and that the power includes a payment of capital directly to a beneficiary, even though he does not require it for any particular purpose at the moment, though the trustees must satisfy themselves that it is a proper case for a payment to be made in that manner.[58] The capital advanced may be resettled in favour of the beneficiary and his or her family and it does not matter that people other than the beneficiary benefit incidentally.[59]

Nevertheless, the section itself contains certain fetters on the statutory power:

(a) The money advanced must not exceed one-half of the presumptive or vested share of the beneficiary in the trust property;

(b) If the person in whose favour the advance is made becomes absolutely and indefeasibly entitled to a share in the trust property the money advanced must be brought into account as part of such share;

(c) No advance may be made so as to prejudice any person entitled to any prior life or other interest, whether vested or contingent, in the money advanced unless such person is in existence and of full age and consents in writing to the advance. The consent of an object of a discretionary trust is not necessary, because such object is not entitled to a vested or contingent prior interest within the section.[60]

The power applies only if and so far as a contrary intention is not expressed in the trust instrument.[61] Thus, for example, it does not apply if there is a trust to accumulate income.[62]

Power to compound liabilities and so forth

The settlement may include a power for the trustees to settle

---

58 *Re Moxon's Will Trusts* [1958] 1 W.L.R. 165.
59 *Pilkington* v. *I.R.C.* [1964] A.C. 612.
60 *Re Beckett's Settlement* [1940] Ch. 279; and see *Re Harris's Settlement* (1940) 56 T.L.R. 429.
61 Trustee Act 1925, s. 69 (2).
62 *I.R.C.* v. *Bernstein* [1961] Ch. 399.

claims, compound liabilities and so forth, though extensive powers conferred for this purpose by statute make it unnecessary to frame the power so widely as formerly, and such a clause may be left out altogether. Amongst other things, the statutory power [63] enables trustees to accept any composition or security for any debt, to allow any time for payment of any debt, and to compromise, compound, abandon, submit to arbitration or otherwise settle any debt, account, claim or other thing relating to the trust.

Power to charge for services in a professional capacity

A trustee may make no profit from his trust and so trustees may not usually charge for any services rendered to the trust in a professional capacity. Thus, a trustee who is a solicitor and acts in that capacity to the trust will be allowed only his out-of-pocket expenses,[64] in the absence of a clause enabling him to charge for his professional services. If it is desired that a trustee should be at liberty to charge for his professional services, for example as a solicitor or an accountant, an express clause to that effect should be inserted in the settlement: such a clause is commonly inserted.

VI. A NOTE ON DISCRETIONARY TRUSTS

We have mentioned the discretionary trust and its advantages in a previous chapter [65] and earlier in this chapter.[66] The following are a few points to bear in mind with regard to the operation of such trusts.

Beneficiaries and trusts

The objects of the discretionary trust will depend on the settlor's wishes. For example, they may be members of his family such as his children and remoter issue and the wives and husbands of such persons. Again, if the settlor is engaged in business, he may set up a discretionary trust for the benefit of anyone who is or has been an employee of such business.[67]

A typical discretionary trust will direct the trustees to hold the capital and income of the fund on trust for such of the discretionary objects as they may during the trust period [68] appoint [69] either absolutely or for limited interests. Subject to any such appointment, they will be directed during the trust period [68] to pay such of the income to such of the discretionary beneficiaries as they shall in their

---

[63] Trustee Act 1925, s. 15.
[64] *Moore* v. *Frowd* (1837) 3 My. & Cr. 45.
[65] See *ante*, pp. 345–349.
[66] See *ante*, p. 372.
[67] The trust will be valid if it can be said with certainty that any given individual is or is not a member of the class, and it is not necessary that a complete list can be drawn up of all possible beneficiaries, at any rate where the discretionary trust concerns income: *McPhail* v. *Doulton* [1971] A.C. 424.
[68] See *post*, p. 382.
[69] See *ante*, p. 372, note 3.

discretion decide. The settlement will contain a power to accumulate income which is not distributed. One of certain specified periods for accumulation can be chosen, and often the period of twenty-one years from the execution of the settlement will be suitable.[70] The trustees will be directed, subject to the foregoing, to hold the capital and income of the fund on trust, say, for such of the settlor's children and remoter issue as are living when the trust period expires, if more than one in equal shares *per stirpes*. The " trust period " is the period for which the settlement is designed, at the longest, to endure. Formerly a " royal lives " clause was commonly used to delineate such period, but now the period of eighty years from the execution of the settlement is generally chosen and the settlement will define the trust period as such.[71] Finally, there will be a provision that, subject to the trusts and powers of the settlement, the trustees are to hold the capital and income in trust, say, for the settlor's children living at the date of the execution of the settlement or (in the event of death) their estates, or perhaps the trust will be for certain charities: such a provision will prevent a resulting trust arising in favour of the settlor.[72]

Trustees' powers

The trustees will usually be given similar powers to those given to trustees of a fixed trust, such as powers of investment and power to charge for professional services.

Exercise of trustees' discretion

Although trustees must, if required, furnish the beneficiaries with information relating to such matters as investments of the fund, and permit them to inspect trust documents such as title deeds, they need not give reasons for exercising in any particular mode a discretionary power reposed in them and they need not disclose documents relating thereto.[73]

---

[70] See Law of Property Act 1925, s. 164, and Perpetuities and Accumulations Act 1964, s. 13.
[71] See Perpetuities and Accumulations Act 1964, s. 1. And *post*, p. 440.
[72] For a typical modern discretionary trust, see *post*, p. 439.
[73] *Re Londonderry's Settlement* [1965] Ch. 918.

CHAPTER 16

WILLS

I. REASONS FOR MAKING A WILL

BEFORE discussing the formalities and contents of a will, it is convenient
to give briefly some of the main reasons for making a will at all:

(a) The testator may not wish his property to devolve according
to the rules applicable on intestacy. For example, the testator's
widow may have her own means and he may wish to leave more
to his children than is provided for them by the intestacy rules.
In this connection, the Inheritance (Family Provision) Act
1938 must be borne in mind. This Act,[1] as amended and
extended, gives the court power, in the case of a person who
dies domiciled in England, to order that reasonable provision
for the maintenance of a dependant be made from the
deceased's estate if it considers that his will or the intestacy
rules do not make such provision. However, the effect of the
Act can be avoided.[2] For example, a man may make an
inter vivos settlement in favour of himself, his mistress and
their children in order to defeat the claims of his estranged
wife; the property thus disposed of will not form part of his
estate on death and so will not be subject to the Act's
provisions. Again, the court will take into account the reasons
why the deceased has not provided for a dependant,[3] which
may be stated in the will or some other document. For
example, the deceased may state that he has already provided
for the dependant in his life. It should be noted that the
reasons should be good ones, for otherwise the court will
ignore them.

(b) The testator may wish to leave his property upon trust for
members of his family or for others, with sophisticated and
complex provisions as to powers of investment and the like.[4]

(c) The deceased can appoint his executor. This has the advantage
that a person or body who is competent and trustworthy can be
put in charge of the estate in place of someone entitled to
administration, who may not have these characteristics.[5] In

---

[1] See Tyler, *Family Provision*. See the Law Commission's Working Paper No. 42
(1971) on Family Property Law.
[2] See Tyler, pp. 24–27; *Schaefer* v. *Schuhmann* [1972] 2 W.L.R. 481.
[3] Inheritance (Family Provision) Act 1938, s. 1 (7). See Tyler, pp. 67–69.
[4] See *ante*, p. 378 and *post*, p. 397.
[5] For the choice of executor, see *post*, p. 392. For grants of representation generally,
see Parry, *The Law of Succession* (6th ed.), Chaps. 5, 9, 10.

the past, an administrator had to give an administration bond while an executor did not. The Administration of Estates Act 1971, ss. 8 and 9, abolishes administration bonds and only requires sureties in certain cases.

(d) The making of a will gives an opportunity to procure certain fiscal advantages, an aspect which is discussed later.[6]

II. CAPACITY

Everyone may make a will, unless he falls within one of the exceptions provided by the law, the most important ones being as follows.

Minors

A will made by a minor is void,[7] unless he is a member of the armed forces and comes within the provisions discussed below.[8]

Mental disorder

A person of unsound mind is unable to make a valid will, though if he makes it in a lucid period it is valid [9] and the fact that he suffers from delusions will not upset the will if they did not influence the making of it.[10] As for the position of those wishing to establish validity, such as beneficiaries under the will, and those wishing to upset it, such as those entitled on intestacy, the position is as follows. It is incumbent on a person seeking to establish the validity of a will to show that it is in fact valid.[11] However, " if a will, rational on the face of it, is shown to have been executed and attested in the manner prescribed by law, it is presumed, in the absence of any evidence to the contrary, to have been made by a person of competent understanding. But if there are circumstances in evidence which counterbalance that presumption, the decree of the court must be against its validity, unless the evidence on the whole is sufficient to establish affirmatively that the testator was of sound mind when he executed." [12]

Illness or old age which impairs the understanding may invalidate a will, and in such circumstances a doctor should be procured to pronounce on the testator's dispositive capacity.[13]

Force or fraud

Force or fraud will invalidate a will, though persuasion of the

---

[6] See *post*, p. 398. For further reasons, see Theobald, *Wills* (13th ed.), pp. 5–6. An alternative to a will as regards certain property, such as National Savings Certificates, is a nomination. Nominations may be made by persons aged over 15. A will cannot revoke a nomination. On nominations generally, see (1967) 31 Conv.(N.S.) 85; [1972] J.B.L. 20.

[7] Wills Act 1837, s. 7; Family Law Reform Act 1969, s. 3.

[8] See *post*, p. 389.

[9] *In the Estate of Walker* (1912) 28 T.L.R. 466.

[10] *Banks* v. *Goodfellow* (1870) L.R. 5 Q.B. 549.

[11] See *Barry* v. *Butlin* (1838) 2 Moo.P.C.C. 480; *Harmes* v. *Hinkson* (1946) 62 T.L.R. 445.

[12] *Symes* v. *Green* (1859) 1 S. & T. 401, *per* Sir C. Cresswell.

[13] See *Thomas* v. *Jones* [1928] P. 162 at p. 166.

testator to make his will in a particular way will not by itself invalidate it.[14]

III. FORMALITIES

Wills Act 1837, s. 9

This provides that " No will shall be valid unless it shall be in writing and executed in manner hereinafter mentioned; (that is to say) it shall be signed at the foot or end thereof by the testator or by some other person in his presence and by his direction; and such signature shall be made or acknowledged by the testator in the presence of two or more witnesses present at the same time and such witnesses shall attest and shall subscribe the will in the presence of the testator but no form of attestation shall be necessary." The various points arising will be considered in turn.[15]

" In writing "

The will may be printed, typewritten or in manuscript and may be written on any material. There is no need to use any particular form of words, and a will which reads merely " all for mother " has been held valid.[16]   However, the word " devise " is generally taken to refer to real estate and " bequeath " to refer to personalty; a legacy or bequest is a gift of personal property, a devise a gift of real property.

" Signed by the testator "

The testator's signature may take the form, for example, of his name stamped on the will [17] or a mark (even a thumb mark in ink [18]) but a seal without more is not sufficient.[19]   And where the name of the testatrix appeared at the commencement of a holograph will (*i.e.* one in the handwriting of the testator), which ended " your loving mother," that expression was held to be a sufficient signature.[20]   The will may be signed by someone else in the testator's presence and by his direction.[21]   This may be done by one of the attesting witnesses [22]; and it will be a good execution if the witness signs his own name, stating in the will that he does so on behalf of the testator, in his presence, and by his direction.[23]

---

[14] *Parfitt* v. *Lawless* (1872) L.R. 2 P. & D. 462. On undue influence, see *Wintle* v. *Nye* [1959] 1 W.L.R. 284; *Re Craig* [1971] Ch. 95.

[15] For wills involving a foreign element, see Wills Act 1963; Parry, p. 14.

[16] *Thorn* v. *Dickens* [1906] W.N. 54; " Probably the shortest will ever known," *per* Gorrell Barnes P.

[17] *Jenkins* v. *Gaisford* (1863) 3 S. & T. 93.

[18] *In b. Finn* (1936) 52 T.L.R. 153.

[19] *Wright* v. *Wakeford* (1811) 17 Ves. 454.

[20] *In the Estate of Cook* [1960] 1 W.L.R. 353. And see *In b. Chalcraft* [1948] P. 222 (testatrix only partially completed signature before losing consciousness; signature held sufficient); *cf. Re Colling, The Times,* June 9, 1972.

[21] Wills Act 1837, s. 9, *supra.*

[22] *Re Bailey* (1838) 1 Curt. 914.

[23] *Re Clark* (1839) 2 Curt. 329.

Position of signature

The Wills Act 1837, s. 9, requires the testator to sign the will " at the foot or end thereof." Non-compliance with this direction formerly made many wills invalid, and so the Wills Act Amendment Act 1852 was passed. This provides that a signature is valid if it is " so placed at or after, or following, or under, or beside or opposite to the end of the will, that it shall be apparent on the face of the will that the testator intended to give effect by such his signature to the writing signed as his will." The Act also in effect provides that the will is not invalidated merely because a blank space comes between the will and the signature, or the signature is placed in the attestation clause or under the signatures of the witnesses or on a page where no clause of the will is written, or there appears to be sufficient space on the preceding page for the signature.[24]

However, nothing following the testator's signature is valid. That part of the will coming before the signature will be admitted to probate, but any part following the signature will not. In one case where the writing was on three pages and the signature at the foot of the first page it was held that the first page was properly executed but that the two following pages were not.[25] But if the will contains words which were clearly intended to join in clauses written after the signature with clauses written before, the whole will may be admitted to probate if it is proved that the whole will was written before the testator signed. In one case the testatrix signed her will, made on a printed form, at the end of the first page, and above the signature were the words " See other side for completion." On the back were the words " Continuation from the other side," followed by further dispositions. On proof that all the words were written before the will was signed, the whole will was admitted to probate.[26] But if there are no such words of incorporation above the signature, words after the signature will not be admitted.[27]

A further point is that a will may incorporate other documents provided that such documents were in existence at the time the will was made,[28] that they are referred to in the will as then existing [28] and that such documents are sufficiently indentified in the will.[29] If these conditions are satisfied, dispositions made in an incorporated document will be valid even though the document does not fulfil the formalities of a will.[30]

---

[24] See *Re Archer* (1871) L.R. 2 P. & D. 252. See also *In the Estate of Long* [1936] P. 166.
[25] *In b. Anstee* [1893] P. 283. And see *In the Estate of Bercovitz* [1962] 1 W.L.R. 321 (will signed at foot but also at top, only signature at top attested; will invalid).
[26] *Palin* v. *Ponting* [1930] P. 185.
[27] *In b. Gee* (1898) 78 L.T. 843; *Practice Direction* [1953] 1 W.L.R. 689.
[28] *In b. Smart* [1902] P. 238.
[29] *Re White* [1925] Ch. 179.
[30] For an example, see *post*, p. 394 (statutory definition of personal chattels).

Witnesses

The testator's signature must be either made or acknowledged by him in the presence of two or more witnesses who must be present at the same time and who must then sign and attest the will in the testator's presence.[31]

(a) If the signature is *made* in the witnesses' presence, it is not necessary that they should actually see the testator write. It is sufficient if they see him in the act of writing something[32] or even if they are in such a position that they may, if they please, see him writing.[33] But a blind person cannot be a witness to a will.[34]

(b) If the testator has already affixed his signature to the will, he can *acknowledge* it in the witnesses' presence. No particular form of acknowledgment is necessary. A request that the witnesses sign beneath the testator's signature[35] or even gestures[36] will be enough, though an express acknowledgment is preferable.

(c) Both the witnesses must be present when the testator makes or acknowledges his signature.[37]

(d) The witnesses must sign (that is, subscribe) the will in the presence of the testator.[38] It is not necessary that the witnesses should sign in the presence of each other,[39] though it is advisable that they should do so and in the ordinary form of attestation it is stated that they did so. The testator need not see the witnesses sign,[40] though he must be in such a position that he can see them sign if he wishes to do so.[41]

(e) The witnesses must not only subscribe the will; they must also attest it, which means signing with the intention of bearing witness to the fact of its having been signed by the testator. Although no form of attestation is necessary,[42] it is always desirable to add an attestation clause to a will, for it is then presumed that the statutory formalities have been complied with and it will be easier to obtain probate.[43] The usual form of attestation clause appears in Precedent 33 in the Appendix.[44]

(f) If a beneficiary or the wife or husband of a beneficiary attests the will, the attestation is good, but the beneficiary can take nothing

[31] Wills Act 1837, s. 9, *supra.*
[32] *Smith* v. *Smith* (1866) L.R. 1 P. & D. 143.
[33] *Newton* v. *Clarke* (1839) 2 Curt. 320.
[34] *In the Estate of Gibson* [1949] P. 434.
[35] *Gaze* v. *Gaze* (1843) 3 Curt. 451.
[36] *In b. Davies* (1850) 2 Rob.Ecc. 337.
[37] Wills Act 1837, s. 9, *supra*; *Re Groffman* [1969] 1 W.L.R. 733.
[38] Presence must be both physical and mental. In *Re Chalcraft* [1948] P. 222 the testatrix was losing consciousness during the attestation. The will was held valid.
[39] *In the Goods of Webb* (1855) Dea. & Sw. 1.
[40] *Shires* v. *Glascock* (1688) 2 Salk. 688.
[41] *Doe* d. *Wright* v. *Manifold* (1813) 1 M. & S. 294.
[42] Wills Act 1837, s. 9, *supra.*
[43] Non-Contentious Probate Rules, r. 10.
[44] See *post,* p. 443.

under the will.[45]   However, in the case of a death after May 30, 1968, so long as there are two witnesses who are not beneficiaries, the attestation of a further witness who is (or whose spouse is) a beneficiary can be disregarded [46]; the beneficiary or his or her spouse can thus take the benefit under the will.   A person who is appointed by the will to be an executor may attest the will [47] and a creditor of the testator may be an attesting witness, notwithstanding that by the will the deceased's property is charged with the payment of the creditor's debts.[48]

A properly drafted will will generally include a charging clause [49] authorising a solicitor or other professional person who is executor or trustee to charge for work done on behalf of the estate.   This is equivalent to a legacy to the executor.   A solicitor trustee who attested the will cannot charge under such a clause.[50]   But a solicitor who is subsequently appointed trustee in place of an original trustee can benefit under such a clause.[51]

Alterations

With respect to changes made in a will after its execution, it is provided that no obliteration, interlineation or other alteration made after the execution of the will is valid or effective, except so far as the words or effect of the will before such alteration are not apparent, unless such alteration is executed and attested in the same manner as a will.[52]   But it is sufficient if the signature of the testator and the subscription of the witnesses are made in the margin of the will near such alteration, or near a memorandum which refers to such alteration and which is written at the end or in some other part of the will.[52]   If, therefore, there is an unattested alteration it will be struck out of the will unless it can be proved to have been made before the will was executed.   Because it will be presumed, in the absence of contrary evidence, that an unattested alteration was made after the execution of the will,[53] it is best to attest every alteration, even if made before the will was executed.

An unattested obliteration or erasure has the effect of revoking that part of the will in so far as it makes that part impossible to read. If the original words or figures can still be read by natural means they stand.[54]

---

45 Wills Act 1837, s. 15.   See *Re Doland's Will Trusts* [1970] Ch. 267.   For exceptions, see Parry, pp. 19–20.
46 Wills Act 1968, s. 1, which reverses *Re Bravda* [1968] 1 W.L.R. 479.
47 Wills Act 1837, s. 17.
48 *Ibid.* s. 16.
49 *Post*, pp. 439, 443.
50 *Re Pooley* (1889) 40 Ch.D. 1.
51 *Re Royce's Will Trusts* [1959] Ch. 626.
52 Wills Act 1837, s. 21.   The initials of the testator and witnesses will suffice: *In the Goods of Blewitt* (1880) 5 P.D. 116.
53 See *In b. Sykes* (1873) L.R. 3 P. & D. 26 at pp. 27–28.
54 *In b. Itter* [1950] P. 130.

Exceptions

An exception to the necessity to observe the above formalities exists as regards wills of personalty or realty of soldiers or airmen in actual military service [55] or sailors who are either at sea or, if they had been soldiers, would have been in actual military service.[56] Such wills may be written without being signed or attested by witnesses or even made verbally before witnesses, so long as there is a testamentary intention,[57] and if the exception applies it matters not that the testator is an infant.[58]

Summary

It will be clear that there are many pitfalls surrounding the formal requirements of a will. The following is the usual way of making a valid will. The solicitor will take instructions from the testator and draw the will up, with a proper attestation clause, as mentioned above. The testator will call his two witnesses together and will then sign the will in their presence. Each witness will then sign below the testator's signature, in the presence of the testator and of each other.

IV. REVOCATION

A will may be revoked at any time until the testator dies. Revocation may take a number of forms.

Revocation by subsequent will or codicil [59]

A will usually commences with a clause expressly revoking all former wills, codicils and testamentary dispositions: or it may revoke part of a former will, leaving the rest of it standing. But a mere statement that " this is my last will " does not revoke a former will.[60] If a revoking clause is not inserted, the will or codicil only revokes a former will in so far as it is inconsistent therewith: thus, if two wills dispose of the same property in different ways, the former disposition is revoked by the latter, but if the first of two wills disposes of property not dealt with in the second, the first is not revoked so far as that disposition is concerned and both wills can be admitted to probate.[61]

Revocation by writing executed like a will

A will may be revoked by a written instrument which makes no disposition, provided it is executed like a will and declares an intention to make a revocation. Thus, where a testator in a letter, signed by

---

[55] See *Re Wingham* [1949] P. 187; *In the Estate of Coleman* [1958] 1 W.L.R. 457.
[56] Wills Act 1837, s. 11, as amended by Wills (Soldiers and Sailors) Act 1918.
[57] *In the Estate of Knibbs* [1962] 1 W.L.R. 852.
[58] Wills (Soldiers and Sailors) Act 1918, s. 1. See *ante*, p. 384.
[59] Wills Act 1837, s. 20. But see (1972) 122 New L.J. 6.
[60] *Simpson* v. *Foxon* [1907] P. 54; *Kitcat* v. *King* [1930] P. 266.
[61] See *e.g. Re Wayland* [1951] 2 All E.R. 1041; *Re Pearson* [1963] 1 W.L.R. 1358.

him and attested by two witnesses, directed his brother to burn his will, it was held that the will was revoked.[62]

Revocation by marriage

A will is automatically revoked by the testator's or testatrix' marriage,[63] except that:

(a) a will made in exercise of a power of appointment, when the property thereby appointed would not, in default of such appointment, pass as on the testator's intestacy is not revoked as regards such appointment,[63] although the will is otherwise revoked[64];

(b) a will made after 1925 and expressed to be made in contemplation of a marriage is not revoked by the solemnisation of that marriage,[65] but it will be revoked by marriage if the will merely states that it is made in contemplation of marriage in a general sense.[66]

It is the duty of a solicitor preparing a will, who knows that the testator intends to get married in the near future, to bring to the testator's attention the effect of subsequent marriage on the will.[67]

Revocation by destruction

A will can be revoked by the testator or some person in his presence and by his direction burning, tearing or otherwise destroying it with the intention of revoking it.[68] This provision is stringent. For instance, a will has been held valid notwithstanding that it was struck through with a pen.[69] But if the testator cuts out his signature the will is revoked.[70]

Again, the destruction must be by the testator or by someone in his presence and by his direction. Thus, where a codicil was destroyed by someone at the request of the testatrix, but not in her presence, it was held that this was not a revocation and probate was granted of a draft copy of the codicil.[71] Finally, the destruction must be accompanied by the testator's intention to revoke. Thus, an accidental destruction by fire does not constitute revocation.[72]

The court will presume that a will which remained in the custody of a deceased person until the time of his death, but which cannot then be found, has been destroyed by him during his lifetime with the intention to revoke it.[73] However, this presumption may be rebutted

---

[62] *In the Goods of Durance* (1872) L.R. 2 P. & D. 406; and see *Re Spracklan's Estate* [1938] 2 All E.R. 345.
[63] Wills Act 1837, s. 18.
[64] *In b. Russell* (1890) 15 P.D. 111; *In b. Gilligan* [1950] P. 32, 38.
[65] Law of Property Act 1925, s. 177.
[66] *Sallis* v. *Jones* [1936] P. 43. See further Parry, pp. 34–35.
[67] *Hall* v. *Meyrick* [1957] 2 Q.B. 455.
[68] Wills Act 1837, s. 20.
[69] *Stephens* v. *Taprell* (1840) 2 Curt. 458.
[70] *Bell* v. *Fothergill* (1870) L.R. 2 P. & D. 148.
[71] *In the Goods of Dadds* (1857) Deane 290.
[72] *Re Booth* [1926] P. 118.
[73] *Eckersley* v. *Platt* (1866) L.R. 1 P. & D. 281.

by evidence to the contrary; in such cases, despite the loss or destruction of the will, it may be proved by producing a copy [74] or by oral statements by a witness who has seen the will and remembers its contents.[75]

Dependent relative revocation

If a testator purports to revoke a will intending to make some other disposition of his property which is never validly made, there is no revocation. Thus, if a testator revokes his will merely in order to substitute another for it, then if the other is not in fact executed [76] or is not properly attested,[77] the will is not in fact revoked. Again, if he destroys his will under the mistaken idea that all his property would pass to his wife on his intestacy,[78] the will must be admitted to probate.[79]

Revival of a revoked will

A will or codicil which has been revoked (otherwise than by destruction) can be revived by the re-execution thereof or by a properly executed codicil showing an intention to revive the same.[80]

V. CONTENTS OF A WILL

What clauses will appear in the will depends, of course, on the wishes of the testator, the nature and value of his estate and so forth. The following are some of the points to be borne in mind.

Revocation [81]

The first clause in a will is usually one revoking all former wills, codicils and testamentary dispositions of the testator. This will avoid the difficulties which may arise from having to read two or more wills together. Of course, the testator must be told the effect of such a clause, for he may wish a former will to stand, in which case a general revocation is inappropriate.

Appointment of executors and trustees

Probate cannot be granted to more than four persons in respect of the same *property*,[82] so that no more than four executors should be

---

[74] *In the Goods of Dadds, supra.*
[75] *Sugden* v. *Lord St. Leonards* (1876) 1 P.D. 154.
[76] *Dixon* v. *Solicitor to the Treasury* [1905] P. 42.
[77] *In b. Davies* [1951] 1 All E.R. 920.
[78] *In the Estate of Southerden* [1925] P. 177.
[79] For a further extension of the doctrine, see *Re Mills* (1968) 88 W.N.(N.S.W.) (Pt. 2) 74; (1969) 32 M.L.R. 447.
[80] Wills Act 1837, s. 22.
[81] See *ante*, p. 389.
[82] Supreme Court of Judicature (Consolidation) Act 1925, s. 160. *Re Holland* (1936) 53 T.L.R. 3.

named. Probate can be granted to one executor alone, but, in such a case, if a minor is interested under the will or the will confers a life interest (by settlement) in any property comprised in it, any person interested may apply to the court for the appointment of an additional personal representative, unless the sole personal representative is a trust corporation.[83] Thus, if there is such a minority or life interest, two executors or a trust corporation should be appointed.

A minor should not be appointed executor because he cannot act until he attains majority.[84] If there are other executors the grant will be made to them, power being reserved to the minor to apply on attaining his majority. If he is the sole executor, administration with the will annexed will be granted to his parents or guardian.

The same persons are usually appointed both executors and trustees where the latter are required because the testator settles property by will.

The testator will have to decide whether to appoint an individual or individuals or a body such as a trust corporation or a bank as his executors and trustees. The advantages of appointing individuals are that they are likely to be able to discharge their duties with more sympathy and understanding to the testator's family than a body such as a bank is[85] and that they may be willing to act without payment. The advantages of professional bodies are that they have the requisite knowledge and experience, that if they do act so as to deplete the estate they have the money to compensate the beneficiaries, and that they do not die. There is much to be gained by appointing a solicitor (usually, of course, the one who drafts the will); he not only has the requisite knowledge and experience but his services will be less expensive than those of the bank.[86]

Legacies

A legacy is a gift of personal property made by will. A *specific* legacy is a gift of a definite thing, such as " my gold watch." A *general* legacy is a gift of something which is not specifically distinguished from all other things of the same type: it may be a sum of money, such as " £1,000 " (a pecuniary legacy) or (less commonly) of something else, such as " a diamond ring." The distinction is important. A specific legacy is adeemed, that is, it fails, if the subject of it is disposed of by the testator before he dies, or changed into something substantially different,[87] but a general legacy is not. On the other hand, if the testator's debts are such that all his gifts cannot

---

[83] Judicature Act 1925, s. 160; Family Law Reform Act 1969, s. 7. For special personal representatives of settled land, see *ante*, p. 367.
[84] Judicature Act 1925, s. 165.
[85] *e.g.* as regards the exercise of a power of appointment.
[86] See " Which? " December 1970, pp. 369–374; (1970) 122 New L.J., p. 1101. For the appointment of a firm of solicitors, see *Re Horgan* [1971] P. 50.
[87] *Re Leeming* [1912] 1 Ch. 828; *Re Kuypers* [1925] Ch. 244; *Re Jameson* [1908] 2 Ch. 111.

be met, general legacies abate, that is, are reduced *pari passu*, before specific ones.[88] A *demonstrative* legacy is a legacy to be met out of a particular fund, such as a gift of " £500 to be raised out of the sale of my Government stock." It is a general legacy in that it is not subject to ademption, so that the legatee is entitled to have it paid out of the rest of the estate if the fund out of which it is payable ceases to exist in the testator's lifetime. But it is a specific legacy in that it is not liable to abate with general legacies if the particular fund does exist at the testator's death.

In drafting a will, consideration should be given to the possibility of the testator disposing *inter vivos* of something which is the subject of a specific legacy, and if he wishes to replace it with something else or with a pecuniary legacy in such a case, provision should be made for this in the will. Again, if it appears that there will be insufficient residue to meet the testator's debts, and if in such event it is desired that specific legacies should abate before pecuniary ones, provision to that effect should be made in the will.

If a legatee (or devisee [89]) dies before the testator the gift will lapse, that is, it will not take effect, unless the will provides for the eventuality. Instead, the property concerned falls into residue or, if there is no gift of residue in the will or if the lapsed gift is itself residue, it devolves as on intestacy. There are certain exceptions [90] to this rule, the most important being:

(a) Where there is a devise in tail and the devisee dies in the testator's lifetime leaving issue capable of inheriting and any of them survive the testator.[91]

(b) Where there is a devise or bequest to a child or other issue of the testator who dies before, but leaves issue surviving, the testator.[92]

These two exceptions are expressed to apply only in the absence of a contrary intention. The surviving issue do not necessarily benefit in either case, for the devise or bequest takes effect " as if the death of [the deceased devisee or legatee] had happened immediately after the death of the testator." [93] Accordingly, the devise or bequest is deemed to form part of the deceased devisee's or legatee's estate and will devolve accordingly. For example, if a testator leaves property to his son, who dies before the testator leaving issue who survive the testator, if the son died leaving his property by will to a friend, he and not the issue will take; again, if the son was an undischarged bankrupt when he died his trustee in bankruptcy will take the property.[94]

[88] Administration of Estates Act 1925, s. 55 (1) (ix); Sched. 1, Pt. 2.
[89] Wills Act 1837, s. 25.
[90] See *e.g. Williamson* v. *Naylor* (1838) 3 Y. & C. Ex. 208.
[91] Wills Act 1837, s. 32. Entails can now exist in personalty: see Law of Property Act 1925, s. 130.
[92] Wills Act 1837, s. 33. See (1971) 115 S.J. 89.
[93] *Ibid.* ss. 32, 33.
[94] *Re Pearson* [1920] 1 Ch. 247.

However, lapse is not avoided in the second of the above situations in certain cases, the most important being:

(i) Where the gift is to a class.[95] Thus, if a testator gives property " to my children," having three children when he makes his will, and one dies before him leaving issue surviving the testator, only the two surviving children of the testator will take.

(ii) Where the gift is not of the testator's own property but is conferred by the exercise of a special [96] (though not a general [97]) power of appointment.

It will be noted that the law of lapse can appear capricious. Accordingly, it is always best to provide expressly in the will what is to happen if a beneficiary predeceases the testator: for example, a gift may be made " to A or, if he dies in my lifetime, to B."

A further rule that must be borne in mind is that references to property in the will speak from the date of the testator's death.[98] Thus, if he makes a gift of all his shares or of all his land, such gifts will include all the shares or land owned by him at his death, even though not owned at the date of the will. But this rule is ousted if a contrary intention is shown. Thus, a gift of " all the shares I *now* own " will be taken to refer only to those owned at the date of the will. The rule does not apply to specific, as opposed to generic, property, for if the specific property referred to is disposed of by the testator in his lifetime the gift is adeemed, as we have seen,[99] and this is so even if it is replaced by other property of the same description before the death. Thus, where a testatrix gave " my piano " by will but later disposed of it and bought another, it was held that the second piano did not go to the donee under the will.[1] Where the rule does have application, it is advisable to make it clear, if so desired, that the date with reference to which the gift is made is that of the will and not that of the death.

It should be noted that if the testator leaves all his personal chattels to someone (the surviving spouse being the usual donee), it is often convenient to incorporate the statutory definition [2] of these, the advantages being that it saves a long list of objects and its meaning is more likely to be ascertainable than any other, it having been clarified in a number of cases.[3]

---

[95] *Olney* v. *Bates* (1855) 3 Drew. 319.
[96] *Holyland* v. *Lewin* (1883) 26 Ch.D. 266.
[97] *Eccles* v. *Cheyne* (1856) 2 K. & J. 676.
[98] Wills Act 1837, s. 24.
[99] See *ante,* p. 392.
[1] *Re Sikes* [1927] 1 Ch. 364.
[2] See Administration of Estates Act 1925, s. 55 (1) (*x*).
[3] However, in *Re Reynolds' Will Trusts* [1961] 1 W.L.R. 19, at p. 22, Stamp J. said " the decision of a judge as regards an article is of no real assistance as to whether another article is within the definition " and referred to " the curious collocation of terms I find in the definition." See also *Re Collin's Will Trusts* [1971] 1 W.L.R. 37.

Devises

A devise of land may be specific or general (for example, " 100 acres of my farmland "), just as a legacy may be. The points about ademption and lapse discussed in connection with legacies apply to devises also, and appropriate provision should be made in the will if desired.[4] A specific devise, like a specific legacy, abates after a general legacy, and again if it is desired to change the order appropriate provision should be made. Again, it must be remembered that the will speaks from death unless a contrary intention is shown, and it should be clear whether the date of the death or the date of the will is the one intended to be referred to. If successive interests are to be created, care must be taken to create a trust for sale and to avoid creating a strict settlement, unless the latter is desired, which will be unlikely, especially in the case of an ordinary dwelling-house.[5]

Commorientes

If two people die in circumstances where it is uncertain which of them survived the other (as in a car accident) the younger will be deemed in the case of deaths after 1925 to have survived the elder.[6] Thus, if the elder had made a gift by will in favour of the younger the gift will be saved from lapse. However, the rule may cause undesired results, as where a husband leaves all his property to his younger wife and both die at the same time in an accident; the wife will be deemed to have survived him and, if she was intestate and without issue, the wife's (not the husband's) parents will benefit. Accordingly, especially in such a case as the one just stated, it is advisable to provide in the husband's will that the wife will only benefit if she survives him for (usually) a month.[7]

Provision of house for widow

Where the testator is the sole owner of a house, which is used as the matrimonial home, he will usually want to enable his widow to continue to live in the house after his death. He can, of course, do this by an absolute gift to her in the will, but, if estate duty saving is material in the testator's circumstances, *inter vivos* action, by a gift to the wife or a transfer into joint names, is to be preferred.[8] Where the property is held by the husband and wife as beneficial joint tenants, the whole property will accrue to the survivor. Assuming *inter vivos* action is not possible, there are four ways in which the testator may

---

[4] *e.g.* if it is desired to take account of the possibility of the testator moving house, he might devise to his wife his house " Blackacre " or any other house which he owns and in which he lives at the time he dies: see Precedent 33 in the Appendix.

[5] See *ante,* p. 344.

[6] Law of Property Act 1925, s. 184. The presumption is modified in the case of husband and wife dying intestate: Intestates' Estates Act 1952, s. 1 (4).

[7] See (1968) 118 New L.J. 700, 711. And see *Re Rowland* [1963] Ch. 1; *Re Figgis* [1969] 1 Ch. 123.

[8] See Pinson, *Revenue Law* (5th ed.), Chap. 25. But note the Finance Bill 1972.

deal with the house, namely (1) trust for sale; (2) strict settlement; (3) lease; and (4) licence.[9] If a strict settlement is created, the widow, as tenant for life, will have power to sell the property.[10] Hence a trust for sale is the usual form in this situation, the exercise of the trust for sale generally being subject to the widow's consent. It is usual to provide that the widow shall be responsible for rent (if any), insurance and other outgoings.

The devise to the trustees should be of the particular house in question or such other house as the testator shall own and occupy as the matrimonial home at his death.[11]

Annuities

Annuities were formerly common, but, because they can lead to unfortunate estate duty[12] and tax[13] consequences, they are not much favoured today.[14] *Inter vivos* provision for the intended beneficiary is usually more advantageous. Furthermore, the terms of the will providing the annuity may give rise to difficult questions of construction.[15]

An annuity is a pecuniary legacy payable by instalments. In the absence of a contrary intention in the will, it will be charged on the residuary estate. An annuitant is entitled to have a fund set aside which will produce sufficient income to meet the annuity. As the income of any appropriated fund may decrease, trustees tend to appropriate more than is needed. The appropriated fund cannot, of course, be distributed until the annuitant's death; thus, the winding up of the estate is delayed. Usually the trustees are given power to appropriate a fund sufficient at the date of appropriation to meet the annuity and the remainder of residue is then exonerated.

An annuity may be " tax free." In this case, if the annuitant is liable to surtax, the trustees must indemnify him in respect of surtax attributable to the annuity. If the annuitant is entitled to any repayment of tax, he must pay back to the trustees so much of the repayment as relates to the annuity.[16]

The capital element in each payment of a purchased life annuity is exempt from tax.[17] Accordingly, it is now preferable for the testator

---

[9] See Hallett's *Conveyancing Precedents,* p. 983; (1966) 30 Conv.(N.S.) 256; (1966) 116 New L.J. 1567, 1591; (1967) 117 New L.J. 103, 777, 863, 889.

[10] *Ante,* Chap. 14.

[11] See *ante,* p. 395, note 4.

[12] Duty will be payable on the testator's death, and, if the annuity is charged on residue, on the slice of the estate supporting the annuity on the annuitant's death (subject to the surviving spouse exemption, see *post,* p. 398): see Pinson, pp. 333, 381, 387, 400.

[13] The annuity may increase the annuitant's tax liability, and, if the amount of the annuity has to be made up out of capital, such capital may be taxable as income; see *Cunard's Trustees* v. *I.R.C.* [1946] 1 All E.R. 159.

[14] See Potter and Monroe, *Tax Planning* (6th ed.), pp. 444–448; Brighouse's *Short Forms of Wills* (9th ed.), pp. 11–13.

[15] See Parry, pp. 304–306; *Re Berkeley* [1968] Ch. 744.

[16] *Re Pettit* [1922] 2 Ch. 765. On tax free annuities, see Pinson, 5–26 *et seq.*

[17] Finance Act 1956, s. 27; now Income and Corporation Taxes Act 1970, s. 230. See Pinson, 5–31, 32; *post,* p. 400, n. 35.

either before his death to purchase an annuity for the annuitant, or to provide by his will a sum with which the beneficiary can himself purchase an annuity. Sometimes wills contain powers or directions for the trustees to purchase the annuity. In either case, the annuitant can call for the capital sum once the trustees have decided to purchase, and spend the money as he likes. Furthermore, in these circumstances the capital element of the annuity is not exempt from income tax.[18]

Settlements

Often a will, after giving legacies, gives the residue of the testator's estate to the trustees to hold it upon trust for his family. The beneficial interests depend on the testator's wishes, but a common form [19] is to give the residue to the trustees on trust to sell, call in and convert it into money, to pay out of such money the funeral and testamentary expenses, debts, general legacies, annuities bequeathed and death duties, and to hold the remainder of the proceeds of sale and the investments representing them upon certain trusts. There will usually be a trust to pay the income to the testator's wife for life or (if desired) as long as she remains a widow. After her death (or re-marriage) the trustees will be directed to hold the capital and income of the fund on trust absolutely for such of the children of the testator living at his death who attain twenty-one or (if female) attain that age or marry under that age. There will usually be a provision [20] that if a child of the testator dies in his lifetime leaving issue, the latter will (if they reach twenty-one or, if female, reach that age or marry under that age) take the share which the deceased child would have taken if he or she had survived the testator and attained a vested interest.

The reader is further referred to the section on settlements made *inter vivos*, the observations there made (for example, on maintenance, advancement, the trustees' powers of investment and the like and taxation) being equally applicable here. The fiscal advantages of a discretionary trust have been noted there and these apply to a settlement created by will as well as to one created *inter vivos*, so that such a trust may be attractive.[21]

Residue

It is wise to provide for the destination of any property not otherwise dealt with in the will, for this will prevent any undisposed of property or property comprised in a gift which fails (as by lapse where

[18] Pinson, *op. cit.* And see (1967) 117 New L.J. 1076; (1968) 118 New L.J. 1081; (1969) 119 New L.J. 28, 39.
[19] See Hallet's *Conveyancing Precedents*, pp. 1023 *et seq.*; and *post*, pp. 441 *et seq.*
[20] If there is no such provision, s. 33 of the Wills Act 1837 will not prevent lapse, because the gift to the children is a class gift; see *ante*, p. 394.
[21] And see *post*, p. 398.

O*

no alternative provision is made) devolving as on intestacy. Often, as just stated, residue is settled.

It should be kept in mind by the draftsman that if debts and estate duty are payable out of residue, this may so reduce it as to make the gift worthless.

VI. TAXATION

The fiscal implications of drawing up a will can be regarded as twofold. First, it affords an opportunity of reviewing the testator's financial position, with a view to mitigating taxation otherwise than by the will. For instance, it may be desirable for the proposed testator to give away some of his property *inter vivos*, either absolutely or by way of settlement, in the hope that he will survive long enough for estate duty to be saved or avoided on his death.[22]

Secondly, as regards such property as he does not give away in his lifetime but leaves by his will, provision can be made in the will itself for avoiding taxation. A few examples follow:

(a) A settlement may be created which procures substantially the same fiscal advantages as can be procured by a settlement created *inter vivos*.

(b) A possible estate duty saving provision arises in the following way. We have seen[23] that it is usually presumed, in circumstances where it is not clear which of two people died first, that the elder died first. But this rule does not apply for estate duty purposes, for where " two or more persons have died in circumstances rendering it uncertain which of them survived the other or others, the property chargeable with estate duty in respect of each death shall be ascertained as if they had died at the same instant and all relevant property had devolved accordingly."[24] Thus, if in such circumstances one of the two deceased persons has left property to the other by his will, there is a charge to duty on the testator's death but not on the beneficiary's death. However, if it is clear that the testator did in fact die, say, an hour before the beneficiary, the above provision does not apply and there is a second charge to duty.[25] Accordingly, if the testator and the beneficiary are likely to be concerned in an accident together, the gift could be made contingently on the beneficiary surviving the testator by, say, one month. If he survives the testator by, say, an hour but not a month, the gift will never vest and so the property will not pass on the beneficiary's death and will not be liable to duty twice.

(c) Advantage is often taken of the exemption from estate duty which in certain circumstances arises on the death of a surviving spouse

---

[22] See *ante*, p. 348.
[23] See *ante*, p. 395.
[24] Finance Act 1958, s. 29 (1).
[25] Subject to quick succession relief: Finance Act 1958, s. 30, as amended.

and which comes about in the sort of case we are discussing as follows. If a testator leaves his property absolutely to his wife, estate duty is payable on his death and again when the property passes on her death. But if he settles the property on his wife for life (with, say, remainder to their children), though the property is liable to duty on his death it is often exempt from duty on her death.[26] The exemption also operates where the wife settles property by her will on her husband for life and he is the surviving spouse. The exemption only operates if certain requirements are observed, one of which is that the surviving spouse must never have been competent to dispose of the property in the settlement. Thus, for example, if a surviving wife is given a general power of appointment (which she might exercise in her own favour), the exemption will not apply, though if she is given a special power of appointment in favour of a class not including herself and if she is not entitled in default of appointment, the exemption can operate.

VII. INCIDENCE OF DEBTS AND ESTATE DUTY

Debts

Reference should be made to the textbooks on wills and succession for the principles which apply to the payment of debts.[27] We would mention here a number of matters for the draftsman's consideration. The order of application of assets in payment of debts is: undisposed-of property, then residue, then property specifically appropriated or charged, then the fund retained to meet pecuniary legacies, etc.[28] This generally means that the deceased's debts will have to be met out of the residuary estate, thus reducing it, or in some cases making the gift of residue valueless. Subject to any contrary intention shown in the will, the first step in administering a solvent estate is to set aside out of undisposed-of or residuary property, as the case may be, a fund to meet pecuniary legacies. Then a second fund will be set aside out of the balance of the undisposed-of or residuary property to meet debts and testamentary expenses. Difficult problems may arise when a share of residue lapses. It is a question of construction of the particular will as to whether the debts will be payable out of the lapsed share or out of residue as a whole before division.[29]

It should also be remembered that, in the absence of an intention to the contrary, debts charged on property must be borne, as between persons claiming through the deceased, by the property on which they are charged.[30]

---

[26] Finance Act 1894, s. 5 (2); Finance (1909–10) Act 1910, s. 55; Finance Act 1914, s. 14. See further Pinson, *Revenue Law* (5th ed.), pp. 400–402. And note the new relief for property given to a spouse up to £15,000 in the Finance Bill 1972.
[27] See *e.g.* Parry, pp. 278 *et seq.*
[28] Administration of Estates Act 1925, s. 34.
[29] See Parry, pp. 293–297.
[30] Administration of Estates Act 1925, s. 35.

Express provisions in the will may alter the statutory order or liability of specific devises to meet debts.[31]

It seems that, in the absence of any provision to the contrary in the will, realty and personalty are liable rateably.[32]

Estate duty

Estate duty payable in respect of property which prior to the 1894 Act did not pass to the executor as such (for example, realty) is a specific charge on such property. Estate duty in respect of property passing to the executor as such (for example, personalty and leaseholds) is a testamentary expense and borne by the deceased's estate in accordance with the general law.[33] The incidence of duty can be varied by the testator by appropriate " free of duty " provisions.[34] The precise meaning and effect of such provisions is a question of construction.[35] Again, the draftsman should keep in mind that by making specific devises "free of duty " he will be increasing the burden on residue.

VIII. ASSENTS

It is not within the scope of this book to discuss probate, the duties of executors or the administration of assets,[36] but one important conveyancing point can properly be made here. When the executors have paid the deceased's debts and estate duty they must distribute his property to the beneficiaries under the will. This is done by making an assent in favour of the particular beneficiary concerned. This is often done informally in the case of personalty—for example, by handing over the subject of a specific legacy or by paying a pecuniary legacy by cheque. In some cases a special form may be necessary, as in the case of shares in a company, where a proper transfer must be used. But an assent to the vesting of a legal estate in land [37] must be in writing, signed by the personal representative, and must name the person in whose favour it is given, otherwise it will not pass the legal estate.[38] Thus, in the case of a specific devise, the personal representatives must assent in writing in favour of the beneficiary in order to pass the legal estate to him. If the will leaves land on trust and appoints trustees who are different from the personal representatives, the latter must assent in writing in favour of the trustees. Moreover, where the trustees are the same persons as the personal representatives they must, as personal representatives, assent

---

[31] See *e.g.* (1970) 120 New L.J. 376, 387.
[32] See Parry, p. 288, 290, 296.
[33] For the rule in *Re Spencer Cooper* [1908] 1 Ch. 130, see *post*, p. 441.
[34] For form of will, see *post*, p. 441.
[35] See Parry, pp. 357–358, Pinson (5th ed.), 23–54 *et seq.*
[36] See, generally, Parry, *The Law of Succession*, 6th ed.
[37] For settled land, see *ante*, pp. 360, 367–368.
[38] Administration of Estates Act 1925, s. 36 (4). It need not be by deed: Law of Property Act 1925, s. 52 (2).

in writing in favour of themselves as trustees before they can deal with the land in the capacity of trustees.[39] Until this has been done they remain personal representatives and cannot appoint a new trustee so as to vest the legal estate in him. This is logical, but unpopular, for, until the law was decided thus, numerous titles had been regarded as good on the assumption that an assent could be implied by an appointment of new trustees; accordingly, titles sometimes have to be perfected by obtaining grants *de bonis non.*

The grant of probate (or the letters of administration) and the assent are links in the title to the land and the purchaser is concerned with these.[40]

39 *Re King's Will Trusts* [1964] Ch. 542. For criticism, see (1964) 80 L.Q.R. 328; (1964) 28 Conv.(N.S.) 298.
40 See *ante,* pp. 136, 145. For registered land, see *ante,* p. 178.

APPENDIX

PRECEDENTS*

---

* See Hallett's *Conveyancing Precedents* (1965) from which many of the forms which follow are adapted; see also the *Encyclopaedia of Forms and Precedents* (4th ed.). On the technique of drafting, see Piesse and Gilchrist Smith, *The Elements of Drafting* (3rd ed.).

LIST OF PRECEDENTS

		Page
1.	Table of Procedure on Sale of Land	406
2.	Abstract of Title	409
3.	Epitome of Title	410
4.	Completion Statement	411
5.	Notice to Complete	412
6.	Conveyance on Sale	412
7.	Conveyance on Sale. Subject to Right of Way and Restrictive Covenants	413
8.	Conveyance on Sale. Grant and Reservation of Rights of Way, Etc.	414
9.	Conveyance by Co-Owners to Co-Owners	416
10.	Transfer of Registered Land	417
11.	Conveyance by Personal Representatives	417
12.	Conveyance by Mortgagee under Statutory Power of Sale .	418
13.	Conveyance by Mortgagor and Mortgagee	419
14.	Assignment of Leaseholds	420
15.	Assignment of Leaseholds. Informal Apportionment of Rent	421
16.	Transfer of Leaseholds	422
17.	Tenancy Agreement for Furnished Flat	422
18.	Long Lease	423
19.	Legal Charge	426
20.	Legal Charge by Co-Owners. Repayment by Instalments .	430
21.	Mortgage by Demise of Freeholds	431
22.	Mortgage by Sub-Demise of Leaseholds	431
23.	Charge of Registered Land	432
24.	Equitable Mortgage. Memorandum under Seal to Accompany Deposit of Title Deeds	433
25.	Transfer of Mortgage	434
26.	Statutory Receipt	435
27.	Release of Part of Mortgaged Property	435
28.	Discharge of Registered Charge	436
29.	Undertaking to Discharge Mortgage	437
30.	Settlement on Named Grandchildren of Settlor at Twenty-one	437
31.	Discretionary Settlement	439
32.	Appointment of New Trustee	440
33.	Will	441
34.	Assent	443

No. 1

TABLE OF PROCEDURE ON SALE OF LAND

Steps to be taken by vendor's solicitor	*Steps to be taken by purchaser's solicitor*
1. Obtain title deeds, or in the case of registered land, land certificate.[1]	
2. Prepare draft contract [2] and submit it to purchaser's solicitor.[3]	
3.	Send preliminary inquiries.[4]
4.	Make local authority searches and inquiries.[5]
5.	Approve or amend draft contract and return to vendor's solicitor.
6. Reply to preliminary inquiries and consider any amendments to draft contract.	
7. When contract approved, send copy to purchaser's solicitor for engrossment [6] and signature by purchaser.	
8.	If satisfied by result of local searches and inquiries and answers to preliminary inquiries,[7] purchaser signs a copy of the contract which is sent or delivered to vendor's solicitor.
9. On receipt of copy of contract signed by purchaser and deposit, vendor signs his part of the contract which is then sent or delivered to purchaser's solicitor.	

[1] If the property is mortgaged, the land certificate will have been deposited at the Registry. In this case, obtain an office copy of the register.

[2] The vendor's solicitor should have previously examined the title, in the case of unregistered land, to ascertain what is to be the root of title and if any restrictive covenants, etc. affect the property. He should also ascertain from the vendor if there are to be any special provisions for fixtures and fittings, etc.

[3] See *ante*, p. 9.

[4] See *ante*, p. 34.

[5] See *ante*, p. 44.

[6] See *ante*, p. 86.

[7] And if he has obtained firm offer of a mortgage advance, where this is required.

Steps to be taken by vendor's solicitor	Steps to be taken by purchaser's solicitor
10.	Protect contract by registration as estate contract, if desirable,[8] and insure property.[9]
11. Give notice of redemption to mortgagee (if any) if not already done so on obtaining deeds.	
12. Send abstract of title [10] or in the case of registered land office copy register and authority to inspect the register [11] to purchaser's solicitor, if not already done so.	
13.	Peruse abstract, etc. and submit requisitions on title.
14. Draft vacating receipt or discharge in respect of mortgage (if necessary).	
15.	Submit report on title to purchaser's building society or submit abstract, etc. to mortgagee's solicitor.[12]
16.	Prepare draft conveyance or transfer and submit to vendor's solicitor.
17. Answer requisitions.[13]	
18. Peruse draft conveyance or transfer and approve or amend.	
19.	Make any observations on answers to requisitions.
20. Answer observations on requisitions or further requisitions.	
21.	When satisfied with title and draft conveyance or transfer approved, engross conveyance/transfer.[14]

---

[8] See *ante*, p. 26.
[9] See *ante*, p. 191.
[10] See *ante*, p. 119.
[11] See *ante*, p. 93.
[12] See further, *ante*, p. 4.
[13] See *ante*, p. 131.
[14] See *ante*, p. 207.

Steps to be taken by vendor's solicitor	*Steps to be taken by vendor's solicitor*
22.	Obtain purchaser's signature to conveyance/transfer (if necessary) and send or deliver conveyance/transfer to vendor's solicitor.
23. Obtain all necessary receipts for production on completion.[15]	
24. Where appropriate, prepare schedule of deeds to be handed over.[16]	
25. Prepare completion statement[17] and send it to purchaser's solicitor.	
26. In the case of unregistered land, if conveyance contains restrictive covenants by the purchaser, enter a priority notice in the Land Charges Register.[18]	
27. Obtain vendor's signature to conveyance. *	
28.	In the case of unregistered land, obtain official certificate of search in register kept at Land Charges Department of the Land Registry dated not more than fourteen days before completion.[19] In the case of registered land, four days before completion requisition for an official search of the register.[20]
29.	On or before completion examine and mark abstract.[21]
30. Completion. Hand over deeds, etc. keys, etc.[22] and (if appropriate) give usual undertaking to discharge mortgage.[23]	Completion. Hand over banker's draft or drafts and authority for agent to hand over deposit to vendor's solicitor.

[15] See *ante*, p. 210. [16] See *ante*, p. 211.
[17] See further, *ante*, p. 210; *post*, p. 411. [18] See *ante*, p. 160.
[19] See *ante*, p. 158. [20] See *ante*, p. 184. 4 days is merely a convenient period.
[21] See *ante*, p. 210.
[22] See *ante*, p. 211. If deeds are retained, a memorandum of the conveyance should be indorsed on the appropriate conveyance or probate.
[23] See *ante*, p. 211 and *post*, p. 437.

Steps to be taken by purchaser's solicitor	*Steps to be taken by purchaser's solicitor*
31. Complete draft conveyance. Repay mortgage. Cancel vendor's insurance. Register restrictive covenants as Class D (ii) land charges referring to priority notice.[26]	See to stamping of conveyance.[24] Apply for registration of title if in area of compulsory registration and not yet registered.[25] If registered, within the period of priority provided by the official certificate lodge application for registration with transfer and other relevant documents.[27]

No. 2

ABSTRACT OF TITLE [28]

ABSTRACT of the TITLE of John Brown to freehold property 5 Gordon Street in the City of Liverpool.

March 28, 1948 — OFFICIAL CERTIFICATE of search of this dt in H.M. Land Registry against HELEN ELIZABETH SMITH revealing no subsisting entries

March 31, 1948
Stamp £1.2.6
P.D. — CONVEYANCE of this dt btwn the sd HELEN ELIZABETH SMITH the Vendor (1) and MARGARET BROWN the Purchaser (2) RECTNG seisin of Vndr and agrmnt for sale at £1500

IT WAS WITNSD

Exd. with original at office of Mssrs. ABC & Co. XYZ & Co. 1/2/1972

1. In conson of £1500 paid to the Vndr the rcpt etc. the Vndr as B.O. conveyed unto the Pchsr:

ALL THAT pce of lnd site on the northerly side of Gordon St. in the City of Liverpool contg in the whole 500 sq. yards. or thrbts and deltd with the linear dimensions throf in the plan drawn on a Convynce dated the 8th day of May 1900 and made betwn William Shuttleworth of the one pt and Arthur Williamson of the other pt TOGR with the messge or dwghs thron erected and Nod. 5 in Gordon Street afsd. AND TOGR with the free use and enjoyment of Gordon Street afsd and of the common passes shown on the sd plan TO HOLD unto the Pchsr in fee simple SUBJT to the restve covnts contd in the sd Convce dated the 8th day of May 1900

2. Covnt to obsve and perfm sd covnts and for indemnity

3. Ack for prod of docs in Sched

4. Cert of val £3500

[24] See *ante*, p. 213.
[26] See *ante*, p. 160.
[28] See *ante*, pp. 119 *et seq.*

[25] See *ante*, p. 214.
[27] See *ante*, p. 220.

THE SCHEDULE

May 8, 1900	CONVEYANCE
May 8, 1900	MORTGAGE
October 1, 1935	RECONVEYANCE
April 21, 1937	CONVEYANCE
	DULY executed and attested

March 31, 1948
Stamp
£2.10.0.

LEGAL CHARGE of this dt mde btwen the sd MARGARET BROWN the Mtgor (1) and the sd HELEN ELIZABETH SMITH the Mtgee (2)

IT WAS WITNSD

Exd. as above
XYZ & Co.
1/2/1972

1. In conson of the sum of £1000 pd by the Mtgee to the Mtgor the Mtgor covtd as follws:
    i) To repy pcpl and intt by inslmnts
2. For the conson afsd the Mtgor as B.O. thrby charged by way of legal mtge the scheduled prems
3.–6. Usual pvte mtge covts etc.

THE SCHEDULE

ALL THAT the lastly abstd prems
                    DULY executed by Mtgor and attested

July 4, 1962
Stamp 10s.
Exd. as above
XYZ & Co.
1/2/1972

VACATING RECEIPT of this dt endrsd on lastly abstd Legal Charge

January 21, 1971

DEATH of the sd MARGARET BROWN

March 5, 1971

LETTERS OF ADMINISTRATION of ths dt granted to the Vndr out of the Liverpool District Probate Registry

MEMORANDUM of ths dt endrsd on the lastly abstd Grant of the sale of the ppty bfre abstd to the Pchsr.

No. 3

EPITOME OF TITLE [29]

Documents and events constituting title of John Brown to freehold property 5 Gordon Street in the City of Liverpool

No. of Document, etc.	Date	Short description of document and parties, or of event	Evidence now supplied	Whether original document will be handed over on completion
1.	March 28, 1948	Official Certificate of Search against Helen Elizabeth Smith	Photocopy	Yes

[29] See *ante*, p. 121; (1969) 66 L.S.Gaz. 492.

2.	March 31, 1948	Conveyance by Helen Elizabeth Smith to Margaret Brown	Photocopy	Yes
3.	March 31, 1948	Legal Charge by Margaret Brown to Helen Elizabeth Smith	Photocopy	Yes
4.	July 4, 1962	Vacating Receipt indorsed on above mentioned Legal Charge		
5.	Jan. 21, 1971	Death of Margaret Brown		
6.	March 5, 1971	Letters of Administration to estate of Margaret Brown granted to Vendor	Photocopy	No

No. 4

COMPLETION STATEMENT

5 Gordon Street, Liverpool
Brown to Smith

—

COMPLETION STATEMENT [30]

Purchase price	£
Less deposit	

£

Add:

Proportion of general rates at £   per half-year
from   to   (days) [31]
Proportion of water rates at £   per half-year
from   to   (days)

£

Less:

Rentcharge at £   p.a.
from   to   (days) [31]

Balance on completion   £

By draft[s] [32] please in favour of

---

[30] See *ante*, p. 210.
[31] See *ante*, p. 108.
[32] See *ante*, p. 211.

No. 5

NOTICE TO COMPLETE

To [*the other party to the contract or his solicitor*] of [*address*] WE, [*name of solicitors for party giving notice*] of [*address*] as solicitors for and on behalf of [*the party giving notice*] of [*address*] hereby give you notice in accordance with [*the appropriate condition*] [33] as follows:

1. The said [*party giving notice*] is ready [able [34]] and willing to complete the contract dated [*date*] and made between [*name the parties in the proper order*];

2. The date fixed for completion by the said contract was [*date*] and the sale has not yet been completed;

3. You [your client] are [is] required to complete the contract in conformity [accordance] [35] with the above-mentioned condition;

4. If you [your client] fail[s] to complete within twenty-eight days after service of this notice (excluding day of service) [after the day of service of this notice (excluding the day of service)] [35] our client will proceed to enforce the rights powers and remedies conferred on him by the said Condition.

Dated the   day of   197

[*Signature of solicitor for party giving notice*] [36]

No. 6

CONVEYANCE ON SALE

Parties   THIS CONVEYANCE is made the   day of   197 BETWEEN A of [*address and description*] (hereinafter called " the Vendor ") of the one part and B of [*address and description*] (hereinafter called " the Purchaser ") of the other part

Recitals   WHEREAS the Vendor is the estate owner in respect of the fee simple of the property hereinafter described and expressed to be hereby conveyed free from incumbrances [37]

---

[33] *i.e.* Law Society's Condition 19 or National Condition 22. If neither set of Conditions is incorporated a similar notice (with suitable amendments) may be given; see *ante*, pp. 110–111. Express reference to the particular condition in the notice is probably no longer required, but is included here *ex abundante cautela.* The notice should reflect so far as possible the special wording of the particular condition.

[34] We have seen that under the Law Society's Condition the party giving notice must be " ready, able and willing " or " not so ready, able and willing " by reason of the default or omission of the other party to the contract; *ante*, p. 111. The National Conditions require the party giving notice to be " ready and willing."

[35] The alternative wording is appropriate for a notice under the Law Society's Conditions, reflecting as it does the different wording in Law Society's Condition 19 from that in National Condition 22.

[36] For precedents of forms of notice to complete, see 18 *Encyclopaedia of Forms and Precedents*, pp. 809 *et seq.*, and revised forms in service volume.

[37] For alternative forms of recital of seisin, see Hallett, p. 192.

and has agreed with the Purchaser for the sale thereof to him for the sum of £ [price]

Consideration NOW in pursuance of the said agreement and in consideration of the sum of £ [price] paid by the Purchaser to the Receipt Vendor (the receipt whereof the Vendor hereby acknow-
Testatum ledges) [38] THIS DEED WITNESSETH as follows:
Operative words 1. The Vendor as beneficial owner HEREBY CONVEYS unto the Purchaser ALL THAT piece of land TOGETHER with
Parcels the messuage or dwelling-house erected thereon or on some part or parts thereof situate and known as [address] and for the purpose of identification only shown edged red on
Habendum the plan annexed hereto [39] TO HOLD unto the Purchaser in fee simple
Certificate of value 2. It is hereby certified that the transaction hereby effected does not form part of a larger transaction or of a series of transactions in respect of which the amount or value or the aggregate amount or value of the consideration exceeds [£10,000] [£15,000] [40]

Testimonium IN WITNESS whereof the vendor [parties hereto] has [have] hereunto set his [their respective] hand[s] and seal[s] the day and year first before written

SIGNED SEALED AND
DELIVERED by the said   [Signature and seal of the
[the Vendor] [41] in the   Vendor]
presence of:

[Signature address and
description of witness] [42]

No. 7

CONVEYANCE ON SALE

SUBJECT TO RIGHT OF WAY AND RESTRICTIVE COVENANTS

THIS CONVEYANCE is made the   day of   197
BETWEEN A of etc. (hereinafter called " the Vendor ") of the one part and B of etc. (hereinafter called " the Purchaser ") of the other part WHEREAS the Vendor is the estate owner in respect of the fee simple of

---

[38] For the purpose and effect of a receipt clause, see *ante*, p. 225. The consideration and receipt clause may be placed in the operative part, if desired; see Hallett, p. 192.
[39] For the parcels, see *ante*, p. 230.
[40] For the certificate of value, see *ante*, p. 239.
[41] The conveyance will be executed by the purchaser where, *e.g.* it contains a covenant by him; see *e.g.* Forms 7 and 8, *post*.
[42] For execution of deeds, see *ante*, p. 207.

the property hereinafter described and expressed to be hereby conveyed subject as hereinafter mentioned but otherwise free from incumbrances and has agreed with the Purchaser for the sale thereof to him (subject only as aforesaid) for the sum of £   [*price*]

NOW in pursuance etc. THIS DEED WITNESSETH as follows:

1. The Vendor as beneficial owner HEREBY CONVEYS unto the Purchaser ALL THAT the property conveyed by a Conveyance dated, etc. TO HOLD unto the Purchaser in fee simple SUBJECT to (and with the benefit of) the right of way and (so far as the same are subsisting and capable of being enforced) the restrictive covenants mentioned in the said Conveyance

2. The Purchaser HEREBY COVENANTS with the Vendor with the object and intent of affording to the Vendor and his representatives a full and sufficient indemnity but not further or otherwise that he will at all times hereafter duly observe and perform the said covenants so far as they relate to the property hereby conveyed and indemnify the Vendor and his estate against all actions proceedings costs claims and demands in respect thereof [43]

[3. *Certificate of value if appropriate*]

IN WITNESS, etc.

[*To be executed by both parties*] [44]

No. 8

CONVEYANCE ON SALE

GRANT AND RESERVATION OF RIGHTS OF WAY, ETC.

THIS CONVEYANCE is made the   day of   197
BETWEEN A of etc. (hereinafter called " the Vendor ") of the one part and B of etc. (hereinafter called " the Purchaser ") of the other part
WHEREAS:

(1) The Vendor is the estate owner in respect of the fee simple of the property hereinafter described and expressed to be hereby conveyed and adjoining property for a legal estate in fee simple in possession free from incumbrances

(2) The Vendor has agreed with the Purchaser for the sale to him for the sum of £   [*price*] of the property hereby conveyed except and reserving and subject as hereinafter provided

NOW in pursuance etc. THIS DEED WITNESSETH as follows:

1. The Vendor as beneficial owner HEREBY CONVEYS unto the Purchaser ALL THAT [*description of the property*] TOGETHER WITH (in

---

[43] The wording of this clause may have to be modified to comply with a condition for a covenant for indemnity contained in the contract; see Law Society's Conditions, Condition 11 (2); National Conditions, Condition 19 (6).

[44] The conveyance will have to be executed by the Purchaser (as well as by the Vendor) where there is a covenant for indemnity.

common with all others entitled to the like rights) the full and free right of passing with or without vehicles at all times over the parts of
Road and the passageway at the back of the property as are not hereby conveyed for all tenantly purposes and of using all sewers drains and watercourses now made or to be made within the period of twenty-one years from the date hereof [45] thereunder EXCEPT AND RESERVING unto the Vendor his successors in title and assigns and all persons deriving title under them like rights of way passage sewerage drainage and watercourse over and under such parts of the said road and passageway as are hereby conveyed TO HOLD the same unto the Purchaser in fee simple subject to the covenants and conditions hereinafter contained

2. For the benefit of the Vendor's said adjoining property and any and every part thereof [46] and so as to bind the property hereby conveyed into whosesoever hands the same may come the Purchaser for himself and his successors in title HEREBY COVENANTS with the Vendor and his successors or assigns that the Purchaser and those deriving title under him will at all times hereafter observe and perform the following stipulations:

That no manufacture trade or business shall at any time hereafter be carried on upon the property hereby conveyed nor shall anything be done or carried on which may be or become a nuisance damage or annoyance to the Vendor his successors in title or assigns or to any property in the neighbourhood now or heretofore belonging to the Vendor or any occupier thereof

[Set out other covenants desired]

3. IT IS HEREBY AGREED AND DECLARED that the walls and fences separating the property hereby conveyed from the property retained by the Vendor shall be deemed to be party walls and fences and shall be repaired and maintained by and at the joint and equal expense of the owners for the time being of the respective properties separated thereby and that the parties hereto shall have the same rights to use the sewers drains pipes ways water light roads chimney stacks flues eaves roofs gutters and other commodities privileges conveniences easements and quasi-easements as the same now exist in or under and form part of either the property hereby conveyed or the property retained by the Vendor as the same are now used and enjoyed or are capable of being used or enjoyed by or for the convenience of the other or all of such properties or any part thereof [47]

4. The Vendor HEREBY ACKNOWLEDGES the right of the Purchaser

[45] Or some other perpetuity period; see *Dunn* v. *Blackdown Properties Ltd.* [1961] Ch. 433; Hallett, p. 211.
[46] See generally on the proper wording to be used, Preston and Newsom, *Restrictive Covenants* (5th ed.), pp. 77 et seq.
[47] As to party walls, see Megarry and Wade, pp. 446–448; (1950) 14 Conv.(N.S.) 380; (1971) 68 L.S.Gaz. 275.

to the production of the documents mentioned in the Schedule hereto (the possession of which is retained by the Vendor) and to delivery of copies thereof AND HEREBY UNDERTAKES with the Purchaser for the safe custody of the same documents [48]

[5. *Certificate of value, if appropriate*]

IN WITNESS, etc.

THE SCHEDULE above referred to

No. 9

CONVEYANCE

BY CO-OWNERS TO CO-OWNERS

THIS CONVEYANCE is made the   day of   197   BETWEEN A of etc. and his wife B (hereinafter called "the Vendors") of the one part and C of etc. and his wife D (hereinafter called "the Purchasers") of the other part

WHEREAS the Vendors are the estate owners etc. and hold the same as trustees [49] upon the trust for sale declared by a Conveyance dated [*date*] and made between etc. and have as such trustees agreed with the Purchaser for the sale thereof to them for the sum of £   [*price*] NOW in pursuance etc.   THIS DEED WITNESSETH as follows:

1. The Vendors as trustees [50] in execution of the said trust for sale HEREBY CONVEY unto the Purchasers ALL THAT [*parcels*] TO HOLD unto the Purchasers in fee simple

2. The Purchasers shall stand possessed of the property hereby conveyed upon trust to sell the same and to stand possessed of the net proceeds of sale after payment of costs and of the net rents and profits until sale after payment of all outgoings in trust for the Purchasers as joint tenants beneficially [as tenants in common in equal shares]

3. Pending the sale of the whole of the property hereby conveyed pursuant to the trust for sale in that behalf hereinbefore declared the Purchasers or other the trustees for the time being hereof shall have the same full and unrestricted power of mortgaging the said property or any part thereof for any purpose and in any manner and of leasing or otherwise dealing therewith in all respects as if they were absolute owners thereof [51]

[4. *Certificate of value, if appropriate*]

IN WITNESS, etc.

[*To be executed by the Vendors and the Purchasers*]

---

[48] For acknowledgments and undertakings, see *ante*, pp. 238 *et seq.*
[49] Alternatively the contract may provide for the vendors to sell as beneficial owners; see *ante*, p. 91.
[50] For the implied covenants where vendors sell as trustees, see *ante*, p. 228.
[51] Clauses 2 and 3 are the so-called "joint tenancy clauses."

No. 10
Transfer of Registered Land
H.M. Land Registry
Land Registration Acts 1925 to 1971

Space   [52]

County, county borough }
or London borough   } ....

Title No. ....

Property ....

Date ....

In consideration of   pounds (£   ) the receipt whereof is hereby acknowledged I, A, of etc. as Beneficial Owner [53] HEREBY TRANSFER to B, of etc., the land comprised in the title above referred to [54]

[*Certificate of value, if appropriate*] [55]

Signed sealed and delivered
by the said A   [*Signature and seal of A*]
in the presence of
Name ....
Address ....
....
Description ....

No. 11
Conveyance
by Personal Representatives

THIS CONVEYANCE is made the   day of   197   BETWEEN A of etc. and B of etc. (hereinafter called " the Vendors ") of the one part and C of etc. (hereinafter called " the Purchaser ") of the other part

WHEREAS the property hereinafter described and expressed to be hereby conveyed is now vested in the Vendors for a legal estate in fee simple in possession free from incumbrances as the personal representatives of X whose Will was proved by them on the   day of   197   in the Principal [District] Registry of the Family Division of the High Court and as such personal representatives have agreed with the Purchaser for the sale [56] thereof to him for the sum of £   [*price*]

---

[52] This space is for the stamp.
[53] For the advantages of introducing the implied covenants for title, see Hallett's *Conveyancing Precedents*, p. 1248.
[54] Or " the land shown and edged red on the plan annexed hereto being part of the land comprised in the title above referred to." If the vendor is retaining deeds, an acknowledgment for production, etc. should be included.
[55] Where part only is sold, grants and exceptions of mutual rights, covenants and provisions as to party walls may be necessary.
[56] For conveyances by personal representatives, see *ante*, p. 222. All the personal representatives who proved the will must join in the conveyance, see *ante*, p. 222.

NOW in pursuance etc. THIS DEED WITNESSETH as follows:

1. The Vendors as personal representatives [57] of the said X deceased HEREBY CONVEY unto the Purchaser ALL THAT etc. TO HOLD unto the Purchaser in fee simple

2. The Vendors HEREBY DECLARE that they have not previously hereto given or made any conveyance or assent in respect of any legal estate in the property hereby conveyed or any part thereof [58]

3. The Vendors HEREBY ACKNOWLEDGE the right of the Purchaser to the production of the Probate of the said Will of X deceased (the possession of which is retained by the Vendors) and to delivery of copies thereof [59]

[4. *Certificate of value, if appropriate*]

IN WITNESS *etc.*[60]

No. 12

CONVEYANCE

BY MORTGAGEE UNDER STATUTORY POWER OF SALE

THIS CONVEYANCE is made the   day of   197   BETWEEN A of etc. (hereinafter called " the Vendor ") of the one part and B of etc. (hereinafter called " the Purchaser ") of the other part

WHEREAS:

(1) By a Legal Charge (hereinafter called " the Legal Charge ") dated [*date*] and made between etc. the property hereby conveyed was charged by way of legal mortgage in favour of the [Vendor] to secure the repayment to the [Vendor] of the sum of £   [*principal sum secured*] with interest thereon as therein mentioned

[(2) The benefit of the Legal Charge is vested in the Vendor] [61]

(3) In exercise of the statutory power in that behalf the Vendor has agreed with the Purchaser for the sale to him for the sum of £ [*price*] of the property hereby conveyed for a legal estate in fee simple in possession free from incumbrances

NOW in pursuance etc. THIS DEED WITNESSETH as follows:

1. The Vendor as mortgagee [62] in exercise of the statutory power and all other relevant powers enabling him in this behalf [63] HEREBY

---

[57] For the covenants implied by conveying " as personal representatives," see *ante*, p. 228.

[58] For the purpose of the statement that there has been no previous assent or conveyance, see *ante*, p. 136. The statement may be included in the recitals rather than in the operative part.

[59] Note that no undertaking for safe custody is given; see *ante*, p. 239.

[60] Notice of the conveyance should be indorsed on the grant; see *ante*, p. 137.

[61] This is appropriate where the Vendor is not the original mortgagee and avoids the necessity of reciting transfers, etc. of the benefit of the mortgage.

[62] For the implied covenants, see *ante*, p. 228.

[63] This is not strictly necessary, because a conveyance by a mortgagee after 1925 will be deemed to have been in exercise of the statutory power unless a contrary intention appears: Law of Property Act 1925, s. 104; *ante*, p. 319.

CONVEYS unto the Purchaser ALL THAT [*parcels*] TO HOLD unto the Purchaser in fee simple discharged from all right of redemption and all claims and demands under the Legal Charge

[2. *Certificate of value, if appropriate*]

IN WITNESS etc.

No. 13

CONVEYANCE

BY MORTGAGOR AND MORTGAGEE

THIS CONVEYANCE is made the   day of   197   BETWEEN A of etc. (hereinafter called " the Vendor ") of the first part B of etc. (hereinafter called " the Mortgagee ") of the second part and C of etc. (hereinafter called " the Purchaser ") of the third part

WHEREAS:

(1) The Vendor is the estate owner in respect of the fee simple of the property hereinafter described and expressed to be hereby conveyed subject to the Legal Charge [Mortgage] hereinafter recited but otherwise free from incumbrances

(2) By a Legal Charge (hereinafter called " the Legal Charge ") [*continue as in Form 12*]

(3) The principal sum of £   remains owing upon the security of the Legal Charge but all interest thereon has been paid up to the date hereof

[(4) The benefit of the Legal Charge is vested in the Mortgagee] [64]

(5) The Vendor has agreed with the Purchaser for the sale to him for the sum £   [*price*] of the property hereby conveyed for a legal estate in fee simple in possession free from incumbrances and the Mortgagee has agreed to join herein for the purposes hereinafter appearing

NOW THIS DEED WITNESSETH as follows:

1. This Deed is made in pursuance of the said agreement and in consideration of the sum of £   paid by the Purchaser at the request of the Vendor in manner following namely the sum of £   part thereof [65] to the Mortgagee in full discharge [reduction] of the moneys owing to him under the Legal Charge (the receipt whereof the Mortgagee hereby acknowledges) and the sum of £   the residue thereof to the Vendor [with the consent of the Mortgagee] [66] (the payment in the manner aforesaid and the receipt of which respective sums the Vendor hereby acknowledges) [67]

---

[64] This is appropriate where the mortgagee is not the original mortgagee; see n. 61: *ante*, p. 418.

[65] If the mortgage is being wholly repaid, a statutory receipt will generally be used, see Hallett, p. 270.

[66] The alternative wording should be used where the mortgagee is not wholly repaid.

[67] A separate receipt clause is used here as a matter of preference only.

2. The Vendor as beneficial owner HEREBY CONVEYS and the Mortgagee as mortgagee by the direction [at the request] [66] of the Vendor HEREBY SURRENDERS AND RELEASES unto the Purchaser ALL THAT etc. TO HOLD unto the Purchaser in fee simple freed and discharged from the Legal Charge and all principal moneys and interest thereby secured and all claims and demands thereunder

[3. *Acknowledgment for production, if appropriate*]

[4. *Certificate of value, if appropriate*]

IN WITNESS etc.

No. 14

ASSIGNMENT OF LEASEHOLDS

THIS ASSIGNMENT is made the   day of   197   BETWEEN A of etc. (hereinafter called " the Vendor ") of the one part and B of etc. (hereinafter called " the Purchaser ") of the other part WHEREAS:

(1) The Vendor is the estate owner of the property hereinafter described and expressed to be hereby assigned for the residue of the term of years granted by the Lease short particulars of which are set out in the Schedule hereto subject to the rent and the covenants and conditions thereby reserved and contained but otherwise free from incumbrances and has agreed with the Purchaser for the sale thereof to him (subject only as aforesaid) for the sum of £   [*price*]

[(2) The consent of the Lessor (as required by the said Lease) to this Assignment has been duly obtained] [68]

NOW in pursuance etc. THIS DEED WITNESSETH as follows:

1. The Vendor as beneficial owner [69] HEREBY ASSIGNS unto the Purchaser ALL THAT the property described in the Schedule hereto and comprised in and demised by the Lease TO HOLD unto the Purchaser for all the residue of the said term of years and subject henceforth to the said rent covenants and conditions [70]

[*Certificate of value, if appropriate*] [71]

IN WITNESS, etc.

THE SCHEDULE

Lease dated [*date*] and made between etc. for the term of [*number*] years from [*date*] at the yearly rent of £   [*rent*] ALL THAT [*parcels as in Lease*] [72]

---

[68] See *ante*, p. 261.

[69] These words imply the usual covenants for title; see *ante*, p. 226.

[70] A covenant to pay the rent and observe and perform the covenants and for indemnity is sometimes included, but such a covenant is implied on an assignment for a monetary consideration by s. 77 (1) (C) of the Law of Property Act 1925; see *ante*, p. 269. The conditions of sale will usually modify the implied covenants.

[71] See *ante*, p. 239.

[72] The assignment should be executed by the Vendor and (preferably) also by the Purchaser. For assignments generally, see *ante*, p. 268.

No. 15

ASSIGNMENT OF LEASEHOLDS

INFORMAL APPORTIONMENT OF RENT [73]

THIS ASSIGNMENT is made the   day of   197   BETWEEN A of etc. (hereinafter called " the Vendor ") of the one part and B of etc. (hereinafter called " the Purchaser ") of the other part
WHEREAS :

(1) The Vendor is the estate owner of the property comprised in and demised by the Lease short particulars of which are set out in the First Schedule hereto for the residue of the term of years granted by the said Lease subject to the rent and the covenants and conditions thereby reserved and contained but otherwise free from incumbrances

(2) The vendor has agreed with the Purchaser for the sale to him for the sum of £   [price] of the property described in the Second Schedule hereto (part of the said property) for the said legal estate subject as hereinafter mentioned
NOW in pursuance, etc. THIS DEED WITNESSETH as follows:

1. The Vendor as beneficial owner HEREBY ASSIGNS unto the Purchaser ALL THAT the property described in the Second Schedule hereto TO HOLD unto the Purchaser for all the residue of the said term of years and subject henceforth to the payment of the informally apportioned rent hereinafter mentioned and to the said covenants (other than for payment of the said entire yearly rent of £   [rent]) and conditions so far as the same relate to the property hereby assigned [74]

2. It is hereby agreed and declared that the said yearly rent of £   [rent] reserved by the Lease shall henceforth be apportioned between the property hereby assigned and the remainder of the property comprised in the Lease as to £   [apportioned rent] to the property hereby assigned and as to £   (the balance thereof) to the property retained by the Vendor (being the remainder of the property comprised in the Lease) [75,76,77]

[3. *Acknowledgment and undertaking*]

[4. *Certificate of value, if appropriate*]

IN WITNESS, etc.

---

[73] An informal or equitable apportionment is an apportionment made without the consent of the lessor. A formal or legal apportionment is made if the lessor joins in. Formal apportionments are not common, save in those cases when the rent has been formally apportioned by order of the Minister of Housing and Local Government under the Landlord and Tenant Act 1927, s. 20.

[74] Reference should be made to the precedent books for more complicated apportionments, *e.g.* an apportionment after an earlier apportionment.

[75] For the implied covenants on an apportionment under an assignment for value, see Law of Property Act 1925, s. 77 (1) (D).

[76] Mutual charges to secure payment of the apportioned rents may be included, if the contract so provides or the parties otherwise agree.

[77] Mutual rights of way, etc. and an agreement and declaration as to party walls (see *ante*, p. 415) may be included if appropriate.

P

THE FIRST SCHEDULE

Lease dated, etc. [*See Form 14*]

THE SECOND SCHEDULE

[*The property assigned*] [78]

No. 16

TRANSFER OF LEASEHOLDS

[*See Form 10*]

Where it is intended to negative the covenants implied by section 24 of the Land Registration Act 1925,[79] *add*:

It is hereby declared as follows:

(1) The covenants implied by section 24 of the Land Registration Act 1925 are hereby expressly negatived [save in so far as they do not apply nor extend beyond the terms of the covenants implied in assignments of leasehold interests by sections 76 and 77 of the Law of Property Act 1925] [80]

[(2) *Charges to secure money payable under implied covenants under sections 76 and 77 of the Law of Property Act 1925 if desired*] [81]

[*Certificate of value, etc., if appropriate*] [82]

[*To be executed by both parties and attested*]

No. 17

TENANCY AGREEMENT

FOR FURNISHED FLAT [83]

AN AGREEMENT made the   day of   197   BETWEEN A of etc. (hereinafter called " the Landlord ") of the one part and B of etc. (hereinafter called " the Tenant ") of the other part

WHEREBY IT IS AGREED as follows:

1. The Landlord lets and the Tenant takes ALL THAT the floor flat known as [*number*] (hereinafter called " the Flat ") being part of the property [*address*] from the   day of   197   until the tenancy shall be determined as hereinafter provided at the [*weekly*] rent of £   [*rent*] payable on the   day of each week

[2. The Tenant shall have the use (in common with all others entitled thereto) of the bathroom and lavatory on the   floor of the said property] [84]

---

[78] The assignment should be executed by both parties.
[79] See *ante*, p. 178. See generally Hallett, pp. 1303 *et seq.*
[80] See *ante*, pp. 226, 269.
[81] See *ante*, p. 421, note 76.
[82] See *ante*, Form 10.
[83] For tenancy agreements generally, see *ante*, p. 245.
[84] Other facilities might be a common kitchen, use of a common telephone, etc.

[3. The Tenant shall have the use of the furniture and effects in the Flat specified in the inventory attached hereto]

4. The Tenant shall be responsible for all gas and electricity consumed by him

5. The Tenant shall replace or make good or (at the option of the Landlord) pay reasonable compensation (to be assessed by Messrs of   at the cost of the Tenant) for all damage (including accidental damage) done to the Flat or the said furniture and effects or to any part of the said property which the Tenant is entitled to use and any furniture and effects therein and shall take reasonable care thereof

6. The Landlord shall keep the Flat and any other part of the said property which the Tenant is entitled to use and all pipes wires drains and installations in the said property in good repair and condition

7. The Tenant shall permit the Landlord or his agent at all reasonable times to enter the Flat and examine the condition thereof and repair the same

8. The Tenant shall use the Flat as a private dwelling-house only for the sole occupation of himself and members of his family and household and shall not assign the benefit of this agreement nor assign or sub-let the Flat or any part thereof nor (subject as aforesaid) share the same with any other person or persons

9. The Tenant shall not do or suffer in the Flat or in any other part of the said property which the Tenant is entitled to use any act or thing which may be or become a nuisance or annoyance to the owners or occupiers of any other flats in the said property

10. This tenancy may be determined:

(1) By the Landlord forthwith if any rent or part of the rent shall be more than [7] days in arrears or if the Tenant shall be in breach of any of the foregoing stipulations [85]

(2) By the Tenant if the Landlord shall be in breach of any of the foregoing stipulations on his part for more than [14] days after receipt of a written notice by the Tenant specifying such breach

(3) By either party upon giving four weeks' written notice to that effect

AS WITNESS, etc.

[INVENTORY]

No. 18

LONG LEASE

Parties   THIS LEASE is made the· day of   197   BETWEEN A of etc. (hereinafter called " the Lessor " which expression where the context admits shall include the persons for the time being entitled in reversion immediately expectant

[85] Four weeks' notice to quit will be required: Rent Act 1957, s. 16.

upon the term hereby granted) of the one part and B of etc. (hereinafter called " the Tenant " which expression where the context admits shall include the Tenant's successors in title and assigns) of the other part
WITNESSETH as follows:

1. In consideration of [the sum of £   paid by the Tenant to the Lessor (the receipt whereof the Lessor hereby acknowledges) and in consideration of] the yearly rent hereinafter reserved and of the covenants by the Tenant hereinafter contained the Landlord as beneficial owner HEREBY DEMISES unto the Tenant ALL THAT etc. TOGETHER with etc. EXCEPT AND RESERVING etc. TO HOLD the same (hereinafter called " the demised premises ") unto the Tenant for the term of [Nine hundred and ninety-nine] years from the   day of   197

YIELDING AND PAYING therefor unto the Lessor during the said term hereby granted the yearly rent of £   by equal [half-yearly] payments on the   day of   in every year clear of all deductions the first of such payments to be made on the   day of   next and to be for a proportionate part of a [half-year's] rent in respect of the period then elapsed from the date hereof

2. The Tenant HEREBY COVENANTS with the Lessor as follows:

(1) To pay the yearly rent hereby reserved on the days and in manner aforesaid without any deductions

(2) To pay all rates taxes charges duties obligations assessments and outgoings of every description now or hereafter to be assessed charged or imposed upon the demised premises or any building thereon or on the owner or occupier in respect thereof

(3) To maintain and keep in good order condition and repair the messuage or dwelling-house hereby demised or other building or buildings in lieu thereof and in case of destruction of the same or any part thereof forthwith to reinstate the same with other such like good buildings so that at all times during the term hereby granted there shall be erected upon the demised premises a good and substantial dwelling-house

(4) That the Lessor and his agents surveyors servants or workmen may at all reasonable times during the said term enter upon any part of the demised premises or any building or erection for the time being thereon and inspect the state and condition thereof

(5) That the Tenant will at all times during the said term keep the buildings for the time being standing on the

(margin notes:) Demise / Parcels / Habendum / Reddendum / Tenant's covenants

demised premises insured against loss or damage by fire in some fire insurance office of repute to be previously approved by the Lessor in full value thereof and will from time to time upon request of the Lessor or his agents produce the receipt for the premium on such insurance for the current year and in default of such insurance being effected or such receipt or receipts being so produced as aforesaid it shall be lawful for the Lessor to insure or cause to be insured in the manner hereinbefore mentioned the said buildings and to pay the premium payable in respect thereof and to charge the Tenant with the amount thereof and that the Tenant will reimburse the sum to the Lessor from time to time on demand

(6) That no act matter or thing which shall or may be or become or grow to be a public or private nuisance or a damage annoyance grievance or inconvenience to the Lessor or any occupier of adjoining neighbouring or other land or buildings or which may lessen the value of any such land or buildings shall be made carried on or done or suffered on the demised premises

(7) That every building for the time being on the demised premises shall be used only as a private dwelling-house or an outbuilding of or to a private dwelling-house on the same land and that so much of the demised premises as shall not form the site of a building shall be used only as a yard garden or pleasure ground of or to the dwelling-house on the demised premises

(8) That the Tenant will within two months after every assignment or underlease for a term exceeding twenty-one years (including an underlease or legal charge by way of mortgage) of the demised premises or any part thereof or any share therein give notice in writing to the Lessor or to his solicitors and pay to the Lessor or his solicitors a fee of [one pound] for the registration of such assignment underlease or devolution

(9) That the Tenant will at the expiration or sooner determination of the term hereby granted surrender and deliver up to the Lessor or his successors in title peaceable and quiet possession of the demised premises and the buildings for the time being thereon and all other the premises in such good and substantial repair order and condition as aforesaid

Covenant by Lessor for quiet enjoyment
3. The Lessor HEREBY COVENANTS with the Tenant that the Tenant paying the yearly rent hereby reserved and performing and observing the covenants on the part of the Tenant and conditions herein contained shall and may

during the term hereby granted peaceably and quietly possess and enjoy the demised premises without lawful interruption from or by the Lessor

Proviso for re-entry

4. PROVIDED ALWAYS AND IT IS HEREBY AGREED AND DECLARED as follows:

If and whenever the said yearly rent hereby reserved or any part thereof shall be in arrear and unpaid for twenty-one days after the same shall have become due (whether legally demanded or not) or if and whenever default shall be made in the observance or performance of any of the covenants by the Tenant hereinbefore contained then and in any of the said cases the Lessor may at any time thereafter and notwithstanding any receipt of rent at any time subsequent thereto and after notice thereof or any actual or constructive waiver of any previous cause or right of re-entry re-enter upon any part of the land demised premises and the buildings thereon in the name of the whole and thereupon the term hereby granted shall absolutely determine

[5. *Agreement and declaration as to party walls etc. if appropriate*]

[6. *Joint tenancy clauses if appropriate*]

IN WITNESS, etc.

No. 19

LEGAL CHARGE

Parties

THIS LEGAL CHARGE is made the   day of   197
BETWEEN A of etc. (hereinafter called " the Borrower " which expression shall where the context admits include persons deriving title under the Borrower [86] or entitled to redeem this security [87]) of the one part and B of etc. (hereinafter called " the Lender " which expression shall where the context admits include persons deriving title under the Lender [86]) of the other part

WHEREAS:

Recital of title of Borrower

(1) The Borrower is the estate owner etc. of the property described in the Schedule hereto (hereinafter called " the mortgaged property ") [subject as mentioned in the said Schedule but otherwise] free from incumbrances [*as appropriate for freehold or leasehold*]

---

[86] The statutory definitions of " mortgagor " and " mortgagee " (see the Law of Property Act 1925, s. 205 (1) (xvi)) apply only in respect of the statutory powers, etc. If, as is usual, additional powers are included, this express definition clause is necessary.

[87] A person may be entitled to redeem, although he has not derived title under the mortgagor, *e.g.* a surety who has paid the debt.

Agreement for loan

(2) The Lender has agreed to lend to the Borrower the sum of £ [*advance*] upon having the repayment thereof with interest at the rate hereinafter mentioned secured in manner hereinafter appearing

Testatum

NOW in pursuance of the said agreement and in consideration of the sum of £ [*advance*] paid by the Lender to the Borrower (the receipt whereof the Borrower hereby acknowledges) THIS DEED WITNESSETH as follows:

Covenant to pay principal and interest

1. The Borrower hereby covenants with the Lender to pay to the Lender on the day of [88] next the sum of £ [*advance*] with interest thereon from the date hereof at the rate of per cent. per annum And further if the said sum shall not be so paid to pay to the Lender (as well after as before any judgment [89]) interest at the rate aforesaid by equal [half-yearly] payments on the day of and the day of in every year

Charge by way of legal mortgage

2. The Borrower as beneficial owner hereby charges by way of legal mortgage ALL THAT the mortgaged property with the payment to the Lender of the principal money interest and other money hereby covenanted to be paid by the Borrower

Proviso for discharge

[3. If the Borrower shall on the day of [90] next pay to the Lender the said sum of £ with interest thereon from the date hereof at the said rate the Lender will at the request and cost of the Borrower duly discharge this security]

Borrower's Covenants

4. The Borrower HEREBY COVENANTS with the Lender:

(1) To pay all outgoings and keep the mortgaged property free from any charges taking priority over the money hereby secured

(2) To observe and perform all covenants provisions and regulations affecting the mortgaged property

(3) To keep the buildings for the time being comprised in or subject to this security insured against loss or damage by fire in the name of the Lender to the full value thereof with some insurance office or underwriters approved by the Lender and duly and punctually to pay all premiums and other payments required for effecting and keeping up such insurance as and when the same shall become due and when required by the Lender to produce to him the policy or policies of such insurance and the receipt for each such payment [91]

[88] Generally six months from the date of the charge.
[89] For the purpose of this, see *ante*, p. 306.
[90] The same date as in the covenant for repayment. For this proviso see *ante*, p. 311.
[91] For provisions in mortgages for insurance, see *ante*, p. 312.

(4) That all moneys received by the Borrower under any insurance on the buildings for the time being comprised in or subject to this security not effected or maintained under the foregoing covenant shall if the Lender so requires be applied in making good the loss or damage in respect of which the moneys shall have been received or be paid to the Lender and be applied by him in or towards the discharge of the money for the time being owing hereunder [92]

(5) To keep all buildings for the time being comprised in or subject to this security in repair and to permit the Lender and his agents with or without workmen or others to enter and inspect the said buildings at all reasonable times for the purpose of ascertaining the state of repair thereof (without the Lender being thereby rendered liable to account as mortgagee in possession [93]) and to make good all defects and wants of repair of which notice in writing shall be given by the Lender to the Borrower And if the Borrower shall fail to keep the said buildings in repair or if default shall be made by the Borrower in making good for one month after receipt of such notice as aforesaid the Lender and his agents with or without workmen or others shall thereupon be entitled to enter upon the mortgaged property or any part thereof and execute such repairs as in the opinion of the Lender may be necessary (without the Lender thereby becoming liable to account as mortgagee in possession) [93]

Modification of statutory powers, etc.

5. PROVIDED ALWAYS:

(1) The statutory power of sale shall be exercisable at any time after the principal money hereby secured shall have become due and section 103 of the Law of Property Act 1925 shall not apply to this security [94]

(2) The Borrower shall not be entitled (without the consent in writing of the Lender) to exercise any powers of leasing or accepting surrenders of leases conferred on a mortgagor in possession by the Law of Property Act 1925 [95]

(3) Section 93 of the Law of Property Act 1925 (restricting the Lender's right of consolidation) shall not apply to this security [96]

Covenants as to planning matters

6. The present use of the mortgaged property is a permitted use thereof under the provisions of the Town

[92] For the purpose of referring to *any* insurance, see *ante*, p. 312.
[93] For the liability of a mortgagee in possession, see *ante*, p. 324.
[94] For modification of the statutory power of sale, see *ante*, p. 316.
[95] For modification of the statutory power of leasing, see *ante*, p. 314.
[96] For consolidation, see *ante*, p. 325.

and Country Planning Acts 1962 to 1971 and orders and regulations made thereunder and the Borrower will not use the mortgaged property for any other purpose except with the consent in writing of the Lender and the relevant planning authority and will deliver any such consent of the relevant planning authority to the Lender but shall be entitled to a copy thereof If the Borrower persists in such use after a refusal of consent on the part of the Lender all and every or any of the powers and remedies conferred on mortgagees by the Law of Property Act 1925 (as hereby varied and extended) shall become immediately exercisable by the Lender

And the Borrower will forthwith produce to the Lender any order or notice or other matter whatsoever affecting the mortgaged property and served on the Borrower but the Borrower shall be entitled to a copy thereof

Charge of costs and expenses

7. The Borrower will on demand repay to the Lender all money properly paid and all costs charges and expenses properly incurred hereunder by the Lender (as to such costs charges and expenses on a full indemnity basis) [97] together with interest thereon from the time of paying or incurring the same until repayment at the rate aforesaid and until so repaid such costs charges and expenses shall be charged upon the property for the time being subject to this security and shall be added to the principal money hereby secured and interest thereon as aforesaid shall be charged upon the same property and shall be payable by equal [half-yearly] payments on the respective dates hereinbefore appointed for payment of interest on the said principal money [98]

Attornment clause

8. The Borrower hereby attorns tenant to the Lender of the mortgaged property during the continuance of this security at the yearly rent of a peppercorn if demanded but nothing in this clause shall prevent the Lender from at any time entering on and taking possession of the mortgaged property and so determining the tenancy hereby created [99]

IN WITNESS, etc.

THE SCHEDULE

[Description of mortgaged property]
[To be executed by both parties and attested]

---

[97] It is useful to provide for a full indemnity basis, otherwise the full costs will not be recoverable.

[98] Without this clause the costs and expenses mentioned may be added to the principal, but do not form a debt for which the mortgagor may be sued.

[99] For the attornment clause, see *ante*, p. 325.

Q*

No. 20

LEGAL CHARGE

BY CO-OWNERS

REPAYMENT BY INSTALMENTS

THIS LEGAL CHARGE is made the   day of   197 BETWEEN
A of etc. and his wife B (hereinafter called " the Borrowers " which
expression etc.) of the one part and C of etc. (hereinafter called " the
Lender " which expression etc.) of the other part

WHEREAS:

(1) The Borrowers are the estate owners etc. of the property
described in the Schedule hereto etc. [*as appropriate for freehold or
leasehold*] and hold the same as trustees etc. [*continue as in Form 9*]

(2) The Lender has agreed to lend to the Borrowers etc.

NOW in pursuance etc. THIS DEED WITNESSETH as follows:

1. [*Covenant for payment of principal and interest*] [1]

2. [*Charge*]

3. If the Borrowers shall pay to the Lender on the   day of
next and thereafter every   week [month] instalments of combined
principal and interest of £   each the Lender will apply the balance
if any of the total of such payments made in each period of   months
after deduction therefrom of such an amount as is required to discharge all interest due for the time being on this security at the
commencement of each such period of   months in reduction of the said
principal sum hereby secured [2]

[*Or* 3. If the Borrowers shall pay to the Lender on the   day of
      next and thereafter for the next subsequent [*number of instalments*]
weeks [months] instalments of combined principal and interest of £
each (apportioned as to £   of principal and as to the balance to
interest)] [3]

[*Or* 3. If the Borrowers shall pay to the Lender on the   day
of   next and thereafter every   [month] the sum of £   on
account of the principal sum due hereunder and also shall pay to
the Lender on the   day of   next and thereafter every   [month]
interest at the rate aforesaid on the principal money for the time being
unpaid [4]]

And if the Borrowers shall in all respects comply with the conditions
of the deed then the Lender shall accept payment of the said principal
sum hereby secured and the interest thereon by the instalments at the

---

[1] This is the method of drafting an instalment mortgage to be preferred (*i.e.* the
covenant for repayment by instalments is preceded by a traditional covenant for
repayment). This should be compared with the " direct covenant " method; see
ante, p. 308.

[2] This is the flat rate method; see *ante*, p. 308.

[3] This is suitable for cases where a lump sum representing interest is added to
the advance to form one sum; see *ante*, p. 308.

[4] This is the fixed instalment method; see *ante*, p. 308.

times and in manner aforesaid

4. Notwithstanding that any instalments may have been paid pursuant to Clause 3 hereof the balance of the principal sum hereby secured shall continue to be due for all the purposes of the exercise of statutory or other powers on the   day of   .[5]

[*Add Borrower's covenants, etc., as desired*]

IN WITNESS, etc.

THE SCHEDULE

[*Description of mortgaged property*]
[*To be executed by both parties and attested*]

No. 21
MORTGAGE BY DEMISE OF FREEHOLDS

THIS MORTGAGE is made the   day of   197   BETWEEN A of etc. and B of etc.

WHEREAS:

[*Recitals*]

NOW in pursuance etc. THIS DEED WITNESSETH as follows:

1. [*Covenant for payment*]

2. The Borrower as beneficial owner HEREBY DEMISES unto the Lender ALL THAT the mortgaged property TO HOLD the same unto the Lender for the term of [3,000] [6] years from the date hereof without impeachment of waste [subject as mentioned in the said Schedule] and subject to the proviso for cesser [7] hereinafter contained

[3. Provided that if the Borrower shall on the said   day of next pay to the Lender the said principal sum of £   with interest thereon from the date hereof at the said rate then the term hereby created shall cease] [7]

[*Other clauses, see Form 19*]

IN WITNESS, etc.

THE SCHEDULE above referred to

No. 22
MORTGAGE BY SUB-DEMISE OF LEASEHOLDS

THIS MORTGAGE is made the   day of   197   BETWEEN A of etc. and B of etc.

WHEREAS:

[*Recitals*] *and also* (*where appropriate*)

(3) The Lessor's consent hereto has been duly obtained

---

[5] The date mentioned in Clause 1. Without this clause it may be that the lender cannot call the mortgage-moneys in if the borrower is not in default.
[6] The term is usually 3,000 years. See generally *ante*, p. 293.
[7] For the proviso for cesser, see *ante*, p. 311.

Q**

NOW in pursuance etc. THIS DEED WITNESSETH as follows:

1. [*Covenant for payment*]

2. The Borrower as beneficial owner HEREBY DEMISES unto the Lender ALL THAT the mortgaged property TO HOLD the same unto the Lender for the residue now unexpired of the term created by the Lease except the last [10] days thereof [8] [subject as mentioned in Schedule] and subject also to the proviso for cesser [9] hereinafter contained

[3. Provided that if the Borrower shall on the said   day of next pay to the Lender the said principal sum of £   with interest thereon from the date hereof at the said rate the sub-term hereby created shall cease] [9]

[*Other clauses, see Form 19*]

IN WITNESS, etc.

THE SCHEDULE above referred to

No. 23

CHARGE OF REGISTERED LAND

H.M. LAND REGISTRY

LAND REGISTRATION ACTS 1925 TO 1971

County, county borough ⎫
or London borough   ⎭ ....

Title No.[10] ....

Property ....

Date ....

In consideration of   pounds (£   ) (the receipt whereof is hereby acknowledged) I, [*the borrower*] of etc. (hereinafter called " the Borrower " which expression etc.) [11] as beneficial owner hereby charge [12] the land comprised in the above title [13] with the payment to [the lender] of etc. (hereinafter called " the Lender " which expression etc.) of the principal sum of £   with interest thereon at the rate of   per cent. per annum payable (half yearly) on the [*dates*] in every year

The following provisions shall have effect in respect of this charge:

1. The Borrower hereby covenants with the Lender [14]:

[*Set out covenants, provisos, etc.*] [15]

---

[8] Or " the last day thereof." The " 10 days " allows for several mortgages of the property each being for one day longer than the previous one. See generally. *ante*, p. 293.

[9] For the proviso for cesser, see *ante*, p. 311.

[10] Leave blank if not already registered.

[11] See Form 19.

[12] The words " by way of legal mortgage " are not required: *Cityland Property (Holdings) Ltd.* v. *Dabrah* [1968] Ch. 166; see *ante*, p. 311.

[13] Or " the land edged red on the accompanying plan being part of the land comprised in the above title," or, if the land is not yet registered, describe the land by reference to the deed inducing registration.

[14] See *ante*, p. 298.

[15] As in Form 19.

SIGNED SEALED AND DELIVERED
by the said [*the borrower*]
in the presence of   [*Signature and seal of borrower*]

No. 24

EQUITABLE MORTGAGE

MEMORANDUM UNDER SEAL [16] TO ACCOMPANY DEPOSIT OF TITLE DEEDS
TO [*the lender*] of, etc.

In consideration of the sum of £   advanced by you to me (the
receipt whereof I hereby acknowledge) I, [*the borrower*], of etc.
HEREBY DECLARE that I have this date deposited with you the documents
specified in the Schedule hereto to secure the repayment to you on
demand of the said sum of £   [*the advance*] with interest thereon
at the rate of   per cent. per annum [17] from the date hereof payable
by equal [*quarterly*] payments on the [*dates*] in each year

I HEREBY UNDERTAKE when so required by you at my own cost to
execute a legal mortgage of the property to which the said documents
relate in your favour in such form and containing such covenants and
provisions as you may reasonably require including provisions excluding
section 93 (relating to consolidation) and section 99 (1) (relating to
mortgagor's power of leasing) of the Law of Property Act 1925 for
further securing repayment of the money secured by the said deposit.[18]

AND I FURTHER HEREBY DECLARE that I shall henceforth hold the
said property as trustee for executing such charge or mortgage as
aforesaid and the statutory power of appointing a new trustee in my
place shall be exercisable by you and the persons deriving title under
you who shall have full power to make such appointment and to
remove me from such trusteeship at your or their sole and unfettered
will and pleasure notwithstanding that none of the events referred to
in the said statutory power as conditions precedent to its exercise
shall have occurred and further that on any such exercise of the
statutory power the party or parties exercising the same may appoint
himself or themselves to be the new trustee or trustees.[19]

AND I HEREBY IRREVOCABLY APPOINT you and the persons deriving
title under you to be the attorney and attorneys of me and the persons
deriving title under me and in my or their names and on my or their
behalf and as my or their act or deed or otherwise sign seal and
deliver and otherwise perfect any such legal or formal mortgage or

---

[16] The memorandum being under seal the mortgagee will have the statutory power
of sale, etc.; see *ante*, p. 296.

[17] If no rate is specified, interest will be at 4 per cent. per annum: *Re Drax* [1903]
1 Ch. 781.

[18] An equitable mortgagee by deposit is entitled to call for a legal mortgage even
in the absence of express agreement. This undertaking should be registered as
an estate contract; see *ante*, p. 154.

[19] For the purpose of the declaration of trust, see *ante*, p. 297.

registered charge as aforesaid or (without executing any such mortgage) any deed assurance or act which may be required or may be deemed proper on any sale by you of the said property or of any part thereof under the power of sale conferred by this security in order to vest in the purchaser the legal estate and all other my or their estate and interest in the said property or such part thereof as the case may be.[20]

IN WITNESS, etc.

THE SCHEDULE

No. 25

TRANSFER OF MORTGAGE

THIS TRANSFER OF MORTGAGE is made the   day of   197

BETWEEN A of etc. (hereinafter called "the Mortgagee") of the one part and B of etc. (hereinafter called "the Transferee") of the other part

SUPPLEMENTAL to a Legal Charge dated the   day of   and made between etc.

WHEREAS:

(1) The said [the original mortgagee] died on the   day of and Probate of his Will dated the   day of   was granted to the Mortgagee out of the Principal [District] Registry of the Family Division of the High Court on the   day of

or

(1) By a Transfer of Mortgage dated the   day of   and made between etc. the benefit of the said Legal Charge was transferred to the Mortgagee as therein stated

or

(1) The benefit of the said Legal Charge is now vested in the Mortgagee

(2) The principal sum of £   remains owing upon the security of the said Legal Charge but all interest thereon has been paid up to the date hereof

(3) The Transferee has agreed to pay to the Mortgagee the sum of £   upon having such transfer of the benefit of the said Legal Charge as is hereinafter contained [21]

NOW in pursuance of the said agreement and in consideration of the sum of £   now paid by the Transferee to the Mortgagee (the receipt whereof the Mortgagee hereby acknowledges) THIS DEED WITNESSETH that the Mortgagee as mortgagee [22] [*or* as personal representative of the said [the original mortgagee] deceased] HEREBY CONVEYS AND TRANSFERS to the Transferee the benefit of the said Legal Charge

[20] For the purpose of the power of attorney, see *ante*, p. 297.
[21] For transfers of mortgages generally, see *ante*, p. 331. For transfers of registered charges, see statutory form 54.
[22] This implies a covenant that the mortgagee has not incumbered: Law of Property Act 1925, s. 76 (1) (F), Sched. 2, Pt. VI.

Where the transfer is by a personal representative add [23]:

AND HEREBY DECLARES that he has not previously hereto given or made any conveyance or assent in respect of any legal estate in the mortgaged property or any part thereof

AND HEREBY ACKNOWLEDGES the right of the Transferee to the production of the Probate of the Will of the said [*the original mortgagee*] deceased (the possession of which is retained by the Mortgagee) and to delivery of copies thereof

IN WITNESS, etc.

No. 26
STATUTORY RECEIPT [24]

I, [*the original mortgagee or transferee*], of etc. HEREBY ACKNOWLEDGE that I have this   day of   197   received the sum of £   [25] representing the [balance remaining owing in respect of] principal money secured by the above-written Legal Charge [26] together with all interest and costs the payment having been made by the above-named [*the original mortgagor*] [*or the present mortgagor*] [27] of etc.

[This receipt does not operate as a transfer] [28]

AS WITNESS, etc.[29]

No. 27
RELEASE OF PART OF MORTGAGED PROPERTY

THIS SURRENDER AND RELEASE is made the   day of 197   BETWEEN A [*the mortgagee*] of etc. (hereinafter called " the Mortgagee ") of the one part and B [*the mortgagor*] of etc. (hereinafter called " the Borrower ") of the other part

SUPPLEMENTAL to a Legal Charge [Mortgage] dated the   day of   19   and made between etc.

WHEREAS:

(1) The principal sum of £   remains owing upon the security of the said Legal Charge [Mortgage] together with the sum of £   for interest thereon [*or* but all interest has been paid up to the date hereof]

23 For the following clauses, see Form 11.
24 For discharge of mortgages generally, see *ante*, p. 334. For discharge of registered charges, see *post*, p. 337.
25 An indorsed receipt only effects an automatic reconveyance when it is for the whole of the moneys secured; see Law of Property Act 1925, s. 115 (1).
26 The receipt will be indorsed on the Legal Charge.
27 Where the payment is made by the personal representatives of the mortgagor the receipt may, but need not, state their capacity and that the repayment is made out of a fund properly applicable for the discharge of the mortgage; see Law of Property Act 1925, s. 115 (2) (*b*).
28 This statement prevents the receipt operating as a transfer where the money appears to have been paid by a person not entitled to the immediate equity of redemption; Law of Property Act 1925, s. 115 (2) (*a*); see *ante*, p. 336.
29 The receipt may be under hand, unless made by a building society under the Building Societies Act 1962, s. 37.

(2) The Mortgagee has agreed with the Borrower that in consideration of the payment by the Borrower to the Mortgagee of the sum of £   in part discharge of the said sum of £   [*amount owing for principal and interest (if any)*] the Mortgagee shall surrender and release to the Borrower such part of the mortgaged property as is described in the First Schedule hereto [30]

NOW in pursuance of the said agreement and in consideration of the sum of £   paid by the Borrower to the Mortgagee (the receipt whereof the Mortgagee hereby acknowledges) in reduction of the said mortgage debt THIS DEED WITNESSETH as follows:

1. The Mortgagee as mortgagee HEREBY SURRENDERS AND RELEASES unto the Borrower ALL THAT the property described in the First Schedule hereto TO HOLD the same unto the Borrower discharged from all principal moneys and interest secured by and from all claims and liabilities under the said Legal Charge [Mortgage] [*add if mortgage by demise* and to the intent that so far as regards the property hereby surrendered and released the term created by the said Mortgage shall merge and be extinguished in the reversion immediately expectant thereon] PROVIDED ALWAYS that nothing herein contained shall operate to prejudice or affect the security of the Mortgagee under the said Legal Charge [Mortgage] in respect of so much of the property comprised therein as is not hereby surrendered and released from the payment to the Mortgagee of so much of the said principal money [and interest] as remains owing thereunder.

2. The Mortgagee HEREBY ACKNOWLEDGES the right of the Borrower to the production of the documents mentioned in the Second Schedule hereto (the possession of which is retained by the Mortgagee) and to delivery of copies thereof [31]

IN WITNESS, *etc.*

THE FIRST SCHEDULE above referred to

[*Particulars of property released*]

THE SECOND SCHEDULE above referred to

[*Documents retained by mortgagee*]

No. 28
DISCHARGE OF REGISTERED CHARGE
H.M. LAND REGISTRY
LAND REGISTRATION ACTS 1925 TO 1971

County, county borough   ⎫
or London borough   ⎬ ....

---

[30] Where the whole of the mortgaged property is to be released to enable the mortgagor to sell free from the mortgage either the mortgage should be released by statutory receipt (*ante*, p. 335) or the mortgagee should join in the conveyance to surrender and release the property (*ante*, p. 419). Where a sale is not contemplated, a statutory receipt is only available if all the moneys secured by the mortgage are repaid; see *ante*, p. 335.

[31] No undertaking for safe custody is given; see *ante*, p. 239.

Title Number ....

Property ....

Date ....

I, B [*the mortgagee*] of etc. hereby admit that the Charge dated and registered on the [*date*], of which I am the proprietor, has been discharged [32]

[*To be signed by the proprietor of the charge and attested*] [33]

No. 29

UNDERTAKING TO DISCHARGE MORTGAGE

To [*the purchaser or his solicitor*]

In consideration of your today completing the purchase of
                                              we hereby undertake
forthwith to pay over to [*the mortgagee*] the money required to redeem the Mortgage [Legal Charge] dated   and to forward the receipted Mortgage [Legal Charge] to you as soon as it is received by us from [*the mortgagee*] [34]

No. 30

SETTLEMENT ON NAMED GRANDCHILDREN OF SETTLOR AT TWENTY-ONE

THIS SETTLEMENT is made the   day of   197   BETWEEN A of etc. (hereinafter called " the Settlor ") of the one part and X of etc. and Y of etc. (hereinafter called " the Trustees " which expression shall where the context admits mean the survivor of the Trustees or other the trustee or trustees for the time being hereof) of the other part

WHEREAS :

(1) The Settlor is desirous of making such provision for his grandchildren [*names of grandchildren*] (hereinafter called " the Beneficiaries ") as hereinafter appears

(2) The Settlor has previously hereto paid or transferred to the Trustees the money and investments specified in the Schedule hereto to be held by them upon the trusts of this deed

NOW THIS DEED WITNESSETH as follows :

1. The Trustees shall stand possessed of the said money and investments and the moneys investments and property from time to time representing the same and any property hereafter transferred to the Trustees upon the trusts hereof (hereinafter called " the Trust Fund ") upon such trusts and with and subject to such powers and provisions for the benefit of all or any one or more exclusively of the

[32] The discharge may be made as to part of the land only, by adding at the end " as to the land shown and edged with red on the accompanying plan, signed by me, being part of the land comprised in the above title," or as to part of the money only by adding " to the extent of £   part of the moneys secured thereby."

[33] See generally, *ante*, p. 337.

[34] See (1971) 68 L.S.Gaz.; (1971) 35 Conv.(N.S.) 3; *ante*, p. 211.

others or other of the Beneficiaries as the Trustees shall in their absolute discretion from time to time by any deed or deeds revocable or irrevocable appoint before [date] [35] (hereinafter called " the Specified Date ") Provided Always that the Trustees may at any time by deed extinguish or restrict the future use of this power [36]

2. Subject as aforesaid the Trust Fund and the income thereof shall be held by the Trustees in trust for such of the Beneficiaries as shall attain the age of twenty-one years and if more than one in equal shares

3. If any of the Beneficiaries shall die under the age of twenty-one years leaving a child or children (including an adopted child or children) [37] him or her surviving such child or children who shall attain the age of twenty-one years shall take by substitution and if more than one in equal shares the share the deceased beneficiary would have taken had he or she attained the age of twenty-one years

4. Notwithstanding the trusts hereinbefore declared of and concerning the income of the Trust Fund the Trustees may during the period of twenty-one years from the date hereof accumulate the same or any part thereof by investing it in any of the investments hereby authorised and shall hold such accumulations as part of the capital of the Trust Fund [38]

5. The provisions of section 31 of the Trustee Act 1925 [39] shall apply to this deed subject to the following variations:

(a) the words " may in all the circumstances be reasonable " shall be omitted from paragraph (i) of subsection (1) thereof and the words " the trustees shall in their absolute discretion think fit " shall be substituted therefor and

(b) the proviso to subsection (1) thereof shall be omitted

6. The Trustees may allow any investments transferred to them upon the trusts hereof to remain in their actual state of investment or may realise the same or any part thereof and shall invest the proceeds of any such realisation and any cash held by or transferred to them upon the trusts hereof in any investments hereby authorised with power to vary or transpose investments for or into others of a nature hereby authorised

7. Money to be invested under the trusts hereof may be applied or invested in the purchase or at interest upon the security of such investments shares securities or other investments or property of whatsoever nature and wheresoever situate (including the purchase

---

[35] The date when the youngest grandchild attains 21 years of age.
[36] This overriding power of appointment allows for greater flexibility if, *e.g.* one of the grandchildren is better off than the others.
[37] Unless specifically mentioned adopted children are not included. Unless expressly excluded illegitimate children are included: see Family Law Reform Act 1969, s. 15.
[38] Income which is accumulated is not treated as belonging to the infant's parent; see generally, Potter and Monroe, *Tax Planning* (6th ed.), p. 87; but note Finance Act 1971, s. 16 (1).
[39] *i.e.* the statutory power of maintenance.

or improvement of a freehold or leasehold dwelling-house situate in the United Kingdom or elsewhere for use as a residence) and whether involving liabilities or not or upon such personal credit with or without security as the Trustees in their absolute discretion shall think fit and to the intent that the Trustees shall have the same powers in all respects as if they were absolute owners beneficially entitled [40]

8. Any trustee being a solicitor or other person engaged in any profession or business shall be entitled to be paid all usual professional or proper charges for business transacted time expended and acts done by him or by any partners of his in connection with the trusts hereof including acts which a trustee not being in any profession or business could have done personally [41]

9. No discretion or power conferred upon the Trustees by this deed or by law shall be exercised in such manner as to cause or permit any part of the capital or income of the Trust Fund to be paid to or applied for the benefit of the Settlor or any wife [husband] of the Settlor [42]

10. The power of appointing new trustees is vested in the Settlor during his lifetime

IN WITNESS, etc.

THE SCHEDULE

[Particulars of money and investments]
[To be executed by the Settlor and the Trustees and attested]

No. 31

DISCRETIONARY SETTLEMENT

THIS SETTLEMENT is made the   day of   197   BETWEEN A of etc. (hereinafter called " the Settlor ") of the one part and X of etc. and Y of etc. (hereinafter called " the Original Trustees ") of the other part

WHEREAS the Settlor is desirous of making such provision as hereinafter appears and has previously hereto transferred to the Original Trustees etc. *[continue as in Form 30]*

NOW THIS DEED WITNESSETH as follows

1. In this Deed the following expressions have where the context admits the following meanings:

" The Trustees " means the Original Trustees or other the trustee or trustees for the time being hereof

" The Trust Fund " means the said money and investments and any property hereafter transferred to the Trustees upon the trusts hereof and the moneys investments and property from time to time representing the same

---

[40] For investment powers, see Hallett, p. 774; Potter and Monroe, p. 115.
[41] For trustee charging clauses, see *ante*, p. 381; Hallett, pp. 774, 775.
[42] The Settlor must be excluded from any benefit under the settlement; see Hallett, p. 781; Potter and Monroe, p. 78.

" The Beneficiaries " means the children and grandchildren of the Settlor and their wives and husbands or their widows and widowers until remarriage. An adopted child or grandchild shall be treated as a child or grandchild of the Settlor for the purposes of this Deed

" The Specified Period " means the period of seventy-nine years commencing from the date hereof which period shall be the perpetuity period applicable to this Deed for the purposes of section 1 of the Perpetuities and Accumulations Act 1964

" The Accumulation Period " means the period of twenty-one years from the date hereof

2. The Trustees shall stand possessed of the Trust Fund and the income thereof upon such trusts for all or any one or more to the exclusion of the others of the Beneficiaries as the Trustees in their absolute discretion shall at any time or times during the Specified Period by any deed or deeds recoverable or irrevocable appoint [43]

3. Notwithstanding the trusts hereinbefore declared and contained of and concerning the income of the Trust Fund the Trustees may during the Accumulation Period accumulate the same or any part thereof by investing it in any of the investments hereby authorised and shall hold such accumulations as part of the capital of the Trust Fund [44]

4. Subject as aforesaid the Trustees shall during the Specific Period stand possessed of the Trust Fund upon trust to pay or apply the income thereof unto or for the benefit in any manner of all or any one or more to the exclusion of the others of the Beneficiaries as the Trustees shall think fit and from and after the expiration of the Specified Period the Trustees shall hold the Trust Fund upon trust for such of the children or grandchildren of the Settlor as shall be living at the expiration of the Specified Period and if more than one in equal shares per stirpes [45]

5. Subject as aforesaid the Trustees shall stand possessed of the Trust Fund in trust for [*names of beneficiaries* or *beneficiary entitled in default*] [46]

[*Other clauses as Clauses 6* et seq. *in Form 30*]

No. 32

APPOINTMENT OF NEW TRUSTEE

THIS DEED is made the   day of   197   BETWEEN A of etc. (hereinafter called " the Continuing Trustee ") of the one part and B of etc. (hereinafter called " the New Trustee ") of the other part

---

[43] For the advantages of this overriding power of appointment and on the general framework of a discretionary trust such as this, see Hallett, pp. 771 *et seq.* And see *ante*, p. 438, note 36.
[44] For the accumulation period, see *ante*, p. 382.
[45] Or *per capita*, if preferred.
[46] This is the so-called " long-stop " clause, which is inserted to prevent a resulting trust to the Settlor.

SUPPLEMENTAL to a Conveyance (hereinafter called "the Conveyance") dated the   day of   and made between etc. of the one part [*the deceased trustee*] and the Continuing Trustee of the other part (whereby the property specified in the Schedule hereto was conveyed to the said [*the deceased trustee*] and the Continuing Trustee upon trust for sale with power to postpone the sale [47])

WHEREAS:

(1) The said [*the deceased trustee*] died on the   day of
(2) The property specified in the Schedule hereto is vested in the Continuing Trustee
(3) The Continuing Trustee is desirous of making the appointment hereinafter contained

NOW THIS DEED WITNESSETH that in exercise of the statutory power in that behalf [48] and all other relevant powers the Continuing Trustee HEREBY APPOINTS the New Trustee to be a trustee of the Conveyance in the place of the said [*the deceased trustee*] and to act jointly with the Continuing Trustee [49]

IN WITNESS, etc.

THE SCHEDULE
[*To be executed by both parties and attested*]

No. 33

WILL

I, John Smith, of etc. hereby revoke all wills codicils and other testamentary dispositions heretofore made by me and declare this to be my last will which I make this   day of   19

1. I appoint A of etc. and B of etc. (hereinafter called "my Trustees") to be the executors and trustees of this my Will [50],[51]

2. I Bequeath the following pecuniary legacies free of duty [52]
(1) To X the sum of £500
(2) To Y the sum of £100 [53]

3. I Bequeath to my wife W absolutely free of duty all my personal chattels as defined by the Administration of Estates Act 1925 [54]

4. I devise to my Trustees in fee simple free of all duty [55] my

47 This assumes that there were originally two trustees of a conveyance one of whom has now died.
48 For the statutory power, see *ante*, p. 373.
49 For the implied vesting declaration, see *ante*, p. 375.
50 For the comparative advantages and disadvantages of trust corporations as executors, see *ante*, p. 392.
51 Declarations as to the use of the body for medical purposes (see (1968) 118 New L.J. 486; (1970) 33 M.L.R. 353), cremation, etc. should really be contained in another document, as the will may not be found until after the funeral.
52 This avoids the rule in *Re Spencer Cooper* [1908] 1 Ch. 130, under which a pecuniary legacy in so far as it is paid out of residuary realty must bear the duty attributable to that realty.
53 Where substantial absolute gifts are made a *commorientes* clause should be considered; see *ante*, p. 395.
54 See *ante*, p. 394.
55 The draftsman should keep in mind that by exonerating specific devises from estate duty, residue will be reduced; see *ante*, p. 400.

freehold dwelling-house Blackacre or such other dwelling-house as I shall own and which shall be the principal matrimonial home of myself and my said wife at my death [56] Upon trust (with the consent in writing during her life of my said wife) to sell the same with full power to postpone the sale for so long as they shall in their absolute discretion think fit and to hold the net proceeds of sale and other moneys applicable as capital and the net rents and profits until sale in trust for my said wife during her life And from and after her death in trust for my sons P, Q and R in equal shares absolutely And I empower my trustees during the life of my said wife to permit her to have the use and enjoyment of the said property (or any other property for the time being subject hereto) for such period or periods as they shall in their absolute discretion think fit pending postponement of the sale she paying the rates taxes and other outgoings in respect of the said property and keeping the same in good repair and insured against fire to the full value thereof in some office of repute nominated by my Trustees in the joint names of herself and my Trustees [57]

5. I Devise and Bequeath all the real and personal estate of or to which I shall be possessed or entitled at my death or over which I shall then have a general power of appointment or disposition by will except property otherwise disposed of by this my will or any codicil hereto unto my Trustees Upon the trusts and with and subject to the powers and provisions hereinafter declared of and concerning the same that is to say Upon Trust that my Trustees shall sell call in collect and convert into money the said real and personal property at such time or times and in such manner as they shall think fit with power to postpone the sale calling in or conversion of the whole or any part or parts of the said property during such period as they shall think proper and to retain the same or any part thereof in its actual form of investment

6. My Trustees shall out of the moneys to arise from the sale calling in and conversion of or forming part of my said real and personal estate pay my funeral and testamentary expenses (including all estate duty leviable at my death in respect of my estate) and debts and the legacies given by this my will or by any codicil hereto and the rules of equity known as the rules in *Allhusen* v. *Whittell* and *Re Chesterfield* shall be disregarded [58]

7. My Trustees shall invest the residue of the said moneys in or upon the investments hereinafter mentioned with power to vary or transpose such investments for or into others of a nature hereby authorised

8. My Trustees shall pay the income of the investments above directed to be made or authorised to be retained and the investments

---

[56] For ademption, see *ante*, p. 395.
[57] For the provision of a house for a widow, see *ante*, p. 395.
[58] For further clauses to exclude the rule in *Dimes* v. *Scott* (1828) 4 Russ. 145 and other apportionment rules, see Hallett, pp. 1031, 1032.

for the time being representing the same (hereinafter called " the Trust Fund ") to my said wife during her life [59]

9. After the death of my said wife my Trustees shall stand possessed of the Trust Fund and the income thereof In Trust for such of my children who shall be living at the death of my said wife and if more than one in equal shares but so that if any child of mine shall die in the lifetime of my said wife leaving a child or children (including an adopted child or children [60]) who shall attain the age of twenty-one years or marry such child or children shall take and if more than one in equal shares the share in the Trust Fund that my child so dying would have taken had he or she survived my wife

10. [*Power of investment as in Form 30, Clause 7*]

11. The power of appropriation conferred by the Administration of Estates Act 1925 shall be exercisable by my Trustees as well after as during the administration of my estate without any of the consents required by that Act [61]

12. Notwithstanding the provisions hereinbefore contained my Trustees may in their absolute discretion at any time or times advance out of the capital of the Trust Fund any sum or sums [not exceeding in the aggregate £] and pay the same to my said wife for her own benefit [62]

13. [*Trustees' charging power*] [63]

14. My wife during her life shall have power from time to time to appoint a new trustee(s) of this my Will

IN WITNESS whereof I the said John Smith have hereunto set my hand the day and year first above written

Signed by the above named Testator John Smith as his last Will in the presence of us both present at the same time who in his presence and in the presence of each other have hereunto subscribed our names as witnesses [64]

No. 34

ASSENT

BY EXECUTORS OF FREEHOLDS IN FAVOUR OF PERSON
ABSOLUTELY ENTITLED

WE, A of etc. and B of etc. the personal representatives of X late of etc. who died on the   day of   and whose Will was proved by

[59] For the surviving spouse exemption, see *ante*, p. 398.
[60] Unless specifically mentioned adopted children are not included. Unless expressly excluded, illegitimate children are included; see Family Law Reform Act 1969, s. 15.
[61] For the advantages of an express power of appropriation, see *ante*, p. 138.
[62] But such a power should not be exercised regularly; see *ante*, p. 396, note 13.
[63] As in Form 30, clause 8, substituting " executor or trustee " for " trustee."
[64] See *ante*, p. 387.

us on the   day of   in the Principal [District] Registry of the
Family Division of the High Court do this   day of   hereby:

1. As such personal representatives [65] assent to the vesting in C [66]
of etc. of ALL THAT the property described in the Schedule hereto for
all the estate and interest of the said X at the time of his death

2. Declare that we have not previously hereto given or made any
assent or conveyance in respect of any legal estate in the premises or
any part thereof

3. Acknowledge the right of the said C to the production of the
Probate of the said Will (the possession of which is retained by us)
and to delivery of copies thereof

AS WITNESS whereof we the said A and B have hereunto set our
respective hands

THE SCHEDULE

SIGNED by the above-named
A in the presence of:
[*Signature, address and
description of witness*]   [*Signature of A*]

SIGNED by the above-named
B in the presence of [67]   [*Signature of B*]

---

[65] These words imply a covenant that the personal representatives have not themselves
  incumbered the land; see *ante*, p. 228.
[66] For the need for an assent, even by an executor in favour of himself, see *ante*,
  pp. 136, 401.
[67] This assent is under hand only and stamp duty is therefore not payable. In some
  cases it will be preferable to have the assent under seal, *e.g.* on an assent of
  leaseholds, when the beneficiary should enter into an indemnity covenant in respect
  of the lessee's covenants in the lease. Stamp duty will be payable in some cases, *e.g.*
  where there has been an appropriation under the statutory power; see *ante*, p. 138.

INDEX

ABSTRACT OF TITLE, 119 *et seq.*
  contents of, 121 *et seq.*
  defined, 119–120
  delivery of, 101, 124
  form, 120–121, 409–411
  marking, 210
  " perfect," 101–102, 119
  presumptions, 130
  proof of documents, 124 *et seq.*
  proof of facts, 128 *et seq.*
  root of title. *See* ROOT OF TITLE.

ACKNOWLEDGMENT AND UNDERTAKING,
  238–239, 242, 415–416

ADVANCEMENT, POWER OF, 380

AGREEMENT,
  offer and acceptance, 8–9
  And see CONTRACT FOR SALE.

AGREEMENT FOR LEASE, 24, 245 *et seq.*

AGRICULTURAL TENANCY, 287 *et seq.*

ALL THE ESTATE CLAUSE, 234, 242

ANNUITIES IN WILL, 396, 397

APPOINTMENT OF TRUSTEES, 356 *et seq.*,
  372 *et seq.*, 440–441

APPORTIONMENT,
  of rent, 421
  on completion, 107–108, 210

ASSENTS, 136–138, 400–401, 443–444

ASSIGNMENT OF A LEASE,
  covenant against, 261 *et seq.*
  form, 420, 422
  generally, 267 *et seq.*
  title to be shown on, 60, 99–100,
  187–188

ASSIGNMENT OF REVERSION, 269

ATTESTATION,
  deed, of, 207, 208, 267, 413
  transfer, of, 242, 417
  will, of, 287, 288, 443

ATTORNEY, POWER OF, 125–127, 138

ATTORNMENT CLAUSE IN MORTGAGE,
  323, 325–328, 429

AUCTION, 11, 87–88

BANKRUPTCY,
  lease, forfeiture of, on, 265–266
  of parties pending completion, 192–
  193
  registered land, 179
  registration of land charge, 151–152
  search in, 187
  settlements, 346–347
  voluntary settlement, effect on, 148

BENEFICIAL OWNER,
  covenants for title, 225 *et seq.*

BOUNDARIES, 37, 72
  And see IDENTITY OF LAND *and*
  PARCELS.

BREACH OF CONTRACT. *See* REMEDIES.

BUILDING SCHEMES, 238

BUILDING SOCIETY,
  mortgages to, discharge of, 337

BUSINESS PREMISES, LEASES OF, 281
  et seq.

CAPITAL MONEY. *See* STRICT SETTLE-
  MENTS.

CERTIFICATE OF SEARCH,
  land charges, 158
  local land charges, 42
  registered land, 184

CERTIFICATE OF VALUE, 239, 242, 413

CHARGE BY WAY OF LEGAL MORTGAGE,
  293 *et seq.*, 426

CHARITIES,
  title of, 138

COLLECTION,
  covenant for, of apportioned rents,
  123

COMMORIENTES, 131, 395

COMPANIES,
  liquidation of, 139
  title of, 139

COMPANY SEARCH, 163, 330

COMPENSATION,
  for misdescription, 74
  town and country planning, 53

COMPLETION, 108 *et seq.*, 206 *et seq.*
  acceptance of title, 206
  completion statement, 210, 411
  date for, 108, 206
  execution of conveyance, 207 *et seq.*
  failure to complete, 110, *et seq.*
  matters subsequent to, 213–214
  meaning of, 206
  merger of contract in conveyance,
    212–213
  notice to complete, 110–111, 412
  payment of purchase-money, 210–
    211
  place of, 111, 210
  preparation of conveyance, 104, 206–
    207
  registration of title, 214 *et seq.*
  title deeds, rights of purchaser to,
    211
  undertaking to discharge mortgage,
    211–212
  what amounts to, 206

COMPULSORY PURCHASE, 116–118
  compulsory purchase order, 116
  conveyance, 117
  general vesting declaration, 117–118
  notice to treat, 117
  purchase by agreement, 116

CONDITIONAL CONTRACT, 13–14

CONDITIONS OF SALE, 84 *et seq.*
  abstract and requisitions, 101–104
  apportionment of receipts and out-
    goings, 107–108
  auction, 87–88
  completion, 108–111
  condition of property, 96–97
  conveyance, preparation of, 104
  deposit, 88–90
  easements, etc., 99
  exchange of contracts, 90
  fixtures, fittings, etc., 90–91
  general conditions, 85
  generally, 84
  identity of property, 94–95
  insurance, 104
  interest on purchase-money, 105–107
  Law Society's, 84
  leases, 99–100
  local land charges and inquiries, 97–
    98
  misdescription, 95–96
  National, 84
  occupation pending completion, 104–
    105
  remedies on default, 111–113
  requisitions and abstract, 101–104
  special conditions, 85
  tenanted properties, 101
  title conditions, 91–94
  town and country planning, 98–99
  usual, the, 87 *et seq.*
  vacant possession, 97
  vendor's capacity, 91
  void by statute, 86–87

CONSIDERATION,
  statement of, in conveyance, 224–
    225, 412

CONSOLIDATION OF MORTGAGES, 325

CONTRACT FOR LEASE, 24, 245–248

CONTRACT FOR SALE, 8 *et seq.*
  assignment of benefit of, 195
  auction, 11
  collateral contracts, 14–15
  conditional contracts, 13–14
  correspondence, by, 10
  effect pending completion, 189–199
  estate agents. *See* ESTATE AGENTS.
  exchange of contracts, 15
  existence and validity, 8–15
  form, 15 *et seq.*
  formal. *See* FORMAL CONTRACTS FOR
    THE SALE OF LAND.
  informal. *See* OPEN CONTRACT.
  inquiries before contract. *See* IN-
    QUIRIES OF LOCAL AUTHORITIES
    and PRELIMINARY INQUIRIES.
  local searches. *See* LOCAL SEARCHES.
  offer and acceptance, 8–9
  open contracts. *See* OPEN CON-
    TRACT.
  options. *See* OPTIONS.
  oral, 11
  part performance, 22
  particulars of sale. *See* PARTICULARS
    OF SALE.
  preparation of, 2, 9
  rectification, 25
  registered land, of, 24
  registration, 25–28
    estate contract, 25–26
    non-registration, effect of, 26–27
    registered land, 27–28
    vacating of, 27
  remedies. *See* REMEDIES.
  statutory requisites, 15–23
    land or interest in land, 16–17
    memorandum, 17 *et seq.*
      absence of, effect of, 21–22
      concluded contract necessary, 21
      consideration, 18–19
      form, 20
      not essential, cases where, 22–23
      parties, 18
      several documents, 20–21
      signature, 19–20
      special terms, 19
      subject-matter, 18
      terms, must contain all, 21
  subject to contract, etc., 11–13
  variation, 24–25

CONVERSION,
  doctrine of, 17–31

CONVEYANCE, 221 *et seq.*
  acknowledgment, 238–239
  adverse rights, 238
  all the estate clause, 234
  appurtenant rights, 238

CONVEYANCE—*cont.*
  certificate of value, 239, 413
  commencement, 221
  consideration, 224, 413
  contents of, 221 *et seq.*
  co-owners, by and to, 416
  covenants for title. *See* COVENANTS
    FOR TITLE.
  date, 221
  exceptions and reservations, 234–235
  execution, 207 *et seq.*, 240
  forms of, 412 *et seq.*
  general words, 231–233
  habendum, 235–236
  mortgagee, by, 418
  mortgagor and mortgagee, by, 419
  operative part, 224–230, 413
  parcels, 230–231, 413
  parties, 221–222, 412
  personal representatives, by, 417
  positive covenants, 236
  preparation of, 206–207
  receipt clause, 225, 413
  recitals, 223–224, 412
  restrictive covenants. *See* RESTRIC-
    TIVE COVENANTS.
  testatum, 224, 413
  testimonium, 240, 413
  undertaking, 238–239
  words of, 229–230

CONVEYANCING,
  costs, 5–6
  future of, 5 *et seq.*
  scope of, 1 *et seq.*

CORRESPONDENCE,
  contracts, by, 10, 65 *et seq.*
  contracts, otherwise than by, 59
    et seq.

COVENANTS FOR TITLE, 225–229
  beneficial owner, as, 226–227
  benefit of, 227
  breach of, 229
  burden of, 227
  committee, as, 228
  " conveys and is expressed to con-
    vey," 228
  express limitation or variation, 228–
    229
  limitation period, 229
  mortgage, by way of, 227
  mortgagee, as, 228
  order of court, under, 228
  personal representative, as, 228
  qualified, 227
  receiver, as, 228
  settlor, as, 228
  trustee, as, 228

COVENANTS IN LEASES, 100, 256–263,
  268–269, 424, 426

COVENANTS IN MORTGAGES, 305 *et seq.*,
  427–429

DAMAGES FOR BREACH OF CONTRACT,
  203

DEATH,
  of parties pending completion, 191

DEBENTURE, 301–302, 340–341

DECLARATION,
  as remedy, 205
  statutory, 95, 128

DEDUCING TITLE, 119

DEED OF DECLARATION, 357–358

DEED OF DISCHARGE, 369–370

DEFECTIVE PREMISES, 81–83

DEFECTS,
  vendor's duty to disclose, 78 *et seq.*

DEFERRED PURCHASE, 197

DELIVERY OF DEED, 209

DEPOSIT,
  forfeiture of, 112, 204
  generally, 3, 22, 88

DISCHARGE OF MORTGAGE, 43 *et seq.*,
  333 *et seq.*

DISCHARGE OF SETTLEMENT, 369–370

DISCLAIMER,
  by trustee, 372–373

DISCLOSURE,
  duty of, 78

DISCRETIONARY TRUSTS, 345–348, 348–
  349, 372, 381–382, 397
  advantages of, 346–348
  beneficiaries, 381–382
  form of, 439
  trustees' discretion, exercise of, 382
  trustees' powers, 382
  trusts of, 381–382

DISPUTES,
  boundary, 72
  And see VENDOR AND PURCHASER
    SUMMONS.

EASEMENTS, 37, 71, 72, 80. 99, 140,
  231–235, 413–415
  latent, 80–81

ENDORSEMENT. *See* INDORSEMENT.

ENFRANCHISEMENT. *See* LEASEHOLD
  ENFRANCHISEMENT.

ENGROSSMENT, 3, 86, 104, 207
  meaning of, 3, 207

EPITOME OF TITLE, 121, 410

EQUITABLE CHARGE, 293

EQUITABLE INTERESTS,
overreaching, 363, 378
registered land, 168–169

EQUITABLE MORTGAGE, 140, 293, 295–
297, 320, 330, 332, 334, 337, 433

EQUITY OF REDEMPTION, 292, 309, 311

ESCROW, 209

ESTATE AGENTS, 31–33
commission, 32–33
deposits, 32
misrepresentation by, 31–32

ESTATE CONTRACT, 25 et seq., 154, 246–
247, 330

ESTATE DUTY, 141, 143, 348–349, 384,
396, 398–399, 400

ESTOPPEL, 72
by recital in deed, 223
tenancy by, 203

EXAMINATION OF TITLE, 131 et seq.

EXCEPTIONS AND RESERVATIONS, 234–
235, 414–415

EXCHANGE,
of contract, 3, 15, 90

EXECUTION OF DEEDS, 207 et seq.
meaning, 207

FEE SIMPLE,
words of limitation, 235–236

FIRST REGISTRATION OF TITLE, 166 et
seq., 214 et seq., 243

FIXTURES,
condition of sale, as to, 90
generally, 16, 37

FLATS AND MAISONETTES, 141

FLOATING CHARGE, 142, 163, 302, 330

FORFEITURE,
deposit, 112, 204
lease, 263 et seq.
tenant for life's interest, 346–347,
365, 368, 369

FORMAL CONTRACTS FOR THE SALE OF
LAND, 9–10, 59, 71 et seq.
conditions of sale. See CONDITIONS
OF SALE.
generally, 9–10, 59
particulars of sale. See PARTICULARS
OF SALE.

FRAUD, 35, 80, 142, 148
conveyance to defraud creditors, 148

GENERAL WORDS, 231–233

GIFT, 142–143

HABENDUM,
in conveyance, 235–236
in lease, 253–256

HUSBAND AND WIFE,
conveyance to, 243–244, 416

IDENTITY OF LAND, 94–95

IMPROVEMENTS TO SETTLED LAND, 366–
367

INCOME TAX, 107, 269–270, 339–340,
349–350, 396, 398

INDEMNITY,
covenant for, 207, 269, 414

INDORSEMENT,
on conveyance etc., memorandum of
sale, 213, 410

INFANTS,
advancement to, 379
maintenance of, 379
settled land, 352

INFORMAL CONTRACTS FOR THE SALE OF
LAND, 59 et seq.

INQUIRIES BEFORE CONTRACT. See
INQUIRIES OF LOCAL AUTHORITIES;
PRELIMINARY INQUIRIES; TOWN
AND COUNTRY PLANNING.

INQUIRIES OF LOCAL AUTHORITIES, 42–
43

INSPECTION OF PROPERTY, 186–187

INSTALMENT MORTGAGES, 308

INSTALMENT SALES, 196

INSURANCE,
between vendor and purchaser, 104,
190–191
leases, in, 260, 424–425

INSURANCE POLICY,
mortgage of, 301, 339–340

INTERESSE TERMINI, 253–254

INTEREST,
mortgages, on, 306–309
purchase-money, on, 105–107

INTESTACY,
proof of, 129

INVESTIGATION OF TITLE. *See* TITLE, investigation of.

INVESTMENT,
capital money under Settled Land Act 1925, 366
trustees' power in respect of, 378–379

JOINT ACCOUNT CLAUSE, 309–310

JOINT OWNERS, 91, 143–144, 416, 430

JOINT TENANCY CLAUSES, 416

JOINT TENANTS,
sale by survivor of, 143–144

LAND CHARGES,
criticism of registration system, 161–162
registration, mode of, 158
vacating the registration, 27
And see LAND CHARGES SEARCHES.

LAND CHARGES SEARCHES, 43–44, 150 *et seq.*
against whom made, 150
annuities, 151
deeds of arrangement, 152
land charges, 152 *et seq.*
Class A, 152
Class B, 152–153
Class C, 153–155
Class D, 155–156
Class E, 156
Class F, 156–158
method of search, 158–160
official search, 158–159
pending actions, 151
priority notice, 160–161
registration, mode of, 158
when made, 43, 44
writs and orders, 151–152

LAND REGISTRY, 165–166

LAND REGISTRY SEARCH, 44, 153 *et seq.*

LAPSE, 393–394

LAW SOCIETY'S CONDITIONS OF SALE, 84

LEASE, 245 *et seq.*
agreement for, 24, 245 *et seq.*
formal, 245–246
open, 245–246
registration of, 26, 246–247
writing, 245
agricultural holdings, 287–291
compensation, 290–291
deterioration, for, 291
disturbance, for, 290–291
improvements, for, 291
control of rents, 291
definition, 287–288
security of tenure, 288–290

LEASE—*cont.*
assignment, 267–269
lease of, 268–269
reversion, of, 269
business premises, 281–287
compensation, 286–287
disturbance, for, 286
improvements, for, 286–287
defined, 282
security of tenure, 282–286
certainty of term, 253, 254–256
consideration, 252–253
covenants, 256–263, 424–425
assignment or underlet, not to, 261–263
insure, to, 260
pay rent, to, 256
pay taxes, to, 257
quiet enjoyment, for, 250, 267
repair, to, 257–259
restrictive of user, 260
" usual," 245–246, 248–249
duration, must be fixed, 253, 254–256
duration of the war, 254–255
enfranchisement. *See* LEASEHOLD ENFRANCHISEMENT.
exceptions, 253
express contents, 252–267
forfeiture. *See* proviso for re-entry and forfeiture.
form, 423 *et seq.*
formalities, 247–248
furnished premises, 275–276
control of rents, 275–276
security of tenure, 276
habendum, 253–256, 424
implied terms, 248–252
interesse termini, 253–254
internal decorative repairs, 259
licences, in, 253
life or lives or until marriage, 255
long tenancies of dwellings, 276–277
operative part, 252–253
parcels, 253, 424
parties, 252, 423
perpetually renewable, 255–256
premises, 252–253
proviso for re-entry and forfeiture, 263–267, 426
bankruptcy of tenant or his interest being taken in execution, 265–266
breach of covenant other than for payment of rent, 265
generally, 263–264
non-payment of rent, 264
underleases, 266–267
waiver, 267
quiet enjoyment, landlord's covenant for, 250, 267
recitals, 252
reddendum, 256, 424
re-entry and forfeiture. *See* proviso for re-entry and forfeiture.
registered land, 166–168, 174 *et seq.*
Rent Act. *See* unfurnished premises.
reservations, 253–256

LEASE—*cont.*
  reversion, assignment of, 269
  reversion, lease of, 254
  reversionary leases, 254
  taxation, 269–270
    income tax, 269–270
    stamp duty, 270
  tenancy agreement, 245–248, 422
  testimonium, 267
  unfurnished premises, 271–275
    controlled tenancies, 272–273
    death of tenant, 275
    protected tenancies, 271–272
    regulated tenancies, 273
    rent control, 274–275
    security of tenure, 273–274
    statutory tenancies, 272
  " usual covenants and conditions,"
    245–246, 248–249

LEASE-BACK, 270

LEASEHOLD,
  examination of title to, 187–188
  words of demise, 253

LEASEHOLD ENFRANCHISEMENT, 113–
    116, 277–281
  action by landlord, 114–115
  completion, 115–116
  death of tenant, 278
  deduction of title, 115
  exercise of tenant's rights, 278–280
  form of conveyance, 115
  landlord's overriding rights, 280–281
  procedure, 113 *et seq.*
  requirements, 277–278
  tenant's desire notice, 113–114
  withdrawal by tenant, 116

LEGACY. *See* WILL.

LEGAL CHARGE. *See under* MORT-
  GAGES.

LICENCE, 282, 288

LIEN, 193–194
  purchaser's, 194
  vendor's, 193–194, 305

LOCAL AUTHORITIES, inquiries of, 42–43

LOCAL LAND CHARGES, 39 *et seq.*, 97–
  99

LOCAL SEARCHES, 39–42
  generally, 39
  local land charges register, 39–40
  registration, 40–41
  searches, 41–42

MATRIMONIAL HOME, 147–148, 156–158,
  243–244

MEMORANDUM,
  of contract, 17 *et seq.*
  of conveyance, 213, 410

MERGER,
  of contract in conveyance, 212–213

MINOR INTERESTS, 168–169

MISDESCRIPTION, 73–78, 95–96

MISREPRESENTATION, 2, 31, 35, 78, 200–
  201

MISTAKE, 200
  effect on contract, 25, 200

MONEYLENDERS, 304–305

MORTGAGEE,
  power of sale, 317–319
  sale by, 319–323

MORTGAGES, 292 *et seq.*
  attornment clause, 325–327, 429
  building society receipts, 337
  charge, legal, 293–295, 426 *et seq.*
  chattel mortgages, 300–301
  choses in action, 301
  collateral advantages, 311–312
  company borrowing powers, 301
  consolidation, power of, 325
  contents of mortgage, 303–327, 426
    et seq.
  covenant against letting, 313
  covenant for repayment, 305–306
  covenant not to call in the loan, 309
  date, 303
  debentures, 301–302, 340–341
  demise or charge, 310–311
  discharge of equitable mortgages,
    337
  discharge of registered charge, 337,
    436
  discharge of sub-mortgages, 388
  endowment mortgages, 339–340
  equitable charges, 297
  equitable mortgages, 295–297, 433
  equity of redemption, 292
  extension of statutory powers, 315–
    316, 320
  floating charge, 142, 302
  form, 292–302, 426 *et seq.*
  freeholds, of, 292, 293
  further advances, 325
  instalments, 308, 430
  insurance, 312–313
  interest, 306–309
  joint account clause, 309–310
  leaseholds, of, 292, 293
  leases, power to grant, 314–316
  legal charge, 293–295
  mortgage protection policy, 304
  mortgagee, sale by, 316–323
  notices, 320
  obtaining mortgage, 341
  option mortgage scheme, 307, 339
  parties, 303–305
  possession, right to, 322–323
  postponement of redemption, 309
  proviso for redemption, 311, 427
  re-assignment of life policies, 338

MORTGAGES—*cont.*
  receipt operating as transfer, 336
  receiver, appointment of, 323–325
  recitals, **305**
  registered charges, 298–299, 432
    company charges, 298
    priority of charges, 299
    second charge, 299
  registered land, 297–300
    deposit of certificate, 300
    equitable mortgage, 299–300
    first registration, 297–298
    forms, 298–300
    mortgages off the register, 299–300
    registered charge, 298–299
  registration of charges, 329–331
  repair, 313
  sale, power of, 316 *et seq.*
  satisfied terms, 334–335
  second mortgages, 295, 327–328
    disadvantages, 328
    form, 327–328
    use, 327
  shares and other choses in action, 301
  statutory mortgages, 295
  sub-mortgages, 328–329
    effect, 329
    form, 328–329
    generally, 328
    sub-charges of registered charge, 329
  tax relief, 339
  termination of mortgages, 333–338
    after 1925, 334–338
    before 1926, 334
  transfer of mortgages, 331–333
    concurrence of mortgagor, 331
    form of transfer, 331–333, 434–435
    notice of transfer, 333
    transfer after mortgagee's death, 333
    transfer of equitable mortgages, 333
    transfer of registered charge, 333
    transfer of sub-mortgages, 333
  undertaking to discharge, 211–212, 437
  use of mortgages, 338–341
    consumer credit, 339
    debentures, 340–341
    endowment mortgages, 339–340
    generally, 338
    house purchase, 338–339
    investment property, 340
    restrictions on tax relief, 339
  vacating receipt, 335, 435

NATIONAL CONDITIONS OF SALE, 84

NATIONAL HOUSE-BUILDERS' REGISTRATION COUNCIL SCHEME, 83

NON-DISCLOSURE, 78–81

NOTICE, 148–150
  actual, 149
  constructive, 149–150

NOTICE—*cont.*
  generally, 148–149
  imputed, 150
  registration, 150

NOTICE OF ASSENT, ETC., 136, 213

NOTICE OF ASSIGNMENT, 213

NOTICE OF SEVERANCE, 143

NOTICE TO COMPLETE, 110–111, 412

OPEN CONTRACT, 10–11, 59 *et seq.*
  advantages and disadvantages, 69–70
  correspondence, made by, 65–69
    apportionment of outgoings, 66
    date fixed for completion, 66
    delivery of abstract, 67–68
    interest on purchase-money, 66–67
    place for completion, 66
    possession, 66
    power for vendor to resell after notice, 69
    power to rescind, 68–69
    preparation of conveyance, 69
    requisitions, 68
  correspondence, made otherwise than by, 59–65
  defined, 10–11, 59

OPERATIVE WORDS IN CONVEYANCE, 224 *et seq.*, 413

OPTIONS,
  assignment of benefit of, 30
  burden of option runs with land, 30
  conversion, 31
  exercise of, 30–31
  nature of, 28
  types of, 28
  validity, 29
    perpetuities, 29
    registration, 29
  when used, 28

OVERREACHING,
  strict settlement, 363
  trust for sale, 378

OVERRIDING INTERESTS, 170–171, 186–187

PARCELS, 230–231, 412

PART PERFORMANCE, 22–23, 296

PARTICULARS OF SALE, 71–83
  contents, 71 *et seq.*
  defective premises, 81–83
  misdescription, 73–78
  non-disclosure, 78–81

PARTIES,
  conveyances, 221–222
  leases, 252
  mortgages, 303–305

PARTY WALLS, 231, 415

PERPETUALLY RENEWABLE LEASE, 255–256

PERSONAL REPRESENTATIVES,
assents by, 136–138, 400–401, 443
conveyance by, 417
covenant for title by, 228
powers of,
joint or several, whether, 145–146
purchaser's protection, 136–138
sale by, 145–146, 222, 417
settled land, in respect of, 367
special representatives, 367

PERSONALTY, TRUST OF, 343, 345, 371, 437 et seq.

PLANNING. See TOWN AND COUNTRY PLANNING.

PLANS ON CONVEYANCE, 230

POWER OF ATTORNEY, 125–127

PRELIMINARY INQUIRIES, 34–38
inquiries, the, 36–38
practice points, 38
purpose of, 34–35
remedies for incorrect answers, 35–36

PREPARATION OF CONVEYANCE, 69, 104, 206–207

PRESUMPTIONS, 130–131, 230–231

PRINCIPAL VESTING DEED, 360

PRIORITY NOTICE, 160–161

PROBATE, 128, 136–138, 400

PROOF OF DOCUMENTS, 124 et seq.

PROOF OF FACTS, 128 et seq.

PROPERTY, INSPECTION OF, 186–187

PROTECTIVE TRUSTS, 347

PROVISO FOR REDEMPTION, 295, 311, 427

PURCHASE-MONEY,
condition as to interest on, 105–107
payment of, 210–211
receipt for, 225, 413

QUIET ENJOYMENT,
covenant for, 226 et seq.

RECEIPT,
conveyance, in, 225, 413
mortgage, repayment of, 334–338

RECEIVER,
appointment by mortgagee, 302, 323–324
powers and duties of, 324

RECITALS,
in conveyances, 223–224, 412–413 et seq.
in mortgages, 305, 426–427 et seq.

RECTIFICATION,
of contract, 25, 200
of conveyance, 25, 229, 233
of register, 172–173

REDDENDUM IN LEASE, 256, 424

REGISTRATION,
agreement for lease, 26, 163, 330

REGISTRATION OF TITLE, 163 et seq., 214 et seq.
absolute title, 175, 183
bankruptcy of registered proprietor, 179
cautions, 181–182
certificates, 174
charge certificate, 174
charges. See MORTGAGES.
charges register, 172
compulsory registration, 166–167
conversion into absolute or good leasehold title, 176–177
death of registered proprietor, 178
examination of title by registrar, 176
first registration, 184
generally, 163–164, 184–186
good leasehold title, 176
inhibitions, 182
investigation of title, 183–184
land certificate, 174
maps and indexes, 172
minor interests, 168–169
mirror principle, 185–186
notices, 180–181
objects, 164–165
official searches, 184
overriding interests, 170–171
possessory title, 175–176, 183
property register, 171–172
proprietorship register, 172
qualified title, 175, 183–184
rectification of the register, 172–173
register, the, 171–173
registrable interests, 167–168
registries, the, 165–166
restrictions, 182–183
rules, land registration, 166
settled land, 179–180
State guarantee 184–185
transfers. See TRANSFERS OF REGISTERED LAND.
trust for sale, land held upon, 180
unregistered transfer of registered land, 178

REMEDIES, 200, 205
damages, 203–204

REMEDIES—*cont.*
 declaration, 205
 Greenwood v. *Turner* motion, 202
 misdescription, 74–75
 misrepresentation, 200–201
 mistake, 200
 non-disclosure, 80–81
 rescission, 204
 specific performance, 201–203
 summary judgment, 202

RENT,
 collection of apportioned rents, 123
 covenant to pay, 256, 268–269, 424
 forfeiture of lease for non-payment,
 263 *et seq.*

RENTAL PURCHASE, 196–197

REPAIR, COVENANT FOR, 246, 249, 250–
 252, 257–259, 423
 in lease 257–259, 424
 in mortgage, 313, 428

REQUISITIONS ON TITLE, 131 *et seq.*
 condition of sale, as to, 101–104
 generally, 131–135
 waiver, of, 135

RESCISSION, 201, 203, 204
 for misdescription, 74, 95
 for requisitions, 102–104

RESERVATIONS, 234–235, 414, 415

RESTRICTIVE COVENANTS, 236–238
 benefit of, 237–238
 burden of, 237
 drafting of, 237–238, 415

RETIREMENT OF TRUSTEES, 375–376

RIDER, MEANING OF, 85

ROOT OF TITLE, 121 *et seq.*
 defined, 121–122
 examples of, 122
 generally, 121 *et seq.*
 recital as root, 123

SALE OF LAND, USUAL PROCEDURE, 2–5,
 406, 409

SEARCHES,
 searches generally, 150 *et seq.*
 See also COMPANY SEARCH; LAND
 CHARGES SEARCHES; LAND REGIS-
 TRY SEARCH; LOCAL SEARCHES;
 TOWN AND COUNTRY PLANNING;
 YORKSHIRE DEED REGISTRIES.

SECOND MORTGAGES, 327–328

SETTLEMENTS OF LAND, 342 *et seq.*, 371,
 437 *et seq.*
 generally, 342–345
 strict settlements, 351 *et seq.*

SETTLEMENTS OF PERSONALTY, 342 *et
 seq.*, 371–372, 437 *et seq.*

SPECIAL REPRESENTATIVES FOR SETTLED
 LAND, 367

SPECIFIC PERFORMANCE, 201–203

SPOUSE,
 rights in property, 147–148, 243–244
 rights of occupation, 156–158

STAMP DUTY,
 assent, 138
 certificate of value, 329, 413
 contract, 197–198
 conveyance, 213–214, 239, 270
 lease, 95

STATUTORY DECLARATION, 95, 128

STATUTORY FORM OF CONDITIONS OF
 SALE, 65 *et seq.*

STRICT SETTLEMENTS, 342 *et seq.*, 351
 et seq.
 capital money, 366
 change of ownership, 367–369
 conveyance by tenant for life or
 statutory owner, effect of, 363–364
 creation of, 358–361
 death of tenant for life, 367–368
 deed of declaration, 357
 deed of discharge, 369–370
 documents, two, 358 *et seq.*
 duration, 353
 history of, 342 *et seq.*
 improvements, 366–367
 infant attaining majority, 368
 leasing, power of, 364
 mortgage, power to, 364
 ownership, change of, 367–369
 powers of tenant for life, 361–367
 consent needed, when, 366
 enlargement of, 365
 notices before exercise of, 365–366
 release of, 365
 restriction of, 365
 principal vesting deed, 360
 purchase-money, payment of, 363
 purchaser's investigation of title,
 362–363
 sale, power of, 362–364
 " settled land," meaning of, 353
 " settlement," meaning of, 351–353
 statutory owner, 355–356, 361 *et seq.*
 meaning of, 355–356
 powers of, 361 *et seq.*
 subsidiary vesting deed, 360
 tenant for life,
 assignment of interest, 368–369
 death of, 367–368
 forfeiture of interest, 368–369
 infancy of, 355
 lack of, 355–356
 meaning of, 353–355
 position of, 358
 powers of, 361–367
 surrender of interest, 368–369
 trust for sale, contrast with, 343 *et
 seq.*
 trust instrument, 361

STRICT SETTLEMENTS—*cont.*
  trustees of the settlement, 356–358
  vesting assent, 360–361

SUB-MORTGAGE, 328–329

SUB-SALE,
  conditions as to, 195
  conveyance on, 195
  stamp duty, on, 195

" SUBJECT TO CONTRACT," 11–13

SUBSIDIARY VESTING DEED, 360

SURRENDER OF LEASE, 144

TACKING,
  of further advances, 325

TAXATION,
  annuities, 396–397
  certificate of value, 239, 413
  estate duty. *See* ESTATE DUTY.
  income tax and surtax, 269–270,
    349–350, 396
  leases, 269–270
  settlements, 349–350
  stamp duty. *See* STAMP DUTY.
  wills, 398–399

TENANCY AGREEMENT, 245, 422

TENANT FOR LIFE. *See* STRICT SETTLE-
  MENTS.

TESTATUM, 224

TESTIMONIUM,
  conveyance, 240, 413
  lease, 267
  transfer of registered land, 242, 417

TIME,
  completion, for. *See* COMPLETION.
  whether " of the essence," 108–109

TITLE,
  conditions, 59 *et seq.*, 91–94
  deducing, 119
  investigation of,
    assents, 136–138
    attorney, 125–127, 138
    charities, 138–139
    companies, 139–140
    easements, 140
    equitable mortgages, 140–141
    estate duty, 141
    flats and maisonettes, 141–142
    floating charges, 142
    gifts, 142–143
    joint owners, 143–144
    leaseholds, 144, 187–188
    mortgagee, investigation by, 187
    mortgagee, power of sale, 144
    mortgages, 144–145

TITLE—*cont.*
  personal representatives, 145–146
  restrictive covenants, 146–147
  settled land, 147, 362–363
  spouse's rights, 147–148
  trustees for sale, 148
  voluntary conveyances, 148
  See also ABSTRACT OF TITLE;
    INSPECTION OF PROPERTY;
    NOTICE; REGISTRATION OF TITLE;
    REQUISITIONS ON TITLE;
    SEARCHES.
  prior to root, 63
  requisitions on. *See* REQUISITIONS
    ON TITLE.
  See also ROOT OF TITLE *and* TITLE
    TO BE SHOWN

TITLE DEEDS,
  acknowledgment as to, 238–239, 242,
    415–416
  mortgagor's right to return of, on
    repayment, 338
  purchaser's right to, 64–65, 211
  undertaking as to, 238–239, 242,
    415–416
  vendor's right to retain, 64–65, 238

TITLE TO BE SHOWN, 59 *et seq.*, 91–94
  conditions of sale, as to, 91–94
  freeholds, 60
  generally, 59 *et seq.*
  leases, 60–62
  length, 60–62, 92

TOWN AND COUNTRY PLANNING, 44 *et
  seq.*
  adverse planning decisions, 57–58
    blight notice, 57–58
    purchase notice, 57
  building preservation notice, 47
  building preservation order, 46–47
  compensation, 53–56
  conservation areas, 47
  development, 46
  enforcement action, 51–52
    certificate of established use, 52
    enforcement notice, 51–52
    stop notice, 51
  highways, stopping up and diversion,
    47
  inquiries, 44 *et seq.*
  listed building consent, 47
  planning permission, 47–50
    advertisements, 50
    application for planning permis-
      sion, 48–49
    conditions, 49
    industrial and office development,
      50
    lapse, etc., 49–50
    outline permission, 49
    personal, not generally, 50
    register of permissions, 50
    temporary permission, 49
  planning proposals, 52–53
    development plans, 52–53
    structure plans, 53
  searches, 44 *et seq.*

TOWN AND COUNTRY PLANNING—*cont.*
tree preservation orders, 47
use, 44–45
description of, 77–79

TRANSFER OF MORTGAGE, 331–333, 434–435

TRANSFERS OF REGISTERED LAND, 177–178, 240–243
effect of registered transfer, 177–178, 242–243
form, 240–242, 417, 422
registration of transferee, 242
rule 72, 243
unregistered transfer of registered land, 178

TRUST CORPORATION, 363, 378, 392
as executor, 392

TRUST FOR SALE, 342 *et seq.*, 371 *et seq.*
consents to sale, 377
form of, 371
history of, 342–343
land, of, 342–343
mode of sale, 377–378
personalty, of, 345
power to postpone sale, 376–377
registered land, 179–180
sale under, 376–378
strict settlement, contrast with, 343–345
trustees for sale. *See* TRUSTEES.
trusts, the, 371–372

TRUST INSTRUMENT, 361

TRUSTEES,
appointment of, 372 *et seq.*, 440
covenants for title, 228
disclaimer by, 372–373
powers of, 376 *et seq.*, 378 *et seq.*
advancement, 379–380
charging for services, 381
compounding liabilities, 380–381
investment, 378–379, 438–439
maintenance, 379
removal, 376
retirement, 375–376
settlement, of. *See* STRICT SETTLEMENTS.
vesting property in, 372 *et seq.*

TRUSTEES CHARGING CLAUSE, 381, 439

TRUSTS. *See* PROTECTIVE TRUSTS; SETTLEMENTS OF LAND; SETTLEMENTS OF PERSONALTY; STRICT SETTLEMENTS; TRUST FOR SALE; TRUSTEES.

UNDERTAKING TO DISCHARGE MORTGAGE, 211–212, 437

VACANT POSSESSION, 97

VACATING RECEIPT, 335–337, 435

VARIATION,
of contract, 24–25

VENDOR AND PURCHASER, 189 *et seq.*
bankruptcy of either party, effect of, 192–193
benefit and losses, purchaser's position with regard to, 190
death of either party, effect of, 191–192
effect of contract pending completion, 189–199
instalment sales, 196–197
insurance, 190–191
liens of vendor and purchaser, 193–194
position of parties generally, 189–191
stamp duty on contract, 197–198
sub-sales, 195–196
trustee, vendor as, 189–190

VENDOR AND PURCHASER SUMMONS, 198–199

VENDOR'S COVENANTS FOR TITLE, 225 *et seq.*

VERIFICATION OF TITLE, 124, 210

VESTING ASSENT, 360, 367–368

VESTING DECLARATION, 375

VESTING DEED, 359, 360, 367–368

VOLUNTARY CONVEYANCE, 148

WAIVER,
objection and requisitions, of, 105, 135
right of entry, of, 267

WILL, 383 *et seq.*, 441
abatement, 392–393, 395
ademption, 392–393, 395
alterations, 388
annuities, 396–397
assents, 400–401
attestation, 387–388
capacity to make, 384–385
commorientes, 395
contents of, 391–398
dependent relative revocation, 391
destruction, 390–391
devises, 395
dwelling-house, provision of, for widow, 395–396
executors, appointment of, 391–392
force, 384–385
formalities, 385–389
fraud, 384–385
incidence of debts and estate duty, 399–400
incorporation of documents, 386
infants', 384
lapse, 393–394, 395

456   INDEX

WILL—*cont.*
  legacies, 392–394
    demonstrative, 393
    general, 392–393
    specific, 392–393
  marriage, effect of, 390
  mental disorder, 384
  personal chattels, 394
  reasons for making, 383–384
  residue, 397–398
  revival of revoked will, 391
  revocation, 389–391
  settlements, 397
  signature of testator, 385–386

WILL—*cont.*
  soldiers, etc., 389
  subsequent will or codicil, **revocation**
    by, 389
  taxation, 398–399
  trustees, appointment of, 391–392
  witnesses, 387–388
  writing executed like a will, revoca-
    tion by, 389–390

WORDS OF LIMITATION, 235–236

YORKSHIRE DEED REGISTRIES, 162–163